D0070754

Wayward Contracts

Wayward Contracts

THE CRISIS OF POLITICAL OBLIGATION
IN ENGLAND, 1640–1674

Victoria Kahn

PRINCETON UNIVERSITY PRESS

PRINCETON AND OXFORD

Copyright © 2004 by Princeton University Press
Published by Princeton University Press, 41 William Street,
Princeton, New Jersey 08540
In the United Kingdom: Princeton University Press,
3 Market Place, Woodstock, Oxfordshire OX20 1SY

All Rights Reserved.

Library of Congress Cataloging-in-Publication Data
Kahn, Victoria Ann.
Wayward contracts : the crisis of political obligation
in England, 1640–1674 / Victoria Kahn.
   p. cm.
Includes bibliographical references and index.
ISBN 978-0-691-17124-1 (acid-free paper)
1. English literature—Early modern, 1500–1700—History and criticism.
2. Politics and literature—Great Britain—History—17th century. 3. Great
Britain—Politics and government—1642–1660. 4. Great Britain—Politics
and government—1660–1688. 5. Contracts—Great Britain—History—17th
century. 6. Political obligation—History—17th century. 7. Social contract—
History—17th century. 8. Contracts in literature. I. Title.
PR438.P65K34 2004
820.9′358′094109033—dc22   2004042850

British Library Cataloging-in-Publication Data is available.

This book has been composed in Sabon

Printed on acid-free paper. ∞

pup.princeton.edu

Printed in the United States of America

10 9 8 7 6 5 4 3 2 1

For Helene

You sense that something is not right. If matters were otherwise, then you would have a sense of well-being. Or you cannot make another person's circumstances right.
   —Ernst Bloch, *Natural Law and Human Dignity*

As empirically constructed and produced objects, works of art, even literary ones, point to a practice from which they abstain: the creation of a just life.
   —Theodor Adorno, "Commitment"

There is an element of the world-building capacity of man in the human faculty of making and keeping promises.
   —Hannah Arendt, *On Revolution*

Contents

Acknowledgments   xi

Abbreviations   xiii

CHAPTER 1. Introduction   1

    From Virtue to Contract   8
    The Psychology of Contract   13
    Poetics and the Contract of Genre   15
    The Usual Story   20
    The Road Ahead   25

PART I
An Anatomy of Contract, 1590–1640   29

CHAPTER 2. Language and the Bond of Conscience   31

    Natural Rights Theory: The Social Contract and the
        Linguistic Contract   33
    The Common Law: Magna Carta and Economic Contract   41
    Covenant Theology: Divine Speech Acts and the
        Covenant of Metaphor   48

CHAPTER 3. The Passions and Voluntary Servitude   57

    The Slave Contract   60
    The Law of the Heart   64
    Free Consent   73

PART II
A Poetics of Contract, 1640–1674   81

CHAPTER 4. Imagination   83

    Five Knights: From Promise to Contract   85
    Shipmoney and the Imagination of Disaster   90
    Henry Parker and the Metaphor of Contract   95
    Falkland, Chillingworth, Digges, and the Fiction
        of Representation   104

CHAPTER 5. Violence   112

    Prophesying Revolution   113
    The Metaphorical Plot   120

CHAPTER 6. Metalanguage   134
  The Problem of Essex   138
  Hobbes's Critique of Romance   141
  The Contract of Mimesis   147
  Hobbesian Fictions   151
  Method and Metalanguage   154
  Hobbes's Readers or Inescapable Romance   166

CHAPTER 7. Gender   171
  Political Contract and the Marriage Contract   174
  The Politics of Romance   177
  Passion and Interest   180
  Contract on Trial   185
  The Sexual Contract   189
  The Paralogism of Romance   192

CHAPTER 8. Embodiment   196
  Resistless Love and Hate   198
  Paradise Lost *and the Bond of Nature*   207
  Pity or Fear of Violent Death   214

CHAPTER 9. Sympathy   223
  Wise Compliance   227
  The Politics of Pity   234
  Sympathy between Men   241

CHAPTER 10. Critique   252
  Reason of State   254
  Samson as Exception   262
  Reasoning about the Exception: Dialectic and Equivocation   264
  Taking Exception to Pity and Fear   270
  Political Theology and Tragedy   276

CHAPTER 11. Conclusion   279

Notes   285

Index   365

Acknowledgments

THIS BOOK IS THE PRODUCT of a happy period at the University of California at Berkeley and at Irvine. I want to thank my colleagues at both campuses for the lively intellectual environment that was crucial to the completion of the book. At Berkeley, I am particularly grateful to David Bates, Lorna Hutson, and Nancy Ruttenburg for their lunchtime conversation, advice, and commentary on the early chapters of the manuscript. Louise George Clubb first invited me to visit Berkeley in 1996 and I have benefited from her generosity ever since. Thanks are due to Carol Clover for suggesting the title of this book and for her passing comment that voluntary servitude seemed like a good thing to write about. At Irvine, I owe a special debt to Brook Thomas for reading early drafts of some of my thoughts on Hobbes and natural rights, for timely bibliographical suggestions, and for his exemplary collegiality. Also at Irvine, Jane Newman and Patrick Sinclair were delightful midweek companions.

It seems appropriate for a book on contract theory that I should have discovered a community of readers in the process of writing it. Constance Jordan, Catherine Gimelli Martin, Jason Rosenblatt, and Nancy Struever read a large chunk of the manuscript and gave me encouraging responses when I most needed them. Catherine Martin and David Bates heroically read the same chapters several times and offered invaluable advice. For their comments on individual chapters or parts thereof, I want to thank Marshall Grossman, Jeffrey Knapp, A. A. Long, Lois Potter, J. P. Sommerville, Tracy Strong, and David Quint. I was very fortunate in my readers for the press, Don Herzog and Steven Zwicker, whose engagement and astute criticism helped to sharpen my argument. Mary Murrell was a loyal and supportive editor, and Brian MacDonald was a scrupulous copyeditor. In the process of writing this book, I have had many occasions to be grateful to Liz Huyck, my research assistant at Princeton many years ago, who is personally responsible for my large xerox library of obscure seventeenth-century texts. At Berkeley, Robyn Marasco was a splendid research assistant on some last-minute tasks. The project received financial support in the form of a grant from the NEH, as well as a UC President's Fellowship, and a UC Berkeley Humanities Research Grant. I am grateful to Constance Jordan, Kathy Eden, and David Quint, for their letters of recommendation. Marsha Silverberg was the Gracious Guardian of the East Coast Diskettes. As always, Nancy Troy was an inspiring example and a supportive friend, as was my sister Lisa Davenport, whose regular telephone salutation was "Are you working?"

The subject matter of this book has followed the career of Helene Silverberg who, in the course of its writing, moved from Political Science to the Law. This book, and life in general, are better in every way because of her.

Abbreviations

CD   John Milton, *Of Christian Doctrine*, ed. Maurice
            Kelley, in *CPW*, vol. 6.

CPW   John Milton, *Complete Prose Works of John Milton*,
            general ed. Don M. Wolfe, 8 vols. (New Haven,
            1953–82).

Behemoth   Thomas Hobbes, *Behemoth or the Long Parliament*,
            ed. Ferdinand Tönnies, with an introduction by
            Stephen Holmes (Chicago and London, 1990).

De cive   Thomas Hobbes, *On the Citizen*, ed. and trans.
            Richard Tuck and Michael Silverthorne (Cambridge,
            1998).

De jure belli   Hugo Grotius, *De jure belli ac pacis libri tres*, ed. James
            Brown Scott, trans. Francis W. Kelsey with the col-
            laboration of Arthur E. R. Boak, Henry A. Sanders,
            Jesse S. Reeves, and Herbert F. Wright, 2 vols.,
            Classics of International Law (Oxford, 1925).

Elements   Thomas Hobbes, *Elements of Law*, in Thomas
            Hobbes, *Human Nature and De Corpore Politico*,
            ed. J. C. A. Gaskin (Oxford, 1994).

Leviathan   Thomas Hobbes, *Leviathan*, ed. Richard Tuck
            (Cambridge, 1991).

PL   John Milton, *Paradise Lost*, in *Complete Poems and
            Major Prose*, ed. Merritt Y. Hughes (Indianapolis,
            1957).

State Trials   *Cobbett's Complete Collection of State Trials*, ed.
            T. B. Howell, 33 vols., (London, 1809–20).

All works of Cicero and Seneca are quoted from the Loeb Classical
Library, published by Harvard University Press.

CHAPTER 1

Introduction

> To breed an animal with the right to make promises—is not this
> the paradoxical problem nature has set itself with regard to
> man? and is it not the real problem of man?
> —Nietzsche, *The Genealogy of Morals*

> A worthy person of our age was accustomed to say, that con-
> tracts in writing were invented only to bind villains, who
> having no law, justice, or truth, within themselves, would not
> keep their words, unless such testimonies were given as
> might compel them.
> —Algernon Sidney, *Discourses concerning Government*

THE SEVENTEENTH CENTURY is the period in which scholars have located
the emergence of a distinctively modern conception of political obligation. From Maine and Weber through Macpherson and Walzer, they have
recorded the shift from a world of status to one of contract—from a
world, that is, of hierarchical feudal relations to one made up of autonomous individuals who rationally consent to their self-imposed government. In contrast to the medieval pact of subjection, in which a corporate
body of the people subjects itself to the sovereign, the new discourse of
obligation yielded a protoliberal subject who freely enters into a social
and political contract.[1] It is the aim of this book to reconstruct the discourse of contract in the making and, in doing so, to revise this story of
political obligation. Specifically I show that seventeenth-century contract
theory was defined by a struggle over the role of language and representation, and of the passions and interests, in binding and releasing the political subject. Instead of presupposing a rational and autonomous individual
who consents to the political contract, seventeenth-century contract theorists were compelled to create a new political subject ex nihilo. Rather
than assuming that government was natural and only needed to be legitimated by consent, early modern writers argued that the state was an artifact that was brought into being by a powerful, if sometimes fictional,
speech act. For these reasons, I argue, early modern contract theory is
best thought of as a radically new poetics of the subject and the state,

one that was manifest across a wide range of texts and genres in mid-seventeenth-century England.

In revising the usual accounts of contract theory, I take a cue from Nietzsche's skeptical remarks in *The Genealogy of Morals*. "I assume," he commented acerbically, "we have got over that sentimentalism that would have [the state] begin with a contract." According to Nietzsche, the emergence of the contracting subject coincided with the development of Judeo-Christian notions of conscience, subjectivity, and ethical responsibility. Contract theory was implicated in the ongoing battle between Rome and Israel, between the warrior ethos and the slave mentality, which involved the sublimation of the warrior's aggression into the new faculty of conscience. This battle was replayed in the Renaissance between Machiavelli on the one hand and Luther and Calvin on the other. Against this mystified discourse of conscience and contract, Nietzsche counterposed a demystified discourse of power. In Nietzsche's alternative account, which sounds not coincidentally like Burckhardt in *The Civilization of the Renaissance in Italy*, both the state and the contracting subject were instead the product of the "hammer blows" of the creative artist. Nietzsche was not contesting the emergence of contract theory in the early modern period but rather exposing the violent conditions of its emergence. As I show in the following chapters, Nietzsche was far closer to the truth—far closer, that is, to the historically specific imaginative experience of mid-seventeenth-century Englishmen and women—than most modern scholars. In these tumultuous years, early modern men and women experienced at first hand—and argued intensely about—the violence and artistry required to fashion the contracting subject.[2]

For men and women of all political persuasions, the outbreak of civil war in 1642 set off a dramatic crisis of political obligation. All of a sudden, a majority of English subjects were confronted with a choice—king or parliament?—that they had not previously encountered. This choice in turn required that individuals examine, discover, or refashion the bonds of obligation. As Philip Hunton observed in his *Treatise of Monarchy* of 1643, when the king and the people came into conflict, "the individual would be left alone with his conscience to guide him." Both in 1642 and after the execution of the king in 1649, the forging of individual obligation was the urgent political task. This political crisis proved to be uniquely fertile ground for thinking about political obligation as an agreement individuals entered into voluntarily. And, in fact, parliamentary debates, sermons, and theological tracts show an explosion of the language of contract in these years. In this light, the juridical murder of the king in 1649 appears less as an anomaly than as the logical conclusion of the new discourse of contract and, in particular, of the king's perceived breach of contract in taking up arms against his subjects in 1642. By 1652 Robert Filmer would claim disapprovingly that "original power by nature in the people . . . is the only theme now in fashion."[3]

Although accusations of broken promises and breach of contract were hurled from all sides, contemporaries did not always agree—in fact, this was at the heart of the conflict—what kind of agreement had been broken. Was political obligation best thought of in terms of a marriage contract between sovereign and subject, an economic contract, a theological covenant, or the implicit contract of the common law or the ancient constitution? Were human beings naturally sociable, in which case only government was formed by a contract, or was a social contract the precondition of a political contract? Was the contract of government a consequence of natural law, according to which humans are equal in the state of nature; or a consequence of the illegibility of natural law, which in turn dictated a purely conventional agreement among individuals and the arbitrary imposition of sovereignty?

The slightest inflection of the new language of contract could signal a radically different view of human nature, natural law, and society. When the parliamentary pamphleteer Henry Parker argued that government was formed by a contract among men to set up a sovereign, he assumed that contract was grounded on the authority of reason and natural law. To reestablish the contract of government was thus, ironically, to return government to its basis in human nature. Hobbes argued, in contrast, that individuals were by nature asocial, even bellicose, and that fear of violent death would move them to consent to a political contract. Filmer, whose *Patriarcha* articulated an altogether different notion of government, ridiculed this notion of the political contract as a preposterously artificial conception of human relations. And he mocked Hobbes's implicit equation of contract with consent: "I *consent* with him," he wrote in his *Observations* on Hobbes, "about the rights of exercising government, but I cannot agree with him to his means of acquiring it."[4]

Mid-seventeenth-century writers disagreed about whether the discourse of contract was a sign of political anarchy or a remedy for the chaos of civil war. The royalist pamphleteer Dudley Digges satirized the contractualist fiction of self-determination as a kind of anarchist fantasy of self-creation: "As for Power inherent in the People, how should we imagine such a thing? unlesse also he would imagine People to be *juvenes aquilone creati*; men like *grashoppers* and *locusts* bred of the winde, or like *Cadmus* his men sprung out of the earth; where none deriving from any pre-existent Parents, had all of them equall originall and power, and therefore subject to no civill Power but what by agreement they themselves ordained?"[5] In contrast, in *The Tenure of Kings and Magistrates*, Milton argued that a republican government based on "power inherent in the people" was the solution to the faction and discord of civil war. Although Hobbes rejected republicanism, he too presented a political contract as the solution to political anarchy: while lamenting the pervasive reduction of aristocratic glory to petty self-interested calculation, he argued that it was precisely the calculation of self-interest, and the resulting contract of sovereignty, that would check the self-aggrandizing heroic virtue that was one source of violent conflict.

The outbreak of civil war made seventeenth-century men and women reexamine the motives for obedience to the sovereign power. In the preceding decades, supporters of the king had analogized the political contract to the marriage contract as a way both of naturalizing allegiance and legislating the affections. But, to the extent that the language of contract conjured up the new world of self-interest and economic exchange, it seemed to threaten the view that political or domestic obedience was based on the subject's or wife's affections.[6] In the 1640s, critics of the king drew on the marriage contract as an analogy for the political contract but inverted it, arguing that the king was the wife or servant of the people. Milton famously invoked the affective ideal of companionate marriage as a justification for political as well as domestic divorce. By contrast, Hobbes rejected the usual domestic analogies and suggested a different passion—the fear of violent death—as the motive for political obligation. The crisis of allegiance was thus inseparable from what we might call a crisis of the affections.

It was also inseparable from the increasing secularization of conscience. In this period of loyalty oaths, such as the oath of allegiance or the engagement to the new Cromwellian government, political obligation often turned on how one construed linguistic promises or verbal contracts. Seventeenth-century men and women wondered whether a verbal promise was legally binding, and if so, whether because of conscience or because of some material evidence—some "consideration" or benefit—which established the secular validity of a contract. For many writers the appeal to the moral law of conscience was incendiary because it licensed exceptions to positive law. This anxiety was a powerful spur to recasting conscience in terms of the common law discourse of contract or in the everyday language of interest. For some contemporary writers, interest replaced conscience altogether. In 1642 the Reverend Charles Herle, an outspoken parliamentarian, remarked that "Every experience tells us that *interests* are better state security than oaths." The royalist Samuel Butler was even more cynical: "Oaths and obligations in the affairs of the world are like ribbons and knots in dressing, that seem to tie something, but do not at all. For nothing but interest does really oblige."[7]

The perceived unreliability of both conscience and interest in turn precipitated an intense concern with the binding force of language. In *Levia-*

than, Hobbes declared optimistically that "words are wise mens counters, they do but reckon by them"—as though, by saying so, he could bring about this utopian state of linguistic equivalency and transparent calculation (4.28–29). But he also worried that "Metaphors, and senslesse and ambiguous words, are like *ignes fatui*; and reasoning upon them, is wandering amongst innumerable absurdities; and their end, contention, and sedition, or contempt" (5.36). In contrast, Milton and his associates exploited the resources of linguistic indeterminacy to argue for a different construction of the social and political contract, a different conception of political agency and responsibility. In their hands, the openendedness of metaphor—its capacity to effect semantic transfers and establish new, polyvalent relationships of meaning—became a way of exploring the continuously creative power of the political contract. Along with this heightened sense of the poetic capacities of the political agent came an insistence on the revocability of the political contract, the ongoing revision of political obligation.

If we adopted one traditional narrative of the 1640s, we might say that one version of the contracting subject gave priority to a religious notion of covenant and the other to a secular notion of contract; one emphasized the claims of individual conscience, while the other stressed the role of calculation, self-interest, and the natural right of self-preservation. In the first case, contracts were governed by the divine and natural law that promises must be kept; in the second case, contracts were to be kept if there had been some exchange of "consideration" or benefit. If the contract of conscience was associated with casuistry, the contract of self-interest was linked to the language of reason of state. These two different strains of contract corresponded to divergent conceptions of the passions, divergent histories of natural law. As linguistic events or verbal artifacts, they conjured up different conceptions of metaphor and granted a different place to literature in the ties that bind. The forerunner of the first might be Luther, with his assertion of justification by faith; the forerunner of the second, Machiavelli, with his recommendation that princes break their promises and his redefinition of political virtue as *virtù*. If we had to choose, we might say that the mid-seventeenth-century English representative of the first was Milton; of the second, Hobbes.

In fact, however, the political crisis of the civil war brought these discourses—and their speakers—into explosive contact. On the parliamentary side, covenant theologians and Independents such as Milton joined with lawyers and natural rights theorists to declare their individual right to resist the king. In the process, covenant theology radicalized natural rights theory by virtue of its exclusive emphasis on the individual conscience, while natural rights theory contributed to the secularizing of conscience by virtue of its emphasis on passion, self-interest, and purely human agreements. On the opposing side, Hobbes and those royalists who were influenced by him marshaled these same discourses of covenant and contract (sometimes ironically) in defense of voluntary but absolute obedience to the sovereign. In the process, natural rights theory worked to undermine the claims of conscience, even as the divine speech act of covenant theology was adopted as a model by the secular absolute sovereign. Although the stated political goals of the two sides were antithetical, each side contributed separately and in conversation with the other to the English "radical imagination" of a new kind of political subject—a subject located between the discourses of conscience and natural rights, promise and contract.[8] This was a subject motivated not only by the claims of conscience but also by his passions and interests. This was a subject who could bind himself (the pronoun is part of this history), but only because he was first bound by the social and linguistic agreement that promises must be kept.

The publication of *Leviathan* in 1651 proved to be a watershed in the construction of the new political subject. After 1651 many of those who wrote on contract or political obligation were responding, implicitly or explicitly, to arguments associated with Hobbes. *Leviathan* was the turning point because it emphasized the fictional dimension of contract to a greater degree than before, because it offended contemporary beliefs on both sides of the political divide, and because it was more powerfully argued than any other account of contractual obligation. Hobbes used his fiction of the state of nature and the political contract to trump the competing versions of contract that derived from constitutionalism, covenant theology, and natural law jurisprudence. At the same time, Hobbes presented his readers with a dramatically compelling fiction of the state of nature, an eloquent story of how obligation came to be, and a vivid illustration of the poetic power of contract to bring political obligation into existence ex nihilo. If Hobbes's materialist psychology of the passions and interests demanded a response from his opponents, his frankly ahistorical hypothesis about the origins of the political contract provided them with new resources. *Leviathan* opened up ways of looking at human contracts, history, and nature as contingent constructs, that is, as merely probable fictions or narratives rather than universal facts. In so doing, it prompted not only counterarguments but counternarratives.

In the decade immediately following the civil war, royalists in particular struggled to make sense of the recent conflict and to provide new, more compelling accounts of political obligation. Many of these writers were eager to address the obvious role of the passions and interests in causing civil war. Some were eager to respond to contemporary arguments, associated with Hobbes, about the role of the passions and interests in precipitating the transition out of the state of nature. Margaret Cavendish married Hobbesian self-interest to the passion of love in an effort to redefine the basis of obligation to Charles II. Royalist writers of prose romance countered Hobbes's argument about fear of violent death with an emphasis on the role of the aesthetic emotions of pity and fear in contributing to the Restoration. In the aftermath of the Restoration, Milton tried to save the critical potential of literature, and of pity and fear, from the politically conservative, royalist response to Hobbes.

In the seventeenth-century story of contract presented here, Milton is the mirror image of Hobbes. In the mid-seventeenth-century, I argue, Milton and Hobbes looked more alike than they do now. Although Hobbes defended absolutism, and Milton espoused republicanism, both were seen as radical materialists and contractualists, whose emphasis on consent and the artifice of government undermined conventional notions of obligation. Hobbes was shocking to contemporaries because his version of the political contract authorized consent to de facto political power. Milton was equally shocking because his version of contract justified revoking consent from an ostensibly legitimate ruler. Hobbes's *Leviathan* scandalously included no mention of the recent regicide, while Milton's *Tenure of Kings and Magistrates* just as scandalously urged the execution of the king.

But Hobbes and Milton also articulated different versions of the new discourse of contract. Like Hobbes, Milton was interested in presenting his readers with a dramatically compelling fiction of the state of nature; a vivid narrative of the psychology of obligation; and a forceful illustration of the power of language to bring obligations into existence ex nihilo. But, for Milton, the state of nature was the biblical Eden; his materialist psychology was predicated on love rather than fear; and his conception of the creative dimension of contract was predicated on the violation of precedent, the destruction of custom, and the right of an individual to break his covenant and form a new one—arguments all anathema to Hobbes. Together, then, Hobbes and Milton articulate the two poles of the new contractualism in mid-seventeenth-century England.

As a result of the political and discursive struggle from the 1640s through the Restoration, both politics and literature decisively changed. The midcentury emphasis on the constructive power of covenant and contract helped create the secular subject of politics. At the same time, the reconceptualization of political theory as a science helped to relegate the poetics and passions of contract theory to the new discipline of aesthetics. The intersection of the religious discourse of conscience and the secular discourse of natural right created the secular right of conscience, but the revolutionary fusion of Protestant subjectivity with the natural rights discourse of passion and interest yielded to the new sentimental subject or effeminized man of feeling, defined primarily by his capacity for aesthetic appreciation rather than political judgment. The seventeenth century witnessed a broad cultural shift from a discourse of innate obligations to those based on the shared conventions of language and a pragmatic negotiation of the passions and interests. But it also saw a shift from the moral or political justification of literature to aesthetic interest as the basis of a new kind of sociopolitical contract.[9]

In the early eighteenth century, there were still debates about the relationship between politics, linguistic convention, and literary form, but the terms of the debate had changed. The multifaceted discourse of contract had separated into Locke's emphasis on rational consent, on the one hand, and Hume's critique of rationalism, on the other. Locke expounded a version of contract that retreated from the heroic construction of Hobbes. Hume argued that the idea of the political contract was implausibly artificial and that obligation should instead be understood in terms of custom, consensus, the passions, and linguistic convention—all easily assimilated to an ostensibly depoliticized, aesthetic cult of sentimentality. At the same time, as scholars of the eighteenth century have argued, the emerging discipline of aesthetics also became the place where the sources and bonds of social and political association were reimagined or reconceived. One of the goals of this book is to recover the moment before the historical division of the political contract and what we might call the aesthetic contract, and to make this division seem less of a foregone conclusion.

FROM VIRTUE TO CONTRACT

This book explores how the metaphor of contract emerged as the locus of a culture-wide debate about the grounds of political obligation, and how contract came to articulate some of the most radical innovations of early modern political thought. It focuses on the various discourses of contractual obligation that arose in the aftermath of the Protestant Reformation and the emerging system of nation-states, at the intersection of what the influential puritan minister William Perkins called "the discourse of conscience," and what the Dutch humanist and jurist Hugo Grotius called the "laws of war and peace." The late sixteenth century saw an explosion of the twin discourses of casuistry and reason of state, that is, the art of resolving individual cases of conscience and an art of reasoning specific to politics.[10] At a time of such intense cultural ferment about issues of obligation both in the personal and political sphere, it was clear to all that the relationship between the individual and the state needed to be reconceived. As we will see, contract theory is the place where the arts of casuistry and reason of state, of conscience and calculation, form a new compound and together articulate a new concept of the subject and a new understanding of the state.

The novelty of the seventeenth-century preoccupation with the artifice of political contract and the linguistic act of consent can best be appreciated when considered against the two most prominent authorities on politics in the early modern period. Neither Aristotle nor Aquinas accorded any role to contract in the establishment of government. Although Aristotle recognized the role of consent in some forms of government, he did not put forward a contractual view of political association. Virtue and a natural disposition to the political life, rather than contract and the constitutive power of language, were at the center of Aristotle's account of citizenship. Although Aquinas, unlike Aristotle, occasionally used the language of *pactum* to describe the relationship of sovereign and subjects, he essentially subscribed to an Aristotelian account of natural sociability and the virtues. Contracting was not a part of Aquinas's discussion of political obedience. Subjects obeyed not because they were supposed to keep their contracts but because it was according to divine and natural law that there be a political hierarchy.[11]

A few late medieval neoscholastic writers, such as Vitoria, Molina, De Soto, and Suárez, did conceive of government in terms of consent to a political contract. Some of these figures imagined consent as the consent of a community as a whole and so took the existence of community for granted. Others imagined the consent of an individual but explained the binding force of contracts—including the political contract—in terms of the Aristotelian virtues of liberality and commutative justice, and the natural law that promises must be kept.[12] In general, the late scholastics subscribed to Aristotle's view that human beings are naturally political. For these writers, consent was not so much the source of government and legitimacy as the vehicle by which a people instituted a government in accordance with the law of nature.[13]

At least in theory, early modern subjects did not so much *consent* to political order as *assent* to a natural order the way we assent to a statement of fact.[14] In the reigns of Elizabeth and James I, Englishmen were repeatedly asked to swear oaths of allegiance, a fact that might seem to indicate the importance of consent.[15] Such consent, however, did not entail a contractual view of the origins of government. Rather, Tudor and Stuart apologists represented the political subject as assenting to what was already the case: his divine, natural, and historical subjection to the sovereign. The Thirty-nine Articles of the Anglican Church (1563) located the authority of government in "the queen's majesty"—that is, the "prerogative, which we see to have been given always to all godly princes in

Holy Scripture by God himself, [to] rule all estates and degrees committed to their charge by God."[16] Even those sixteenth-century writers who did imagine a contractual view of the origins of government often presented consent as compatible with assent, or even coercion. Thus, the great Anglican apologist Richard Hooker described government as founded on the "common consent," but he also advanced the "historical" argument that conquest could be legitimated by subsequent consent: by such "after-agreement," Hooker argued, "it commeth many times to pass in kingdoms, that they whose ancient predecessors were by violence and force made subject, do grow little and little into that most sweet form of kingly government which philosophers define to be 'regency willingly sustained and endured, with chiefty of power in the greatest things.' "[17] Perhaps not surprisingly, Hooker also asserted that "the command of an absolute monarch may be taken to represent the assent of the people."[18]

There were, of course, sixteenth-century figures such as the Marian exile John Ponet, who argued not only that legislation required "the consent of the people," by which he meant Parliament, but also that individuals could revoke their consent and violently resist a tyrant. There was also a well-developed tradition of counsel and the protorepublican theory of the ancient constitution, influenced in part by the fifteenth-century writer John Fortescue, who had defended the notion of a mixed or limited government, the *dominium politicum et regale*. In sixteenth-century England, none of these arguments amounted to a full-fledged contractualist theory of government, according to which individuals in a state of nature joined together to create the artifacts of society and government.[19] In the 1580s French Huguenot resistance theorists such as Beza, Hotman, and the author of the *Vindiciae contra tyrannos* put forward the idea of a contract of government between the king and the people. But, like their English contemporaries, they did not yet conceive of the creation of the state as wholly artificial. Instead, they conceived of political obligation as arising "from the nature of things and the will of God."[20]

In the Tudor and Stuart periods, the family was a far more common analogy for political order than was contract. The affective bonds presupposed by such putatively natural relations were a mainstay of contemporary arguments for political authority. When Elizabeth described herself as married to her subjects, and James I presented himself as the loving father of his people, they intended to convey their natural affection rather than anything like a legally sanctioned relationship. And the sentiment was reciprocated, at least in theory. Contemporary manuals of casuistry and "domesticall duties" regularly analogized the relation of sovereign and subject to father and child, or husband and wife. According to both the domestic and the royalist rhetorics of obligation, the political subject consented to his natural subordination out of love and affection for the sovereign, just as the wife consented to her husband.[21]

In the 1620s the conflicts between the Stuart monarchs and Parliament over Magna Carta, taxation, unjust imprisonment, and property rights placed great stress on traditional rhetorics of obligation. The perception that the king was acting in an arbitrary fashion must have crystallized for many in 1629. After an unsuccessful attempt to wrangle subsidies from Parliament, Charles dismissed both houses. During the following decade of "personal rule," Charles attempted to govern by royal prerogative and to raise the funds needed for the unpopular war against the Scots without the consent of Parliament. Such extralegal action mobilized the parliamentary opposition and intensified the struggle over the language of economic political obligation in relation to positive, divine, and natural law.

In the state trials resulting from royal prosecution of those who refused to pay the subsidies imposed by royal prerogative, critics of Charles began to use the language of economic contract to describe the political relation of sovereign and subject. Increasingly, the common lawyers, some of whom were members of Parliament, joined forces with other parliamentary critics of the crown. Together, they defended the "notion that the king had a contractual obligation to rule in the public interest" and that the commonwealth "had the right to resist its king in certain circumstances."[22] Time soon yielded the harvest of this way of thinking: in March 1642 Parliament passed the Militia Ordinance, which deprived Charles of his authority over the militia, thereby implicitly asserting the right to take up arms against the king. During the spring of 1642 the king was twice denied entry to the munitions magazine in Hull. In the autumn, royal and parliamentary forces encountered each other at Edgehill, the first important battle of the civil war.

The Putney debates of 1647 and the debates at Whitehall in 1648 illustrate the explosion of the language of contract during the civil war. They also dramatize the metalinguistic struggle to control the meaning of contract. In October 1647 the officers and soldiers of the parliamentary army met at Putney Church to debate the Leveller Agreement of the People, a proposal that, had it been signed and ratified, would have amounted to a political contract by which the people determined their representatives and their form of government.[23] But, even before the debate about the Agreement could begin, Oliver Cromwell raised the question of whether the army was bound by any prior engagements that rendered the discussion of the Leveller proposals moot. The first third of the debate, then, turned on the question of what constituted a binding agreement. As all parties recognized, this was not merely a procedural issue. It was the central question of the civil war, the "great war about breach of trust," in the Leveller John Lilburne's words.[24]

Some soldiers represented themselves as divinely inspired individuals who were not bound to observe their contracts if they determined at some later point that these contracts were not just. A soldier by the name of Everard declared, "Whatsoever hope or obligation I should be bound unto, if afterwards God should reveal himself, I would break it speedily, [even] if it were an hundred [times] a day." Others adopted a rhetoric of natural law that was equally incendiary. The civilian John Wildman pronounced that "the first thing is to consider the honesty of what is offered; otherwise, it cannot be considered [that] any obligation [binds us]."[25] According to Wildman, what made a contract binding was the individual's interpretation that it conformed to "the law of nature and of nations," to justice, *salus populi*, and the right of self-preservation.

In contrast, the army officers put forward a view of the political contract that stressed its conventionalism. In the officers' view, the soldiers' religious enthusiasm could only lead to interpretive relativism—to each individual interpreting for himself. General Ireton expressed his concern in this way: "[W]hen I hear men speak of laying aside all engagements to [consider only] that wild or vast notion of what in every man's conception is just or unjust, I am afraid and do tremble at the boundless and endless consequences of it." For Ireton, contracts were the bulwark against antinomianism and unconstrained passion: "[T]he necessary thing, that which *necessarily* leads all men into civil agreements or contracts, or to make commonwealths, is the necessity of it for preserving peace. Because otherwise, if there were no such thing, but every man [were] left to his own will, men's contrary wills, lusts, and passions would lead every one to the destruction of another, and [every one] to seek all the ways of fencing himself against the jealousies of another." According to Ireton, the only protection against this interpretive and affective anarchy was to assert the secular authority of convention, including the conventional understanding of justice and of contracts. "But when we talk of just," Ireton asserted, "it is not so much of what is sinful before God," but what is "just according to the foundation of justice between man and man." He then went on to invoke "the great foundation of justice . . . that we should keep covenant one with another."[26] By distinguishing between justice before man and before God, Ireton suggested that the keeping of covenants was not so much a divine law as a moral principle or human institution deriving entirely from human interaction. In striking contrast to classical notions of man as a political animal, Ireton presented the artificiality of government as a guarantee of its effectiveness and legitimacy. With this argument, we have come a long way from Aristotelian and Thomist notions of virtue and of politics.

THE PSYCHOLOGY OF CONTRACT

Even as early modern thinkers emphasized consent to the political contract as the criterion of legitimacy, they worried about the waywardness of the will. Although Ireton saw contract as the antidote to men's "contrary wills, lusts, and passions," others were not so sure. The new fiction of the autonomous political subject, a subject not bound by traditional notions of status or hierarchy, raised the question of what could possibly motivate such an individual to consent to the political contract and to remain bound by it—what would make the political subject both conscientious and dependable. In *De cive* Hobbes depicted a version of this new subject, with a touch of self-irony, as a "mushroom," which "had just emerged from the earth . . . and grown up without any obligation" to others. But, like his contemporaries, Hobbes also worried that it was "not possible for any person to be bound to himselfe; because he that can bind, can release; and therefore he that is bound to himselfe onely, is not bound."[27]

To resolve this problem of motivation, civil war writers turned their attention to the self-regarding passions that were in evidence everywhere around them. For these writers, the passions of self-love and fear of violent death—in short, the desire for self-preservation—were defining characteristics of human nature. This reduction of human nature to its basic passions or drives, and of society to discrete individuals, then set the stage for reconstituting political obligation. Although these passions could be an obstacle to contract, they could also, it was argued, serve as a powerful motive for individual consent. The goal was to turn the problem into a solution: to recast self-love as the spur to self-interest, to join fear of violent death and rational consent, channeling the one and promoting the other. In the process, the most volatile passions were reimagined as some of the most dependable and calculable.

Here we see that, for some midcentury contract theorists, the concern with motivation dictated an interest in materialist accounts of human nature. The seventeenth-century attack on Aristotelian accounts of causation and of ethics had given rise to explanations of human motivation primarily or initially in terms of passion and action rather than virtue and vice. In the work of Hobbes, Milton, Spinoza, and even Descartes, we can see how, for a brief historical moment, it seemed possible to explain the virtues by—or reduce the virtues to—a materialist discourse of the body or a material calculus of the passions and interests.[28] This new materialism was seen to be more responsive to the scientific discoveries of the seventeenth century. At the same time, it seemed to offer new political resources to those attempting to reforge the bonds of obligation on a more secure foundation than that of violently contested religious beliefs or the abstract injunctions of the moral law.

Of course, the appeal to the passions raised as many problems as it solved. Some civil war writers wondered whether the individual would rationally consent to the good or irrationally enslave himself to his passions. Others worried that passion and interest, self-aggrandizement and self-preservation, would of necessity supplant moral virtue as the motive and purpose of political association. In *De cive* Hobbes observed that individuals "give their consent out of hatred, fear, hope, love or any other passion rather than reason."[29] In *The Doctrine and Discipline of Divorce* Milton argued that passion was the source of genuine consent, so that its absence was grounds for breach of contract. For Hobbes, the regicide advocated by Milton in *The Tenure* was one of the symptoms of the passionate misconstruction of contract. For Milton, the absolute subjection to the sovereign advocated by Hobbes in *Leviathan* was another.

In the evolving vocabulary of the period, a passion that was dependable came to be called an interest.[30] But, in time, interest too came to be seen as volatile. In the chaos of civil war, many believed that the interests that served as a motive for contract would also generate casuistry, lying, and deception. In *The Tenure of Kings and Magistrates* Milton worried that the Presbyterians' perception of their self-interest would lead them casuistically to evade moral responsibility for the regicide of Charles I. During the Engagement controversy, when Parliament sought to secure allegiance to the new, de facto government, contemporaries feared that the appeal to self-interest would lead to the pretense of consent. In *Leviathan*, Hobbes worried about "the fool" who says in his heart there is no God and that to "not keep Covenants, was not against Reason, when it conduced to ones Benefit" (15.101). Marchamont Nedham, notorious in his own time for switching from the royalist to the parliamentary side (and then back again), complained in the parliamentary news sheet, *Mercurius Politicus*, of the royalists' "violation of Faith, Principles, Promises and Ingagements, upon every turn of time and advantage."[31] For Nedham and others, interest was a powerful motive but an unreliable one. It was just as likely to lead to breach of contract as to keeping one's contracts. It could just as well foster the pretense of agreement as genuine consent.

In these seventeenth-century reflections on the voluntarist and affective dilemmas of contract theory, the lover and slave, the tyrant and regicide, the fool and the liar emerge as some of the central, if wayward, protagonists of the new theory of political obligation. While the first four of our cast of characters call attention to the violence of the passions, the last two show how the artifice of contract in its primary seventeenth-century sense of construction or workmanship begins to shade into artifice in its secondary sense of guile or trickery. These protagonists dramatize what we might call the underworld of contract. At the same time, they illustrate the dialectic between the recourse to the new materialist psychology and the realm of fabrication, including linguistic fabrication.

Scholars of the seventeenth century have neglected the place of artifice and the passions—and their relationship—in seventeenth-century debates about political obligation. There is no sustained account of the emergence of contract theory in these terms. Although a few scholars have analyzed the antinomies of contract theory, very little attention has been devoted to seventeenth-century writers' active rhetorical fashioning of the new psychological and linguistic subject of contract.[32] Almost none has been paid to the narratives and poetry in which seventeenth-century men and women imagined and commented upon the dilemmas of this new contracting subject.

In the following chapters I show that seventeenth-century writers of both literary and political texts were explicitly concerned with artifice and the passions, matter and making, as the two poles of any effort to re-conceive the grounds of political obligation. Skepticism about the persua-siveness of an older normative discourse of virtue led at one and the same time to a new, naturalistic anthropology of the passions, and to the preoc-cupation with the possibility of reconstructing society from the ground up, on the basis of consent. Rather than being the unwitting victims of logical incoherence, these writers were preoccupied with the tensions be-tween matter and method. They wondered what it meant to make or construct the matter of obligation, to what extent materialism could be the basis of morality, which passions could authorize or legitimate politi-cal obligation, and what the role of language and artifice was in forging new social and political bonds. The embodied subject of passion and in-terest on the one hand and the artificial construction of obligation on the other were two sides of the same coin.

POETICS AND THE CONTRACT OF GENRE

Early modern contract theory was distinguished from its predecessors by its emphasis on the power of the political contract to bring new obliga-tions into existence. This emphasis on the constitutive power of contract, I argue, makes the new politics part of the history of poetics. In particular, in the seventeenth century the poet as maker was regularly invoked as an analogue for the political agent, and government was imagined as the product of a contractualist poetics, of mimesis construed not simply as imitation but also as the productive capacity of the human imagination to create new artifacts.[33] What this meant in practical terms was that, from thinking of politics as a prudential activity, an activity very often linked to a normative conception of virtue, many seventeenth-century men and women came to think of politics as a realm of poetics, even fabrication. The fiction of the political contract was the single most important example of this new way of thinking about politics in the early modern period.[34]

The best seventeenth-century illustration of this is the introduction to *Leviathan*, where Hobbes compares the creation of the state to God's creation of the world. "For by Art is created that great *Leviathan* called a *Common-Wealth*, or *State* . . . which is but an Artificiall Man." In particular, "the *Pacts* and *Covenants*, by which the parts of this Body Politique were at first made, set together, and united, resemble that *Fiat*, or *Let us make man*, pronounced by God in the Creation." Of course, Renaissance writers were used to comparing the creative powers of man to God's, the role of the artist to that of the divine creator.[35] But it was much less common to think of government as being created by a specifically human fiat or speech act, one modeled on the divine act of creation.

In the modern period, we are familiar with a wide range of arguments equating the transition to modernity with a linguistic turn.[36] In *Les mots et les choses* and elsewhere, Foucault argued that the modern episteme, which he dated to the eighteenth century, was defined by the priority of representation to the objects represented and that the modern subject was itself a product of this discursive regime. In *Sources of the Self*, Charles Taylor also equated modernity with "the new centrality of constructed orders and artifacts in mental and moral life," and a new understanding of language as constructing not only the object of knowledge but also the subject who knows.[37] In a similar vein, historians of science have located a "maker's knowledge" tradition in the seventeenth century: influenced by medieval nominalism and voluntarism, seventeenth-century writers argued that individuals can have knowledge of the external world because they construct that world themselves. For these early modern thinkers, "truth lies only in propositions, and to be true is the same as to be constructible." The signs by which individuals represent their knowledge may derive from nature, but "inasmuch as they are part of our language, they are always arbitrary, disregarding their own origin."[38]

Although the new science provided one model for the construction of the commonwealth, I believe that the humanist tradition of poetics taught to every Renaissance schoolboy offered a more widely diffused and more influential account of the human capacity to create new artifacts. Moreover, this tradition encompassed not only literary but also legal and political activity and so helps to explain the perceived analogies between these activities in the early modern period. This is because Renaissance poetics was fundamentally shaped by the rhetorical tradition stemming from Aristotle, Cicero, and Quintilian. For these classical writers, rhetoric or persuasive argument was primarily a practical skill needed by politicians and lawyers, one that drew on the resources of the poet. When Cicero and Quintilian instructed the classical rhetorician in the practical use of the tropes and figures, they also educated early modern writers about the political uses of poetry. Even in antiquity, however, the commerce between poetry and rhetoric flowed in the opposite direction as well: in the *Poetics* Aristotle specifically discussed those rhetorical techniques of argumentation that would help the poet produce the illusion of verisimilitude. In addition, both the poet and orator were concerned to solicit the passions and interests, and move the will. Renaissance schoolboys first learned about the political uses of "the passions and the interests" not from political theory—as Albert Hirschman's influential account would have it—but from Aristotle's *Rhetoric*, Cicero's *De oratore* and *De officiis*, and Quintilian's *Institutio oratoria*.

In the minds of early modern writers, it was the shared task of the poet, the forensic orator, and the political orator to create plausible fictions that would engage the listener or spectator in an activity of probable reasoning that would in turn result in an equitable judgment. These fictions could involve rhetorical syllogisms, which drew their force from common opinions rather than the logical sequence of events.[39] Both for the poet and the orator, the notion of the plausible or probable was, by definition, socially constructed. The illusion of mimesis or verisimilitude was inextricable from social conventions of truth, from an implicit social contract. In a similar fashion, early modern writers and readers recognized genre as a kind of social contract, a set of shared assumptions to which each party consented.[40]

In the early modern period, the inflection of poetics by rhetoric and social convention could be construed negatively or positively. In the negative view, rhetoric insinuates the ever present possibility of deception and coercion, force and fraud. The elements of the rhetorical syllogism that are extrinsic to the logic of a plot hint at the arbitrariness of the final resolution.[41] The moment of "recognition," which Aristotle required of tragedy and which later critics extended to other genres as well, could result not from the cause-and-effect sequence of the plot but from paralogism or faulty reasoning. The resolution of the plot could depend on what Aristotle in the *Rhetoric* called atechnical or inartistic proofs: vows, oaths, contracts, and marks such as Odysseus's scar in the famous recognition scene in the *Odyssey*.[42] In this negative view, the conventions of mimesis would be a vehicle of coercion or social control.

In the positive view, the rhetorical syllogism pushes plot and argument "away from the certitudes of a teleological metaphysics towards an emphasis on the more contingent constraints of social context, within which the artist has to 'persuade' an audience in large measure by the cultural frames of meaning to hand."[43] Here, narrative as social knowledge affirms and maintains the collective identity of author and reader.[44] Whether the social contract of mimesis is construed negatively or positively, the idea that readers enter voluntarily into such a contract from some prior, undetermined state is a heuristic fiction, but in the first case the fiction of contract masks the coercive or disciplinary function of culture, while in the second case this contract is the condition not only of subjectivity but of genuine agency and community.

Early seventeenth-century writers and readers were aware that particular genres could be construed as beneficial social contracts or coercive ideological fictions. They were acutely aware of the role that genres played in the "criticism and compliment" of the Stuart court. They understood the struggle over the cultural meanings of epic, romance, and tragedy as part of the ongoing political struggle.[45] Charles and Henrietta Maria had appropriated the conventions of romance in support of Stuart ideology; in response, Milton famously redefined the Stuart romance as an ideological fiction in *Eikonoklastes* (1650) when he accused Charles of stealing a prayer from Philip Sidney's prose romance, the *Arcadia*. Defenders of the king portrayed the regicide as a tragedy. In *The Tenure of Kings and Magistrates*, Milton celebrated Senecan tragedy as a model for that same regicide. Royalists such as Davenant and Cowley wrote epics in an effort to reclaim heroism for the Stuart cause, while Hobbes composed a preface to Davenant's *Gondibert* in which the neoclassical criteria of verisimilitude and perspicuity served as the poetic equivalent of the Hobbesian contract—a way of chastening potentially subversive political enthusiasm.[46]

Civil war writers explicitly analogized the reader's consent to the literary contract to an individual's consent to the political contract, and vice versa. There had, of course, been earlier examples of authors' calling attention to the literary contract, but this contract was compared with a legal document rather than with the contract of government. A well-known example is Ben Jonson's Induction to *Bartholomew Fair* (1614), in which the Scrivener speaks of the legal "Articles of Agreement" between the spectators and the author. But in 1642, when Milton referred to his "covenant" with the "knowing reader" in *The Reason of Church Government*, readers would have understood the political overtones of this covenant, not only because of Milton's own discussion of the relationship of church government to political government, but also because of the widespread political and religious use of this metaphor in the preceding decades. And the analogy worked the other way as well. In the Introduction to *Leviathan*, Hobbes made it clear that consent to the political contract depended on consent to a literary contract: a prior agreement about the dangers of romance, the limits of metaphor, and the right construction of analogy. And in chapter 13 of *Leviathan* he invited his readers to consent to a powerful narrative about the state of nature and the origins of government.

Of course, *Leviathan* has not traditionally been read in terms of what it has to say about metaphor and narrative. Hobbes famously claimed to have modeled his construction of the commonwealth on Euclidean mathematics, and most modern commentators have followed his cue. Ernst Bloch's comment on the epistemological assumptions of early modern contract theory is typical: "This is an essential trait of modern bourgeois thought since its inception: It knows only that which has been rationally produced, and it must be able to be reconstructed logically from its elements and foundations. . . . Here mathematics provided the model."[47] Although there is some truth to this claim, it is clear that seventeenth-century writers thought of contract as a metaphor and consent as a speech act. They knew that, in imagining a new, voluntary, and therefore contingent beginning of obligation, they were rewriting traditional accounts of obligation as a story that "could have been otherwise."[48] They understood the metaphor of the political contract as requiring a narrative, even as they differed on the meaning of consent and on the larger story they wished to tell.

In composing their own narratives, Hobbes, Milton, and their contemporaries drew on the existing narratives of covenant and contract in Scripture and classical literature. They did not simply accept these narratives at face value, but instead used them as the raw material of their own accounts of obligation. In the covenants of the Hebrew Bible and the New Testament, early modern readers found a powerful metaphor for the voluntary relation of creature to creator, one that in turn generated a providential narrative of exile and redemption.[49] In classical Roman moral and rhetorical treatises, early modern readers found an alternative account of a social contract that resulted from individuals coming together in a state of nature to set up society. In Roman law they encountered the *lex regia* by which the people had transferred their power to the emperor, a law that had historically been interpreted to support both absolutism and popular sovereignty.[50] All midcentury writers understood that the political struggle between royalists and parliamentarians was in part a struggle over the interpretation of these authoritative texts.

In the ferment of the 1640s, these biblical and classical narratives were appropriated and recast by those seeking to intervene in the crisis of political obligation. Hobbes, who was troubled by the parliamentary use of the language of contract to justify revolution, combined the classical fiction of the state of nature with the covenant of the Hebrew Bible to argue for an irrevocable political contract. Milton, who supported the parliamentary cause, combined the classical narrative of a state of nature with the discourse of covenant theology to authorize the violent breach of the political contract. Together, Hobbes and Milton represented two versions of the heroic moment of contract theory, with its emphasis on the creative fiat and the speech act of consent.

In the aftermath of the civil war, writers such as Margaret Cavendish, Milton, Percy Herbert, Richard Brathwaite, and William Sales turned to romance, tragedy, and epic to provide new narratives about the causes of the civil war and the nature of political allegiance. In these years, royalist writers in particular attempt to respond to the heroic discourse of contract by reemphasizing the natural affective bonds between subject and sovereign. Some of these authors departed from the humanist emphasis on equitable judgment to explore the political uses of the specifically aesthetic pleasures associated with the work of art. If contract theory imagined a subject, motivated by his passions, who consents to bind himself, these works solicited the reader's or spectator's aesthetic passions of pity and fear in an effort to induce consent to a new social and political contract. In these responses to contract theory, we begin to see the lineaments of the eighteenth-century discourse of aesthetics.

THE USUAL STORY

The multifaceted story of contract I wish to tell differs from the usual accounts of political historians and the preoccupations of literary scholars. In particular, it challenges the division of labor between political theory and literary criticism, Hobbes and Milton, that other scholars have taken for granted. In the story I have to tell, Hobbes is as preoccupied with literary questions as Milton is with politics; and contract theory is not an abstract, legalistic discourse but is instead at the center of a cultural debate about the contingency of obligation, the political role of the imagination, and the motivating power of the passions. Modern critics, who approach the seventeenth century through anachronistic spectacles, miss the richness and complexity of debates about obligation in the mid-seventeenth century.

Many historians and political philosophers look to the seventeenth century as the formative period of liberalism, with its ideals of autonomy, equality, and individual freedom. In the usual story, these are the characteristics of the Hobbesian or Lockean individual in the state of nature, who then consents to the establishment of government and, by consenting, confers legitimacy. One needn't accept Macpherson's argument about the economic origins of Lockean "possessive individualism" to buy into this picture of seventeenth-century contract theory. The important point is that, in assuming that contract theory is already liberal, modern critics miss the struggle over its meaning. Instead, they anachronistically read the triumph of the secular, protoliberal, linguistically and phenome-nologically thin subject of modern contract theory back into the seven-teenth-century debates about political obligation. They attribute to mid-seventeenth-century writers such modern ideas as the formal equality of the contracting parties, the incompatibility of coercion and consent, and the equation of contract with a kind of procedural or instrumental ratio-nality. Finally, they impose upon these debates the disciplinary division between politics and literature that is in part the product of these debates. In other words, both historians and political philosophers take for granted an outcome that needs to be explained.[51]

There is, of course, an alternative interpretation of early modern political thought that stresses the republican tradition of virtue, citizenship, and public participation, rather than natural rights and individual consent. This is the interpretation advanced most famously by J.G.A. Pocock, who traced its genealogy to Italian civic humanism and to Machiavelli. Pocock's seven-teenth-century English heroes are accordingly the republican theorists James Harrington and Algernon Sidney. As Isaac Kramnick remarked of Pocock's republican revisionist reading of the seventeenth and eighteenth centuries, "Locke and possessive individualism in this scheme . . . obvi-ously had to go." But Hobbes and the English revolution had to go as well. This is because in *The Machiavellian Moment* Pocock reads Hobbes primarily as a politically conservative thinker. He fails to mention that Hobbes's discourse of natural rights and contract was equally available for revolutionary uses, which is one of the reasons Hobbes provoked so much anxiety in the seventeenth century. Such a thematic reading of Hobbes can't explain why both contemporary and modern readers have seen Hobbes as inaugurating a revolution in early modern political thought.[52]

Recently, historians of political thought have begun to complicate this traditional dichotomy of liberalism and republicanism. Joyce Appleby, Isaac Kramnick, Quentin Skinner, Alan Houston, and Jonathan Scott, among others, have pointed to the inextricability of questions of right and virtue for early modern thinkers.[53] These scholars have reminded us that a single writer in the seventeenth century could use the language of rights and virtue, interest and morality, contract and republicanism. At times, these terms appear in tandem without any hint of contradiction. At other times, they are used separately and strategically with a more acute aware-ness of the different traditions out of which they emerge. These are helpful cautions, but they do not begin to address the full range of complex issues encompassed by early modern contract theory. The struggle, in the early modern period, was not between liberalism and republicanism, not least of all because liberalism did not yet exist. If we want to rethink the con-tested origins of liberalism, we need to revisit the struggle over the new language of contract.

Although I criticize the anachronistic projection of the thin modern subject of liberalism back into seventeenth-century debates, my point is not that seventeenth-century contract theory is irrelevant to the later history of liberalism. To the contrary, the book argues for what we might call a reverse anachronism, that is, a genuine dialogue between the early modern and modern periods. I believe that recovering the seventeenth-century contest over the new language of rights and individual consent, including the kinds of questions and anxieties that it provoked, can shed light on some of the limits and deficiencies of modern liberal thought. It can also illuminate the contribution of early modern poetics to modern political thought, including above all the antifoundationalist view that contract can bring into existence new obligations that had no prior existence. The specific advantages of focusing on the discourse of "contract"—rather than liberalism or republicanism—are twofold. First, unlike liberalism, which only emerged as a political label in the nineteenth century, the language of contract was widespread in the seventeenth century. Second, attending to the shifting uses of this word in seventeenth-century texts keeps us from prejudging its meaning in liberal or republican terms. Contract was at the intersection of a wide variety of existing discourses, including natural law theory, covenant theology, the common law, economic exchange, genre, and gender relations.[54] One of the things that will become clear in the following chapters is that contract emerged as a central term in the struggle over political legitimation and obligation in the 1640s precisely because it could be inflected in a variety of ways.

In contrast to historians of political thought, literary historians have shown little or no interest in the seventeenth-century discourse of the political contract.[55] Despite the political turn of much recent literary scholarship on this period and the widespread interest in the emergence of something like a public sphere, the focus has tended to be on republicanism or radical religious thought rather than on contract theory or liberalism. An important recent exception is Annabel Patterson's *Early Modern Liberalism*, an exemplary account of the contribution of both literary and political texts to the creation of "liberal" rights. But, perhaps as part of her effort to present a less abstract and legalistic account of liberalism, Patterson does not even mention contract in her index. The literary works of Milton and the literary dimension of Locke figure prominently, but Hobbes has no significant role to play.[56] I think Patterson is wrong to dismiss Hobbes's contribution to liberalism. But, however one sees Hobbes in relation to the liberal tradition, neglecting Hobbes means neglecting the fears provoked by the new language of rights in the seventeenth century. As a result, Patterson's analysis misses a crucial part of the psychology or affective dimension that was so central to early modern debates about obligation.

Literary scholars interested in the psychology of the new political subject have also tended to focus on Milton to the exclusion of Hobbes. In *The Imaginary Puritan*, Nancy Armstrong and Leonard Tennenhouse argued that the literature of the English civil war—in particular Milton's *Paradise Lost*—was crucial to the emergence of a new conception of personal life and intellectual labor.[57] According to this conception, the new protoliberal subject was produced in writing before he appeared in reality; more important, he was defined by the activity of writing rather than by aristocratic status or real property. I think Armstrong and Tennenhouse are correct about the centrality of writing to the modern conception of the subject. But, while claiming to expose the fault line between the early modern and modern periods, Armstrong and Tennenhouse conceal the very real struggle over the nature of the new political subject by marginalizing Hobbes. They do so by claiming that Hobbes is affiliated "with a cultural moment that was passing away rather than with one that was emerging" and that Hobbes "lacks a semiotic . . . that would account for the production of interior (personal) and exterior (political) discursive worlds." As we will see, not only did Hobbes not lack a semiotic; his semiotic account of personal and political worlds decisively shaped every genre of prose narrative and political theory in the decades and arguably centuries that followed. In contrast to Armstrong and Tennenhouse, who take the postlapsarian domestic life of *Paradise Lost* as the model of bourgeois subjectivity, I argue that the production of the new bourgeois subject cannot be explained without also attending to Hobbes.

Here I should mention an older tradition of scholarship that noted both the constructive dimension of contract theory and the contribution of Hobbes to the psychology of the new political subject.[58] But, in sharp contrast to the argument presented here, this tradition emphasized the losses entailed by contract theory. In *The Political Philosophy of Hobbes*, Leo Strauss stressed Hobbes's concern with the construction of the commonwealth, and he linked Hobbes's voluntarist account of political obligation to his "study of the passions." According to Strauss, in taking the passions as his point of departure and in advancing a voluntarist conception of the good—according to which the good is subjectively determined by human desires, volition, and agreement—Hobbes broke with the rationalism of classical political philosophy. He thus anticipated the modern loss of confidence in reason that one finds in Rousseau's general will and the noncognitive judgment of taste in eighteenth-century aesthetics. As Strauss remarked, "It is thus not a matter of chance, that *la volonté générale* and aesthetics were launched at approximately the same time."[59] The crucial point for Strauss was that Hobbes's voluntarist, relativist, and proto-aesthetic notion of the good contributed to the death of the classical notion of politics.

A similar argument was elaborated from a different political perspective but with equally grim conclusions by Hannah Arendt and Jürgen Habermas, both of whom stressed the loss entailed in the new emphasis on construction. In *The Human Condition* Arendt argued that the early modern preoccupation with constructing the commonwealth was a consequence of skepticism. Human beings despaired of attaining objective knowledge of the external world and so retreated to a world of man-made objects. The paradigm of fabrication was then extended to action. Doing was subordinated to making, and politics was eclipsed by a new emphasis on "society," the realm of work and homo faber.[60] In *Theory and Practice*, Habermas seconded Arendt's account of the demise of the classical conception of politics in the early modern period. Once the Reformation led to "a positivization and formalization of the prevailing Thomistic natural law," morality was separated from legality. An outgrowth of this new legal positivism, contract theory was the political vehicle of the "commerce of bourgeois private individuals."[61] Contract theory thus contributed to the rise of an instrumental conception of reason, whose counterpart was the discipline of aesthetics, construed not only as the study of human artifacts but also of the affective response to such artifacts. As such, contract signaled a "loss of [the] hermeneutic power" that had once been associated with classical notions of rationality and political agency.[62]

Strauss, Arendt, and Habermas are right to think that the early modern notion of contract breaks with classical notions of rationality by virtue of its emphasis on construction, and that, in doing so, it anticipates certain features of the eighteenth-century discourse of aesthetics. But, against their narratives of decline, I argue that seventeenth-century debates about political obligation are defined not by a loss of hermeneutic power but by its intensification. Early modern writers may no longer conceive of politics in classical terms, but they also do not yet subscribe to the division between political science and aesthetics, instrumental reason and sensibility, that Strauss and others locate in the eighteenth century. Nor are they as backward-looking as some of their modern commentators. From J.G.A. Pocock's complaint about contract theory's incoherent account of character and motivation to Arendt's celebration of the ancient Greek polis, accounts of early modern contract theory are afflicted by a nostalgia for Aristotelian, medieval, or republican virtue.[63] And yet, what is most impressive about seventeenth-century debates are the innovative attempts to rethink obligation in the absence of such shared Aristotelian assumptions. The early modern derivation of political obligation from the social contract is, in this sense, always "after virtue," if by virtue we understand the ethical and teleological assumptions informing the *Summa theologica*.[64] It is also, crucially, after the Reformation and the flowering of Renaissance humanism, both of which redirected the attention of early modern thinkers to the power of language to solicit the passions and transform the will. This book is not a story of decline, nor is it the Whiggish story of the triumphal emergence of the liberal subject. Rather, it is a story about the contest over the ownership of the new language of contract, as well as the contribution of poetics to the rethinking of political obligation in antifoundationalist terms.

The Road Ahead

Part I of the book explores the building blocks of mid-seventeenth-century contract theory, focusing in particular on the early seventeenth-century discourses of natural rights, covenant theology, and the common law. Hugo Grotius represents the new discourse of natural rights, while William Perkins serves as a representative spokesman for covenant theology. Chapter 2 analyzes the attention to artifice, particularly linguistic convention, that is characteristic of these discourses, while chapter 3 turns to the interest in the passions and the dilemma of voluntary servitude that accompany early modern attempts to liberate the individual will from the constraints of nature, social hierarchy, and custom.

Part II presents a poetics of contract, beginning with the civil war and ending with the publication of the second edition of *Paradise Lost* in 1674. Chapters 4 through 6 present a series of case studies of the discourse of contract in the making. With the emergence of a public sphere in the decades leading up to the civil war, and particularly with the explosion of publication in the 1640s, contemporary writers elaborated their political views in newsbooks, fast sermons, pamphlets, and published speeches. These works were governed by their own formal conventions and deserve close analysis just as do the literary works of the period. In these texts, we see how the assumptions of natural rights theorists, covenant theologians, and common lawyers are reorganized and radicalized in the context of specific legal and political disputes. We also see that midcentury political writers were as aware of the poetic, rhetorical, and linguistic dimension of their arguments as poets were of the politics of genre.

Chapter 4 analyzes the state trials and parliamentary debates leading up to the English civil war and then examines civil war pamphlets debating the right of the subject to take up arms against the sovereign. The central figure here is Henry Parker, the most important parliamentary pamphleteer, propagandist, and contract theorist of the 1640s. Chapters 5 and 6 present the animating antithesis of the book as a whole: the contrasting views of Hobbes and Milton. Chapter 5 explores the link between prophecy, metaphor, and contract in Milton's justification of regicide in *The Tenure of Kings and Magistrates*. Chapter 6 takes up Hobbes's interpretation of the political contract, an interpretation that depends on enforcing an antithetical regime of metaphor, mimesis, and the passions in defense of absolute sovereignty. Hobbes then serves as a linchpin between the political texts explored in chapters 4 through 6, and the literary works of chapters 7 through 10. In *Leviathan* we begin to see that the discourse of contract is designed to solve what we might call the problem of romance. In the Renaissance, romance plots involved broken vows, as well as wayward passions and interests. Renaissance literary critics also identified the genre of romance with improbability, feigning, and what Aristotle called paralogism. Romance so conceived was the dark side of contract, a place of ostentatious fictions and violent stratagems, shifty characters and unreliable witnesses. But romance also provided new affective resources, new motives for entering into a contract, for those aiming to counteract the Hobbesian emphasis on fear.

Chapters 7 through 10 explore the ways in which literary authors of the period intervene in the crisis of political obligation precipitated by the civil war. Chapter 7 reads Margaret Cavendish's prose romances as a response to the engagement controversy and to Hobbes's analysis of political obligation in *Leviathan*. In these romances, Cavendish exposes the sexual contract at the basis of the marriage contract and political contract. Chapter 8 analyzes Milton's very different politics of the marriage contract and theological covenant in *The Doctrine and Discipline of Divorce* and in *Paradise Lost*. Chapter 9 presents the voluminous royalist prose romances of the 1650s as a response to the Hobbesian critique of the passions and an attempt to make the aesthetic passions of pity and fear the ground of the Restoration. Finally chapter 10 reads *Samson Agonistes* as a critique of the royalist aestheticizing of politics—an aesthetics of reconciliation—in favor of a revolutionary view of the literary contract, as well as the political contract and the theological covenant. All of the writers explored in these chapters engage contemporary arguments for the countervailing force of the passions, the use of one passion—or interest—to counteract the harmful political effects of another. But in contrast to modern accounts of these arguments, which stress the political or economic origins of the argument from interest, seventeenth-century writers were attuned to the role of mimesis and aesthetic interest in educating the reader's political interest. While one aim of chapters 4 through 6 is to show that early modern reflection on political obligation was inseparable from a heightened consciousness of the shaping power of metaphor, chapters 7 through 10 demonstrate that the aesthetic interest in literary representation was a crucial part of early modern debate about political interest.

It is generally agreed among historians and literary scholars that the political crisis of the English civil war precipitated a crisis in literary genre. Blair Worden comments: "On the one side of the civil wars lie metaphysical and Cavalier poetry, the alliance of thought and the imagination, the apparent harmony of power and 'antient Rights.' On the other side lie the reaction of reason against inspiration, the heroic couplet, the utilitarian prose of the Royal Society, Hobbesian politics." In a similar vein, Steven Zwicker has characterized the Restoration as a response to the linguistic absolutism and visionary frenzy of the puritan revolutionaries. According to Zwicker, the antidote to revolution was the recognition that there was "no divine and hence fixed relationship . . . between words and things" and that political differences could be papered over with linguistic fictions, even deceit. For both Worden and Zwicker, this preoccupation with the social uses of deceit is apparent in the Restoration revision of genre: "in comedy that seems to prize deception in new and exalted ways; in epic whose most characteristic expression is in travesty and translation; in the dominance of satire whose social role is revolution."[65]

Although the literature of the postwar years certainly differs in its preoccupations from that of the prewar decades, this standard account needs to be refined. The notion that there is no fixed relationship between words and things is available much earlier in the century and is, in fact, at the heart of the contractual theory of the state. At the same time, contemporaries recognized that the radically nominalist view of the relation of language to things could produce a new absolutism of its own. Whereas Zwicker believes Restoration writers attributed linguistic absolutism to the puritan revolutionaries, some seventeenth-century readers seem to have felt such absolutism was much more characteristic of Hobbes. Moreover, although Milton may have been demonized as an enthusiast by some of his Restoration readers, his own literary efforts in this period suggest that he was far more interested in promoting a republican contractualist poetics, one that could compete with the absolutist version advanced by Hobbes.

In chapters 7 through 10, I read the literature of the postwar decades less as a rejection of puritan enthusiasm than as a response to the new contractualism. In the account offered here, the midcentury discourse of contract gave rise to fears of lying and deception; but it also promoted a reevaluation of the passions. It encouraged a concern with the social and linguistic uses of probability, at the same time that it contributed to the elevation of sentiment. The literary works of the 1650s and 1660s tell the story of the civil war breach of contract, but they also dramatize the necessity of a new affective basis of government. Contract theory helped to unmoor seventeenth-century individuals from the constraints of custom, but it also instructed them in the use of artifice to solicit what Hume called "the common and natural course of our passions."[66]

Many years ago, Ernest Barker wrote that the social contract was "a way of expressing two fundamental ideas or values to which the human mind will always cling—the value of Liberty, or the idea that will, not force, is the basis of government, and the value of Justice, or the idea that right, not might, is the basis of all political society and every system of political order." Barker also noted that "even if there had never been a contract, men actually behaved 'as if' there had been such a thing" and, in so doing, made the fiction of contract the ground of a new social and political reality.[67] Early modern contract continues to fascinate us, I suggest, not only because it raises fundamental questions about the relation of freedom and justice but perhaps even more because it lies at the threshold of a purely human construction of obligation. Seventeenth-century men and women were just beginning to struggle with the question of the source of obligation in the absence (or illegibility) of any transcendental guarantees of morality. This is our question, we have inherited it from them, and we can still learn from the texts in which they chose to represent their hopes and fears.

PART ONE

An Anatomy of Contract, 1590–1640

CHAPTER 2

Language and the Bond of Conscience

> Syllables govern the world. . . . [*All Power is of God*] means
> no more than *Fides est servanda*. When St. *Paul* said this,
> the people had made *Nero* Emperour. They agree, he to
> command, they to obey.

> If our Fathers have lost their Liberty, why may not we labour
> to regain it? *Answ.* We must look to the Contract, if that be
> rightly made we must stand to it. If we once grant we may
> recede from Contracts upon any inconveniency that may af-
> terwards happen, we shall have no Bargain kept. . . . Keep your
> Contracts, so far a Divine goes, but how to make our Con-
> tracts is left to our selves. I tell you what my Glove is, a plain
> Glove, and pretend no virtue in it, the Glove is my own, I
> profess not to sell Gloves, and we agree for an hundred pounds.
> I do not know why I may not with a safe Conscience take it.
> The want of that common Obvious Distinction of *Jus praecep-
> tivum*, and *Jus permissivum*, does much trouble men.
> —John Selden, *Table Talk*

IN THE EPIGRAPHS to this chapter, Selden muses on the language of political obligation. *Fides est servanda* was a tag familiar from classical rhetoric, Roman law, the church fathers and canon law, and articulated the
principle that we have a moral obligation to keep our promises, an obligation that seventeenth-century jurist and antiquarian John Selden elsewhere traced to a divine command. *Fides est servanda* meant that one's
bare promise or word was binding, even in the absence of any written
documentation or tangible proof of exchange; the technical term in civil
and canon law was *nudum pactum.*[1] But Selden, who was a preeminent
scholar of the common law and always kept in mind the practical reali-
ties of human interaction, was less interested in bare promises than in
how a moral obligation becomes a legal one. Thus he insisted that contracts needed to be *made* correctly, according to convention and positive
law. God tells us to keep our promises but "how to make our contracts
is left to ourselves."

This concern with convention inflects Selden's question about the political contract. Characteristically, Selden answers his own question about regaining political liberty with a discussion of economic contracts and the necessity of keeping one's bargain. This move is authorized by the theological distinction, familiar from Suárez, Grotius, and others, between divine precept and permission. Although God commands us to keep our promises, he permits human discretion about the manner in which we promise and thus the definition of binding promises. So if we want to understand whether a contract is binding, it is not enough to look to the *nudum pactum* principle of *fides est servanda*; we must look instead to the particular contract, to see if "that be rightly made." If God is the remote cause of binding contracts, by virtue of his power to punish, convention is the proximate cause, not least of all the conventions of legal language. In this case, it is not conscience that authorizes the bargain; rather, conscience is freed from any reservations about shady deals by the fact that the seller has acted according to the conventions of exchange and has, moreover, "pretend[ed] no virtue" in the glove he wishes to sell.[2]

Selden immediately makes it clear that the principle that we must keep our promises does not mean that we cannot change our minds. Contracts by definition concern changeable human experience, contingent negotiations, not universal laws: "This is the Epitome of all the Contracts of the World, betwixt man and man, betwixt Prince and Subject, they keep them as long as they like, and no longer."[3] In the charged political climate of the early seventeenth century, "keep them as long as they like, and no longer" might suggest that Selden thought of contracts in revolutionary terms. But, although Selden was an outspoken defender of parliamentary liberties in the 1620s and a critic of Charles during the Long Parliament, he insisted on the binding power of public and private contracts alike. "Every law," he remarked, "is a Contract between the King and the People, *and therefore to be kept.* An hundred men may owe me an hundred pounds, as well as any one man, and shall they not pay me because they are stronger than I? *Object.* Oh but they lose all if they keep that Law. *Answ.* Let them look to the making of their Bargain."[4] Contracts for Selden were not merely expedient human arrangements to be broken when they no longer served private interest. Rather, contracts stood between men and brute force, between the individual and the hundred stronger men; they stood as well between society and the potentially subversive force of enthusiasm, the individual unrestrained by social agreements but empowered by his assurance of a heavenly contract. For Selden, this possibility was represented by the Anabaptist, of whom Selden asked rhetorically, "If we once come to leave that out-loose, as to pretend Conscience against Law, who knows what inconvenience may follow?"[5]

This chapter explores the discourses that Selden and his contemporaries drew on in elaborating their arguments about the new contracting subject: a continental and chiefly Protestant discourse of natural rights, a native tradition of covenant theology, and a heightened consciousness of the common law as a bulwark against the royal prerogative and a repository of ancient liberties. Each of these discourses came into its own in the early decades of the seventeenth century and each developed its own view of the relationship of the individual conscience to social and linguistic convention. To the construction of the contracting subject, natural rights discourse contributed both a minimalistic account of obligation and a Ciceronian narrative about the power of language to bring into existence new rights and obligations. The common law elaborated a legal fiction of the contracting subject that illustrated a new confidence in the adequacy of human agreements to secure or constrain intention. Covenant theology contributed the enabling fiction of the heavenly contract, a biblical narrative of the role of the covenant in history, and a theologically charged interpretive activism. Each of these discourses meant something different by "contract," and each provided a different account of the subject who consents to a contract. In the decades leading up to the civil war, however, these discourses fed on and borrowed from each other to produce a heightened sense of the artifice, conventionality, and eventually the arbitrariness of political obligation.

NATURAL RIGHTS THEORY: THE SOCIAL CONTRACT AND THE LINGUISTIC CONTRACT

In the late sixteenth and early seventeenth centuries, a new conception of natural law emerged in response to the legitimation crisis brought about by the Reformation, the consolidation of nation-states, and the outbreak of religious wars. These wars dramatically illustrated the dangers of religious enthusiasm, the potential violence of acting on one's conscience, and the manifold exceptions to the moral law that promises should be kept. All of a sudden it became necessary to rethink the basis of political association, political obligation, and the respective duties to God and sovereign. Aiming to provide a nonconfessional basis of social harmony and political order, continental writers resorted to the time-worn language of natural law and natural rights. But in contrast to older Aristotelian, Stoic, and canon law conceptions of natural law as the moral law or the objective law of reason, they elaborated a minimalist conception of natural law centered on sociability, self-interest, and the subjective right of self-preservation.[6] In the minds of its proponents, this "minima moralia" offered a new, artificial method for generating political association. Whereas older doctrines of natural law were predicated on the belief in a natural moral order dictated by God, these newer doctrines drew nearer to "the developing scientific view of the world as totally neutral with respect to value."[7] God was still the creator of the world, but man was the proximate creator of value by virtue of his voluntary social and political arrangements. Chief among these was the contract to transfer one's rights to the sovereign and to establish government.[8]

In the early seventeenth century, the preeminent treatment of natural law for the new world of nation-states and confessional differences was Hugo Grotius's great treatise of natural law jurisprudence, *De jure belli ac pacis*, first published in 1625. A Dutch humanist scholar who was sympathetic to the Arminians and who had escaped to Paris after the Statholder Prince Maurice threw his weight to the Calvinists, Grotius was responding to the religious wars raging on the continent, wars that were the occasion of intense interest and foreign policy debate in England in the 1620s.[9] In *De jure belli*, Grotius's English readers found the new minimalist theory of natural law, a contractual account of political association, and an analysis of the right of resistance. These arguments were of interest to royalists and republicans alike. We know that Filmer was reading Grotius in the 1630s. Hobbes certainly knew his work; and Milton, impressed by Grotius's learned arguments, sought him out in Paris in 1638. Robert Sidney, the second earl of Leicester (and father of Algernon), also met Grotius in Paris in the 1630s and recorded his thoughts on Grotius's theories in his commonplace book. With the outbreak of civil war in England, Grotius's arguments would become directly relevant to the conflict at home. As Jonathan Scott has remarked, between 1640 and 1670 Grotius was "pre-eminent as a modern European influence upon English political thought."[10] This influence, I suggest, cannot be separated from Grotius's humanist confidence in the power of language to subdue irrational conflict. In *De jure belli*, the social and political contract necessarily involved reflection on what we might call a linguistic contract and on the social construction of rights and obligations.[11]

Cicero is the most important classical source for Grotius's attention to the social and linguistic contract. In his moral and rhetorical works Cicero provided two accounts of the contractual origins of society. In *De inventione*, Cicero painted a picture of men wandering in a state of nature until they were brought together by the powerful eloquence of a single individual.[12] Only then did they establish communities and "give shape to laws, tribunals, and civil rights." In this version of the original social contract, Cicero described asocial individuals voluntarily subjecting themselves to the new social order. By contrast, in *De officiis*, the most influential Latin work of moral philosophy in the early modern period, Cicero advanced a Stoic view of man's natural sociability and natural disposition to form contractual political associations. According to Cicero, nature is the source of the principles of community among men, who are joined together "naturali quadam societate" (1.16.50), "in a certein naturall fellowship," as one sixteenth-century translation has it. *Societas*—the Latin term for a legal partnership—is Cicero's metaphor for this distinctively human community, this willed but natural association.[13]

Cicero also invited his readers to think about language in contractual terms. At times, Cicero presented rhetoric as the handmaiden of natural sociability. At other times, Cicero argued that rhetoric rather than sociability, convention rather than nature, formed the basis of social and political organization. But in both cases, a precondition of justice or what Cicero called the "societas juris" is the bond or "societas" of language.[14] Language is both a precondition of obligation and itself a source of obligation. In *De inventione* Cicero famously celebrated the power of language to create different forms of association: "[M]any cities have been founded, . . . the flames of a multitude of wars have been extinguished, and . . . the strongest alliances and most sacred friendships have been formed not only by the use of reason but also more easily by the help of eloquence" (1.1). And in *De officiis* he described language itself as a common bond or form of association: "[N]ature, likewise by the power of reason, associates man with man in the common bonds of speech and life [orationis et . . . vitae societatem]" (1.4.12).[15] He alternately presented the gift of speech as reflecting human rationality or bringing it into being. The first account was predicated on natural law as the source of right reason, whereas the second implied the conventional establishment of rights and the imposition of political order.

In *De jure belli ac pacis*, Grotius did not simply use the prestige of Ciceronian rhetoric and moral philosophy to make neoscholastic arguments about contractual association more palatable, as has sometimes been argued. Instead, he drew on Cicero to recast earlier arguments about contractual association as powerful secular and rhetorical fictions appropriate to the early modern crisis of foundationalism. Cicero provided Grotius both with a secular narrative of political association and with a conviction that language can itself create the association it presupposes. Grotius, in turn, updated Cicero for the new world of nation-states and confessional differences by presenting natural law as first and foremost a matter of individual rights.

In the prolegomena, Grotius threw down the gauntlet by declaring that natural law was binding on all, regardless of religious belief or even the existence of God: "[W]hat we have been saying [about the existence of a natural law of justice] would have a degree of validity even if we should concede [*etiamsi daremus*] that which cannot be conceded without the utmost wickedness, that there is no God, or that the affairs of men are of no concern to Him."[16] Grotius's "etiamsi daremus" could be described as a hypothetical, strategic, or artificial skepticism, designed to respond to irrational dogmatism and religious wars. As such, it was arguably the grandfather of all such strategic fictions in natural rights discourse, including that of the social contract itself.[17] Following upon this initial hypothesis, Grotius focused on natural rights. Whereas natural law referred to an objective order of duties, natural right referred to subjective faculties and powers—such as the freedom to defend oneself and one's property.[18] Along with natural sociability, Grotius argued, the natural right of self-preservation provided the lowest common denominator for individuals of conflicting religious beliefs and thus a particularly compelling motive for entering into a political contract.[19]

This minimalism in turn focused attention on the human realm of conventional agreements, the realm of the secondary law of nature. Although the principles of primary natural law—including the law that individuals should keep their promises—are by definition unchanging, the precise form they take in individual choices and in the law of nations may vary.[20] In reality, human beings have a great deal of discretion in implementing their own social and political arrangements, and promises and contracts are the vehicles by which they do so.[21] This explains the very large place given in *De jure belli* not to Aristotelian and neoscholastic virtues but to what we might call the social and linguistic mechanisms of obligation, including verbal and written promises, oaths, contracts, vows, treaties, and professions of political allegiance.

For seventeenth-century readers, the centerpiece of *De jure belli* was Grotius's contractualist account of property, society, and government. Like some of his medieval predecessors, Grotius asserted that there was initially no property in the state of nature: all things were held in common. As population increased, people became less trustful and their needs more elaborate. At this point private property or *dominium* was introduced by agreement or contract (*pactum*).[22] But once it was brought into being by human agreement or secondary natural law, humans were morally and legally obliged to respect the property rights of others. Grotius made a similar argument about society: men joined together "to form civil society not by command of God, but of their own free will."[23] They then transferred their rights of self-protection and dominion in exchange for protection, security, and what Hobbes would later call "commodious living."[24] Although conceding that some governments have their origin in conquest or inheritance and others in the will of the people, Grotius described government primarily in Ciceronian terms as a voluntary association: "The state is a complete association [*coetus*] of free men, joined together for the enjoyment of rights and for their common interest."[25] Still later, he insisted that, for those "who unite to form a state" by a "voluntary compact" (*voluntate contractum*) sovereignty cannot be alienated without the people's consent."[26]

Grotius's contractualism leads to the second influential aspect of *De jure belli*, its attention to the right of resistance. As contemporary readers were well aware, Grotius's account of how individuals consent to the political contract in exchange for protection provided grounds for the breach of contract in those exceptional cases where protection was no longer assured. Drawing on Cicero's famous defense of *salus populi* in *De legibus*—"salus populi suprema lex"—Grotius argued that in cases of "extreme and imminent peril" individual resistance to the sovereign was justified. In support, he also cited the example of how the Jews were allowed to break the Sabbath and eat the shewbread in exceptional cases of hunger.[27] This example had already figured prominently in English manuals of casuistry and would become shorthand for *salus populi* or reason of state in English parliamentary treatises on the right of resistance. In books 2 and 3 Grotius argued that war against one's sovereign, breach of the political contract, and obedience to a usurper were all justified for reasons of self-preservation.[28] Grotius tried to constrain the constitutionalist implications of his remarks about promises and contracts by arguing that the proof that one owns something—including the right to resist—is the ability to transfer it irrevocably to someone else. He also tried to bind the conscience of the individual subject by recourse to a kind of social contract of language, represented by custom and usage. But this emphasis on convention inevitably heightened awareness that obligation was constructed rather than natural and thus capable of alteration.

This brings us to Grotius's Ciceronian concern with linguistic convention. The obvious question raised by the notion of a political contract was why do individuals remain bound by it when the sovereign acts contrary to their interests? Why should and do they keep their promises? Like his neoscholastic predecessors, Grotius cited the maxim of divine and natural law that "promises must be kept." In support, he cited the biblical example of Joshua who kept his oath to the Gibeonites, even though it had been obtained by fraud.[29] But Grotius also pointed to speech as evidence of humans' natural reason and sociability—and thus of the natural obligation to keep one's promises.[30] Beginning with the assumption that language is a distinctively human capacity that is essential for the founding of society, Grotius gradually articulated the insight that language itself entails certain obligations. On the basis of this normative view of language, he then argued that a linguistic contract—a contract about the meaning and right use of language—is the precondition of all other contracts.

Like Cicero, Grotius sometimes confidently asserted that man has "an impelling desire for society, for the gratification of which he alone among animals possesses a special instrument, speech [*sermonem*]."[31] He spelled out the implications of this view in his discussion of good faith in book 3. Here Grotius went so far as to criticize Cicero's opinion that promises could be broken in exceptional cases.[32] Although lying might be permitted in wartime, promises have a special status as a sign of our rationality: "From the association of reason and speech arises that binding force of a promise with which we are dealing" (3.19.1.3).[33]

At other times, however, Grotius gave greater emphasis to the indispensable role language played in *eliciting* the capacity for reason and sociability. Here Grotius drew on, among others, Cicero's account of the linguistic origin and preservation of society in *De inventione* where the eloquence of one man was necessary both to transform irrational "wild savages into a kind and gentle folk" and to induce "those who had great physical strength to submit to justice without violence." Moreover, Cicero went on to argue, eloquence also has a role to play in regulating violence. In a passage that could describe Grotius's own ambitions, Cicero tells us that, after "eloquence came into being and advanced to greater development, . . . in the greatest undertakings of peace and war [*in rebus pacis et belli*] it served the highest interests of mankind."[34] In the prolegomena, Grotius proposed a similar role for eloquence with regard to his savage and irrational contemporaries. Here Grotius made it clear that the goal of his ambitious treatise was to subdue irrational force—to subdue war itself—to the constraints of rational discourse.[35]

Although Grotius pointed to speech as evidence of natural reason and sociability—and thus of a natural obligation to keep one's promises— he also argued that a political contract was necessary because a natural disposition to sociability was not enough to ensure peaceful and faithful interaction. In *De jure belli*, reflection on political obligation is always shadowed by the conviction of sin or by its secular equivalent, the recognition that humans are naturally prone to breach of promise. Thus it was a short step from Grotius's observations on the distinctively linguistic nature of human society to the insight that a linguistic contract logically preceded the social or political contract. Because political and other contracts are forged in language, part of what is involved in making a contract is making language itself dependable or calculable. A contract in language is inevitably also a contract about the use of language—one that proscribes deceit, equivocation, and, in most cases, coercion. The possibility of binding signification then becomes the precondition of binding oneself politically, the precondition of the irrevocable transfer of rights.[36]

The centerpiece of Grotius's argument about the relation between right linguistic usage and right government appears in book 2, chapter 16, of *De jure belli*, "On Interpretation." Here we see that Grotius was particularly anxious to establish criteria regarding the "objective" or socially determined meaning of words, criteria that would then serve to constrain the speaking subject. The chapter thus registers Grotius's difference from his scholastic predecessors, who generally felt no such anxiety about the lack of fit between subjective intention and objective meaning. At the same time, it signals his debt to earlier humanist legal scholars who, in their effort to codify the norms of interpretation gave increased attention to the rules for the interpretation of Roman law found in *Digest* 50.16, "de verborum significatione."[37] Even more than his predecessors, however, Grotius was acutely aware of the political implications of the norms of interpretation. In particular, he argued that the meaning of an individual's consent to a contract, including a political contract, was constrained by a prior agreement regarding the use of language. This linguistic contract would be a bulwark against the anarchy of multiple, conflicting interpretations on the one hand and the tyranny of the sovereign as unique interpreter on the other.

Thus, to the fundamental question regarding political obligation, Must we mean what we say? Grotius answered a resounding yes:

> If we consider only the one who has promised, he is under obligation to perform, of his own free will, that to which he wished to bind himself. "In good faith what you meant, not what you said, is to be considered," says Cicero. But because internal acts are not of themselves perceivable, and some degree of certainty must be established, lest there should fail to be any binding obligation, in case every one could free himself by inventing whatever meaning he might wish, natural reason itself demands that the one to whom the promise has been made should have the right to compel the promisor to do what the correct interpretation suggests. For otherwise the matter would have no outcome, a condition in which morals is held to be impossible.[38]

In this passage Grotius both acknowledged and departed from the widespread medieval view that internal acts are perceivable by God and morally binding for that reason.[39] Instead, he imagined a world in which morals are secured in the realm of interpersonal communication. Confronting the ever-present possibility of deception and equivocation, he asserted a public standard of meaning and accountability: words should be understood "according to current usage" (2.16.2: "populari ex usu"). That is, while appealing to the independent authority of natural reason, Grotius also located that authority in common linguistic practice—in the hope that language itself might provide the ethical and interpretive guidelines that are "not of themselves perceivable," and for which there is no more obvious foundation. In light of the arguments we have surveyed, we can now recast Grotius's formulation, "etiamsi daremus": even if we were to imagine that God did not exist, language would still permit the transfer of rights and would still dictate certain rational obligations.[40]

Although Grotius saw himself as elaborating in a systematic fashion the laws of international conflict, it was his voluntarism, contractualism, and concern with problems of interpretation that most impressed his contemporary English readers. One of these readers was Robert Filmer, who recorded his thoughts on *De jure belli* in *The Originall of Government* (1652). Filmer associated Grotius with Hobbes and Milton, whom he also attacked in this work. Despite their very different political orientations, Filmer saw all three as contractualists, and thus as enemies of the patriarchal account of political order. He was particularly agitated by Grotius's account of property, an account that presupposed a dangerous freedom of interpretation. Grotius's two main assumptions—that "the use of things in common was natural" in the state of nature and that "property as it now exists was introduced by human will"—produced "divers dangerous and seditious conclusions." For they amounted to a distinction between the law of nature and subsequent voluntary human arrangements—whether property or government—and according to Filmer this implied that "the moral law depends upon the will of man." As Filmer read Grotius, all forms of government were by consent, which meant that individuals had the right to resist their governors. Filmer was particularly dismayed by Grotius's response to the argument that divine law commands obedience. In *De jure belli* Grotius had argued, in a passage quoted by Filmer,

> If any man shall say that this rigid doctrine of dying rather than resisting any injuries of superiors is no human but a divine law, it is to be noted that men at first, not by any precepts of God, but by their own accord, led by experience of the infirmities of separated families against violence, did meet together in civil society, from whence civil power took beginning. Which therefore St Peter calls an human ordinance, although elsewhere it be called a divine ordinance, because God approveth the wholesome institutions of men. God in approving a human law is to be thought to approve it as human, and in a human manner.[41]

One implication of this genealogy of society was that God permitted the exercise of human volition and discretion, not only in establishing and preserving government but in resisting threats to the commonwealth. (Selden was commenting on the same scriptural passage—1 Peter 2:13—when he asserted in one of the epigraphs to this chapter that "syllables govern the world.") In the next passage cited by Filmer, Grotius explicitly linked this possibility of resistance to equitable interpretation: "The greater the thing is which is to be preserved [e.g., the state as a whole], the greater is the equity which reacheth forth an exception against the words of the law." According to Grotius, "necessity"—which contemporaries equated with reason of state—legitimized the potentially revolutionary, equitable interpretation of the law.[42] It legitimized, that is, resistance to the sovereign.

According to Filmer, such a license to interpret amounted to the destruction of both property and the state because Grotius did not explain "who should be judge of the greatness and certainty of the danger." Moreover, he did not explain where the force of obligation lies. "It must be remembered," Filmer cautioned, "that is not sufficient for men to have a will to bind, but it is necessary also to have a power to bind." "If it were a thing so voluntary and at the pleasure of men when they were free to put themselves under subjection, why may they not as voluntarily leave subjection when they please, and be free again?" According to Filmer, it is not possible for an individual to bind himself; obligation cannot be self-imposed. For, if Grotius's account is right, "then it will be lawful for every man, when he please, to dissolve all government, and destroy all property."[43] Because consent involves interpretation and is revocable, it poses a fundamental threat both to government and to property, to government as the property of the sovereign. As Filmer noted, this fundamental lesson from *De jure belli ac pacis* had been put to contrary but equally dangerous uses by both Hobbes and Milton in the 1640s.

THE COMMON LAW: MAGNA CARTA AND ECONOMIC CONTRACT

The common law proposed its own secular theories of binding the conscience in the late sixteenth and early seventeenth centuries that contributed to the creation of the individualized, denaturalized subject of contract and the focus on human agreements and arrangements. It did so both through a native tradition of constitutionalism and through specific developments in the common law of contract. Constitutionalist arguments were sharpened by specific conflicts between James and his parliaments, while contract law developed in response to the increasing commercialism of English society and the astonishing explosion of legal actions for debt. Moreover, in the minds of some seventeenth-century writers, these two areas converged. The economic theorist Edward Misselden summed up the perceived connection between these two realms of activity when he asked rhetorically: "Is it not lawfull for merchants to seeke their *Privatum Commodum* in the exercise of their calling? Is not gaine the end of trade? Is not the publique involved in the private and the private in the publique? What else makes a commonwealth but the private wealth . . . of the members thereof in the exercise of *Commerce*?' " (204).[44]

In the early seventeenth century, Edward Coke and other common lawyers actively promulgated the theory of the ancient constitution, according to which the institution of parliament, the common law, and the ancient rights and liberties of Englishmen preceded the Norman Conquest or, as it was often called, the Norman Yoke. In so doing, they provided Parliament with a powerful rhetorical weapon for binding the king's conscience or the royal prerogative. Drawing on historical and legal documents, Coke argued that Magna Carta simply ratified these ancient liberties, and the coronation oath sworn by every monarch thereafter testified to the sovereign's willingness to respect the ancient traditions. According to the theory of the ancient constitution, kingship was an office rather than a personal attribute, and Magna Carta was a contract between sovereign and subject, one that declared rather than made the law. The respect for history evident in this recourse to immemorial custom did not preclude an activist political agenda. As Corinne Weston reminds us, the common lawyers in Parliament "were at least as interested in lawmaking as [they were] in the common law viewed as fundamental law."[45] In addition, members of Parliament increasingly began to think of themselves as the legal representatives of the people. The Commons MP Robert Mason spoke for many of his colleagues when he declared in 1626 that "we sit not here as private men but as public [persons] vested for the commonwealth's service." The refusal of the House of Commons to accede to Charles's imperious requests in 1628 and 1640 was in part a consequence of these views.[46]

In the early decades of the seventeenth century, Coke was also codifying the common law in his series of *Reports*. These written records of case law provided new ammunition to those seeking to argue from precedent against the "innovations" of royal absolutism. Against the Roman legal maxim, *Rex est lex loquens*, favored by James and his supporters, Coke argued that only the judges—with their "artificial" or professionally educated reason—could declare the law.[47] In 1628 Coke, who by this time had been dismissed from the bench and the Privy Council but held a seat in Parliament, published his commentary on Littleton's *Tenures*, a legal textbook on land law. As Richard Helgerson has remarked, "in Coke's account tenancy takes a long step towards outright ownership," and ownership of land in turn "becomes the basis for and a type of the liberty of the subject." Not surprisingly, Charles suppressed the next three parts of Coke's *Institutes of the Laws of England*. In 1641, however, in an obvious affront to the king, Parliament arranged for their publication.[48]

In the course of the sixteenth century, developments in the law of economic contract also contributed to the ability to imagine a contracting political subject. Although contract law as we know it came into existence in the nineteenth century, in the late sixteenth century the legal jurisdiction of breach of contract shifted from the ecclesiastical courts to the common law courts. These changes registered a wider cultural crisis of faithfulness in early modern England, a crisis precipitated by a shift from an older economy of obligation, predicated on informal networks of kinship, to one in which economic transactions were, increasingly, between strangers.[49] The common law responded to these changes by arrogating to itself jurisdiction over breach of promise (formerly a matter for the ecclesiastical courts) and by placing greater emphasis on the intention of the contracting parties. Conscience itself thus came under secular jurisdiction and in the process was reconceived—at least for the purposes of legal disputes—in common law terms. As we will see, changes in contract law were not the main source of the rhetoric of political contract but, as political obligation seemed increasingly to involve an agreement among equals—a relationship of association as well as or instead of one of subordination—the economic contract of exchange came increasingly to seem one appropriate way of thinking about the political contract. The common law notion of the economic contract itself underwent a sea change, according to which the trust reposed in an individual on the basis of membership in a small community became less important than the legal analysis of the circumstances of the promise. With this change, economic contract came to speak not only to the equality of the contracting parties but also, increasingly, to the conventional nature of all contractual agreements.

In order to understand these developments, we need to turn first to the most influential early modern English treatise on the common law, St. German's *Doctor and Student* (1530). This dialogue between a canon lawyer and a student of the common law, which became "the standard textbook in legal theory almost until the time of Blackstone," was written during the period of Henry VIII's break with the Catholic Church.[50] St. German, who was sympathetic to the Reformation parliament and to church reform, argued that the common law rather than canon law should have jurisdiction over the consciences of Englishmen. Drawing on Aristotle's authoritative treatment of equity in the *Nicomachean Ethics*, St. German argued for a well-established common law tradition of equitable interpretation.[51] In light of this tradition, he asserted, Chancery was competent to adjudicate those matters of conscience that had previously been the purview of the ecclesiastical courts, in particular cases involving breach of promise or contract.[52] Furthermore, Chancery should have jurisdiction over "parole" contracts, informal verbal contracts without witnesses, of the sort that were increasingly frequent with the explosion of commercial activity during the second half of the sixteenth century.[53] The introduction of an Aristotelian notion of equitable interpretation in England thus went hand in hand with development of the common law of contract, and both of these were tied to the idea that the common law should bind in conscience.

As his editors Plucknett and Barton argue, St. German's definitions were conventional, derived not only from Aristotle but also from Aquinas, Gerson, and medieval manuals of casuistry; but the political uses to which he put them were not. We see this in particular in St. German's double-edged use of equity. In defending a common law tradition of equitable interpretation, St. German aimed not only to legitimate the chancellor's equitable jurisdiction over against that of the ecclesiastical courts but also to constrain the chancellor's jurisdiction vis-à-vis the common law. Thus, the Student asserts that "the lord chancellor must order his conscience after the rules and grounds of the law of the realm."[54] This emphasis on the superiority of the common law to the chancellor's equitable judgment would have far reaching political consequences in the 1620s and 1630s.

St. German's treatment of the mutually enforcing relationship between conscience and the law of the realm was echoed in his treatment of promises and contracts, in particular, contracts regarding the sale or transfer of property. In sixteenth-century English law, legal actions involving debt were separate from those concerning breach of contract. The former were treated in common law, the latter by the ecclesiastical courts. What was legally actionable in breach of contract was not the existence of a debt but the failure to keep one's promise. St. German's Student argues, as part of his secularizing approach to conscience and equity, that breach of contract could also come under the jurisdiction of the common law. In addition, he states that what determines the enforceability of a sworn verbal promise is not mere intention (as at least some canon lawyers thought) but the evidence of some kind of exchange. Against the canon lawyers' defense of the binding nature of the *nudum pactum*, or what the Student calls the "nude contract" (a verbal promise without any token of exchange), the Student argues that no one can have access to a bare intention or promise, "For it is secret in his own conscience whether he intended for to be bound or nay. And of the intent inward in the heart, man's law cannot judge." It is for this reason that a promise needs to be "clothed" in some "recompence." Just as conscience was constrained by common law, so intention was legally bound by some "consideration" or material proof of exchange.[55] St. German thus stands on the cusp of an older common law doctrine of contract (a transaction involving the transfer of property or the creation of debt, but not one in which the notion of mutual promises was central) and a gradually evolving common law conception of contract as a mutual promise with consideration.[56]

St. German's innovations were apparent in other ways as well. For example, he adopted Gerson's distinction between the primary and secondary law of nature or reason and identified the latter with human institutions, but he did so in order to argue that what had been established by human law could also be revoked by human law. St. German offered the standard example of private property, which in turn gives rise to contracts. Such contracts are themselves a human invention and the laws concerning them may be changed by statute. But St. German also applied the argument to the temporal rights of the clergy, which, he argued, could be revoked by an act of Parliament. In both cases, the potential reversibility of decisions based on the secondary law of reason could be used—as they were against the clergy—to potentially revolutionary ends.[57]

Doctor and Student is an important example of the complicated intersection of legal, economic, and political contract in the common law. Motivated by his religious and political allegiances as well as by his profession, St. German proposed a shift of jurisdiction for cases of conscience involving secular affairs, including economic transactions. This solution involved the elaboration of a common law tradition of equitable interpretation that was to have long-term consequences not only for the common law of contract but also for the political disputes of the early seventeenth century. In particular, St. German's treatment of equity was prophetic of the dual reception of equity in the decades leading up to the civil war. If in *Doctor and Student* questions of jurisdiction were bound up with the struggle between state and church, in the years that followed they were increasingly bound up with the struggle between the king and Parliament. On the one hand, equity was associated with the prerogative courts, such as Chancery and the Star Chamber, and thus with royal supremacy; on the other hand, equity was appealed to by parliamentarians and common lawyers in their fight against the abuses of the royal prerogative. In particular, the relevance of St. German's insistence that the chancellor order his conscience by the common law was not lost on critics of Charles I in the 1620s and following.[58]

The common law jurisdiction over breach of contract was codified at the beginning of the seventeenth century by the decision in Slade's Case (1602), the most important early modern case in the historical development of contract law. The facts of the case are simple. In 1595 John Slade sold some wheat and rye to Humphrey Morley, who promised to pay for it at a specified time after receiving the goods. Although the grains were delivered, Morley refused to pay, and Slade brought a common law suit not for the recovery of debt, the usual action given the facts, but for breach of promise. The legal action of debt would have put Slade at a disadvantage since, in the absence of written evidence of a contract, an accusation of debt could be answered by the defendant's "wager of law," that is, by his swearing an oath of compurgation along with eleven or twelve character witnesses that he was innocent. There was no chance Slade would recover his losses under such a system. But if he brought the case as breach of promise, Slade could argue that the circumstances of the case (the delivery of the wheat and rye, and so the existence of debt) amounted to "consideration." That is, they provided good reason to assume that Morley had, implicitly, promised to pay for the goods received.[59]

The lower court found for Slade but referred the question of whether debt could be treated as breach of promise to a higher court. Sir Francis Bacon argued for Morley and Edward Coke represented Slade. The court found that breach of promise was a legitimate action since any verbal (parole) contract with consideration presupposed the intention or promise to perform what one had contracted to perform. As Coke wrote in his summary of Chief Justice Popham's decision, "every contract executory imports in itself an *assumpsit*, for when one agrees to pay so much money, or deliver any thing, thereby he assumes or promises to pay, or deliver it." One could legally assume, in other words, that the defendant "super se assumpsit"—had taken it upon himself—to perform certain actions (such as delivering a sum of money) in exchange for consideration (a crop of wheat).[60] With the decision in Slade's Case, which permitted the action of breach of promise, oaths of compurgation became irrelevant.

In breaking with the wager of law or oath of compurgation, the legal principle of *assumpsit* amounted to an increased concern on the part of the common law not just with the intentions of the contracting parties but also with the formal means of deducing them. If character and status fell by the wayside (at least as far as legal procedure was concerned), intention became both a relevant consideration and a necessary deduction from the facts at hand.[61] These facts included the motive or reasons for entering into a contract. In mandating the consideration of circumstances, the doctrine of consideration amounted to a doctrine of equity.[62] In opposition to the view that a mere verbal promise (*nudum pactum*) was binding, the doctrine of consideration held that promises were actionable when circumstances existed (e.g., when some prior relationship existed, something had been exchanged, or some action had taken place) that provided a reason for a promise.[63]

Although there is general agreement that the modern law of contract, with its emphasis on intention, promissory liability, and consideration, takes its point of departure from Slade's Case, the precise legal and larger cultural meanings of the case have been disputed.[64] Some scholars emphasize the way Slade exemplifies early modern ways of thinking about obligation, which differ in crucial respects from the modern "will" theory of contract; others stress the continuity between Slade and modern contract law. Some have argued that the doctrine of consideration was consistent with the older economy of obligation, whereas others have seen consideration and assumpsit as facilitating a newer protocapitalist economy, in which the courts needed to "hold commercial agreements actionable" for trade to be calculable.[65]

For our purposes, it is precisely the slipperiness of Slade—its uneasy joining of conscience and calculation—that is significant. Here I take issue with the legal historian A.W.B. Simpson, who has argued that we should avoid the temptation to ask, anachronistically, whether contractual obligation at the time of Slade was moral or legal. According to Simpson, early modern men and women made no such distinction; they believed that "commerce, like other areas of life, must be conducted morally if the general good is to be furthered, and there is no special set of principles of commercial morality."[66] But, judging from contemporary comments, in the early seventeenth century assumpsit and consideration were not always seen as ratifying or codifying an existing moral obligation. Although something like these principles had been sporadically articulated in earlier legal discussion and common law, the decision in Slade was also represented as something new—a necessary and equitable reform of existing actions for debt. And part of what was new was that Slade articulated a new basis of obligation. Coke went so far as to suggest that together assumpsit and consideration seemed more suited to the modern world of self-interest, if not exactly commerce: assumpsit is superior to the wager of law because "experience now proves that men's consciences grow so large that the respect of their private advantage rather induces men to perjury."[67] In the new world of market relations, interest will induce men to swear false oaths, making the use of compurgation or the character witness inadequate; however, it will also induce them to keep their contracts—hence, the value of substituting contracts for oaths.

Slade thus stands at the crossroads of what Max Weber called the status contract and the purposive contract, of older and newer ways of thinking about intention and obligation. If in the older view of obligation, promises were to be kept because of a transcendent moral law ("pacta sunt servanda"), in Slade promises were to be kept because they had been articulated in the shared medium of language and ratified by the exchange of other material signs. In relying on consideration, rather than character witness and religious oath, Slade dramatized a pervasive skepticism about older ways of determining or guaranteeing intention, specifically the intention of the parties to a contract.[68] But, from another perspective, Slade exemplified a new confidence in the adequacy of human agreements—and of individual self-interest—to secure intention. Whether such agreements were primarily moral or legal, whether they were based on conscience, calculation, or some combination of the two, remained open to debate. But, it was clearly possible to suggest—as Coke did—that keeping one's promise was not so much a moral obligation as a legal one. Specifically, the legal codification of the doctrines of assumpsit and consideration provided for legal sanctions for breach of contract, which the fear of divine punishment did not reliably provide. As James Morice, a Middle Temple lawyer, argued in *A briefe treatise of Oathes* (c. 1590), "Know we not that all, or the moste part of men will rather hazard their soules [by perjury] then put their bodies to shame and reproach."[69] The legitimate power of the state—the force of law—provided the element of coercion necessary to the enforcement of contract. This insight about the cultural and political conditions of a binding contract, implicit in Slade, were to become explicit in mid-seventeenth-century political debate.

Covenant Theology: Divine Speech Acts and the Covenant of Metaphor

At the same time that natural rights theorists were advocating a secular notion of the social and political contract, and common lawyers were codifying the economic notion of contract, puritan theologians were developing their own distinctive version of contractualism. Covenant theology—the offspring of Protestant scripturalism, Hebraism, and in England more immediate conflicts arising out of the Elizabethan religious settlement—offered an alternative to the ceremonies of High Church Anglicanism, focusing instead on the two covenants of Scripture and the fallen sinner's unmediated relationship to God.[70] Although the notion of the heavenly contract was not simply a response to new economic and political circumstances, covenant theologians drew on both realms to make their view of the heavenly contract accessible to their readers and parishioners. In the process, they also radicalized the insights of those two domains: in covenant theology we find an even more radical linguistic turn than in natural law jurisprudence and an even more radical emphasis on individual intention than in the common law. In the words of the influential puritan minister William Perkins, "God is the author and worker of faith, so God hath appointed a means whereby he works it and that is his word."[71] For Perkins and his followers, the Word was the vehicle of the divine covenant, and this in turn meant that the moral subject—the subject of conscience—was created through an activity of interpretation.

Of course, the language of the covenant had always been a part of Jewish notions of faith and political obligation; the Word had always been at the center of Christian religion. But with the Reformation came a renewed concern with the unmediated word of Scripture as God's covenant with man. The Reformation had both liberated the individual conscience from the oversight of the Catholic Church and condemned it to perdition without the assistance of grace. For the fallen Christian, obligation, including above all the obligation of faith, was strictly speaking unnatural, outside the capacity of fallen human nature. The central "case of conscience" for Protestants of all persuasions was accordingly how to know whether they were damned or saved, bound to the devil or to God.[72] Covenant theology thus included a powerful narrative dimension by virtue of its attention to the divine workings of the covenant in history, that is, the biblically sanctioned providential narrative of redemption. At the same time, the focus on the bond of the individual conscience produced an interpretive activism, beginning with an intense preoccupation with the artificial arrangements— or covenants—established by the voluntarist God of Calvinism. For covenant theologians, Scripture did not simply inform the reader of the spiritual covenant; as God's word, Scripture was itself the prime instance of the covenant. And this meant that the first obligation—the obligation that trumped all others—was the individual obligation to interpret Scripture. Paradoxically, the centrality of the Word did not amount to a new determinism, but an optimism about the power of language to shape, make, or induce obligation. At the extreme, covenant theology reimagined fixed status or, rather, the ontological relations of man and God, in terms of the voluntary relations of contract.[73] This in turn was to have profound implications for the relation of subject and sovereign.

By the 1580s in England covenant or "federal" theologians (from the Latin *foedus* or covenant) characteristically distinguished between the law and the gospel in terms of a covenant of works and a covenant of grace.[74] God's covenant with the Hebrews was a covenant of works: the Jews' destiny as the chosen people was conditional upon their fulfillment of the moral and ceremonial law. Christ canceled the covenant of works and substituted a covenant of grace—a paradoxical covenant in which God's grace enabled the faith of the individual believer. Covenant theologians stressed that the covenant of grace was already available in the Old Testament. In particular, God's postlapsarian covenant with Abraham was a covenant of grace, made in Perkins's words "not for the merit of his worke, but for the merit of Christ."[75] This covenant, which was not only with the individual believer but also with "the entire nation of Moses" and with "the new Israel centered on Christ," was progressively realized in history: "promised in the Garden to the fallen Adam, made more explicit in the dealings with Abraham, given added substance in the covenant of Sinai, and sealed and certified in the death of Christ, so that now men are incorporated under that New Covenant made most certain by him."[76]

In the interpretation of puritan theologians, the covenant thus served as an emblem of both the fall and redemption, a way of making human incapacity the occasion of divine accountability. This understanding of the covenant extended to the language of covenant itself: covenant theologians argued that God's use of the metaphor of the covenant was an accommodation of divine truths to human understanding. Influenced in part by New Testament metaphors of spiritual debt and in part by the increasing prominence of contracts in everyday life, puritan ministers glossed the covenant in terms of civil and common law notions of economic contract, debt, and indenture. As Richard Sibbes noted, "God will argue with us from our traffic and commerce with men."[77] According to covenant theologians, although the language of debt and redemption made salvation imaginable, it also dramatized the incommensurability of human and divine transactions. In particular, economic metaphors of accounting very often functioned ironically to indicate an infinite debt, a debt that could never be repaid. God's purpose in employing comparisons familiar from everyday business transactions was, paradoxically, to indicate a legal obligation that the individual was incapable of fulfilling. In *A Treatise of the Vocations or Callings of Men*, William Perkins glossed the parable of the good steward in terms of "the account that every man must make of the works of his calling," only then to show that such "even reckoning" was impossible. By attempting to reckon their debts, sinners discover "that they are utterly unable" to repay them. Their only assurance lies in God's being "content to account of Christ his satisfaction as payment for [their] sins."[78] As William Gouge noted, "By covenant [God] is bound to man, but his covenant is established upon his own promise . . . there never was, nor could be anything in man to move God to enter into covenant with [him]."[79]

At the same time, the impossibility of a mutual covenant was a source of consolation. Although human beings could not of themselves fulfill the covenant, God bound himself to fulfill it and, in so doing, became reliable and calculable. The irony or paradox of the heavenly contract was that God bound himself to become a debtor to the human sinner. Thus, the covenant was regularly compared with an indenture, bond of debt, or "earnest" by which God assured the believer of his salvation. In *A Golden Chain* Perkins asserted: "This covenant is also named a testament, for it hath partly the nature and properties of a testament or will. For it is confirmed by the death of the testator. Secondly, in this covenant we do not so much offer or promise any great matter to God, as in a manner only receive: even as the last will and testament is not for the testator's but for the heir's commodity." Unlike a contract, a testament is a pure gift. It is legally binding on the giver but not on the beneficiary, who is not obligated to promise anything in return. There is, and can be, no quid pro quo. Thus Jeremiah Burroughs compared the covenant of grace with "God's insurance offer," for which the sinner pays no premium.[80] In his *Marrow of Theology*, Perkins's follower William Ames described the believer's redemption through Christ in similar terms: spiritual redemption "was not primarily effected by power, nor by prayers . . . but by the payment of a just price."[81]

In the logic of covenant theology, Christ's payment transformed the covenant from a unilateral transaction to a bilateral one: God's gift of grace rectified human incapacity and made a place for the will. Accordingly, along with the Calvinist notion of the covenant of grace as "God's promise to man," which God has obligated himself to fulfill, some English and continental federal theologians conceived of the covenant as "a conditional promise on God's part, which had the effect of drawing out of man a responding promise of obedience, thus creating a mutual pact or treaty. The burden of fulfillment rest[ed] upon man."[82] God's conditional promise, in other words, turned what might simply have been passive assent into what George Downame called "a true, willing, and lively assent," "not forced, as that of the devils."[83] Although the distinction between assent and consent is not always clear in this period, Downame seems intent on making a distinction between passive assent to an existing state of affairs and active consent, which helps to realize the new covenant.

Once the heavenly contract was reconfigured as a mutual pact or divinely authorized exchange of redemption for obedience, it made sense to compare this exchange with a political contract. Peter Bulkeley analogized the divine covenant to the covenant "which passeth between a king and his people; the king promiseth to rule and govern in mercy and righteousness, and they again promise to obey in loyalty and faithfulness." In their attempts to explain the workings of covenant theology, other writers borrowed from contemporary understanding of the magistrate or member of Parliament as a "public person" or legal representative of the people. Thus Perkins described the way humankind sins with Adam to the way a county or shire is represented by an MP: "[A]s in a Parliament whatsoever is done by the burgess of the shire is done by every person in the shire." John Preston similarly described Christ as a "public person" or legal representative of the faithful. Christ, in this view, is not only an attorney but a model MP, one who is related to the people not as their spiritual father but as their elected representative. Even more than covenant theology's emphasis on consent, this view of Christ as representative was obviously difficult to square with the Stuart rhetoric of inherited right and patriarchalism.[84]

Arguably, the most unusual aspect of covenant theology's treatment of the heavenly contract was its equation of performance with faith. Here we begin to see the different constructions of contract in natural rights theory and the common law, on the one hand, and covenant theology, on the other. In the first two cases, a contract involves a quid pro quo and faith enters into the equation insofar as each party to the contract relies on the other's performance. In contrast, covenant theologians used the metaphor of the contract to turn faith itself into what is required of the contracting party. In *Life Eternall* (posthumously published in 1631),

John Preston articulated the paradoxical status of a covenant with the Almighty, when he spoke of a "double covenant" in which "God doth not onely promise for his part, but makes a covenant to inable us to performe the conditions on our part."[85] According to Preston, the legal condition of God's promise was man's faith: what was required before God's promise could be fulfilled was a belief in God's promises. As the puritan minister John Ball remarked in his *Treatise on the Covenant of Grace* (1645), "That therefore Man should enter into Covenant with God, it was necessary that men should first give credit to the Word of God."[86] The believer's faith in turn enabled his "free and willing obedience."[87]

We can see this complex negotiation between God's promise and man's faith reflected in the contemporary analysis of the covenant as a divine speech act—an analysis that in turn heightened awareness of the interpretive activity and speech acts of the covenant theologians themselves. In his extraordinarily influential treatise of theology, *A Golden Chain*, William Perkins defined "God's covenant" as "his contract with man concerning the obtaining of life eternal upon a certain condition."[88] He then went on to analyze the two covenants as different kinds of speech acts. The covenant of works is identical with the moral law, "that part of God's word which commandeth perfect obedience unto man." By virtue of this command, the law reveals sin and "denounce[s] eternal damnation." "This sentence the law pronounceth against offenders, partly by threatening, partly by terrifying, it reigneth and ruleth over man." The covenant of grace, in contrast, is not a commandment but both a conditional promise and a testament. "The covenant of grace is that whereby God freely promising Christ and his benefits, exacts again of man that he would by faith receive Christ and repent of his sins. This covenant is also named a testament, for it hath partly the nature and properties of a testament or will."[89] Later covenant theologians such as George Downame and John Preston echoed Perkins's description of the covenant of grace as both an unconditional testament and conditional contract. These different linguistic forms solicit different responses. The legal covenant of the Old Testament demands that the believer fulfill the commands of the law; the covenant of grace is both an absolute gift and contingent upon faith—what we might call bona fides.[90]

This emphasis on faith in turn had the potentially revolutionary effect of licensing the individual's equitable interpretation of the law. In the axiom of covenant theology, God accepts the will for the deed.[91] In *A Treatise Tending unto a Declaration Whether a Man Be in the Estate of Damnation, or in the Estate of Grace* (1595), Perkins explained the consolations of covenant theology's focus on intention: "If any humbled Christian find not this measure of sanctification in himselfe, yet let him not bee discouraged. . . . And though he faile greatly in the action of obedience, yet God will accept his affection to obey, as obedience acceptable to him." In the sublime process of accounting outlined by Perkins, intention substitutes for the deed, faith for works, equity for strict law. Like Perkins, Ball linked intention to equity, construed both as a principle of interpretation and a disposition of the affections—both God's and man's. Commenting on the representation of God in the Psalms, Ball stated in his *Treatise of the Covenant of Grace*, "His will is the most certaine rule of equity and rectitude; and our hearts are then upright, when they stand in conformity" with it. "And herein is implied . . . an holy disposition of mind, will and affections." "For God regards not so much the matter, as the forme of obedience: nor so much as the thing done, as the affection wherewith we doe it."[92] In *The New Covenant* John Preston also stressed the crucial importance of "uprightness" or "sincerity" in all the believer's dealings with God. The covenant is the "ground of all our sincerity" and sincerity is all that is required by the covenant. "In this sense," Preston tells his readers, "*faith* is said to be *accounted for righteousness*." Preston went on to describe the transformative effects of the new covenant, which alters the sinner's "disposition and affection": "he looks not on God now as upon a hard and cruell Master, but he lookes upon him now as a *God* exceeding full of mercy and compassion":

> [N]ow hee sees another way, his apprehension is altered, even as a servant when it is revealed to him that he is a son, and that those hard taskes that are laid on him, are the best way to leade him to happinesse . . . *the case is altered*, hee lookes now not upon the Law of God as an enemy, or as a hard bondage, but he lookes upon all the Law of God, as a wholsome and profitable rule of direction, that hee is willing to keepe for his owne comfort: now, when the heart is thus softened, then the Spirit of God is sent into his heart, and writes the Law of God in his inward parts.[93]

This passage clearly exemplifies the links between the new covenant, right intention, and equitable interpretation in covenant theology. Together, they were part of a new way of seeing that read the letter of the law metaphorically and so transformed the law into an internal disposition, into the law of the heart. Particularly striking is Preston's use of "the case is altered," a common phrase for the casus omissus, the case not covered by existing law and thus requiring equitable judgment.[94] Preston used the phrase to signal God's equitable dealing with man and the believer's understanding of the Law. The New Covenant transformed the sinner's desperate case and ensured merciful treatment; it also instructed the believer to read the Old Covenant metaphorically and equitably as the New Covenant, a better covenant that took one's intentions for one's deeds.[95] Equitable interpretation was both a principle of divine mercy and a hermeneutical imperative.

Reading the law metaphorically revealed not only that covenant and contract were God's metaphors but that metaphor itself could be a kind of covenant. Thus in his enormously popular *A Golden Chain*, in language that echoed discussions of the mutual assent necessary to a covenant, William Perkins described figurative language in Scripture as a kind of "mutuall, and as I may say, sacramentall relation."[96] William Ames in turn read the sacraments of Baptism and the Eucharist as figures of the covenant.[97] Both effectively equated the covenant of grace with figurative understanding. In *Of the New Covenant*, John Preston drew out the implications of this equation when he presented metaphor as a promissory or conditional contract that enjoined a labor of interpretation on the faithful reader. Discussing the "similitude" between the Christian life and a journey, Preston commented:

> I finde not any metaphor in the Scriptures used more frequently, and therefore it should teach us some thing: for a metaphor, you know, is but a similitude that is contracted to one word, it is but a short similitude, folded up in a word, and somewhat is to be taught us, some resemblance there is that wee will labour to expresse, and make some short use of it. (181)

The metaphor of the journey dictated a labor of interpretation which was in turn part of the working out of one's own salvation. That is, the believer performs his part of the covenant by interpreting.

According to Preston, this equation of metaphorical walking and hermeneutical working was made explicit in God's covenant with or promise to Abraham:

> When the *Lord* sayth to *Abraham, I am All-Sufficient*; therfore *walke perfectly before me*, it is as if he had sayd, *Abraham*, I meane to be a good Master to thee, I meane to give thee sufficient wages, thou shalt want nothing thou needest; now be thou carefull to doe thy worke, be not idle, sit not still, but be working (that is intimated by *walking*), to *walke* is still to be acting some thing, still to be working, to be in employment, and not sit still. (181–82)

Preston glossed the covenant not only as a promise but also a contract of "wages" for interpretive labor. His own activity of interpretation then served as an example of walking/working with God.[98] In the words of William Ames's injunction in *Conscience with the Power and the Cases thereof* (1639), "the interpretation of the Scriptures, or a judgement to discerne Gods will for a mans selfe, in his owne Conscience, belongs to every man."[99] In this way, Preston dramatized the analogy between the covenant of grace and figurative or equitable interpretation. The individual activity of interpretation was itself one of the ways in which the covenant was realized.

Covenant theology thus made room for human agency, even as it seemed to deny it. It authorized scrupulous analysis of the intentions and dispositions of the individual believer; it enabled the fallen sinner through the divine gift of a contract; it made the activity of interpreting Scripture an obligation of faith; and it licensed the metaphorical or equitable interpretation of the law. If the divine covenant as testament suggested a saving legalism, according to which God was more calculable and dependable than Calvinist theology might at first suggest, the covenant as mutual contract implied "the partial rehabilitation of natural man," the partial legibility of natural law, and thus the meaningfulness even to sinners of the notion of moral obligation.[100]

As we will see in the following chapters, it was a short step from imagining the covenant with God to having the covenant of grace dictate a revocable social and political contract. In the early seventeenth century covenant theologians, like most everyone else, did not think to question the institution of monarchy.[101] Over the next few decades, however, covenant theology began to provide critics of the king with a powerful weapon. As Perry Miller has observed, "Charles I was tyrannical [not only] because he broke the compact, violated immunities, and invaded rights sealed in the agreement," but also because "he pretended to a prerogative to which only God was entitled, but which God himself scorned to exercise."[102] By definition, the contract with God trumped all merely human contracts and thus authorized not only passive but, in some cases, active resistance to secular power. If the immediate effect of the metaphor of contract was to make God more calculable, its ultimate effect was to make the individual less calculable, less predictable, by virtue of the role it granted to intention and consent. In this way, covenant theology came to underwrite political contractualism of the sort we have seen in natural law jurisprudence and the common law.

In concluding this first part of my anatomy of the tributary discourses of contract, a few general remarks are in order. In their predominant seventeenth-century meanings, covenant is a theological concept, whereas contract is a secular one; and the history of political thought usually charts a shift from one to the other. There is an obvious truth to this account but it misses features that are equally and, arguably, more characteristic of early modern debates about obligation: a widespread preoccupation with the linguistic dimension of contract, a concern with the linguistic character of the bond of conscience, and a related interest in the human capacity to create and enforce contractual agreements. There was, of course, no single view of the relationship between conscience and language, the *nudum pactum* and the contingent circumstances of our agreements. Yet, if the "poetics" of contract could be aligned with no one set of political or religious beliefs, the focus on the linguistic dimension of contract served to denaturalize and demystify the grounds of political obligation. Obligation was coming to be seen as a human artifact, a product of human artifice. This pervasive concern with artificial bonds in turn dictated an interest in the supplementary role of the passions, equitable interpretation, and imaginative literature in the new economy of political obligation.

CHAPTER 3

The Passions and Voluntary Servitude

> Man himself has a conscience; consequently the subjection
> required of him is a free allegiance.
>
> —G.W.F. Hegel

> Lady *Kent* Articled with Sir *Edward Herbert*, that he should
> come to her when she sent for him, and stay with her as long
> as she would have him, to which he set his hand; then he Arti-
> cled with her, That he should go away when he pleas'd, and
> stay away as long as he pleas'd, to which she set her hand. This
> is the Epitome of all the Contracts of the World, betwixt
> man and man, betwixt Prince and Subject, they keep them as
> long as they like, and no longer.
>
> —John Selden, *Table Talk*

IN THE EARLY DECADES of the seventeenth century, the discourses of covenant and contract solved some problems, but they also created new problems of their own. Precisely because they called attention to the artifice
and voluntarism of divine and human arrangements, they were a source of
great anxiety. For the first time in history, there was a cultural conversation
about the consent of the individual subject as a crucial aspect of political
legitimacy. Yet there was also a widespread perception that consent was
an unstable basis on which to build a government. Early modern men and
women recognized that the language of contract endowed the will with a
new authority but also wondered what could possibly motivate the will to
consent to its own subordination. They worried that the will was a source
of arbitrariness and artifice and that the fiction of contract might contami-
nate other, putatively natural relations in society.

The new language of contract was thus accompanied by an intense
interest in the motives of the contracting subject. In the eyes of some,
the religious conflicts on the continent and social upheaval at home were
evidence that the moral law was illegible or insufficient to bind the conscience. For many seventeenth-century writers, human beings were mani-
festly, even primarily motivated by passion and interest.[1] In contemporary
discussions of political obligation, invocations of the moral law gave way
to discussions of psychology. Concern with binding the conscience gave

way to binding the will, and self-love and fear of violent death emerged as more compelling motives for political obligation than duty or love of the sovereign. Reasoning about these self-regarding passions and natural rights, it was argued, dictated the individual's consensual or voluntary subjection to a political contract. In this scenario, the individual's natural appetites provided the motive for consent, and consent in turn legitimated the state's coercive power. Seventeenth-century discussions of political contract thus signaled a shift in the libidinal economy of political obligation, according to which consent based on the self-regarding passions and interests supplemented or replaced the subject's filial love of the sovereign.

This new psychology of consent itself raised a host of problems. Some worried that the will could not serve as the lasting foundation of government; others worried that the will would subject itself to the wrong authorities or that consent might be subject to coercion. As we saw in the preceding chapter, Robert Filmer complained that voluntary subordination was by definition subject to change when he asked rhetorically in *The Originall of Government*, "If it were a thing so voluntary and at the pleasure of men when they were free to put themselves under subjection, why may they not as voluntarily leave subjection when they please, and be free again?" John Selden, as quoted in the epigraph, rendered Filmer's observation in comic terms when he stated that political obedience was as voluntary—or arbitrary—as sexual preference. And Hobbes articulated the pervasive fear of a different sort of arbitrariness when he trenchantly observed that people "give their consent out of hatred, fear, hope, love or any other passion or emotion rather than reason."[2] For Filmer, the contingency of contractual relations implied chaos; for Selden, the voluntarism of contract suggested the inherently changeable desire for sexual pleasure; while for Hobbes this same linking of passion and the will raised the specter of irrational subordination. Together, these writers pinpoint the central dilemmas of the new psychology of contract: Filmer and Selden isolate the paradox of a will free to bind itself, whereas Hobbes is concerned with the passions as unreliable sources of motivation.

This chapter explores the role of the will and the centrality of the passions in the tributary discourses of contract in the early seventeenth century. It focuses in particular on the role the passions played in contemporary efforts to distinguish between the rational act of voluntary *subjection* and the irrational act of voluntary *servitude*. All the writers discussed here recognized the crucial role of the passions in motivating the subject of contract. They also fully recognized that, carried to its logical and perhaps affective extreme, the contractual account of obligation implied the legitimacy of voluntary enslavement for reasons of "fear, hope, love, or any other passion." Although in the seventeenth century consent was not necessarily incompatible with coercion, not all instances of coercion were thought to be equal. Hence the necessity of distinguishing between better and worse passions, better and worse reasons for consenting. Thus natural rights theorists contrasted legitimate and illegitimate passions and interests. Covenant theologians went to great lengths to distinguish the filial fear of God from servile fear and proper subjection from willful enslavement. Common lawyers developed their own language of the Norman Yoke, and construed the feudal past as a period of partially self-imposed bondage against which genuine consent and contractual relations with the king might be measured.

In the account offered here of the tributary discourses of contract, wives, slaves, and feudal villeins emerge as the shadows of the contracting subject. There is an important difference, however, in the respective treatments of slavery in these discourses. Whereas common lawyers rejected the slavery of the Norman Yoke, natural rights theorists and covenant theologians reinstated a different kind of enslavement in their efforts to avoid it. On the threshold of a purely conventional account of political subjection, they drew back and reasserted, by analogy, the natural subordination of the political subject. Faced with the problem of voluntary servitude, they illustrated the right sort of subjection by comparing the political contract or the theological covenant to the marriage contract, the voluntary subjection of the contracting subject to the voluntary subjection of the wife in marriage. In so doing, however, they unwittingly feminized the subject of contract. In their retreat to a more conventional analogy for political obligation, these thinkers only further aggravated the instability of the new discourses of contract. In natural rights theory and covenant theology, contract thus became an explicit fault line in early modern discussions of gender—a place where gender difference was not simply reinforced but also questioned.[3]

As I show in this chapter, the idioms and ideas elaborated by natural rights theorists, covenant theologians, and common lawyers did not form a stable theory of political obligation. Even in their own minds, the vocabularies they proposed could be mobilized to support arguments for allegiance or resistance to the sovereign. Their works illustrate the great uncertainty provoked not only by contemporary religious and political events but also by the new languages used to conceptualize them. It was unclear to all concerned whether the voluntarism of consent could be effectively contained within acceptable limits, whether the passions could be reconceived as a stable basis of voluntary subjection, and, not least, whether relations between master and servant, or husband and wife, would remain uncontaminated by the new voluntarism. Finally, the instability of these discourses was intensified by the very public nature of the conversation: the very fact of debating the nature of the will, the lability of the passions, and the meaning of consent, insinuated the possibility of individual agency and constructive change even when the ostensible topic was the bondage of the will.

THE SLAVE CONTRACT

Grotius's account of the laws of war and peace was marked from the outset by a concern with wayward passions and voluntary servitude. As he described his motives for writing in the prolegomena to *De jure belli ac pacis*: "Throughout the Christian world I observed a lack of restraint in relation to war, such as even barbarous races should be ashamed of; I observed that men rush to arms for slight causes, or no cause at all, and that when arms have once been taken up there is no longer any respect for law, divine or human; it is as if, in accordance with a general decree, frenzy had openly been let loose for the committing of all crimes."[4] In response, Grotius aimed to provide an account of political association that would be persuasive to individuals of different religious beliefs, bring about voluntary subjection to political authority, and thus establish peace on the continent.

This pragmatic political goal shaped Grotius's account of human nature. In the prolegomena he argued in Stoic and Thomist fashion that human beings are motivated to form peaceful associations by "an impelling desire for society," a natural *appetitus societatis*, rather than by egotistical self-interest. But he added that "the law of nature nevertheless has the reinforcement of expediency [*utilitas*]":

> [F]or the Author of nature willed that as individuals we should be weak, and should lack many things needed in order to live properly, to the end that we might be the more constrained to cultivate the social life. But expediency afforded an opportunity also for municipal law, since that kind of association of which we have spoken, and subjection [*subjectio*] to authority, have their roots in expediency.[5]

It was thus not only reason or the natural law of sociability that impelled individuals to consent to the social contract but also weakness, vulnerability, and fear for one's self preservation: "[M]en joined themselves together to form civil society not by command of God, but of their own free will, being influenced by their experience of the weakness of isolated households against attack."[6]

Paradoxically, this less sociable view of human nature—which Grotius associated with the development of more sophisticated forms of social interaction—was Grotius's best argument for the necessity of peace. Discussing the primitive ownership of all things in common later in *De jure belli*, Grotius observed, "This primitive state might have lasted if men had continued in great simplicity, or had lived on terms of mutual affection such as rarely appears." Instead, men acquired knowledge, engaged in cultivation and trade, and in the process succumbed to vice, ambition, acquisitiveness, "a passion for pleasure" and "unlawful loves." "From the difference in pursuits arose rivalry, and even murder; and at length, since the good were corrupted by contact with the wicked, there came the kind of life ascribed to the giants, that is given over to violence."[7] This violent condition was not simply a declension from the Golden Age; as Grotius's remarks in the prolegomena make clear, it also described the bloody state of Europe in the 1620s. In the context of religious war, then, sociability was not so much a fundamental condition of human nature as a construct or artifact: by arguing that fear of attack was a motive for cooperation, Grotius turned a pessimistic account of human passions into an argument for sociability and peace. Fear of violence and the desire to protect one's property led individuals to transfer their rights and their allegiance to the sovereign.

In his brief comments on fear and property, Grotius adumbrated a new psychology of political obligation that contrasted sharply with the continental and English rhetoric of married or familial love between subject and sovereign. According to the new psychology, the passions were at once an irreducible feature of human nature and an expression of individual self-interest, but this fact was less of a problem than a resource. Although the passions could lead to violence, they could also, he argued, serve as a powerful motive for rational calculation. The goal, accordingly, was to join appetite and rational consent, and thus to shore up the obligation of natural law with the appeal to legitimate self-interest. Rational consent was figured as consent to one's own passions; and the subjects of contract were imagined as both voluntarily binding themselves and voluntarily submitting to the external coercion of the state.

At least since Plato, of course, the passions and affections had been central to discussions of securing and maintaining political power. Political theorists had argued not only that the tyrant's passions needed to be controlled but also that the citizen's or subject's needed to be solicited. In his rhetorical works Cicero had advised the would-be orator how to move the people's passions, and in *De officiis* Cicero had instructed the reader in the morality of self-interest and self-preservation.[8] In this work, Cicero had also explicitly advised the statesman that "of all motives, none is better adapted to secure influence and hold it fast than love; nothing is more foreign to that end than fear" (2.7.23). In early modern manuals of "domesticall duties," readers were regularly instructed in the duty to love their superiors. Contemporary political rhetoric was filled with protestations of love for the sovereign. In Grotius's work, however, instead of being educated concerning his *duty* to love, the political subject was instructed about his *right* to fear—specifically, his right to fear violent death, his right of self-preservation. Arguments for the right of self-defense had, of course, existed earlier but had not been a central part of arguments for political obligation.

The novelty of Grotius's argument is most apparent to modern eyes in his willingness to pursue it to its logical conclusion: the slave contract. Initially, for Grotius, the slave contract logically followed from the notion that one has property in one's person and that one may enter into a contract for reasons of self-preservation. Such contracts (for which Grotius cited both classical and modern examples) were either economically motivated and took the form of indentured servitude, or entered into by captives in war in exchange for their lives. In both cases, the motive was self-preservation and in both cases fear for one's self-preservation was construed as legitimate duress. Although such an argument could be used to justify obedience to de facto political power,[9] Grotius made his own political preferences clear when he used the validity of the slave contract as an argument for absolute sovereignty. Against the position of those who located sovereignty in the people "so that it is permissible for the people to restrain and punish kings whenever they make a bad use of their power," Grotius reasoned

> To every man it is permitted to enslave himself to anyone he pleases for private ownership, as is evident both from the Hebraic and from the Roman Law. Why, then, would it not be permitted to a people having legal competence to submit itself to some one person, or to several persons, in such a way as plainly to transfer to him the legal right to govern, retaining no vestige of that right for itself?[10]

Just as individuals may sell themselves into indentured servitude out of fear for their self-preservation, so they may irrevocably transfer their right to govern themselves.

Yet, as both Grotius and his readers recognized, this argument for voluntary subjection to the sovereign also provided a justification of political resistance and defensive war. As we saw in chapter 2, Grotius conceded that in cases of "extreme and imminent peril" resistance to one's sovereign and obedience to a usurper were justified.[11] It was in this context that Grotius cited the passage from Aristotle's *Nicomachean Ethics* that was central to all early modern discussions of coercion, whether in everyday contracts or a political contract. In the *Ethics*, "Aristotle . . . has rightly stated, the man who throws his property overboard because of the fear of a shipwreck would wish to save it conditionally, if there was no danger of a shipwreck. But, considering the circumstances of the place and time, he is willing to lose his property absolutely."[12] Similarly, in Grotius's account, an individual genuinely consents to transfer his property in his liberty—that is, he consents to a political contract—when he fears for his life. Such arguments were of immediate contemporary relevance in Europe in the 1620s, especially in war-torn Holland and Bohemia. In this context Grotius was concerned both to justify legitimate subjection to absolute political rule and to condemn illegitimate servitude, however voluntary. The burning question of the day was how to tell the difference between them.[13]

The focal point of Grotius's anxiety about this problem was the slave contract. Although Grotius represented the slave contract as the paradigm of voluntary subjection to an absolute monarch, he also condemned voluntary slavery as the most extreme instance of irrational conduct. "The basest form of voluntary subjection is that by which a man gives himself into complete slavery, as those among the Germans who staked their liberty on the last throw of the dice. 'The one who lost,' says Tacitus, 'went into voluntary slavery' [*voluntariam servitutem*]." Even worse than those Germans who risked their freedom on a throw of the dice were those, cited in an example from Dio of Prusa, who voluntarily enslaved themselves by contract (*ex contractus*). Grotius then offered his own explanation of Dio's remarks: "That is complete slavery which owes lifelong service in return for nourishment and other necessaries of life." And he went on to cite supporting examples from the Stoic Posidonius regarding those who enslave themselves, and from Plautus's *Casina* about the runaway slave who voluntarily returns to his master.[14] Grotius did not go as far as Rousseau, who argued that the slave contract was an oxymoron because, in binding the will absolutely, it extinguished the very condition of voluntary subjection. But he did seem to feel that necessity and fear were servile and base motives, characteristics of comic lowlife rather than of rational political subjects. In this view, voluntary servitude was no longer the logical extension of the political contract but its irrational other.

Faced with the contingency and irrationality of the individual will, the uncertainty and anxiety provoked by the possibility of voluntary servitude, Grotius understandably looked backward to an older model of political obligation: the marriage contract. This had two advantages. First, in contrast to the slave contract, which instituted a relationship of dominance and subordination, seventeenth-century marriage—as described in contemporary manuals of domestic duties—simply ratified a prexisting natural hierarchy. Arguing against the claim that the person who invests power in another has the greater authority (which would mean that the people have authority over the sovereign), Grotius observed that this "does not hold true of a situation brought about by an act of will, from which a compulsory relationship results, as is the case of a woman giving authority over herself to her husband, whom she must ever after obey."[15]

Second, and equally important, Grotius argued that the marriage relationship was characterized not by servile fear but by affection, close friendship, and "association."[16] The implication of this comparison to marriage is that, like the wife, the people are naturally subordinate to the sovereign, whom they affectionately consent to obey. The marriage contract thus answered some of Grotius's anxieties about the slave contract but only by reimporting status into the purposive contract of political subjection. And yet, in using the language of association, Grotius also suggested, in spite of himself, that husband and wife, sovereign and subject, might be natural equals rather than unequals.

Precisely because Grotius was poised on the threshold of a new way of thinking about political obligation, because he was operating in uncharted linguistic and psychological space, he was unusually attuned not only to the logic of contract but also to its voluntarist and affective dilemmas. In the contrast between wives and slaves, slaves stood for servile fear and the illegitimate consent to coercion, whereas wives stood for the right interpretation of the affections, the right motives for entering into the political contract. The problem with this argument—a problem subliminally registered by Grotius's rapidly alternating images of wife and slave, in a kind of rabbit-duck effect of contract theory—was that it ended up either feminizing the political subject or empowering the wife. In the first case, the subject was a docile, naturally subordinate creature whose consent could only ratify a state of natural subjection and whose sphere of activity was restricted to the private or domestic realm. In the second case, the position of wife was denaturalized and she became—at least theoretically—a political agent capable of acting in her own right. Although neither of these possibilities was fully cognized by Grotius, both would be played out in subsequent political theory in England.

The Law of the Heart

For Reformation theologians, voluntary servitude was not simply one of the possible directions in which a voluntarist theory of obligation might lead; it was instead the naturally fallen condition of humankind. At the heart of this theology was Romans 7:14, "I am carnall, sold under sinne," where Saint Paul described the sinner as sold into slavery, and Galatians 4:22, where he explicitly compared the two covenants to bondage and freedom.[17] Although Paul, and after him Luther, found comfort in the notion of the enslaved will, which was liberated from the impossible task of saving itself, others saw predestination as a potentially demoralizing doctrine, one that could lead to a paralyzing despair or to an antinomian disregard for human laws and social conventions. The task of covenant ministers in the 1590s and after was to elaborate a pastoral message that gave some hope to individual believers and some role to individual agency, even as it respected the omnipotence of the divine will. At the heart of covenant theology was an account of how the individual conscience voluntarily subjected itself to God; but this emphasis on the voluntary subjection of the revivified will was itself a new source of contingency. The language of moral obligation and duty appeared in this context, but it was fundamentally destabilized by the internalization of the New Covenant "in the affections of the heart."

William Perkins analyzed the problem of voluntary subjection in his treatise on the most difficult case of conscience, *Whether a Man Be in the Estate of Damnation or the Estate of Grace* (1595).[18] According to Perkins, even when the believer "willingly subject[s]" himself to God, he worries about whether he is himself reliable, whether he subjects himself for the right reasons, whether he has a "sound" or "unsound heart." Perkins identified the right reasons for voluntary subjection with the right passions. The reprobate cannot "answer and be obedient to the calling of God" because he experiences servile fear.[19] In contrast, the elect are characterized by "sanctified affections": a righteous fear of God, a hatred of sin, and a joyful heart. These passions are the sign of the intention to obey God's will, despite the absence of any independent ability to do so: "And though [the believer] faile in the action of obedience, yet God will accept his affection to obey, as obedience acceptable to him. God will approve of thee for his owne worke which he hath wrought in thee."[20] The passions are thus the locus of the paradoxical agency of the sinner who can do nothing to effect his own salvation but with God can do all things.

In the same collection of treatises, Perkins addressed the experience of servile fear and despair which many of his readers felt, faced with the doctrine of predestination. In *Consolations for Troubled Consciences*, Perkins offered advice to those who find themselves "voyde of all grace and goodnes, froward and rebellious to any good work; so that [they] feare least Christ have quite forsaken [them]."[21] In particular, he addressed the experience of "spirituall desertion," the loss of "the inward assurance and certificate of [God's] love and favour in Christ, with a sense and feeling of the same in heart." Such spiritual desertion, he argued, is the complicated result of both human and divine action. First, desertion occurs because the sinner "voluntarily forsaketh and refuseth grace." Second, by deserting the sinner God demonstrates that "he is not bound to any; and hee may doe with his owne whatsoever he will."[22] Third, and ultimately, God uses desertion as a divine rhetorical ploy: it is his way of terrifying "drowsie Protestants" into belief, righteous fear, and absolute reliance on grace.

In his *Discourse of Conscience* (1596) Perkins offered a more elaborate analysis of the passage from the servile state of voluntary servitude to the liberated state of voluntary subjection. Here we begin to get a sense of the violence involved in renewing the will. Perkins repeatedly described the action of conscience not only as self-accusation but as self-wounding. In the first metaphor, conscience is the lawyer for the prosecution, and in accusing the sinner it "stirre[s] up sundrie passions and motions in the heart," especially shame, "sadnes and sorrow," "feare" (the attribute of a guilty conscience), "desperation," and "perturbation."[23] In the second metaphor, conscience is a wild beast that inflicts wounds on the soul, or is itself a body that is wounded, and these wounds include "secret pangs and terrours," "the apprehension of the feare and anger of God in conscience." The fear of God, in this analysis, is equivalent to the recognition of sin or the infinite debt of guilt. Conscience creates this sense of debt by what Nietzsche will later describe as a violent mnemotechnics—by wounding, rending, stabbing. The wound of conscience creates an ethical subject who can be indebted, who can recognize the possibility of obligation in the very failure to live up to it.[24] This recognition of failure is the precondition of grace. As a result of the violent operation of grace, the accusing conscience becomes the excusing conscience, the passions of sin are replaced by confidence and joy, bondage becomes freedom, and coercion becomes consent: "[O]ur libertie most of all appears in our service and obedience; because the service of God is perfect freedom: as on the contrarie in the disobedience of Gods commaundements, stands our spirituall bondage."[25]

Perkins dramatizes this spiritual and affective dialectic throughout the *Discourse* in his equivocal rhetoric of bonds. To be bound is to be commanded and obligated; it is also to be in bonds, enslaved, fearful or guilty. Hence the lapidary, dialectical statement: "[T]he bond of conscience is guiltiness."[26] Guilt is the bond of conscience because it is the pivotal passion, the passion that precipitates the sinner from a condition of servitude to one of voluntary subjection. Until then, conscience "hath libertie and is not bound either to accuse or excuse: but is apt to doe either of them indifferently." "Like silly wretches," sinners "neither see nor feele the constraining power, that Gods word hath in their consciences." Perkins thus imagines conscience as both "free" (in the sense of fallen and undetermined) and bound (positively constrained by God). Such undetermined freedom is paradoxically a form of slavery, whereas the bond of conscience—forged initially by guilt, fear, and sadness—is true freedom. Although "nothing can stanch or slay the terrours of conscience, but the blood of the immaculate lambe of God," that is, "the satisfaction of Christ," this is still a bond or sacrifice to which the believer must willingly "assent."[27]

In other treatises on covenant theology, the distinction between the two covenants, between servitude and subjection, was also rendered in terms of the opposition between good and bad passions, consent and coercion, subjection and rebellion. According to John Preston in *The New Covenant*, "The Covenant of Workes begets bondmen, and slaves, not sonnes and freemen." This covenant "brings onely a servile feare," while the covenant of grace disposes to the "true feare" of sin and the word of God.[28] Elsewhere, commenting on the lability of the passions, Preston noted that "there is a double desire in the heart of man," a natural desire and "an inordinate desire" or "a work of fancy." God satisfies the first kind of desire; the second is a sign of what Hobbes would call our restless seeking after power, which can never be satisfied, but only eliminated by faith.[29] In his *Treatise on the Covenant of Grace*, John Ball observed that "the old Covenant did beget to servitude, and so did compell and restraine by force, as when we leave undone what we would doe, or doe what we would not for feare." In contrast, the new covenant was written "in the affections of the heart."[30] The internalization of God's word transformed servile fear into love, the coercion of the sinner into the "voluntary subjection of his creature."[31] In *The Covenant of Grace* George Downame was even more forceful: "From this spirit of fearfullness, which is also called the spirit of bondage, Christ hath freed us, that as a voluntary people. . . . Zelous of good works . . . we may worship God *aphobos*, . . . without servile fear." And he went on to contrast this servile fear to the "filial fear" of the sinner "under grace," who does not fear punishment so much as he fears to offend God. In *The Faithful Covenanter*, a commentary on Genesis 17:7 (1639), Richard Sibbes remarked that believers know they have made God their own if they have given him obedience and their "affections." And he made it clear that this voluntary, affective subjection was the means by which conscience itself became sovereign: "God disposeth of it so that he that keeps a good conscience shall always be king, and rule over the world; and therein he performs his promise."[32]

This rhetoric of voluntary subjection was a source of tension within covenant theology and seventeenth-century English society. Although covenant theology was espoused by defenders of the status quo, it also provided critics of church and state with a powerful idiom through which to voice dissent. Intended to console the sinner, it fostered an attention to the individual's own passions, intentions, and will that was potentially at odds with ecclesiastical structures of authority. At the same time, covenant theology encouraged a metaphorical interpretation of servitude and subjection that threatened the existing social hierarchy. In both psychological and hermeneutic terms, its account of voluntary subjection to God made all other contracts of absolute subjection void.

Thus, in his *Discourse of Conscience* Perkins stated that "humane lawes binde not simply of themselves, but so farre forth as they are agreable to Gods word, serve for the common good, stand with good orders, and hinder not the libertie of conscience. The necessitie of the lawe ariseth of the necessitie of the good thereof." And he went on to cite what was one of the standard examples of the exercise of discretion in a case of necessity:

> And this [assertion that human laws are not binding in themselves] stands even by the equitie of Gods word. God made a law, that the priests onely should eat of the shew bread: now David being no priest, did upon urgent occasion eate of it without sinne. If this be true in Gods lawe, then it may also be true in the lawes of men, that they may in some cases be omitted without sinne against God.[33]

The crucial question in all such exceptional cases was whether rebellion was allowed against the sovereign power, and whether discretion in such cases was the prerogative of the individual or of what Calvin called "lesser magistrates." No casuist, whether of Anglican or puritan persuasion, allowed the individual actively to resist sovereign authority; yet, every casuist asserted that the bond of conscience was superior to mere human laws. Perkins declared that the "proper binder" of conscience was God's word, while the "improper binder" was "Humane lawes, an Oath, a Promise."[34] In cases where "God commaunds one thing, & the magistrate . . . the flat contrarie," God must be obeyed.[35] Thus God's commandment to Abraham to sacrifice Isaac took precedence over the commandment, "Thou shalt not kill."[36] And God's law that "priests onely should eat of the shew bread" was ignored "without breach of conscience" by David, who "did upon urgent occasion eate of it without sin." This is because "the soveraigne power of binding and loosing, is not belonging to any creature, but is proper to Christ."[37] Manuals of casuistry thus both insisted on the necessity of keeping one's promises and the necessity of breaking them in those exceptional cases where they conflicted with the divine covenant. In instructing the reader in a habit of reasoning and reading, they helped to construct the conscientious subject—but it was unclear whether such a subject would be rebellious or obedient.[38] The resolution of this dilemma was to insist that the subject obey positive law not because it is binding in itself but because God enjoins the believer to obey civil power. Yet, as the passage from Perkins shows, God does not always dictate obedience to his own positive laws, let alone those of men. Moreover, the "equitie of Gods word" licenses a similar equitable interpretation of human laws.

Ames's remarks in *Conscience with the Power and the Cases thereof* (1639) about the position of the political subject are exemplary in their ambiguity. On the one hand, Ames's contrasted the individual's everyday transactions, which involved commutative justice, to his relation to the sovereign, which could not be thought of as a contract or agreement between equal parties. Instead, it was best analogized to the hierarchical relation of father and child, husband and wife, in which the inferior honors and obeys the superior.[39] On the other hand, Ames's emphasis on the sovereignty of conscience had implications for the individual's relation to positive law. Although he argued that believers were bound in conscience to obey the law, his insistence that "nothing but the law of God doth properly, directly, and immediately, and by it selfe bind the conscience" made room for conscientious objection to mere human law.[40] Ames asserted that legitimate "power" and "subjection" are "correlatives," with the superior requiring the consensual subordination of the inferior. Commenting on the sovereign's power, Ames asserted: "[T]his power is not absolute, but carries a double limitation, one from the will of God, whose Minister every Magistrate is, *Deut.* 17. 18. 2. Another from the will of man, which is included in those conditions and Lawes, in which the power of rule is founded."[41] Ames conceded that some people, "compelled by necessity, may so sell them selves over to a King, that they may be all justly his slaves, *Gen.* 47.23." But, he added,

> wee must not presume this, because it is not evident, because it is against custome, & against all natural inclination: neither can it be lawfully or justly bee aymed at by any Prince: because it is his duty to have an eye upon the common advantage of his subjects: Neither would such a government constitute a City or Body Politick, but rather a Lordly Domineering, and a monstrous slavery.[42]

This was a conclusion that could be, and was, endorsed by a staunch royalist such as Jeremy Taylor, who stated in *Ductor Dubitantium* that "a king rules over a free people, but a Lord rules over slaves."[43] But the rhetoric of voluntary subjection and voluntary servitude would be put to revolutionary uses in the tumultuous years of the 1640s.

Although Perkins, Ames, and their confederates believed that any given form of government was "the device of men," and that the king's lawful rule required the people's consent, they drew back from some of the more radical implications of their emphasis on the righteous fear of God and the metaphorical interpretation of subjection.[44] Thus, for example, William Allen distinguished between servile and filial fear in *A Discourse of the Two Covenants*, but he also warned about their incalculable social and political effects. He noted that the "Sons and Heirs" of the New Covenant "serve their Father with a free and ingenuous Spirit, though they have but little for the present, in confidence of what he will do for them hereafter in another world, when they shall come to age. But those under the Old Covenant were like Servants, who serve with a servile Spirit, because they do it with expectation of present pay." In the appendix to this work, Allen described how the "assent" of the believer to God's promise requires the "consent of the Will," which in turn presupposes the "operative and affecting influence [of faith] upon the passions of Hope, Fear, and Love, the powerful Principles of Action in Man."[45] Like Preston, Allen stressed the lability of the passions. God has implanted in his creatures a principle of self-love, a desire for happiness, which leads them to love and fear God as the means to that end. But Allen also acknowledged that "assent" to these same passions of self-love and filial fear, now glossed as the desire for the afterlife and the fear of divine punishment, might not always conduce to voluntary political subjection or obedience.[46]

Perkins articulated a similar fear of voluntarism in his influential *Treatise of the Vocations or Callings of Men*.[47] In a sense, the whole treatise was designed to argue that Christians should consent or voluntarily subject themselves to their God-given status in life. Its purpose was thus to harness and control the voluntarism of covenant theology. But by distinguishing between the calling of the Christian believer, which is determined by God's general providence, and the individual calling or profession (king, subject, merchant, plowman), which is determined by God's specific providence, Perkins also revealed the potential conflict between these two callings. This fault line is particularly apparent in Perkins's treatment of the callings of slave and wife. Whereas Grotius identified wives and slaves with the proper and improper affective dispositions of the political subject, Perkins's main anxiety in dealing with these two callings was the correct interpretation of Scripture's message of freedom, the correct ratio of literal and figurative understanding.

Perkins took up this challenge on the very first page of his treatise by addressing the scriptural question of whether a man who is a slave or "bondman when he is called [to Christianity] must then leave his calling." Perkins answered that, according to Saint Paul, he must not only remain in his calling but labor in it diligently. Paul's answer binds men to their God-given callings by helping them to see how the freedom granted by faith transforms even slavery into a higher subjection. This higher subjection, Perkins insisted, need not conflict with literal or actual servitude. To the objection that actual "servitude is against the law of nature," Perkins replied, "It is indeed against the law of nature as it was before the fall, but against the law of corrupted nature since the fall, it is not." To the objection that "Christ hath purchased liberty to believers," Perkins responded, "Only a spiritual liberty in this life, and a corporal only in the life to come. For though the servant in regard of faith and the inner man be equal to his master, because in Christ Jesus there is neither master nor servant, bond nor free, yet in regard of the outward man and civil order amongst men, the master is above the servant and the servant is and must be subject to the master." Just as consent should not be taken too far, Christian liberty should not be taken too literally. The Christian's metaphorical slavery to Christ should not be allowed to disrupt literal bondmanship, which functions in Perkins's treatise as a synecdoche for the social order of specific callings.

Describing the Christian "duties of love," Perkins then developed the paradox of voluntary servitude so as to implicate all believers:

> A Christian is the freest of all men in the world. For in that respect he is the child of God in Christ, he is truly freed from hell, death and condemnation; yea, and in part from sin and Satan and that in this life: and yet, for all this, he must be a servant unto every man. But how? By the duties of love, as occasion shall be offered, and that for the common good of all men. . . . Let us therefore in the fear of God be careful to learn this duty, for the practice of it is the special ornament of Christ's holy gospel.[48]

The duty of love, or what Perkins also calls the "bond" of love, preserves society by disposing individuals to accept domestic, social, and political hierarchy. In addition to accepting their general calling as Christians, believers must accept their individual calling or given social position. Perkins describes personal callings as "all such as be of the essence and foundation of any society, without which the society cannot be: as in a family, the calling of a master and the calling of a servant, the calling of a husband and wife, of parents and children, and in the commonwealth the calling of magistrates and subjects; and in the church the calling of the minister and the people."[49] In each case, the willing subordination to one's calling, including the calling of wife or slave, is part of the heavenly contract of covenant theology that transforms bondage into freedom.[50]

In the *Treatise of Callings* and elsewhere, however, Perkins's resolution of the tensions between specific and general calling, literal and metaphorical interpretations of subjection, was not entirely successful. He was not able to circumscribe fully the voluntarism he had so well analyzed. First, the slave escaped from his control, and then the wife. After insisting that the bondman must labor in his calling, Perkins conceded that "where this kind of servitude is abolished, it is not to be again received [since] servitude proceedeth not of nature, but hath his original from the laws of nations and is a consequent of the fall." Slavery describes a relationship of subjection, from which the slave might eventually be liberated: "For all men are equally and indifferently free, none more or less than others." Insofar as they are only contingently bound, then, slaves threaten to expose the arbitrariness of their calling; they risk encouraging a literal interpretation of the scriptural promise of Christian liberty.[51]

A different instability afflicted Perkins's treatment of the calling of wife. On the one hand, in contrast to slaves, wives were—at least ideally—both naturally and voluntarily subordinate. They illustrated the more conservative contractualism of irrevocable consent to one's subordinate nature. Accordingly, both in Perkins's *A Golden Chain* and in *Christian Oeconomie*, his manual of domestic life, marriage exemplified a subjection that was at once natural and voluntary or contractual. "Now the duties of the wife are principally two. The first is to submit herself to her husband. . . . The second duty is to be obedient unto her husband in all things, that is wholly to depend on him in judgment and in will."[52] So much was perfectly traditional and familiar in the early seventeenth century.

On the other hand, the wife was metaphorically implicated in the whole system of scriptural hermeneutics in a way that threatened traditional gender relations. Perkins not only adopted the New Testament's equation of the Old Testament covenant with bondage and the New Covenant with freedom, he also associated the slave with servile literalism and marriage with charitable interpretation.[53] Thus in *Epieikeia* Perkins argued,

> Indeed a kingdom may be obtained by force and arms, by violence and cruelty, but it cannot stand or continue without this equity and Christian moderation betwixt man and man. Nay, civil society and common dealing betwixt man and man cannot continue unless one man yield to another. In a word, there can be no peace in families, no sound or lasting love betwixt man and wife, nor comfortable quietness where one doth not yield to the other and bear with another in many things. And if it be so in marriage which is the nearest conjunction and the most excellent and perfect society which is in this world, then it is much more true in all other societies of men.[54]

Perkins obviously intended marriage to illustrate the coexistence of equity with political inequality and charitable interpretation with the literal status quo. In the same way, when he discussed the literal and figurative interpretation of slavery in *Christian Oeconomie*, he made it clear that the charitable or metaphorical understanding of freedom was perfectly compatible with actual subordination. Only the person enslaved by literal understanding could think that the gospel promised literal freedom. And yet, like the biblically charged figure of the slave, the equation of a good kingdom or a good marriage with equitable interpretation was potentially explosive: it could sanction "literal freedom," as it would for Milton, in the form of divorce and political resistance. Moreover, the metaphorical system of scripture could also suggest a greater hermeneutic and actual freedom for the wife—or the "Associate sole" (*PL*, 9.227).[55]

The scriptural hermeneutics of covenant theology had the potential to liberate not only the believer who was metaphorically enslaved to sin but the bondman who was enslaved to his master, the wife who was subordinate to her husband, the subject who was enslaved by an absolute monarch. As specific callings, both wives and slaves were exemplary of the right kind of voluntary subjection; but, in their metaphorical registers, both wife and slave began to suggest what it might mean to take the liberating message of the New Testament—the New Covenant—literally. Just as the wife might claim her spiritual equality in reality, so the actual slave might interpret his condition metaphorically as slavery to Christ. For Perkins the slave represented not so much the logical extreme of the voluntarism of contract—irrevocable subordination—as the contingency of one's "calling" and the possibility of perfect freedom. Seeping around the edges of the doctrine of the calling was a more radical contractualism, which turned one's social status and one's political position into a matter of interpretation.

FREE CONSENT

Common lawyers and members of Parliament were also preoccupied with the problem of slavery and the meaning of consent in the early decades of the seventeenth century. But, rather than seeing these as two sides of the same coin, they tended to see them as strictly opposed. Slavery was associated with the Norman Conquest of England by William in 1066, while the people's consent to government was linked to the notion of fundamental laws or to an evolving tradition of constitutionalism. According to Christopher Hill, the idea of the Norman Yoke had probably long had an underground life in the popular imagination but it gained new life beginning with Thomas Starkey in the 1530s, who wrote of the " 'tyrannical customs and unreasonable bonds' imposed by the conqueror 'when he subdued our country and nation.' " In his defense of absolutism, *The Trew Law of Free Monarchies*, written when he was James VI of Scotland, James I defended the conquest as providing discipline to the "the dissolute Anglo-Saxons." In response to James's account of the benefits of conquest, the antiquarians John Selden, John Spelman, and Robert Cotton attacked feudal tenures as villeinage, slavery, or bondage. William Perkins also represented William as a conqueror and tyrant whose rule became lawful only when the people ratified it by their consent. As the new lecturer on history at Cambridge in 1627, Isaac Dorislaus informed his audience that Tacitus had "placed the right of monarchy in the [Germanic] people's voluntary submission."[56] Writers such as these were clearly less preoccupied with the slippery slope between the people's voluntary subjection and their voluntary servitude than they were with the king's arbitrary exercise of his royal prerogative. The voluntarism they feared was the king's, as well they might, given James's view in *The Trew Law* that kings are "the authors and makers of the Lawes, and not the Lawes of the kings," and though a good king would be bound by the laws, "yet is hee not bound thereto but of his good will." In James's account of the relation between sovereign and subject, the sovereign was the only party capable of free—that is, revocable—consent to the laws.[57]

James's wayward passions also strengthened Parliament's desire to curb the royal prerogative. For many critics of the crown, George Villiers, duke of Buckingham, literally embodied the problem. The object of James's inordinate, even sacrilegious affection (James once remarked that as Christ had his John, James had his George), Buckingham eventually also controlled the corrupt system of court patronage. The puritan Lucy Hutchinson later spoke for many when she described "the court of this king [as] a nursery of lust and intemperance."[58] Although subjects and sovereign alike described their relationship as one of love and affection, James was increasingly perceived as violating the rights of his subjects. In response to these abuses, which were not concealed by James's rhetoric of paternal love for his subjects, critics insisted on a more austere relationship of sovereign and subject. Increasingly, the implied contract of the common law and the ancient constitution came to be seen as the antidote to the propaganda of the royalist romance and to the actual corruption at court.[59]

In the early decades of the seventeenth century, Coke and the common lawyers also sought to constrain the king's arbitrariness by insisting on the necessity of "artificial reason" or professional judgment to interpret the common law. In Calvin's Case or the case of the Post-Nati (1608), concerning the rights of Scotsmen to own land in England if they were born after the accession of James I, Coke defined artificial reason as "the legal and profound reason of such as by diligent study and long experience and observation are so learned in the laws of this realm, as out of the reason of the same they can rule the case in question."[60] Later, in his twelfth *Report* (published posthumously), Coke would recount how he had rebuked James for claiming he could interpret the law as well as any judge. Although the king was well endowed with natural reason, legal cases "which concern the life or inheritance or goods or fortunes of his subjects are not to be decided by natural reason but by artificial reason and judgment of law, which law is an act which requires long study and experience before that a man can attain to the cognizance of it." This view of the common law, and of the role of judges in interpreting it, severly limited the king's authority.[61] The fact that many members of Parliament were common lawyers (Coke himself would become an MP in 1621) and that Parliament was in fact a High Court contributed to the increasingly widespread view of Parliament as the defender of the common law against the encroachments of the royal prerogative.[62]

One of the most important early seventeenth-century cases concerning the arbitrariness of the royal prerogative was Bates' Case (1606), which turned on the king's right to levy impositions. Bates was a merchant who had refused to pay an import tax on currants from Venice, claiming that the tax "was imposed unjustly, and unduly against the lawes of the land."[63] Chief Baron Fleming argued that the very willingness of James to have the case heard in the court of the Exchequer (which was concerned with "matters of the kings prerogative, his revenue and government") was a sign of his gracious attention to his subjects' grievances: "It is a great grace in the king to the merchants, that he will command, and permit this matter to be disputed between him and his subject, and the most fit place is in this court, and the best rules herein are the precedents hereof, and pollitick reasons."[64] In referring to precedents and politic reasons, Fleming was reiterating a distinction made earlier, that "in these cases of prerogative the judgment shall *not be according to the rules of the common law*, but according to the precedents of this court, wherein these matters are disputable and determinable."[65] And he went on to distinguish between the common law and the king's prerogative in terms of the king's ordinary and absolute power:

> The kings power is double, ordinary and absolute, and they have several lawes and ends. That of the ordinary is for the profit of particular subjects, for the execution of civil justice, the determining of *meum*; and this is exercised by equitie and justice in ordinary courts, and by the civilians is nominated *jus privatum* and with us, common law: and these laws cannot be changed, without parliament. . . . The absolute power of the king is not that which is converted or executed to private use, but is only that which is applied to the general benefit of the people, and is *salus populi*; as the people is the body, and the king is the head; and this power is guided by the rules, which direct only at the common law, and is most properly named Pollicy and Government; and as the constitution of this body varieth with the time, so varieth this absolute law, according to the wisdom of the king, for the common good.[66]

In this striking passage, Fleming used a distinction from medieval nominalist theology concerning God's absolute and ordinary powers in order to defend an interpretation of the royal prerogative as a matter of will rather than law. Just as God's absolute powers were unconstrained by the ordinary workings of nature and the moral law, so James's prerogative was not bound by the ordinary workings of the common law. (James himself would later make similar arguments in his speeches to Parliament.)[67] At the same time, Fleming identified the whole sphere of common law with Roman private law, thereby implying that the common law had no purchase on public matters of state. According to Fleming's casuistical distinction, the king had imposed a tax on Venetian currants, not on Bates, whose private property or *meum* remained intact. James had thus not infringed on the common law but had simply exercised his prerogative to "regulate commerce and affairs with forrainers" by levying "customs." Moreover, he had done so for "the general benefit of the people . . . [the] *salus populi.*"

Although Sir Francis Bacon had the rhetorical savvy to argue that the prerogative to levy customs taxes was itself granted by "the fundamental laws of this kingdom," other lawyers for the king developed Fleming's argument in a way that brought out the darker implications of *salus populi.* Thus Sir John Davies asserted that the king was

> the fountain of all justice, as well commutative as distributive. The first is exercised chiefly in the ordering and government of trade and commerce; wherein he is to do justice, or procure it to be done, not only to his subjects who make contracts real or personal within the land, but to his merchants also, who trade with foreign nations, and to strangers who traffick in his dominions.

The king's prerogative to regulate foreign as well as domestic commerce was not only the source of justice, and thus the fundamental guarantor of the possibility of "contracts real or personal." It was also necessary for reasons of state: "[F]or commerce is not to be held with all persons. Else enemies might discover the secrets of the realm, and corrupt religion or the manners of the people."[68] In this way, Davies turned a commonplace argument about the king's power to regulate foreign commerce into a much more troubling argument about his power to oversee religion, manners, and the secrets of the realm.

In response to these arguments, the Commons MP William Hakewill charged James with breach of promise. Hakewill described how he was at first reluctant to call "his majesty's right of imposition into question," especially since "we had his majesties promise never to lay any more [impositions] but in parliament time, by the *advice and free consent* of his subjects." Moreover, he was initially persuaded by the arguments of Fleming and others when he heard them in court. But when the House of Commons employed him to review the Exchequer precedents, he was forced to conclude "that his majestie hath no right to impose," since such a right was "against the Great Charter of our liberties." Impositions were instead "due by the common-law." This meant they required "the subjects *free and voluntary assent*, and that in parliament." To admit anything else "were by consequence to bring us into bondage."[69] With the repeated addition of "free" to "consent" and "assent," Hakewill both acknowledged and refuted the contemporary view that the people's consent was compatible with coercion. Hakewill might have been thinking of James's *Trew Law*, where the king argued that the people consented to their conquest and thus to the king's absolute rule.[70] Or he might have been thinking of John Cowell's notorious legal dictionary, *The Interpreter* (1607), which defended the view that the Norman Conquest had introduced a new legal system and that parliamentary taxes were "not free gifts but debts owed to the king 'in recompense or consideration, that whereas the Prince of his absolute power might make laws of himself, he doth in favour admit the consent of his subjects therein.' " As Johann Sommerville comments, "For Cowell . . . there had been a conquest and it had made William and his successors absolute rulers."[71] This meant that the people could only consent by the "favour" of the king, a view Hakewill vociferously rejected.

The Commons MP Sir Henry Yelverton endorsed Hakewill's understanding of consent, arguing that the substance of the case was "whether we shall have any thing or nothing; for if there be a right in the king to alter the property of that which is ours without our consent, we are but tenants at his will of that which we have." The idea that subjects were mere tenants called up the specter of the Norman Yoke, which Yelverton then cleverly dismissed by asserting that a king with mere tenants was no king at all:

> And if you give this power to the kings patent, you subject the law, and take away all rules and bounds of settled government, and leave in the subject no property of his own, neither do you by this advance the kings power and prerogative, but you make him no king; for as Bracton saith . . . "Rex est, ubi dominatur lex, non voluntas." [The king is where the law rules, not will.][72]

Finally, Yelverton adduced the petitions "exhibited by the commons in parliament": "[T]he very knot of their griefe, and the principal cause of their complaint, hath been expressed in those petitions that the impositions have been without assent of parliament; by which is necessarily inferred that their griefe was in point of right, not of burden."[73] The complaint, that is, was not that the taxes were financially burdensome but that they had been imposed without consent. In this account, the passions were clearly not a motivation for consent but rather a reason for dissent.

Although MPs and common lawyers did not have precisely the same concerns about the voluntarism of the contracting subject as natural rights theorists and covenant theologians, they all participated in the cultural conversation about the meaning of consent. Even as they worried about the dangers of voluntary servitude, the fact that they did so out loud or in print furthered the possibility of dissent. As Thomas Wentworth remarked in 1610, "if we shall once say that we may not dispute the prerogative, let us be sold for slaves." In their comments and petitions, in other words, we see the Commons claiming its rights through disputation. According to Yelverton, it was not ultimately James's gracious condescension but the Commons' assertion of its right to dispute the prerogative that laid the ground for other rights—such as the right of habeas corpus—that would be articulated and defended in the decades that followed.[74] A similarly charged discussion occurred in local parishes where ministers were advising the faithful that consent to the heavenly contract both served as a model for and trumped consent to the contract of government. At the same time, John Selden and other parliamentary students of natural rights were voicing their own views of the free consent of the governed. In his famous speech to Parliament in 1610 James warned his subjects not to discuss the prerogative. He must have known—or he would not have insisted—that it was already too late.

In concluding this anatomy of the early seventeenth-century discourses of contract, it's worth emphasizing how far we've come from the usual accounts. To modern ears, contract is a legalistic conception of obligation that presupposes the formal equality of the contracting parties before the law. Accordingly, most historians of political thought stress these features of early modern contractual thinking; they present the seventeenth-century language of contract as a fairly unproblematic theory of consent, motivated by a new optimism in the power of individuals to determine the form of their governments. Coercion, bondage, slavery to the passions as well as to another person do not figure in the usual accounts.[75] But in the early decades of the seventeenth century, I have argued, the idea of a political contract was a source of anxiety as well as optimism: anxiety about voluntary servitude, on the one hand, and about the refusal of voluntary subjection, on the other. Absolute bondage and absolute contingency were viewed as two sides of the same coin.

In the first case, contemporaries were afraid that an individual freed from the constraints of status and custom—an individual freed to act on his passions and interests—might simply, perhaps irrevocably, enslave himself. Traditional bonds would give way to new forms of bondage. Absolute freedom would, paradoxically, result in absolute servitude—whether to passion, irrationality, political and religious tyranny, or some combination of these. In the second case, contemporaries were afraid that, instead of becoming the calculable, dependable subject of political obligation—the subject who could stand surety for himself and his promises—the subject of contract might instead be filled with anger and resentment, rebellious and unruly passions, and refuse subjection to authority altogether. Here the threat was religious antinomianism, enthusiasm, domestic rebellion, and civil war.

In both cases, as we will see, the voluntarism of contract posed a threat to traditional conceptions of gender. The attention to the affective dimension of contract risked making wives the paradigmatic political subject, with pejorative implications for the husband's consent. The emphasis on consent to the political contract risked empowering the wife to question her natural subordination to her husband in marriage. In the early seventeenth century, John Selden's blithe acceptance in one of the epigraphs to this chapter of a world in which women negotiated contractually with men regarding their sexual passions and interests, and subjects negotiated with sovereigns regarding their political passions and interests, was the exception rather than the rule. But in linking the contingency of contractual political negotiations to the vicissitudes of the passions, Selden had tapped some the deepest fears of his contemporaries.

PART TWO

A Poetics of Contract, 1640–1674

CHAPTER 4

Imagination

> The causes and motives of seditions are: innovations in reli-
> gion, taxes, alteration of laws and customs, breaking of priv-
> ileges, general oppression, advancement of unworthy persons,
> strangers, dearths, disbanded soldiers, factions grown des-
> perate, and whatsover in offending people joineth and knitteth
> them in a common cause.
> —Francis Bacon, "Of Seditions and Troubles"

> Not only the imprudent *Commissions*, but also voluntary
> *Omissions* of *King James* [were] so much instrumentall in
> the promotion of our present evills, as it may justly be said,
> He, like *Adam*, by bringing the Crown into so great a Neces-
> sity through a profuse prodigality, became the originall of his
> Son's fall: who was in a manner compel'd to stretch out his hands
> towards such gatherings and *Taxes*, as are contrary to Law: by
> which he fell from the *Paradise* of a Prince, to wit, The *hearts*
> of His People.
> —Francis Osborne, *Memoirs of King James*

IN THE YEARS LEADING UP TO the civil war, conflicts between the Stuarts
and Parliament brought the language of contract to the fore in the political sphere. Although members of Parliament first marshaled the language
of contract in the context of financial negotiations over subsidies, the
recourse to this language in the 1620s and 1630s also reflected a growing
perception that Charles I was morally unreliable. In the early years of his
reign, Charles had earned Parliament's distrust by marrying the Catholic
Henrietta Maria, adopting his father's political rhetoric of the divine right
of kingship, refusing to intervene in behalf of the Protestant cause on the
continent, and engaging in a host of other actions that were perceived to
be crypto-papist, absolutist, and tyrannical. In his demands for subsidies,
Charles was perceived to be acting in bad faith and without regard for
Magna Carta and the common law. Increasingly, the notion of a political
contract was proposed as the antidote to the king's breach of promise in
all areas of negotiation.[1]

In 1628, as in previous years, Charles offered "promises and assurances" in exchange for Parliament's grant of subsidies. Specifically, he promised that Parliament's timely supply would "bind [him] in an obligation of thankfulness."[2] John Selden and others replied in the language of fundamental rights and liberties, the law of nature and of nations. To Charles's "I give you my word," the Commons replied that the king's right to promise was itself bound by the common law. To Charles's half-threatening offers of clemency and oblivion—his promise to "forget" his subjects' failings—they answered that their obligation did not follow from "thankfulness" but from their legally protected "rights." Here, as so often in the years leading up to the civil war, an older language of noblesse oblige, trust, thankfulness, and affection confronted a newer language of rights and legally binding promises. Although the Commons MPs protested their "love and affection" for the king's "favours," they also insisted that property, the subject's "meum," was a condition of the people's affection. "How can we show our affections whilst we retain our fears?" Sir Francis Seymour inquired, adding with revolutionary common sense, "how can we think of giving subsidies till we know whether we have anything to give or no?" Selden drew the obvious conclusion: the right to property, like all other rights, is nothing without legal remedies.[3]

In this chapter I explore two moments in this developing seventeenth-century debate about the nature of political obligation. The first encompasses the state trials involving the subjects' rights and liberties in the decade and a half before the outbreak of war. In response to the king's empty promises, Parliament's discussion of political obligation began to shift. From a vaguely defined sense of some kind of mutual obligation, MPs began to invoke the common law notion of contract as a mutual exchange of promises accompanied by some reliance, expectation, or consideration. Parliament also invoked the notion of contract in response to Charles's arbitrary exercise of the royal prerogative, with his imaginary claims of reason of state and equitable interpretation. In both cases, the common law notion of an economic contract came to seem the right way to think about the implied contract of Magna Carta, and in both cases the rhetoric of contract was an attempt to make Charles accountable to Parliament.

The second moment in the debate about political obligation concerns the pamphlet war touched off by the parliamentarian Henry Parker's response to *His Majesties Answer to the Nineteen Propositions* (1642). In this pamphlet, "Charles" abandoned his absolutist rhetoric and spoke—fatally, to the minds of some historians—the language of the mixed constitution, the people's "rights," and the "fundamental laws" of the kingdom. He even went so far as to hint at the parliamentary notion of political contract, according to which the sovereign guarantees "protection"

in exchange for the subject's "obedience," a contract that is in the "interest" of both parties to uphold.[4] In response, Parker began to draw on the
language of necessity and *salus populi* that had characterized the arguments of the crown in the late 1620s and 1630s. He also appealed to the
imagination and to equitable interpretation, in support not of the royal
prerogative but rather of the right of Parliament to take up arms against
the king. The rhetoric of contract here was no longer part of an argument
for royal accountability; it was instead shorthand for the people's legitimate breach of contract. In response to these arguments, Parker's critics
explicitly condemned the parliamentary "fiction" of contractual political
representation. In the course of these struggles, both sides came to understand contract as a powerful metaphor that could be used to loose as well
as bind, to justify resistance as well as allegiance. Both sides also revealed
their awareness that the power of contract to construct new social and
political relations was inseparable from the power of the imagination.

FIVE KNIGHTS: FROM PROMISE TO CONTRACT

As previous chapters have begun to suggest, in the early modern period
the moral act of promising and the legal act of contracting were analyti-
cally distinct, even as the promise was commonly seen to be the moral
foundation of the contract.[5] In canon law, promises were made before
God and binding because of the natural and moral law that "pacta servanda sunt." Early modern manuals of ethics and casuistry state that written and parole (informal verbal) contracts should be kept because of this
moral law. On the other hand, the separate existence of ecclesiastical and
common law courts in England meant that the moral and legal—the
promise and the contract—also had separate jurisdictions. As we have
seen, the common law did not treat broken contracts as breach of promise
until Slade's Case in 1602. Prior to this time, the common law courts
treated broken contracts in terms of the action of debt, while actions for
breach of promise were brought in the ecclesiastical courts. In the course
of the sixteenth-century, however, the precise nature of the link between
a promise and a contract was increasingly a contested legal issue—a contest that reflected the expansion of trade and the increasing number of
legal actions for debt, as well as the turf wars between the ecclesiastical
and common law courts, and the changing balance of power between
church and state.

In the state trials and parliamentary debates of the 1620s and 1630s,
the contest over the relationship between a morally binding promise and
a legally binding contract became an explicitly political issue involving
the relationship between king and Parliament, sovereign and subject. Al-

though Parliament was not the only important arena of political conflict in these years, the trials and Commons debates illustrate a dramatic transformation in these political relationships. In this transformation, the absolute sovereign (who was, at least in theory, the only autonomous subject in this period) was himself subjected, and the sovereign act of promising was redefined in terms of the social conventions of contracting. Rather than the divinely authored natural law that promises must be kept, we have something like the common law notion that promises may be inferred when there has been some consideration, reliance, or expectation. As a result, the sovereign individual and the ability to promise come to be seen to be an effect of convention and of human institutions as much as their cause. The secularization of promises coincides with a developing awareness of the legal, social, and linguistic construction of both ruler and subject.[6]

In the reign of Charles two state trials occurred that are crucial for understanding this development. The first is the Five Knights Case of 1627, with its repercussions in the Commons Debates and Petition of Right of 1628–29. The second is the Shipmoney Case of 1637–38. The issues in the two cases are similar: although the first turned on the right of habeas corpus or freedom from unjust imprisonment and the second on taxation without parliamentary consent, both were set off by Charles's unpopular forced loans; both involved the relation of the royal prerogative to the common law and to the rights and fundamental liberties of the subject, including the right to property. Both thus addressed the relationship between the king's promises and the implicit contract of Magna Carta. But the political consequences of the second case were more serious than the first, not least of all because the issues had been rehearsed ten years before; Charles, it seemed, was incapable of learning from his mistakes. "Looking back from 1641," Glenn Burgess writes, "MPs accorded key significance to the Shipmoney case.... [T]his was undoubtedly the climactic political event of the pre–Civil War period."[7]

In the 1620s and 1630s Charles I was widely seen as imposing taxes on his subjects without their consent in order first to fund military action against France and Spain, and then to pay for his unpopular war against the Scots. This was in conflict with Magna Carta, which, in the discourse of early modern constitutionalism, was understood to guarantee not only property in one's person but also in one's lands and goods. Of particular relevance was the clause in chapter 29 that stipulated that a man's property could not be taken nor his person imprisoned *nisi per legem terrae*, unless by the law of the land. (One important point of contention was whether "law of the land" included the king's command, or whether the phrase meant "by due process.") These "native liberties" came into conflict with the royal prerogative in the Five Knights Case, in which five

MPs who were imprisoned for refusing to pay a forced loan sought bail and release from imprisonment through a writ of habeas corpus. (Selden was the lawyer for one of the MPs, Edmund Hampden, a cousin of the more famous Commons MP John Hampden.) The court ruled in favor of the crown, refusing to grant bail, although it did not address the legitimacy of the forced loan. Instead the judges accepted the crown's interpretation of the royal prerogative, including the king's right of discretionary imprisonment for "reasons of state."

Attorney General Heath summed up the reasoning of the crown when he used the king's power to coin as a metaphor for the royal prerogative:

> No doubt but the king's power is absolutely over his coins; if then he shall command his coin shall be turned to brass or leather, I confess it were inconvenient; but if the king would do it, the answer that I can make is, that he would not undo the kingdom: but can your lordship hinder it, as being an inconvenience, if he would do it? . . . and therefore we are too wise, nay we are too foolish, in undertaking to examine matters of state, to which we are not born.[8]

As Heath made clear, at the center of this case and the Shipmoney Case was the king's right of interpretation, specifically his right to determine exceptions to the law. Parties on both sides of the dispute agreed that the king could exercise his royal prerogative in matters that fell outside the common law. What was at issue, then, was whether the prerogative could also be applied to matters which did come under common law jurisdiction.[9] By arguing from the king's prerogative right to coin money Heath essentially collapsed this distinction. He assumed, in short, what he needed to prove.

In response, critics of the crown emphasized that the royal prerogative was a *part* of the common law and that it had been granted to the king by the people in an original contract. In a parliamentary debate about the "liberties of the subject," which was occasioned by the Five Knights Case, Sir Robert Phillips (or Phelips) asserted

> It is well known, the people of this state are under no other subjection, than what they did voluntarily consent unto, by the original contract between king and people; and as there are many prerogatives and privileges conferred on the king, so there are left to the Subject many necessary Liberties and Privileges, as appears by the common laws and acts of parliament. (3:65)

These liberties and privileges included the right not to be imprisoned arbitrarily or taxed without consent. Thus Coke, who was in favor of supplying the king, "yet with some caution," reminded his audience that "the [feudal] lord may tax his villein high and low, but it is against the franchise of the land, for freemen to be taxed but by their consent in parliament" (3:63). Cresswell concurred, arguing that "almost every leaf and page of all the volumes of our Common-Law prove this right of propriety, this distinction between *meum* and *tuum*, as well between the King and subject, as one subject and another" (3:73). In the minds of the Commons MPs, economic rights were inseparable from political rights, which helps to explain why the political contract of Magna Carta was increasingly analogized to the common law understanding of an economic contract between one subject and another.

In defense of these political and economic rights the House of Commons, led by Wentworth and Coke, drew up the Petition of Right.[10] Although the Lords tried to include a clause "saving" the king's prerogative, this clause was ultimately rejected. The commons MP John Glanville explained this exclusion in terms of the opposition between trust and the common law:

> [O]ur petition is uppon the Common lawe and statutes, there is in the King concerning some statutes and lawes, a trust, but in some there is not, there is noe trust whatsoever to bee above the Common lawe, for the statutes in them that are paenall that prohibit *male prohibita* and are paenall, for those lawes the Kings of England have dispensed with the breach of them, *non obstante*, but those statutes that are not under anie penaltie, but absolute commaunds according to the Common lawe and of the nature of the Common lawe, I never heard any trust to dispince with them.

The king, that is, could exercise his trust or prerogative to "dispense in statute with his own rights but not with his subjects' rights."[11]

Thus, when, in his original reply, the king gave his "Royal Word" that he would respect the provisions of the Petition of Right (3:172, 176), his critics responded that such a promise was insufficient in the absence of a legally binding contract. Without such a contract, there was no reason to trust the king. Trust, the MPs seemed to be saying, is not something that an individual grants to or inspires in another. Trust is instead the effect of institutions and specifically legal arrangements. Once these mechanisms become the subject of explicit discussion, trust is fundamentally riven by distrust. Speaking like a modern-day contracts lawyer, Glanville cautioned: "The word 'trust' is of great latitude and large extent, and therefore ought to be well and warily applied and restrained, especially in the case of a king: there is a trust inseparably reposed in the persons of the kings of England, but that trust is regulated by law" (3:206). The king's "promise" or noblesse oblige was not in itself sufficient. His prerogative—his right to promise or give his royal word—was itself granted by the same contract that ensured the ancient rights and liberties, including the property rights, of free men.[12]

John Pym, a leader in the House of Commons, made this case with reference to Magna Carta. In forwarding the Petition of Right, the Commons was "not suing for any new [rights and liberties]," he asserted, but simply demanding those that had been established in the contract between William the Conqueror and his subjects. According to Pym, William had obtained the throne by "composition, in which he bound himself to observe these and the other ancient laws and liberties of the kingdom, which afterwards he likewise confirmed by oath at his coronation." Robert Mason argued that royal sovereignty in England was not absolute but limited: the king derived his power from the people and ruled "by contract" (*ex pacto*). According to Mason, "the extent and limit of the king's power . . . depend on human will and on the ancient agreement or contract between the kings and the kingdom."[13]

Others also tried to transform the king's language of promises and royal word into the language of contract, construed not simply in terms of ancient rights and liberties but contemporary common law. Invoking something like the reliance theory of promissory liability, Edward Coke argued, "if we rest upon his majesty's promise, we may assure ourselves of the performance of it; *we bind his majesty, by relying on his word*" (3:180).[14] Coke was not simply asserting that promises should be kept, but that verbal promises amount to legally binding contracts when one party acts on the promise of another. In this way one's reliance on what might be a deceitful promise became a source of strength rather than weakness; the king's promise—however badly intentioned—became the fulcrum that transferred his power to bind to Parliament.[15] Thomas Wentworth performed an analogous operation when he turned the king's request for trust on its head:

> [N]ever house of parliament trusted more in the goodness of their king, for their own private account, than the present; but we are ambitious that his majesty's goodness may remain to posterity, and we are accountable to *a public trust*: and therefore seeing there hath been a public violation of the laws by his ministers, nothing will satisfy him but a public amends; and our desires to vindicate the Subjects Right by Bill, are no more than are laid down in former laws, with some modest provision for instruction, performance and execution. (3:180)

The difference between the trust of private individuals and "a public trust," with all of its legal connotations of fiduciary responsibility, would be exploited in the parliamentary pamphlets of the 1640s.[16] But already in 1628 trust had bifurcated into public and private, general and particular, a trust based on right or one based on affection. Secretary Cook urged the House to rely on the king's promise, which binds not only his "conscience" but also his "affection, which is the greatest bond between king and subject" (3:188). In response, Coke returned to the issue of trust in promises, insisting with Wentworth that they be construed according to legal norms:

> Was it ever known . . . that general words were a sufficient satisfaction to particular grievances: Was ever a verbal declaration of the king *verbum regni*? When Grievances be, the parliament is to redress them. Did ever parliament rely on Messages? They put up Petitions of their Grievances, and the king ever answered them: the king's answer is very gracious, but what is the law of the realm, that is the question? . . . All succeeding kings will say, Ye must trust me as you did my predecessors, and trust my Messages; but messages of love never came into a parliament. Let us put up a PETITION OF RIGHT: not that I distrust the king, but I cannot take his trust, but in a parliamentary way. (3:188)

In passages such as these we can see the unraveling of the old bonds of nobility and trust, the old notion that a gentleman's—or king's—word is his bond. According to his critics, the king cannot grant to the people by his gracious favor what is already theirs legally, by right. Moreover, even the king's word needs to be "assented to by the king in parliament," that is, by the Lords and Commons, before it can be made the basis of a binding obligation (3:189).[17]

SHIPMONEY AND THE IMAGINATION OF DISASTER

Even more important for understanding the developing political crisis was Hampden's Case or the Shipmoney Case of 1637–38. Shipmoney was a tax imposed on coastal towns for the provision of ships or money for defense of the coastline. The tax, which could be imposed without parliamentary consent when the king judged there was an external threat, had been in existence since the fourteenth century. In 1635 Charles extended the tax to inland counties as well.[18] John Hampden, an influential and wealthy member of the House of Commons, refused to pay on the grounds that the new tax amounted to a breach of contract, specifically the provision of Magna Carta concerning the subject's property rights. (Hampden had also refused to pay the forced loan of 1626 and had been imprisoned with his cousin Edmund for most of 1627.)[19] In arguing the case against Hampden, Charles's lawyers invoked reason of state, citing the "imminent danger" of war, which demanded that new ships be built to protect England's coastline. They also presented a purely economic argument for the tax, based on the threat posed by pirates to seafaring

English mechants.[20] In response, Hampden's lawyers replied that there was no real danger; the king was simply trying to squeeze money out of his subjects without calling Parliament. In so doing, Charles posed a fundamental threat to the rights and liberties of Englishmen. Many of those who spoke for the crown or Parliament in the debate over Ship-money remarked on the high stakes of the case. "I say it is a great case," pronounced Sir William Jones, one of the justices of the King's Bench, "It concerns the king in his royal prerogative, and the subject in his interest, in his land and goods, and liberty of his person" (3:1182).[21]

In Shipmoney, just as in Five Knights, political issues were inseparable from economic issues, and both in turn gave rise to a conflict over the right to interpret. To ask what price—if any—the king could equitably exact without the consent of his subjects was to cast disputes about property and political contract as disputes about equitable interpretation. In both cases, defenders of the crown argued that it was the king's prerogative to exercise his discretion in matters of state, that is, matters pertaining to *salus populi* or the safety of the commonwealth. If the king judged it necessary to impose a tax for reasons of state, the subject was obliged to trust his judgment. "You will believe that there is a great reason of state so to do, or else they [the king and his ministers] would not do it," Attorney General Robert Heath had asserted in Five Knights.[22] In arguing for the crown in Shipmoney, Sir Edward Littleton followed suit, invoking the maxim of reason of state, *salus populi suprema lex*, which he glossed as "positive laws are abrogated by reason, when the safety of the kingdom and the people are in danger" (3:926). And, like defenders of the crown in Five Knights, he equated such discretionary judgment with equity.[23]

In response, critics of the king made it clear that they did not trust his judgment. Thus they did not simply argue that the royal prerogative was limited by law, beginning with "the original contract between king and people." Nor did they simply rebuke the king for treating his free subjects as "slaves" or feudal "villeins," without fundamental rights of liberty and property.[24] Critics also accused the king of fancy, in the sense of arbitrary interpretation. And they described the king's references to matters of state, equity, *salus populi*, and imminent threat as dangerous metaphors, feigning, and equivocation. To the king's argument that "imminent danger" to the commonwealth kept the king from seeking parliamentary consent to taxation, Commons MPs objected that this imminent danger had already lasted for many years.

This naturally led to a debate about how to interpret *salus populi*, about how and when the fear of danger could legitimate extralegal action. Some of those who spoke for Hampden did not dispute that, in genuine cases of danger, the king had the right to take a subject's property without his consent. Others did not dispute the king's right to demand that the subject at least defend the commonwealth in person. What both sorts of critics did dispute was Charles's "metaphorical" version of "necessity," along with his equally metaphorical—or, more properly, proleptic— "fear" for the safety of the commonwealth. "We that are judges are bound," declared Sir George Crooke, justice of the King's Bench, "according to the law, not according to our own imaginations."[25] Against the king's imagination, Crooke asserted the authority of statute law and the common law.

Sir Edward Littleton, the king's solicitor general, had argued in defense of the king, using the timeworn "storm at sea" example of necessity from Aristotle and Cicero: "Necessity is the law of the time and action, and things are lawful by necessity, which otherwise are not; . . . If a storm arise at sea, to cast out goods into the sea is lawful for the safety of the other goods; and they whose goods are not lost, shall be sharers with the others" (3:927). This superficial appeal to the principle of necessity did not persuade critics of the crown, who objected that "necessity," "salus populi," and other such justifications, were, like "trust," of too "great latitude and large extent." They were, in short, equivocal metaphors designed to facilitate the king's breach of contract.

Addressing the crown's appeal to "salus populi," Holborne commented, "the word 'salus,' being only proper to a physical and natural body, is applied here to a body politic. It is but a metaphor, which the law will not endure in writs, for it would bring in great mischiefs. In writs and in pleadings, metaphors are dangerous: We know not how to take issue upon it, and therefore it is not regularly allowed" (3:966). Sir John Banks, the king's attorney general, replied that *salus* commonly meant safety as well as health, and in any case "Metaphors are usual in writs" (3:1061). To the objection that the king's phrase "salus populi periclitabatur" (the safety of the people was in danger) is "metaphorical," Banks asked with obvious irritation, "Will you bind the king to the language of J. S.? May [the king] not express himself in what legal manner he pleaseth?" (3:1086). J. S. or John à Stiles was the John Doe of the common law whose manner of speaking, Banks claimed, could not be a model for the king. Instead, Banks equated the king's prerogative to exercise his discretion in extraordinary cases with a specifically linguistic prerogative: the license of metaphor.

Related to Holborne's objection to metaphor was the charge that the king's judgment of "imminent danger," his "fear" for the commonwealth, was hasty at best and a mere "pretense" for arbitrary taxation at worst. Edmund Waller sarcastically accused the king of a "pretended necessity," "supposed necessity," "supposititious [sic], imposed necessity"—in short, a fictional necessity whose magical effect was to change "our real property into a shadow of a property, so of a feigned it is made a real necessity"

(3:1302–3). Waller's riff was an acerbic display of wit, but the issue was serious. How was either a king or a subject to judge the legitimacy of his fears when fear was, almost by definition, bound up with the imagination? Holborne argued more soberly for Hampden that the appeal to necessity was only legitimate

> in such a danger . . . as in case of fire; there must not only be fear of fire, for our house must be first actually on fire, before the house can be pulled down. . . . If there be a storm, or a leak in a ship, that the danger be actual, it is justifiable for the master to throw out the goods; but if he sees a cloud arise, and out of fear of a storm he threw out the goods, I doubt on a jury which way this will go with the bargeman. . . . It is not enough there be but an apprehension. (3:1012–13)

Moreover, the king must not be sole judge of the difference between apprehension and just fear.[26] If he is, Oliver St. John, Hampden's principal lawyer, argued, the king's fears or rather his desires "may be multiplied *in infinitum.*" Such an unregulated sovereign "will," he cautioned, would amount to royal—or Roman—absolutism, "imperium legibus solutum" (3:1266).[27]

In defense of the king, Sir John Banks pointed out that there was little or no distinction between fear and apprehension, between the imagination of disaster and the protection against it: "If a man be in fear, that another man lieth in wait for him to do him a mischief, shall he stay until he receive a wound? . . . and shall not the common law provide for the king, that he in his expectation of danger, may make his preparation against it?" (3:1037, 1038). In a similar vein, Edward Crawley, justice of the Common-Pleas, argued that the king was only reasoning according to the principles of equity:

> It much concerns the king, the head of the commonwealth, to be circumspect in the prevention of public danger; conjectures and probabilities are to be regarded. Now put the case upon a probable and violent presumption; a potent enemy is prepared and ready to come. Is it not fit there should be a defence prepared instantly? Besides, there may be just reason of state, why an enemy is not fit to be revealed in parliament; for if great preparations be, and very probably against us, then to discover them to be an enemy, is to give them occasion to become a challenger. No man can know the certain event of things. (3:1083)[28]

Crawley himself exemplified equitable reasoning in these remarks by hypothesizing a case of danger and then reasoning about the best way of preparing for it. He rejected the charge that "violent presumption" itself did violence to the commonwealth; a master of paradiastole, he recast presumption as foresight, and secrecy as caution. And he went on to cite

St. German's *Doctor and Student* on equity by way of clarifying Charles's invocation of reasons of state:

> [S]aith Doctor and Student, To follow the words of the law, were, in some cases, injustice, and against the good of the commonwealth; wherefore, in some cases, it is necessary to leave the words of the law, and to follow that which reason and justice requireth: and to that intent equity is ordained, which is not other but an exception of the law of God, or law of reason, from the general rules of the law of man: Which exception is tacitly understood, in every general law. This imposition without parliament appertains to the king originally, and to the successor *ipso facto*, if he be a sovereign in right of his sovereignty from the crown. You cannot have a king without these royal rights, no, not by act of parliament. (3:1085)

But St. German could also be quoted to defend the subject's rights.[29] Justice Crooke, who eventually ruled for Hampden, cited St. German "That the law doeth vest the absolute property of every man's goods in him, and that they cannot be taken from him but by his consent" (1162). And he went on to cite Coke's reasoning in Slade's Case that precedents (in this case, those cited by the crown) should not be regarded unless "confirmed by judicial proceedings, in courts of record" (1167). It would later be said in the Inns of Court "that the King had Ship-Money 'by hook but not by Crooke.' "[30]

Although a majority of the judges ruled in favor of the king, Charles's already strained relations with Parliament were further damaged by the Shipmoney trial. Not only were the king's prerogative and secrets of state subjected to public discussion; the "vizor of necessity" was torn from his face (3:1302). In the process, MPs increasingly found themselves speaking the language not of trust, love, and affection, or simply of the common law, but also of the fear of self-preservation and the implied contract between subject and sovereign, a contract that made the sovereign subject to the law like anyone else. Thus it was that, much later, in his *History of the Rebellion* Edward Hyde, earl of Clarendon, singled out Shipmoney as an extraordinary lapse of judgment on the part of the crown. It was one thing to invoke the royal prerogative; it was quite another to mix idioms by invoking reason of state in a court of law.[31] Such a staging of the prerogative in the theater of the common law was bound to backfire, by suggesting that the law should take precedence even over the king's rightful prerogative:

> [W]hen [the MPs] heard this [Shipmoney payment] demanded in a court of law, as a right, and found it, by sworn judges of the law, adjudged so, upon such grounds as every stander-by was able to swear was not

law, and so had lost the pleasure and delight of being kind, and dutiful to the king; and, instead of giving, were required to pay, and by a logic that left no man any thing which he might call his own, they no more looked upon it as the case of one man, but the case of the kingdom.[32]

In this condensed and characteristically brilliant passage, Clarendon summed up the crisis of political obligation that led to the English civil war—at one and the same time a crisis of the common law and of the affections.[33] According to one dominant fiction of Charles's reign the king ruled by love and affection rather than fear and coercion. In return, his subjects lovingly and voluntarily subordinated themselves and their property to their sovereign. Clarendon describes this original relationship in terms not of contract and consent but of an older economy of gift giving that produces "pleasure and delight." Charles's mistake in the Shipmoney Case was thus not only to demand what his subjects understood to be a gift but to demand it as a legal right. In doing so, he unmasked the coerciveness behind the Caroline politics of love and, by asking that such coercion be ratified in a court of law, threatened the very distinction between law and force.[34] It was maneuvers such as this that helped to make the language of contract, natural law, natural right, and even the royalist rhetoric of reason of state seem more promising idioms in which to conduct the business of government. As time would tell, they were also more promising idioms in which to justify the conduct of war.

HENRY PARKER AND THE METAPHOR OF CONTRACT

The outbreak of civil war saw the publication of a series of pamphlets by both royalists and parliamentarians that debated the war as a case of conscience and a dispute over the rights of the subject. For our purposes, several related characteristics of these tracts are noteworthy. Even more than the speakers in the Five Knights Case, Shipmoney, and the parliamentary debates of 1628, the authors were acutely self-consciousness about the language in which they chose to discuss political obligation. They understood that the political contest about sovereignty was a contest of interpretation and analogy, one that raised questions of intention, equitable interpretation, imagination, and reason of state. The writers of these pamphlets frequently recurred to the metaphor of contract, which was intertwined—as it was in the culture at large—with discussions of covenant, oaths, and promises. And, as elsewhere, the meaning of contract was not taken for granted; its definition was precisely what was at issue.

For parties of all political persuasions, the debate about the nature of the political obligation involved questions about the relation of natural right and duty, right and natural law, in the establishment of government.

How much was obligation a matter of conscience and how much a matter of calculation? Was it moral or prudential? Was political obligation dependent on the theological covenant, analogous to economic contract or the marriage contract, distinct from the slave contract, and if so how? How one answered these questions determined whether one could transfer one's right to self-preservation absolutely, whether the political contract should instead be construed as conditional, whether and how conscience was bound, whether conscience licensed arguments and actions based on reason of state. Ironically, in debating these issues, parliamentary pamphleteers began to put forward arguments from natural law, "imminent danger," and reason of state, while royalists appropriated the earlier parliamentary language of positive or common law.[35]

We can begin to get a sense of the different strands in the discourse of political obligation by turning to Henry Parker's *Observations upon Some of His Majesties Late Answers and Expresses* of 1642. Parker, a lawyer by training, was the most important parliamentary pamphleteer of the 1640s.[36] When Parliament convened in 1640, he published *The Case of Shipmony briefly discoursed*. The relevance of the case to present circumstances was obvious. Not only was the Shipmoney decision still a source of outrage, but the question it purported to answer was current as well: "whether the king should be sole judge of the danger to the kingdom and the means to be taken for its preservation."[37] In this pamphlet, which proved to be a kind of trial run for his *Observations*, Parker conceded that *salus populi* was the supreme law, but he rejected the king's argument that Shipmoney was a case of necessity or imminent danger. The fact that Charles thought or pretended it was pointed only to his fallible human nature, even perhaps to his restless seeking after power. "If this ambition and desire of vast power were not the most naturall and forcible of all sinnes," Parker wrote, "Angels in heaven, and man in Paradise, had not fallen by it; but since it is, Princes themselves ought to be more cautious of it."[38] This appropriation of the royalist language of *salus populi*, along with a denigration of Charles's ability to determine which situations warranted reason of state, would recur in the *Observations*.

By most accounts the *Observations*, a response to Charles's *Answer* to the Nineteen Propositions, was one of the most influential pamphlets of the civil war period; "its impact," according to Ernest Sirluck, "was enormous." In the *Observations* Parker made two powerful and related arguments. First, building on Grotius and French monarchomach theorists, he advanced a theory of the popular, contractual origins of government. Second, he appropriated the royalist language of imminent danger or emergency circumstances to defend a theory of "parliamentary absolutism" and reason of state. The first move allowed Parker to link Parliament to the rule of law, to derive the royal prerogative from law, and to criticize

Charles for his own illegal actions. The second move allowed Parker to use the language of natural or fundamental law to justify Parliament's own violations of positive law. Together, these arguments amounted to the first English use of the discourse of natural rights and the political contract to claim parliamentary sovereignty.[39]

According to Parker, "power is originally inherent in the people" and is transferred to the sovereign, for reasons of self-preservation, by "the Pactions and agreements of such and such politique corporations."[40] But the same natural or fundamental law of self-preservation that informs the political contract of government also legitimates the breach of contract, in the form of extraordinary measures to preserve the state. In defense of Parliament's own recent extralegal actions (in particular, the ordinance granting Parliament oversight of the militia and Sir John Hotham's refusal to allow the king access to the munitions at Hull), Parker argued that natural or fundamental law trumped positive law: "[F]or since all naturall power is in those which obay, they which contract to obay to their owne ruine, or having so contracted, they which esteeme such a contract before their owne preservation are felonious to themselves, and rebellious to nature" (8). But Parker went still further. Although the state had its origins in contract, the essence of sovereignty, he argued, was ultimately arbitrary power: "[E]very man has an absolute power over himself; but because no man can hate himself, this power is not dangerous; So every State has an Arbitrary power over it self, and there is no danger in it for the same reason." It is as though Parker were advancing the republican model of contractual obligation *and* saying, with Hobbes and Filmer, that "it is not power except it be arbitrary."[41] In the *Observations* contract and violence, contract and the emergency measures of reason of state, emerge as two sides of the same coin.

In the course of elaborating these arguments for the contractual basis of the state, Parker also anatomized some of the problems of the new language of contract. The first difficulty was to determine how exactly the political contract between subject and sovereign should be construed. For Parker, contract did not need to be between equals, nor was it incompatible with subordination. But if monarchy was to keep from sliding into tyranny, there had to be limits to consent. Thus Parker conceded that the people contract to obey but asserted that they cannot do so against their interests (7). They consent to be ruled, but "to consent is more than to counsell, and yet not always so much as to command and to controll" (9).

The second, related problem regarding contract concerned the relationship of reason and the will. Political contract is necessary because "Man is by nature of restlesse ambition; as the meanest vassall thinks himself worthy of some greatnesse, so the most absolute Monarch aspires to something above his greatnesse" (39). In this Hobbesian world of vain-glory, human beings need artificial constraints to keep the restless seeking after power from spiraling out of control. Accordingly, government has its origin in an act of volition (13); but this emphasis on the will raises the question of how to distinguish mere will from legitimacy, might from right. And this in turn raises the question of who shall judge? Parker laid out the problem in the following way:

> [W]e see consent as well as counsell is requisite and due in Parliament and that being the proper foundation of all power (for *omnia Potestas fundata est in voluntate*) we cannot imagine that publique consent should be any where more vigorous or more orderly than it is in Parliament. Man being depraved by the fall of *Adam* grew so untame and uncivill a creature, that the Law of God written in his brest was not sufficient to restrayne him from mischiefe, or to make him sociable, and therefore without some magistracy to provide new orders, and to judge of old, and execute according to justice, no society could be up-held. Without society man could not live, and without lawes men could not be sociable, and without authority somewhere invested, to judge according to Law, and execute according to judgement, Law was a vaine and void thing. It was soon therefore provided that lawes agree-able to the dictates of reason should be ratified by common con-sent. . . . *Twas not difficult to invent Lawes, for the limiting of supreme governors, but to invent how those Lawes should be executed or by whom interpreted, was almost impossible.* (13; emphasis added in this last sentence)

The illegibility of natural law necessitated the "invention" of positive laws, but this in turn threatened an infinite regress of interpreters.[42] Such an infinite regress ultimately dictated the arbitrary imposition of sover-eignty. According to such reasoning, sovereignty itself is the "exception" to or foundation of the law. But not all forms of sovereignty are equal. Because the sovereignty of Parliament does not rely on a single judgment, it is less dangerous than monarchy. The king rules as an individual whose reason and conscience are "meere private opinion." In contrast, Parlia-ment rules as a representative body (by what Parker called the "virtue of representation"), whose "interests" can never conflict with those of "the people."[43] Parliament is not governed by "meer pleasure" but by the dic-tates of "natural law."[44] And yet, as we have seen, in cases of self-preserva-tion, natural law may look very arbitrary indeed. Moreover, the problem of arbitrariness is compounded by the illegibility of natural law. Parker drew the obvious—but, at the time, radical—conclusion: the power to interpret the law is the same as the power to make or "invent" the law

(44); or, what amounts to the same thing, Parliament's "right of declaring and interpreting Law" may take the form of reason of state (35).[45]

It is worth pausing here to emphasize the two prongs of Parker's radical argument. First Parker uses the language of natural law to justify Parliament's violations of positive law; he then uses Parliament's "invention" of positive laws to supplement the illegibility of natural law. In either case, where the preservation of the state is at risk, the law is imagined as actively or tacitly "consenting" to its own abrogation. As one of Parker's contemporaries put it, in a fiction in which even natural law is imagined as a party to a contract, "where Necessity commandeth, the Lawes of Nature and Nations give their consent, and all positive Lawes are silent and give place."[46]

This association of the "inventive" or constitutive power of contract and the threat of arbitrariness or violence is dramatized in the linguistic self-consciousness with which Parker conducts his argument. Thus Parker attacks the king's vocabulary of "trust" and "conscience," redefining the first in legal terms (a trust), identifying the latter with illegality, and substituting contract for both.[47] But he also calls attention to his own construction of the new language of obligation by subjecting the timeworn metaphors for political obligation to new scrutiny. In this way, Parker shows that the metaphors one uses to talk about sovereignty are themselves a matter of politics. For example, the people's consent to subordination suggests the usual analogies, but these in turn prompt reflection on their limitations: "Princes are called Gods, Fathers, Husbands, Lords, Heads, &c. and this implyes them to be of more worth and more unsubordinate in end, then their Subjects are, who by the same relation must stand as Creatures, Children, Wives, Servants, Members, &c. I answer, these termes do illustrate some excellency in Princes by way of similitude, but must not in all things be applyed" (18). In particular, Parker argues, the marriage contract and servant contract are not analogous to the political contract: "[T]he wife is inferiour in nature, and was created for the assistance of man, and servants are hired for their Lords meere attendance; but it is otherwise in the State betwixt man and man."

Parker also dismantles the usual metaphor of the body politic, arguing that "the head naturally doth not more depend upon the body, than that does upon the head . . . but it is otherwise with the Head Politicall, for that receives more subsistence from the body than it gives, and being subservient to that, it has no being when that is dissolved, and that may be preserved after its dissolution" (19). In Parker's view of government, the sovereign exists only by virtue of the political contract "betwixt man and man." One consequence of this view of sovereignty, as Parker makes clear elsewhere in the *Observations*, is that the king's person is separate from his office—a distinction that means that one can challenge the king's public actions without threatening his person but which, as in the metaphor just cited, might also suggest that the king's person cannot be preserved once his office is dissolved. (Milton would develop this logic to its lethal conclusion in *The Tenure of Kings and Magistrates*.) In all these examples, the issue of the subject's consent prompts the exercise of interpretive discretion, which in turn yields an argument for limited monarchy. Prior to the right of self-preservation, it seems, lies the potentially violent right of interpretation.

Parker's achievement in the *Observations*, then, was to use the language of natural law and the political contract not only to defend the people's sovereignty but also to justify Parliament's own violation of positive law in the interests of the higher law of self-preservation. But in doing this, Parker also called attention to the underside of contract, the problems of interpretation and fiction, of reason of state and the exception. In particular, the *Observations* exposed the arbitrariness at the foundation of political contract. Parker did not refer this arbitrariness to God's inscrutable will, however, but to the conventional arrangements of individuals, to individuals who create their obligations by means of the social, political, and linguistic contract.

Parker elaborated on and defended the *Observations* in *Jus Populi* (1644). The aim of this treatise was to argue that all government presupposes the people's ongoing consent and thus "the right of the people" to resist.[48] Parker interpreted Old Testament instances of covenant as political contracts that show that divine law is not incompatible with human consent; instead, the divine origin of political power authorizes the human institution of particular forms of government. He then cleverly appropriated the arguments of two "assertor[s] of absolute monarchy," Grotius and Barclay, to demonstrate the link between consent and the right of resistance: "And hereupon *Grotius* takes a good difference between *imperium* and *imperii habendi modus* [rule and the manner of rule], and as for the manner of qualification of rule, that he accounts *so meerly humane*, that if the King seek to alter it, he may be (as he acknowledges) *opposed by the people*" (7).[49] For Parker resistance was thus both a matter of conscience and self-preservation. Given the sanctity of the individual conscience, Parker's dispute with his adversaries "is not about obedience, but the measure of obedience; for if the Kings will be the sole judge thereof, wee cannot disobey God in obeying the King, but this we know is false" (12). Parker then argued that the right of self-preservation is, by definition, incompatible with enslavement and thus with the "remedilesse servitude of non-resistance" (67–68).[50]

Even more than Parker's *Observations*, *Jus populi* highlights the problem of political obligation predicated on conscience and natural right. At the same time that Parker grounded legitimate government in conscience and natural right, he was acutely aware that neither the moral law informing conscience nor the natural right of self-preservation was a strong enough bond to "keep the world from dissipation":

> We must insist upon Necessitie therefore, as the main ground and end of Policie; And besides Order, and the Lawes of God and Nature, we must finde out some more particular constitutions, to cement us, and to hold us fast bound together. Though the times of *Adam* were not uncouth, as ours now are, yet even then the common consent of Mankinde (that which we now call, *Jus Gentium*) was too slack and loose a bond, to keep the World from dissipation. (43)

Moral bonds—bonds of natural law or natural right—are thus merely heuristic:

> Bounds are set, by God and Nature, to the greatest and most absolute Monarchs, as well as to the least, and most conditionate: but those Bounds seem but as imaginary Lines, or as meer stones, not reall Trenches, or Fortifications: They serve onely to discover to the Subject what his Right is, but they have no strength at all to protect him from wrong. Those slaves that are sold, and forfeited to the worst of Bondages, as we have proved before, have a Divine and Naturall claim to safety, and freedom from abuses; as other Subjects have; yet want of some Politicall remedy, exposeth them to miseries far worse then death. . . . there is no safety nor freedom from abuse which depends upon meer will, as an Arbitrary power, but the poorest slave is as capable of it as the freest Subject. (51)

In this remarkable passage Parker concedes the imaginary status of natural right. In doing so he points out that it is not enough to have the right or will to do something—as, for example, slaves do—one must also have the power. Protection accordingly requires a "political" solution, it requires positive laws and the power to enforce them. Such a government, Parker argues in proto-Lockean fashion, is not arbitrary because it is consensual. But in another sense this power is arbitrary because it is not subject to positive law but rather guided by "the extraordinary law of generall necessity" (64).

As in the *Observations*, Parker's heightened sense of political artifice and the arbitrary is reflected in the linguistic artifice of *Jus populi*. In particular, his sense that human order is made rather than found is registered in a self-conscious dislocation of the traditional analogies for political obligation: husband-wife, father-son, master-slave. Thus Parker does not simply propose a new interpretation of these analogies. Instead, he highlights his discomfort with the usual comparisons, especially with their suggestion of a "natural" basis of subordination. He makes it clear to the reader that such metaphors are always contested, always themselves a matter of political negotiation and consent. This metaphorical instability is, we might say, the linguistic condition not only of genuine consent but also of reason of state and equitable judgment. It is the linguistic price of an exercise of discretion that by definition exceeds the strict economy of the law.

We can see this instability at work in Parker's treatment of the royalist analogies between sovereign and husband, subject and wife. In response to his opponents' argument that all power is derived from God, Parker cites the example of "matrimony" as a "bond" that is instituted both by God and by "humane consent" (4). Whereas royalists had used the marriage analogy to argue for the willing subordination of the subject to absolute monarchical rule, Parker presents marriage as a model for mixed monarchy:

> Is there not in conjugall Jurisdiction (notwithstanding the divine establishment of it) a strange kind of mixture, and coordination, and may not the Spouse plead that divine right as much for sweet equality, as the husband does for a rigorous inequalitie? . . . There may be a parity even in the disparity of the matrimoniall bond. (4)

Here the political subject is in the position of the wife who, despite her subordinate position, is nevertheless equal in some respects to her husband. In drawing the appropriate political moral, however, Parker immediately inverts the analogy by describing the position of the sovereign as one of wifely subordination: "And if men, for whose sakes women were created, shall not lay hold upon the divine right of wedlock, to the disadvantage of women: much lesse shall Princes who were created for the peoples sake, chalenge any thing from the sanctity of their office, that may derogate from the people" (5). The inversion becomes even more explicit some pages later: "The woman is coruscant by the rayes of her husband, borrowing resplendence like the Moon from the Suns aspect, without losse or diminution to the fountain and cause of that coruscance. In the same manner also Princes derive honour and power from their Subjects, yet drain not at all the scource [source] that derives it" (17). Here too princes play the wife to the subject-husband. Still later, however, Parker abandons the analogy altogether. He admits that the first species of absolute power was marital but denies that this has any relevance whatsoever to current politics, because "we see in all nations the power of Husbands is regulated by the publick civill power" (31). Therefore "nothing can be rightly extracted out of it, for the licensing of arbitrary rule in the State" (32). From an argument about the divine and natural subordination of wife to husband, Parker moves to a conception of marital relations as socially and politically constituted—"regulated by the publick civill power." Parker's own gloss then implies that, like the political subject, the wife may legitimately claim equal rights.

Here and elsewhere in *Jus populi* Parker exposes the radical implications of his own contractual model of obligation. His diametrically opposed interpretations of the marriage analogy imply that marriage cannot be the natural term that grounds our understanding of political obligation. Rather, all contracts—including marriage—are civil artifacts, that is, a matter of negotiation and consent, with everything that that implies for political resistance and divorce.[51] Parker's resistance to this insight about marriage replicates the tension between will and legitimacy in other contemporary instances of the language of contract. Although Parker appears willing to entertain what looked, to many of his contemporaries, like the radical ungroundedness of political contract, he shared their anxiety about a similar ungroundedness of domestic relations. This is undoubtedly one reason he abandoned the analogy. Contract, as Charles II's chaplain George Hickes was to observe, is sexually disquieting. (I return to Hickes later.)

After demonstrating the inadequacy of the marriage analogy, Parker proceeds in a similar fashion to dismantle the argument that based absolute rule on natural, patriarchal power: not only do sons naturally become fathers but "in all Civill Countries, where Government is established, there are Lawes to over-rule Parents as well as Children" (33). Finally, Parker takes up the argument that some men are naturally incapable of governing themselves, are naturally slaves, and so require absolute rule: a natural slave, he argues, is a contradiction in terms because slavery "rob[s men] of that naturall interest which they have in themselves" (38). Or, to put it another way, "no nation yet ever did voluntarily or compulsorily embrace servitude" (66).[52] In contrast to Grotius, for whom slavery was the logical extreme of contract, Parker presents slavery and contract as incompatible: not only are there no slaves in nature, not only did Christ himself make slaves and free men equal in the sight of God (40), but it is a contradiction of our nature and our right of self-preservation to bind the will absolutely—hence the right of resistance, a right based on both conscience and the calculations of self-interest.

But what if there were no agreement about how to construe this right and when to exercise it? In most of *Jus populi* Parker represents conscience and self-interest as compatible motives for consent. There is no suggestion that they might be at odds, that conscience might unaccountably lead one to act against one's self-interest, or that the desire for self-preservation might lead one to act dishonorably or against conscience—issues that will be very much on Milton's mind, for example, in *Samson Agonistes*. Moreover, there is no suggestion that the "people" might disagree among themselves, that conscience does not necessarily produce consensus (although it was that very fact which had led to the crisis of civil war). Yet, there is one important exception in *Jus populi*—an exception, we might add, that stands as a synecdoche for the royalist position and that explains the occasion of the treatise in the first place:

> If a Nation by solemne oath, or otherwise has ingaged it self to submit to the will of a Prince absolutely, affirmatively reserving no priviledges, I shall not seek to destroy such agreements. I onely say such agreements are not the effects of Nature, and tis not easie to imagine how right reason should ever mingle with such a morall principle, as gave being to such an agreement. (17–18)

In some cases, the people may unaccountably construe the political contract as irrevocable. (Such a people, Rousseau was to argue more than a century later, must be forced to be free.) In making this concession, Parker once again exposed one of the dilemmas at the heart of contract: that of reconciling will and legitimacy, the free exercise of discretion with the constraints of reason—or unreason. This is the problem of voluntary servitude, a problem, Parker has vainly argued, that has no right to exist.

Falkland, Chillingworth, Digges, and the Fiction of Representation

Even before the publication of *Jus populi*, Parker's *Observations* had spawned a pamplet war of its own. Two pamphlets in particular, the *Answer to a Printed Book, Intituled Observations . . .* (1642) by the royalists Falkland, Chillingworth, and Dudley Digges (the younger), and Digges's *The Unlawfulnesse of Subjects taking up armes against their Soveraigne in what case soever* (1643), adopt Parker's language of contract but propose a diametrically opposed interpretation of obligation. (In developing this interpretation, Falkland and Chillingworth, who were friends of Hobbes, may have been influenced by Hobbes's *Elements of Law* in manuscript and by *De cive*, which had been published in Paris early in 1642.)[53] As in Parker's treatises, the metaphor of contract in these tracts is the locus of conflicting discourses of conscience and calculation, law and right. In striking contrast to Parker's arguments, however, the authors argue for the legitimacy of voluntary servitude, while also raising questions about the role of the passions and the imagination, "affection" and "fancy," in the realm of politics.[54]

According to the *Answer*, it is entirely rational to "contract" to give up one's power once and for all. Such absolute subjection is an obligation dictated by both Scripture and self-interest. We are obliged to obey the king for "conscience sake" and because the sovereign is better able to protect us than we can ourselves (1–2). "No question, rule and subjection . . . did spring from reason directing man-kind to its greatest convenience" (13–14). What Parker calls "slavery," the authors call "consent, from which an obligation naturally followes, for it is, as with him in the Comoedy, *voluntate coactus sum mea*" (22–23). They even go on to argue "there may be reasonable motives why a people should consent to [actual] slavery . . . if in danger of a potent enemy . . . or if reduced to extream want. . . . The Gibeonites bought their lives of the children of Israel with the price of their liberty, and they thought they had a cheap purchase" (23). That is, we have a right to give up our right to self-preservation "if reason tells us, we shall thereby obtain a more excellent good, the benefit of peace and society" (44). But even if the king were incapable of protecting us, we would still be obliged by God to keep the covenant or contract we had made. Here too the example of the Gibeonites, which appeared prominently in Grotius's *De jure belli*, is relevant: "That covenants should not be violated, will appear by the revenge God took in behalf of the *Gibeonites* [who tricked Joshua into promising to make peace with them, a promise he felt obliged to keep (Joshua 9:15)]. . . . Thus we see what speciall care God takes to preserve the faith of contracts" (9).[55]

This argument about irrevocable contract obscures the ever-present right of interpretation, and thus the ever present possibility of dissent. And this, according to the *Answer*, is all to the good. For if the civil law maxim *quod omnes tangit, ab omnibus approbari debet* (what touches everyone must be approved by everyone) "be understood in its full latitude, without all limitation, it will dissolve the bonds of Government, by reducing us to that primitive state, wherein every one had absolute right, to dispose of his own as he pleased."

> Therefore we must take into consideration, that multitudes finding a necessity of Government, did restraine this native right by positive Constitutions, so that in the best governed States, the greater part of men were presumed by a *fiction of law*, to handle and approve such things as they never heard of. The ground of which fiction is very reasonable; for the people though they are not advised with, *may well be said to consent* to what their rulers doe, because they have entrusted them with their safety. (29, emphasis added)

In this striking passage, the authors call attention to the fiction of political representation. The people's consent, they argue, is a fiction and does not bind Parliament: the MPs "represent [the people] only to some purposes, and ends" (36). But Parliament's own views are similarly nonbinding on the king: "[T]he trust committed to both Houses, cannot bind Him to assent, to what ever they propose . . . nor absolve Him in point of conscience" (36–37). In extraordinary cases, the king must exercise his con-science—which, in political terms, amounts to his "reason of state" (49).

If the king's conscience cannot be bound by any prior oath or contract, what about his subjects? When we recall that subjects are obliged, as Joshua was, to keep their contracts for reasons of *conscience*, we begin to see the authors' problem. In contrast to Parker, for whom "it is not just nor possible for any nation [irrevocably] to inslave it selfe," the *Answer* implies that it is a characteristic of the will to be able to bind itself abso-lutely.[56] But it also defines conscience as that which cannot be bound when circumstances change. Contracts should make subjects calculable, but cal-culability, the authors tell us, is a function of conscience. And, although in one sense conscience assumes a prior contract with oneself, it appears that this internal contract is a "fiction" of the moral law, which may be no more binding on the king in practice than an actual political contract.

The *Answer* attempts to deal with this dilemma by distributing the cal-culable and the conscientious to subjects and sovereign respectively. Thus, while the authors construe the king's not being bound by law as a function of his conscience, they read Parliament's claim that it is similarly not bound as deception or craft: "For if they can make it appeare, they are not bound to keep any law, no man can accuse them for the breach of any. What obligation can justice lay on them, who by a strange vertue of repre-sentation, are not capable of doing wrong?" (113). By "strange vertue of representation" the authors appear to be alluding to the representative function Parker attributed to Parliament; by marking it as "strange" they undoubtedly want to convey that Parliament does not in fact represent the people. In this second case, the word "vertue" suggests the power of representation to bring things into being ex nihilo: "It will become justice," they mockingly assert of Parker's Parliament, "because they did it" (113). Here the *Answer* identifies the parliamentary political contract not with conscience but with a contract of mimesis, according to which power dic-tates—or constructs—likeness (in this case, the likeness of justice).

This objection leads to a further consideration of Parliament's methods. Like papists, Parliament is guilty of using "fained stories" of imminent disaster in order to "insinuate themselves into [the people's] affections" (104, 105). Such feigned appeals to self-preservation work "upon our understanding by our affection" (72). In particular, the people's passions have been stirred up by "pretence of apparent danger" at Hull, the north-ern town with a store of munitions to which the king and his army de-manded access early in the civil war (67). But it is not only private subjects but also members of Parliament who are governed by "private interest"; both groups are motivated by ambition, covetousness, hatred, and af-fection to their friends (59).[57]

Ironically, given its characterization of the people as erratic and excitable, the *Answer* too must appeal not to conscience but to passion and self-interest. Like their parliamentary opponents, the authors use the imagination of disaster to excite the people's "affections." Addressing Parliament's demand to approve the king's counselors, they write, "If not out of duty to their King, and a just sense of His honour, yet *out of love to themselves*, and a naturall care of their own safety, Subjects are bound in all legall ways to expresse their dislike of [Parliament's] proposition [to approve the king's counselors]. For they must expect to suffer all those evills which Faction can produce; . . . This were the ready way to kindle a fire in our own bowells" (108; emphasis added). But what kind of bond is the bond of self-love? And what does it mean, given the previous distribution of conscience and self-interest, when the *Answer* invites its readers to attribute the same calculation of self-interest to the king as to the people: "[I]f the people hearken to reason they must needs think, His Majesty will be more ready to prevent all reall danger, then any Subject whatsoever, because He is sure to beare the greatest share in the losse" (117)? The *Answer* has no answer to these questions. For all their attempts to isolate conscience from calculation, the authors end up dramatizing their inseparability. We make political contracts out of self-interest, they seem to be saying; we are expected to keep them for conscience's sake, but we actually keep them just as much or more out of fear or self-love. But this, as Parker had argued, is also an argument for breach of contract.

Like the *Answer*, Digges's *Unlawfulnesse* dramatizes the tension between conscience and calculation, law and right. In arguing for an irrevocable political contract, he both appeals to the subject's self-interest and condemns self-interest in favor of an argument from conscience. But in neither case does Digges find a sure standard of judgment or guarantee of political obedience. Even more than in the *Answer*, the calculations of self-interest and the dictates of conscience alike are affected by what we might call the incalculable tropological force of conscience, the passions, and the imagination, to turn the dependable and obedient subject into a disobedient one.

Throughout the treatise, Digges concedes the natural right of self-preservation. But he cautions the reader that self-interest and the passions are not easily separable from "phancy." The people are persuaded to accept political innovation because "they have the strongest phancies to those things of which they have the least experience"; thus the common people are "craftily prevailed upon" to identify their interests with Parliament's.[58] Reason of state is made to seem a romance—"Populi salus, suprema lex, is the Engine by which the upper roomes [of state] are torne from the foundation, and seated upon fancy onely, like Castles in the aire" (7)—and the people are induced to "fall in love with a bare sound, and court [the] name of freedome, which duely examined, will be found to signifie nothing" (25). In every case, Digges observes, the imagination affects the passions and thus the perception of self-interest. And this is true not only of the love of freedom but also of the fear for one's safety. To Parliament's "endeavor to justifie [their actions] by reason of State, and plead the necessity of it, as being the onely cure of *feares* and *jealousies*," Digges replies:

> The recovery of this Kingdome were certainely desperate, if His Majesty too should grow fearfull and jealous, who hath been more unanswerably tempted to give admitance to these unhappy passions. . . . If this [Law of feares] should once prevaile, peace and justice were lost to mankinde; for it would still be some-bodies turne to be afraid. . . . There is no other way to get out of this maze and confusion—to which their wild feares inavoydably betray a State, but by prevailing with our reason, not to suspect those whom the Lawes have not suspected.[59]

As Hobbes would argue in *Leviathan*, fear and jealousy, passion and suspicion—in short, the imagination of disaster—will themselves produce the disaster we fear. Hence the necessity of constraining passion and imagination by the exercise of reason or the prudent calculation of self-interest, which dictates voluntary, irrevocable subjection to the sovereign and positive law.

Like the other writers we have examined, Digges is fully aware that a corollary of binding the will is the binding of signification. In defending the sanctity of contracts in *The Unlawfulnesse*, Digges recurs not only to the distinction between law and right but also to a kind of modified patriarchalism, to the binding "knot" of the marriage contract, and to a politically conservative interpretation of Romans 13. Yet what is most striking from a rhetorical perspective about these traditional royalist arguments is not Digges's advocacy of an irrevocable political contract but—like Parker—his intuition that such a contract presupposes a prior contract about metaphor. "For the King is *Pater patriae*, a common Father to all without a Metaphor," Digges asserts, where "without a Metaphor" seems to be a metaphorical way of talking about irrevocable consent or a binding contract. Thus Digges goes on to argue that "it was our owne act which united all particular paternall powers in Him, and . . . these are *truly transferred*, and now really in Him" (61). If we recall that metaphor means transport in Greek, we might say that a true transfer is a real metaphor, even a literal or corporeal one, and this is what allows the king to be a real or literal *Pater patriae*.

A similar anxiety about the political instability of metaphor attends Digges's argument that the king is inseparable from his office (88–96). In Digges's view, the king does not represent but is actually identical with the body politic.[60] The division of the king from his office is part of the logic of parliamentary representation. Citing the example from Plutarch's *Lives* of Tiberius Gracchus, who hypocritically "court[ed] the Commons by all popular Artes," Digges cautions: "[T]he same Artes [of rhetoric] which made Rome miserable, are visible in our calamities" (94, 96). Along with rhetoric, Parliament's claim of representation—with its implied division between sign and signified—is now made to seem responsible for the divisions of civil war, even, potentially, for the death of the king.

Digges's treatment of the marriage analogy is similarly self-conscious about the need to bind signification. Digges wants to fix the way we interpret the analogy; and this, in turn, presupposes the possibility of fixing one's intention in an act of consent:

> There are many resemblances in matrimony which will afford great light to the better understanding the duty of Subjects. The consent of the woman makes such a man her husband, so the consent of the people is now necessary to the making of Kings (for conquest is but a kind of ravishing, which many times prepares the way to a wedding, as the Sabine women chose rather to be wives, then concubines, and most people preferre the condition of Subjects though under hard lawes to that of slaves). . . . As in marriage, so in monarchy there are two parties in the contract; though without a mutuall agreement there could be no covenant, yet after it is once made the dissent of the inferiour party, let it not be upon fancyed, but reall discontents, cannot dissolve the compact. (113)

As in the later example of the Norman Conquest (116), consent is not incompatible with coercion (here figured as ravishment), nor with an irrevocable binding of the will. The voluntary acceptance of such coercion transforms rape into marriage, slavery into subjection. In a similar fashion, Digges deftly does away with the problem of distinguishing real and fanciful discontents: even real discontents cannot legitimate divorce.

In his most brilliant move, Digges then uses the argument from self-interest—or natural right—to defend the right we have to forfeit our rights.

> *Selfe preservation is justifiable by the law of nature.* I grant this; hands were given to men for this purpose. . . . But this will nothing advantage them in the present case. For by that which they call *Law* of nature is meant onely *right* of nature, which is not command, but a permission onely, and therefore it may be, and indeed it is actually restrained by positive constitutions, whether divine or civill. For example, all things were common *iure naturali*, by the right of nature, and yet the lawes of property are now binding to us. Hence is discovered the hollowness of their discourses upon this principle. (120)

Digges builds here on the distinction (found in Grotius and Perkins, among others) between command and permission, primary and secondary natural law. In particular, by distinguishing between law and right as different kinds of "speech acts," Digges turns Parker's argument about the civil constitution of marriage and sovereignty to his own ends. Laws command or oblige, rights permit or allow. Thus, although "humane power is not above the law of nature,"

> humane power is above the *law* or rather the *right* of nature, which doth permit a freedome of doing or not doing according to discretion. *Else no contracts could be of force* [emphasis added], because by the law of nature men were free, and the obligation is positive, as arising from promise, which it was in our power not to make, but having once made it, we have tied our hands from using native liberty. Of this permissive law *Aristotle* spake pol. 7. cap. 12 [13]. . . . *some things of nature depend upon our choyse and cease to be of force, when we please, to part with our naturall rights, not all things.* (121)

As the equivocation on "law" illustrates, the achievement of this passage is to make natural law a matter of right, and right a matter of discretion. Because we are free according to natural law, we are free to choose whether to exercise our rights. Moreover—and here is the jab at Parker—if natural right always trumped positive law, if it were not possible voluntarily to cede one's rights and to bind the will, there could be no contracts at all. The *ceding* of natural rights in contract thus becomes an example of the *power* or natural right to contract in general. For contract to work, it must be possible voluntarily to give up one's right of self-preservation. It must be possible, as Grotius argued, to transfer or alienate one's rights and to bind the will absolutely. Here Digges brilliantly turns the argument from self-interest against itself, by showing that all contracts presuppose something like the bond of conscience. The role of conscience becomes explicit shortly after this when Digges argues that, although the natural right of self-preservation does not forbid killing another in self-defense, "yet the Gospell doth" (122). Obedience to "Christs praecepts" may require us "to resigne our lives . . . out of conscience" (123). Here conscience does not act in tandem with the right to self-preservation to justify resistance to the king; rather, conscience dictates obedience to the king even at the risk of self-preservation. It was precisely this argument that both Hobbes and Milton would attempt to demolish in their different ways.

Some forty years after the outbreak of the English civil war, George Hickes, chaplain to Charles II, commented on the disquieting aspects of the language of contract in his *Discourse of the Soveraign Power* (1682).[61] "The opinion that I am speaking against is this, that the People are the fountain and foundation of all power and dominion, which is understood to be derived from them even upon those whom Custom calls sovereign Princes, who are but their *trustees*, or *fiduciary ministers*; with whom they have at least a *virtual* contract" (20). In addition to calling attention to the fiction of a "virtual contract," Hickes isolates two problems with this theory of obligation. The first problem is that "such Kings are only equivocal Kings, Kings in name, but in reality Subjects" (20). The second problem is the difficulty of determining where exactly sovereign power lies: "They cannot tell us upon this hypothesis [that power derives from the people], whether the supreme Power belongs to all the people promiscuously, that have the use of reason, without any regard to Sex or condition, or onely to qualified persons, to Men onely, and men of such a condition and sort. If men onely have a share and interest in the supreme Power, by whose order and authority, or by what Salique law of Nature were Women excluded from it, who are as usefull members of the Commonwealth, and as necessary for humane society as men?" (22). Needless to say, this was not an argument for gender equality but against it. But Hickes's insight points to those aspects of the discourse of contract which made Parker so obviously uncomfortable, and with which Hobbes and Milton would struggle from the 1640s through the 1660s. At times, this disquiet appeared as the possibility that women too might be parties to the contract. At times, it appeared as the possibility that contract might involve both coercion and consent, ravishment and will, slavery and freedom, thereby feminizing the male subject of contract. And in either case, this possibility of crossing boundaries, this unstable identity of the subject of contract, took the form of a metaphorical instability as well—an instability in the very metaphor of contract.

CHAPTER 5

Violence

> Though we kill him, it is no fault, because violence was offered
> only to his person, not to his authority.
> —Dudley Digges, *The Unlawfulnesse of Subjects taking up
> armes against their Soveraigne in what case soever*

> The Light of humane minds is Perspicuous Words, but by exact
> definitions first snuffed, and purged from ambiguity; *Reason*
> is the *pace*; Encrease of *Science*, the *way*; and the Benefit of
> man-kind, the *end*. And on the contrary, Metaphors, and
> senslesse and ambiguous words, are like *ignes fatui*; and rea-
> soning upon them, is wandering amongst innumerable ab-
> surdities; and their end, contention, and sedition, or contempt.
> —Hobbes, *Leviathan*

THE PREVIOUS CHAPTER has considered debates on the role of the imagination and equitable judgment in determining threats to the commonwealth. In this chapter, I turn to the potential for violence inherent in
contractual arguments for political obligation. My first exhibit involves
the "fast sermons" preached in Parliament, which argued that the heavenly covenant dictated the violence of civil war. My second is Milton's
Tenure of Kings and Magistrates, which urged that keeping one's covenant dictated the execution of the king. In their different ways, each contributed to the beheading of Charles I, that strange coincidence of legal
procedure and bloody consequence, that gripped the attention of the nation in the last months of 1648.

In the state trials and parliamentary debates of the 1620s and 1630s,
we saw a redefinition of the king's promise or "royal word" in terms of
the ancient constitution and the common law of contract. The king's right
to promise was itself seen as a consequence of legal institutions, while his
reason of state and imagination of disaster were censured as fantasies
of autonomy. In the fast sermons and Milton's *Tenure*, in contrast, we
encounter a different sort of argument. In these texts, covenant and contract are enormously empowering models of agency, both for the nation
and the individual. In the first case, they authorize prophetic narratives
of national redemption; in the second, they authorize the individual's

right to prophetic interpretation, the right to determine the violent exception to law and precedent.

PROPHESYING REVOLUTION

One of the many ironies of the civil war was that the fatal juxtaposition of law and reason of state in the Five Knights and Shipmoney cases recurred—this time to the detriment of Parliament—in the trial of Charles I. Summoned before the high court of Parliament, Charles resolutely refused to answer the charges. Instead, he called attention to the illegality of the proceedings on several fronts. The court represented only a small fraction of the Commons, not Parliament as a whole. Moreover, by definition the king had no peers and so could not be judged even by a lawfully constituted jury. Finally, the court had no legitimacy to try a divinely anointed, hereditary sovereign—a sovereign who received his "trust" not from the people but from God.[1] In his references to legality, Charles seemed finally to have understood the lesson of the state trials, too late to save his own skin but not too late to embarrass the MPs who sat in judgment on his case.[2]

John Bradshaw, the judge appointed by Parliament, argued from precedent for the justice of the sentence. He referred to the depositions of Edward II and Richard II; he also adduced the coronation oath and cast the relation of subject and sovereign in terms of the feudal obligations of liege lord and liege subjects. At the same time, he called attention to the calculus of protection and obedience by describing this oath and bond as "a contract and a bargain." And he made it clear that this contract did not simply ratify preexisting relations of sovereignty and subjection. Instead, the contract was *constitutive* of these relations: no protection, no king:

> There is a contract and a bargain made between the King and his people, and your oath is taken: and certainly, Sir, the bond is reciprocal; for as you are the liege lord, so they are liege subjects. . . . This we know now, the one tie, the one bond, is the bond of protection that is due from the sovereign; the other is the bond of subjection that is due from the subject. Sir, if this bond be once broken, farewell sovereignty![3]

Bradshaw's remarks capture the complicated interweaving of precedent and breach of precedent in all aspects of the trial and execution of the king. In their rapid flickering back and forth between the language of coronation oath and bargain, feudal obligation and rational calculation, they alert us to the discursive crisis of those seeking to justify the legal murder of the king. As C. V. Wedgwood remarked, in bringing the king to trial the Commons faced the problem of "how to reconcile their wholly unprecedented action with the English Common Law, a law rooted in the practice and precedent of centuries. . . . They might have done better to assert, even to boast of, the novelty of their procedure."[4]

As we have seen in previous chapters, there was an available discourse of bonds and obligations that lent support to the argument from novelty—the argument for a radical departure from customary ways. And that was the language of spiritual covenant. By the 1640s both the divine Word of covenant theology and its emphasis on the moral obligation to interpret Scripture were bearing unexpected fruit. From John Ball's description of the divine covenant as "a perpetuall speech," it had been a short step to thinking of the preacher's verbal communication of the divine promise as itself a form of the covenant.[5] Thus George Downame declared: "the preaching of his word is the covenant of grace" and John Angier argued that "we renew our covenant in every sermon, for God declared what he will be unto us and what he requires of us back again."[6] Initially espoused by conservative puritans such as Perkins, Preston, and Downame, this divine speech act theory came to underwrite the political activism of parliamentary preachers such as Cornelius Burges, Jeremiah Burroughs, and Stephen Marshall.

Beginning with the Long Parliament in November 1640, the House of Commons commissioned a number of clergymen to deliver sermons on national days of fasting and repentance in the difficult time of political struggle. For the Presbyterian and Independent preachers of these "fast sermons," the cause of church reform was intimately bound up with the struggle against tyranny. Along with Parliament, they believed that Charles I was tyrannical not only because he had broken the implicit contract of Magna Carta but also because he "pretended to a prerogative to which only God was entitled."[7] As we saw in chapter 3, by insisting that the contract with God trumped all merely human contracts, covenant theologians had authorized passive resistance to secular power. In the hands of the fast preachers, the heavenly contract authorized active resistance to the contract of government.

In the first fast sermon of 1640, preached on a text from Jeremiah 50 ("Let us join ourselves to the Lord in a perpetual covenant. . . . My people hath been lost sheep: their shepherds have caused them to go astray"), Cornelius Burges urged Parliament, which he striking apostrophized as "the Representative Body of this whole Kingdome," to renew its covenant with God:

> This if we doe, we need not care much for other Covenants: God will provide for that . . . he will make our Exactors peace, and our Officers righteousness, violence shall no more be heard in the Land, nor wasting, nor destruction within our border . . . . He will be a God of Cove-

nants, and take care for our estates, Lawes, Liberties, lives, children and all that belong to us, when once this is done.[8]

He continued, in a language that would be echoed by Hobbes and Milton,

But alas! what Good, in the issue, hath followed, or can be yet hoped for so long as men continue *Philistines*, enemies to God & his Church, Anti-Covenanters (even with Hell) rather than true Covenanters with God? Whether is our Condition any what better now than heretofore, when those *Leviathans* were alive, and in their height?[9]

At the time Burges was preaching, the Scottish army had invaded northern England. As one modern commentator notes, "[Burges's] point could hardly have been missed, either by puritan sympathizers in parliament or by those who supported the policies of Archbishop Laud. Scotland, a nation in covenant with God, was a judgment upon England whose shepherds (the bishops) had been leading the people from true religion."[10] A modern day Jeremiah, Burges warned his contemporaries that the dire state of England was owing to their breach of covenant with God; it was only by renewing that spiritual covenant that England could be saved.

In this and other sermons, Burges offered a "Deuteronomic" interpretation of history. Drawing on the prophetic books of the Hebrew Bible, especially Joshua, Judges, I and II Samuel, and I and II Kings, "the Deuteronomist discerned God acting in the events of Israel's history. He saw disaster as a judgment of God upon Israel's idolatries, and he interpreted prosperity to be God's blessing upon a nation whose people and leaders had 'returned to the Lord.' "[11] This view of history allowed England's trials and tribulations to be integrated into a providential narrative of exodus from "Egypt" and entry into the promised land. In this first fast sermon Burges did not discuss whether such a renewal of the spiritual covenant dictated a breach of the political contract; but this issue very quickly became the question of the day. Increasingly, the preachers of these sermons called on the nation not only to pray for the kingdom but also to take up arms against Charles I.

Just as Burges's Deuteronomic interpretation of history illustrates the link between the divine covenant and providential narrative, so these arguments for armed resistance tie the individual's obligation to interpret Scripture to the construction of a plot. As we saw in chapter 2, covenant theologians interpreted the figurative dimension of Scripture as a kind of covenant with the reader. In this hermeneutic, metaphor dictated an equitable activity of interpretation, and this activity then served as an example of the agency granted to the believer by God's saving grace. The right interpretation of metaphor presupposed equitable judgment on the part of the author and facilitated it in the reader. In both cases, covenant

theology appears as an early modern example of the way in which metaphors contain narratives in little and produce what Patricia Parker has
called "the metaphorical plot."[12] Metaphor generates a plot because, as
Terence Cave has argued, "*Metaphora* is a linguistic mode of disguise or
temporary deception leading to the revelation of likeness and difference."
Metaphor is also linked to narrative because, like the recognition plot,
it involves a process of inference.[13] Finally, metaphor generates a plot
because the interpretation of scriptural metaphor yields new insights and
new obligations to act in the world. Scriptural hermeneutics does not
just take a prophetic and ethical narrative as its object; it produces one
in turn.

Burges's associate Stephen Marshall also preached the necessity of renewing the spiritual covenant with God, along with the political moral
that "the glory and happinesse of a nation stands in the presence of God
in his Covenant."[14] But like Burges, he charged that England in 1640 was
not "with God"; it had "abus[ed] God in the poynt of his Worship,"
thereby "defiling . . . the marriage bed betwixt God and his people.[15] In
particular, the Laudian Church was guilty of Arminianism, an excessive
"Philistine" confidence in the believer's ability to contribute something to
his salvation: "when you hear, that God will be with his people as they
are with God, take heed you understand it not as some, who . . . set up
the rotten *Dagon* of mans free-will, above the Arke of Gods free-grace."
Although God's covenant is conditional, it is not Arminian: he "work[s]
in us the Condition which he himself requireth of us. . . . he works both
the will and the deed."[16] As with earlier covenant sermons, such a message
was ultimately empowering: if Parliament takes "the Lord's side," it
chooses "that side which must and shall have the victory at the long run."
This message was also self-referential and self-reinforcing: because the
"Word" is the "Scepter whereby Christ rules," this victory is dependent
on Parliament's establishment of a "preaching Ministry."[17]

The fast sermons became more strident in December 1641, after the
House of Commons presented the king with a Grand Remonstrance.[18]
The Remonstrance enumerated the causes of the recent difficult relations
between king and Parliament, urged the king to reject his "evil counsellors," defended the actions of the Long Parliament, clarified the Commons' demands, all the while protesting allegiance to the crown. Among
the causes of discontent listed in the Remonstrance were the Five Knights
and Shipmoney cases, the "extravagant censures" of the prerogative
Court of Star Chamber, the common law courts' "straying beyond their
bounds, under pretense of equity, to do injustice," the foisting of "Popish
superstitions and innovations" upon Scotland, the earl of Strafford's levying the Irish Catholics against the Scottish Presbyterians, and taxation
"without consent in Parliament."[19] When Parliament only narrowly

passed the Remonstrance, Charles was emboldened to indict a peer and five MPs, including John Hampden, for high treason. The two houses refused to cooperate and shortly thereafter Charles broke with Parliament and left London for the north of England.

On February 23, 1641/42 Marshall preached a sermon entitled "Meroz Cursed," on the text of Judges 5:23, which tells the story of the inhabitants of Meroz who refused to come to the aid of Deborah and the Jews against Sisera and the Canaanites. The curse of Meroz was part of Deborah's song celebrating the slaying of Sisera by Jael. In his *History of the Rebellion*, Clarendon described "Meroz Cursed" as the most seditious sermon preached during the civil war.[20] Marshall's message was clear: God has no patience for "neuters," for those who refused to choose sides and do the work of the Lord against oppression and tyranny. The interests of the kingdom and of the church were inextricable and both were better served by Parliament than by Charles.

Ultimately, however, the church took precedence over the state, as in Marshall's new maxim, *Salus Ecclesiae suprema lex*, a riff on the Roman *salus populi suprema lex*. Marshall portrayed the church as a mystical body whose corporate *salus* or spiritual health depended on the cooperation of all. Drawing on secular arguments for *salus populi* as self-preservation, Marshall compared the church to the ship of state: "[T]he good or gaine of the whole is the gaine of every member, and whatsoever tends to the dissolution of the whole, cannot but be destructive to all the parts . . . as it is with a company of passengers in the same Ship, and every mans Cabbin is cast away. Now this is a more prevailing argument than reason can make, it is grounded in nature which must prevail with all."[21] Natural law justifies preservation of the physical body; all the more so of the mystical body.

Further on in "Meroz Cursed," Marshall returned to the metaphor of the spiritual ship of state, now described as one in which the passengers refuse to jettison their wealth to preserve themselves and the common good. Drawing a page from Roman history, Marshall argued:

> It is ever well with the Church, when the members of it, doe preferre the Churches good above their owne. Polititians and Historians observe this of States and Empires, that they usually thrive when the Subjects are *Common-wealths men*, every one endeavouring to promote the publick good. Livie observes this of Rome, that so long as men would leave their trades, farmes, and merchandise, Ladies part with their Jewels and ornaments, rather than any detriment should come to the Citie, all Nations were subdued to them: But when they grew *private wealths men*, every one labouring to preserve and adorn his owne Cabbin only; the ship presently was endangered and went to decay. This is as true of the Church.[22]

As in his earlier sermons, the immediate "publick good" Marshall had in mind was the work of preaching and praying. But in the political climate of February 1641/42 his savvy comparison of the Roman Republic and the Presbyterian cause also amounted to a declaration of total war against the king.

This rhetoric of divine covenant and commonwealth found its preeminent expression in the Solemn League and Covenant, which Parliament signed with the Scottish Presbyterians in 1643 in order to win them over to the parliamentary cause. (Marshall was one of the members of the Westminster Assembly of Divines who took part in the negotiations in Scotland regarding the Covenant.)[23] Probably more than any other document, the Covenant articulated "the interrelated religious, political, and social goals of the Long Parliament."[24] Parties to the Covenant swore to preserve reformed religion in England, Ireland, and Scotland; to "extirpate" popery and prelacy (ecclesiastical government by bishops); to "endeavor with our estates and lives mutually to preserve the rights and privileges of the Parliament, and the liberties of the kingdom," to defend other parties to the Covenant, and not to give oneself to "a detestable indifference or neutrality in this cause." Sandwiched in between these fervent declarations—as a testimony of their good intentions—was one clause that was to prove troublesome in 1648/49: "We shall [endeavor] . . . to preserve and defend the King's Majesty's person and authority . . . that the world may bear witness with our conscience of our loyalty, . . . that we have no thoughts or intentions to diminish His Majesty's just power and greatness."[25] It was this clause, above all others, that linked the Solemn League and Covenant to the "tragy-comedy" of Charles's trial and execution.[26]

At the request of the House of Commons, Joseph Caryl, a future leader of the Independents, preached a sermon at Westminster "Of the Nature, Solemnity, Grounds, Property, and Benefits of a Sacred Covenant" (1643) in which he urged the Solemn League and Covenant on his countrymen. Alluding perhaps to Burges's and Marshall's first fast sermons, he argued that England's condition and the necessity of reformed religion had been prophesied in Jeremiah 50. And, in a comparison that looks forward to *Samson Agonistes*, he constructed a mini-narrative about the Covenant by comparing it to Samson's vow in Judges:

> This Covenant . . . hath beene [Scotland's] *Sampson's Locke*, the thing (in sight) wherein their strength lieth. And why should not we hope, that it will be ours; if we can be wise, as they, to prevent or overcome the flattering enticements of those *Dalilahs*, who would lull us asleepe in their laps, onely for an opportunity to cut or shave it off?

But if Englishmen did not keep their vows, Caryl warned, God would "utterly depart" from them, "for [their] falseness and unfaithfulnesse in this Covenant."[27] In "The Saints Solemne Covenant with their God" (1644), John Brinsley also urged the Covenant on his readers, arguing that the civil war was punishment for England's religious "lukewarmness," its breach of its spiritual contract.[28]

In a more melancholy key, the Erastian Thomas Coleman preached "The Christians Course and Complaint, both in the pursuit of Happiness desired, and for Advantages slipped in that Pursuit" (1643) on another theme from Jeremiah (8:20): "The Harvest is past, the summer is ended, and we are not saved."[29] In a striking passage in the "Epistle dedicatory," Coleman described the voluntary servitude of the English, refusing to be freed:

> Moses, Exod. 21. 1, 2, 3, 4 leaves to his people an ordinance, that when an Hebrew servant hath served sixe years, he should then be free, but if he be one of such a servile temper, that had rather be a slave still; Oh, I love my Master, I will not be free; then shall he be brought to some publique place, and there have his eare bored with an awl, and brandished for a slave, and so let him be a slave for ever. We have been many sixe yeares in service, a doore is opened for our freedome; if continuance under bondage, have so naturalized slavery to our disposition, that we desire no better condition; though you would thinke it uncharitable, to wish that all such might have their eares bored, as a brand of an ignoble heart: Yet I hope I may without prejudice say, that had you lived under the Judicials of Moses, you may see how you should have been used. But God hath given you (Honourable, and respected) a more noble, and Christian spirit, which I beseech God to continue, and increase.

To those who had found God "a promising God" but not yet "a performing God," Coleman urged patience and the "needfull dutie of waiting" (as Milton would at various points in his career). Teaching a lesson that would be of particular relevance to Milton's Samson, Coleman warned against drawing "wrong inferences" when God's promises are not immediately fulfilled. He asserted that God's delayed performance means that "God dislikes the meanes we use," but he also cautioned against discouragement and backsliding.[30] And he alerted his reader that God speaks to man not only through events but also in figurative, indirect ways: especially "in accidental passages, God sometimes by words casually spoken, without any intention in the speaker, may sometimes appear in that word to the apprehensions of his people." While urging patience, Coleman also invited his listeners and readers to engage in their own potentially revolutionary interpretation of God's intentions for England.[31]

The Independent minister Jeremiah Burroughs was even more forthright. In 1643 Burroughs preached two sermons vindicating the right of subjects to take up arms, and dedicated their publication to the earl of Essex, then commander of the parliamentary armies.[32] Following the lead of Grotius, Selden, and others, Burroughs distinguished between the divine origin of political power and the human institution of particular forms of government. Like Parker and later Milton, Burroughs saw the individual right of resistance as the counterpart of the "covenant or compact" of government. He argued that in new political situations or "cases" for which there were no "precedents," Parliament should be the judge and its criterion of judgment should be the law of nature, especially *salus populi*. Resistance was not extralegal so much as it was the only lawful thing to do in certain extraordinary circumstances. Here too Samson was offered as an example of justified disobedience. In a passage that summed up all of Hobbes's fears concerning the contribution of religious zeal (and the belief in an afterlife) to civil war, Burroughs declared:

> Those are fittest to venture their lives in fight, who are able to see beyond life, to see what is on the other side of the shore of this mortality, even eternall life and glory: All the Saints, especially in these days, should be ful of spirit, strong in the might of the Lord, because Jesus Christ is about to pul down that great enemy of his, That man of sin, and in his conquest, he is said to come with his garments dipt in blood, *Apoc.* 19.[33]

With an image from Revelations 19:13 that would also figure in contemporary accounts of the regicide, Burroughs celebrated the example of Christ victor, "the Word of God," with his "garments dipt in blood." It is not surprising, then, that in the hindsight of Hobbes, Milton, and many of their contemporaries, the regicide appeared to be the logical outcome of the rhetoric of these sermons.[34] With their emphasis on national repentance and the glorious work of reformation, these sermons helped forge a revolutionary consciousness.[35] In contrast to Luther and Calvin, who had distinguished between the spiritual and political kingdoms, Marshall, Burges, and their contemporaries drew on the scriptural language of covenant to undermine this very distinction.[36] Specifically, they argued that the covenant with God must in some circumstances supersede the covenant with the king. In hermeneutical terms, they linked scriptural interpretation to prophetic narrative. In practical terms, they legitimated the violence of taking up arms against Charles I.

THE METAPHORICAL PLOT

For two of the most brilliant commentators on the civil war, Hobbes and Milton, the violence of the civil war and the eventual regicide were directly related to the prophetic interpretation of Scripture exemplified by Marshall, Burges, and Burroughs. When Hobbes expressed his fear that the "inconstant signification" of words would precipitate rebellion, and when he devoted two books of *Leviathan* to the dangers of scriptural interpretation, he was responding in part to the fast sermons and their revolutionary, public demonstrations of scriptural exegesis.[37] In their incendiary interpretation of the divine covenant, the fast preachers had encouraged the seditious interpretation of political obligation as well. They had shown how the metaphorical interpretation of Scripture could give rise to antinomianism, false prophecy, and political anarchy. Hobbes reiterated these concerns in *Behemoth*, a history of the civil war written in the 1660s: Christian sovereigns should exercise more control over preaching, Hobbes cautioned, since "the interpretation of a verse in the Hebrew, Greek, or Latin Bible, is oftentimes the cause of civil war and the deposing and assassinating of God's anointed."[38]

In *The Tenure of Kings and Magistrates* Milton also linked the prophetic interpretation of Scripture to the revolutionary cause, although his aim in doing so was in sharp contrast to Hobbes's.[39] First, Milton interpreted Scripture to argue against absolute sovereignty. Second, Milton believed that the individual's right (or obligation) to read and interpret Scripture for himself dictated a form of government that would support rather than undermine this free and open encounter with the Bible. As he would explain in *On Christian Doctrine*, Milton conceived of God's relationship to man as involving persuasion rather than coercion, and this in turn informed his understanding of prophecy: "So we must conclude that God made no absolute decrees about anything which he left in the power of men, for men have freedom of action."[40] This meant that God's covenant was a conditional rather than an absolute covenant, dependent on the goodwill of the believer who strives "to love him and keep his commandments." And this was true not only of the covenant of works but also of grace, whose condition or "work" is "faith in Christ."[41] In a memorable phrase that also appears in *Paradise Lost*, Milton claimed that the gospel frees men "from the works of the law" so that they may engage in "works of faith."[42]

One of the most important works of faith for Milton—one of the most important manifestations of the "new covenant"—was the work of reading, specifically reading and interpreting Scripture. As he put it in *Christian Doctrine*, "all true believers either prophesy or have within them the Holy Spirit, which is as good as having the gift of prophecy and dreams and visions." He who interprets under the new covenant interprets according to the spirit rather than the letter: "[O]n the evidence of scripture itself, all things are eventually to be referred to the Spirit and the unwritten word."[43] Reading is a prophetic and ethical activity precisely because meaning is not simply or literally given but must be spiritually construed. The work of prophecy or interpretation is thus inseparable from attention to the figurative dimension of Scripture. Conversely, the figurative language of Scripture functions as a conditional covenant that demands the reader's interpretive and ethical response.[44]

In *The Tenure of Kings and Magistrates*, Milton dramatized the political implications of such interpretive individualism. In reasoning about the scriptural metaphor of covenant, as well as the secular metaphors of tenure and contract, Milton made metaphor itself the basis of a new contract with the reader, the aim of which was to further the figurative and actual violence that Hobbes called "contention, sedition, or contempt." Although Milton began by arguing that monarchy involves a contractual relationship between the subject and the sovereign, he concluded that monarchy is itself a metaphor for which there is no literal, earthly referent. In the process, *The Tenure* shows how attention to the figurative or more precisely metaphorical nature of sovereignty dictates not only republicanism but also the regicide of Charles I.

The immediate occasion of *The Tenure*, which was written between the trial and execution of Charles I, was the backsliding of the Presbyterians. From the beginning of the Long Parliament, the Presbyterians had supported the parliamentary cause against the king. Yet in 1648/49, in *A Serious and Faithful Representation* addressed "to the General and his Council of War," a number of Presbyterian ministers had urged mercy for Charles on the eve of his execution. Arguing that they were bound by The Solemn League and Covenant to preserve the person of the king, they attacked the army's "intent of framing and contriving a new model . . . of the laws of government"; and, in language that eerily foreshadowed the dilemma of Milton's Samson, charged Cromwell and his followers with trusting in their own judgment rather than divine law: "Nor is it safe to be guided by impulses of spirit or pretended impressions in your hearts without or against God's written word; for by this means the temptations of Satan and the motions of God's Spirit will be put in equal balance."[45] In response to this charge of antinomianism and the Presbyterians' own backsliding. Milton's paradoxical task in *The Tenure* was to *make the case* for regicide: to reconcile the rule of law and the exception, the political contract and the violent breach of contract, in the minds of the English people. He did so by foregrounding the activity of interpretation—the distinction between literal and figurative meaning and their metaphorical equivalents, slavery and freedom. Drawing on arguments from natural law, Scripture, and positive law, Milton argued that the right sort of metaphorical interpretation dictated the violent plot of regicide, whereas the wrong sort would produce a tragic narrative of voluntary servitude. *The Tenure* was, in short, Milton's lesson in the politics of reading for the year 1649.

In his case for regicide, Milton adopted two strategies of interpretation. On the one hand, he argued—as Bradshaw, who tried the case against Charles I, did—from positive law, authority, and precedent; on the other, he argued—as Bradshaw failed to do—from natural law, natural right, and the lack of precedent. In the first case, he claimed that the regicide followed from historical precedent and the Presybterians' own earlier actions. In the second, he redescribed the regicide as a uniquely creative act. In asserting that the regicide was the "necessary consequence" of previous events, Milton used the logic of narrative to domesticate a shocking act of violence. But in arguing that the regicide needed no precedent, and that prophetic interpretation was creative and constitutive of political authority, Milton told a different story: one in which precedents were a form of slavery and the violent exception was the motor of history.

What united these diverse and, in somes cases, contradictory arguments was Milton's powerful sense of the constitutive power of covenant and contract: their metaphorical power to transform existing relations or to create new relations ex nihilo. First, Milton construed the biblical covenant and political contract in similar terms: both were structured as rational, open-ended, and revocable agreements that depended for their realization on the performance of the contracting parties. Second, and consequently, biblical examples of God's covenant with the Jews were cited not so much as authoritative precedents for political contract as instances of the kind of God-given rational deliberation that should inform men's political covenants with each other.[46] Third, Milton's understanding of covenant and contract was rooted in the interest of the people and, for that reason, compatible with strategic considerations of equity and reason of state. Finally, covenant and contract were not only objects of interpretation for Milton but also models of interpretation. Like scriptural prophecy and metaphor, they were conditional and performative rather than predictive. If in his explicit justification of violence Milton borrowed from the fast sermons and radical pamphlets, the covenant theology and the contract theory, of the 1640s, he went further than almost all of his contemporaries in equating the natural law of justice with the productive power of metaphor and the activity of prophecy with the individual's natural right to interpret.

Milton's first hermeneutical lesson in *The Tenure* concerned the precedent set by the Presbyterians themselves. The Presbyterians' backsliding, he argued, was the result of an interpretive error, a faulty inference or misrecognition of their own earlier actions. In pleading for clemency in 1648/49, they were being disloyal to their previous deeds. Although shortly after this, Milton would argue that the trial and regicide were justified by natural law, right reason, and the right of self-preservation because Charles had broken the Covenant first, at the outset he focused on the Presbyterians as interpretive agents, agents whose prior actions should be construed as a kind of legally binding promise. The legal proceedings against the king were "the necessary consequences of thir own former actions."[47] Thus the Presbyterians were failing to follow the outlines of their own plot. Loyalty, properly construed, dictated breaking with the Covenant; contract properly construed dictated violence against the king. By "shifting and relapsing," the Presbyterians had not only disavowed their own previous good intentions; they had effectively rescripted their earlier actions as rebellion.[48]

Milton described the interpretive failures of the Presbyterians as slavish literalism and "fals prophecy." His chief example involved the clause of the Solemn League and Covenant binding Parliament to respect the safety of the king. Milton mocked the Presbyterians for their literal-minded desire to preserve the "meere useless bulke" of Charles's person. He then demystified this desire by charging that the clause had only been included for reasons of self-preservation: in the event that they lost the war, the Presbyterians could pretend they had always defended the king's person. The Presbyterians' "seeming to sweare counter almost in the same breath Allegeance and no Allegeance" was "evidence of thir feare, not of thir fidelity."[49]

This fear in turn was the real motive for the Presybterians' "dissembl'd and seditious pity":

> [T]hey plead for him, pity him, extoll him. . . . But certainly if we consider who and what they are, on a soddain grown so pitifull, wee may conclude, thir pitty can be no true, and Christian commiseration, but either levitie and shallowness of minde, or else a carnal admiring of that worldly pomp and greatness, from whence they see him fall'n; or rather lastly a dissembl'd and seditious pity, fain'd of industry to begett new discord. As for mercy, if it be to a Tyrant, under which Name they themselves have cited him so oft in the hearing of God, of Angels, and the holy Church assembl'd, and there charg'd him with the spilling of more innocent blood by farr, then ever *Nero* did, undoubtedly the mercy which they pretend, is the mercy of wicked men; and their mercies, wee read are cruelties.

In attributing pity as well as fear to the Presbyterians, Milton called to mind the Renaissance debate about these two passions, a debate precipitated by the catharsis clause in Aristotle's *Poetics*. In implicitly comparing Charles with Nero, Milton also alluded to Seneca's *De clementia*, written for his recalcitrant imperial pupil. In commentaries on Aristotle's *Poetics*, sixteenth-century writers worried about how to reconcile the purgation of pity with Christian ethics. In *De clementia*, Seneca provided one answer by distinguishing between genuine mercy and theatrical, effeminizing pity.

Mercy for a tyrant, Milton argued, can only be a feigned, seditious, self-regarding pity based on fear for one's life. This fear naturally leads to enslavement or voluntary servitude to a tyrant. Milton would return to this attack on pity from a slightly different but related vantage point in *Eikonoklastes*, in response to the pathos-ridden narrative of the king's sufferings in *Eikon Basilike*, which sought to evoke sympathy for the royalist cause.[50] The point to note in *The Tenure* is that the accusation of false prophecy and breach of contract brings in its wake an accusation about false or feigned passions as well.

Just as Milton demystified pity as slavish fear, so he called attention to the Presbyterians' figurative reading of the Bible only to show that it too was a form of slavish literalism: the "turnes" and tropes they discerned in Scripture were incapable of producing narratives of liberation. "Ridling" divines such as Stephen Marshall had "gloss'd and fitted [Scripture] for thir turnes with a double contradictory sense, transforming the sacred verity of God, to an Idol with two Faces." Under the "latitude and shelter of ambiguous interpretation," they had casuistically pursued their own self-interested ends.[51] Such an idolatrous preoccupation with self-interest involved not only slavery to mere life but also the slavish inability to generate a new plot. This interpretive slavery had as its corollary political slavery: the Presbyterians' backsliding was the modern version of the "ancient slavery" the English knew under the Norman Yoke.[52] In disowning their own actions, they had effectively ceded their power to interpret—and thus their political power—to the king. Accordingly, Milton turned the example of Meroz against Marshall and other Presbyterians, inviting God to visit upon the heads of the Presbyterians "that *curse ye Meroz*, the very *Motto* of their Pulpits, wherwith so frequently, not as *Meroz* but more like Atheists they have blasphem'd the vengeance of God and [traduc'd] the zeale of his people." Like Meroz, the Presbyterians were "neuters" who refused to interpret, and thus to fight, in God's cause.[53]

Milton devoted the middle section of *The Tenure* to illustrating this hermeneutical lesson with an energy and single-mindedness unmatched by any of his contemporaries. Although he claimed to offer a defense of tyrannicide with reference to "autorities and reasons . . . fetch't out of the midst of choicest and most authentic learning," his real goal was to show that all precedents, all historical and textual authorities, were really examples of the "right" to interpret. This right, guided by the natural law of justice, preceded and informed all other rights and obligations.[54]

The section begins with a narrative about the contractual origin of government. After the fall, men first agreed "by common league to bind each other from mutual injury." When they discovered "no faith in all was . . . sufficiently binding," they chose a single Hobbesian authority to protect themselves. This in turn led to the recognition of "the danger and inconveniences of committing arbitrary power to any," and the consequent re-definition of the covenant as conditional rather than absolute and irrevo-cable: first, "the law was set above the magistrate."

> When this would not serve, but that the Law was either not executed, or misapply'd, they were constrain'd from that time, the onely remedy left them, to put conditions and take Oaths from all Kings and Magis-trates at thir first instalment to doe impartial justice by Law: who, upon those termes and no other, receav'd Allegeance from the people, that is to say, bond or Covnant to obey them in execution of those Lawes which they the people had themselves made, or assented to. And this ofttimes with express warning, that if the King or Magistrate prov'd unfaithfull to his trust, the people would be disengag'd.[55]

Milton then proceeded to demystify the logic of Hobbes's account of the subject's transfer of allegiance to the sovereign. In *The Tenure* the contract between subject and sovereign is a conditional contract that is continually subject to renegotiation: "It being thus manifest that the power of Kings and Magistrates is nothing else but what is only derivative, transferr'd and committed to them in trust from the People to the Common good of them all, in whom the power yet remains fundamentally and cannot be tak'n from them without a violation of thir natural birthright."[56] It thus stands to reason that when the common good is not realized the power of the sovereign may be revoked and reassumed by his subjects.

Scripture is then adduced not, as in Hobbes, to underwrite the argu-ment for an absolute sovereign but rather as evidence of the historical revision of the original contract and of the impossibility of any such per-manently binding agreement. Milton quotes Deuteronomy 17:14 and 1 Samuel 8—both of which had been cited by Grotius against popular rights—in support of "the right of choosing, yea of changing [one's] government":[57]

> It follows, lastly, that since the King or Magistrate holds his autoritie of the people, both originaly and naturally for their own good in the first place, and not his own, then may the people, as oft as they shall judge it for the best, either choose him or reject him, retaine him or depose him, though no Tyrant, meerly by the liberty and right of free born Men to be govern'd as seems to them best. This, though it cannot but stand with plain reason, shall be made good also by Scripture. *Deut.* 17.14. *When thou art come into the land which the Lord thy God giveth thee, and shalt say, I will set a King over mee, like as all the Nations about mee.* These words confirme us that the right of choosing, yea of changing their own Goverment is by the grant of God himself in the People.[58]

Scripture teaches that God's covenants with Abraham and Moses were revised by David, Samuel, and others—both for good and for ill. As Milton remarked of the Jews' request for a king in Samuel, "God himself joyn'd with them in the work; though in som sort it was at that time displeasing to him." The choice of a king was evidence of the rational—though faulty—exercise of free will that is the central tenet of Milton's Arminianism. As Milton observed in *Christian Doctrine*, "God made his decrees conditional . . . for the very purpose of allowing free causes to put into effect the freedom which he himself gave them," including, as God sourly remarks in *Paradise Lost*, the freedom to err.[59] Scripture and reason are not only compatible; Scripture is itself a record of the trials and errors of God-given reason.

The charged biblical example of Ehud, "whom God had raysd to deliver Israel from *Eglon* King of *Moab*," was part of this argument about the natural right to interpret. In *De jure belli ac pacis* Grotius had warned against interpreting Ehud as a warrant for tyrannicide.[60] In *The Tenure* Milton methodically dismissed all the objections that might be made to Ehud's exemplarity, including Grotius's view that he "had special warrant from God." This, Milton replied, "cannot be granted, because not expressd; tis plain that he was raysd by God to be a Deliverer, and went on just principles, such as were then and ever held allowable, to deale so by a Tyrant that could no otherwise be dealt with." And even in those cases where a divine command is evident, tyrannicide is "not the less imitable for that; for where a thing grounded so much on natural reason hath the addition of a command from God, what does it but establish the lawfulness of such an act."[61]

In asserting the compatibility of divine and human ordinance, Milton made the whole realm of politics coextensive with that of human judgment. In striking contrast to many of his contemporaries who distinguished between the express commandments of God and the invention and the ordinance of man, Milton equated them: the power that is ordained by God is the same power that is ordered by man.[62] He then developed the implications of this analysis by calling attention to the rhetorical dimension of sovereignty. Just as Romans 13 is open to interpretation, so the rule of a sovereign is open to interpretation by the people, who create legitimacy by their linguistic act of consent. Thus, if Romans 13 may be cited to support obedience to kings, it may also be cited to support resistance; similarly

if the peoples act in election be pleaded by a King, as the act of God, and the most just title to enthrone him, why may not the peoples act of rejection, bee as well pleaded by the people as the act of God and the most just reason to depose him? So that we see the title and just right of raigning or deposing, in reference to God, is found in Scripture to be all one; visible onely in the people, and depending meerly upon justice and demerit.[63]

As in Hobbes's *Leviathan*, authority is constituted by the metaphorical transfer of allegiance and power to the sovereign. But Milton's account differs in one significant respect: just as for Milton consent is not meaningful without the possibility of dissent, so the ability to transfer power to the sovereign is evidence of the "right" to revoke allegiance. Milton stressed what Hobbes labored to conceal: that political contract involves only a metaphorical transfer, because power remains fundamentally with the people. In this light, we might strengthen Hobbes's caution in *Leviathan* against allowing metaphors into political deliberation: metaphors are not less dangerous to absolute sovereignty "when they openly profess their own inconstancy"—their own metaphoricity—but rather more.[64]

In characteristic fashion, Milton dramatized this metaphorical understanding of covenant and contract in the metaphors of his treatise. The opening of *The Tenure of Kings and Magistrates* encapsulated his hermeneutic lesson about the logic of interpretation, the way plots are generated from good and bad metaphors:

> If men within themselves would be govern'd by reason, and not generally give up thir understanding to the double tyrannie, of Custom from without and blind affections from within, they would discerne better what it is to favour and uphold a Tyrant of a Nation. But being slaves within doors, no wonder that they strive so much to have the public State conformably govern'd to the inward vitious rule, by which they govern themselves. For none can love freedom heartilie but good men.[65]

It is striking that the opening sentence of this treatise on the literal tyranny of Charles I should use tyranny and government as metaphors. But this is precisely Milton's point: metaphorical tyranny within gives rise to literal tyranny without. Charles's tyranny would be impossible without the voluntary servitude of the Presbyterians.[66]

Milton then harnessed the ethical logic of metaphor to argue for a different sort of conformity, a different political narrative. In Milton's view, kingship was itself simply a metaphor—that is, the name of a contract or relation between two terms: "We know that King and Subject are relatives, and relatives have no longer being then in the relation."[67] This conception was not original with Milton. Both Grotius and Perkins had used it to argue for obedience to the sovereign.[68] But Milton spins a whole bloody narrative from this premise of relation. According to Milton's metaphorical logic, "King is a name of dignity and office, not of person: Who therfore kills a King, must kill him while he is a King. Then they certainly who by deposing him have long since tak'n from him the life of a King, his office and his dignity, they in the truest sence may be said to have killed the King." Although such a distinction between the king's "two bodies" would seem to imply that there was no point in killing Charles once he had been deposed, Milton drew the opposite conclusion: he claimed that since the Presbyterians had figuratively or metaphorically killed the king, they were logically and morally obliged to do so literally as well.[69] It was precisely such an equivocal—or casuistical—understanding of "king" that Hobbes feared, and with good reason. For, in a kind of parody of the scriptural distinction between the spirit and the letter, the figurative murder of the king is prior to and dictates his literal murder as its lethal consequence. Or, to put it another way, the king's official body proves to be fatally indistinguishable from his personal body. The contract of sovereignty and the metaphor of "king" are thus prophetic in the sense of generating new meanings and actions, including the execution of the king himself.[70]

The language of "tenure" also figures prominently in the metaphorical logic of the treatise. "Tenure" in this period could mean "the action or fact of holding a tenement," "the condition of service, etc., under which a tenement is held of a superior; the title by which the property is held; the relations, rights, and duties of the tenant to the landlord," and by extension, a "title" or "authority."[71] As we saw in chapter 2, in 1628, the same year that saw the Petition of Right, Edward Coke published his commentary on Littleton's *Tenures*. Coke, who had already been dismissed from the bench by James for his insistence that the law made the king rather than vice versa, construed the law of tenancy as just such a limit to royal power.[72] In so doing, Coke was inspired by Magna Carta, which made the freehold or free tenure of property a defining characteristic of the free subject as opposed to the king. Significantly for our purposes, in his discussion of the definitions of tenure in the *Institutes*, Coke called attention to the connection between tenure and a legal contract: "Also, *tenere* signifieth performance; as in the Writ of Covenant, Quod teneat conventionem, that is, That hee hold or performe his Covenant. . . . And likewise it signifieth to be bound, as it is sayd in every common Obligation, teneri et firmiter obligari." He argued further that all the meanings of tenant could be linked in the following formula: "For (1) he hath the estate of the land, (2) he holdeth the land of some superiour Lord, (3) and is to performe the services due, and (4) thereunto he is bounden (5) by doome and iudgement of Law."[73]

Milton used this constellation of meanings to develop a revolutionary logic of political obligation in *The Tenure*. From its first metaphorical reference in the title of Milton's tract to the authority or office of "kings and magistrates" (a phrase that equates and thus undermines the distinction between two hierarchically distinct positions of power), tenure gradually regains its literal meaning of feudal tenure. Milton played on this meaning to suggest first that the people do not hold their land in a grant of tenure from the king so much as the king is a bondsman who holds his office or "tenure" from the people on the condition that he fulfill his covenant with them; he then argued that the tenure of kingship—regardless of whether the king was a good ruler—reduced the people to the status of feudal subjects.[74]

For the king to hold his subjects in feudal subjection is to arrogate to himself divine authority: "[T]o say that Kings are accountable to none but God, is the overturning of all Law and government. . . . for if the King feare not God, as how many of them do not? we hold then our lives and estates by the tenure of his meer grace and mercy, as from a God."[75] This, of course, was precisely the claim royalist defenders of divine right wished to make. But Milton drew the republican conclusion. A free nation, without "the natural and essential power" or "just right" of deposing its ruler, must "be thought no better then slaves and vassals born, in the tenure and occupation of another inheriting Lord. Whose goverment, though not illegal, or intolerable, hangs over them as a Lordly scourge, not as a free government; and therfore to be abrogated." In this slippage of meaning, tenure comes to stand not for the legitimate authority of the king but for the Presbyterians' and royalists' idolatrous interpretation of political contract and their voluntary servitude.[76]

In literalizing the meaning of tenure, Milton once again activated the language of the Norman Yoke and the ancient constitution.[77] In seventeenth-century political discourse, as we have seen, parliamentarians often referred to the so-called ancient constitution of immemorial custom, which rooted power in the people and subjected the king to the law. Royalists, in contrast, insisted that the king made the law and was thus above it; and they pointed for support not only to Scripture but also to the institution of hereditary feudal tenure introduced with the Norman Conquest.[78] As Pocock and others have shown, some puritans and Presbyterians combined the idea of the ancient constitution with that of England's divine mission as the Elect Nation, arguing that the ancient constitution was a sign of England's covenant with the Lord: godly rule reached its culmination with the restoration of the ancient constitution.[79] In passages such as the one quoted immediately preceding, we can see Milton using the Presbyterians' language to argue against their interpretation of the Covenant. In Milton's view, a rational and revocable political contract *is* the form of God's covenant with the English people. And this in turn means that the historical "rights" of the ancient constitution are effectively the same as the natural rights of resistance granted to men at birth: "Whence doubtless our Ancestors who were not ignorant with what *rights either Nature or ancient Constitution* had endowed them, when Oaths both at Coronation, and renewd in Parliament would not serve, thought it no way illegal to depose and put to death thir tyrannous Kings." In this way Milton equated the historical precedent of the ancient constitution with the individual right to interpret, the right to interpret metaphorically or equitably according to the natural law of justice.[80]

Milton then applied this logic of metaphor to his own definition of sovereignty. By the end of the treatise Milton was no longer simply justifying tyrannicide; he was arguing for the abrogation of monarchical government even when it was "not illegal or intolerable." And lest his reader think this argument applied only to absolute monarchs, he turned sovereignty itself into a metaphor without any literal referent except God: the purpose of the trial of Charles I was "to teach lawless Kings, and all who so much adore them, that not mortal man, or his imperious will, but Justice, is the onely true sovran and supreme Majesty upon earth."[81] In the conclusion of the treatise, Milton made the exclusive identification of monarchy and God explicit:

> Therfore he who is our only King, the Root of *David*, and whose Kingdom is eternal righteousness, with all that Warr under him, whose happiness and final hopes are laid up in that only just & rightful kingdom (which we pray uncessantly may com soon, and in so praying wish hasty ruin and destruction to all Tyrants) eev'n he our immortal King, and all that love him, must of necessity have in abomination these blind and lame Defenders of *Jerusalem* [the Jebusites, who are biblical precursors of the Presbyterians].[82]

Like covenants, metaphors could be used to oblige or disoblige, to engage or disengage: the metaphorical contract of tenure obliged subjects to abrogate hereditary kingship; the metaphorical contract of sovereignty engaged subjects to take up arms against Charles, whose literal pretensions to absolute monarchy had proved to be blasphemous.

Milton's demonstration of the power of interpretation to manufacture a new narrative of political obligation leads us to the most radical argument of *The Tenure*. At the same time that he appealed to authority and precedent, Milton also argued that the very lack of precedent should be a powerful incentive to kill the king.[83] In his most extreme defense of the regicide as an action "above the form of Law or Custom," Milton courted the charge of antinomianism he was ostensibly rebutting.[84] Declaring that "the Sword of God [is] superior to all mortal things, in whose hand soever by apparent signes his testified will is to put it," he risked arguing tauto-

[handwritten margin note: "The reversal of priority ("first shall be last") in Milton's typology makes all earthly sovereignty into a figure for divine authority"]

logically that violence was its own justification. Even here, however, Milton insisted that the absence of precedent was an occasion for virtuous interpretation and action, an occasion to make precedents rather than being enslaved by them:

> And if the Parlament and Military Councel doe what they doe without precedent, if it appear thir duty, it argues the more wisdom, vertue, and magnanimity, that they know themselves able to be a precedent to others. Who perhaps in the future ages, if they prove not too degenerat, will look up with honour, and aspire towards these exemplary, and matchless deeds of thir Ancestors, as to the highest top of thir civil glory and emulation.[85]

In such pronouncements Milton advanced the inextricability of justice and violence, positive law and the exception.

Here we see Milton drawing on the arguments of Henry Parker and others for the compatibility of the political contract with reason of state. In his justification of the regicide, as well as in his account of the origin of monarchy, Milton appealed to the "autoritie and power of self-defence and preservation" which is "originally and naturally" in all individuals. "Present necessitie" and "the Law of nature justifies any man to defend himself, eev'n against the King in Person." The same was true of the state: "[J]ustice done upon a Tyrant is no more but the necessary self-defence of a whole Common wealth," the preservation of "the public good."[86] Although in *Paradise Lost* Milton acknowledged that such appeals to necessity and the public good could be used for the purposes of tyrannical self-aggrandizement,[87] for Milton in *The Tenure*, and for other defenders of Cromwell and the New Model Army, such appeals to the preservation of the commonwealth were perfectly consonant with conscience and true justice.[88]

Well after Milton's defense of Parliament and the army, the question of who could claim to represent and thus defend the commonwealth remained a subject of intense debate; the danger of a satanic abuse of conscience and reason of state remained constant. The army chaplain William Sedgwick drew on the language of reason of state and illustrated its ambiguity when he argued in *A Second View of the Army Remonstrance* (1649), "What makes a public person above a private but that he hath the civil sword in his hand to administer justice?" "This Army is truly the people of the kingdom, in which the common interest most lies."[89] In the seventeenth century, a "public person" was generally defined as a legitimate representative of the people, a legitimate administrator of justice. Marshall and Burges had presented Samson as such a public person when they defended taking up arms against the king in the early 1640s. Yet the view that justice and the sword, or justice and the trial of Charles I, were perfectly compatible was certainly a minority position in 1649.[90] It would be a radical fringe position by the time Milton revisited these issues in *Samson Agonistes* in 1670.

In the preceding pages I have argued that in *The Tenure* Milton was concerned not simply with the physical violence of regicide but also with the power of metaphorical interpretation to generate new narratives, new relations of political obligation. In particular, Milton was preoccupied with the regicide as an event for which there was no simple precedent, which was "above the form of law or custom" and thus required equitable interpretation. For Aristotle, Roman law, and canon law, an equitable judgment was often a merciful one, a judgment designed to mitigate the rigors of the law. But as a supplement to or transgression of positive law literally construed, such metaphorical interpretation could also license violence. In *The Tenure* Milton was eager to appropriate this interpretive power—the power of "the sword" or Word—for the revolutionary cause. In the process, he also presented a genealogy of the revolutionary subject.

In the *Genealogy of Morals*, Nietzsche provides a helpful modern gloss on *The Tenure*. In Nietzsche's genealogy, the ability to keep one's promises presupposes a kind of internal contract that constitutes the conscientious and "calculable" ethical subject.[91] Although the discourse of contract appears to be antithetical to any notion of force or coercion, the contract with oneself that we call memory involves a kind of originary violence, a mnemotechnics predicated on pain and asceticism.[92] According to Nietzsche, one of the consequences of such self-violence is that will to power is manifest as a will to interpretation—not least of all the Protestant will to interpret Scripture. In *The Tenure* Milton provides us with an early modern genealogy of morals in the sense that the ethical subject—the subject who can keep his promises to himself as well as others—emerges by means of a potentially violent activity of interpretation. The Presbyterians equivocated about this responsibility. Milton, by contrast, put it center stage. As Hobbes feared, Milton's account of regicide was intended to teach its readers "a better fortitude, to dare execute highest Justice on them that shall by force of Armes endeavour the oppressing and bereaving of Religion and thir liberty at home."[93] In Milton's account, the regicide—like the right interpretation of the Covenant—was a good metaphor, a "troubler of stability."[94]

CHAPTER 6

Metalanguage

> How many Rebellions have been caused by the doctrine that it
> is up to private men to determine whether the commands of
> Kings are just or unjust, and that his commands may be rightly
> discussed before they are carried out, and in fact ought to be dis-
> cussed? . . . I think that those ancients foresaw this who pre-
> ferred that the knowledge of Justice be wrapped up in fables
> rather than exposed to discussion. Before questions of this kind
> began to be debated, Princes did not lay claim to sovereign
> power, they simply exercised it.
>
> —Hobbes, *De cive*

> Though nothing can be immortall, which mortals make; yet, if
> men had the use of reason they pretend to, their Common-
> wealths might be secured, at least, from perishing by internall
> diseases. For by the nature of their Institution, they are designed
> to live, as long as Mankind, or as the Lawes of Nature, or as
> Justice it selfe, which gives them life. Therefore when they come
> to be dissolved, not by externall violence, but intestine disorder,
> the fault is not in men, as they are the *Matter*; but as they are
> the *Makers*, and orderers of them.
>
> —Hobbes, *Leviathan*

IF HOBBES was not thinking of Milton's defense of regicide, he was certainly thinking of similar arguments when he proposed his radically dys-
topic account of the origins of government in *Leviathan*. Prior to government and the motive for it, according to Hobbes, human life is "solitary,
poore, nasty, brutish and short" (13.89). Human beings in such a world
are motivated by calculations of self-interest and the fear of aggression;
they act on their own judgments, producing chaos and conflict, until—
spurred by the fear of violent death—they recognize that they can only
achieve their own ends by contracting to set up a sovereign power to
guarantee peace and security. Contract for Hobbes is the degree zero of
obligation, cut loose from scholastic natural law, from ostensibly natural
hierarchies of government, family, and marriage, as well as from covenant
theology and the promise of the afterlife. In the Hobbesian counterplot

to the Miltonic plot of regicide, fear of violent death is the motive for contract, and contract is the antidote to civil war.

Hobbes's counterplot was a response to the contemporary imagination of a new kind of political subject—a subject capable of joining with others in revolution. As we have seen in the preceeding chapters, this subject was first created in discourse, specifically the new discourse of contract, an unstable compound of natural rights theory, covenant theology, and the common law. But, as I have argued, what allowed the new political subject to emerge was not simply a thematic shift in the vocabulary of political obligation. Equally important was the metalinguistic dimension—the metalinguistic self-consciousness—of mid-seventeenth-century discussions of political obligation. These discussions—which occurred in pamphlets, public pronouncements, treatises, and actual debates—repeatedly dramatize an acute awareness on the part of the writers and speakers of the way in which language shapes their political opportunities. In these metalinguistic moments we see the revolutionary awareness of the possibility of creating new political obligations ex nihilo. In some cases this sense of the artifice of obligation empowered the individual interpreter to exercise his natural right of dissent; in other cases it made individuals aware of the necessity of constraining natural right by conventional agreements.

No one understood the linguistic causes of the English civil war better than Hobbes, the greatest political theorist of seventeenth-century Europe, and the thinker who has the greatest claim to having inaugurated the revolution in early modern political thought. Hobbes's revolution was a revolution in method, as Hobbes himself declared in the preface to his *Elements of Philosophy* when he stated that "civil philosophy" was "no older . . . than my own book *De Cive*."[1] In interpreting this claim, scholars have usually pointed to Hobbes's borrowings from contemporary science: his adoption of Galileo's scientific method of resolution and composition, that is, learning about an object of study by dividing it into its constituent parts and then reassembling it; or his adoption of a "mathematical" model of construction, according to which we can only know what we make ourselves.[2] But when we look at Hobbes's explanation for the causes of the English civil war and at Hobbes's own methodological solution to the problem of political obligation, we can't help being struck by his preoccupation with language, metalanguage, and genre rather than mathematics or geometry. Hobbes explained the causes of the civil war in terms of linguistic abuse and dysfunction. In response, his method of political science was metalinguistic and literary through and through.

In *Leviathan* Hobbes blamed the civil war on the contemporary discourses of covenant theology, the common law, and natural rights theory. In particular, Hobbes complained about the seditious preaching of the

Independents and Presbyterians, who incited their listeners to interpret Scripture according to their individual consciences. He was sarcastic about the common lawyers who criticized the royal prerogative while arrogating to themselves the equitable interpretation of the law. And he was skeptical of interpretations of the "unwritten Law of Nature": "though it be easy to such, as without partiality, and passion, make use of their naturall reason . . . yet considering there be very few, perhaps none, that in some cases are not blinded by self love, or some other passion, it is now become of all Laws the most obscure; and has consequently the greatest need of able Interpreters." In Hobbes's view, such discourses were quite literally revolutionary, since they had recently led to "Disputes, Controversies, and at last War."[3]

Above all, Hobbes was concerned with the deleterious effects of metaphorical thinking and of the imagination, which he witnessed in the political and military exploits of the 1640s. Hobbes associated this world of vainglory in particular with the literary genre of romance. But romance for Hobbes did not simply conjure up the self-aggrandizing passions of the aristocracy; it also served as a kind of shorthand for the dilemma of mimetic desire—the mediation of our passions by our own and others' imaginations—shared by nobleman and commoner alike.[4] By extension, the critique of vainglory did not simply apply to the aristocratic activities of "love and duel" but to the crown's chief competitors in the production of ideological fictions: the common lawyers, natural rights theorists, Presbyterians, Independents, and radical sectarians.[5] Well before Hegel analyzed the link between the law of the heart and the frenzy of self-conceit, Hobbes saw in conscience and vainglory, the Calvinist officeholder and the knight errant, two sides of the same coin, two manifestations of the same politically troublesome link between the passions, the imagination, metaphorical thinking, and rebellion.[6]

Hobbes's response to the contemporary state of discursive anarchy was to present in *Leviathan* "the true and onely Moral Philosophy," which he defined as "the Science of what is *Good*, and *Evill*, in the conversation and Society of man-kind." In this definition of moral philosophy, Hobbes made it clear that *Leviathan* is metadiscursive: it is a rhetoric, in the Aristotelian sense of an analysis of prevailing ways of speaking.[7] It is also a new ethics and politics of discourse. Hobbes did not want simply to dissect contemporary discursive errors or even to explain the reasons for their widespread acceptance. His goal was to rectify improper discourse by deducing the rights and duties of subjects and sovereigns from the correct analysis of the "passions of men."[8] Both in his critique of prevailing ways of speaking and in his reconstruction of political obligation, Hobbes made linguistic convention and artifice central to his method. For Hobbes, the constitutive parts of the commonwealth were discursive; and this meant that the reconstitution of the political subject involved refashioning "the conversation and Society of man-kind."

Many readers have wondered about the compatibility of Hobbes's focus on linguistic convention and his materialism, or his voluntarism and his appeal to the passions, but Hobbes clearly perceived these as inseparable.[9] This was not only because discourse was the "matter" of Hobbes's analysis, but also because, in Hobbes's view, the matter of human nature was itself fundamentally discursive. In *Leviathan* matter is shot through with the restless seeking after power; the passions are mediated by an individual's understanding of the desires, opinions, and imagination of others; and understanding is dependent on both genre and linguistic convention. The restless seeking after power produces dysfunctional romance plots of conscience and vainglory; but such a radically constructed social world proves to be the remedy for dysfunction as well. Mimesis—the human capacity for imitation, construction, and emulation—is in Hobbes's analysis simultaneously a matter for the police and the source of a utopian blueprint for the perfect commonwealth: "For by Art is created that great LEVIATHAN called a COMMON-WEALTH, or STATE . . . which is but an Artificall Man" (9).[10]

Hobbes's strategy in *Leviathan* is, accordingly, twofold. On the one hand, he diagnoses the pathology of mimetic desire that underlies the plots of vainglory and conscience, and offers an austere counterplot in which the state of nature and the fear of violent death are motives for entering into the political contract. On the other hand, he dismantles the competing discourses of obligation, by showing that no discourse can be effective unless authorized and enforced by the sovereign. In the first case, he counters the fictions of romance with a minimalist psychology that portrays human life in the state of nature as solitary, poor, nasty, brutish, and short. In the second case, he elaborates a metalinguistic critique of his opponents, in part by arguing that consent to the political contract involves consent to a linguistic contract, that is, to the sovereign's determination of linguistic usage. In both cases the human capacity for construction is the link between a materialist account of desire and a radically voluntarist account of natural law and obligation as the products of linguistic agreements: precisely because humans have no natural inclination to justice and virtue, these must be artificially created by means of human institutions and inventions, including the "profitable invention" of speech (4.24). Reasoning from the elementary "matter" of human nature, Hobbes believes, allows one to arrive at the proper way of speaking about rights and duties, and thus the proper way of reconstructing government from the ground up.

The Introduction to *Leviathan*, in which Hobbes famously compares the political contract with the divine "*Fiat*, pronounced by God in the

Creation," serves as a manifesto for Hobbes's heroic conception of mimesis; but Hobbes was also acutely aware of the darker side of voluntarism. Throughout *Leviathan*, artifice is shadowed by arbitrariness, contract is threatened by contingency. In his intensely ambivalent preoccupation with human fictions, including his own fictions of contract and of the state of nature, Hobbes not only opened up the possibility of producing new accounts of political obligation; he also captured for his contemporaries the frightening contingency of human relationships in the brave new world of passion and interest. In so doing, Hobbes prompted his readers to develop not only counterarguments but also counternarratives.

THE PROBLEM OF ESSEX

The political dangers of romance are well illustrated by a real-life example known to Hobbes and his readers: the career of the third earl of Essex. In 1606 the young earl married Frances Howard; yet, in 1613, in what became one of the most notorious scandals of the seventeenth century, James had the marriage annulled by impugning Essex's virility in order to bestow Frances Howard on his then favorite and her lover, Robert Carr. In 1630 Essex remarried and here too he proved unfortunate: his second wife also committed adultery. Then, with the outbreak of civil war in 1642 Essex became general of the parliamentary armies and was celebrated in parliamentary broadsides as a chivalric knight, a romance hero who was motivated by honor and virtue. Essex's real-life opponents were not convinced. On the battlefield, the royalist army carried banners that taunted Essex with the line "Cuckold, we come."[11] And in *Behemoth*, his history of the civil war, Hobbes conjectured that Essex was driven to insurrection by his wounded pride or vainglory: "But I believe verily, that the unfortunateness of his marriages had so discountenanced his conversation with the ladies, that the court could not be his proper element, unless he had had some extraordinary favour there, to balance that calamity."[12]

This account of Essex's motives illustrates one of the central problems confronted by *Leviathan*. Although Hobbes famously characterized the state of nature as one in which life is nasty, brutish, and short and in which people fear violent death at the hands of their fellow men, Essex and his bellicose contemporaries obviously felt no such compelling fear. Rather, they were motivated by the pursuit of glory or, more often, vainglory: the restless seeking after power and reputation at the expense of self-interest, even the interest of self-preservation.[13] But Essex's case was more complicated still. Although elsewhere in *Behemoth* Hobbes wrote respectfully of the commander of the parliamentary armies, here he implied that it was not so much manly valor as the fear of being perceived not to have it that caused Essex to risk violent death on the battlefield. Essex's military role was inescapably tied to his imagination of others' perception of him; his chivalric persona was itself a product of his mimetic desire. For Hobbes and his contemporaries, the problem of mimetic desire was the problem of romance. As Hobbes was well aware, any account of political obligation needed to address the role of the romance imagination in fostering the secular vainglory of soldiers like Essex or the vainglory of those seeking eternal life.[14]

A word about the cultural significance of romance in early modern England is pertinent. Romance was an immensely popular set of literary conventions, which could take the form of court masque, pastoral drama, or prose fiction. The formal elements of romance included idealizing Neo-platonic fictions, the ethical extremes of good and evil, a tendency toward allegory, a plot often modeled on the quest. As Kevin Sharpe, Lois Potter, and others have argued, these conventions provided an important vehicle of political debate at the Jacobean and Caroline court. The romance themes of love and honor were amenable either to praise or criticism of the monarch, either to the celebration of peace and prosperity or to arguments for military intervention abroad.

In the 1630s and 1640s, both critics and supporters of the crown saw romance as a particularly royalist genre. This was in part because it was the genre favored by court patronage: Charles I was known for his love of chivalric romance, as Queen Henrietta Maria was for her love of pastoral romance. Romance was also perceived to be the genre of royal behavior. Judging from contemporary poems, letters, and the masque roles they themselves performed, Charles I and Queen Henrietta Maria were seen as exemplifying the pastoral romance of domestic love. Their subjects, however, appeared to yearn for a romance that was composed equally of love and chivalric adventure. In the the poems of Edmund Waller and the drama of Sir Walter Montague, Prince Charles's trip to woo the Spanish Infanta was cast as such a romance adventure; the poet William Davenant similarly used romance conventions in a poem about Prince Rupert's trip to Madagascar, a venture that Charles opposed.[15]

Although royalist writers emphasized the idealizing components of romance, the romance plot in this period could also dramatize the theme of delusion and the dangers of imitation. Seventeenth-century readers would have been familiar with the works of Ariosto, Spenser, and Sidney, in which the digressive and episodic plot structure of the romance mirrored the moral error of the knight errant, his succumbing to the temptations of the senses, especially the temptation of erotic love. They would also have encountered characters both in love and war engaged in potentially deadly activities of imitation and emulation.[16] One consequence of the formal and thematic association of romance with delusion and emulation was that the term "romance" began to be used more widely in sixteenth and seventeenth-century England to connote not only errant passion but also imitation in the sense of fiction, deception, and paralogism.

With the obvious failure of Stuart cultural politics and the outbreak of civil war in the 1640s, these pejorative connotations of romance appeared increasingly in poems, plays, broadsides, and pamphlets. The word "romance" began to serve as a kind of shorthand for the delusions of love and the problem of imitation which—in the minds of many contemporaries— had helped precipitate the crisis of political obligation. The old trope of romance error—of the knight errant as a figure of errant passion and imagination—began to be used to describe Charles I and the future Charles II. The anonymous *The None-Such Charles* remarked that the king's "soule was more fixt on . . . Romances, during the time of his imprisonment, then on those Holy Writs."[17] Milton famously made a similar charge in *Eikonoklastes*. In the republican newsbook, *Mercurius Britanicus*, John Hall described the 1648 escape of Charles I from his parliamentary captors as "that late fine *Romance* of the Isle of Wight, a business that carries as much probability as anything that we read of *King Arthur* or the *Knights* of the *round* table."[18] Romance here conjured up not only chivalric love and adventure, but also a world of feigning and improbability.

Essex, who had supported the king and later defected, illustrated all three meanings of romance in this period: the idealizing plot of love and adventure, the theme of delusion, the dangers of imitation. Thus, some contemporaries understood Essex's fighting on the side of Parliament against the king to be motivated and excused by a romance conception of love and honor shared by Charles I. Others clearly viewed Essex as a quixotic figure, misled by the delusions of chivalry. But, as we have seen, Hobbes went even further, for he suggested that Essex's charging into battle illustrated not so much his unmediated love of honor as his mimetic desire, his desire to prove his virility to the women of the court and perhaps also—or even more—to other men by engaging them in murderous conflict on the battlefield. Essex's honor, in short, was motivated by his imagination of others' perceptions rather than by a love of chivalric virtue for its own sake.

Leviathan is in dialogue with the contemporary problem of romance, construed both as the cultural politics of the Stuart court and as an analysis of the inextricability of the passions and the imagination. For the royalist and romance emphasis on the passion of love, Hobbes substituted fear. For the romance problems of delusion and rampant imitation, Hobbes substituted contract. But the problems that Hobbes associated with romance inform Hobbes's solution to the problem of political obligation as well. For all of the passions as Hobbes described them are implicated in the delusions and fatal imitation that he associated with romance. In this sense, the genre of romance does not only signal the problems of vainglory and conscience to which Hobbes responded with an argument about fear of violent death; romance also names the structure of the imagination that posed a problem for Hobbes's own politics of fear. This in turn means that the first contract of *Leviathan* is a contract about mimesis, and that this mimetic contract is the precondition of the political contract that founds the Hobbesian commonwealth. Once we attend to this link between passion and the imagination, *Leviathan* emerges as one of the great meditations in the history of political thought on the relation of imitation to politics. Mimesis—the human capacity for imitation, metaphor, and emulation—is in Hobbes's analysis both a source of conflict and a solution to the problem of political obligation. The Hobbes who emerges from this interpretation is in some ways more traditional and in other ways more radical than one might guess from the scholarly reception of his work: a political philosopher for whom the problem of mimesis is still central, yet one who imagines that the mimetic impulse and the passions can themselves be the object of contractual definition.

HOBBES'S CRITIQUE OF ROMANCE

A glance at Hobbes's early work shows that he thought of romance both as a genre and as a problem of the imagination. Moreover, these two forms of romance were most often inextricable. Thus, romance referred to narratives of chivalric love and honor but also to the abuse of the imagination to which these romances gave rise. In *The Elements of Law*, composed in 1640, Hobbes compared the deceptions of sense and of the imagination to the fictions of romance: "[T]he brain . . . stirred by divers objects" may perceive "castles in the air, chimeras, and other monsters which are not in *rerum natura* . . . . And this composition is that which we commonly call FICTION of the mind" (28). He then went on to describe the linguistic manifestation of such romance deception in terms of the "paralogism" or faulty reasoning that Aristotle analyzed in the *Rhetoric* and *Poetics*:

> If we consider the power of those deceptions of sense . . . and also how unconstantly names have been settled, and how diversified by passion . . . and how subject men are to paralogism or faulty reasoning, I may in a manner conclude, that it is impossible to rectify so many errors of any one man, as must needs proceed from those causes, without beginning anew from the very first grounds of all our knowledge, sense; and, instead of books, reading over orderly one's own conceptions: in which meaning I take *nosce teipsum* for a precept worthy the reputation it hath gotten. (39)

I will return to this proposed solution to the problem of error later in this chapter. For the moment it is important to note that Hobbes describes both faulty inference and the deceptions of sense in the debased generic terms of romance.

Romance is also Hobbes's preferred analogy for wayward passions in *The Elements.* For example, Hobbes described glory as "that passion which proceedeth from the imagination or conception of our own power, above the power of him that contendeth with us" (50). "Vainglory," in contrast, is an inaccurate imagination or conception of our power, which derives from the "fame and trust of others" rather than from our own actions. In both cases, passion is relative and socially constituted. But in the first case, our passion corresponds to our ability and actions, in the second not. This second, bad form of mimetic desire Hobbes linked to the imitation of romance:

> [T]he fiction (which also is imagination) of actions done by ourselves, which never were done, is glorying; but because it begetteth no appetite nor endeavour to any further attempt, it is merely vain and unprofitable; as when a man imagineth himself to do the actions whereof he readeth in some romant, or to be like unto some other man whose actions he admireth. And this is called VAIN GLORY: and is exemplified in the fable by the fly sitting on the axletree, and saying to himself, What a dust do I raise![19]

In this passage, imitation does not so much lead to further rivalry as to a delusional self-satisfaction that is relatively harmless "because it begetteth no appetite nor endeavour to any further attempt." Yet, a slightly different picture of the link between imitation, vainglory, and romance appears in the next chapter:

> First we have had the example of one that preached in Cheapside from a cart there, instead of a pulpit, that he himself was Christ, which was spiritual pride or madness. . . . The gallant madness of Don Quixote is nothing else but an expression of such height of vain glory as reading of romants may produce in pusillanimous men.

Here, as so often in the history of the genre, romance does not simply narrate the story of emulous desire but also excites the desire for imitation in the reader. In particular, listening to "false prophets" or reading romances may contribute to the disregard of one's personal safety, a contempt for violent death.[20]

Hobbes's criticism of the genre and effects of romance also appears in his exchange with the poet William Davenant. In 1651 Davenant dedicated his unfinished epic romance, *Gondibert,* to Hobbes. In addition to the fact that Hobbes had been an assiduous reader of earlier drafts, Davenant must have thought of *Gondibert* as a Hobbesian poem because martial deeds are at a minimum, the hero's rival is killed off in the first canto, and the hero himself retreats into a life of contemplation. *Gondibert*, in short, presented "the Spenserian synthesis of love and a quest for glory [as] a pernicious mistake." In drawing this line between love and politics, Davenant signaled his "departure from earlier epic romance" and thus seconded—at least thematically—Hobbes's wariness about mixing romantic passion with politics. But Davenant's prefatory letter to Hobbes told a different story. In many ways a traditional humanist statement about the force of poetry, Davenant's credo must have seemed as much a symptom of, as a response to, the problems Hobbes was trying to address in his political works. Although Davenant criticized politicians, lawyers, and divines for contributing to the current political crisis, his own solution was to argue that poetry could instill political obedience by inspiring the reader with love. Romance was not simply a powerful generic influence on *Gondibert*, it was also Davenant's model for the poet's relation to the reader.

To Davenant's praise of love, Hobbes responded with a critique of romance. Against the majority of his contemporaries who thought that the sovereign needed to appeal to the subject's affections, Hobbes believed that love was erratic and subversive, not least of all when it took the form of emulous identification. In his analysis of the passions in *The Elements* Hobbes made it clear that, like romance vainglory, love gives rise to the desire to imitate and master others, and such emulation is itself a potential threat to civil order. For this reason, Hobbes insisted, "love" needs to be replaced by "contract . . . or fear" or both (57). Accordingly, while he praised Davenant for his chaste representation of love in the female character Birtha in *Gondibert*, he also cautioned Davenant against the improbabilities and extravagances of the typical romance plot. Less volatile than love or fancy—indeed, a bulwark against them— were the neoclassical criteria of perspicuity, propriety, and decency. To these Davenant had adhered, avoiding the "exorbitancy of . . . fiction" traditionally associated with romance. Hobbes then proceeded to criticize less careful poets, those who are seduced by the trappings of chivalric romance: "There are some who are not pleased with fiction, unless it be bold, not onely to exceed the *work* but also the *possibility* of nature: they would have impenetrable Armors, Inchanted Castles, invulnerable bodies, Iron Men, flying Horses, and a thousand other such things, which are easily feigned by them that dare." If *Gondibert* is a romance, Hobbes implied, it is a properly chastened one—a Hobbesian poem in which the author adheres to the truths of history and philosophy and excludes all supernatural machinery.[21]

When we turn to *Leviathan*, we see that the problems Hobbes associates with romance are features of the imagination in general. And because the imagination is inseparable from the passions, this in turn means that the passions are inevitably implicated in a romance structure of imitation and emulation. Already in chapter 1, Hobbes defines thought as "a *Representation* or *Apparence*, of some quality, or other Accident of a body without us" and "Sense" as "*seeming*, or *fancy*" (1.13, 14). In Hobbes's epistemology, humans know representations rather than objects, and these representations or sense perceptions are fundamentally colored by the individuals who receive them. In the chapters that follow, we begin to see how this displacement of the object by the subject's imagination or fancy means that nature itself is the product of our imaginative construction, that our social relations are the product of mimetic desire, and that these relations need to be controlled by an artificial authority.

We can begin to understand this inextricability of passion and imagination by looking at Hobbes's analysis of simple and compound imagination. In chapter 6 of *Leviathan*, Hobbes explains the relation between the passions and the simple imagination. He distinguishes between those vital motions which we share with animals such as "the *course* of the *Bloud*, the *Pulse* . . . &c; to which Motions there needs no help of the Imagination"—and voluntary motions such as "to *go*, to *speak*, to *move* any of our limbes, in such manner as is first fancied in our minds." It is because we can first imagine something that we can intend it. Fancy or "the Imagination is [thus] the first internall beginning of all Voluntary Motion"—of all passions, desires, appetite, or aversion (6.37–38). And while Hobbes has explained that simple imagination is simply decaying perception, he also insists that our perception of particular things as desirable "proceed[s] from Experience, and triall of their effects upon [us], or other men" (6.39). Accordingly, there is "nothing simply or absolutely" desirable or hateful; rather, there are only things that we call good or evil based on our changing perceptions of their relative usefulness to us:

> The names of things as affect us, that is, which please, and displease us, because all men be not alike affected with the same thing, nor the same man at all times, are in the common discourses of men, of *inconstant* signification. For seeing all names are imposed to signifie our conceptions; and all our affections are but conceptions; when we conceive the same things differently, we can hardly avoyd different naming of them. (4.31; see 6.39)

Even simple imagination, as it turns out, is inseparable from the "tincture of our different passions" and thus the contamination of "inconstant signification" (4.31).

Passion and imagination are even more tightly linked in the case of compound imagination. Whereas simple imagination, according to Hobbes, is the imagination of something "formerly perceived in sense" (2.16), compound imagination involves the combining of sense perceptions into something new. It is thus more closely allied to metaphor and the poetic imagination—a not altogether good thing. For, in the example Hobbes gives here, as in *The Elements*, compound imagination is compared with romance. "So when a man compoundeth the image of his own person, with the image of the actions of an other man; as when a man imagins himself a *Hercules*, or an *Alexander*, (which happeneth often to them that are much taken with reading of Romants) it is a compound imagination, and properly but a Fiction of the mind" (2.16). In this mini-narrative, the very use of this faculty is confounded with its abuse: it is natural to combine sense impressions into more complicated representations, but this natural ability may be allied to fiction rather than truth, to the all-too-human desire to imagine oneself other and greater than one is. The danger here is not simply that the reader of romance will imagine himself a lover and knight errant (like the Don Quixote of *The Elements*), but that the reader of romance will imagine himself a Hercules or Alexander, that is, a military hero of epic proportions. Epic action is the deviant offshoot of romance imagination, rather than the other way around (as it was usually judged to be in Renaissance poetics). Romance vainglory is not simply unprofitable but dangerous, as it is when the parties to the civil war begin to imagine that their honor demands that they engage in violent conflict. Thus the errant activity of the imagination—and specifically of metaphorical thinking (the perception of a false likeness between oneself and Hercules)—is not simply associated with moral and epistemological error, or with what Hobbes calls "paralogism" or faulty reasoning.[22] It is also associated with political error—with what Hobbes called "sedition and contempt."

For all these reasons, it is tempting to read the comparison of romance and compound imagination as an illustration of mental error. Yet, as Hobbes makes clear, romance error also illustrates a fundamental principle of Hobbesian psychology: all specifically human desires are mediated by the imaginative activity of comparing ourselves with others. The imagination in turn is shaped by our passions—and not only with respect to objects we desire. In a kind of metacommentary on the inextricability of passion and imagination, Hobbes even describes superior compound imagination—or the intellectual virtue of wit—in terms of our passionate rivalry with others.[23] In other words, wit is not an absolute quality but a superiority to others in an ability they admire. We desire wit not simply because of its absolute scarcity but because other people desire it. And, just as the intellectual virtue of wit is defined by "comparison" to others, so power is a matter of "eminence," of having or being thought to have more than others.[24] What counts as power also is socially determined, and is at least in part a matter of opinion or convention: "[T]he Reputation of Power is Power" (10.62). Thus, by Hobbes's own account, our passions and imagination are implicated in a romance plot of emulation.

As in his earlier work, so in *Leviathan* Hobbes attributes the dysfunctional romance plot of mimetic desire to conscience as well as vainglory. Thus, in the chapter on compound imagination, Hobbes argues that religion is also tainted by metaphorical thinking and romance error.[25] And in book 4 of *Leviathan* Hobbes uses the language of romance to describe the delusions of the "Kingdome of Darknesse." Hobbes's target includes all those preachers, whether puritan or Presybterian, who have convinced their auditors to fear damnation more than physical death and thus to construe political disobedience as a matter of conscience. In conjuring up hellfire, the preachers have promoted "the Daemonology of the Heathen Poets"; in combating their errors Hobbes redescribes the demons as "ghosts" and "faeries," based on "false, or uncertain Traditions, and faigned, or uncertain History" (44.418)—precisely the charges brought against romance by its critics. Similarly, he describes the pagan images and idols appropriated by the church as "meer Figment[s], without place, habitation, motion, or existence, but in the motions of the Brain" (45.446), and remarks further on, "A man can fancy Shapes he never saw . . . as the Poets make their Centaures, Chimaeras, or other Monsters never seen" (45.448). Such fictions are politically dangerous when their fictive quality is masked and when claims are made for their validity or efficacy that pose a threat to the absolute authority of the sovereign. In *Leviathan* the Roman Catholic Church and, closer to home, the English Presbyterians are the chief promulgators of such ideological fictions, and Hobbes's task is to demystify these fictions *as* romance and *as* ideology.

Vainglory and conscience, however, do not simply produce alternative romance plots; they are also versions of each other. Criticizing those who speak prophetically of the life to come in order to stir up rebellion on earth, Hobbes remarks sarcastically, "If the Kingdome of God . . . were not a Kingdome which God by his Lieutenants, or Vicars, who deliver his Commandements to the people, did exercise on Earth; there would not have been so much contention, and warre, about who it is, by whom God speaketh to us" (35.284). No one, in Hobbes's view, would quarrel over a merely spiritual or metaphorical kingdom. In their ambition to rule, churchmen are guilty of a kind of secular vainglory. Hobbes expands upon this insight in the next chapter, remarking, "he that pretends to teach men the way of so great felicity, pretends to govern them" (36.297). Precisely because all men are naturally ambitious to govern, we should be suspicious of the claim to speak prophetically on the basis of a personal covenant with God.[26] Scripture itself warns us of this danger in the figure of Micaiah: "[T]hat there were many more false then true Prophets, appears by this, that when Ahab [1 *Kings* 12] consulted four hundred prophets, they were all false Imposters, but onely one Michaiah" (36.298). Contemporary politics illustrates even more powerfully for Hobbes the dangers of false prophecy:

> For when Christian men, take not their Christian Soveraign, for Gods Prophet; they must either take their owne Dreames, for the Prophecy they mean to be governed by, and the tumour of their own hearts for the Spirit of God; or they must suffer themselves to bee lead by some strange Prince; or by some of their fellow subjects, that can bewitch them, by slaunder of the government, into rebellion. (36.299–300)

Ultimately, for Hobbes, conscience is itself a product of vainglory and metaphorical thinking. Although conscience originally meant witnessing or "knowing together," "afterwards, men mayde use of the same word metaphorically, for the knowledge of their own secret facts, and secret thoughts. . . . And last of all, men, vehemently in love with their own new opinions (though never so absurd,) and obstinately bent to maintain them, gave those opinions the reverend name of Conscience" (12.48).[27] Conscience in this account is simply another form of self-love and self-aggrandizement, whose practical political effects can only be catastrophic.

THE CONTRACT OF MIMESIS

Hobbes announces his remedy to the problem of mimetic desire—his alternative use of mimesis—at the very outset of *Leviathan*:

> NATURE (the Art whereby God hath made and governes the World) is by the *Art* of man, as in many other things, so in this also imitated, that it can make an Artificial Animal. For seeing life is but a motion of Limbs, the beginning whereof is in some principall part within; why may we not say, that all *Automata* (Engines that move themselves by springs and wheeles as doth a watch) have an artificiall life? For what is the *Heart*, but a *Spring*; and the *Nerves*, but so many *Strings*; and the *Joynts*, but so many *Wheeles*, giving motion to the whole Body, such as was intended by the Artificer? *Art* goes yet further, imitating that Rationall and most excellent worke of Nature, *Man*. For by Art is created that great LEVIATHAN called a COMMON-WEALTH, or STATE, (in latine CIVITAS) which is but an Artificall Man. (9)

Although Hobbes begins with the timeworn conceit of nature as the art of God, in the course of his elaboration life itself comes to seem artificial: the heart is a spring, the nerves are strings. The creation of the state then figures as an extension of this constructed body, as though bodies and states did not occupy two realms—nature and art—but a single realm of artifice. Hobbes then calls attention to the constructive power of artifice when he compares "the *Pacts* and *Covenants*, by which the parts of this Body Politique were at first made" to the divine "*Fiat*, or the *Let us make man*, pronounced by God in the Creation." Hobbes here draws on familiar comparisons between the poet and the divine creator, as well as between the poet and the legislator. But he does so in order to illustrate how human agreements bring the commonwealth into being ex nihilo. Covenants have the power to create the commonwealth not *because of* the prior existence of God (as Hobbes's critics thought); rather, they are constitutive, *like* God's creation ex nihilo. Likeness here licenses mimesis in the sense of making something new.[28] Hobbes further reinforces the identity of matter and artifice in his description of the first part of *Leviathan*: First, he will discuss "the *Matter* thereof, and the *Artificer*, both [of] which is *Man*. Secondly, *How*, and by what *Covenants* it is made; what are the *Rights* and *just Power* or *Authority* of a *Soveraigne*; and what it is that *preserveth* and *dissolveth* it." Man is both matter and maker, and covenants are his art.

How should we understand the linguistic covenant that is *Leviathan*? In *The Political Philosophy of Hobbes*, Leo Strauss argued that "the antithesis between classical and modern political philosophy, more accurately between [Plato] and . . . Hobbes, is that the former orientates itself by speech and the latter from the outset refuses to do so" (163).

> This refusal arises originally from insight into the problematic nature of ordinary speech, that is, of popular valuations, which one may with a certain justification call natural valuations. This insight leads Hobbes, just as it did Plato, first to the ideal of an exact political science. But while Plato goes back to the truth hidden in natural valuations and therefore seeks to teach nothing new and unheard-of, but to recall what is known to all but not understood, Hobbes, rejecting the natural valuations in principle, goes beyond them, goes forward to a new *a priori* political philosophy, which is of the future and freely projected. (163)

Although from one perspective it is true that Hobbes rejects orientation by speech, from another he adopts an even more radical linguistic orientation than Plato. This is the orientation of someone for whom the possibility of political contract is founded first and foremost on a linguistic contract. In *The Elements of Law* Hobbes defines science as

> the remembrance of the names or appellations of things, and how every thing is called, which is, in matters of common conversation, a remembrance of the pacts and covenants of men made amongst themselves,

concerning how to be understood of one another. And this kind of knowledge is generally called science, and the conclusions thereof truth. (170)

In *De cive*, Hobbes refers to science "whose truth is drawn out by natural reason and Syllogisms from human agreements and definitions."[29] And in chapter four of *Leviathan*, Hobbes declares that the "first use of Speech" is—or should be—metalinguistic: it consists in "the right Definition of Names" or words, that is, a single definition, based on an agreement among individuals to use words in the same way (4.28). This argument will lead Hobbes eventually to argue that definitions need to be enforced by a sovereign power; and that when we consent to the political contract, we consent as well to a linguistic contract, that is, to the sovereign's regulation of "the use of words" (32.255).[30]

In the Introduction to *Leviathan* as well, political contract depends on our subscribing to a linguistic contract. This is a contract regarding the passions—but it does not simply stipulate, as Strauss would have it, "the natural right only of the fear of death."[31] A precondition of this stipulation is the contract to redescribe the potentially dangerous social construction of the passions as a matter of "fixed similitude." Hobbes's goal in the Introduction is not only to introduce the reader to the notion of the commonwealth as an "Artificiall man," made by "pacts and covenants," but also to set up a contract with the reader specifying the protocols for interpreting *Leviathan*. Crucial to this contract is a clarification of the relation of passion to the imagination—a clarification, that is, regarding mimetic desire. Contract in the Introduction then is a metaphor for both the Hobbesian commonwealth and the process of analogical reasoning that checks the errant activity of the Imagination.

Accordingly, Hobbes moves from his sublime elaboration of the contract of government to a discussion of what it means to read metaphorically, thus explicitly addressing and limiting his implied contract with the reader:

> [T]here is . . . [a] saying not of late understood, by which [men] might learn truly to read one another, if they would take the pains; and that is, *Nosce teipsum*, *Read thy self*: which was not meant, as it is now used, to countenance, either the barbarous state of men in power, towards their inferiors; or to encourage men of low degree, to a sawcie behaviour towards their betters; But to teach us, that for the similitude of the thoughts, and Passions of one man, to the thoughts, and Passions of another, whosoever looketh into himself, and considereth what he doth, when he doth *think, opine, reason, hope, feare*, &c., and upon what grounds; he shall thereby read and know, what are the thoughts and Passions of all other men, upon the like occasions.

In this passage, Hobbes warns against what we might call the Miltonic plot of metaphor, according to which the linguistic transport of meaning serves as a model for political usurpation (something Hobbes worried about elsewhere in *Leviathan*).[32] While using the metaphor of "reading oneself" and recommending that the reader analogize from his self-knowledge to knowledge of others, Hobbes explicitly cautions us against interpreting the metaphorical activity of comparison as emulation, since the latter sort of reading threatens social and political hierarchy and thus the peace of the commonwealth. Thus he contrasts metaphor conceived of as a stable contract between individuals who agree to ignore their differences—to imagine themselves as equal parties to the contract—and metaphor as overreaching and transgressive and as articulating relations of hierarchy and inequality (imagining oneself a Hercules). Bourgeois diffidence, the simple perception of likeness, is proposed as the remedy for aristocratic self-aggrandizement or metaphorical usurpation. Hobbes's goal is to eradicate this danger by subordinating the transgressive activity of emulation to the putatively stable contract of comparison. In so doing, he produces the likeness he asks the reader to recognize.[33]

Hobbes thus makes it clear from the outset that the argument of *Leviathan* depends on a process of metaphorical identification that involves a chaste revision of the bad mimetic desire he associates with the reading of romance. For the typical romance appeal to eros as a motive of obligation, Hobbes substitutes the desire to "know [in] oneself" the "thoughts and passions" of other men, the desire to recognize oneself as like others. To shore up this perception of likeness in the Introduction, Hobbes eliminates the diverse objects of the passions and, while recommending comparison, he also eliminates other human subjects, as though in tacit recognition that mimetic desire feeds on the imagination and perception of others, and generates not only rivalry but dissimulation:

> I say the similitude of *Passions* [he continues from the passage quoted earlier] which are the same in all men, *desire, feare, hope,* &c; not the similitude of the *objects* of the Passions, which are the things *desired, feared, hoped,* &c.: for these the constitution individuall, and particular education do so vary, and they are so easie to be kept from our knowledge, that the characters of mans heart, blotted and confounded as they are, with dissembling, lying, counterfeiting, and erroneous doctrines, are legible onely to him that searcheth hearts.

Hobbes's distinction between the similitude of the passions and the objects of the passions is designed to respond to obvious objection that we do not all desire or fear the same things. According to Hobbes, this is not an obstacle to peace once we see that we are alike in wanting what we individually desire and in disliking the frustration of those desires. By thinking in such formal terms about desire, Hobbes implies, we can avoid the problems raised by vainglory and conscience—not only competition for scarce resources but also dissembling, lying, counterfeiting, and erroneous doctrines. Only if we think in such formal terms, can we achieve the proper combination of imaginative identification and distance, the proper ratio of passion and interest. Only then will Hobbes have succeeded in replacing the plot of mimetic desire with the plot of political science; only then will he have succeeded in creating the abstract liberal subject, whose interior life has been relegated to the private sphere, and who has been made—at least in theory—calculable and dependable.[34]

Hobbesian Fictions

As the Introduction makes clear, Hobbes's goal in *Leviathan* is not simply to deflate the self-aggrandizing subject of conscience and vainglory. It is also to create a new political subject, one who is not only calculable but absolutely subordinate. The fictions of the state of nature and of the political contract are Hobbes's attempt to construct a counternarrative to the plots of conscience and vainglory and to extricate the reader from the restless seeking after power, the drama of mimetic desire. Hobbes notoriously paints a much more pessimistic picture of the motives for entering into a contract than his contemporaries. Human beings in the state of nature are not naturally sociable. Rather, the state of nature is characterized by "continuall feare, and danger of violent death." But precisely because the fear of violent death renders the state of nature so unpleasant, it is an excellent motive for leaving it. Hobbes's pessimism is tinged by a corresponding optimism, for by choosing the lowest common denominator of human experience as the motive for contract, Hobbes hoped to render passion calculable. Although fear of violent death would in the short run exacerbate distrust and conflict, once individuals reasoned about this fear, they would recognize that rivalry and suspicion—what Hobbes called competition and diffidence—would in the long run be only self-defeating. In this way, the fundamental insecurity of the state of nature would dictate the first law of nature, "to seek peace" through setting up a political contract. Fear of violent death would dictate consent.

Hobbes's claim about the compatibility of fear and consent is buttressed by a crucial assumption regarding the passions: the Hobbesian subject can consent to fear because the passions, in Hobbes's analysis, are voluntary and allied with the faculty of deliberation.[35] Moreover, Hobbes makes deliberation itself a sequence of appetites or passions, and defines the will as "the last appetite in Deliberating." The will is no longer a separate faculty that links cognition and action. Rather, every action motivated by appetite or passion is by definition voluntary.[36] Individuals may deliberate about their passions incorrectly and thus will to act in irrational ways; but they cannot conclude from this that the passions are the source of involuntary actions. The passions are thus ideally the source not only of both legitimate coercion and consent but also of their compatibility.

As the previous paragraphs have begun to suggest, although the Hobbesian state of nature is an "Inference from the passions," Hobbes also makes sure that this state contains the seeds of its own destruction. For the very representation of the state of nature as nasty, brutish, and short—as one in which everyone fears violent death—is, ironically, both a vivid illustration of the horrific effects of the imagination and an idealistic portrait of a world in which the imagination (in particular, the imagination of the afterlife) has already been contained. One of the rhetorical functions of the state of nature is to single out fear of violent death as an exceptional passion, a passion that is not really vulnerable to the contagion of the imagination. Chapter 13 enacts this marginalization of mimesis in little, turning mimesis against itself to produce the calculable passion of fear.

In place of the romance plot of mimetic desire, Hobbes substitutes a minimalist psychology in which individuals are all equally motivated by the desire for self-preservation and commodious living, and in which conscience has been reduced to this-worldly calculation. He even mimics this world on the level of syntax, for the parataxis of nasty, brutish, and short suggests the additive reasoning or reckoning that Hobbes recommends to his reader.[37] It suggests as well the new minimalism of contemporary natural rights discourse. In Hobbes's counterplot, chapter 13 is not only a powerful fiction in its own right; it is also the hinge that transports the reader from the fantasies of conscience and vainglory to the stripped down juridical discourse of rights and duties in subsequent chapters.

From the outset, Hobbes portrays the state of nature as one in which the imagination is central. This is true whether the state of nature is characterized as one of scarcity (competition for the same objects), diffidence (the desire to secure what one already has), or vainglory (the desire for recognition and power). Scarcity in Hobbes's account is not a simple empirical matter but a matter of opinion, specifically the opinion that one has an equal right to the object in question.[38] Then, from the opinion of equality, diffidence, or fear of one's fellow men arises diffidence or the imagination of some future harm—at the worst, violent death. And this in turn leads to another kind of imagination, which Hobbes calls "Anticipation," by which one seeks to secure what one already has by acquiring ever more.

Passion and imagination are also intimately linked in the state of nature in the case of vainglory, which does not so much seek to secure what one has, as what one thinks one is. Vainglorious men take "pleasure in contemplating their own power in the acts of conquest, which they pursue farther than their security requires" (13.88). Here the imagination has a double role: precisely because "the reputation of power is power," the vainglorious man can only imagine himself as powerful if he is recognized or imagined as such by others.

It should be clear from this description that, although Hobbes sometimes distinguishes between "moderate" men who would be satisfied with subsistence were it not for vainglorious men, and vainglorious men who are always seeking "power after power" and thus undermining the security of the moderate, the distinction cannot be maintained. Whether men in the state of nature are vainglorious or moderate, they are restless and self-aggrandizing. Whereas the former desire power for its own sake, the latter desire some guarantee of protection. This desire amounts to a passion for self-aggrandizement that, however motivated by bourgeois considerations of security, mimics the aristocratic passion of vainglory. Clearly, then, it is not enough to fear violent death to get out of the state of nature, for the fearful individual perpetuates this state by miming the behavior of those he fears.[39] By definition, such restless seeking after power can never be satisfied, for it is socially and linguistically constructed. Construed in this way, the passions become "particular ways of striving after precedence and recognition." They become, in short, the vehicle of a romance "absorption in the world of [the] imagination."[40]

Hobbes then uses the recognition of the mimetic impulse to argue for its expulsion altogether. In his description of the state of nature, Hobbes simultaneously acknowledges that fear of violent death may mimic the effects of vainglory, insofar as it sets off a restless seeking of power after power; and argues from that shared mimetic tendency to the necessity of a "common Power to feare" (13.90). Here Hobbes's claim is that the recognition of the logic of mimetic desire will persuade you to give up mimesis. Precisely because the fear of violent death *can* take the form of courage (competition, diffidence, vainglory), you are persuaded it *should* take the form of obedience, of contracting to obey a higher power. Only in this way will we be able to achieve a state of peaceful and "commodious living" (13.90). To "reckon upon" the fear of violent death in the state of nature, then, is to reason about its unreliability, whereas to reckon upon it in the commonwealth is to count on the sovereign power of the sword to terrify everyone into obedience. But what enables the passage from one to the other is not fear of violent death per se but rather the recognition that even that passion which would seem to be most dependable—the passion for life, the fear of violent death—is subject to contamination by vainglory. It is only as a result of this recognition that the passion of fear can be redescribed and contained: such fear is no longer simply a passion like any other but rather the locus of reason.[41] Such predictable, calculable fear and diffidence are now not "dishonorable," as Hobbes had earlier said they were, but rather the beginning of wisdom.[42] To put it another way, the passion of fear is not simply a given from which Hobbes deduces political contract; rather, the passion of fear needs to be constructed. Fear, as Hobbes comes to define it, and the resulting political contract are a consequence of a prior dismantling and reassembling of the imagination, a prior contract to limit mimetic desire.

Method and Metalanguage

If one task of *Leviathan* is to counteract the romance plots of conscience and vainglory, an equally important task is to dismantle the competing discourses of obligation: natural law, covenant theology, and the common law, on the one hand; patriarchalism and divine right theory, on the other. In this section, I turn first to Hobbes's metalinguistic critique of the dominant parliamentary languages of obligation and then examine his assault on royalist arguments for the natural subordination of the political subject.

In the conclusion to chapter 13, Hobbes uses his own self-consciousness about fiction as a transition from the state of nature to the new world of rights and duties. As if to call attention to the artificiality of the state of nature, Hobbes ventriloquizes one possible objection: "It may peradventure be thought, there was never such a time, nor condition of warre as this; and I believe it was never generally so, over all the world: but there are many places, where they live so now"—not only in "*America*," but also in those places where "men that have formerly lived under a peacefull government" have degenerated into "a civill Warre" (13.89–90). The state of nature is a metaphor for civil war, that is, for that condition in which there is no justice. Hobbes then signals his departure from the available discourses of obligation by his gloss on this apparently uncontroversial point: "Justice and Injustice" are "Qualities, that relate to men in Society, not in Solitude," and the "Lawes of Nature" are "convenient Articles of Peace, upon which men may be drawn to agreement" (13.90). The laws of nature are suggested by reason but they are no longer written on the solitary heart or inscribed in the solitary conscience. They come into being as a result of human interaction and are agreed to like any other conventional, mutually beneficial arrangement. Borrowing from the contemporary world of international conflict, Hobbes compares these laws with a peace treaty; but, as he makes clear in the next chapter, the laws of nature could just as well be conceived of as human contracts—as the product rather than the presupposition of conventional agreements. In contrast to Grotius, who distinguished between primary and secondary natural law, Hobbes turns even primary natural law into a human invention, one whose effectiveness depends on the will of the sovereign. This subversion from within is characteristic of Hobbes's attack on contemporary discourses of political obligation.

Nowhere is Hobbes's dismantling and reassembling of the available discourses of obligation more dazzling than in chapters 14 and 15 of *Leviathan*, "Of the first and second NATURALL LAWES, and of CONTRACTS," and "Of other Lawes of Nature." At first glance, we are in a familiar world of natural law treatises and manuals of casuistry. We are instructed that a covenant about something impossible is invalid; that intention is relevant to determining breach of contract; that we should keep our covenants; even that we should strive to act in conformity with the moral virtues. Like other seventeenth-century writers, Hobbes takes his examples from the obligations incurred in everyday contracts of buying and selling. He tells us, unexceptionally, that there is a difference between a contract of exchange in the present, and a wholly or partially executory contract (when one party agrees to perform in the future). As we will see, Hobbes's language even suggests something like the common law doctrines of assumpsit and consideration articulated in Slade's Case.[43]

And yet, for seventeenth-century readers, these lucid, straightforward, and, in some ways, modest chapters were among the most shocking in the book. For the reader interested in obligation, covenants, and promises—and what contemporary reader was not?—all the pieces are there, but strangely rearranged. The contemporary discourses of natural law covenant theology, and the common law all appear, but each is systematically undermined. Natural right takes precedence over natural law; the argument from self-preservation is used to disable the casuist's appeal to conscience; and the authority of the sovereign trumps the independent authority not only of the common law but also of natural law and divine commandments.

The effect of these chapters is to hollow out the traditional discourses of moral and political obligation, to bracket them, to reproduce them as though Hobbes were simply quoting rather than referring, to render them pure "theorems" or what the speech act theorist J. L. Austin designated as fiction.[44] This suspension of reference is an important aspect of Hobbes's method, an important aspect of his argument regarding political obligation. For Hobbes was convinced that conflicting interpretations of the referent or content of traditional moral discourse were one of the main causes of civil war. As we will see, however, this "hollowing out" is just the first step. Hobbes's ultimate achievement is to make this emptying out of obligation dictate the sovereign's absolute authority. For only in the context of the commonwealth does the fiction or theorem of contractual obligation become law. We might then call this law a speech act in Austin's sense. In *Leviathan* natural laws are speech acts because they need to be performed or put into practice and enforced by a sovereign power.[45]

Hobbes begins his assault on conventional wisdom by redefining the relationship between natural right and natural law. It was traditional to think of natural right and natural law as the subjective and objective parts of a single, divinely instituted moral law. In contrast, Hobbes defines natural right as the individual right of self-preservation and the laws of nature as "precepts of reason" or deductions from natural right. If we want to preserve ourselves (as natural right dictates), we should (here are the first three laws of nature) seek peace, make a contract to transfer our rights to a sovereign power, and keep our contracts. In practice, this argument amounts to an emphasis on the individual's subjective judgment rather an objective moral law and thus to the derivation of natural laws from the individual fear of violent death and the individual perception of self-interest.[46] The laws of nature become means rather than ends, instruments rather than goods in themselves. They become discursive in Hobbes's sense: they are conclusions derived from reasoning or "reckoning" about "names." They appear in short as the logical and linguistic consequence of Hobbes's definition of natural right. Thus Hobbes tells us that once we have willed to transfer our rights to the sovereign, we are "obliged" or have a "duty" not to cancel that voluntary act. Obligation here follows from the linguistic definition of "renouncing a right." It would be a logical and linguistic "absurdity" to go back on one's word. We are obliged to keep our contracts as a matter of definition.

To define breach of contract in formal terms as a logical and linguistic absurdity would have been shocking enough to Hobbes's contemporaries. In Aristotle and Aquinas, the idea that promises should be kept was a maxim of the moral law. This maxim was absolutely binding in conscience, that is, before God. But Hobbes goes even further in his assault on traditional notions of binding obligation by depriving even his own logical definition of any practical force. First, he tells us that although we are logically obliged to keep our covenants in the state of nature, we are not obliged to do so in practice. In this perilous state, contracts to perform at some future time raise particular problems: it could never be consistent with self-preservation to endanger oneself by performing one's part of the covenant first. Because the moral law that promises must be kept is only a means to the end of self-preservation, it can make sense to perform first only when one is sure that the other party will perform second. According to Hobbes, this security cannot be guaranteed by the moral law; it can be effected only by the fear of punishment, that is, the sovereign's power of the sword. Only this power can create the conditions in which keeping one's covenants is sensible; and this means that only the sovereign can create the conditions in which observance of the moral law is binding:

> If a Covenant be made, wherein neither of the parties performe presently, but trust one another; in the condition of meer Nature (which is a condition of Warre of every man against every man,) upon any reasonable suspition, it is Voyd: But if there be a common Power set over them both, with right and force sufficient to compell performance; it is not Voyd. For he that performeth first, has no assurance the other will performe after; because the bonds of words are too weak to bridle mens ambitions, avarice, anger, and other Passions, without the feare of some coercive Power; which in the condition of meer Nature, where all men are equall, and judges of the justnesse of their own fears, cannot possibly be supposed. . . . But in a civill estate, where there is a Power set up to constrain those that would otherwise violate their faith, that feare is no more reasonable; and for that cause, he which by the Covenant is to perform first, is obliged to do so. (14.96)

In this brilliant ellipsis, Hobbes utterly erases God, conscience, and the moral law as independent reasons for keeping one's word. It is no longer enough to pronounce that "promises must be kept." One needs to explain the conditions under which it is reasonable to do so, and these exist only when a sovereign can enforce the performance of the other party. This is because fear of one's fellow men is generally a stronger motive than fear of God: "The Passion to be reckoned upon, is Fear; whereof there be two very generall Objects: one, The Power of Spirits Invisible; the other, The Power of those men they shall therein Offend. Of these two, though the former be the greater Power, yet the feare of the latter is commonly the greater Feare" (14.99). Thus contracts that are made for reasons of fear are binding (an issue debated in contemporary works of jurisprudence and casuistry); for most individuals, moreover, they are binding only for that reason.[47] The effect of this argument is to make natural law a fiction that only comes into existence along with the coercive power of the sovereign.

Hobbes drives this point home in chapter 15 where he deduces the third law of nature, *"That men performe their Covenants made."* Here too Hobbes wants to convince his reader that promises should be kept, but he does not think that referring to the moral law is the most convincing argument one can make. Thus, when he comments that "in this [third] law of Nature, consisteth the Fountain and Originall of JUSTICE," what he means by this equivocal statement is that justice is natural only in theory; in practice justice is the product of our covenants (15.100).[48] If we want to live in a just social and political order, we will have to keep our covenants; however, most people's motive for doing so is not that it is a priori or naturally just, but that it is in their interest. Contract is thus constitutive of obligation in several senses: it creates the sovereign and the "artificiall person" of Leviathan ex nihilo; it creates the new obligation to obey the sovereign; and it allows for the actual as opposed to merely theoretical existence of justice, which Hobbes defines as the "keeping of valid covenants" (15.101).

By this logic, the sovereign emerges as the authoritative interpreter of natural law, including the natural law that promises should be kept, because only the sovereign has the power to make that law actual. As Hobbes writes in chapter 26 of *Leviathan*:

> The Interpretation of the Lawes of Nature, in a Common-wealth, dependeth not on the books of Morall Philosophy. The Authority of writers, without the Authority of the Common-wealth, maketh not their opinions Law, be they never so true. That which I have written in this Treatise, concerning the Morall Virtues, and of their necessity, for the procuring, and maintaining peace, though it bee evident Truth, is not therefore presently Law; . . . For though it be naturally reasonable; yet it is by the Soveraigne Power that it is Law. (26.191)

Truth is, in short, subordinate to power. To put it another way, the truth of natural law must be produced even if it already, in some abstract sense, exists.

In chapter 14 Hobbes dismantles the independent authority of covenant theology as well. First he asserts that "to make Covenants with bruit Beasts, is impossible; because not understanding our speech, they understand not, nor accept of any translation of Right; nor can translate any Right to another: and without mutuall acceptation, there is no Covenant" (14.97). Here Hobbes is drawing on his argument in chapter 4 of *Leviathan* that reasoning depends on speech, and that without speech "there had been amongst men, neither Common-wealth, nor Society, nor Contract, nor Peace" (4.24). Arguments such as this are reminiscent of the celebration of the powers of speech in Cicero, Grotius, and Renaissance rhetoric handbooks. But in chapter 14 Hobbes emphasizes the human conventions of speech, contracts, and covenants specifically to disable the claims of covenant theology: given the requirements of language and mutual consent, "To make Covenant with God, is impossible, but by Mediation of such as God speaketh to, either by Revelation supernaturall, or by his Lieutenants that govern under him, and in his Name: For otherwise we know not whether our Covenants be accepted, or not" (14.97). Not knowing whether our covenants are accepted by God might be a good definition of faith, but Hobbes's point is that covenants are human agreements, made between men; thus no claim of revelation can trump the human agreements dictated by "naturall reason."[49]

Hobbes further undermines covenant theology in chapter 15 when he explicitly attacks the independent authority of conscience. Borrowing the vocabulary of canon law and manuals of casuistry, he pronounces, "The Lawes of Nature oblige *in foro interno* ["in Conscience," as Hobbes writes the margin]; that is to say, they bind to a desire they should take place: but *in foro externo*; that is, to the putting them in act, not alwayes." As we have seen, this is because it would be contrary to the natural right of self-preservation that is "the ground of all Lawes of Nature" to endanger oneself by performing first. Accordingly, we are obliged "onely to a desire, and endeavor" to perform the obligations of conscience. In a convincing imitation of the casuist's or covenant theologian's emphasis on right intention, Hobbes excuses his reader from feeling obliged to act on his conscience in the real world: "[H]e that endeavoureth their performance, fulfilleth them; and he that fulfilleth the Law, is Just" (15.110). In one swift move, Hobbes divorces conscience from performance; or, to put it another way, he makes the performance of one's promises dependent not on conscience and natural law but on sovereign power. In so doing, he redescribes the problem of binding the conscience as a problem of self-interest and so turns the problem, he believes, into a solution.

Hobbes also draws on common law thinking about contracts in order to recast the discourses of natural law and moral obligation in more pragmatic terms. Although Hobbes defines the third law of nature as "*That men performe their Covenants made*" (15.100), he also insists that some kind of "consideration" or quid pro quo is crucial to the validity of a contract. This is as relevant to a political contract as it is to an economic contract: the consideration for the subject's obedience is the sovereign's protection, and when the latter is lacking, the subject is no longer bound. Accordingly, Hobbes defines the "mutuall transferring of Right, . . . which men called CONTRACT," in terms of the common law notion of consideration formalized in Slade's Case: "Whensoever a man Transferreth his Right," Hobbes writes, "or Renounceth it; it is either in consideration of some Right reciprocally transferred to himselfe; or for some other good he hopeth thereby. For it is a voluntary act; and of the voluntary acts of man, the object is some *Good to himselfe*" (14.93). He then uses this notion of consideration—which infers intention from the terms of a contract (rather than the validity of a contract from the intention of the parties)—to control the potentially subversive understanding of contract as a matter solely of individual promises, conscience, and consent. Consideration helps to explain why subjects of a commonwealth may be assumed to have consented to transfer their rights:

> [H]e that promiseth onely, because he hath already received the benefit for which he promiseth, is to be understood as if he intended the Right should passe: for unlesse he had been content to have his words so understood, the other would not have performed his part first. And for that cause, in buying and selling, and other acts of Contract, a Promise is equivalent to a Covenant; and therefore obligatory. (14.95)

This notion of consideration explains why some rights are inalienable: the individual cannot "lay down the right of resisting them, that assault him by force, to take away his life" (14.93). But it also explains why the subject is legally bound to obey the sovereign from whose protection he has benefited. (Hobbes makes the same argument in the Conclusion to *Leviathan*, when he asserts that soldiers may be assumed tacitly to have consented to defend the sovereign in wartime since they have benefited from his protection in peace.) Political obligation, Hobbes implies, is best thought of not so much as a moral obligation but as a business transaction. But it is a business transaction that is enabled and enforced by the sovereign, not by the common law.[50]

Hobbes also draws on the common law language of equity and artificial reason to shore up the sovereign's authority. This is at first glance surprising, given what Hobbes has to say in *Leviathan* and elsewhere about Edward Coke and the encroachment of the common lawyers on the royal prerogative.[51] But here, too, Hobbes's goal is to appropriate the language of the common law for his own purposes while undermining its independent authority from within. In a discussion of commutative and distributive justice in chapter 15, Hobbes scoffs at the belief in a fixed standard of justice in matters of contract: "As if it were injustice to sell dearer than we buy."[52] Hobbes then uses the relativeness of economic contract to get at something important about political contract: there is no abstract, a priori standard of justice or, in the language of everyday exchange, "The value of all things contracted for, is measured by the Appetite of the Contractors: and therefore the just value, is that which they be contented to give." In this arbitrary or conventional world of value, "Commutative Justice, is the Justice of a Contractor," and "Distributive Justice, the Justice of an Arbitrator; that is to say, the act of defining what is Just." According to Hobbes, such "Just Distribution" or distributive justice is properly called "Equity."[53] Although equity in matters of economic and other contracts may be a law of nature, its ultimate interpreter, according to Hobbes, is the sovereign. In an explicit attack on the common lawyers, with special mention of Coke, Hobbes asserts that it is not the antiquity or the customary nature of the law that makes it authoritative but the sovereign's command: "For in [i.e., with respect to] the differences of private men, to declare, what is Equity, what is Justice, and what is morall

Vertue, and to make them binding, there is need of the Ordinances of Soveraign Power." These ordinances alone can counteract the interests, "dreams, and fancies" of private men who, "when they have, or think they have force enough to secure their unjust designes, and convoy [*sic*] them safely to their ambitious ends, may publish for Lawes what they please, without, or against the Legislative Authority."[54]

By identifying the sovereign-interpreter and legislator, Hobbes puts his own absolutist spin on the traditional view that the equitable meaning of the law is the "sense of the Legislator" (26.190). As in his later *Dialogue Between a Philosopher and a Student of the Common Laws of England* (1681), where the Student voices the opinions of Coke and St. German, and the Philosopher those of Hobbes, Hobbes undermines both the independent authority of the common law and St. German's conception of equity as based in natural law.[55] He also offers an unusual solution to the problem of arbitrary interpretation. He makes the potential arbitrariness of equitable interpretation a necessary virtue, one that is able to resolve any hermeneutical contradiction: "[I]t is not that *Juris prudentia*, or wisedom of subordinate Judges [as his adversary Coke thought]; but the Reason of this our Artificiall Man the Common-wealth, and his Command, that maketh Law: And the Common-wealth being in their Representative but one Person, there cannot easily arise any contradiction in the Lawes; and when there doth, the same Reason is able, by interpretation, or alteration, to take it away" (26.187).[56]

Hobbes knew that the dismantling of natural law, covenant theology, and the common law in chapters 14 and 15 would be shocking to his contemporaries, and he anticipated their resistance. In his most brilliant metadiscursive move in these chapters, Hobbes turns his analytic powers on his own argument. Just when we might be tempted to conclude that Hobbes does not believe in morality or justice, he ventriloquizes our objections, alluding to Psalm 14: "The Foole hath sayd in his heart, there is no such thing as Justice." This fool, who has also said "there is no God" and so no cause to fear divine punishment, reasons that it might be in his interest to break a covenant "when it conduceth to such a benefit, as shall put a man in a condition, to neglect not onely the dispraise, and revilings, but also the power of other men" (15.101). The fool, in other words, is the person who refuses to recognize or read himself in the new plot of *Leviathan*. Hobbes's response is indirect: he imagines the fool reasoning in a similar way about the kingdom of God, and in this way Hobbes displaces objections to his own argument onto those of his adversaries: "[T]he Kingdome of God is gotten by violence: but what if it could be gotten by unjust violence: were it against Reason so to get it, when it is impossible to receive hurt by it? and if it is not against Reason, it is not against Justice, or else Justice is not to be approved for good."

This is Hobbes ventriloquizing the radical sectarians, such as Burges and Marshall in 1642, or Milton in 1649, who believed that it was necessary to break their covenants and take up arms against the king in order to hasten the kingdom of God. But Hobbes was no secular fool, and no covenant breaker. To the contrary, he conceived of his argument as rebutting both kinds of foolishness. Thus he first piously distances himself from the unjust violence of those seeking the kingdom of God: "From such reasoning as this, Successfull wickedness hath obtained the name of Virtue." Then, tacitly conceding the secular fool's point about the absence of divine justice, Hobbes argues that it can still never be reasonable to break a covenant since one cannot count on worldly success. But even if one could, a reputation for unreliability would mean one could not "be received into any Society" and would thus be vulnerable to "destruction" by others.

Hobbes then draws the obvious conclusion for contemporary politics. Breach of covenant can help neither those motivated by secular vainglory nor those motivated by conscience; neither those who wish to attain "Soveraignty by Rebellion" nor those who hope to attain "an eternall felicity after death." In a sly rhetorical move, he then conflates the two. Although Hobbes first asserts that we should keep our "Covenant[s]" if we wish to gain "the secure and perpetuall felicity of Heaven," it quickly becomes apparent that he is not thinking of the spiritual covenant with God. "Because there is no naturall knowledge of mans estate after death," those who think they will be rewarded for their breach of faith in the afterlife are simply relying on "other mens sayings." We have no unmediated knowledge of a spiritual covenant; this is the reason justice depends on our keeping our earthly covenants.[57] By the end of this response to the fool, covenant theology and worldly cynicism have been equated and both have been sent packing.

In the rest of chapter 15, Hobbes swiftly deduces the remaining "laws of nature," that is, the rules of conduct we should follow if we wish to live peacefully together. These laws are, in essence, the "Morall Vertues" and can even be summed up in a negative version of the golden rule, "Do not that to another, which thou wouldest not have done to thy selfe." From the perspective of our often cynical reading of Hobbes, this endorsement of the golden rule may seem strange. But Hobbes undoubtedly considered his deduction of the virtues ex nihilo, or, more properly, from our passions and interests, his greatest achievement.[58] Here, he seems to be saying to the fool and to all those motivated by self-interest, is an argument for keeping one's contracts that even you can follow. The golden rule is best conceived of not as a moral law, a dictate of conscience, or divinely given command of reciprocity (even though it is all three),[59] but rather as the first rule of self-preservation, the first quid pro quo.

In the conclusion to this chapter, Hobbes justly calls attention to his methodological achievement—his artificial production of the laws of nature:

> These dictates of Reason, men use to call by the name of Lawes, but improperly: for they are but Conclusions, or Theoremes concerning what conduceth to the conservation and defence of themselves; wheras Law, properly is the word of him, that by right hath command over others. But yet if we consider the same Theoremes, as delivered in the word of God, that by right commandeth all things; then are they properly called Lawes. (15.111)

This is Hobbes's version of Grotius's "etiamsi daremus": even if we were to assume that God did not exist, the natural laws derived from human passions and interests would still be binding. Unlike Grotius, however, Hobbes articulates his concession in positive terms: "[I]f we consider the same Theoremes, as delivered in the word of God. . . ." For those who care, Hobbes explains, his argument is compatible with the existence of God. This way of phrasing the matter makes God far more hypothetical than Grotius's hypothesis of his nonexistence could ever do. For Grotius still insisted that the enforcement of natural law depended ultimately on God's command, whereas Hobbes makes the validity of natural law dependent on the artifice of contract, "the Constitution of a Civill Power."[60]

In basing his argument for political contract on the fear of violent death and the right of self-preservation, Hobbes believed he had solved the problem of obligation: for the laws of nature, including the obligation to seek peace and keep our covenants, are deduced from the right of self-preservation. This is a natural desire—a natural interest—and thus the best possible basis for establishing government and legitimating its coercive force. With the consent to the political contract, fear of violent death in the state of nature is transformed into the specific fear of the sovereign's power of the sword. Only this fear of the sovereign, which alone grants us the security to perform our obligations without fear of others, saves us from the conflict of rights in the state of nature and allows us to institute "natural law."

Hobbes's new method of deducing natural law in turn had consequences for other competing discourses of obligation, especially those that stressed the divine and patriarchal authority of the sovereign. As the preceding analysis has shown, one of the effects of this method was to highlight both the waywardness of mimetic desire and the artifice of the political contract. That is, it was less the language of contract per se than Hobbes's emphasis on arbitrariness and artifice that distinguished his defense of absolutism from his royalist contemporaries. James I had rooted absolute monarchy in patriarchialism and divine right.[61] Grotius had argued for voluntary subjection to a political contract based on natural sociability as well as natural right. In contrast to both, Hobbes argued that absolutism was a response to contingency: because the moral law is "contrary to our naturall Passions," because contracts without coercion are mere "breath," we need to set up an absolute sovereign to compel us to obey.[62] The arbitrariness of the human will and waywardness of human passions necessitate an absolute sovereign whose will is not subject to "dispute" (21.144, 145). But the absolute sovereign is not just the remedy for contingency; he is himself marked by contingency. The Hobbesian sovereign does not simply inherit his authority by patrilineal descent or divine right. He is himself an "artificall person," established voluntarily by the consent of individuals; and this consent, in turn, authorizes the sovereign's arbitrary will. In his arbitrary rule, the secular Hobbesian sovereign draws near to the voluntarist God of Calvinism.[63] At the same time, he undermines any conception of human relationships as natural.

Part II of *Leviathan* spells out the implications of Hobbes's emphasis on arbitrariness both for the commonwealth and for the relations of sovereign and subject. First, Hobbes declares that there is no significant difference between the commonwealth established ex nihilo by "institution" and the commonwealth established by "acquisition" or conquest; in both cases, the subjects willingly consent out of fear for their self-preservation (20.138). Hobbes elaborates on this point in a discussion of "Dominion PATERNALL, and DESPOTICALL." He explains that there are two ways of acquiring dominion or absolute rule: by generation or conquest. But by generation, Hobbes does not mean the natural process of fathering a child, as the adjective "paternal" might seem to suggest. Dominion "is not so derived from the Generation, as if therefore the Parent had Dominion over his Child because he begat him; but from the Childs Consent, either expresse, or by other sufficient arguments declared" (20.139). In this way, the distinction between paternal and despotical maps onto that between institution and conquest. In equating these two kinds of commonwealth, Hobbes collapses the distinction between a legitimate government and a de facto government—which helps explain why his defense of absolutism was offensive to his royalist contemporaries.

Second, Hobbes argues that the subject's consent to set up a sovereign means that "every particular man is Author of all the Soveraigne doth" and so can never complain of any injury from the sovereign (18.124). Here Hobbes co-opts the parliamentary language of representation to shore up his defense of absolutism: "[W]here there is already erected a Soveraign Power, there can be no other Representative of the same people."[64] This absolute identification of subject and sovereign serves paradoxically to disable any claim on the part of the subject to control, let alone resist, the sovereign: instead, the subject's consent authorizes the sovereign's arbitrariness, even his tyranny. Hobbes flaunts this conclusion: "And though of so unlimited a Power, men may fancy many evill consequences, yet the consequences of the want of it, which is perpetuall warre of every man against his neighbor, are much worse" (21.144–45).

Third, Hobbes equates fear and liberty, liberty and necessity. In the process, he undermines both the contemporary republican discourse of "liberty" and the royalist rhetoric of the king as a loving father or husband to his people. Both prior to government and under government, "Feare, and Liberty are consistent; as when a man throweth his goods into the Sea for *feare* the ship should sink, he doth it neverthelesse very willingly, and may refuse to doe it if he will" (21.146). "*Liberty* and *Necessity* are consistent; as in the water, that hath not only *liberty*, but a *necessity* of descending by the Channel; so likewise in the Actions which men voluntarily doe: which, because they proceed from their will, proceed from *liberty*" (21.146). Like a good casuist, Hobbes parses the meanings of liberty and in the process makes the liberty of the subject an effect of voluntary subjection to an absolute power. Like a Reformation theologian, Hobbes makes the "free will" of the creature a gift of the divine omnipotence of God.[65]

Arguments such as these led the clergyman George Lawson later to complain that Hobbes's goal in *Leviathan* was to have his readers "know themselves to be absolute slaves."[66] But, as in his earlier rebuttal of the charge of immorality, so here too Hobbes anticipates the objection. Specifically, Hobbes uses his equation of fear and liberty, coercion and consent, to argue that the slave contract is an oxymoron. "Slaves," who are "kept in prison, or bonds," he pronounces, "have no obligation at all; but may break their bonds, or the prison, and kill, or carry away captive their Master, justly" (20.141). Such slaves are physically constrained, and physical constraint is incompatible with genuine consent. Fear, however, is not. If the slave were to come to his senses and accept his master without such compulsion, if he reasoned about his fear and decided voluntarily to transfer his right to the sovereign, he too would be a subject.

Hobbes's attitude toward the slave contract explains his unorthodox characterization of the marriage contract in *Leviathan*. Because Hobbes denies the validity of the slave contract, he does not need to introduce the marriage contract (as Grotius and Perkins did) to explain the difference between the right and wrong kind of consent. At the same time, because he sees all contracts as instituting artificial relations, the marriage contract comes to look remarkably like the political contract. Thus, to the extent that the marriage contract appears at all in *Leviathan*, it illustrates the conventionality of the contract of subordination rather than its naturalness. In the state of nature, Hobbes tells us, mothers have dominion over their children; fathers acquire this dominion by subjugating mothers by force. Because Hobbes thinks force is compatible with consent, the point of the argument about a mother's dominion over the child is "to show that the power of the *father* was derived from the consent of the mother" rather than by virtue of natural superiority, as patriarchalists such as Filmer thought. Hobbes's treatment of women thus follows from a rigorous application of his political principles, his belief that political relationships are conventional rather than natural.[67] In contrast to other contract theorists, Hobbes makes marriage a fully conventional and thus fully political relationship.[68] But he does not draw the obvious conclusion that the political contract should therefore be gender neutral.

Hobbes's treatment of women reveals both a logical inconsistency at the heart of Hobbes's political theory, and a gender instability in his characterization of the political subject. Given what Hobbes has said about the physical equality of men and women in the state of nature, and the unenforceability of contracts in this state, there is no reason why women should consent to be coerced—should consent to fear—while still in the state of nature. Conversely, if women are capable of entering into contracts in the state of nature, why should they not also be capable of entering into the political contract to set up the commonwealth?[69] The Hobbesian political subject is thus, irrationally, exclusively male. At the same time, Hobbes's critique of the manly cult of military glory and his emphasis on the fear of violent death destabilize the gender identity of the political subject. Ironically, as a subject who is motivated by fear rather than vainglory, desire for self-preservation rather than self-aggrandizement, the Hobbesian subject is also—in the traditional terms set out by manuals of domestic duties—conspicuously feminized. Although Hobbes himself did not draw the obvious conclusion that women, too, should be parties to the political contract, his radical conventionalism made it possible for others to begin to imagine this possibility.

HOBBES'S READERS OR INESCAPABLE ROMANCE

One of the ironies of Hobbes's reception is that his argument against the revolutionary discourses of his time was perceived to be more revolutionary, more seditious and incendiary, than any of its targets. A further, perhaps unintended irony is that, in their effort to disarm Hobbes, seventeenth-century readers often imitated him, not only by parodying his argument but also by mimicking his wit. Far from accepting Hobbes's claim to have constructed a truly rational account of obligation, critics complained that the voluntarist Hobbes left "reason . . . dejected at the feet of affection."[70] As this phrase suggests, Hobbes's readers were more impressed by his portrayal of mimetic desire and his heroic artifice than they were convinced by his new minimalist conception of the political subject. Hobbes's attempt to check the arbitrariness of human fancy was itself perceived as arbitrary; his effort to harness the restless seeking after power was condemned as a romance.

Hobbes's seventeenth-century readers objected both to his materialist account of the passions and to his artificial conception of natural law. And, like Hobbes, these critics saw materialism and artifice as two sides of the same coin. According to the Cambridge Platonist Ralph Cudworth, Hobbes based his argument on "certain Counterfeit Laws of Nature, of [his] own devising, that are Nothing but meer Juggling Equivocation; they being but the Laws of Fear, or [his] own Timorous and Cowardly Complexion." He condemned Hobbes's theory of contract as a "vain Attempt, by Art to Consociate, what Nature hath Dissociated, like tying Knots in the Wind or Water. Their Artificial Obligation, or Ligaments, by which the Members of their Leviathan are held together, [are] more slender then Cobwebs."[71] But, Cudworth objected, "A man cannot apprehend himself as a being standing by itself, cut off, separated and disjointed from all other beings . . . but looks upon himself as a member lovingly united to the whole system of intellectual beings."[72] By contrast, if civil sovereignty is conceived of as "wholly Artificial," it will also of necessity be "violent": "[B]ecause every man being a Judge of [Private Utility] for himself, it would then be Lawful for any Subject, to Rebel against his Sovereign Prince, and to Poyson or Stab him, whensoever he could reasonably perswade himself, that it would tend to his own Advantage." Cudworth here associates the artifice of the Hobbesian contract with arbitrariness, the relativism of individual judgment with the "fool's" rebellion and tyrannicide, which Hobbes had sought to combat.[73]

Bishop Bramhall also called attention to the artificiality of Hobbes's conception of natural law. Bramhall charged that Hobbes's radical voluntarism undermined *synteresis*, the repository of moral law in the individual human conscience. He noted that Hobbes derived "Even the law of nature it self from the civil law," and commented on the world turned upside down of Hobbes's method: "God help us into what times we are fallen, when the immutable laws of God are made to depend upon the mutable laws of mortal men, just as if one should go about to controle the Sun by the authority of the clock."[74] James Tyrrell asserted in a similar vein that there is a natural law before civil law, and he complained that Hobbes's method turned the actual into the metaphorical: "[T]his Law of endeavouring the common Good, is really and indeed, and *not metaphorically a Law*."[75] With this metalinguistic comment, Tyrrell signaled his awareness that the effect of Hobbes's deduction of natural law was to make that law a mere fiction, without the authority of the sovereign power.

Other seventeenth-century readers also objected to the artificiality and implausibility of Hobbes's account of contracting; and in the course of objecting, they began to construct their own anti-Hobbesian mini-narratives. In *Mr Hobbs's State of Nature Considered* (1672), John Eachard imagined a dialogue between one Timothy and the aptly named Philautus who, with his self-love and distrust of others, was an obvious stand-in for Hobbes. Eachard specifically ridiculed Hobbes's identification of society with linguistic contracts. Parodying Philautus-Hobbes's logic, "Timothy" notes "you only observe that we are children before we are men, and children can't speak; and where no speech, there can be no bargain or engagement, or treaty for termes of peace, and where no bargain, &c. There must needs be the Devil, & war." And he went on to mock the idea that we make such contracts out of mutual fear rather than natural sociability. In a delightful example that recalls us to the commonsense world of everyday contracts, Timothy imagines Philautus buying a pair of shoes out of fear and the shoemaker taking his money out of fear he won't see Philautus again. According to Eachard, Hobbes simply constructed his fictional state of nature in order to generate his own dubious principles of absolute sovereignty.[76]

Like Eachard, Bramhall charged Hobbesian psychology with offending common sense: "[A]ll other Writers of Politicks do derive Common-wealths from the sociability of nature, which is in mankind, most truely. But he will have the beginning of all humane society to be from mutual fear: as much contrary to reason as to authority." Hobbes's account of the passions was a self-confirming prophecy, one that prompted Bramhall to his own flights of fancy: his "perpetual suspicions and causeless jealousies, which have no ground, but an universal suspicion of the humane nature, (much like the good woman's fear, that the log would leap out of the fire, and knock out the brains of her child) do beget perpetual vexations to them that cherish them, argue a self-guiltinesse, teach them who are suspected, often to do worse than they imagined, and ordinarily produce hostility and war." Hobbes's version of contract was correspondingly thin: his universal suspicion of human nature led him to rule out love and trust as motives for political association. Whereas others were able to imagine the contract of subject and sovereign as a marriage contract, "it seemeth *T. H.* did take his soveraign for better, but not for worse." Whereas others saw the covenant between subject and sovereign as one of mutual defense ("the subject ought to defend his King, as well as the King his subject"), Hobbes made the subject's obedience contingent upon his protection by the sovereign, his "fidelity and loyalty" contingent upon his "self-interest."[77] Such self-interest could never be the basis of lasting obligation.

While insisting that they themselves were not convinced, seventeenth-century critics worried that Hobbes's powerful depiction of the new world of passion and interest would carry conviction with his other readers. That is, they were less concerned with Hobbes's logical prowess than with his rhetorical skill, his powerful fiction-making and seductive wit. James Harrington was not alone in describing Hobbes as the best writer of his day. In his *Survey of Leviathan*, Edward Hyde, earl of Clarendon, expressed his fear that "there are many [readers of *Leviathan*], who being delighted with some new notions, and the pleasant and clear Style throughout the Book, have not taken notice of those down-right Conclusions, which overthrow or undermine all those Principles of Government, which have preserv'd the Peace of this Kingdom through so many ages."[78] Particularly dangerous to Clarendon's mind was Hobbes's metalinguistic habit of "making . . . merry with . . . proper and devout custom[s] of speaking," such as that good thoughts are "inspir'd, or infus'd" by God. Clarendon feared that Hobbes's ironic treatment of Scripture would induce readers "by degrees to undervalue those other conceptions of Religion and Piety, which would restrain and controul the licentious imagination of the excellency of their own understandings." Hobbes's licensing of the imagination, Clarendon asserted, would in turn "corrupt the natural motives" of men, and bring about "the dissolution of Allegiance, and [the] eluding the obligation of all Oaths."[79]

Still other critics suggested that, in portraying the world of power politics and mimetic desire in such graphic detail, *Leviathan* too presented the reader with a prose romance, a world governed by passion and interest, rampant imitation and emulation.[80] Thus James Tyrrell, in his *Confutations of Mr. Hobb's Principles*, complained that Hobbes's natural man required more strength and cunning than "our Modern Romance-makers can feign in their Heroes." As Tyrrell suggests, the Hobbesian individual, with his restless seeking after power, is a kind of the picaresque hero; and the paratactic world of contingency he inhabits suggests the episodic adventures of Renaissance prose romance.[81]

But if the world of *Leviathan* is similar to the contingent world of prose romance, what about Hobbes's proposed solution? Ralph Cudworth argued that Hobbes's solution was pure romance as well: in a world in which covenants do not bind in conscience, the atheist politician must shift "from Art to Force and Power," including the power of "political enchantment," in a futile effort to secure allegiance to the sovereign. Hobbes becomes a fiction-maker like Spenser's romance magician Archimago, and his commonwealth becomes a mere "Artificial Thing," "made by the *Enchantment* and *Magical Art* of *Policy*."[82]

Taking a cue from Cudworth, we can press this romance analogy even further and begin to anticipate some of the narratives examined in the following chapters. Although *Leviathan* is presented as a logical argument, it may also be read ironically as a romance of political obligation.[83] Like his literary compatriots, Hobbes's narrative tells the story of an initial broken vow (let's say, the Oath of Allegiance to Charles I), followed by a critique of the errant adventures of the imagination and, finally, the restoration of the bond of subject and sovereign on a more secure basis, that of contract. And like the typical romance plot, the dénouement of *Leviathan* depends on a moment of recognition—here the self-recognition of Hobbes's "Nosce teipsum, Read thy self."[84] Fear is important in this narrative, but equally important is the invitation to "know oneself" by reading oneself in "the thoughts and passions" of other men. Crucially, however, the addressee of this invitation is not the male hero of chivalric romance. Precisely because manly mimetic desire is synonymous with the state of war, the ideal Hobbesian reader and subject is closer to the female subject of romance or of seventeenth-century domestic manuals, the wife who consents to be bound by her own passions to a hierarchical, inequitable, irrevocable marriage contract. And if the ideal Hobbesian subject is the docile, effeminized political subject of an absolute sovereign, the fear of the sovereign may be construed as a gendered fear—what seventeenth-century manuals called the "fear" of one's husband that leads to appropriate subordination and reverence rather than insubordination and emulation.[85] In *Leviathan*—the canonical text of rational theories of contractual obligation—lurks a parody of the romance plot that Hobbes's criticism of mimetic desire would appear to exclude.[86] In the decades following the publication of *Leviathan*, Hobbes's radical fiction-making would prompt parliamentary and royalist writers alike to propose their own anti-Hobbesian narratives of political obligation, their own accounts of the motives for political contract. These literary responses to the midcentury crisis of political obligation are the subject of the following chapters.

CHAPTER 7

Gender

All things by war are in a Chaos hurl'd
But love alone first made,
And still preserves the world.

—Alexander Brome

I have heard [William Cavendish] say several times, that his love to his gracious master King Charles the Second was above the love he bore to his wife, children, and all his posterity, nay, to his own life.

—*The Life of William, Duke of Newcastle*

IN MAY 1640 Hobbes dedicated his *Elements of Law, Natural and Politic* to William Cavendish, earl of Newcastle, soon to be general in the royalist army as well as a great financial supporter of Charles I. Cavendish had been a governor to the young Prince of Wales and was a member of the king's privy council. In his epistle dedicatory, Hobbes explained to his patron that his goal in the *Elements* had been to articulate "principles" of political obligation that "passion not mistrusting may not seek to displace."[1] Yet, Hobbes's isolation of self-interest and fear of violent death as motives for obedience to the sovereign was rejected by many of his royalist contemporaries. In response, supporters of Charles II both in England and abroad attempted to revive the royalist rhetoric of love and affection between subject and sovereign and to retell the story of obligation as one of loving rather than fearful subjection. But the times had changed. Charles II was in exile on the continent; the new Cromwellian government required male citizens to declare their "engagement" or allegiance to the new regime; and *Leviathan* itself was construed as a contribution to the engagement controversy and a legitimation of de facto political power. Many Englishmen subscribed to the engagement and justified breaking their earlier oath to Charles I with arguments from the casuistical literature that accompanied the engagement. In this climate, it was obvious to many that the bonds of affection were not enough to guarantee life and limb. And yet, it was equally obvious that arguments from self-preservation were not enough to secure lasting obedience. The arguments of Hobbes and others needed to be acknowledged, but they could not be fully accepted if Charles II was to be restored to the throne.

In this chapter, I turn to Margaret Cavendish's response to the crisis of political obligation in two short prose romances, *The Contract* and *Assaulted and Pursued Chastity*. In these works, Cavendish uses the resources of romance to counter the Hobbesian response to the crisis of political obligation. At the same time, she also draws on the genre of romance to anatomize more fully than any author explored so far the implications of contract theory for gender relations. As Cavendish shows, the notion of a political contract, even—or especially—one based on the marriage contract, was disturbing to traditional conceptions of gender. Some four hundred years before modern feminist critics of contract theory, Cavendish exposes the illogical exclusion of women from the political contract. She also shows how the political contract presupposes something like a sexual contract.[2]

The Contract, published in 1656 in a volume entitled *Natures Pictures*, tells the story of a young woman who, orphaned at birth, is betrothed in childhood by her uncle and guardian to the son of a friend.[3] The contract of the title is thus a spousal contract, and the issue from the outset is whether the contract is binding, given that the young girl was not old enough to consent and the young man only "seemed to consent, to please his father." Some years later, when the young lady comes of age, the young man (now a duke) marries someone else. He subsequently meets the young lady at a masque, and they fall in love. The question the narrative then seeks to answer is whether and under what conditions the original contract is valid, and under what conditions a contract may be broken.

Assaulted and Pursued Chastity, published in the same volume, tells the story of a young woman in exile from her homeland because of civil war and the consequent threats to her chastity. From the outset, the violation of the social and political contract is explicitly paralleled to the violation of the sexual contract: the romance plot of "assaulted and pursued chastity" is a consequence of civil war. Miseria/Affectionata disguises herself as the page "Travellia" and, in a series of predictably improbable romance adventures, travels to foreign lands inhabited by people with purple skin, is captured by pirates, escapes, and ends up serving as a general in the army of the Queen of Amity, who is herself resisting the unwanted advances of the King of Amour. In the course of these adventures, Cavendish takes up the right of self-preservation, the meaning of consent, and the legitimacy of politic dissembling.

As Cavendish was well aware, these were topical issues not only for men and women in their domestic relations but for all adult male citizens who were being asked to consent to the new Cromwellian government. They were topical as well for women who were assumed to consent to the marriage contract but precluded from participation in the political sphere. In *The Contract* Cavendish uses the language of contract both to argue for a more equitable relationship between husband and wife, and to present an account of political obligation that is based on love rather than on filial obedience, wifely subordination, or a Hobbesian account of self-interest. In love, Cavendish finds an alternative motive for political subordination, an alternative version of interest, and thus, indirectly, an argument for allegiance to Charles II. In *Assaulted and Pursued Chastity* as well, Cavendish makes the case for love but, throughout the narrative, she also raises questions about what it means to consent under the threat of violence or enslavement and about the relative political value of fear and love in inducing voluntary subjection.

As we will see, if Cavendish's initial arguments about domestic and political obligation are mutually reinforcing, they turn out to be at odds with each other. This is because Cavendish's emphasis on romance grants more importance to the ongoing consent and affection of the partners to a contract than do royalist or Hobbesian conceptions of political obligation—both of which involve an initial but irrevocable act of consent. Thus, in striking contrast to previous royalist writers, who had occasionally used the analogy between the marriage contract and the political contract to justify absolute sovereignty, Cavendish's emphasis on "true romance" threatens to undo the hierarchical, inequitable relationship between the contracting parties—not only husband and wife but also sovereign and subject. Although such an equitable relationship in marriage might be desirable even to a royalist, it could never be the basis of a subject's oath of allegiance to an absolute sovereign. In her critique of the marriage contract, the royalist Cavendish ironically draws near to the parliamentarian theory of an original and revocable contract between the people and their ruler.

Cavendish's romances are potentially even more subversive: in undoing the hierarchical relation of husband and wife in *The Contract*, Cavendish also intimates the fallacy of assuming that only men are parties to the political contract. In *Assaulted and Pursued Chastity* Cavendish goes further and suggests that a sexual contract is the basis of the patriarchal political contract. This critique of traditional political and gender relations is intricately related to Cavendish's manipulation of the genre of romance. In contrast to Hobbes's view that contract is the solution to the problem of romance, Cavendish presents true romance as the positive outcome of a broken contract and the basis of a new one. Specifically, both narratives equate the broken contract that initiates the romance plot with the heroine's opportunity for action, deliberation, and the equitable consideration of motives and circumstances, including above all her own desires. But Cavendish's stories also ultimately raise the question of the compatibility of romance and contract. This is because, like other early modern romances, these stories call attention to the "scandal" of romance and perhaps of fiction more generally: they flaunt precisely those elements of the plot that challenge shared assumptions of verisimilitude or probability.[4] In this way the generic contract of romance invites reflection on the social and political contract. It forces us to question some of the dominant fictions of early modern patriarchalism and contract theory alike: the fiction of male superiority and the fiction of legally binding the affections. In order to understand Cavendish's intervention in contemporary debates, we need first to explore the analogy between the marriage contract and the political contract and then to consider Cavendish's own understanding of the politics of romance.

POLITICAL CONTRACT AND THE MARRIAGE CONTRACT

As we have seen in earlier chapters, in seventeenth-century England, as on the continent, the political relationship of subject and sovereign was regularly compared with marriage. This model of contract preserved an older sense of status and natural hierarchy while simultaneously addressing contemporary arguments for the voluntary nature of political obligation. According to this model, the relationship between subject and sovereign was not based on fear or coercion but on love and unadulterated consent: the best analogy for sovereignty was the affectionate relationship of marriage. If, in the Hobbesian model contract responded to and reconfigured the passions and the interests, construed as the baser elements of human nature, in this model it was ostensibly not base human nature but the most elevated affections that underwrote the contract of political obligation.[5]

Precisely because marriage in the seventeenth century was understood to be a natural political relationship involving the sovereignty of husband over wife, the marriage contract was an important ideological weapon in Caroline propaganda for absolute monarchy. While emphasizing mutuality, such an analogy did not preclude inequality; in fact, one could say that the point of the analogy was to naturalize and romanticize absolute sovereignty by making it seem that the subject, like the wife, was both naturally inferior and had consented to such inferior status out of affection. Yet, while such a contract was originally predicated upon consent of the governed (or the wife), once it had been agreed to, the contract was irrevocable. Accordingly, the royalist Henry Ferne described the king as "sponsus Regni [bridegroom of the realm], and wedded to the kingdom by a ring at his Coronation," and he used the analogy to argue that resistance to the king was as illegitimate as divorce: "[W]hat our Saviour said of their light and unlawfull occasions of Divorse, *non suit ob initio*, it was not so from the beginning, may be said of such a reserved power of resistance, it was not so from the beginning."[6]

It quickly became clear that this analogy could work both ways: devised at first to justify royal absolutism, the analogy between marriage and sovereignty could also be inverted to suggest that the king was the wife of his subjects and so subservient to their wills.[7] As we saw in chapter 4, in his *Observations upon some of his Majesties late Answers and Expresses* (1642), Henry Parker remarked that the comparison of king and husband, along with that of king and father, was an imperfect "similitude." Taken literally, it might seem to suggest—since the king occupied the position of husband—that his male subjects were to be thought of as "wives." But such an inference would be incorrect, for just as "the wife is inferiour in nature, and was created for the assistance of man," so "the Head Politicall . . . receives more subsistence from the body than it gives, and being subservient to that, it has no being when it is dissolved."[8] Accordingly, in *Jus populi* (1644), Parker inverted the analogy by comparing the king with the wife rather than the husband: "*Man* (saies the Apostle) *was not made of the woman, but the woman of the man*: and this is made an argument why the woman should pay a due subjection to man"; so, Parker argued, "*Princes were created by the people, for the peoples sake, and so limited by expresse Laws as that they might not violate the peoples liberty.*"[9] One N. T., author of *The Resolver Continued*, explained "When my *Wife* turneth *adultresse*, my *Covenant* with her is broken, And when my *King* turneth *Tyrant*, and continueth so, my *Covenant* with him also is broken."[10] And Milton, in the famous "Preface to Parlament" appended to the second edition of *The Doctrine and Discipline of Divorce*, argued the case for divorce by referring to the parliamentary argument for government by consent.

As these quotations suggest, well before Hobbes elaborated his version of the original political contract the language of the marriage contract was appropriated by both royalists and parliamentarians in their debate over the conditions of legitimate sovereignty. For both, in contrast to Hobbes, love rather than fear was the ostensible key to lasting political union; for both, the hierarchy of the marriage relationship had important (if diametrically opposed) political implications. Precisely because of this difference, as Mary Shanley has argued, parliamentarians eventually abandoned the metaphor of the marriage contract altogether, correctly perceiving that it was deleterious to their argument for contractual obligation predicated not only on consent but also on equality.[11]

In the seventeenth century the marriage contract, in addition to serving as a vexed metaphor for political obligation, could itself occasion conflicts of allegiance. In particular, the moral and legal status of marriage contracts *per verba de praesenti* and *de futuro* was a frequent topic of discussion.[12] This was no doubt in part because there was genuine confusion about the relative weight of canon law and common law in disputed cases; but it was also because spousal contracts and the state of marriage were themselves the locus of casuistical dilemmas. All commentators agreed that parents arranging for the marriage of their children should ask their consent; they also agreed that children should not act against the wishes of their parents. Almost by definition, then, marriage contracts posed questions regarding the relation of coercion and consent, conflicts regarding obedience to one's own conscience and to one's superior, whether one's father or husband. Even in cases where no parents were involved, it was not always clear how to define consent or how to distinguish between a promise to marry and the act itself. As Keith Thomas has noted, "Next to politics and religion, the most persistent source of cases of conscience [in the seventeenth century] was to be found in the domestic sphere."[13]

The engagement controversy also was an important context for understanding the relationship between the political contract and the marriage contract in this period. Readers of *The Contract* in the 1650s would not only have recognized it as a domestic case of conscience concerning the validity of spousal contracts *de futuro*; they would also have had in mind the casuistical dilemma brought about by the change of regime. The statement of engagement, which was eventually required of all male citizens aged eighteen or over, gave rise to a fast and furious pamphlet war debating the legitimacy of declaring allegiance to the new government when one had previously sworn obedience to the king. Thus, like the duke's breach of the original marriage contract, the engagement presented its would-be subscribers with a case of conscience—of conflicting moral allegiances and legal obligations. Of particular concern to the pamphleteers were the conditions that would allow one to argue that an earlier oath was invalid or still binding. Casuistical concerns of another sort entered into the debate as well, for parliamentarians were anxious that those who declared allegiance not engage in any sort of equivocation by—in Cavendish's words—*seeming* to consent. This dilemma was relevant not only to *The Contract* but also to *Assaulted and Pursued Chastity*, which repeatedly raised the question of whether one should seem to consent in order to preserve one's life or chastity.

The royalist Cavendish, who was married to William Cavendish, was certainly aware of the drama of the engagement and the more general crisis of royalist ideology precipitated by the civil war. When William was defeated at Marston Moor in 1644, the Cavendishes went into exile on the continent (first in Paris, then in Rotterdam and Antwerp), where they remained until the Restoration. Margaret Cavendish and her brother-in-law Charles Cavendish traveled to England in 1651 and remained until 1653, attempting to negotiate with Parliament on behalf of William's sequestered estates. When these negotiations failed and Cavendish applied to the Council of State for a pass to return to Antwerp in 1653, she was asked to take the engagement but refused to do so.[14] This experience, along with her exile and the failure to secure her husband's estates, could only have made her more acutely aware of the costs—both personal and financial—of allegiance to the king.

Finally, Cavendish undoubtedly confronted the issues of allegiance and engagement through her acquaintance with Hobbes, whom Sir William had patronized in the 1630s and with whom the Cavendishes associated during their exile in Paris. Although in her *Philosophical Letters* of 1664 Cavendish asserted that she did not read those parts of *Leviathan* that discussed politics (a subject inappropriate for women), she went on in the same letter to give some of her opinions on government; and in a later letter she briefly alluded to contemporary debates about political obligation, criticizing those who "endeavour to cut between command and obedience to a hairs breadth."[15] Here too Cavendish signaled her awareness of the political case of conscience confronting her compatriots in England.

THE POLITICS OF ROMANCE

Like Hobbes, though for different reasons, Cavendish turned to the genre of romance to comment on the contemporary crisis of political obligation. Whereas romance for Hobbes conjured up the world of aristocratic vainglory or the fantasies of the afterlife, for Cavendish romance suggested married chastity and true love, both in the domestic and the political sphere. This can be explained in part by Cavendish's biography. As lady-in-waiting to Queen Henrietta Maria, Cavendish would have been attuned to the "politics of love" at the Caroline court. She would also have been aware of the specific prominence of romance conventions in court entertainments, both in England and at the Parisian court in exile.[16]

The court masque provides a salient example of the ideological function of romance during the early reign of Charles. As in discussions of the marriage contract between subject and sovereign, here too marriage was a charged political metaphor: the masque's idealizing Neoplatonic fictions included celebrations of the royal marriage as an emblem of political harmony and stability. In a time of peace and prosperity, the Caroline masque suggested, marriage rather than warfare is the preoccupation of princes; romance rather than epic is the chief genre at court.[17] So much, of course, had been implicit in the political language of the marriage contract. Yet, even more than the metaphor of the marriage contract, romance conventions allowed for the representation of the royal marriage as a marriage of love rather than political expediency. For example, the performance of Walter Montague's *The Shepherd's Paradise* in 1633 allegorized away the embarrassing fact that Charles had sought to marry the Spanish Infanta rather than the French Henrietta Maria, by suggesting that the former marriage negotiations had failed because Charles had already fallen in love with the French princess, whom he met in France on his way to Spain. In a typical romance plot that includes many of the twists and turns we find in *The Contract*, love triumphs over or, at the very least, obfuscates contractual negotiation.[18] The same was true of the many court masques celebrating the royal marriage.

While Montague used the plot of romance to revise the political past, royalists in the 1640s and after were particularly interested in using the romance narrative of love and adventure both to stage and to deny any significance to the crisis of the civil war. In their hands, the romance plot represented the contingent realm of fortune, to which parliamentary models of contract were also trying to respond; but the romance narrative also served as the vehicle of the ultimate reconciliation of coercion and consent, pleasure and virtue, destiny and choice. In the course of the narrative, characters who were originally coerced into a marriage contract came to love each other "of their own free will," and contingency was simultaneously canceled and preserved in that illusion of self-determination. Here we begin to see why seventeenth-century prose romance has traditionally been associated with the assimilation (and hence decline) of the formal discipline of casuistry and the rise of a new ideal of autonomous moral character; we also begin to see how romance could contribute to the "disciplining" in the Foucauldian sense of a political subject, who internalizes coercion in the form of his very own passions.[19]

This strategy describes the work of Sir Richard Fanshawe, who translated Guarini's pastoral romance, *Il pastor fido* (The faithful shepherd) and dedicated it to the future Charles II. *Il pastor fido* must have attracted Fanshawe not only because it begins with a coerced vow (or, as Fanshawe translates, "contract") that is broken off only to be reestablished as a "happy Royall Marriage," but also because it tells a story of a faithfulness that endures in the face of deception and misfortune.[20] In one sense the plot served both to represent the trials and tribulations of the suffering prince and to deny that they could have any possible effect on his constancy;[21] in another sense the plot dramatized the royalists' fantasy that the relation between sovereign and subject could never be one of simple coercion, but would always—also—be one of affection and consent. The contingency of the romance plot was thus the narrative equivalent of the ideological message that the subject consents, of his own free will, to be coerced: by a series of apparently fortuitous events and individual choices, the protagonists bring about the marriage that has been decreed by an oracle even before the opening of the play.[22] Similarly, Fanshawe implied, if the relation between sovereign and subject must be conceived of as contractual, it should not be imagined as the Hobbesian or parliamentary contract of equal parties but rather the marriage contract of husband and wife.

In the poems and prose appended to his translation of *Il pastor fido*, Fanshawe was even more explicit about the relevance of the nicer passions of pastoral romance to the events of the civil war. Writing "To His Highnesse [The Prince of Wales] in the West, Ann. Dom. 1646," Fanshawe urged,

> That which the murdring *Cannon* cannot force,
> Nor plumed Squadrons of steel-glittering *Horse*,
> *Love* can. In this *the People* strive t' out-doe
> *The King*; and when they find they're lov'd, love too.
> They serve, because they need not serve: and if
> A good *Prince* slack the reins, they make them stiffe;
> And of their own accords invite that yoke,
> Which, if inforc't on them, they would have broke.

Fanshawe's solution to the crisis of civil war, in which everyone acts according to self-interest, was to replace the language of interest with that of passion or affection—and thus to make a rhetoric of the passions serve the interest of the king. It was in the interest of the king to love rather than directly to coerce his subjects because, freed from the enforcement of political obligation, they would then begin to love him in return. In Fanshawe's anti-Hobbesian romance, in short, it is better to be loved than feared; although there is a suggestion of quid pro quo of the sort that Margaret Cavendish would have appreciated ("when they find they're lov'd, [the people] love too"), Fanshawe also clearly states that consent predicated on the affections—on what Rousseau called the law of the heart—is more binding than coercion or than even the Hobbesian perception of self-interest could ever be. The affections are transmuted to obligation in the form of a self-imposed, internalized discipline: "if / A good *Prince* slack the reins, they make them stiffe." Thus Charles is invited to construct a romance plot along the lines of *Il pastor fido* in which "ama, se piace" (love if you like) is reconciled with "ama, se lice" (love lawfully). Fanshawe thus offers us an unusually explicit account of the politic use of romance to obscure the relations of power between sovereign and subject.[23]

Fanshawe's gloss on *Il pastor fido* foreshadows the 1650s and 1660s, which saw the appearance of a form of romance narrative that was neither chivalric nor pastoral but closer to the Greek romances of Heliodorus, "a form that allowed for adventure and coincidence but not for the improbably supernatural 'marvels' of the old chivalric narratives."[24] Here, too, romance was very often construed as a vehicle of royalist ideology—although, the message was no longer the celebration and justification of domestic and foreign policy of the 1630s but rather (as with Fanshawe's "faithful shepherd") the depiction of the "travails" of the royal protagonists and their ability to withstand the vagaries of fortune through strength of character.[25] Crucially important for the revival of this form of romance narrative were the translations of French romances by Madeleine de Scudéry, de la Calprenède, and others: along with contemporary romances of English authors such as William Sales and Percy Herbert which stressed the aptness of romance adventures to allegorize the political upheavals of the civil war, the French works satisfied the reader's desire both for "strange actions" and for the analysis of the passions and development of character, in part through casuistical debate. Such an emphasis, Annabel Patterson has suggested, provided "a role, both in political life and in the new literature, for women" and may have contributed to the popularity of these romances with female readers.[26] Margaret Cavendish undoubtedly had some familiarity with these popular romances in their English translations; as we will see, her own romantic critique of romance involves a similar emphasis on character, casuistry, and women's agency, and a similar concern with travels and travails.

Passion and Interest

As a woman writer, Cavendish was sensitive to the "feminization" of romance, its association with women readers, fantasy, and escapism. At the same time, like Fanshawe, she wanted to use the conventions of romance to present an argument for allegiance to the Stuart monarchy, one that engaged contemporary Hobbesian arguments about contract, passion, and self-interest in order to reform romance from within. In the preface to *Natures Pictures* (the volume including *The Contract* and *Assaulted and Pursued Chastity*), she signals her ambivalence about the genre of romance and, in so doing, attempts to revise the contract of genre she shares with the reader:

> Though some of these Stories be Romancical, I would not be thought to delight in Romances, having never read a whole one in my life; and if I did believe that these Tales should neither benefit the Life, nor please the Mind, more than what I have read in them, did either instruct or satisfie me; or that they could create Amorous thoughts in idle brains, as Romances do, I would never suffer them to be printed, and would make Blots instead of Letters. But Partiality persuades me otherwise; and I hope that this Work will rather quench Passion, than enflame it.[27]

Simultaneously declaring and denying the romance elements of the stories that follow, Cavendish alerts us to her dialectical critique of the genre most prominently associated with the court and with royalist political propaganda from the 1630s to the 1660s. Her goal, she tells us, is to use romance's representation of the passions in order to quench passion or, at the very least, to redirect erotic passion to political obligation. In *The Contract* and *Assaulted and Pursued Chastity*, Cavendish does not oppose romance and contract in the Hobbesian manner, but neither does she simply conflate them in a royalist politics of love. In the process of making what appears to be a traditional royalist argument for the role of love in securing political obligation, Cavendish parodies the Hobbesian picture of the passions and the interests, of power seeking after power, and uses romance to revise the absolutist model of the marriage contract. In so doing, she suggests a feminist critique of arguments for the political contract as well.[28] In the following pages I turn first to *The Contract* to explore Cavendish's critique of the contract of genre, her anatomy of the contemporary language of contract, and her defense of true romance. I then take up Cavendish's more jaundiced view of the royalist rhetoric of romance and its implicit patriarchalism in *Assaulted and Pursued Chastity*.

Cavendish's intention to reform romance is apparent early on in *The Contract* from various moments of generic self-consciousness: the uncle keeps his young charge away from "courts, masques, plays, [and] balls," and forbids her to read "romancies," substituting instead moral philosophy and history. She in turn adopts a Jonsonian strictness about the masque of life, disparaging spectacle when it is unaccompanied by "the rational and understanding part."[29] Although the uncle eventually takes the lady to a court masque, where she strikes the assembled courtiers with Spenserian "amaze," this romance victory is achieved at the expense of the court culture of romance. The uncle's description of the masque reads like the famous account of opera in Tolstoy's *War and Peace*, an account that Russian formalist critics used to exemplify the device of "making strange." To his niece's inquiry, "Pray . . . what is a masque?" he answers

> it is painted scenes to represent the poet's heavens and hells, their gods and devils, and clouds, sun, moon, and stars; besides, they represent cities, castles, seas, fishes, rocks, mountains, beasts, birds, and what pleaseth the poet, painter, and surveyor. Then there are actors, and speeches spoke, and music; and then lords or ladies come down in a scene, as from the clouds; and after that, they begin to dance.

In this deliberate reduction of the symbolic world of the masque to its material components, the uncle dismantles the contract of genre. In his paratactic description of "speeches spoke," he ridicules the way the allegorical program of the masque was often received by members of the royal audience. By pointing up the superficiality of the spectacle and the audience's response, he trivializes the rhetorical effect of the masque and, implicitly, the courtly society of which it is an emblem. At the same time, he points to the primacy of event over characterization in the masque for which a number of Cavendish's contemporaries criticized prose romance. In the preface to the English translation of Mlle de Scudéry's *Ibrahim* (1652), we read, "to make them [the heroes] be known perfectly, it is not sufficient to say how many times they have suffered shipwreck, and how [many] times they have incountered robbers, but their inclinations must be made to appear by their discourse." In the best romances, the author implies, intention and motive distinguish heroes more than their superficial actions.[30] And this is what happens in *The Contract*.

Although the court masque itself is criticized for its superficial display, it is also the occasion of "true romance," for here the lady and the duke meet and fall in love. It is also here that the uncle meets the elderly viceroy to whom he hopes to marry his niece. These events then motivate the rest of the plot, for the newly amorous duke must extricate himself from his current marriage; the lady must negotiate her conflicting allegiances to her uncle and her new love; and the uncle must be convinced that the new marriage contract he is negotiating on his niece's behalf with the elderly viceroy is invalid. One thing is clear: a contract that was originally broken for lack of consent begins to be validated through romance, specifically romantic love.

Cavendish then develops her views about the relationship of contract to consent, morality and "nice scruples" to love, in a number of exemplary scenes. These scenes amount to a kind of interregnum anatomy of contract, specifically in relation to the passions and interests that contract is intended to reconfigure or represent. In simultaneously stressing the importance of consent and its irrelevance, these scenes suggest that precisely this contradiction is the heart of the royalist argument about irrevocable political contract; at the same time, they dramatize Cavendish's attempt to use the conventions of romance to reconcile necessity and consent in an argument for political obligation that is modeled on romantic love. In the end, however, *The Contract* also illustrates the paradox of using the passions to counter those arguments for the engagement and political obligation that emphasized the rational calculation of self-preservation—the paradox, that is, of using the passions to provide a securer foundation for contract. As Hobbes himself had noted in making fear of violent death a cornerstone of his commonwealth, the passions are themselves a source of interest; and, as he acknowledged in the conclusion to *Leviathan*, the interest of self-preservation may ultimately give rise to the same sorts of casuistry and broken contracts that the original contract was designed to avoid. The final scene of *The Contract* shows us that the same is true of "true love."

In the first exemplary scene (really two in quick succession), both the lady and her uncle see contract as an agreement that is based on love and consent. Thus, in trying to persuade his niece to marry the viceroy, the uncle resorts to persuasion rather than coercion. Although the lady suspects her uncle's "design" to marry her against her affections, the uncle initially has no such intention. Instead, he urges the lady to put aside passion and to marry "a discrete and sober man," and he tells the viceroy that "he could not force [his niece's] affection," although he would try "to get her to consent to marry." When he then tries to persuade the lady of the viceroy's virtues, she protests that they are ill-suited—for he is old and she is young, he will be jealous and she will be restrained "like a prisoner." Obviously, the partner she has in mind is one who will be like her in age as well as station; the contract she envisions is one that will preclude coercion both before and during the marriage. Nevertheless, at the end of this scene, she reiterates that she is "bound in gratitude and duty to obey" her uncle's will, thereby calling attention not only to the case of conscience posed by the uncle's proposed contract but also to the difficulty of making consent a meaningful act in the context of a relationship that is hierarchical and inequitable.[31]

Shortly after this, the lady experiences pangs of conscience about replying to the duke's love-letter, both because her uncle would disapprove if she responded and because the duke would think her "malicious" if she did not. This case of conscience is explicitly "resolved" by an appeal to her own experience of "charity and love," which persuade her that the duke "speaks the truth" when he claims her indifference will kill him: "I would be loath to murder him with nice scruples [about replying to his letter], when I am neither forbade by honour nor modesty, religion nor laws. Well, I will adventure, and ask my uncle pardon when I have done." In her reply to the duke, the lady similarly conflates conscience and love: "[I]f you have wars with your conscience, or fancy, or both, interrupting the peace of your mind, as your letter expresses, I should willingly return to your side, and be an arbitrator; yet the fates have determined it otherwise." In these and other scenes in which the lady both acknowledges and casuistically evades the authority of her uncle, Cavendish seems to be suggesting that consent in accordance with one's conscience is required for a contract or any other "law" (including the moral law) to be binding.[32] And that consent is figured as love.

In the second exemplary scene, by contrast, the duke describes the original marriage contract in terms of a model of political obligation that is hierarchical, inequitable, and irrevocable, and to which consent is irrelevant. He does so in response to the news that the lady has been betrothed to the viceroy after all. Here and in the following episode, we see the narrative explicitly take up the central question of the engagement controversy: under what conditions is a contract no longer binding? Although the match was arranged "without the young Lady's consent," "the uncle told her afterwards, she must prepare herself to be the viceroy's bride; and, said he, if you consent not never come near me more." We know that she does tacitly consent because, immediately after this, the duke who has heard of the match appears in the lady's chamber to protest, and she responds that if she were to disobey her uncle she would prove herself "a traitor to gratitude." The duke then argues that the original marriage contract between the two of them is still in effect:

> [Y]ou cannot want an owner whilst I live, for I had, nor have no more power to resign the interest I have in you, than Kings to resign their crown that comes by succession, for the right lies in the crown, not in the man, and though I have played the tyrant, and deserved to be uncrowned, yet none ought to take it off my head, but death, nor have I power to throw it from myself, death only must make way for a successor.

Contrary to what we might expect, the duke is not claiming that the original contract is now valid because his consent has finally been secured, but that it has continued to be valid regardless of his consent. Thus, in describing his situation, he draws an analogy between his condition and that of the absolute monarch who remained sovereign even when he was a tyrant. The implication seems to be that, as Hobbes argued in *De corpore* and *Leviathan*, contracts are legally binding as long as the contracting parties are in a position to perform their obligations (whether they do or not).[33] The application of the analogy to contemporary politics is obvious: Charles I was king and therefore deserved his subjects' allegiance. What complicates this reading is that the motive for the duke's argument is his passionate love for the lady. To focus on the domestic drama is to see that passion is figured as sovereign, and that the duke now defends the marriage contract because he is in love and it is in his interest to do so.

That Cavendish believes love is a more powerful basis for obligation than coercion and self-preservation is dramatically illustrated by the third scene, a parody of the Hobbesian account of contract, which mediates between the lady's emphasis on consent and the duke's insistence on its irrelevance. In this scene, the duke confronts the viceroy at sword point and insists that he swear in writing not to marry the lady. When the viceroy very reasonably asks why, the duke informs him that "she is my wife, and I have been married to her almost nine years." The duke thus argues that the viceroy's contract is invalid because of a prior contract. It is not the force of logic that persuades the viceroy, however, but mere brute force: not until the duke tells him "If you do not [swear], you shall die a violent death," does the viceroy agree. The scene reads as a textbook illustration of the question at the heart of the engagement controversy— the question of whether one can break a prior contract and sign a new one for reasons of self-preservation. Whereas Hobbes had answered in the affirmative and had used such arguments to justify the legitimacy of de facto political power, Cavendish strikingly uses the argument for engagement to justify a prior contract and the status quo ante. Here, too, what the scene with the viceroy appears to illustrate for Cavendish is that contracts based on fear and self-interest are weaker than those based on love, for they will always be broken when the contracting party is threatened with force. In marked contrast to the nascent view that a person pursuing his own interest becomes "transparent and predictable" and that "interest will not lie," Cavendish shows us that interest—at least the interest of self-preservation—is the source of inconstancy.[34] The viceroy is forced to "unswear" his recent oath to marry the lady, with the result that the earlier oath of engagement between the duke and the lady is reaffirmed—and thus, indirectly, the earlier oath of obedience to the king.

CONTRACT ON TRIAL

While in the encounter between the duke and the lady, the duke argues that contracts are binding even without consent and the episode with the viceroy shows that contracts may be broken for reasons of self-preservation, in both cases these arguments are in the service of preserving the original engagement of the duke and the lady, one now infused with true love. The final scene of *The Contract*, however, seems to dramatize some of the problems of granting the affections such a role by linking the royalist interest in true romance with the engagers' worst fears of royalist deception and manipulation.[35] In this last scene the duke and the lady have consented to marry, but the duke must still extricate himself from his current marriage. Accordingly, the lady and the duke decide "to conceal their agreement . . . , and to cover it by the duke's *seeming dissent*"—a phrase that echoes his "seeming consent" to the first contract at the very beginning of the narrative.[36] Lest he seem to have deliberately contracted to marry two women, the lady agrees to pretend to sue for his hand in court. This way the duke can seem to be "coerced" by justice to consent to the original contract.

More than any other scene in *The Contract*, the final "trial" scene dramatizes the generic self-consciousness of Cavendish's fiction. At the same time, the scene raises questions about the political and gender implications of Cavendish's manipulation of genre. From Heliodorus's *Aithiopika*, where the heroine Chariclea is her own defending counsel, to Shakespeare's Portia, female characters have used the courtroom to present equitable arguments for the satisfaction of their desires.[37] In *The Contract* as well, the lady uses the courtroom to present a plausible case for her marriage to the duke; at the same time, her forensic oratory makes the case for women's place in the public sphere. What is politically troubling about this final scene, however, is the obvious casuistry involved in the lady's pleading before the judges. By casuistry I do not mean a case of conscience, for the duke and the lady appear to have no scruples at all about their mock suit, but rather casuistry in the sense of equivocation and deceit—of romance, we might say, in the sense of improbability and fiction. Here the legal dispute about the contract gives rise to a scene of probabilistic reasoning designed to reveal the intentions of the contracting parties to the judges. But this scene of probabilistic reasoning—which is, after all, the activity of the reader of romance as well—proves to be inseparable from coercion and deception, force and fraud. The politically charged casuistry of the trial scene in turn raises questions about the nature of the literary, social, and gender contract to which the reader has consented.

First, the lady insists that she was "married" to the duke according to common law (if not canon law), and that her legal status as a minor is irrelevant now that she has consented to the marriage as an adult.[38] She then argues in Hobbesian fashion that the duke was old enough to consent when the original contract was made and "if a coward make a promise through distracted fear, laws that carry more terrors, than the broken promise [carries] profit, will make him keep it. . . . For a promise must neither be broken upon suspicion, nor false construction, nor enticing persuasions, nor threatening ruins, but it must be maintained with life, and kept by death, unless the promises carry more malignity in the keeping them, than the breaking of them." As a result, the duke's "vows" to his current wife could only be "love's feignings, [rather] than really true": "for where right is not, truth cannot be." Affection, the lady argues, cannot justify a new marriage contract when an old bond is still in force. In such situations, the new contract will instead be a cause of "feigning," including the pretense of freedom to contract a new marriage; yet "he cannot be free, unless he hath my consent, which I will never give."[39]

The lady then protests that (unlike the duke) she is incapable of deceit:

And for dissembling, I have not have had time enough to practice much deceit; my youth will witness for me, it is an art, not an inbred nature, and must be studied with pains, and watched with observation, before any can be master thereof. And I hope this assembly is so just, as not to impute my innocent simplicity to a subtle, crafty, or a deceiving glass, to show the mind's false face, making that fair, which in itself is foul.[40]

Yet that is precisely what the trial is designed to do: to make the duke's past foul behavior seem fair—or fairer than it might otherwise seem—through the artful dissembling of his knowledge of the validity of the prior contract and of his desire to be rid of his present wife. And part of the lady's casuistry is to invoke the Hobbesian argument for the validity of covenants made for reasons of fear, although the reason for the trial is that the contract is now motivated by love.

This casuistical sacrifice of love to the law only in order to enforce "the law of the heart" is then replayed by the duke, who confesses that in his licentious youth he sought pleasure more than virtue: "but experience hath learned me stricter ways, and nobler principles, insomuch as the reflection of my former actions, clouds all my future happiness, wounds my conscience, and torments my life; but I shall submit to what your wise judgements think fit." The duke portrays himself as a "wounded conscience"—a common phrase from casuistical manuals and treatises concerning political obligation—not because he is faced with a conflict of allegiances (as in the engagment controversy) but rather because his wayward passion and infidelity have been revealed to him by the law. A few lines later, the lady reiterates the fiction that passion forced the duke to break his prior vow, when she urges that the court "excuse the faults of the duke, since he was forced by Tyrant Love to run in uncouth ways." And yet, as the reader knows, the law that reveals the wounded conscience is also the instrument that reconciles "pleasure" and "virtue." Not surprisingly, when the court rules that the lady is his "lawful wife," he "willingly submit[s]," thereby making his legal destiny his choice.[41]

One way to read this last scene is as Cavendish's final attempt to rebut arguments such as Hobbes's and the engagers': whereas in *Leviathan*, irrevocable political contract is predicated on consent and validated by coercion, for Cavendish such coercion will, ideally, always be staged, because the real relationship between contracting parties is not only one of consent, but also of true love. This argument has obvious gender implications as well: just as the lady in the trial scene recalls the enterprising, independent-minded heroine of Shakespearean comedy—a woman such as Rosalind or Portia who is capable of acting in her own interest—so the contract she defends is one that fulfills her own desires just as much as her husband's.

This fiction of satisfied desire has potentially revolutionary implications in the political sphere. As we have seen, romance in Cavendish's work is the motor and motive of narrative: the narrative of coming to understand one's obligations as willed—not as a matter of self-preservation but of fantasy, desire, and self-fulfillment. Yet, to the extent that self-fulfillment requires the greater equality—to adopt Eve's oxymoron in *Paradise Lost* (9.823)—of the contracting parties (in the first instance husband and wife, but also sovereign and subject), it threatens not only the traditional understanding of the marriage contract but also the royalist's use of the marriage contract as a justification of political subordination. After all, it is not the wife but the husband who "willingly submit[s]" at the end of the trial, a gesture (however feigned) that recalls the pejorative analogy between obedient and effeminized subjects that parliamentarians such as Henry Parker had used to argue against absolute sovereignty. Intentionally or not (or perhaps both, given her characteristically ambivalent claims for the equality of the sexes in the many prefaces to her works), Cavendish's defense of a more equitable marriage contract may in the end bring her closer to parliamentary critics of the king than she would have liked.[42] While using romance to justify the "marriage contract" of subject and sovereign, she exposes the problem at the heart of the royalist marriage-sovereignty analogy, for she shows almost in spite of herself that true romance is as much a justification of personal and political divorce as it is of marriage. Finally, Cavendish's brief for women's agency also hints at the illogic of excluding women from the political contract. Specifically, in making the lady's marriage contract the central issue of her politically charged romance, Cavendish may imply that if women are capable of consenting to marriage, they must also be capable of consenting to a political contract. At the very least, the logic of the plot exposes this antinomy in contract theory.

But there are other aspects of the final trial scene that are at odds with the radical gender and political possibilities I have just sketched. In particular, the obvious casuistry of lady and duke leaves us with a feeling of discomfort reminiscent of Shakespeare's problem plays—a feeling of the incompatibility of law and romance, coercion and consent, both in the domestic and the political spheres. This incompatibility is illustrated by the fact that the fictions of the final scene—that love is tyrannical and contracts are binding without consent—are at odds with the implicit argument of earlier episodes according to which contract is a vehicle of true, that is, consensual romance. In the end Cavendish's romance justification of sovereignty dramatizes some of the same problems we saw in *Leviathan*. For to the extent that she emphasizes the consensual aspect of romance, she runs the risk of justifying parliamentary critics of absolute sovereignty; and, to the extent that she sees romance as a figure of coercion, she runs the risk of apologizing for de facto political power.

There are other ways as well in which the fiction of true romance and thus the implicit contract of genre are contaminated by coercion and dissembling at the end of *The Contract*. As I noted earlier, for the duke "the wounded conscience" is less a matter of principle than of psychology; it does not involve an application of moral judgment but an experience of guilt (18–19). Yet this psychologizing of conscience is not a move that inspires confidence in the duke's reformed character, since we know that he is acting the part of the penitent rake for the benefit of his judges. This dissembling then seems to call into question the resolution of the plot. In particular, our discomfort with the duke's sudden "conversion" and his marriage to the lady is aggravated by the fact that the elderly viceroy makes what appears to be a purely expedient proposal at the last moment to the duke's first wife—"since the law has given away your husband, I will supply his place"—and by the fact that the new marriages seem likely to be as unsatisfactory as the old (43). In gender terms, Cavendish would then be pointing to both the conventionality of traditional gender relations and the violence required to enforce them.

The Sexual Contract

While this violence is only implicit in *The Contract*, it is quite explicit in *Assaulted and Pursued Chastity*, beginning with title. Married chastity was, as we have seen, a highly politicized virtue at the Stuart court. Early modern readers would also have been familiar with the political implications of chastity from examples such as the rape of Lucretia or the rape of Dinah in Genesis 34 (which Cavendish mentions in her prefatory note). Jerome had argued that the threat to chastity, like the threat to self-preservation, justified self-defense. And Grotius had made a similar argument in book 2 of *De jure belli ac pacis*, citing the example of Heliodorus's Chariclea to illustrate the justifiable warding off of rape by means of murder.[43] But Cavendish's take is somewhat different.

As the romance plot develops, we see that chastity is threatened not only during civil war but also during peacetime. When the young lady tries to return home, she is thrown off course by the proverbial romance tempest and lands in the Kingdom of Sensuality, where she is sold to a bawd. Attention quickly shifts from the broken political contract to the sexual contract of prostitution; yet Miseria (as she is called) reveals her familiarity with the notion of property underlying both, when she rebuts the advances of a customer—a prince who is described as a "grand monopolizer of virgins"—by appealing to the notion of property in one's person: "And it is an injustice to take the goods from the right owners without their consent. . . . and none but base or cruel tyrants will lay unreasonable commands, or require wicked demands to the powerless, or virtuous."[44] The prince, however, refuses to be persuaded by this appeal to the right of property. When his passions become "more violent" and he threatens to assault her, Miseria shoots him—a refreshing twist in the typical romance plot (even though the prince survives) and a sign that Cavendish wants to endow her romance heroine with greater resources than simple constancy of character. The use of force is clearly justified for reasons of self-defense.

Whereas in the scene with the prince Miseria is threatened with outright violence, in the romance adventures that ensue Cavendish repeatedly exposes the coercion at the heart of ostensible moments of consent. Through a series of twists and turns, Travellia is adopted by a sea captain and the two of them are shipwrecked on an island inhabited by purple people with white hair. (This is Cavendish's idea of ethnographic detail.) Here Travellia quickly learns the language of the islanders and delivers a number of orations in which she displays a Machiavellian cunning about the use of religion to induce political obedience. Rhetorical fraud becomes an indirect means of coercion: the people's consent is predicated on their deception. Then, in case we missed this point about the coercion underlying their consent, Cavendish has Travellia fatally shoot the chief priest with her pistol and command the people outright to obey.

Consent and coercion are also implicated in the subsequent encounter between Travellia and the prince who has, in the meantime, become head of a band of pirates. When Travellia and the sea captain are shipwrecked on the prince's island, he recognizes her and tells her he will rape her unless she "consent[s] to live with him as his wife." At which point, realizing the predicament she is in, Travellia thinks "it best to dissemble and give a seeming consent" (83). By dissembling, Travellia manages to escape to the Kingdom of Amity; but the prince, who in the meantime has established "a new and small monarchy" on his island, uses the absence of women as an argument to his fellow pirates to invade the Kingdom of Amity where Travellia has taken refuge. For without procreation and offspring, the prince argues, the pirates will be unable to maintain their commonwealth. Here, in what reads as a parody of Filmer, Cavendish exposes what Carole Pateman calls the "sex-right" that is the condition of political right in the prince's patriarchal kingdom. There can be no political order or government if there are no subjects to rule, and for these to exist women must first be subjected to men by force. By making the prince who asks for Miseria's consent also the would-be father of the patriarchal kingdom, Cavendish implicitly suggests that this sex-right is not limited to patriarchy but underlies the Hobbesian or parliamentary political contract as well.[45]

As part of her critique of domestic and political tyranny, Cavendish also repeatedly calls attention to the difference between slavery and voluntary subjection. In line with the affective logic of *The Contract*, slavery is aligned with the passion of fear and voluntary subjection with love. The kingdom of the purple people, we learn, keeps "a great store of slaves, both males and females, to breed on." "As for their government, it was tyrannical for all the common people were slaves to the royal." When the lady and the sea captain leave this kingdom, they instruct the king and the people both to love each other and to grant liberty to their slaves. Later in the text, the distinction is made between a prisoner of war, who is by definition enslaved, and a political subject, who is not. The former is characterized by fear for his life, whereas the latter is defined by love of the sovereign and thus by voluntary subjection.[46] Finally, Travellia, speaking to her troops, delivers a stirring speech with obvious relevance to the enslavement of the royalists during the interregnum:

> [I]f we let our enemies become our masters; they will give us restless fears, unreasonable taxes, unconscionable oaths, whereby we shall lose . . . the liberty of a subject, the royalty of your government, and the company and rule of our gracious, virtuous, and beautiful Queen: . . . All noble spirits hate bondage, and will rather die than endure slavery. (97–98)

The only kind of slavery that is tolerated by Travellia and the other main characters is slavery to one's passions, by which one voluntarily subjects oneself to one's beloved or to one's sovereign.

A different kind of voluntary subjection—this time to circumstance— is also recommended in the course of the narrative. Although Travellia herself is somewhat of an idealist in matters of love and war, one of her older counselors instructs her in the necessity of policy:

> [T]hat we call policy in a public state, is called discretion in a private family; and it is not, as the vulgar think it, a cheat or mere deceit, but a wise prudence, to prevent the worst of ills, or to keep peace, and get tranquility. . . . policy will rather choose the oars of patience, and take the tides of time, than venture where the doubts are more than hopes, or hazards more than gains: then let us try to make a prudent peace, not trusting to Fortune's favour, unless she were more constant. (104)

Ironically, such prudent deceit is precisely what Travellia has been engaged in throughout her adventures as a page and a general. Her romance stratagems, including her feigned consent to the prince, are her politic response to inconstant fortune. As in *The Contract*, the message—which sounds remarkably like William Cavendish's own political advice to the future Charles II—has obvious relevance to the exiled royalists attempting to make their peace with present circumstances, while hoping for the restoration.[47]

In the end, like *The Contract, Assaulted and Pursued Chastity* performs a delicate balancing act between the imperatives of female emancipation and those of political restoration.[48] Travellia subjects herself to her husband, but she also insists that she will govern the kingdom. She thus articulates the standard resolution of the conflict inherent in the position of a female ruler who is also a wife.[49] At the same time, she lays claim to the one sphere of female agency in which the husband had no jurisdiction: that of the female ruler. Like *Il pastor fido*, the romance plot of *Assaulted and Pursued Chastity* ultimately reconciles the law and desire, but not without exposing the coercion at the heart of the marriage contract, dramatizing the socially constructed asymmetry of gender in both the political and the domestic realm, and offering a brief for politic feigning or prudent deception.[50]

The Paralogism of Romance

In their foregrounding of coercion and deception, both of Cavendish's romances repeatedly call attention to what Terence Cave has described as the scandal of fiction, a scandal particularly associated with the genre of romance in the early modern period. In Aristotelian terms, the scandal is that the illusion of mimesis or verisimilitude may depend on paralogism or faulty reasoning. The resolution of a plot may be brought about by what Aristotle called inartistic means: mistakes, accidents, coercion, and deception, rather than by the logical entailment of events. In Cave's reading, paralogism may include the characters' own fraudulent fictions. Such crafty manipulators of the plot "serve as a focus for reflections on the way fictions as such are constituted, the way in which they play with and on their reader, their distinctive marks *as* fictions—untruth, disguise, trickery, 'suspense' or deferment, the creation of effects of shock or amazement, and so on."[51] Paralogism so conceived disrupts the illusion of verisimilitude or what I have called the contract of mimesis. And, in doing so, it calls attention not only to the social construction of genre but also to the conventionality of the social contract more generally. In some cases, this insight can be liberating by pointing to the capacity for change. In other cases, it invites a darker reading of the contracts of genre and society as vehicles of coercion and social control.[52]

Both *The Contract* and *Assaulted and Pursued Chastity* invite such a reading. According to this reading, the final trial scene of *The Contract* is less a simple rebuttal of Hobbes and the engagers than an adaptation of their arguments concerning the power of self-interest. The collusion of the duke and the lady then appears as a commentary on the difference between the reign of Charles I and the Protectorate: in the later period, the law can no longer be infused with romance but can instead only be casuistically manipulated. This is true not only of the generic contract of romance but also of the marriage contract and the political contract: in all three cases, as Cavendish shows and as Hobbes feared, contract is predicated on and fosters a kind of pretense, even dissimulation. What is worse, this dissimulation taints royalists as well as parliamentarians. This ironic treatment of the royalist romance is even more fully dramatized in *Assaulted and Pursued Chastity*, where the royalist romance of patriarchalism is demystified as a matter of force and fraud, and the heroine resorts to violence and deception to preserve herself against the predations of the prince. In such a world, Cavendish may be suggesting, true romance must be supplanted by tragicomedy or the problem play.[53] This instability of genre, which we might describe thematically as an uncertainty about the relationship between coercion and consent, passion and interest, would then signal a breakdown of the social and political contract during the years of the Protectorate.

The instability of genre returns us to the relationship of the marriage contract to political contract. As I have already suggested, not the least of the "problems" staged by the final scene of *The Contract* is the very incompatibility of Cavendish's critique of the marriage contract with her royalist argument for allegiance to the king—the incompatibility, that is, of the more radical gender argument and the argument for traditional political obligation. Whereas *Assaulted and Pursued Chastity* negotiates this tension by making Travellia the ruler of the kingdom,[54] *The Contract* ends on a note of diminished female agency. For example, although the lady demonstrates great resourcefulness in winning over the duke and satisfying her own desires, nothing in the plot suggests that her marriage will challenge the conventional hierarchical relation of husband and wife. As she remarks earlier in response to her uncle's plans to marry her to the viceroy, "you give your power, authority, and commands, with my obedience, away; for if my husband and your commands are contrary, I can obey but one, which must be my husband." And, as she remarks somewhat later to the duke, "it is an unheard of malice to me . . . neither to own me yourself, nor let another": self-ownership is apparently not a permanent option for women in this text. It is precisely for this reason, I suggest, that the plot of *The Contract* is taken up with the dilatory, casuistical space of debating the conditions of contract rather than with married life; and the plot of *Assaulted and Pursued Chastity* is similarly taken up with the adventures and achievements of the unmarried heroine. Focusing on the time before marriage allows the lady some portion of equity, some degree of autonomy, however unrepresentative of the married state, not to mention the political state, that lies before her. It may also be for this reason that Cavendish protests in the preface to *Natures*

Pictures that she never read "a whole [romance]" in her life: it is not good for women to have romances end, for romantic closure is antithetical to female independence.[55]

As Cavendish's romances illustrate, in mid-seventeenth-century England the genre of prose romance was a vehicle for debates about the proper role of coercion and consent in establishing political obligation. Romance plots fascinated seventeenth-century readers because their paratactic narratives of love and adventure conjured up a world of the passions and interests, of broken vows and deferred marriages, to which the language of contract was also trying to respond; and they fascinated royalist writers in particular because, in their ultimate validation of the romantic affections, they offered a possible alternative to—or revision of—the parliamentary and Hobbesian languages of contract. If, as Sheldon Wolin has argued, Hobbes saw himself as the hero of a new kind of epic, combating the Kingdom of Darkness with the weapon of "right method,"[56] Cavendish imagined herself as the heroine of a new kind of philosophical romance—a chaste "She-Anchoret" (the title of one of the other works in *Natures Pictures*) pronouncing on the central political and philosophical issues of the day. Like Hobbes, Cavendish was concerned to describe a model of obligation that was both irrevocable and consensual; unlike Hobbes, I believe, she was eager to justify the original oath of allegiance to Charles I. To Hobbes's motives of fear and self-preservation, Cavendish opposed romantic love as a stronger foundation for irrevocable contract. In the process, she also appropriated and revised the language of interest. Ideally, she suggests, self-interest need not underwrite a Hobbesian account of life as nasty, brutish, and short: for, in Cavendish's hands, romantic love is both a passion (one might even say, a form of coercion) to which we readily consent; and an interest that allows us to be faithful to our contractual obligations, even in the face of threats to our self-preservation. In contrast to William Cavendish, who sacrificed his interest to the king's and whose love was unrequited,[57] Margaret Cavendish suggests that passion and interest may together underwrite the contract of political obligation and that honor and loyalty may not be incompatible with "politic designs."

While apparently at odds with such ostentatiously demystified accounts of contract as Hobbes's *Leviathan*, Cavendish's prose romance helps us to see that the languages of romance and contract are dialectically related in contemporary debates about political obligation. If the legalistic manipulation of contract by the duke and the lady exposes romance as a matter of interest and calculation, their romance simultaneously reveals the fictional and affective dimension of contract. One might even say that Cavendish's conception of romance amounts to an internalization of the Hobbesian theory of contract, according to which we consent to be coerced: whereas in Hobbes's account coercion takes the form of the sovereign's power of the sword, in Cavendish coercion takes the form of our very own passions. We are coerced, in short, by ourselves. Such coercion would be the equivalent to the disciplining, in the Foucauldian sense, of the political subject who paradoxically experiences such constraint as the most authentic—because most inward and self-imposed. Such a reading would make the projected marriage contract compatible with the argument for allegiance to the king. As we have seen, however, in Cavendish's hands romance is also at odds with the demands of political obligation. This is both because romance dramatizes the instability of the passions, the necessarily figurative dimension of any so-called binding contract, and because contracts are predicated on and foster a kind of pretense, paralogism, or even dissimulation.[58] At the extreme, *The Contract* demystifies the romance of contract, exposing the lability of the passions and the interests, while *Assaulted and Pursued Chastity* demystified the romance of patriarchy, which was as bad for women as the interregnum was for royalists.

In dramatizing the intersection of romance and contract, Cavendish's work contributes to a revised history of theories of political obligation in the seventeenth century. Not only does *The Contract* illustrate the general principle that seventeenth-century political debate was often carried out in terms of competing uses of the same genre; it also suggests that romance was particularly well suited to staging the problematic coexistence of coercion and consent, passion and interest, in contemporary theories of contract. This is no doubt because, as Hobbes feared, the world of politics is itself "concerned with the imaginary and the fantastic," with "lived romance."[59] In *Patriarcha* Filmer had argued that the notion of the original contract was a ridiculous fiction. Cavendish suggests, with considerably more sympathy, that contract is one of the seventeenth century's most powerful forms of romance.

CHAPTER 8

Embodiment

> Metaphor is an affair between a predicate with a past and an
> object that yields while protesting.
> —Nelson Goodman

IN *Christian Doctrine* Milton tells us there was no theological covenant of works or of grace in prelapsarian Eden. The first was not necessary because there was no work Adam and Eve were required to do; the second was unnecessary because Adam and Eve were not yet fallen.[1] For the same reason there was no civil government, no realm of the specifically political, and thus no contract of political obligation. Thus the language of covenant and contract is missing from the scenes of prelapsarian life in *Paradise Lost* just as it is from biblical Eden. And yet more than any other seventeenth-century text, *Paradise Lost* reads as a sustained meditation on the intersection of the theological covenant, marriage contract, and political contract, a profound psychological analysis of the problems of voluntary servitude and breach of trust. And, more brilliantly than any other contemporary text, *Paradise Lost* invites us to reflect on the relation of these contracts to the contract of mimesis—whether we construe this as the order of likeness established by God's creative word or as the poet's contract with the reader.

Milton's shifting remarks about the divine covenant in *Christian Doctrine* provide a window onto the contractual dimension of Eden. Although a covenant of works was not necessary because Adam and Eve were "naturally disposed to do right," this natural law made their "obedience" invisible. It was for this reason that God issued his "command" not to eat of the Tree of Knowledge—a command that "had nothing to do with the law of nature" but was instead an instance of "positive right" (*jus positivum*). Although Milton insisted that God's command was "a declaration of power" rather than a covenant or mutual agreement, this declaration also enabled Adam and Eve to prove or "pledge" their obedience. Milton here touches on the theological dilemma that it must be possible to transgress a divine command for free will or obedience to make any sense. This divinely instituted possibility of transgression makes the relationship to God not simply a matter of primary natural law but of what Grotius, Selden, and others called secondary natural law, the realm of contracts and covenants. Milton acknowledged as much when later, in *Christian Doctrine*, he contradicted his earlier remarks and referred to God's command as a "foedus" or covenant. In *Paradise Lost*, postlapsarian Adam seconds this view when he complains to God that the "terms" and "conditions" of life in Eden were "too hard."[2]

In *Paradise Lost*, Milton presents an anti-Hobbesian account of the contracting subject, one in which an analysis of the heavenly contract serves, as Hobbes feared, to authorize the breach of the political contract. As a biblical epic, *Paradise Lost* tells the theological story of the fall and lapse into voluntary servitude. At the same time, *Paradise Lost* allegorizes the failure of the English revolution and the voluntary servitude of the English people to the Restoration. Like Hobbes, Milton attempts to imagine the subject of these stories as a fully embodied subject, one whose passions are a crucial part of the reasons for action, a crucial dimension of natural right. And like Hobbes, Milton is attuned to the relationship between material embodiment and artifice, between primary natural law and the secondary realm of human institutions. In contrast to Hobbes, however, whose narrative of the state of nature was designed to justify consent to an irrevocable political contract, Milton's narrative serves not only to make sense of the fall but also to justify dissent.

In *Paradise Lost*, Milton also addresses the relationship between contract and dissent formally in his self-conscious manipulation of genre and his relation to the reader. In *The Elements of Philosophy* Hobbes had pronounced that political science was no older than his *De cive*. In the invocation to book 1 of *Paradise Lost*, Milton also claims originality for his undertaking—"Things unattempted yet in Prose or Rhyme"—though he does so ironically in words cribbed from Ariosto. Complicating the question of Milton's relation to the epic tradition is that of Milton's relation to biblical narrative itself. How free could Milton be to "covenant" with the reader given the preexisting authoritative narrative of Scripture? If we recall John Preston's understanding of biblical metaphor as a promissory or conditional contract that enjoins a labor of interpretation on the faithful reader, we can see *Paradise Lost* as exemplifying Milton's covenant with God in the form of an equitable activity of interpretation. In contrast to Hobbes's strictures about scriptural interpretation—his insistence that the sovereign is the only authoritative interpreter—Milton's goal is to create revolutionary readers, readers who will understand their covenant with God as a matter of interpretation.

At the same time, *Paradise Lost* also explores the limits of contract and consent. At the center of Milton's analysis of obligation in *Paradise Lost* is the marriage contract, with its widely accepted metaphorical connotations of the theological covenant and the political contract. For Milton's royalist contemporaries, as we have seen, the marriage contract was a compelling analogy for the hierarchical but affectionate relationship of subject and sovereign; for his puritan allies, marriage figured the theological covenant between Christ and the believer. In *Paradise Lost*, Milton subjects these analogies to scrutiny. Like Hobbes, Parker, and Cavendish in their different ways, Milton sees that the logic of the political contract dictates greater freedom for women in the civil contract of marriage.[3] Like Parker, he draws back from the radical conclusions of his own voluntarism and, in doing so, makes the affective bond of marriage a locus of determinism as well as free will. Marriage is a metaphor for the theological covenant but not in the way that covenant theologians intended. Instead, for Milton, both marriage and the divine covenant raise the question of how free the individual really is to contract for himself. The tension between voluntarism and determinism in the theological covenant is not so much the "other" of the marriage contract or the political contract as a vivid illustration of the problems that afflict all attempts to imagine a radically decontextualized subject who enters into a state of obligation from one of absolute freedom. By foregrounding coercion as well as consent, by focusing on the role of love and fear in Adam and Eve's differing accounts of their union and fall, Milton invites us to reflect on what motivates individuals to bind themselves to another and what legitimates their breach of contract. In the process he does not simply offer an Arminian defense of free will and dissent; he also dramatizes the limits of the contracting subject and of his own theodicy. These paradoxes are at the center of Milton's earlier analysis of the psychology of the contracting subject, *The Doctrine and Discipline of Divorce*.

RESISTLESS LOVE AND HATE

The relevance of *The Doctrine and Discipline of Divorce* to a discussion of political obligation is signaled by Milton himself in the preface to the second edition: "He who marries, intends as little to conspire his own ruine, as he that swears Allegiance: and as a whole people is in proportion to an ill Government, so is one man to an ill mariage. If they against any authority, Covnant, or Statute, may by the soveraign edict of charity, save not only their lives, but honest liberties from unworthy bondage, as well may he against any private Covnant, which hee never enter'd to his mischief, redeem himself from unsupportable disturbances to honest peace and just contentment" (229). This ostentatious proportional metaphor announces *The Doctrine* as one of Milton's earliest attempts to imagine the subject of contract—the male subject of the marriage contract who is also, for Milton, a party to the heavenly contract and the political contract.

The revolutionary arguments of *The Doctrine* had their roots in the political and military conflict of 1642–43.[4] Milton drew, in particular, on the debates between royalists and parliamentarians about religious tolerance, "defensive arms," and the nature of supremacy, which we explored in chapter 4. As we saw, while Charles and his supporters were appealing to positive law in defense of royal supremacy, parliamentarians such as Henry Parker were arguing that the postlapsarian natural law of self-preservation and *salus populi* justified resistance. The increasingly radical uses to which parliamentary pamphleteers were putting arguments about natural law and self-preservation, conscience and equity, directly influenced Milton's own conflation of natural law with the equitable interpretation of conscience in *The Doctrine*.[5]

These arguments had important consequences not only for Milton's conception of the marriage contract but also for his understanding of the political contract. In the passage just quoted from the preface to the second edition, Milton applied the argument about the natural law of self-preservation (fortified by the theological allusion to "charity") to the domestic institution of marriage. The possibility of divorce was a condition of what we might call spiritual self-preservation. But, as is clear from the introduction to *The Doctrine* and even clearer by the time we reach *Tetrachordon*, Milton intended the argument to work in the other direction as well. In discussing marriage, Milton aimed to free his readers—including Parliament, to whom *The Doctrine* is addressed—from voluntary servitude to "Custome," a servitude that was manifest not only in a literal understanding of Christ's prohibition but also of all other obligations.[6] These newly liberated, equitable readers were the ideal subjects of the political contract—citizens who would voluntarily subject themselves on the basis of their own reason.

At the same time, Milton's application of parliamentary arguments to companionate marriage did not leave those arguments unchanged. Milton did not simply equate conscience and equity, but also equity and the passions. In Milton's analysis, the husband's affective disposition was the psychological equivalent of the theological and hermeneutical principle of charity, which dictated the equitable interpretation of the law. The husband's affection, his "resistles . . . love or hate," was the motive for and legitimation of marriage or divorce (347). In contrast to contemporary manuals of domestical duties, which stressed that a husband "should" love his wife, Milton made passion itself a source of obligation rather than having obligation dictate passion. In doing so, Milton sought to provide a rational account of the marriage contract, which "passion not mistrusting may not seek to displace."[7] Like Hobbes, in short, he gave new prominence to the role of the passions in motivating the subject of the contract.

Milton's argument about the passions is played out as a drama of interpretation, specifically the interpretation of Christ's prohibition of divorce. If the husband does not love his wife, he is allowed—according to a charitable interpretation of Christ's prohibition—to divorce her. Milton thus makes the husband's affective disposition the psychological equivalent of the theological and hermeneutical principle of charity, which dictates the equitable interpretation of the law. In so doing, he complicates the distinction between Old Testament law and New Testament spirit by conflating the law with its own conscientious, equitable interpretation, which is itself based on the passions, "the resistles sway in love or hate" (347).

This argument about the passions as both the object of law and the source of equity is modeled on the hermeneutical dilemmas Milton confronted regarding natural law and Scripture. In *The Doctrine* Milton illustrates the paradox of all appeals to natural law or what he calls blameless nature—for if nature were truly a self-sufficient or self-evident criterion of judgment or action, there would be no need to discuss it, let alone instruct one's readers about it. But natural law is obscure and needs to be construed. Hence the necessary intervention of what we might call the "filial" labor of interpretation, which Milton distinguishes from the servile yoke of literalism (see, e.g., 242, 342).

Accordingly, Milton emphasizes the labor of gathering scriptural passages—the difficulty of interpreting Christ's words—because the self-evident meaning of his pronouncements is against divorce. But, as in his glosses on natural law, Milton stresses that this interpretive labor is itself a function of equity or the hermeneutical principle of charity. In contrast to the effortful marriage of two unsuited partners, the labor of interpretation is a labor of love. *The Doctrine* is thus structured as a chiasmus, according to which laborious married love is a form of enslavement, whereas interpretive labor is a form of charity. In the first case, labor signals a kind of coercion: "grind[ing] in the mill" (258); in the second case, labor is the means by which the law is assimilated to one's own disposition.[8]

In illustrating a tension between the labor of interpretation and the "resistless sway" of one's passions, between ethical (or interpretive) voluntarism and psychological determinism, *The Doctrine* captures and attempts to recast the dilemmas of the new language of contract. On the one hand, seventeenth-century contract—whether a marriage contract or a political contract—presupposed a rational act of consent. In equating charity with equitable interpretation, Milton stressed the rational dimension of contract and the agency of the intepreter. On the other hand, a theory of contractual obligation needs to explain not only that it is rational to contract but also why we might be moved to do so. In psychologizing charity, Milton both answered the question of motive and introduced an element of psychological determinism that was in tension with his emphasis on free will. In *The Doctrine* the passions are not just a motive for obligation but an obstacle as well—as in the case of the husband such as John Milton who cannot find it in his heart to love his wife. This linking of passion and equity provided a new argument for domestic and political divorce; at the same time, it announced the limits of the contracting subject, limits Milton would explore more powerfully in *Paradise Lost*. Before turning to that text, we need to look more closely at the two steps of Milton's argument, the equation of conscience with equity, and the link between equitable interpretation and the passions.

Milton argues that the interpretation of the marriage contract (and thus of Christ's prohibition of divorce) depends on a prior understanding of God's intention. This intention has been revealed in the covenant of grace, that is, in God's contract with man. Drawing on the natural law theories of Grotius, Selden, and Parker; the Presbyterian defenders of religious toleration in the early 1640s; and the covenant theology of Perkins and Ames, Milton proposes his own unorthodox, rationalist interpretation of the covenant of grace.[9] In this covenant, according to Milton, God binds himself to the natural law of reason: "The hidden wayes of his providence we adore & search not; but the law is his reve[a]lled wil, his complete, his evident, and certain will; herein he appears to us as it were in human shape, enters into cov'nant with us, swears to keep it, *binds himself* like a just lawgiver to his own prescriptions, gives himself to be understood by men, judges and is judg'd, measures and is commensurat to right reason" (292). Milton reiterates this point a few pages later when he insists, with Perkins and other covenant theologians, that "God is no covnant breaker, he cannot doe this" (297). What God cannot do is violate the law of nature and the principle of equity: "God . . . hath plain anough reveal'd himself, and requires the observance therof not otherwise then to the law of nature and of equity imprinted in us seems correspondent" (297).[10]

It's worth pausing here to reiterate that Milton has essentially conflated the covenant of grace and the rule of charity with natural law of reason and the principle of equity. God binds himself to abide by the law of reason, which authorizes our equitable interpretation; that is, he binds himself to allow us to to interpret for ourselves.[11] Milton then applies the rule of equitable or charitable interpretation to Christ's own prohibition against divorce. In contrast to the "servile literalism" that wrongly insists that the contract of marriage is irrevocable, Christian liberty and the rule of charity license metaphorical interpretation of the prohibition (242, 342). In this way, the equitable principle of charity makes the possibility of *breaking* one's contract the true measure of *consent*: "And it is a lesse breach of wedlock to part with a wise and quiet consent betimes, then still to soile and profane that mystery of joy and union" (258).

Milton's equation of the new covenant of charitable interpretation with equity and natural law is even more apparent in his description of conscience. Conscience is a function of the "Law not onely writt'n by *Moses*, but character'd in us by nature . . . which Law is to force nothing against the faultles proprieties of nature" (237). Against the "letter-bound servility of the Canon Doctors" (342), conscience takes into account the intention of the lawgiver as well as the circumstances of the particular case. This equation of the law with its equitable interpretation means that "every command giv'n with a reason, binds our obedience no otherwise then that reason holds" (308). Obedience that runs counter to reason would be "mis-obedience" (309); so the standard of conformity to the law is not the law but reason. Like the subject of the heavenly contract, the male subject of the marriage contract and, by implication, the political contract binds himself through an equitable activity of interpretation and consent. In the divinely authored law of nature, law and nature are reconciled in a way that seems almost not to require any sacrifice, even positively to prohibit it.

Here we come to the second axis of Milton's argument—the appeal to human nature, in particular, to the affections. For, in the course of his remarks about charitable interpretation, conscience itself begins to look very different from the usual portrayals of it in Protestant theological treatises. Whereas in Perkins's *Discourse of Conscience*, conscience functions as a surveyor, accountant, or judge of the erring individual, in *The Doctrine* conscience is much less a judge of sin than an agent of satisfaction.[12] Moses's law, Milton continues, is not only "full of moral equity" but also "full of due consideration towards nature, that cannot be resisted" (306). Because human nature is both irresistible and "blameless" (279, 355), the function of conscience is not to constrain but to enable our natural desires (310). Milton draws the obvious conclusion about bad marriages:

> [T]here is no Christian duty that is not to be season'd and set off with cherfulness; which in a thousand outward and intermitting crosses may yet be done well, as in this vale of teares, but in such a bosom affliction as [a bad marriage], crushing the very foundations of his inmost nature, when he shall be forc't to love against a possibility, and to use dissimulation against his soul in the perpetuall and ceaseles duties of a husband, doubtles his whole duty of serving God must needs be blurr'd and tainted with a sad unpreparednesse and dejection of spirit, wherein God has no delight. Who sees not therefor how much more Christianly it would be to break by divorce that which is more brok'n by undue and forcible keeping. (259)

In this passage Milton articulates a traditional Christian view of patient suffering only to reject it. In matters of love, there can be no "duty," for duty implies putting up with "*outward* and intermitting crosses" whereas a bad marriage is "a bosom affliction" (emphasis added). In other words, love is both a passion over which we have no control—we cannot "be forc't to love against a possibility"—and part of our "inmost nature." We are a long way here from assuming, as does Perkins, that husbands have "a duty to love" and that they need to be instructed in it. Instead of prescribing our duty, Milton condemns canon law for subjecting

> that ancient and naturally domestick prerogative ["which God from the beginning had entrusted to the husband"] to an external & unbefitting judicature. For . . . differences in divorce about dowries, jointures, and the like, besides the punishing of adultery, ought not to passe without referring, if need be, to the Magistrate. . . . (344)

> But to interpose a jurisdictive power upon the inward and irremediable disposition of man, to command love and *sympathy*, to forbid dislike against the guiltles instinct of nature, is not within the province of any law to reach. (346)

These passages are important for understanding the link between passion and consent in *The Doctrine*: here we see Milton implicitly reject the notion of property in one's person in favor of a conception of the self still more inward.[13] Disputes about dowries, jointures, and other such transactions may be adjudicated by the magistrate, but love or hate are part one's disposition. Not alienable property but the irremediable and resistless passion is the source of—and model for—the husband's rights, including the right not only of divorce but of political resistance to positive law.

As in his earlier remarks about equitable interpretation, the result of this argument about the passions is to identify nature and law, the compulsion of the natural order and rational consent—"for that Law may bandy with nature, and traverse her sage motions, was an error in *Callicles* the Rhetorician, whom *Socrates* from high principles confutes in *Plato's Gorgias*. If therfore divorce may be so natural, and that law and nature are not to goe contrary, then to forbid divorce compulsively, is not only against nature, but against law" (346). Just as covenant theologians distinguished between servile and filial fear, so Milton invokes the possibility of illegitimate compulsion ("to forbid divorce compulsively") to define by contrast the legitimate compulsion of the husband's love. True freedom is to act in accordance with one's natural passions, to be compelled by them. The effect of Milton's argument up to this point is thus to identify divine law with equity, and equity with the affective disposition of the contracting subject.

This alliance of the hermeneutical and affective is dramatized in Milton's metaphorical play with marriage. Milton assumes the traditional view of the marriage covenant as a metaphor for the covenant of grace. He then argues that the covenant of grace governs our interpretation of likeness and liking in marriage. To be created in the image and likeness of God is to be capable of rational consent. Uncoerced love or "liking" is an aspect of this divine likeness, whereas coercion is antithetical to our true nature, a sign, as it were, of unlikeness.

> Mariage is a covnant the very beeing whereof consists, not in a forc't cohabitation, and counterfeit performance of duties, but in unfained love and peace. And of matrimoniall love no doubt but that was chiefly meant, which by the ancient Sages was thus parabl'd, That Love, if he be not twin-born, yet hath a brother wondrous like him, call'd *Anteros*: whom while he seeks all about, his chance is to meet with many fals and faining Desires that wander singly up and down in his likenes. (254–55)

This meditation on the "likeness" of partners to a marriage contract leads to a proliferation of metaphors for unlikeness in which the central image is one of force: "needless thraldome" "this labyrinth of servitude," "a minde unreasonably yoakt," a "mis-yoaking marriage" that "links violently together." And most strikingly: "[I]nstead of being one flesh, [a mismatched husband and wife] will be rather two carkasses chain'd unnaturally together; or, as it may happen, a living soule bound to a dead corps."[14] In these phrases, one is tempted to hear an anticipation of Samuel Johnson's disparaging remark about metaphysical poetry—"the unnatural yoking of violent images together"—and rightly so. For Milton's meditation bears as much on the contract of metaphor as it does the marriage contract. These metaphors—which testify to the human capacity to create likenesses (and to convey unlikeness)—are as much a sign of our likeness to God as the covenant of marriage is an image of the divine covenant. As in manuals of covenant theology, our hermeneutical disposition is a sign of our spiritual disposition—hence Milton's repeated attacks on the "letter-bound servility of the Canon Doctors, supposing mariage to be a Sacrament," and thus making "a fair shew [out of] the fleshly observance of matrimony" (342).

But in dramatizing the connections between the contract of metaphor and the contract of marriage, this mini-narrative also insinuates the problem of sexual deception and coercion. In Milton's allegory, Love, "partly out of the simplicity, and credulity which is native to him, often deceiv'd, imbraces and consorts him with these obvious and suborned striplings," which he wrongly believes to be "his Mothers own Sons" (255). Love is misled, that is, by the false perception of likeness and tricked into "bondage" (256). Although the allegory would have us believe this bondage is the result of fraud, it also suggests (as allegory tends to do) that the false and feigning desires we encounter are not simply others' but, more important, our own. The allegory thus dramatizes the problem of voluntary servitude, the negative counterpart of our voluntary subjection to the resistless sway of good passions.

Milton hints here at two problems for the contracting subject. The first problem, which he will explore more fully in *Paradise Lost*, is that the subject of contract is not—cannot be—a creature of pure reason but, by the same token, this subject cannot be a creature of pure volition either. There are limits to what we can will, limits of our natural dispositions and passions. These limits are our context, they provide our motivation, and they cannot be fully controlled. The second problem (a version of the first) is that nature might very well be illegitimately compelled, and that this coercion may be internal as well as external. Moreover, although this coercion may take the form of misguided erotic passion, it does not always do so. Despite arguing for "the resistles sway in love," Milton does not take self-love for granted. Instead, he warns the reader against the "self-cruelty"—what Nietzsche would later call asceticism—that results from the misapplication of conscience or the misunderstanding of Scripture.[15] Although the husband cannot be coerced to love, he might coerce himself to remain within a loveless marriage. This in turn would amount to self-cruelty, self-hatred, or what we might call the coercion of despair. These are compelling passions but not ones to which we rationally consent.

In attempting to distinguish between legitimate and illegitimate compulsion, Milton could be said to reencounter—even as he tries to resolve—the antinomy between nature and law within the realm of the passions. Passion is the locus of consent but also of coercion, and not simply the beneficent coercion of self-love but also the coercion of self-hatred. Hence the necessity of distinguishing between two antithetical affective states—resistless love and self-cruelty—by aligning the first with nature and second with law, now construed as legalism and literalism. It is not the case, Milton argues, that conscience must always be bad conscience, although the legacy of Catholicism and of Calvinism—which Milton identifies with the "tyranny of usurpt opinions"—suggests as much (343). Instead, the discipline of conscience should be productive rather than coercive or restrictive, a matter of passion rather than legislation, love rather than the law. The problem is that this "should" reintroduces an element of obligation (the paradoxical obligation to be true to one's nature) that Milton's equitable interpretation of Scripture was designed to avoid.

This destablization of Milton's argument occurs as well when we look closely at the gender dimension of *The Doctrine*, for Milton famously sees self-cruelty as a trap specifically for the husband. Although he differs from contemporary manuals of "domesticall duties" in describing love exclusively in terms of rights rather than obligation, he follows Perkins and others in attempting to make the freedom of interpretation (which love licenses) specifically male. In other words, the standard of equitable interpretation is itself inequitably applied since, while the legitimate reason for divorce—"fornication"—is interpreted charitably to mean disobedience, disobedience is then ascribed inequitably to the wife alone (335–36). In the context of this masculinist hermeneutic, the wife becomes a dangerous supplement, at once necessary and superfluous, superfluous but still threatening to the status quo.[16]

This superfluity is particularly obvious when Milton articulates the hermeneutic "axiom" of the text—that no law "should bind against a prime and principall scope of its own institution."[17] As we see in the following passage, the wife is first conspicuously absent from the discussion of covenant and then conspicuously subordinate:

> For all sense and equity reclaimes that any Law or Cov'nant how solemn or strait soever, either between God and man or man and man, though of Gods joyning, should bind against a prime and principall scope of its own institution, and of both or either party cov'nanting: neither can it be of force to ingage a blameless creature to his own perpetuall sorrow, mistak'n for his expected solace, without suffering charity to step in and doe a confest good work of parting those whom nothing holds together, but this of Gods joyning, falsly suppos'd against the expresse end of his own ordinance. And what his chiefe end was of creating woman to be joynd with man, his own instituting words declare, and are infallible to informe us what is mariage and what is no mariage; unlesse we can think them set there to no purpose: *It is not good*, saith he, *that man should be alone; I will make a help meet for him.* (245–46)

Milton's failure explicitly to name "man and wife" in the first sentence describing the parties to a covenant is striking; it suggests that the marriage covenant is for Milton essentially a covenant between "man and God" or even (to borrow Carole Pateman's argument) a covenant between men.[18] This is not surprising when we remember that the model of covenant Milton invokes in the preface to the second edition *is* a covenant between men: the political covenant of male citizens. Hence Milton's focus on the specifically political consequences of enforced marriage: "[I]f natures resistles sway in love or hate be once compell'd, it grows careless of it self, vitious, useles to friend, *unserviceable and spiritles to the Common-wealth*" (347, emphasis added).

The seventeenth-century natural rights theorist Samuel Pufendorf noticed the homoerotic tendency of Milton's argument when he asked rhetorically, "And surely if a happy association had been the primary purpose of God, what need would there have been of different sexes?"[19] Different sexes were divinely created for the purpose of procreation; if companionship is what Milton wants, he should associate with other men. In response to Pufendorf, we can say that Milton's tendency to eclipse the other sex—as in the myth of Eros and Anteros—is part of an effort to internalize contract, in the sense of making it a contract with oneself and thus a symbol of ethical and political self-determination rather than a matter of negotiation with or dependence upon another.[20] In contrast to manuals of domestic duties that analyze the contractual and affective relationship of husband and wife, Milton is more concerned with the contractual and affective relationship to himself. As I have argued, this is a relationship not only between the husband's conscience and the moral law but also between his conscience, conceived of as a principle of interpretation, and his passions. Together, these two relations articulate a new conception of right—both personal and political—that moves beyond traditional conceptions of natural law. The male subject of the marriage contract is ideally for Milton the autonomous political subject who

> discovers the law in the depths of [his] own free identity, rather than in some oppressive external power. The liberated subject is the one who has appropriated the law as the very principle of [his] own autonomy, broken the forbidding tablets of stone on which that law was originally inscribed in order to rewrite it on the heart of flesh. [For this subject] to consent to the law is thus to consent to one's own inward being.[21]

And yet, what Milton discovers in his own inward being—or what Milton's prose discovers—is not simply the autonomous subject but a subject who is at once voluntary and involuntary, for whom consent to contract is not always so readily distinguished from voluntary servitude to one's passions. This dilemma lies at the heart of *Paradise Lost*—Milton's fullest anatomy of obligation, his most extended treatment of the subject of the marriage contract, the theological contract, and the political contract.

Paradise Lost and the Bond of Nature

Even more than in *The Doctrine*, the subject of contract in *Paradise Lost* is a passionate, embodied subject rather than the ascetic subject of Weberian Protestantism or Nietzschean ressentiment. The exchanges that occur between Adam and Eve in prelapsarian Eden are Milton's attempt to imagine a subject motivated by passion as much as by reason, but who is yet able to distinguish between good and bad passions, voluntary subjection and voluntary servitude. In a series of set pieces, Adam, Eve,

Raphael, and Satan debate the conditions of legitimate subjection, the correct ratio of coercion and consent, in relation to God and to each other. In taking up the question of obedience to God, they also engage the arguments about self-preservation, self-aggrandizement, servile fear and filial fear, that were central to the midcentury pamphlet wars and political theories of contractual obligation.

As in *The Doctrine*, the problem of the contracting subject is played out both in the realm of the affections and in the realm of interpretation. In *Paradise Lost* the order of creation—the effect of God's creative Word—is the original contract. This contract is at once unilateral and mutual. It is unilateral in the sense that it is only within this divinely authored linguistic community, this fellowship of the Word, that it is possible to reason, to speak, and thus to be a contracting subject.[22] It is mutual, in the sense that the believer is invited to accept the divine Word. The prohibition against eating from the Tree of Knowledge makes this contractual dimension of the Word clear.[23] As in *Christian Doctrine*, the prohibition is God's promise—his "pledge" or "sign"—to Adam and Eve that they are rational and moral creatures and it exacts a promise from them to the same effect. Without this prohibition, there would be no such thing as an occasion for a distinctively human morality, a distinctively human exercise of the rational will. The prohibition enables Adam and Eve to realize (both to understand and to enact) their creation "in the image and likeness" of God. For this reason every temptation to disobedience or voluntary servitude in *Paradise Lost* is accompanied by a series of questions about what constitutes not only the right passions but also true likeness.[24] In the exchanges between Adam and Eve, and in the narrative as a whole, Milton the poet imitates the equitable judgment of Perkins's God who deferred "the full execution" of Adam and Eve's punishment after the fall.[25] Mimesis and narrative are examples of human artifice and human rationality. They are vehicles of making sense of the heavenly contract as an equitable contract, and of man's judgment as an equitable judgment.[26] For these reasons, the question of obligation is metatextual as well textual, formal as well as thematic, a matter of the poet's covenant with his reader as well as his covenant with God.

In Eve's narrative of coming to self-consciousness and her submission to Adam, Milton gives us one version of the contracting subject. This narrative has been read as an emblematic though unwitting account of the the sexual contract that is the precondition of the political contract between men. I want to suggest, in contrast, that this drama of duress is deliberate on Milton's part and that it is part of his self-conscious exploration of the relation of coercion and consent, passion and subjection, in contractual obligation. In Eve's case, self-love does not lead to contract without the supplement of a coercive power, one that forcefully instructs Eve in the right perception of likeness.

Eve describes how, upon waking, she found herself near a

> Smooth Lake, that to me seem'd another Sky.
> As I bent down to look, just opposite,
> A Shape within the wat'ry gleam appear'd
> Bending to look on me, I started back,
> It started back, but pleas'd I soon return'd,
> Pleas'd it return'd as soon with answering looks
> Of sympathy and love; there I had fixt
> Mine eyes till now, and pin'd with vain desire,
> Had not a voice thus warn'd me, What thou seest,
> What there thou seest fair Creature is thyself,
> With thee it came and goes: but follow me,
> And I will bring thee where no shadow stays
> Thy coming, and thy soft embraces, hee
> Whose image thou art, him thou shalt enjoy
> Inseparably thine, to him shalt bear
> Multitudes like thyself, and thence be call'd
> Mother of human Race: what could I do,
> But follow straight, invisibly thus led?
> Till I espi'd thee, fair indeed and tall,
> Under a Platan, yet methought less fair,
> Less winning soft, less amiably mild,
> Than that smooth wat'ry image; back I turn'd,
> Thou following cri'd'st aloud, Return fair *Eve*,
> Whom fli'st thou? whom thou fli'st, of him thou art,
> His flesh, his bone; to give thee being I lent
> Out of my side to thee, nearest my heart
> Substantial Life, to have thee by my side
> Henceforth an individual solace dear;
> Part of my Soul I seek thee, and thee claim
> My other half: with that thy gentle hand
> Seiz'd mine, I yielded, and from that time see
> How beauty is excell'd by manly grace
> And wisdom, which alone is truly fair.
>
> (4.459–91)

This narrative involves two moments of pedagogical intervention, two related lessons regarding liking and likeness, self-love and right judgment. In the first lesson, Eve must be taught how to perceive likeness and difference. To the "unexperienc't" Eve, a lake seems just like "another Sky," while her own reflected image seems completely different, another person.

The perception of true likeness, it seems, is not a natural faculty; it re-quires, instead, the intervention of language, specifically, instruction by a warning "voice." In the second lesson, Eve fails naturally to perceive her likeness to Adam; as a result, she fails to "like" him as much as she loves herself. It is only after Adam "seizes" her hand that she yields; and only then does she come to "see," in the sense of understand, the superiority of "manly grace / And wisdom." Here too the correct perception of like-ness is not natural but rather a function of the divine fiat by which God created man in his "image and likeness." However, in this second instance it is not language but rather physical force that makes Eve "see" that her likeness to Adam dictates her voluntary subjection.[27]

Milton, of course, did not need to dramatize this moment of reluctance and "gentle" coercion. The fact that he chose to do so suggests he under-stood the remarks in some contemporary manuals of casuistry about the resentment women feel toward the "natural" hierarchy of husband and wife. William Gouge, the author of *Domesticall Duties* (1622), dismissed this resentment by attributing it to the widespread, self-aggrandizing delu-sion that wives feel equally capable of rule.[28] Eve's recalcitrance, however, is not a function of resentment or self-aggrandizement but of her naive self-love and her resulting misrecognition of Adam. Moreover, Milton does not simply mention this moment in passing but gives it center stage. Eve's turning away from Adam is deliberately presented as a moment in the general development of her consciousness and so is not limited to the question of domestic relations. Embedded in this drama of likeness and difference, the moment of coercion she describes functions like Odysseus's scar, the contingent sign of identity that enables Odysseus—or Adam—to be recognized. It tears at the fabric of verisimilitude, revealing that likeness (like marriage) is not a fact of nature but a product of the divine covenant and, in Eve's particular case, as much a result of coercion, how-ever gentle, as of consent.

This reading of the scene in terms of likeness or mimesis is reinforced if we recall the cautions against metaphor in early modern rhetoric text-books where, in the words of Dudley Fenner, the tropological "change of signification must bee *shamefest*, and as it were *maydenly*, that it may seeme rather to be led by the hand to another signification, then to be driven by force unto the same." Whereas Fenner distinguished between being led and being forced, Milton deliberately blurs this boundary: Eve dramatizes the unstable ratio of coercion and consent, being led and being forced, in the metaphorical perception of likeness and in her recognition of Adam. The scene suggests that, in some cases, recognition is not so much a cause as an effect of forceful subordination—of Eve to Adam, of both to the divine order of mimesis.[29]

The scene is not just Milton's way of telling us that divine order is made rather than found, that it is artificial rather than natural. Rather, Milton's representation of the intervention of force in the drama of recognition calls into question the meaning of consent in the marriage contract and, by extension, in the theological covenant and the political contract as well. On one level, Milton takes the gender asymmetry of the marriage contract as something that needs to be explained (and gently enforced), given the equality of Adam and Eve in the sight of God. Here, the foregrounding of coercion suggests the degree to which Milton's political convictions may have shaped his conception of Edenic marriage. From a republican point of view, only coercion could explain how one individual could agree to "see" another as both "like" herself and absolutely superior. On another level, the uneasy coexistence of coercion and consent in Eve's case stands for the antinomies of theological covenant and political contract, in which the subject voluntarily consents to divine law or the law of reason. In this case, the inequitable relation of the sexes in marriage would figure the problematic subject of contract in other realms as well.[30]

This inequitable relation is dramatized in Adam's own distinctive experience of the artifice of likeness. In contrast to Eve, who has to learn how to perceive likeness, Adam gets to experience the poetic activity of creating likeness out of his own desires. In his experience, Eve is a product of his fancy—of both his imagination and his desire. It is fitting, then, that in his first encounter with Eve, he does not consent to external force but to the force of his own passions. As a result, whereas Eve illustrates forcible subjection, Adam dramatizes the problem of voluntary servitude.

In book 8 of *Paradise Lost*, Adam engages God in conversation, arguing from a deeply felt lack of companionship for the creation of an equal partner. Although God, being God, has planned everything before the beginning of time, Adam experiences the creation of Eve as motivated by his desire and his reasoning about it with God:

> But Man by number is to manifest
> His single imperfection, and beget
> Like of his like, his Image multipli'd,
> In unity defective, which requires
> Collateral love, and dearest amity.
>
> (8.422–26)

In contrast to Hobbes but like the cavalier poets Milton disliked, here the passion to be reckoned upon is love, specifically desire as a sense of lack. In the colloquy between God and Adam, we see that the reconciliation of God's foreknowledge ("Thus far to try thee, *Adam*, I was pleas'd" [8.437]) and Adam's free will ("Thus I embold'n'd spake, and freedom us'd" [8.434]) is the theological equivalent of the reconciliation of the law and desire, of the preordained order of mimesis and individual consent.

Immediately after this, however, Adam voices concern about his own incompleteness, his desire for Eve, which he now sees as a form of coercion and subordination:

> here passion first I felt,
> Commotion strange, in all enjoyments else
> Superior and unmov'd, here only weak
> Against the charm of Beauty's powerful glance.
> Or Nature fail'd in mee, and left some part
> Not proof enough such Object to sustain,
> Or from my side subducting, took perhaps
> More than enough; at least on her bestow'd
> Too much of Ornament, in outward show
> Elaborate, of inward less exact.
> For well I understand in the prime end
> Of Nature her th' inferior, in the mind
> And inward Faculties, which most excel,
> In outward also her resembling less
> His Image who made both, and less expressing
> The character of that Dominion giv'n
> O'er other Creatures; yet when I approach
> Her loveliness, so absolute she seems
> And in herself complete, so well to know
> Her own, that what she wills to do or say,
> Seems wisest, virtuousest, discreetest, best;
> All higher knowledge in her presence falls
> Degraded, Wisdom in discourse with her
> Loses discount'nanc't, and like folly shows.
>
> (8.530–53)

Adam experiences the force of passion as a personal deficiency: desire is experienced as a lack. In Adam's scarcity economy of desire, moreover, what Adam has lost, Eve has gained. This disproportion is rendered as a crisis in the order of mimesis: according to Adam, Eve's "outward show" does not correspond to her "inward"; more important, both inwardly and outwardly Eve resembles God's "Image" less than does Adam. And yet, she appears to be "wisest, virtuousest, discreetest, best."

The problem, in short, is one of reading likeness. Adam has been told he is supposed to construe "likeness" in marriage as an argument for his dominion over Eve, likeness to God as an argument for his subjection. In marriage, Adam knows he is the "superior"; in his relation to God, the "inferior." Yet the fancy—the desire and imagination—that is one sign of his specifically human capacities induces voluntary servitude to Eve, and voluntary insubordination to God. This potential insubordination prompts Raphael to warn Adam, "weigh with her thyself; / Then value: Oft-times nothing profits more / Than self-esteem" (8.570–72).[31]

In the ensuing exchange with Raphael, however, this simplistic, quantitative notion of self-esteem and likeness to God is quickly abandoned.[32] When Raphael rebukes Adam for confusing love and "subjection" (8.570), Adam responds by revising his account of his feelings for Eve. He does not experience them, he now claims, as external coercion but as internal self-determination. The law is now experienced as the law of the heart.

> Neither her out-side form'd so fair, nor aught
> In procreation common to all kinds
> (Though higher of the genial Bed by far,
> And with mysterious reverence I deem)
> So much delights me, as those graceful acts,
> Those thousand decencies that daily flow
> From all her words and actions, mixt with Love
> And sweet compliance, which declare unfeign'd
> Union of Mind, or in us both one Soul;
> Harmony to behold in wedded pair
> More grateful than harmonious sound to the ear.
> Yet these subject not; I to thee disclose
> What inward thence I feel, not therefore foil'd,
> Who meet with various objects, from the sense
> Variously representing; yet still free
> Approve the best, and follow what I approve.
>
> (596–611)

In Adam's vacillating account of his relation to Eve in these two speeches, Milton psychologizes the antinomies of contract. If in the first speech we see the tie between the passions and voluntary servitude, in the second we see the link between reason and voluntary subjection or following what one approves. These two speeches offer two different accounts of mimesis as well. In the first, Adam assumes a Platonic hierarchy of imitation, and he dramatizes in his own response to Eve Plato's fears of the erotic effects of mimesis. As "all higher knowledge in her presence falls / Degraded," Adam becomes the effeminized political subject criticized in Plato's *Republic*, the subject who has been erotically unmanned by mimesis. In the second, Adam displays a more positive, Aristotelian appreciation of the realm of appearances and an Aristotelian sense of mimesis as an occasion for equitable judgment. This second speech suggests that, as Adam's sense of mimesis and of the realm of sensuous appearances becomes more complicated, so his sensual love for Eve becomes more discriminating: sense impressions "subject not"; Adam's passion for Eve is perfectly compatible with freedom of rational judgment. This second speech represents, I think, Milton's highest hopes for his own narrative as a contract of mimesis to which we can voluntarily consent and which provokes equitable judgment on the part of the reader. But it is obviously only half of the story, half of our story, and Milton in *Paradise Lost* has undertaken to explain why.

PITY OR FEAR OF VIOLENT DEATH

I now want to turn to two later moments in *Paradise Lost* that play out the implications of Eve's and Adam's contrasting accounts of passion and obligation, coercion and consent. The first is the separation colloquy, the second is Adam's consenting to fall with Eve. In the separation colloquy Milton engages Hobbesian arguments about self-love and self-aggrandizement as motives for disobedience, while in Adam's soliloquy Milton proposes a non-Hobbesian interpretation of self-love as the bond of imaginative sympathy—a bond that underwrites not only human society and the political contract but also the possibility of political resistance. These two scenes sketch the lineaments of the Miltonic subject of the political contract, who is motivated not by the fearful interest of self-preservation but by ambition or by empathy. In proposing an altogether different conception of the bond of nature from that of Hobbes, Milton adumbrates an alternative genealogy of the contracting subject.

By the opening of book 9 Adam and Eve have been instructed about God's prohibition regarding the Tree of Knowledge and the threatened punishment of death. They have been instructed, that is, about the implicit contract with God, according to which Eden is theirs in exchange for their obedience. Raphael has also warned them about the "foe" who "seeks to work . . . woe and shame / By sly assault" (9.255–56). So, from the outset, although the Garden of Eden is not the Hobbesian state of nature, and the fear of divine punishment is not the same as the Hobbesian fear of violent death, nevertheless Adam and Eve's fear of death is presented as a possible motive of obedience, a spur to fulfilling their obligations. What I want to suggest by looking closely at the separation colloquy is that this fear can be read in two opposed ways. Although from one theologically correct perspective the fear of God is the beginning of wisdom, from another Miltonic perspective fear amounts to a kind of Hobbesian coercion. Milton rejects this negative passion of fear. He seeks to locate consent not in what Isaiah Berlin called negative liberty—freedom from others, including their threats—but rather in the positive exercise of one's freedom and in what we might call the positive passions of ambition and love. And yet, as in *The Doctrine and Discipline of Divorce*, the passion of love in particular proves to be a constraint as well as a motive, or—to put it another way—love proves to be a motive because it is grounded in the specific constraints of being human.

In the course of elaborating her arguments for working in the Garden apart from Adam and in her later encounter with Satan, Eve illustrates the the problem of how to tell self-preservation from self-love or self-aggrandizement. In fact, Eve enacts within herself the mimetic frenzy of the Hobbesian state of nature. Initially, by her own account, she is motivated by both fear and vainglory: she is the Hobbesian individual who, in seeking to be better prepared against the vainglorious aggressor, becomes vainglorious herself. "How are we happy," she asks Adam, "still in fear of harm?" Immediately after this, however, she rejects her fear and opts for what she calls "honor": "then wherefore shunn'd or fear'd / By us? who rather double honor gain / From his surmise prov'd false, find peace within, / Favor from Heav'n, our witness from th' event" (9.331–34). Here and later in her remarks about the Tree of Knowledge, Eve thinks of faith as a matter of heroic deeds that need to be "approved" (9.1140), both proved to God and appreciated by him.[33]

The narrator makes it clear that Eve's seeking approval is the kind of self-aggrandizement Hobbes criticized in *Leviathan*. Out of her sense of lack, her desire for an audience, perhaps even her sense that cooperative gardening was not quite what she had in mind as "proof" of her faith, Eve generates her own vainglorious plot of adventure. Eve's Christian demonstration of her faith is touched by elements of emulation and display, rivalry and theatricality, rivaling above all an older, more exciting idiom of chivalric faith and honor. In her musings, this romance plot of adventure eventually encompasses Adam. Specifically, by offering Adam a "glorious trial of exceeding Love" (9.961), Eve tries to get Adam to imitate her own restless seeking after power.

In *The Revolution of the Saints* Michael Walzer remarked on the potentially subversive connection between a voluntary contract and married love: "The critique of the patriarchal conception of family unity thus made the romance of individuals possible. And for the moment, the dangers which romance posed for Puritan family discipline were hidden from the ministers by their idealized conception of love."[34] In this condensed formulation, Walzer also summed up the seventeenth-century dilemmas of the theological covenant and the political contract. If one goal of *Paradise Lost* is to produce the subject of the heavenly contract, the subject who rationally consents to subordination (Eve to Adam, Adam to God's ways), in its emphasis on voluntarism and on the passions *Paradise Lost* also licenses the "romance of the individual." Milton is not a critic of the patriarchal conception of family unity, but Eve may be: borrowing from the chivalric idiom of individual valor, she extends the logic of voluntary consent and romantic love in marriage to "the romance of the individual," substituting heroic deeds for the voluntary subjection of the marriage contract.

Here we begin to see the relevance of Milton's experimentation with genre for his meditation on religious and political obligation. As we've seen in earlier chapters, some early modern writers understood how the order of mimesis, both in art and in life, enforces and is enforced by a social contract, a set of conventions to which we tacitly consent. We've also see how, in the Renaissance, the genre of romance conjured up long-standing fears that mimesis might be predicated on purely contingent signs, errant desires, and paralogism or faulty reasoning. Romance, in short, figured the breach of the mimetic contract. But in the early modern period romance also had its defenders, including those Italian commentators who assimilated it to Aristotelian norms. Lodovico Castelvetro allowed that the erotic passion so characteristic of romance could serve as a motive for tragedy, and Giason Denores elaborated on the role of the passions and of human frailty more generally as occasions of hamartia or tragic error. The history of Renaissance epic also bears witness to the dialogue between Aristotle's *Poetics* and the genre of romance, and to the assimilation of the conventions of romance by epic. In its focus on errant passions as well as on adventure, epic romance gave narrative form to what Terence Cave has called a "plot of the psyche."[35]

Milton was famously critical of romance in *Eikonoklastes*, where he castigated Charles I for plagiarizing Pamela's prayer from Sidney's *Arcadia* and for stirring up the romance passion of pity. There Charles's theatrical, pathos-ridden recourse to "heathen fiction" was an index of his feigned religion. But in *Paradise Lost* romance has a more complicated function. In book 9, Milton does not simply condemn Eve's romance desire for a kind of martial glory as Hobbes would, but also asks us to take it seriously. As is well known, he does so by giving Eve his best lines from *Areopagitica* about the necessity of exercising one's will and of not withdrawing from the contest of virtue. Eve's arguments are reminiscent not only of the famous passage in which Milton says he "cannot praise a fugitive and closter'd vertue, unexercis'd & unbreath'd," but also of his description of reason as uncoerced choosing:

> Many there be that complain of divin Providence for suffering *Adam* to transgresse, foolish tongues! when God gave him reason, he gave him freedom to choose, for reason is but choosing; he had bin else a meer artificiall *Adam*, such an *Adam* as he is in the motions. We our selves esteem not that of obedience, or love, or gift, which is of force:

God therefore left him free, set before him a provoking object, even almost in his eyes; herein consisted his merit, herein the right of his reward, the praise of his abstinence. Wherefore did he creat passions within us, pleasures round about us, but that these rightly temper'd are the very ingredients of vertu?[36]

Obedience has to be freely given, otherwise it is "of force"; and Adam will be merely "artificiall," a puppet Adam—an Adam only "in the motions." He will be the sort of Adam, Milton suggests, that Hobbes had in mind when he set out to recreate man as a creature whose chief characteristic was fear of violent death. In contrast, Milton asks us to take Eve's desire for glory seriously by questioning the negative motive of fear. First we are told that Eve is not in fact motivated by fear, and then Satan argues that, even if she were, she shouldn't be.

In the context of book 9 and of *Paradise Lost* as a whole, Eve's initial argument about how fear for her self-preservation requires her to leave Adam is plainly flawed. First, the narrator has already told us that Eve's motive for separation is wounded pride; he describes her as thinking "Less attribúted to her Faith sincere" (9.320). Second, Eve has already told Adam that the real threat is not violent death but deception: "His violence thou fear'st not, being such, / As wee, not capable of death or pain, / Can either not receive, or can repel" (9.283–85). Eve thus anticipates Adam's later argument that the truly fearful coercion is not a matter of violence but of fraud, and that this violence is not external but rather a kind of self-deception. In the words of Adam's caution to Eve, they are "Secure from outward force; within [themselves] / The danger lies, yet lies within [their] power: / Against [their] will [they] can receive no harm" (9.348–50).

Along with Eve, the narrator, and Adam, Satan also rejects the argument from fear of violent death as a motive for Eve's sticking close to Adam. The difference is that, while Eve in the separation colloquy initially speaks of her fear of Satan, Satan argues that God is the source of fear. In doing so, he mixes idioms, improbably combining the legalistic language of duress with the romance language of heroic valor and, even more improbably, making the latter a false deduction from the former. Romance appears here as the paralogistic effect of contract. Satan describes God's prohibition regarding the Tree of Knowledge as a threat of violent death and then proceeds to argue that fear of death amounts to illegitimate duress: "[Y]our fear itself of Death removes the fear," he tells Eve (9.702). It is as though Satan were encouraging Eve by telling her: "You're right not to fall for that Hobbesian argument about fear of violent death or self-preservation as a motive for obedience, a motive for voluntary subjection to Adam and to God. Fear is coercive, and voluntary subjection prohibits coercion." According to Satan, in short, God is a Hobbesian tyrant. What I want to suggest now is that this is true in some ways for Milton, speaking through Eve, as well.

Satan's argument about illegitimate coercion in turn licenses a dangerously metaphorical understanding of the prohibition: "So ye shall die perhaps, by putting off / Human, to put on Gods, death to be wisht, / Though threat'n'd" (9.713–15). Satan's reasoning parodies Reformation biblical hermeneutics—the hermeneutics of *The Doctrine and Discipline of Divorce*—which reads the letter of the law spiritually or metaphorically. In Satan's case, however, such a metaphorical reading of God's prohibition is not the product of faith but of distrust: Satan implies that God's own prohibition is misleading, that the threat of death is a lie. This distrust undercuts the transformative power of metaphor. Satan's reading of God's command does not generate true likeness in the form of divinity, according to which Adam and Eve "shall be as Gods," but rather theatricality and equivocation: they will "put on Gods" (9.708, 714). It does not legitimate obedience but rather the disobedience that Satan craftily redescribes as heroism.

Satan is the true "stranger in the house," to borrow Tony Tanner's phrase, the adulterous other who shadows the marriage contract.[37] Hence his presence at Eve's ear, suggestively whispering to her fancy—her desire and imagination—as she sleeps. Both in that earlier scene and in his explicit temptation of Eve in book 9, Satan figures the link between "feigning" and the sexually disquieting dimension of mimesis—its appeal to the passions, its dependence on contingent signs, its tendency to equivocation, its facilitation of breach of contract. In this way Satan's argument about the romance of heroic deeds ironically foreshadows the very different romance plot in which an initial covenant or contract gives rise to "foul distrust and breach / Disloyal," to romance error and wandering (9.6–7).

Eve repeats Satan's arguments against the fear of death when she reasons about the Tree of Knowledge. In fact, one might say that Satan's achievement is to have persuaded Eve to think of the righteous fear of God as a form of servility or illegitimate coercion. Musing about God's commandment, Eve tells herself: "Such prohibitions bind not" (9.760). Here Eve is obviously trying to make sense of the way in which God's prohibition does bind and she responds to her own question with a kind of Hobbesian literalism: she is not physically constrained and so, she concludes, not actually bound. But, Eve reasons, although she is not physically bound, she *is* unfairly coerced by the threat of death: "if Death / Bind us with afterbands, what profits then / Our inward freedom?" (9.760–62).

For Eve this is a rhetorical question: according to her reasoning, freedom cannot coexist with the threat of force. But what does Milton intend for us to understand by Eve's question? I believe that Eve is not only right in a Hobbesian way that nothing physically "hinders" her from eating from the Tree of Knowledge (9.778). She is also right in a Miltonic way, that is, in terms of Milton's defense of free will: God, Raphael, and Adam all tell us the prohibition is not a tyrant's command but a "sign" of the moral law. The prohibition is in short the sign or seal of a contract to which Eve is supposed implicitly to have consented by virtue of her rationality. But, what kind of contract is it that one may never legitimately break? And what kind of contract is it whose breach is punished by death? These are the questions Eve ventriloquizes for Milton and his contemporaries.

Here we begin to see that Eve's arguments are not simply Satanic and therefore flawed. In addition to dramatizing the Hobbesian and Satanic problem of self-love and self-aggrandizement or the restless seeking after power, they articulate the insight that consent to the heavenly contract might very well feel like coercion or the Hobbesian fear of violent death. They articulate, that is, the felt antinomy between consent and coercion—or, at the very least, voluntarism and rationalism—in the heavenly contract.[38] If this interpretation is correct, there are two possible—and antithetical—conclusions one can draw. The first conclusion is that God is a Hobbesian sovereign, but also the only legitimate absolute sovereign in the universe—and the heavenly contract is the only contract that cannot lawfully be rescinded (this would be the theologically conservative reading of *Paradise Lost*). The second conclusion (it's difficult to say whether this is less or more disturbing than the first) is that God is not a Hobbesian sovereign, and so he must, by the logic of contract, divest himself of his absolute sovereignty. God himself implies as much when says to Christ in book 3 of *Paradise Lost*, "Thou thy regal Sceptre shalt lay by / For regal Sceptre then no more shall need, / God shall be All in All." (3.339–41).[39]

If Eve's deliberations raise the possibility that the moral law involves a kind of coercion, Adam's fall enacts a different drama of consent and coercion. In contrast to Eve's meditation on fear, Adam meditates on love. In contrast to her musings about the constraints of the divine prohibition, Adam debates about his physical and emotional bond with Eve. In these and other ways, Adam has internalized Eve's version of adventure and coercion; he has collapsed her heroic "desire of wand'ring" (9.1136) to simple desire for Eve, which involves a different kind of lack and compulsion: "[T]o lose thee were to lose myself" (9.959).

As in Eve's case, there is an obvious sense in which Adam's reasoning is self-canceling and theologically incorrect. He defends both the moral necessity and the physical inevitability of the fall. On the one hand, Adam's rhetoric echoes manuals of domestic duties, where the husband is enjoined to love his wife as a second self. On the other, he marshals biblical arguments about the "one flesh" of husband and wife to imply that he is physically as well as emotionally bound to Eve (9.914, 959). This conflict between moral necessity and physical inevitability, artifice and nature, appears in the act of narration as well. Adam narrates his fall, as it occurs, as though he were compelled by the "Bond of Nature," "submitting to what seem'd remediless" (9.956, 919). Yet the very fact of his narration and deliberation undermines his argument for the necessity of the fall. Thus, even more than Eve's, his fall reads as a textbook case (*the* textbook case) of voluntary servitude—voluntary enslavement to sin. Adam is "Against his better knowledge, not deceiv'd, / But fondly overcome" (9.998–99); his passions move him to choose voluntarily but irrationally to fall with Eve. At least, this is the theologically correct reading of Adam's fall.

But, as is already apparent, another reading coexists with the theologically correct one, because Milton insists on the antinomies of the theological contract rather than erasing them. In doing so, he invites us to takes seriously Adam's argument that passion—in the form of his love for Eve—dictates obligation, and that he is obliged in the sense of his being tied (from the Latin *ligare*) to Eve: "Our State cannot be sever'd, we are one" (9.958). Here Adam's appeal to the bond of nature is reminiscent of *The Doctrine and Discipline of Divorce*, where Milton opposes the excessive strictness of reason and the law to the legitimate claims of the flesh, the passions, or what he called "blameless nature." And, just as in *The Doctrine* Milton urges the reader to have a "conscionable and tender pitty" for those who have unwittingly enslaved themselves to a loveless marriage (2:240), so in *Paradise Lost* Milton urges a similar pity for Adam's fall. He does so in part by framing Adam's fall not as a predetermined fact of nature but as a response to a kind of theatrical artifice, the theatrical spectacle of Eve's defloration. In Milton's typically Renaissance conception of tragedy ("I now must change / Those Notes to Tragic" [9.5–6]), Adam's fall is a tragic drama that is caused by the moral responses of amazement, pity, and fear as well as giving rise to these emotions.[40] Adam's own pity and fear for Eve then invite our sympathetic identification with Adam. We are sympathetic because we understand that, as Colin Burrow has rightly noted, Adam's choice to fall with Eve does not represent "a purely voluntary choice of mortal union with a sufferer." This is because the absolutely voluntary is the prerogative of God.[41] To put this another way, the power to create and contract ex nihilo—as though obedience and obligation were matters of pure reason or pure will—is a power that not even the unfallen Adam and Eve have in paradise. Such a purely rational or volitional Adam, Milton suggests, would paradoxically be the "meer artificiall *Adam*" of *Areopagitica*, "such an *Adam* as he is in the motions."[42] In making Adam's fall humanly comprehensible in this way, Milton goes a long way toward imagining a purely secular conception of human fallibility and of obligation—one that is not a consequence of the fall but of our natural human embodiment. *Pace* Hobbes, we do not construct ourselves and our obligations ex nihilo. Note that, in this contrast, Hobbes is the radical constructivist, the radical poet or "maker" (to use Sidney's phrase), while Milton insists on the ways in which we come into the world if not fully formed, at least already created. This might seem to be a politically conservative argument. And yet, in Milton's hands and in the drama of the fall, this creatureliness proves to be as much an argument for rebellion as for obedience.

As we have seen, Eve at her worst dramatizes the link between the autonomous will, the self-regarding imagination, and the pursuit of honor that all too easily slides into Hobbes's restless seeking after power. In contrast, Adam illustrates the link between the limits of volition, sympathetic identification, and a powerful sense of obligation.[43] For Eve, self-love leads to self-aggrandizement that cannot imagine itself as bound; for Adam, self-love is inextricable from the bond of nature and the love of another self. Eve illustrates the self-assertion of the will, against which the claims of reason appear arbitrary (as does the divine prohibition). Adam adopts the view that it doesn't make sense to think of himself as a creature of pure volition, but for the same reason he cannot be a creature of pure reason either. Embodiment—in the form of the passions—is the very condition of his rational choices. As a condition, it is both a limit and a motive. Adam's self-love and love of Eve are his motives for consenting to fall.[44]

This is not the same as saying that human beings are fallible, imperfectly or unpredictably capable of Aristotelian virtue, and that one must accordingly lower one's standards or expectations (as Hobbes does). Nor is it the same as saying, as Milton sometimes seems to in *Areopagitica*, that the passions are put in our way as stumbling blocks or tests of our Stoic virtue. *Paradise Lost* instead helps us to see that our passions are also reasons—and not just tests, obstacles, or the lowest common denominator of humanity. Here, we can put Milton's insight in its most paradoxical and historically most specific form by borrowing from Grotius's thought experiment about the nonexistence of God. It's as though Milton were saying through Adam: if there were no God, human nature would be a good defense of the fall.[45] Such a formulation helps us keep in mind and in tension—as Milton did—the competing claims of God and man.

I began this chapter by arguing that Milton's view of the marriage contract is crucial to understanding his view of political obligation. This is not because the marriage contract is perfectly analogous to the contract of male political subjects. Rather, the relationship of husband and wife in marriage figures the relationship of the contracting subject to himself. In Edenic marriage, Milton explores not only the tensions between the marriage contract and the theological contract but also the antinomies of the political contract.

From a theological perspective, as I have argued, Adam's fall is wrong, and so he should have insisted on divorce. But Milton seems to be doing everything in his power to suggest that, from a human perspective, Adam's fall is comprehensible. From this perspective, to justify the ways of men to God is also perhaps to justify the breach of the theological contract. If this is going too far, we can at the very least say that, whereas Hobbes's eloquence was almost always in the service of absolute obedience, Milton's imaginative energies were far more often engaged by breach of contract and dissent. In book 9 of *Paradise Lost* we can almost see Milton imagining the positive postlapsarian uses of Adam's and Eve's arguments about why they needed to fall. We can see him rehearsing the arguments not only for divorce but also for revolution and regicide.

However sympathetically we construe the fall, in the end we are forced to admit that self-love in *Paradise Lost* does not lead to self-preservation but rather to self-destruction. From this perspective, the fall of Adam and Eve could be said to enact the Hobbesian problematic in reverse, dramatizing the breach rather than the establishment of contract. As we will see in chapter 10, in *Samson Agonistes* Milton rewrites the fall of Adam in Samson's revision of his earlier breach of trust. Scorning Hobbesian self-preservation but not obedience to the divine covenant, Samson creates a tragic spectacle whose intended effect is not the aesthetic passions of pity and fear but something more like Kantian respect. But before we can understand Milton's Samson, we need to return to the royalist "romance" of the Interregnum and the Restoration to which Milton's *Samson* was in part responding.

CHAPTER 9

Sympathy

Divers other passions there be, but they want names; whereof some nevertheless have been by most men observed. For example: from what passion proceedeth it, that men take pleasure to behold from the shore the danger of them that are at sea in a tempest, or in fight, or from a safe castle to behold two armies charge one another in the field? It is certainly in the whole sum joy, else men would never flock to such a spectacle. Nevertheless there is in it both joy and grief. For as there is novelty and remembrance of [one's] own security present, which is delight; so is there also pity, which is grief. But the delight is so far predominant, that men usually are content in such a case to be spectators of the misery of their friends.

—Hobbes, *Elements of Law*

You know that Kings are in some sense called Gods, and so they may in some degree be able to look into mens hearts; and God hath given us a King who can look as far into mens hearts, as any Prince alive; and He hath great skill in Physiognomy too, you would wonder what Calculations He hath made from thence; and no doubt, if He be provoked by evil looks, to make further inquiry into mens hearts, and findes those corrupted with the passions of Envy and Uncharitableness, He will never choose those hearts to trust and rely upon. He hath given us a noble and princely example, by opening and stretching His arms to all who are worthy to be His subjects, worthy to be thought English men, by extending His heart, with a pious and grateful joy, to finde all His subjects at once in His arms, and himself in theirs.

—Clarendon[1]

WRITING IN THE AFTERMATH of the English civil war, in his *Certaine Conceptions, or Considerations . . . upon the Strange Change of Peoples, Dispositions and Actions in these latter times* (1650), the Catholic royalist Sir Percy Herbert depicted his contemporaries in terms that would have been recognizable to Hobbes. He noted their restless seeking after power, observing that they "are more taken with hopes of honours to come, then absolutely satisfied with those that are present." He commented on their "roving and unsatisfied nature: which argues, that the very disposition of man cannot be happy with this world."[2] Like Hobbes, Herbert was particularly concerned with the passion of vainglory, that insatiable self-love that "nourish[es] our pride and torment[s] our thoughts, with inconvenient and violent ambitions, by ayming at that which in a manner nothing can arrive unto, but vain imaginations."[3] This pursuit of vainglory accounted for the present vices of ingratitude; disobedience to one's parents, masters, and sovereign; and the widespread contempt for "the strongest bonds of trust." Herbert was so disturbed by this last violation that he devoted a whole section of his treatise to breach of contract, which he filled with counterexamples of virtuous pagans and Christians who kept their word even at cost of life.[4] Where Herbert differed from Hobbes, as these examples begin to suggest, was in the remedy he proposed for this desperate deterioration of social relationships. We must imitate those virtuous men who preferred friendship to "interest and commodity"; we must adopt an attitude of Christian Stoicism in the face of adversity; we must recall the lessons of "romance," including the moral of the faithful dolphin from Pliny: "that the bands of friendship ought not to be broken upon any condition, without impiety & dishonour." Ultimately, Herbert diagnosed the general malaise as a condition of impatience and urged a combination of patience and an active "subjecting [of one's] own will" to Christian authority.[5]

Herbert's *Certaine Conceptions* was part of the outpouring of royalist literature in the 1650s by writers who were attempting to make sense of the civil war.[6] Whether in actual exile on the continent or internal exile at home, supporters of Charles II undertook a period of soul-searching and retrospection. In Herbert's *Certaine Conceptions* we see how romance could serve as a compensatory fiction for these defeated royalists—the fiction of a world in which noble characters remain constant in their affections despite their romance trials and tribulations. This is certainly one important function of royalist literature in England in the 1650s.[7] But in Herbert's own voluminous allegorical romance, *Princess Cloria* (1653–61), as well as in Richard Brathwaite's *Panthalia* (1659), and William Sales's unfinished *Theophania* (1655), we find considerably more skepticism about the arcadian dimension of romance.[8] Instead, romance becomes an analytical tool for reflecting on the causes of the war and the contemporary crisis of political obligation. If Hobbes's solution to the problem of vainglory was to imagine a world of discrete individuals with no incentive to join together except the interest of self-preservation and the fear of violent death, prose romance of the 1650s both records and responds to this Hobbesian solution by proposing a new affective basis for political obligation.

As we saw in chapter 7, in her short prose romance *The Contract* Margaret Cavendish appropriated and revised Hobbesian arguments about self-interest in order to develop a new affective casuistry in defense of Charles II. In this chapter I explore a complementary line of argument, according to which royalist romance of the 1650s responded to Hobbesian self-interest with an account of aesthetic interest and an aesthetic defense of the Restoration. In contrast to Cavendish's protofeminist politics of love, however, these romances articulate an evolving ethos of sympathy between men. Moreover, whereas the staging of the trial scene in *The Contract* linked theater to the paralogism of fiction and to the threat—or uses—of deception, the defenders of sympathy are far more interested in the role of theatrical representation in eliciting and disciplining the passions.

Hobbes's allusion to Lucretius in the epigraph to this chapter suggests why Hobbes was important to later seventeenth-century reflection on theatrical representation and the passions. In the *Poetics* Aristotle had argued both that tragic pleasure derives from the catharsis of pity and fear, and that human beings naturally delight in imitation because they delight in learning from comparisons. This dual account gave rise to two main interpretations of tragic pleasure in the early modern period. According to the first interpretation, the pleasures of tragedy were primarily ethical. Tragedy instructs about virtue and vice both in its explicit plot and in its cathartic effect, by which it purges or moderates those passions that hinder ethical action. According to the second interpretation, we delight in tragedy because we take pleasure in the artist's manipulation of form, that is, in the very fact of artifice or representation. By the middle of the seventeenth century, these explanations were being challenged by Descartes's and Hobbes's materialist accounts of the passions. Followers of Descartes such as Rapin and Dennis explained the effects of tragedy in terms of the natural delight we take in the "sheer physical stimulation of the animal spirits." Hobbes adopted a similar materialist perspective when he explained aesthetic pleasure in terms of the physical distance that ensures the spectator's personal safety. This materialist argument about the link between self-preservation and aesthetic pleasure was regularly associated with Lucretius in the early modern period.[9] Hobbes's argument about self-interest in turn spawned a variety of counterarguments about the pleasures of tragedy, which emphasized the audience's natural sympathy with those who suffer. In this chapter I argue that royalist writers of the 1650s contributed to these arguments by inflecting prose romance in the direction of a specifically sentimental understanding of tragedy, in which the pleasures of tragic representation are explained by fellow feeling rather than self-preservation. Responding to Hobbesian arguments, these writers anticipate the eighteenth-century cult of sentimentality and the new discipline of aesthetics—a discipline less concerned with the formal properties of the work of art than with the spectator's or audience's response.

Like Hobbes, Herbert, Brathwaite, and Sales depict a world of passion and interest, in which the aristocratic pursuit of honor is more often a cloak for factional self-interest and self-aggrandizement than an expression of true nobility. And, like Hobbes, they suggest that a frank recognition of the centrality of interest is the foundation of any secure government. Unlike Hobbes, however, the authors want to resist the complete demystification of the passions—the reduction of the passions to varieties of self-interest. As their choice of genre suggests, like Cavendish they want to hold on to romance, in however revised a form. The narrator of *Panthalia* insists that interest needs to be supplemented by "affection," that the most powerful model of obligation is one in which the Hobbesian quid pro quo is recast as a theatrical one, and that the strategic manipulation of fear needs to be replaced by pity or clemency.[10] The narrator of *Theophania* goes further, suggesting that pity, sentimental identification, or what we would call aesthetic interest can form the basis of a new political settlement. Taken together, Herbert, Brathwaite, and Sales chart a trajectory from a politics of narrow self-interest, which contemporaries identified with Hobbes, to a politics of aesthetic interest: in response to Hobbes's critique of vainglory, they extend an invitation to imaginative or sympathetic identification.[11] As we saw in the introduction, Leo Strauss remarked of Hobbes's attack on rationalism that it was not "a matter of chance, that *la volonté générale* and aesthetics were launched at precisely the same time."[12] In fact, Hobbes was skeptical of this link between political philosophy and aesthetics; it was his royalist contemporaries who were attempting to reforge that link after the death of "the royal aesthete."[13]

The works of Herbert, Brathwaite, and Sales thus bear out Derek Hirst's contention that in the 1650s defeated royalists made culture itself the ground of their political contestation. According to Hirst, while royalist poets and preachers contrived "through the cult of Charles the Martyr . . . to sacralize authority and to render statecraft mysterious," Milton and his fellow republicans "sought to demystify statecraft" by emphasizing the role of interest, "consultation, designs, [and] policies" in the realm of politics. It is in this context, Hirst argues, that we should interpret royalist literature of the 1650s. To deploy "poetry as political statement in itself" was by implication "to assert the philistinism of those in power," and thus "to conduct a fundamental exercise in delegitimation. Not only were the rulers of the new state acting improperly . . .; the state itself was improperly constituted."[14] But, against Hirst's dichotomy of royalist culture and republican statecraft, the royalist prose romances of Herbert, Brathwaite, and Sales show that these authors were more intent on assimilating arguments about craft and interest than in refuting them. Caroline aestheticism failed, they suggest, because it was not interested enough; the aesthetic interest of prose romance is the vehicle of this political insight. A close look at these romances can thus shed light not only on the royalist response to defeat and the distinctive literary culture of England in the 1650s, but also on the neglected role of aesthetic interest in modern treatments of the "passions and interests" in seventeenth-century politics.[15]

WISE COMPLIANCE

Herbert's *Cloria*, in some ways the most Hobbesian of the romances, allows us to see the innovations of *Theophania* and *Panthalia* by contrast. First published as *Cloria and Narcissus* in two parts in 1653 and 1654, by 1661 *The Princess Cloria* had grown to five parts, and some six hundred pages. With Cloria standing for Mary (daughter of Charles I) and William II figured as Narcissus, it offers an elaborate allegory of the English civil war in the context of European politics. Like *Panthalia* and *Theophania*, it is a work of analysis and counsel: analysis of how the royalists should have conducted themselves during the civil war, and counsel regarding what they should do to bring about the restoration of Charles II.

Counsel is in fact an explicit theme of *Cloria* and is manifest in part as an extreme self-consciousness about genre. The romance opens with the figure of Euarchus (Charles I) debating about whether to wage war on the continent. As writers in the employ of the Caroline court had argued, Charles's pacifist inclinations dictated a political romance of love rather than valor, peaceableness or passivity rather than military action. In *Cloria*, however, the characters repeatedly contest this interpretation of the genre both in action and speech. While the future Charles II/Arethusius traipses around Europe in a depressed state— sometimes voicing high-minded sentiments about honor and at other times giving in to self-pity and depression—his younger brother tries to find an occasion to display his martial valor. In a more contemplative mode, Cloria and her maid Roxana debate "whether active valour, or passive courage, were the greater vertue, in that *Euarchus* seemed to possess them both in a high kinde"; Creses (Clarendon) cleverly responds that patient suffering requires more valor than military action: without the diversions of war, the mind needs greater courage to resist the "horrid apprehension" of the "imagination."[16] This self-consciousness about genre is further heightened by the inclusion of comic episodes reminiscent of the parody of chivalric romance in *The Knight of the Burning Pestle*. On one such occasion, Cloria ends up sharing a bed with a country bumpkin who confesses his desire to do "some notable exploit" to avenge the king's death and vindicate the people's "liberties."[17] Whether this is a satire of the ineffectual royalist party or proof of the naiveté of those who believe in a military solution to the royalists' dilemma, it renders a political crisis as a crisis of genre.

The question we are asked to consider is, Do recent events dictate a chivalric romance of martial valor or a romance of love and marriage? Should the protagonists actively seek to determine their fortunes or should they patiently suffer their trials and tribulations? The answer seems to be neither. In the course of the narrative—sometimes in the course of a single episode—the language of military valor and patient suffering gives way to recommendations of wise compliance, strategic calculation, and the theatrical manipulation of the passions. Thus, when Charles II/Arethusius concedes that dissimulation is sometimes necessary, but insists idealistically that "fame is the life and being of a Prince, and that cannot be ruled and governed either by the appetites, or the power of others, but by those demonstrations, that must make us appear as we ought to be, Gods upon earth, never to be terrified, or disobeyed," the Scots commander Meliander brings Charles down to earth with his reply: "I must confess Sir . . . that these are most glorious attributes, fitt to adorn a Princes dignity; but how they can be well attained, without a politick comportment in difficulties, I know not." Similarly, just a page after he has recommended "majestick patience," Creses praises Euarchus's "outward" yielding to his opponents' demands: "So that in my opinion, *Euarchus* hath done like a wise and Politick Prince, in seeming not to contend, where he was not sure to prevail. . . . And besides, it is to be considered, that no Act he shall pass in this condition of constraint, can binde either himself or posterity by all Humane and Divine Laws, if his sword ever become more powerful."[18] Creses's casuistical "seeming not to contend" echoes Roxana's earlier advice to Cloria that she give her "seeming consent" to an unwanted proposal of marriage: "which promise cannot binde at all, not onely in respect of your former obligation to *Narcissus*, but also in regard you are a prisoner, and therefore not tied to any contract made in such a state." Cloria accepts the advice, "wherein she shewed, that her necessities had taught her a craft, that was not at all in her nature, for that she always esteemed it dishonourable to dissemble."[19] For Creses patience and promises are forms of politic dissimulation, and this is a lesson Cloria quickly learns as well.

Cloria's revision of the Caroline romance is also apparent in its treatment of marriage. The marriage of Charles I and Henrietta Maria had served as a charged political metaphor for the harmony and stability of Charles's reign. *Cloria* presents a very different world from that of the Caroline politics of love. Here, in the first sixty pages, we encounter two apparently different stories of marriage contracts. The first concerns the story of Osiris (the younger brother of Louis XIII), who is barred from marriage with his lover Alciana for political reasons. The second concerns the marriage contract of Cloria and Narcissus: "Such contracts made as these, may be / Esteem'd a blessed Unity."[20] In both cases, however, the message seems to be that marriage (like Charles's arcadianism) no longer does its political work in a dependable way. Later, when Osiris (now in love with someone else) becomes king, he is rebuked by his counselors that "it was no time to be amourous, when Memphis was in apparent danger to be lost." Creses provides the appropriate comment. Hearing that the king of Spain has a daughter whom Mazarin wants to marry to Louis XIV, he remarks to Cloria, "neither at all times doth contracted marriages, hinder jealousies procured by reason of National quarrels, and seldom make friendships of a confident nature, when subjection thereby are [sic] feared."[21] In a similar vein, Cloria distinguishes between her marriage contract with Narcissus and the necessity of warfare in support of her father.[22] The marriages in this text are either really based on love or purely political, but not a symbol of the unity of the two. Marriage is no longer an emblem of peace and harmony; at most, it is one instrument among others in the politician's arsenal.

The text evinces a corresponding skepticism about the power of the passions to inspire political obligation. Although numerous characters articulate the view that it is better for a ruler to be loved than feared and that affection is stronger than interest, the passions are on the whole a source of distemper. The people of Lydia (England) are described as having fallen "into so absolute a stupidity or want of courage . . . by reason of their frequent sensualities, that they are content to buy their own slavery at any rate," while Charles II/Arethusius is tossed about by his "exasperated and desperate passions."[23] Particularly striking in this context is the depiction of the future king as a kvetch, one who at the slightest provocation bursts into an aria of passionate complaint about his treatment at the hands of his subjects, fate, even divine providence. The other characters begin to grow tired of his whining, and urge patience, constancy, or "wise compliance."[24] The shift from neo-Stoic "constancy" to "wise compliance" is important for understanding the role of the passions in this text.[25] Ideally, the passions should be the object of moral supervision; practically speaking, however, they have their uses. They should not be simply repressed or even tempered but rather strategically solicited and deployed. Here *Cloria* draws closer to Cicero than Hobbes. First, in contrast to the Hobbesian emphasis on the fear of violent death, the central passion in the newly demystified world of self-interest is, paradoxically, love.[26] Then, passion is not so much a primary motive or incentive for deliberating about self-interest, as part of a strategy of representation that follows from the calculation of self-interest. Thus, for example, the depiction of the restoration of Charles at the end of *Cloria* makes it clear that the outpouring of love on the part of his newly obedient subjects is inseparable from a strategic consideration of their interests. At his entry into England, Charles is

> accompanied by the chiefest Magistrates, [who] met him many furlongs from their dwellings, to shew a loving duty to his person . . .; the Military Discipline being in the streets under curious Banners, both to guard and satisfie his content, when the keys of every gate in the interim were delivered into the possession of his own Officers, that dispersed the command among the Souldiers, as if their natural allegiance belonged onely to King *Arethusius*, as an appearing conqueror of all mens affection.

It is hard to imagine a more qualified representation of the people's affection for their sovereign. "Loving duty" and "natural allegiance" bracket what is arguably the more important point: that Charles has regained control over the militia (an issue of contention in 1642, at the beginning of the civil war). Charles is only "an appearing conqueror" of his subjects' affections. Moreover, the subjunctive "as if" recalls us to an earlier description of Charles viewing these "gallant demonstrations of joy" with "a certain kinde of disdainful aspect, both in regard to his own former usage, as for their want of care in his Sisters [Cloria's] particular; notwithstanding he determined totally to dissemble his passions, either until he was better settled in his Kingdom, or they had procured from him a milder opinion." Although this Charles II is not a quick study, he has by the end of *Cloria* learned to dissemble his passions in a politic way.[27]

Ultimately, the lesson of *Cloria* is one of politic negotiation. The particular message to Charles II, whose father is depicted as partially responsible for the outbreak of civil war, is that the king should not rule absolutely, nor should he attempt to rule simply by love. Rather he should be constrained by the fundamental laws of the kingdom and by a strategic consideration of the power politics of nation-states on the continent.[28] The lesson of politic negotiation is also important for the subject-reader. Although, on the whole, the people in this text are represented as incapable of deliberating about their own interest, their follies are the object of the reader's deliberations. The goal here seems to be to help the reader learn the difference between slavery to one's passions and rational subjection to one's sovereign. This message is conveyed both thematically and formally. Thus, when Charles enters London, he confronts a poem engraved on the city gate which instructs us that "Dark Rebellion's gone." The poem reads in part:

> The Fates have trifled all this time; they knew
> No mortal spight could long contest your due:
> It 'twas their craft to let your Subjects see,
> All were but Slaves, and you have set them free.

(613)

As the quatrain makes clear, the achievement of the romance is to recast contingency as fate.[29] The extended trifling, digressions, and set pieces of the romance plot are now described as a deliberate strategy. What appeared to be randomness was really design, which, the narrator suggests, was as much a matter of providence as artifice. The imposition of a deus ex machina conclusion brings about an aesthetically satifisying, providentially ordained freedom—to which the people and the reader willingly submit. But there is another message for the reader of the text. In attributing craft to the fates, the narrator of *Cloria* calls attention to the conventional romance ending of the narrative and provides a "theological" justification for feigning, construed not only as the duplicity inherent in representation but also as the strategic misrepresentation or wise compliance dictated by politics. In freeing the subjects from their slavery (or, rather, helping them understand that their former "freedom" was really bondage), the narrative encourages not only rational deliberation but also a kind of craft on the part of the reader. In this respect, the reader is invited to imitate the author rather than Charles II.

In alternating between providential and naturalistic explanations of the plot, *Cloria* uncannily reproduces the narrative strategy of Heliodorus's *Aithiopika*, the most popular Greek romance of the early modern period. And in doing so, Herbert, like Heliodorus, foregrounds the author's artistry in reconciling these two explanations of events.[30] As John J. Winkler has observed of the *Aithiopika*, "the novel concludes with a new religious significance read into the romantic events, [but] this religious significance is not religiously meant."[31] In Winkler's account, Heliodorus is chiefly concerned with the way in which "the interplay" of romantic melodrama and providential explanation allows him to display an ironic self-consciousness about literary convention and genre. *Cloria* also alternates between a religious and secular rhetoric, and dramatizes a similar self-consciousness about genre. But in *Cloria* this literary self-consciousness also serves a political function. By inculcating an ironic detachment from the conventions of romance, it also encourages an awareness of the conventions of representation in politics.

Another kind of alternation in *Cloria* cannot be fully assimilated to the alternation between providence and nature: the oscillation between recommendations of wise compliance and a kind of Foucauldian discipline of the passions. We are led to understand that politics requires not only the subject's rational deliberation and craft but also the disciplining of the subject's affections. It is striking in this regard that, while Herbert recommends strategic thinking to the reader, he also claims the upper hand by suggesting that the reader has already been won over through the not entirely rational experience of aesthetic pleasure. If, in the first instance, the genre of romance is associated with a Hobbesian analysis of self-interest, in the second instance it becomes a vehicle of aesthetic delight.[32] This oscillation—this uncertainty about whether aesthetic pleasure promotes or replaces deliberation—is even more characteristic of the other two romances we will explore.

The double message of the plot—the instruction in wise compliance and the eliciting of the passions in order to discipline them—is conveyed in explicit thematic terms in the conclusion to *Cloria*. Just as the people willingly submit to their sovereign, so, the narrator implies, the reader voluntarily submits to *Cloria*: "This now shall finish our Romance, that perhaps hath too long a season troubled the Readers patience; but as Fancies are creations of our own, and therefore for the most part please with some excess; so of the other side, I neither invite or compell any to the exercise." Here the narrator both does and does not take responsibility for the aesthetic pleasure of the text. While admitting that a writer's fancy is by nature extravagant, the narrator also declares that no one is forcing us to read *Cloria* to the end: reading is a form of voluntary subjection to the pleasure of the text, to the pleasure of our own fancy. Unlike the Hobbesian political contract, the contract of genre, in this case the genre of romance, is predicated on a specifically aesthetic interest, a consent, if not to the rules of the genre, at least to the pleasure we take in reading.

The preface to *Cloria* comments at greater length on the discipline that romance can provide the unruly reader. The author tells us that the genre of romance both reflects the tumultuous times of civil war and proposes a solution to this crisis. It is a reflection because recent political events have been as incredible as a romance: "[I]t cannot be denied, but the Ground-work for a *Romance* was excellent; and the rather, since by no other way almost, could the multiplicity of strange Actions of the Times be exprest, that exceeded all belief, and went beyond every example in the doing." It offers a solution since it engages the reader's interest through the lure of aesthetic pleasure, and provides idealized images of virtue "to put persons in minde, what they ought to do." Like other early modern defenders of poetry, the author both subordinates pleasure to instruction and distinguishes between them in terms of the skill of the reader. To intelligent readers, indeed for "any, who have been indifferently versed in the Affairs of *Europe*," *Cloria* presents an easily deciphered political allegory. To "the more vulgar sort, [it offers] a bare *Romance* of Love and Chivalry," which delights without instructing.[33]

It is the former, more skilled reader the author of the preface chiefly has in mind. Thus he goes on to discuss the fanciful portrayal in romance of scenes of probable reasoning, which serve in turn to educate the reader's judgment. As in so many Renaissance defenses of poetry, fancy is now described as conducing to equitable judgment. To the objection that romance's "Invention and Fancies . . . leads [*sic*] peoples thoughts into a dark Labyrinth of uncertainties," the writer replies that fidelity to historical truth precludes the "liberty for inward disputations, or supposed passions to be discovered." In a romance, by contrast, each character's deliberation "stirs up the appetite of the Reader" and provides a model worthy of imitation. *Cloria*'s "Discourses probable . . . may put people in minde of what they may say and do another time, with more advantage to themselves or employment; especially seeing it is impossible otherwise to express inward passions and hidden thoughts that of necessity accompany all Transactions of consequence." This defense of invention sounds in part like Sidney's *Apology for Poetry*, but with an even greater emphasis on the representation of "inward passions and hidden thoughts." Just as important as the representation of virtue is the representation of the psychology and motivation of virtue. Just as crucial as "put[ting] us in minde of Vertues and their effects" is "continu[ing] them constantly in our thoughts and desires; whereby to render them habitual to our natures." This preoccupation with the representation and reproduction of inward passions will be even more pronounced in *Panthalia* and *Theophania*.[34]

In a remarkable turn toward the end of the preface, the writer connects the genre of romance to the question of political origins.

> For Stories of former Ages are no other, then certain kinde of *Romances* to succeeding posterity; since they have no testimony for them but mens probable opinions; seeing the Historical part almost of all Countreys is subject to be questioned; neither is it any great matter, whether they were exactly so or no, provided Bravery be cherished, and Baseness discountenanced to our Instruction; in that all things are but to teach people how to do well, and avoid the contrary; wherefore to be considered, that the Authour had a greater desire to discourse the causes of Accidents, then the truth of Actions.

Here the author conflates history and romance: we have no certain knowledge of the past, only of others' opinions. The origin of all governments is questionable, which in this period is as much to say founded on conquest (as writers as diverse as Marchamont Nedham and James I had argued).[35] In this light, the notion of legitimate authority is a kind of fiction or romance told to "succeeding posterity." The writer of the preface defends these legitimating fictions, as long as they teach the people "how to do well." This conflation of history and romance then provides a defense of *Cloria*. Although in describing the author's "desire to discourse the causes of *Accidents*, then the truth of Actions," the writer of the preface associates both political authority and the contract of genre with the contingent realm of romance, he does not want to discredit either the literary contract or the notion of political authority. For if the non-Aristotelian notion of a caused accident is a good description of the anomalous world of romance, the language of supposition signals the goal of redeeming romance for Aristotelian poetics. In short, the writer of the preface wants to "legitimate" romance by virtue of the reader's participation in the construction of its verisimilitude. By extension, he also makes room for the subject's participation in the construction of political authority.[36] At the same time he reassures us that, unlike other more elaborate romances, *Cloria* does not depend on and will not elicit the paralogism or "false conjectures, which in a *Romance*, is not proper." Instead, he assures us, the romance form of *Cloria* will "stir up the appetite of the Reader to a continuance," not only to continued reading but also to continued equitable reasoning and political allegiance.[37]

Nigel Smith has argued that, to the demise of Caroline arcadian romance, "*Cloria* provides reactions rather than answers, and its arguable insufficiency in this respect points to one reason why post-Arcadian romance faded away. Not only was it associated with royalism, and its fictionality drained by allegorical pressure; it had no answers within itself for the predicament in which many of its readers found themselves."[38] True, the conclusion imposes a providential sanction on the Restoration that the characters had been vainly searching for in the previous six hundred pages; but the real message of that imposition concurs with the narrative as a whole, which offers a remarkably astute analysis of the power politics of the major European states—a politics based on faction, interest, and the dispassionate evaluation of competing military forces. Despite the moralizing rhetoric of the prefatory letter to the reader, supposition and probable reasoning are freed from the constraints of virtue, while political interest is shown to be inseparable from a kind of crafty aesthetic interest, an interest in the uses of representation, including the representation of the passions.

THE POLITICS OF PITY

Like *Cloria*, Richard Brathwaite's *Panthalia: or the Royal Romance* both allegorizes the events of the civil war and reflects on the politics of genre.

This reflection takes the form of a meditation on the use and abuse of romance in domestic and foreign policy from the reign of Elizabeth through the restoration of Charles II. Specifically, *Panthalia* diagnoses the corruption of political passions—the declension from the Machiavellian and Elizabethan dyad of fear and love to the debauchery and uxoriousness of the courts of James and Charles. Like Herbert, Brathwaite redescribes the dangerous passions of love and honor in terms of politic self-interest. And, like Herbert, he makes our interest in aesthetic craft a model for voluntary subjection to the sovereign.[39]

In the seventeenth century, the reign of Elizabeth was the object of nostalgic admiration for the way the queen managed her court and conducted her foreign policy.[40] In both spheres she provided a striking contrast to the reigns of James and Charles. This is the function of Bellingeria (Elizabeth I) in *Panthalia* as well. In particular, Bellingeria is praised for her skill in manipulating the passions: "being no lesse formidable to her Enemies; then infinitely winning and affectionate to her own: as she might appeale to the whole progresse of her flourishing Government, if ever any State were managed with *more Forraigne feare and Domestick love.*" Although Clarentio (Essex) is portrayed sympathetically as a figure out of chivalric romance, Bellingeria's treatment of him (and of "Mariana") is excused by being blamed on her servants and by being psychologized: "But Crowns and Nuptial Beds, as they admit no Competitors, so their enjoyment begets, many times, sundry causeless fears" that end in tragedy.[41] As her name suggests, Bellingeria embodies something of Essex's own martial spirit: while recognizing the political importance of her subjects' affections, she also knows how to distinguish affairs of the heart from affairs of state and is suitably martial in the latter (especially in comparison with her successor).

The respectful treatment accorded Elizabeth is nowhere in evidence when we come to Basilius (James I). In case the name of the misguided ruler of Sidney's *Arcadia* fails to cue the reader's judgment, the narrator tells us that Basilius is taken up with "amorous parlies" rather than state affairs. In the degenerate court of James I, one kind of romance has replaced another: "Tilts and Turnaments . . . became Addresses of too virile a quality"; effeminate courtiers spend their time watching comic and pastoral romance; no one is capable of real employment in "State-service":

> Carpet-Knights were not for Campe-Service: nor Court-Couches convertible to Field-Bedds. Schools and Academies of Love stored with choicest Lectures of pure and attractive Rhetorick, to make their dialect a more powerfull Sollicitor to Fancy, were erected: And Masters of Revells appointed and amply endowed; and these were imployed in

contriving and inventing variety of Comic and Pastorall delights: which were usually represented in their private Court Theaters, purposely erected for such Enterludes and Comicall Inventions. And good opportunity had *Ismenia* with her amorous Ladies to play the Platonick Courtiers: seeing *Basilius* made the Wild Forrest the Place of his solace and recreation.

In this description, Brathwaite contrasts the cult of Platonic love fostered by Henrietta Maria with James's fondness for hunting. Despite the king's poems celebrating the royal romance, Basilius is portrayed as indifferent "to Feminine Objects" owing to his "affection to the contrary Sex," while the Queen Ismenia is rumored to have favorites of her own.[42]

This enervation of romance affects the negotiations over Rosicles/ Prince Charles's marriage. For reasons of personal revenge, Silures/Buckingham, "the Catamite of our time," blocks the Spanish marriage negotiations. The pursuit of pleasure and of self-interest, that is, overcomes state interest.[43] Increasingly in this climate, all professions of love begin to look like hypocrisy. There follows an elaborate allegory of Charles's courtship of Henrietta Maria, who needs to be convinced that Charles has not already been rejected by the Infanta and then that Charles is not inconstant. Commenting on how the hypertrophy of romance conventions mirrors the resentful scheming of figures such as Silures/Buckingham, Irina/Henrietta Maria remarks, "the whole world . . . presents but in a Land-skip, a continued counterfet *Love-mask*; wherein appears variety of Faces, but they are not native nor genuine."[44]

A different—but equally ineffectual—royal romance takes center stage at the court of Rosicles and Irina. Here Brathwaite draws on the numerous contemporary portraits of Charles as uxorious and Henrietta Maria as domineering: "[The] Prince became a Subject to his Queens Command: and she to the pursuit of her own pleasure. A conjugall love injoyned him to obey: and a native affection to Courtly delights begot in her an easie Soveraignty to Command."[45] This inversion of political and gender roles is then aggravated by the king's own confession of a prior contract to the Infanta: "[H]is breach in so high an Interest [was] construed to be a dangerous Omen to his future Success." These breaches of political and affective decorum help to explain why the people "could not Find hearts to believe: where they could find none to love."[46] Genuine love or affection is represented by the narrator as a necessary ingredient to political success, the necessary disciplinary supplement to the law:

Loialty appeares ever an attentive hearer; whereas Sedition proves an indocile Scholar. Lectures of Morall discipline or legall obedience are of hard digestion to such fiery spirits. It is true; The Law is the safeguard; The Custody of all private Interests; Personall Honours, Lives,

Liberties, and Estates are all in the keeping of the Law; without this, no Soveraignty; no Propriety; every man hath a like right to everything.

Yet this Law so necessarily conducing to the Conservation of all Estates is to be moulded after the *Lesbian Rule*: it is to be evenly squared . . . . *If the Prerogative of the King overwhelme the liberty of the People, it will be turned to Tyranny; If Liberty undermine the Prerogative, it will grow into Anarchy.* An even hand is ever fittest to guide the helme of State. But it is *affection* that gives the best Calking to the Vessel.[47]

This extraordinary passage reads as an attempt to use the parliamentary rhetoric of fundamental law for royalist ends, to balance the people's liberty against the royal prerogative, and to advise the king about the necessary supplement of the affections. If law is the bulwark against a Hobbesian state of nature in which "every man hath a like right to everything," affection is the bulwark against "fiery spirits." It is as though Brathwaite wanted to extricate a Ciceronian pragmatism from the Neoplatonic rhetoric of love at the Caroline court. At the same time, the narrator cautions that, while it may be better to be loved than hated, it is not good to have to "beg acceptance" from your subjects. The necessity of love risks putting the sovereign in a position of dependence; besides, affection alone cannot take the place of military force since the people will desert their sovereign when it is in their own interest to do so.[48]

Brathwaite's anatomy of romance—his distinction between the admirable chivalric honor of an Essex and the romance debauchery and delusions of the Stuart court, along with his recommendation of a politic appeal to the affections—is further complicated by the romance insert of "The Pleasant Passages of Panthalia, the Pretty Pedler." This is a miniature prose romance in the tradition of the Italian novella so criticized by Ascham. Panthalia is in love with Acolasto, but Acolasto is a scoundrel who has run off to the wars because he has run out of credit in regular life: he has contracted debts just as he has clandestinely contracted to marry Panthalia. Brathwaite thus links the credit relations of the new market economy to the danger of deception in clandestine marriage;[49] yet, he also shows dissimulation is the motor of the romance plot and a necessary part of our aesthetic interest: Panthalia dresses up as a peddler in order to seek Acolasto in the camps and in this disguise becomes the love object and Platonic "Idea" of one Aretina, whom she pretends to love and then disabuses regarding her apparent sex. This double-edged parody of Platonic love portrays courtly rhetoric as both removed from real life and the vehicle of self-interested deception. The insert then shifts from a parody of courtly romance to allegorical commentary on the causes of the English civil war. Panthalia describes how the king's subjects have grown weary of "Commodity [trade], Liberty and Tranquillity" and analyzes the rea-

sons for Climenes/Cromwell's success. Here we find the negative version
of Bellingeria's masterful rhetoric: Climenes "declared himself a singular
Artizan in the successful pursuit of his own aspiring interest" and he did
so in part by "insinuating himself into [others'] affections."[50]

This dispassionate political analysis then finds fruition in Panthalia's
resolution to leave Acolasto, both because of his inconstant affections and
his probable "Conjugall tyranny." "I have suffered enough," she writes
to him, "I meane not to be unpittiful to my self, as to enlarge sufferings
with fresh feares or inconstant Fancies. . . . Private Contracts being not
accompanied with other Ceremoniall Observances and Conjugall Offices
. . . may legally admit a dispensation."[51] Lacking the legal "consideration" of Acolasto's conjugal offices, Panthalia is justified in acting out
of self-pity, breaking their contract, and joining the contemplative order
of Delia. Although, after a series of twists and turns, Acolasto reconquers
her love and they are married, separated, and reunited (Acolasto enjoys
an "act of Oblivion" regarding his former transgressions), they do not live
happily ever after. We are pointedly told that Acolasto becomes uxorious,
patently as much of a problem as being unfaithful. Clearly Panthalia and
Acolasto—like Charles and Henrietta Maria?—have not found the proper
balance between passion and interest.

In *Panthalia* as a whole, as in this romance insert, Brathwaite seems to
be trying to make sense of the role of the passions in both the domestic
and political sphere. Yet, while the story of Panthalia links the crisis of
the affections to the new world of market relations, the larger narrative
suggests that the crisis is more political than economic: the king's earlier
broken marriage contract implies that his word cannot be taken on credit,
and this doubt of the king's word in turn reinforces the subject's pursuit
of self-interest. As in *Cloria*, although the analogy between the marriage
contract and the contract of sovereignty is still in evidence, it functions
more as a sign of crisis than of harmony and reconciliation. (Basilius's
invocation of this rhetoric of harmony is portrayed as deluded at best,
hypocritical at worst.) An equally disturbing cause of distrust is the king's
failure to support his "faithfull servant," Sophronio/Strafford. Whether
in the public or private sphere, vows and contracts need to be "accompanied with other Ceremoniall Observances and Conjugall Offices." And in
both spheres, interest needs to be balanced with passion, romance artifice
with genuine affection.[52]

It is significant in this light that, in the remainder of the narrative, it is
no longer the Ciceronian and Machiavellian dyad of fear and love but the
aesthetic passions of pity and fear that play a prominent role.[53] In the
early modern period, the history of pity and fear was intertwined with
the reception of Aristotle's *Poetics* and with Stoicism; and in both cases,
pity was associated with a kind of aesthetic pleasure. Although in the

Poetics Aristotle famously argued that tragedy elicits and purges the emotions of pity and fear, in the *De clementia* Seneca claimed that pity and theatricality were mutually enforcing. Specifically, he contrasted pity, the potentially effeminizing emotional response to spectacles of sorrow, and clemency, a rational and helpful response to another's suffering: "Misericodia non causam, sed fortunam spectat; clementia rationi accedit" (pity regards the plight, not the cause of it; mercy is combined with reason). The merciful man "will bring relief to another's tears, but will not add his own."[54] For this reason Seneca argued that mercy or clemency was a kind of equitable judgment (2.7.3). But early modern readers would also have been familiar with counterarguments, which recuperated the aesthetic response of pity as an ethical passion: Renaissance Italian commentators on the *Poetics* had taken issue with the view that pity should be purged, and Calvin had written a commentary on the *De clementia* in which he expressed a similar concern about Seneca's repudiation of pity.[55] These distinctions bear, as we shall see, on Brathwaite's analysis of Charles I's mistakes and his recommendations to the future Charles II. To be an object of pity, he tells us, is a problem; to stage a spectacle of pity—to represent pity—is a source of political power.

Incapable of setting the stage themselves and manipulating the passions of others, Brathwaite's Cromwell and the two Charles are passive before their subjects' gaze: Climenes is pathetically afraid of the people, while Rosicles and Charicles (Charles I and II) are objects of pity. Not surprisingly, the narrator describes the new state as "State-Theatre" and blames this spectacle on the subjects' desire for "innovation" as much as on their rulers' ineptness. As a result, Rosicles and Charicles find themselves playing the role not of chivalric knight so much as suffering damsel in distress. The narrator also repeatedly calls attention to the lost world of chivalric honor and true romance by referring to "mushrump-gallantry" and the "Sprouts of adventitious Honour" who inhabit the present Parliament.[56]

But, by the end of the text, this dangerous aestheticizing, even effeminizing, of sovereignty has been turned on its head. The Restoration occurs in the final pages of the text and is celebrated by a "dance of Sylvans" who enact an "antick" failed coronation of Climenes.[57] With this pastoral interlude Brathwaite simultaneously mocks Cromwell's affected humility and dramatizes the inescapably theatrical dimension of politics. But something has changed. While, up until this point, the question has been what kind of romance hero do you want to be, the final pages attempt to move beyond the romance world of contingency altogether.[58] Crucially, in conclusion Charicles reappropriates the passion of pity, which he now extends to his subjects in the form of clemency. Charicles himself represents his clemency as a complicated theatrical performance. By feigning ignorance (or misrecognition) of his subjects' faithlessness, Charicles claims, he invites them to a kind of closet drama or "bosom-agnition of their own disloyalty." At the same time, he stages the public spectacle of his power: "To have it in ones power to punish, and not to inflict it, I have ever held it Princely," he pronounces, paraphrasing Seneca's *De clementia*.[59] In his treatment of Charicles, in short, Brathwaite illustrates both Seneca's critique of pity and his analysis of the power of clemency, while also associating clemency (as, in fact, Seneca does) with a politically shrewd theatrical staging of one's power.

The public display of clemency also allows Charicles to reestablish the force of the sovereign's word:

> Rely on the reputation of his word [he tells his subjects], under whose Sovereignty you live, that you cannot be more dear to your selves then you shall be unto us, so popular Faction divide you not from us. Nor do we doubt it, for we see that cheerfulness in your faces, as it assures us, that nothing but Characters of loyalty can be writ in your hearts: From which assurance, we have signed your pardon with the Signet Manual of our pity.[60]

Like divine providence, Charicles is now the dispenser rather than the object of pity, the author rather than the character. His subjects'—rather than his own—faithfulness may be subject to doubt (there is a disturbing echo of Duncan's "There's no art / To find the mind's construction in the face" in *Macbeth*), but it is in Charicles's power to resolve the crisis of faithfulness through his own clemency and trust.[61] The metaphor of "characters of loyalty" written on the subjects' hearts is reminiscent of the scriptural image of conscience as the law written on the heart by God. But here the narrator implies that the king is the writer of loyal "characters," that this writing or character is itself the effect rather than the cause of his pity. As in the conclusion to *Cloria*, providential and naturalistic explanations of the plot converge to foreground not only the author's but also the character's artistry. As though to address whatever discomfort we may feel faced with this exposure of the theatrical dimension of politics, Charicles reiterates in conclusion that his resolve is "steered rather by Reason then Passion," that is, by the rational response of "Princely Clemency." Then, as a sign of his confidence in his own judgment, he invites his subjects to "unsheath [their swords] against us, when we act ought deviously, or contrary to the rule of Equity."[62] In his new relation to his subjects, Charicles provides us with a perfect example of controlling the potentially wayward passion of pity by the representation of pity, that is, by clemency. He provides, that is, a perfect image of the link between clemency, equity, and artistry.

SYMPATHY BETWEEN MEN

Like *Cloria* and *Panthalia*, *Theophania* depicts a Hobbesian world in which genuine passion—not least of all the passion for glory—is both a sign of true aristocratic virtue and a cause of civil war. Civil war in turn contributes to a crisis of the affections, an uncertainty about their role in court culture and politics. Depending on who is speaking, passion is either distinguished from the calculation of self-interest and conflated with it, as though the author were trying to find a way to accommodate the old world of chivalric virtue within the new world of "politick maxims."[63] At the same time, like Brathwaite and Herbert, the author resists the reduction of all behavior to interest. Repeatedly in the narrative, chivalric honor is portrayed as a principle of erotic identification—the soldier is above all a man of feeling. Such identification, it is suggested, may in turn become the basis of a new political order of sensibility—or perhaps a newly aestheticized order of sensibility that is less obviously political than the old. The mimetic desire that contributed to civil war may itself provide the basis of the Restoration. (*Theophania* was written in 1645, and published in 1655, so the Restoration is merely hypothetical.)

In conspicuous imitation of Sidney's *Arcadia*, the narrative opens with the shipwreck of two young men, Demetrius (the prince of Orange) and Philocles (Prince Rupert, nephew of Charles I). They are rescued by Synesius (Robert Sidney, the second earl of Leicester) who has retired in wartime to his country estate (Penshurst). After a series of military skirmishes in the surrounding countryside, they are joined by Alexandro, the prince of Wales, and Cenodoxius, the third earl of Essex and erstwhile commander of the parliamentary forces. The remainder of the narrative is then taken up with Synesius's questioning of his visitors about the events of the war and their responses.

The genre of prose romance is well suited to representing the complicated political stance of the author. As scholars have convincingly argued, the romance is a vehicle for the political views of Robert Sidney, second earl of Leicester (1595–1677), who urged negotiation between the royalists and Essex. One of the chief burdens of the text is to justify the actions of Essex without offending the royalist party; equally or more important is the defense of Leicester himself against charges of inconstancy vis-à-vis the king.[64] The typical romance device of the inset narrative serves these purposes by allowing for the rhetorical redescription of the "same" events from different perspectives. For example, in a long inset narrative Cenodoxius/Essex justifies his rebellion in terms of the indignities he and his family have suffered at the hands of their monarchs. He then defends his actions by describing them in terms of the chivalric code of love and honor. In both cases, true passion is a sign of aristocratic virtue and is conspicuously opposed to the conniving self-interest of the crown. In response, Leicester criticizes Essex by redescribing his actions in terms of factional self-interest. Yet Leicester also reprimands the Stuarts for indulging their passions and appeals to politic considerations of interest to urge reconciliation between Essex and the prince of Wales.

In his account of the slights to his family, Cenodoxius portrays his father, the second earl of Essex, as the constant lover and faithful servant of the inconstant Elizabeth, who did not hesitate to abandon him when he no longer served her purposes. Interest, not passion, was the driving force behind Elizabethan policy, as we see in the following depiction of her relationship with her subjects:

> Wherefore knowing that a Prince who will be absolute, must either by an awful terror compel a strict obedience, or else with a show at least of clemencie and vertue gain the affections of the people; and being in her nature cruel and ambitious, she thought severity the most certain means to compass her designs: Nevertheless surpassing even all her sexe in the art of dissembling, she so vailed it over with a mask of affability, that though she were resolved to make her will a law, yet she appeared to the vulgar the most submiss of women, and was believed to have neither affections nor desires, but what tended only to the public good: Insomuch that her most violent proceedings were thought forced by a publike necessity ... and which was most admirable, her profound dissimulations real virtues, and an innate tenderness or affection of the people; by which she so won their hearts, who judge only by outward appearances.[65]

Elizabeth appears here as the Machiavellian prince who knows that it's better to be feared than loved, although ideally both are desirable. Affection is a theatrical effect, designed to win the people, who judge only by appearances, to "slavish obedience." Although there is some suggestion that the queen's feelings for Essex were genuine at one time, Cenodoxius makes it clear that considerations of self-preservation and expediency were always foremost in Elizabeth's mind. Essex, in contrast, lived according to a chivalric code of honor rather than the "politick maxims of the present Government."[66]

A similar opposition between passion and interest appears to govern the life of the third earl of Essex. Like his father, Cenodoxius presents himself as motivated by genuine passion—"the resistless power of love"— and as abused by his sovereigns. Thus he narrates in what must have been, for contemporaries, gripping detail the story of his courtship and clandestine marriage to the notorious Frances Howard, whom James then married to his favorite, Robert Carr. He tells us how, when asked to explain his "pretences of *Interest* in that Lady," he "related at large the birth, growth, and maturation of *our Love, our mutual Vows, our private Contracts*, our formal marriage, and at last the fruition of those joys."[67] (If Cenodoxius echoes Othello here, he must do so in order to appear naive and manipulated.) He describes the insult to his honor when King James arranged for the annulment of the marriage on the grounds it had not been consummated (Cenodoxius tells us the evidence included a faked test of chastity, in which Artemia/Frances Howard was impersonated by her virgin maid). This story of passion and deception is repeated in the reign of Charles, when Essex resolves "once more to become a courtier," again becomes "a slave to love," is again betrayed by his wife, and again insulted by the king, who refuses to punish the guilty parties.[68] Although not as cunning as Elizabeth in her treatment of the second earl of Essex, James and Charles are equally guilty of casting aspersions on the third earl's manhood and aristocratic honor. In doing so, they prime him for the tragedy of vainglory so astutely analyzed by Hobbes in *Leviathan* and *Behemoth*.

According to Essex's own Hobbesian analysis, his passion is not only a sign of aristocratic virtue but also a cause of civil war, for it is on the basis of his many grievances that others can persuade him to take up arms against the king:

> My Fathers blood, *Agnesias* [his mother's] languishing griefs, my violate marriage, and this late contempt, raised several passions, which like so many torrents overthrew all obstacles that withstood the rapacity of their course, where they met the greatest checks, raging with the greatest impetuosity, and though the sacred person of the King, with the holy Office of the Priesthood, seemed secure Ramparts against any violence, they swelled to such a prodigious height, that at last they overflowed them, and have now caused such a vast sea of confusion, in which my self have suffered a miserable shipwreck.
>
> Nevertheless those two considerations of piety and allegiance had perhaps suppressed such unruly thoughts, if the malecontents of the times perceiving my distemper, had not taken that opportunity to enage me in their own designes.[69]

Essex appropriates the proverbial romance tempest and shipwreck as metaphors for his own emotional confusion: his passions, he argues, are both inconstant and genuine—inconstant because genuine—and thus their own apology.

Yet, as in the case of Essex's analysis of Elizabeth's affection for her people, what is passion from one perspective is interest from another. Listening to this narrative, Alexandro (Prince Charles) is suspicious of Cenodoxius's "reformation" and of his offer to assist the royalist cause:

> I had rather to enjoy a divided Empire with [Corastus/Fairfax], then be
> fully restored by the assistance of *Cenodoxius*; for his proceedings
> under specious pretences of reformation, and dissembled protestations
> to advance the interests of the Crown have been so injurious both to
> King and people, that by his wicked practices they are now almost
> irreconicileably [*sic*] engaged in one anothers ruine: Yet I must confess
> if he had avowed his cause, I should not have been so much offended
> with his actions, nor altogether so averse from such a reconcilia-
> tion: For great men that are sensible of their own dishonour, are the
> fittest Ministers for Princes, and being cherished, the chief supports of
> the Crown.[70]

In this complicated analysis, Alexandro recasts Cenodoxius's passionate
defense of his honor as a matter of factional self-interest but he also be-
trays some sympathy for the self-serving pursuit of "greatness." Although, he seems to suggest, love of one's sovereign (as of one's subjects)
can be feigned, love of honor cannot. Thus, the very passion that led Essex
to rebel is potentially just as dependable and calculable in its own way as
self-interest. In fact, there is little or no difference between them, and this
is a source of strength as well as danger for the sovereign who knows how
to "cherish" his nobility.

In his own response to Cenodoxius's narrative, Synesius is less optimis-
tic about the conversion of vainglory to the public interest. Like Hobbes
commenting on the lethal rivalry inherent in chivalric culture, Synesius
recasts Cenodoxius's motivating passions as injured "Vanity and Revenge": "*Cenodoxius*, moved by the sense of his disgraces, finding the
humors of men so congruent to his designs, through Vanity and Revenge,
engaged us all in a miserable war, of which he was himself the first Author,
so himself hath felt first the cruel effects thereof."[71] Mimetic desire has
been rampant in the life of Cenodoxius: out of affection, the king procured Cenodoxius's wife (Artemia/Frances Howard) for his favorite (Robert Carr); as a result, Cenodoxius's honor was offended, and so he found
others similarly offended with whom to join in battle. In both cases, the
courtly bond is first and foremost a bond between men, an erotic bond
that is also the occasion of rivalry and violence. The civil war is itself one
of the "horrid effects of sympathy."

But mimetic desire is not the only problem. Synesius also invites Alexandro to recognize how the Stuarts' neglect of the public interest contributed to the present state of civil war:

> [T]he frequent bloody strife between our Kings and the Nobility . . .
> were the necessary consequences of an ill composed government in the
> first institution, which neither sufficiently declaring in whom consisted

that supream authority, which is necessary to the preservation of every Commonwealth, not yet fully determining the right of succession, left a liberty to subjects to enlarge their privileges by force, and to every one, as he had most power, the arbitrament of his own interest.[72]

Earlier monarchs' reluctance or inability to rule absolutely left a power vacuum in which powerful nobles acted according to their own factional self-interest.[73] Moreover, James and Charles were in turn "inconstant": lenient when it came to their courtiers' private interests and negligent when it came to advancing the public interest. In both cases, this inconstancy was related to unregulated passion. Just as James was "too much byassed by his own affections," especially for Buckingham, so Charles was biased by his affection for Henrietta Maria. This dual misgovernment of passion and interest, Synesius concludes, set the stage for Essex's rebellion:

> Thus, what one built, another presently destroyed, and those active spirits, who sought to prefer themselves, neglecting the interests of their Country, applyed themselves onely to those studies that might render them most gratefull to the present favorites. . . . That Country which is so unhappy to be governed by such depraved Counsels, must of necessity be a nursery of factions and discontents, which through those errors, and defects so abounded amongst us, that it was impossible they should be long contained within the bounds of duty.[74]

The remedy, Synesius argues, is a strong sovereign power, along with attention to "politick maximes" and to the "fundamental laws" that are designed to preserve the public interest. On the basis of England's interest in self-preservation and his own assessment of the unlikelihood of assistance from other European nation-states, Synesius urges reconciliation with Cenodoxius and his followers: Cenodoxius has promised obedience and "a Prince who is deputed by Heaven, to exercise a kingly power upon Earth, ought in this to imitate the supreme Divinity, that though the people only through fear of punishment are obedient to his Laws, yet whilst they perform their duty, he refuseth them not his protection."[75] This advice echoes that of Tacitus, Jean Bodin, and in particular Leicester's friend, Hugo Grotius, whom he had come to know while serving as ambassador to France in the 1630s.[76] In his private papers, Leicester had meditated on the origin of government and the question of political obligation in explicitly Grotian terms: "I [believe] . . . as Grotius sayeth, that men, not by the commandment of God, but of their own [mind] . . . did gather themselves together into civile societyes from whence the civile power hath beginning, and is therefore called a humane ordinance." In other words, "Kings made not themselves by force, but were created in all nations by the people for the public good." The proper response to human weakness and fallibility was for men "to make Laws with consideration of humane infirmity, and for the benefit of the whole." And he concluded, "This is cleare enough in ye mindes of all men, unless it be of such as for their own interests flatter princes in the ruine of theyr country and of all honest men."[77] Alexandro is persuaded by similar politic counsel and promises to relay the argument to his father.

The romance as a whole, however, is not content with the politic solutions of either Alexandro or Synesius. To Alexandro's redescription of the unstable passions of love and honor in terms of calculable interest, and Synesius's proposal of a Hobbesian quid pro quo, Sales adds a number powerful scenes of passion. In a series of erotically charged tableaux, he both dramatizes his sympathy for the older aristocratic values of love and honor and suggests that these passions may become the basis of a new social order. Mimetic desire is still at work in these scenes, but it produces sympathy rather than rivalry. An erotically charged aesthetic interest substitutes for political interest as the characters respond to "spectacles of sorrow" with pity and compassion rather than "vanity and revenge." These sympathetic passions, which differ not only from Synesius's politic counsel but also from the rational clemency recommended by Seneca and Brathwaite, are particularly associated with those figures fighting on the side of the king.

Essex's long, central narrative is framed by the adventures of Alexandro (Prince Charles) and Demetrius (William, the young prince of Orange), as they are narrated to Synesius (the earl of Leicester). Although Alexandro and Demetrius are drawn together by reports of each other's virtue, they do not meet on the battlefield but—for all practical purposes—in bed. Alexandro, who is suffering from battle wounds and even more from lovesickness presents "a spectacle of sorrow" to the Leicester household: even his servant faints for pity on Alexandro's bed. Alexandro tries to revive him and when the doctor Cassianus arrives to check on his royal patient, he is "not a little surprised to find them in such a posture." This ambiguous encounter sets the stage for the meeting of Demetrius and Alexandro a few pages later. Demetrius's eagerness to see Alexandro is referred to as a kind of "courtship."[78] When Alexandro comes to Demetrius's bedroom, Demetrius (who is himself recovering from his exposure at sea) faints at the sight:

> But when he saw *Alexandro*, who presently went to embrace him, instead of returning that civility, all his senses were on a sudden seised with so strange a stupidity, that falling backwards upon his pillow, he fixed his eyes upon him with such a ghastly countenance, that they all thought he was at the same instant yielding up the ghost.

Whereupon the Prince, turned about to [his servant] *Lysander,* cryed out, Is this sympathie, that produces such horrid effects! . . .

But whilst he was speaking, *Demetrius* by degrees began to move his eyes; and raising his body, cryed out, Oh let me for ever gaze upon that glorious object! Some heavenly Deity in commiseration of the languishing *Demetrius* hath assumed that form, to restore him to perfect happiness. When *Alexandro* once more approaching towards him, before he could speak, he proceeded; Disdain not, divine creature, a sacrifice of that heart which hath been so long devoted to thy service: Thy presence hath infused into me a new soul, and I already feel such an overflowing joy, that one pleasing look will enable me not only to overcome this trivial sicknes, but to vanquish even death it self.[79]

And, with the rest of the household looking on, "they flew into each others arms with such a mutual concurrence of affection, that they seemed to breath their souls into each others bosoms. At which sight the standers by were moved with such a tenderness, that they could not refrain from tears."[80] In this scene, the identity of the princes is portrayed not in terms of chivalric combat but erotically charged sympathy. And this sympathy is in turn rendered as an aesthetic effect: the "spectacle" of Demetrius's sorrowful condition moves Alexandro, just as the spectacle of their own tearful recognition scene moves the bystanders. This is the sort of pity Seneca condemns in *De clementia* and that Brathwaite associates with effeminacy in *Panthalia.* In *Theophania,* by contrast, the aesthetic response of pity is tinged with admiration and wonder.[81]

A similarly erotically charged relationship between young men appears at the end of the narrative, along with a similar aestheticizing of passion. In the final romance insert, Cenodoxius, Alexandro, and Demetrius hear the story of two royalist soldiers, Perrotus and Clorimanthes, whose friendship "was paragoned with the best examples of antient times," notwithstanding their love for the same woman, Monelia: "We consorted our selves together in all actions either of danger or recreation: our thoughts were so uniform, that whatsoever pleased the one, was the delight of the other, and even our loves, which it was impossible to separate, by the secret sympathy of our souls, were without jealousies or emulation, directed both to the same object."[82] In *Leviathan* Hobbes had argued, "if any two men desire the same thing, which nevertheless they cannot both enjoy, they become enemies; and in the way to their End, which is principally their own conservation, and sometimes their delectation only, endeavour to destroy, or subdue one another."[83] In contrast to Hobbes's linking of desire to a scarcity economy, this story dramatizes the perfect "regulation" of the passions, the perfect containment of the dangers of mimetic desire: one prince loves Monelia physically, the other worships her platonically, and their shared love of Monelia makes them "more enamoured of each others vertue."[84] And, although the conclusion of the narrative illustrates once again the horrid effect of sympathy, it too manages to contain this effect—again by aestheticizing it. When her physical lover dies in battle (the battle narrated at the opening of *Theophania*), Monelia appears to exhibit Stoic constancy—even impassivity. Yet, when her platonic lover approaches her in her chamber to console her, she stabs herself. The surviving prince describes this last act of her life as a "tragical scene," while praising her "heroick hand"; the narrator of *Theophania* tells us "this sad tragedie moved a wonderfull compassion in the hearers," and that Alexandro urged patience until the perpetrators of the prince's murder could be discovered. By deliberately contrasting Monelia's action to Stoic constancy, the narrator suggests that while passion may be a motive for heroism, it is also a source of tragedy. But tragedy as an aesthetic rather than a political phenomenon may in turn generate compassion rather than "vanity and revenge" in the audience. The "spectacle" of tragedy ideally provokes pity and compassion rather than violent deeds.

In focusing on scenes of pity and compassion, in short, the narrator self-consciously aestheticizes the realm of politics. Political interest is not the only bulwark against the dangerous passions of honor and vainglory. Pity and compassion—which appear in this text as effects of erotic and aesthetic interest—may also serve as a countervailing force to the jealousy and emulation that have given rise to civil war. In this sense *Theophania* too is a kind of metaromance: it self-consciously reflects on the uses of romance (including the long-standing association in romance of erotic and aesthetic interest) to create the kind of distanced engagement characteristic of sympathy rather than rivalry. If such engagement can be sustained, the Restoration may appear as one of the surprising effects of sympathy.[85]

This reading is supported by the prefatory note to the reader, where the stationer singles out *Theophania*'s analysis of the passions as one of the primary achievements of the text:

> You will find Man, and the Passions of Man (the great Engines of our Conversation) and (it may be) traverses of State, set down as in a Mapp or Chart before you.

> [The author's] Designes are natural, correspondent, and effective; his Scenes probable, and suitable; his Loves high and generous (but without extravagancy;) his Passions essential, and real, and such as perfectly limn different souls, in their different agitations; his discourses and reflections solid and mature, and the resultance of all this, so generous and harmonious, that I rather choose to leave you to the consideration of the several beauties you will find in every part thereof, then corrupt your judgements by a previous information in the general.

This is about as near to a defense of aesthetic interest as we will find in these romances. The stationer makes no explicit claim for the power of *Theophania* to inculcate virtue, constancy, or political consent. The adjective "suitable" takes no direct object, unless it is the self-referential "suitable representation." The passions are "real" because perfect imitations. Above all, the stationer recommends "the several beauties" the reader will find in *Theophania*. These remarks capture something of the effect of this strange work. *Theophania* does not so much teach virtue as sympathetic identification. But, in doing so, it transmutes the politically dangerous passion of vainglory into aesthetic interest.

We can measure how far we've come by recalling that, in *Panthalia*, the narrator criticized the court of Basilius/James for its aestheticizing self-regard:

> This graceful and long-continued habit of peace, as it enricht the State with plenty: so it begot in the Inhabitants an incommodious securitie. For those virile & masculine spirits, which formerly proclaimed the Heirs of Honour, were become now strangers to action & exploits of valor, being wholly unexercis'd to those Martial affairs, wherewith their first Assaies of Youth had been insured.

"The court had wars," the narrator goes on to remark, "but they were amourous Encounters: Foes, but they were Corrivals."[86] While Brathwaite condemned the "effeminacy," "amorous Encounters," "Masks, Treats, [and] Balls" of the Jacobean court as obstacles to martial valor, Sales suggests a revival of Caroline aestheticism (in particular, the aesthetic response of pity and fear) as a way of channeling and defusing the passions of war. The pity experienced by both characters and readers will in this respect work very much like the "passion," in Hobbes's words quoted in one of the epigraphs to this chapter, that causes men to "take pleasure to behold from the shore the danger of them that are at sea in a tempest, or in fight, or from a safe castle to behold two armies charge one another in the field." It is not by chance, I think, that this famous image from Lucretius takes the threat to self-preservation (including warfare) as the subject matter, which is both canceled and preserved when perceived as a spectacle. Nor is it by chance that this passage from the opening of book 2 of *De rerum natura* has so often been appropriated as an allegory of art itself. The strongest evidence we have of the shaping power of aesthetic distance is the pleasure we take in viewing those things which we would flee if we encountered them directly. For Hobbes, as for some Renaissance commentators on Aristotle's *Poetics*, such distance could inculcate insensitivity to the misery of one's friends. But, in light of *Theophania*, the passage from Lucretius suggests a different moral: aesthetic distance can make the subject matter of tragedy a source of fellow feeling, not only in art but also in life. It may transform tragedy into tragicomedy or even into the affirmation of society we associate with comedy.

Theophania thus provides a powerful response to Hobbes's argument that consent to the political contract and peaceful coexistence are predicated on the fear of violent death. Instead, Sales suggests, the peace-loving and thus—in the context of aristocratic culture—effeminized political subject is much more likely to be the effect of sentimental identification or aesthetic spectatorship. In this way, *Theophania* anticipates both the political settlement of the Restoration and the sentimental culture of the eighteenth century. As Carol Kay argued in her study of Hobbes's influence on eighteenth-century aesthetics, "the sentimental spectator may be the appropriate incarnation of the timid subject Hobbes was trying to create." According to Kay, "neither Hobbes nor Burke can be described as reducing [political] representation to [a] wholly affective function, but the potential for it in Hobbes's theory is greatly developed by Burke's emphasis on the admiring sentiments with which we regard the 'embodiments' of authority: 'These public affections, combined with manners, are required as supplements, sometimes as correctives, always as aids to the law. . . . To make us love our country, our country ought to be lovely.' " *Theophania* provides one of the missing links between Hobbesian fear and Burkean love.[87]

There are a number of important conclusions to be drawn from these royalist prose romances of the 1650s. First, clear-sighted royalists such as Herbert, Brathwaite, and Sales used the conventions of romance to criticize the "Platonick" obsessions of the Caroline court and to anatomize the contribution of passion and interest to the civil war. While mocking the deluded Caroline politics of love, they claimed a seriousness for their own romances as contributions to contemporary political debate. Second, for all three authors, to varying degrees, the analysis of political interest was intertwined with questions of artistry and aesthetic interest. For Herbert, Brathwaite, and Sales, culture was the ground not only of "political contestation" but also of restoration; in the right hands, they suggested, artistic craft and aesthetic interest could contribute to the hoped-for Restoration of Charles II.

Finally, this defense of the role of aesthetic interest in facilitating political reconciliation invites a revision of Albert Hirschman's influential account of the passions and the interests in the early modern period.[88] Hirschman's great contribution to the early modern history of passion and interest was to argue that the concept of interest was as much political as it was economic in this period: that Hobbes's dispassionate analysis of the passions was itself in the service of the interest—or reason—of state. It was this recognition of the political uses of the passions (the use of one passion to counteract the deleterious effects of another) that eventually gave rise to the argument that greed, or the accumulation of wealth, could itself be of interest to the state by counteracting the self-aggrandizing passions of honor and glory. In this and preceding chapters, I have argued that early modern writers were just as aware of the political uses of *aesthetic* interest, including our interest in the imitation or representation of the passions. Not only does imitation set off the process of rhetorical inference or probable reasoning that helps produce the illusion of verisimilitude and educates our judgment. It also allows for sympathetic identification that may itself be marshaled for political uses. *Cloria, Panthalia,* and, above all, *Theophania* stand at the intersection of these two insights (arguably Platonic and Aristotelian). In these works, to represent and to anatomize the passions are to make them available not only for manipulation but also for solicitation. The passions so conceived become the object of calculation and the vehicle of discipline, both in art and in life. Finally, at the same time that literary representation is conceived as a mode of countervailing passion and thus of political interest, Restoration politics itself is aestheticized. The achievement of royalist romance in the 1650s is to refigure the public interest as a matter not only of Hobbesian calculation but also of sympathy. In this way, Herbert, Brathwaite, and Sales could be said to "redeem" or reinvent romance for the post-Cromwellian settlement.[89] In Clarendon's vision of the Restoration, quoted as an epigraph to this chapter, the newly restored king will both "make Calculations" about the trustworthiness of his subjects' "hearts" and—in an uncanny echo of the embrace of Alexandro and Demetrius in *Theophania*— "finde all His subjects at once in His arms, and himself in theirs."

CHAPTER 10

Critique

More serious is the question whether the law of non-resistance should bind us in case of extreme and imminent peril. Even some laws of God, although stated in general terms, carry a tacit exception in cases of extreme necessity. Such a limitation was put upon the law of the Sabbath by learned men in the time of the Maccabees; hence the well-known saying: "Danger to life breaks the Sabbath." . . . This exception was approved by Christ, as also an exception in the case of another law, which forbade the eating of the shewbread.

—Grotius, *De jure belli ac pacis*

For by the word *Servant* (whether it be derived from *Servire*, to Serve, or from *Servare*, to Save, which I leave to the Grammarians to dispute) is not meant a Captive, which is kept in prison, or bonds . . . for such men (commonly called Slaves,) have no obligation at all; but may break their bonds, or the prison; and kill, or carry away captive their Master, justly. . . . It is not therefore the Victory, that giveth the right of Dominion over the Vanquished, but his own Covenant.

—Hobbes, *Leviathan*

IF ROYALIST ROMANCE OF THE 1650s adumbrates the sentimental culture of the Restoration, in *Samson Agonistes* Milton uses the genre of tragedy to resist the royalist aesthetics of reconciliation, a reconciliation under duress. For Milton and his republican contemporaries, the Restoration amounted to a state of involuntary servitude and coercion in which consent and contract had lost their meaning. Under the new regime, the supporters of the commonwealth were not so much servants as slaves, and not slaves in the sense of captives who had agreed to obey their new masters in order to "save" themselves but rather unwilling captives, prisoners of conscience.[1] In this respect, the tragedy of Samson—bound in chains and refusing to be ransomed—allegorizes the condition of the unwilling republican subjects of Charles II. This portrait of Samson may draw on the arguments of Grotius, Hobbes, and others regarding the status of the captive who has not consented to his conqueror, who has not entered into a political contract, and who accordingly still has the right to resist.[2] In this case, Samson's pulling down the temple would figure the individual right of resistance in exceptional political circumstances.

And yet, as with Samson's own deliberations in his opening soliloquy, the failure of the English republic and the subsequent enslavement of the English people also raise the question of individual responsibility, and thus of a different kind of voluntary servitude and breach of trust. Did the republic fail because of the English people's enslavement to their passions and breach of the heavenly contract? From this perspective, Samson's bondage would represent the failure of the republicans themselves, and the precondition of political agency and a new political contract would be a renewed internal contract or bond of conscience, itself informed by the right passions, the right affective disposition.[3] These in turn would allow Samson to understand his exceptional calling by God and to undertake actions above the form of law or custom.

Samson Agonistes thus revisits the arguments of *The Tenure of Kings and Magistrates* from the perspective of the 1660s. For example, Samson's deliberations about *salus populi* and his own covenant with God take up the questions at the heart of seventeenth-century debates about political obligation: what legitimates the violation of positive law, human or divine? What is the relation of the exception to the rule, of power to legitimate authority, and of the natural law of justice to positive law? And what bearing does the divine covenant have on the political contract? The difference is that, whereas in the earlier work Milton had confidently assimilated the equitable judgments of conscience and reason of state to natural law, in *Samson Agonistes* reasoning about the exception is the problem rather than the solution.[4] In Milton's late drama, the norms of conscientious action, the meaning of natural law, and the sanction for violence are themselves the subject of debate.

As in *The Tenure*, these interpretive issues are affective as well as cognitive, but here too the Restoration marks an important difference. In his defense of regicide, Milton had accused the Presbyterians of "a dissembl'd and seditious pity," as well as an unseemly concern with self-preservation or fear of violent death. From the perspective of the 1660s, it is not only the Presbyterians who are guilty of "a double tyrannie of Custom from without and blind affections within" (*CPW*, 3:190), but all those who have effectively consented to the new regime. Milton's goal in *Samson* is accordingly to purge the politically debilitating responses of pity and fear, to free the reader from his voluntary servitude, and to justify exceptional deeds above the form of law or custom. And, as in *The Tenure*, he does so by dramatizing an activity of interpretation, one diametrically opposed to the understanding of covenant, conscience, natural law, and the fear of violent death—not to mention the role of interpretation itself—that contemporaries associated with defenders of the Restoration and with Hobbes.[5]

In the following pages I begin with the cultural significance of Samson in political debates about reason of state and casuistry in the 1640s; I then show how the problem of interpreting the covenant in *Samson Agonistes* is bound up with the determination of *salus populi* and the exceptional judgments of conscience. Although Milton, unlike Hobbes, was concerned to empower the individual conscience by reference to "the law of nature and of nations," in *Samson Agonistes* he also explores the tragic dilemma of the individual compelled to judge and to act in the absence of cognitive certainty. In this light, *Samson Agonistes* appears as Milton's allegory of antifoundationalism, of the creative fiat of interpretation in the absence of any more secure or more legible foundation. But, whereas Hobbes aimed to preclude the tragedy of civil war by subordinating the heavenly contract to the secular political contract, Milton insists that these two contracts are not homologous. For Milton, conscience by definition cannot be a matter of calculation. This noncoincidence is precisely what makes acts of conscience possible, but it is also what makes room for tragedy.

I then turn to Milton's preface to *Samson Agonistes* in order to show how the problem of the covenant is inseparable from the contract of genre. Both in his choice of genre and in his attention to the passions, Milton indirectly engages the royalist culture of the 1660s. In contrast to the sentimental identification solicited by the theatrical spectacle of the Restoration, Milton stresses the distancing effect of literary representation.[6] This critique of Restoration spectacle bears on Milton's treatment of the passions. Just as Milton had singled out the passion of pity for criticism in *The Tenure*, so in the prefatory note to *Samson Agonistes* and throughout the poem Milton makes it clear that excessive pity and fear have the power to enslave the reader or spectator and must be counteracted and purged by tragic form. The effect of such purgation is not sympathy but something more like Kantian respect: the "pious and just honouring of ourselves." Against the royalist aesthetics of reconciliation, tragedy in Milton's hands offers aesthetics as a form of political critique.[7]

REASON OF STATE

We can begin to get a full sense of the biblical Samson's cultural significance if we recall that Samson regularly figured in seventeenth-century political debate as an illustration of the extraordinary judgments of reason of state and of conscience. In the figure of Samson, we see seventeenth-century writers worrying about the relationship between natural law and the exception, as well as about the relationship between conscience and divine positive law. As an illustration of reasoning about the exception, Samson also raised the question, central to *Samson Agonistes*, of whether Samson's own extraordinary actions could serve as an example, whether they could be imitated by others.[8]

As we have seen in earlier chapters, for Milton and his contemporaries, reason of state was that form of reasoning which deliberated about exceptional political cases in which *salus populi*—the good of the people, the preservation of the state—demanded the violation of positive and/or moral law.[9] Reason of state thus posed distinctive ethical and epistemological problems. According to Carl Friedrich, reason of state emerges as an ethical problem when the preservation of the state is perceived to be at odds with the norms of justice: "[O]nly when there is a clash between the commands of an individual ethic of high normativity and the needs and requirements of organizations whose security and survival is at stake can the issue of reason of state become real."[10] Yet, reason of state also emerges as an ethical problem when true justice seems to require the violation of positive or moral law. These two different interpretations of *salus populi* as self-preservation or the good of the people in turn presuppose different understandings of natural law. When *salus* is construed as safety, as in Hobbes, we find a conflation of natural law with the right of self-preservation; when *salus* is equated with the good, as in Milton, determining the exception depends on the natural law of right reason.

On the royalist side, what Friedrich has described as the ethical issue of reason of state was resolved by assimilating it to the tradition of the *arcana imperii*: the king was privy to the secrets of empire that verged on and were at times explicitly identified with a God-given insight into political matters.[11] Only the king had the knowledge to decide what was in the public interest; his decisions could therefore not be constrained—nor his conscience troubled—by considerations of merely human law. Reason of state was in James I's view not so much a problem as a solution, another name for divine right absolutism. So James argued in a letter to the House of Commons in 1621, defending his discretion in matters of policy, matters that "were of necessity secret, unpredictable, and peremptory."[12] In 1628, in response to the Petition of Right, Serjeant Ashley similarly declared that "kings rule not only by the common law but also by 'a law of state,' and added that 'in the law of state their acts are bounded by the law of nature'" rather than by positive law. In the Commons Francis Nethersole argued that "for reason of state the king could imprison [and tax] without showing cause."[13] Not surprisingly, given this use of reason of state to justify impositions and imprisonment at the king's will, Sir Edward Coke remarked that "a Reason of State is a trick to put a man out of the right way; for, when a man can give no reason for a thing, then he flieth to a higher Strain, and saith it is Reason of State." In the parliamentary debates of 1628, one George (or John) Browne similarly declared that "reason of state is a meere chimera."[14]

By the 1640s parliamentary critics of the king were invoking reason of state in defense of their own policies, identifying it not with divine right absolutism but with nascent constitutionalism. Charles Herle, a Presbyterian clergyman, argued that "mixt Monarchy" was the best form of government and that "*Reason* or *wisdome of State* . . . first *contriv'd* [the mixture]."[15] Reason of state also had the more particular connotation of discretion in matters of necessity and self-preservation, now identified as resistance to the king. For critics of absolute monarchy such as Henry Parker and Milton, God-given reason dictated not only that government be based on an original covenant or contract with the ruler, but that this contract be revocable when the ends of government—self-preservation as well as preservation of the state—were not being served. Thus in *The Contra-Replicant, His Complaint to His Majestie* (1642), Parker justified reason of state as a supplement to contract, one that achieves a kind of sublime—even an imperial—transcendence of the law:

> Lawes ayme at *Justice*, Reason of state aimes at *safety*. . . . reason of State goes beyond all particular formes and pacts, and looks rather to the being, then the well-being of a State. . . . Reason of state is something more sublime and imperiall then Law: it may rightly be said, that the Statesman begins where the Lawyer ceaseth; for when warre has silenced Law, a kind of dictatorian power is to be allowed to her; whatsoever has any right to defend it selfe in time of danger is to resort to policy in stead of Law. (18–19)

Parker's remarks suggest that he recognized reason of state could be a dangerous supplement to any fixed conception of mixed monarchy or government based on law, contract, and consent. Yet, for Parker, precisely because reason of state was concerned with the "right" of self-defense, it proved to be the necessary complement of any legitimate model of contractual obligation.

Milton made a similar argument in *The Tenure of Kings and Magistrates* and the first *Defence*, stressing even more forcefully than Parker the compatibility of natural law and reason of state not simply with "safety" but with true justice. In both texts, government is established and preserved by the exercise of God-given reason in accordance with "that law of Nature and of God which holds that whatever is for the safety of the state is right and just."[16] Thus, in *The Tenure*, Milton argued that the regicide—which violated positive law—was justified by natural law, which dictated above all the safety of the people. And in defending the actions of Parliament and the army, he referred to "the glorious way wherin *Justice and Victory* hath set them; the only warrants through all the ages, next under immediat Revelation, to exercise supream power" (*CPW*, 3:194). In the first *Defence*, Milton asserted that absolute obedience to positive law amounted to an idolatrous submission to tyrannical or de facto political power without concern for justice. In contrast, reason, justice, morality, and the natural law of *salus populi* all demand that tyrants be punished by violence.[17] In both texts, exceptions to or suspensions of positive law are normalized by being referred to right reason and the law of nature. At the same time, in both texts reason of state involves critical judgment rather than an appeal to absolute authority; as such, it transforms the exercise of what Parker called "arbitrary power," making it an instrument of justice rather than mere legality, of revolution rather than the status quo.[18]

Precisely because it required discretionary judgment, contemporaries on both sides of the political divide were acutely aware that reason of state and the necessities to which it claimed to respond could be abused or feigned. In such cases, reason of state was not grounded in God-given reason and natural law; rather, it represented a usurpation of the divine prerogative to suspend the moral law. In these cases, the invocation of reason of state involved equivocation or casuistry in the pejorative sense of the term. In his *Lectures on Conscience and Human Law*, Bishop Sanderson warned in particular against the equivocal interpretation of *salus populi*, promoted by "a class of men [who] have used their leisure in a luckless way, to invent and import a new scheme of *politics* into the *State* . . . under the pretence of *Christian liberty*, or of *liberty of Conscience.*" After explaining that the word *people* is properly understood to include both the king and his subjects, he added, "I have explained these particulars with precision . . . [for two reasons]; the first, that we may not suffer ourselves to be deceived and imposed upon by a fallacious construction of an ambiguous word; the other, in order that there may be no force in the mere sound of the word *people*, to prejudice the sovereign of the community, and the ruler of the nation."[19]

Sanderson might well have had in mind someone like John Goodwin, who in *Right and Might Well Met* (1648) identified the interest of the people with the army and the Independents, and who defended the army's illegal actions on the ground that

> the law of nature, necessity, and of love to their country, . . . being the law of God himself written in the fleshly tables of men's hearts, hath an authoritative jurisdiction over all human laws and constitutions whatsoever, a prerogative right of power to overrule them and to suspend their obliging influences in all cases appropriate to itself. Yea

many of the Lawes of God themselves, thinke it no disparagement unto
them, to give place to their elder Sister, the Law of necessity, and to
surrender their authority into her hand, when shee speaketh.[20]

For Goodwin, as for many of his contemporaries, reason of state could
involve the suspension of divine as well as positive law for reasons of
necessity. To the objection that it is difficult to judge what is necessary,
Goodwin replied that we are obliged by our consciences to do so even
though our judgment may be fallible: "The neglect, or non-exercise of
that judging faculty or power, which is planted in the soules and consciences of men by God, upon such terms, and with references to such
ends as these, draweth along with it that sin, w[hi]ch the Wise man called,
the *despising of a mans wayes.* . . . Every man is bound to consider, judge,
and determine, what is meet, and necessary for him to doe, either to, with,
for, or against, all other men" (16). Whereas Goodwin asserted that the
effort to judge could not be condemned even though a particular judgment might be faulty, contemporary treatises on casuistry stressed that a
right intention could not justify an immoral act. Yet for Sanderson the
problem was not chiefly one of misconstruction but of deception: as
Goodwin himself admitted, necessity could be feigned as well as misinter-
preted; and when it is feigned, the new politics begins to look strangely
like an attempt to use the fiction of necessity to justify merely human
transgressions of divine law.

This dynamic of freedom and necessity, discretion and force, may explain why Samson regularly served as a counter in royalist and parliamentary discussions of this extralegal power to determine the exception. Discussing Bates' Case (1606), which had upheld the king's right to levy
impositions by arguing that the king's power was "supra-legal, so that he
might for reason of state act contrary to the common law," Sir John Davies compared the king's absolute prerogative to Samson:

> [T]he King's Prerogative in this point is as strong as *Samson*, it cannot
> be bound; for though an Act of Parliament be made to restrain it, and
> the King doth give his consent unto it, as *Samson* was bound with his
> own consent, yet if the Philistines come, that is, if any just or important
> occasion do arise, it cannot hold or restrain the Prerogative, it will be
> as thred, and broken as easie as the bonds of Samson.[21]

For Davies Samson was exemplary of sovereign power because his
strength was so great that he could not be restrained by any other force:
he could only be "bound with his own consent," as he was when he agreed
to be bound by the men of Judah in response to his slaughter of the Philistines (see Judges 15:12–14). Yet Davies also noted almost parenthetically
that the occasion of breaking the bonds of Parliament must be "just or

important," thereby suggesting that the king's arbitrary power must be guided by considerations of justice above and beyond positive law. In doing so, he implicitly suggested the rhetorical question that Milton's Samson asks in his first soliloquy: "what is strength without a double share / Of wisdom?" Or, less rhetorically, on the basis of what knowledge should the king or individual subject break his bonds?

In *The Reason of Church Government* (1641), Milton inverted the kind of argument made by Davies by comparing Samson's locks to English law rather than exclusively to royal prerogative:

> I cannot better liken the state and person of a King then to that mighty Nazarite *Samson*; who being disciplin'd from his birth in the precepts and the practice of Temperance and Sobriety, without the strong drink of injurious and excessive desires, grows up to a noble strength and perfection with those his illustrious and sunny locks the laws waving and curling about his god like shoulders. . . . But laying down his head among the strumpet flatteries of Prelats, while he sleeps and thinks no harme, they wickedly shaving off all those bright and waighty tresses of his laws, and just prerogatives which were his ornament and strength, deliver him over to indirect and violent councels . . . and make him grinde in the prison house of their sinister ends and practices upon him.

Whereas Davies compared Samson's strength to Charles's unconstrained prerogative, Milton implies that both strength and prerogative are a function of the law. And he warns that when "Law and Right" recover their "wonted might," they will "thunder with ruin upon the heads of [Charles's] evil counsellors, but not without great affliction to himself." Here too the law is an instrument of critical judgment as well as strength, of justice as well as power. Milton suggests a similar linking of criticism and strength in the first *Defence*, where he describes Samson as a heroic tyrannicide, who "thought it not impious but pious to kill those masters that were tyrants over his country."[22] Yet, in describing Samson as one who "made war single-handed on his masters . . . whether prompted by God or by his own valor," Milton also raises the question of the divine authority for Samson's decision—the question, that is, of his calling. In so doing, he also calls attention to the relationship between the judgments of reason of state and the interpretation of the divine covenant.

Reason of state is often assumed to be a secular rationale of expedient political action, one that is incompatible with the rule of the saints. Yet, as we have seen in previous chapters and as Milton's description of the pious Samson in the first *Defence* suggests, the Protestant doctrines of the covenant and calling proved to be particularly hospitable to reason of state in all its ambiguity.[23] On the one hand, the voluntarism of such doctrines seems to have contributed to a rational view of this-worldly experience, including politics and the exigencies of reason of state.[24] On the other hand, this same voluntarism, along with the notion of the specific calling, served to isolate politics from other kinds of activities and, at least in some cases, to make politics less a matter of shared rational deliberation than of individual conscience and of the will. As we will see, this is particularly the case with Samson the Nazarite, whose struggle to understand his calling—his individual covenant with God—is intimately bound up with his meditation on reason of state.

While all saints were called in general to be conscientious and obedient citizens of the Christian commonwealth, some were called in particular to perform the duties of magistracy or political office. Here the Protestant notion of the vocation isolated the realm of government as a separate calling, one that had its own rules of conduct, its own *ratio* or rationale, separate from the sphere of religious devotion. Luther illustrated this separation when he observed that "I fulfill the commands of the Lord when I teach and pray, the plowman when he listens and does his farm work diligently; and the prince and his officials do not fulfill them, when they cannot be found when needed, but say that they must pray—for that means to withdraw from God's true service in the name of God."[25] What is true of the prince is true of his soldiers as well, whose vocation Luther defends in "Whether soldiers may be in a blessed state" (1526). The occupation of the soldier, including the exercise of violent force, is as legitimate as any other occupation, as long as the soldier realizes that "no one is saved as a soldier but only as a Christian."[26]

Of particular relevance to Samson is the fact that the Protestant notion of the calling could be used to justify not only the social and political status quo but also exceptions to that rule. This was because a calling hovered between vocation and work; or, rather, it made one's work into a vocation by infusing it with faith and conscience. Like the notion of the covenant, it adjudicated between predestination and works, coercion and consent, by making one's vocation appear to be a response to being called.[27] This infusion of conscience—this conversion of work into "works of faith"—made the notion of calling equivocal and unstable; ostensibly a justification of social and political hierarchy, the idea of a calling could also be used to justify extraordinary actions, "above the form of law or custome." Thus, in William Perkins's *Treatise of the Vocations or Callings of Men* (1603), we learn there are two callings—the calling of the Christian believer, which is determined by God's general providence, and the individual calling or profession (king, subject, merchant, plowman), which is determined by God's specific providence. Although the two callings should be performed together, "A particular calling must give place to the general calling of a Christian when they cannot both stand together."[28] Precisely because the doctrine of the calling raises the specter of an individual called to be a "public person," an individual who acts according to conscience rather than according to his place in a social and political hierarchy, it stands at the intersection of norm and exception, contract and reason of state. Like the notion of contract, that of a calling attempts to negotiate a conflict between coercion and consent, divine and human will. Like reason of state, the sense of being "called" can justify exceptions to the rule.

As we have seen, the doctrine of a special calling and of a rationality intrinsic to politics gave rise to a political casuistry.[29] If casuistry is the art of reasoning about difficult moral cases, of adjudicating between conflicting moral principles, political casuistry is the art of reasoning about political cases that are not easily—or usefully—subordinated either to positive law or to the moral law. And one of the goals of this political casuistry was to effect precisely the sort of divorce between public and private persons mentioned previously. Yet, as manuals of casuistry acknowledged, it was often impossible to separate matters of policy from matters of conscience. For, in cases where there was an absolute conflict between obedience to the sovereign and obedience to God, it was the latter that took precedence. It was no doubt for this reason that Luther and Calvin argued that resistance could only be undertaken by public persons who were lesser magistrates, not private individuals acting according to their own consciences. Both seem to have been anxious that, by helping to create conscientious subjects, casuistry might actually foster political resistance.[30]

This dilemma of conscientious action above the form of law or custom is the subject of Luther's tract *On Secular Authority* (1522–23), which takes up the casuistical case of "whether a Christian can even wield the secular Sword and punish the wicked [himself], seeing that Christ's words 'Do not resist evil' seem so peremptory and clear." Luther solves this case of conflicting moral principles as a good casuist would, by distinguishing between contexts: while the sword cannot be used "over or among Christians," "a Christian use" can be made of the sword to punish or restrain the wicked.[31] Similarly, although the sword cannot be used to revenge or benefit oneself, it may be used in "the service of others":

> And so the two [principles] are nicely reconciled: you satisfy the demands of God's kingdom and the world's at one and the same time, outwardly and inwardly; you both suffer evil and injustice and yet punish [the wicked]; you do not resist evil and yet you do resist it. As to you and yours, you keep to the Gospel and suffer injustice as a true Christian. But where the next man and what is his are concerned, you act in accordance with the [command to] love and you tolerate no injustice against him. And that is not prohibited by the Gospel; on the contrary the Gospel commands it elsewhere [cf. Romans 13:4]. (15)

The criterion of Christian usage then raises the further question of whether "I can use the Sword for myself and my own concerns, provided I am not out for my own good, but merely intend that evil should be punished?" (22). According to Luther, this is the case of conscience exemplified by Samson. On the one hand, Samson represents the vocation of "the sword," which, like other callings, can be used in the service of God. On the other hand, Samson stands as a dangerous precedent for ordinary reason because he "used his private concerns as a pretext for declaring war against [the Philistines]," even though he "did not do it to avenge himself or to seek his own advantage, but to help [the Israelites] and punish the Philistines."[32] Thus Luther warns, "Where [ordinary human] reason wants to do likewise, it no doubt pretends that it is not seeking its own advantage, but the claim will be false from top to bottom. The thing is impossible without grace. So if you want to act like Samson, then first become like Samson" (22). As readers of *Samson Agonistes* know, this "becoming like Samson" is something that even Milton's Samson has to achieve.

SAMSON AS EXCEPTION

From the very beginning of *Samson Agonistes*, Samson's task is to interpret God's covenant. Like the covenant theologians we examined in chapter 2, Samson wonders whether God's promise is "assertory" or conditional, whether it is a testament or a mutual contract. But in Samson's case, God's promise is not the general promise of salvation but a promise regarding Samson alone. For Samson, then, understanding God's covenant means understanding himself as an exception, both in the sense of an exceptional individual called to do exceptional acts and as an individual who has singularly failed to live up to his calling. In the first case, Samson addresses the problem of reason of state: the problem of the relationship of the exception to the rule, of power to legitimacy, of justice to positive law.[33] In the second case, Samson confronts the more general problem of voluntary servitude or willful enslavement to his own passions, which keeps him from becoming the deliverer he was prophesied to be.

Samson's reasoning about his exceptional status in both senses is dramatized in his soliloquy on the prophecy of his role as deliverer, a prophecy that he is unable to interpret correctly:

> Promise was that I
> Should *Israel* from *Philistian* yoke deliver;
> Ask for this great Deliverer now, and find him
> Eyeless in *Gaza* at the Mill with slaves,

Himself in bonds under *Philistian* yoke;
Yet stay, let me not rashly call in doubt
Divine Prediction; what if all foretold
Had been fulfill'd but through mine own default,
Whom have I to complain of but myself?

(38–46)

Samson struggles to make sense of his condition by revising his understanding of prophecy: he first interprets the prophecy that he would deliver Israel as a "prediction," a "promise" that God has failed to fulfill. He then reverses his understanding, blaming himself for his fate: "Whom have I to complain of but myself?" No sooner has he done so than he begins to impugn the justice of God's creation: "O impotence of mind, in body strong! / But what is strength without a double share / Of wisdom?" (52–54). He then recoils from this question, asserting that God's will is just, though inaccessible to human reason: "But peace, I must not quarrel with the will / Of highest dispensation, which herein / Haply had ends above my reach to know" (60–62). Struggling to decide between these alternatives, yet incapable of doing so, Samson despairs of making sense of his experience in terms other than those of simple irony: dark amid the blaze of noon, he suffers a living death. He is not so much an exception as an example of the incomprehensibility of God's ways. Irony is here for Samson simply the other side of his either-or mode of reasoning: neither allows him to understand his calling or the conditional nature of God's prophecies and covenants. What Samson fails to understand is that covenants are not predictions because they are not unilateral. On the other hand, because covenants are not unilateral, Samson cannot by himself bring about the fulfillment of the prophecy.[34]

This initial soliloquy sets the pattern for the rest of the play, in which Samson and his visitors struggle to interpret the equivocal signs of his condition. Particularly striking are the repeated failures to recognize Samson as being like his former self (here Samson is the exception to the prophecy), and the repeated attempts to erase the exception by reading Samson as an "example" of some general law or truth of the human condition. In either case, the effect is the same: the reading of Samson as differing from or conforming to some preexisting model curtails efforts to understand Samson's responsibility for his decisions and stifles the possibility of genuine action.

The Chorus unwittingly sums up the problem of turning the exceptional Samson into the rule, when it describes him as a "*mirror* of our fickle state, / Since man on earth *unparallel'd*" (emphasis added); but it goes on to resolve this paradox by seeing Samson simply as an "example" of the reversals of fortune (164–66).[35] Samson describes himself as an "example" of a neglected deliverer (241–276; 290), of fallen pride (532), and of the betrayed husband (765). Like the Chorus, Manoa reads Samson as an example of our fickle state and, like Samson in his first soliloquy, he glosses this state in terms of the simple irony of the "good / Pray'd for, [which] often proves our woe" (350–51). Harapha sees Samson as an example of a fallen hero (1156–67). When it comes to explaining how Samson has come to be enslaved, the Chorus ascribes Samson's condition to fortune (169); Samson complains that he was not given enough knowledge to use his strength correctly (52–54, 206–8), or that he was "overpow'r'd" by Dalila (880); Manoa describes Samson as "ensnar'd" by Dalila and unjustly punished by God (365, 370); and the Chorus exempts Samson of responsibility by pronouncing both that God may dispense with his own laws and that we should not reason vainly about divine justice (293–325, 652–709). In every case, doing away with Samson's decision involves giving up on God's justice or, at the very least, identifying his justice with his absolute authority or arbitrary power.[36]

Samson, however, continues to reason about the exception—both his calling and his weakness of the will. In contrast to his interlocutors, he struggles to make sense both of God's justice and his own actions. In doing so, he explores the equivocal status of reason of state as both reason and decision. As we will see, the dilemma of Samson's calling is not resolved by greater knowledge achieved by the end of *Samson Agonistes*; it is not resolved by choosing one more rationally compelling interpretation over another. Instead, what the conclusion of *Samson Agonistes* dramatizes is the necessity of interpretation. Crucial to our understanding of this necessity are those exchanges in the poem in which Samson discusses his own interpretations and decisions, past and present; and in which he explicitly takes up arguments from conscience and reason of state.

REASONING ABOUT THE EXCEPTION:
DIALECTIC AND EQUIVOCATION

It makes sense that, in reasoning about his past decisions, Samson should explicitly address the argument from reason of state, because he had used this argument to justify his own violation of positive law in marrying an infidel. In reflecting on reason of state in his encounters with Dalila, Harapha, and the Philistine officer, Samson gradually comes to understand that reason of state—reasoning about the exception—involves a critical act of judgment, a negative dialectic that (unlike Hobbes) refuses to equate authority and legitimacy, power and justice.[37] These encounters thus amount to a kind of metadiscourse: an ironic commentary on any discourse that turns the exception into a rule in an attempt to obviate the necessity for an interpretation. Conversely, they show us that interpretation is necessary precisely because arguments from authority (even the authority of natural law) are deeply equivocal and subject to parody, ironic manipulation, and reinterpretation. Finally, as Samson comes to understand, the equivocal signs of experience are not so much to be reasoned away as embraced as the condition of any genuine interpretation: equivocation and interpretation are two sides of the same coin. This in turn means that the covenant is not simply an object of interpretation; it is not something that can be interpreted once and for all. Instead, like the theologians we examined in chapter 2, Samson fulfills the covenant by means of an ongoing activity of interpretation.

Samson first appeals to reason of state in response to a question from the Chorus about his marriages to "*Philistian* women," marriages that violated Jewish law. According to Samson, his marriage to the woman of Timnah was dictated by God's concern for the *salus populi* of the Jews: Samson was "motion'd . . . of God" so that he might "begin *Israel's* Deliverance" (222, 225). This first exception to Jewish law then serves as an authorizing precedent and makes the marriage to Dalila less of an exception than an example: "I thought it lawful from my former act, / And the same end; still watching to oppress / *Israel's* oppressors" (231–33). Yet, by definition, true exceptions cannot be authorized by precedent; nor can they serve as legal precedents if by this we mean authorities that obviate the necessity of an interpretation in the present. It is fitting, then, that Dalila should later throw Samson's argument back in his face, arguing in so many words that she thought her betrayal of Samson was lawful from his former act, his own example. Here, as elsewhere, arguing from precedent and example serves to diminish responsibility: "To what I did thou show'd'st me first the way"; "Ere I to thee, thou to thyself wast cruel" (781, 784). Even Samson's abandoning the woman of Timnah is pressed into the service of Dalila's self-justification: "I saw thee mutable / Of fancy, fear'd lest one day thou wouldst leave me / As her at *Timna*, sought by all means therefore / How to endear, and hold thee to me firmest" (793–96). Finally, Dalila glosses her love for Samson as a kind of erotic reason of state: "These reasons in Love's law have pass'd for good, / Though fond and reasonless to some perhaps" (811–12). The "law" of love excuses reasons that from another perspective violate reason itself.

The next exchange explores further the opposition of authority and interpretation. In justifying her own betrayal of Samson, Dalila once again tries to turn the exception into the rule, this time by explicitly invoking reason of state or "public good" as the authorizing precedent for her actions. Describing the pressure exerted upon her by the Philistine "Magistrates / And Princes" (850–51), she concludes:

> at length that grounded maxim
> So rife and celebrated in the mouths
> Of wisest men, that to the public good
> Private respects must yield, with grave authority
> Took full possession of me and prevail'd;
> Virtue, as I thought, truth, duty so enjoining.
>
> (865–70)

Although Dalila uses the elevated language of public good, she reasons in a fashion that suggests instead the constraints of self-preservation: she "yields" when "grave authority" takes "possession" of her. For Dalila, reason of state does not involve deciding the exceptional case; rather, it functions as the Hobbesian authority of magistrates and princes that usurps judgment and coerces submission.

Samson's reply suggests that he has learned from Dalila's parody of his earlier argument from authoritative precedent. In response to her argument from authority, Samson makes reason of state a matter of critical judgment: he recasts her implicit argument about protection and obedience, contending that Dalila in her married state was no longer a Philistine and therefore owed obedience to Samson rather than to her former countrymen.

> Being once a wife, for me thou wast to leave
> Parents and country; nor was I their subject,
> Nor under their protection but my own,
> Thou mine, not theirs: if aught against my life
> Thy country sought of thee, it sought unjustly,
> Against the law of nature, law of nations,
> No more thy country, but an impious crew
> Of men conspiring to uphold thir state
> By worse than hostile deeds, violating the ends
> For which our country is a name so dear;
> Not therefore to be obey'd.
>
> (885–95)

In this rebuke, Samson makes it clear that Dalila has failed to reason correctly about reason of state: he subjects the terms of her argument—not only self-preservation but also love, justice, nation, and obedience—to an immanent critique. Dalila's nation is not her nation but "an impious crew," both because she has married Samson and because in seeking injustice they have violated the proper ends of nationhood. Thus he distinguishes between positive law and natural law, arguing that the latter cannot be an unquestioned argument for obeying the former.[38] As Catherine Gimelli Martin has pointed out, "while both Hobbes and Milton's Samson claim that 'the Law of Nations, and the Law of Nature is the same thing' (*Leviathan* 2.30)," Hobbes used this identity as "an argument *against* the possibility of appealing to a higher court of law, the very right Samson tries to persuade Dalila that she ought to have exercised in deciding her differing responsibilities to her husband and her people."[39]

Samson's response to Harapha illustrates even more powerfully that natural law cannot serve as a standard of justice and rule of action that obviates interpretation.[40] Although Samson first defends the Hebrews' right of resistance in terms of reason of state and the maxim of natural law—"vim vi licet repellere": force may be repelled with force—he justifies his own particular role as liberator by reference to his calling:

> My nation was subjected to your Lords.
> It was the force of Conquest; force with force
> Is well ejected when the Conquer'd can.
> But I a private person, whom my Country
> As a league-breaker gave up bound, presum'd
> Single Rebellion and did Hostile Acts.
> I was no private but a person rais'd
> With strength sufficient and command from Heav'n
> To free my Country.
>
> (1205–13)

To the argument from natural law the objection could be raised that Samson was merely a private person who had wrongly (according to the standard Protestant argument) arrogated to himself the right to resist that belonged to public persons or "lesser magistrates." The justice of the argument from reason of state—the application of natural law—thus requires an interpretation of Samson's own exceptional status. Here too, in response, Samson does not so much reject his critics' argument as redescribe it: he does not justify his acts by reference to his public position as a judge of Israel but by a claim of individual conscience.[41] As in Luther's description of Samson in *On Secular Authority*, private persons may be public persons and may perform actions for reason of state if they are divinely called to do so.

Samson's deliberations about whether to go with the Philistine messenger dramatize more powerfully than any of his previous encounters the intersection of reason of state and the doctrine of a calling. As in his previous exchanges, here too Samson reasons about reason of state, exploring its equivocal status as the natural law of self-preservation and the determination of justice. But we also see Samson begin to link this equivocal status of reason of state itself to the necessity of interpretation: whereas for Dalila an exception could be subsumed under a rule, Samson has come to understand that an exception resists easy categorization; it

prompts casuistry and equivocation precisely because it is itself equivocal—open to more than one description. In accepting this openness, Samson understands his covenant and calling as exceptions for which there
can be no precedent, if by that we mean an authority that resolves ambiguity and obviates the need for a decision. Reason of state—reasoning about
the exception—becomes an emblem of the equivocal nature of human
attempts to act justly in the absence of authoritative knowledge.

The equivocal nature of reason of state emerges as Samson rehearses
its potential meanings. At first he argues that it is lawful to serve the
Philistines with his labor because they have him "in thir civil power," but
unlawful to be present at "idolatrous rites":

> Where outward force constrains, the sentence holds;
> But who constrains me to the Temple of *Dagon*,
> Not dragging? the *Philistian* Lords command.
> Commands are no constraints.
>
> (1369–72)

The first lines sum up one view of passive obedience—obedience "where
outward force constrains"—with particular attention to the argument
from self-preservation. The next lines draw out one implication of this
view: that one may refuse actively to serve an illegitimate power.[42] Yet,
shortly after this, Samson asserts that God permits an exception to these
rules, an exception that paradoxically identifies active obedience with active resistance:

> Yet that he may dispense with me or thee
> Present in Temples at Idolatrous Rites
> For some important cause, thou needst not doubt.
>
> (1377–79)

God, that is, can equivocate about reason of state, calling his servants to
perform exceptions to the law, which are nevertheless not "forbidden in
our Law" (1409). Immediately after this Samson begins to feel the "rousing motions . . . which dispose / To something extraordinary" and decides
to go to the temple (1382–84), convinced that he will do "nothing . . .
that may dishonor / Our Law, or stain my vow of *Nazarite*" (1385–86).
Whether the reason of state that calls Samson to "go along" with the
messenger is divine or not, it clearly allows Samson to reason dialectically
about the law, to see the law as containing its own negation and higher
preservation, and thus to equivocate.

This equivocation at the heart of reason of state (as obedience or resistance) is nicely dramatized by Samson's own casuistical reply to the
messenger:

Because they shall not trail me through thir streets
Like a wild Beast, I am content to go.
Masters' commands come with a power resistless
To such as owe them absolute subjection;
And for a life who will not change his purpose?

(1402–6)

Practically every word in these lines is ambiguous; even the enjambment
in the first line looks both ways, suggesting the ferocity behind Samson's
"content." The statement that "Master's commands come with a power
resistless / To such as owe them absolute subjection" only raises the question of to whom we owe absolute subjection. Finally, in mocking arguments for self-preservation, Samson also forces us to consider what is
meant by "life" in the line, "And for a life who will not change his purpose?"[43] *Salus populi* in the sense of self-preservation is implicity contrasted to *salus populi* in the sense of salvation.[44]

In linking equivocation to the possibility of rebellion, Milton was articulating the worst fears of many of his contemporaries at the same time
that he was radically revising traditional notions of reason of state.[45] As
we have seen, in the 1650s supporters of the commonwealth feared that
royalists would engage in equivocation or mental reservation when swearing allegiance to the new government; after 1660 supporters of the Restoration suspected a similar equivocation on the part of those who resisted
it. In *Leviathan* Hobbes registered his fears of just such a figurative, other-
worldly understanding of "life" as Samson suggests, observing that the
belief in the "eternal life" was more powerful than the fear that one might
lose one's physical life: thus the belief in metaphorical kingdom of God
could incite rebellion against the literal kingdom of the sovereign.[46] And
Milton justified Hobbes's fears in the first *Defence* when he asserted that
"Christ . . . took upon himself . . . the form of a slave, so that we might
be free. I do not speak of inward freedom only [but also] political freedom."[47] In this light, Samson's response to the messenger is not so much
a simple rejection of Dalila's reason of state as it is a dialectical revision:
a purposeful equivocation that subjects the notion of literal or corporeal
self-preservation to an ironic critique while suggesting a more sublime
conception of what it might mean to preserve the self—a more sublime
conception of reason of state.

This more sublime conception of reason of state is one that cannot be
fully grasped by reason. Samson reasons up to a point, recognizing that
God "may dispense with me or thee / Present in Temples at Idolatrous
Rites / For some important cause" (1377–79). But his decision to go to
the Philistine temple does not follow upon the conclusion that God has
in this case dispensed with him; rather, it follows upon the "rousing mo-

tions . . . which dispose / To something extraordinary" (1382–83). In the end, Samson's about-face in going to the Philistine temple suggests that, while rules can be instantiated, and examples can be imitated, an exception must be decided. A decision is necessary precisely because exceptions are by definition equivocal: there is no single, a priori rule of interpretation—whether the belief in antinomianism or in absolute obedience to de facto political power—that will allow us to reason them away. Decisions are also deeply equivocal since they require that we act in the absence of certainty and in ignorance of the full meaning of our acts.[48]

In this light, *Samson Agonistes* is a tragedy precisely because the exception and the will as the locus of decision are deeply implicated: the exception is the condition of any meaningful decision, at the same time that its incoherence (its availability to contradictory interpretations) dramatizes the violence, including self-violence, involved in any decisive imposition of sense. Hell, Saint Augustine said, is not being able to decide;[49] tragedy, for the late Milton, is having to—is what our decisions look like.

This was the case in part for historical reasons, for the Restoration was a tragedy to Milton, a stage on which the armed saint was compelled to act alone, without fellow citizens. But the act of deciding the exception also looks like tragedy because Milton was not content, as Hobbes was, to equate justice with de facto authority. Precisely because justice is not simply a matter of authority, there is room for the conscientious individual to reason about the exception—specifically, about the justice of our individual acts; but because, in the words of *Areopagitica*, truth has been "hewed . . . into a thousand pieces," there is also room for the tragedy of the will. *Samson Agonistes* thus gives us a tragic version of *Areopagitica*'s "reason is but choosing."

Taking Exception to Pity and Fear

The preceding pages have explored the dilemmas of conscience and reason of state, divine covenant and political contract, in Milton's tragedy. I now want to argue that the tragedy of *Samson Agonistes* does more than simply dramatize a crisis of interpretation and the will; in Milton's hands, tragic form is also a political resource. Milton does not simply declare the Restoration a tragedy by virtue of writing one. *Samson Agonistes* also renders the political and theological problem of interpreting the covenant as a poetic problem of interpreting the contract of genre. Both for Milton's reader and for Samson, then, the answers to the theological problem of how to interpret the divine covenant and the political problem of how to justify the exceptional actions of reason of state are bound up with the correct understanding of tragic mimesis, in particular the imitation of the passions. Artifice—here construed as the artifice of genre—emerges as one answer to the problem of voluntary servitude.

In the polemical prefatory note to *Samson Agonistes*, Milton defends his imitation of ancient rather than modern tragedy, even as he revises the Aristotelian definition of tragedy: "[T]ragedy, as it was anciently compos'd, hath been ever held the gravest, moralest, and most profitable of all other Poems: therefore said by *Aristotle* to be of power by raising pity and fear, or terror, to purge the mind of those and such like passions, that is to temper and reduce them to just measure with a kind of delight, stirr'd up by reading or seeing those passions well imitated." In this definition, Milton shifts Aristotle's definition of tragedy from the imitation of action to the imitation of the passions.[50] In so doing, he reorients our attention from action per se to the subjective, affective conditions of action and to what I have called the psychology of the contracting subject.

At the same time, in his gloss on the effects of tragedy, Milton also enters the Renaissance debate concerning the political effects of catharsis. Although Aristotle had made no particular, explicit claims for the political uses of tragedy, Italian Renaissance commentators regularly discussed its social and political consequences. Central to the debate was whether catharsis purged or merely tempered the passions, and whether purgation created quiescence or something more like Stoic resolve. Giacopo Mazzoni, whom Milton mentions in *Of Education*, took a conservative position on the political effects of tragedy, which he saw as moderating the hubris of the great, extinguishing sedition, and preserving peace. In his *L'arte poetica* of 1564 Antonio Minturno argued for the more complicated effect of patience and resourcefulness: "[T]he recollection of the grave misfortunes of others makes us not merely quicker and better prepared to support our own, but wiser and more skillful in escaping similar evils."[51] Tragedy in this view could both purge and moderate the passions; it could encourage both "patience" and heroic acts of "invincible might," to quote the Chorus of *Samson Agonistes* (1282, 1271). But whereas Minturno argued that this occurs when pity and fear purge other, harmful passions, Milton—like his contemporary, the Dutch Aristotelian Daniel Heinsius—believed that the imitation of pity and fear should temper and reduce pity and fear.[52] In a fundamental way, then, the plot of *Samson Agonistes* is *about* the aesthetic responses of pity and fear.

Milton's gloss on Aristotelian mimesis is important both as an exemplary act of interpretation and in terms of its precise content. First, like Hobbes in the Introduction to *Leviathan*, although to different ends, Milton shows by his own practice that mimesis is not simply a matter of repetition but of productive interpretation. This notion of productive interpretation is, as we have already seen, an important part of Samson's eventual understanding of his covenant with God. Second, Milton argues specifically for the link between imitation and purgation. According to Milton, purgation achieves its effects not simply through pity and fear but through the pleasure we derive from the imitation of pity and fear, the pleasure, that is, of tragic form.[53] In this account, it is not simply that one passion purges another but that the representation of passion purges or moderates passion. Seeing or hearing the passions "well imitated" has a countervailing effect on our perturbations. We might even say, anticipating Samson's decision to go along with the Philistine messenger, that imitation transforms passion from a state of passivity to one of rousing motions. Milton, in other words, doesn't simply foreground the passions as a symptom of Samson's voluntary servitude and as a cause of Samson's inaction. Rather, he dramatizes a theory of countervailing passions in which the activity of imitation is crucial: Samson's being purged of pity and fear through representation is a condition of his final action.

Of course, critics regularly observe that the catharsis of *Samson Agonistes* occurs on stage rather than being experienced by the audience or reader. But the point I wish to make is, I believe, a different one. Rather than seeing *Samson Agonistes* as a mimesis of the government of the passions by reason, I want to suggest that Milton's tragedy is *about the power of mimesis or representation to turn passion into action*.[54] By this, I am not suggesting the humanist commonplace articulated by the Chorus at the end of the play—the notion that the text imitates exemplars of virtue and vice and presents these examples to the reader to be imitated; rather, my argument is that in *Samson Agonistes* Milton dramatizes the way the formal principle of imitation creates a kind of theatrical alienation effect, which is the condition of action, including interpretive action.

Samson Agonistes can thus be read as an extended meditation on the relationship of aesthetic form to politics, one in which Milton enlists the pleasure we derive from imitation in the service of a radical critique of the debilitating responses of pity and fear. In this light, critics who observe that we don't feel pity for Samson or fear for the Philistines at the end of the tragedy are right on target.[55] For like his contemporary Rapin, Milton believed that tragedy "rectifies the passions by the passions themselves," that it cures pride and hardness of heart; "but because man is naturally timorous, and compassionate, he may fall into another extreme, to be either too fearful, or too full of pity; *the too much fear may shake the constancy of mind, and the too great compassion may enfeeble the equity.*"[56] This lesson is learned by both Samson and the reader. Samson sees his own passions represented by others and gains a kind of theatrical distance from them; the reader, similarly, experiences Milton's representation of the passions as a kind of sublime obstacle that provokes interpretive activity. The foregrounding of representation displaces activity from thematic action to interpretive action.

Samson's opening soliloquy is filled with self-pity, lamentation, and despair; however, the ensuing encounters with Manoa, Dalila, and Harapha enable Samson to reject these and other passions by seeing them represented. Manoa represents the response of pity: "O miserable change!" he proclaims upon seeing Samson (340). In response, Samson rejects Manoa's pity. He insists on not being ransomed, on not being "to visitants a gaze, / Or pitied object" (567–68). But, not finding a real outlet for action, Samson succumbs again to a Hamlet-like despair: "My hopes all flat, nature within me seems / In all her functions weary of herself" (595–96). Although he glosses his condition in theatrical terms, he does so in a way that suggests that he still thinks of imitation at this point simply as a matter of repetition: Samson complains that God has "reserv'd [him] alive to be *repeated* / The subject of [Philistine] cruelty, or scorn" (645–46; emphasis added).

Dalila arrives, announcing not only her "tears" (735), but also her repentance. She then puts forth various versions of the theory of countervailing passions as part of her argument for Samson's pardon. She claims that she learned her passions from Samson and the two should cancel each other out: "Ere I to thee, thou to thyself was cruel. / Let weakness then with weakness come to parle / So near related, or the same of kind, / Thine forgive mine" (784–87). She urges her fear: "I saw thee mutable / Of fancy, fear'd lest one day thou wouldst leave me" (793–94). Above all, she solicits Samson's pity: "And Love hath oft, well meaning, wrought much woe, / Yet always pity or pardon hath obtain'd" (813–14). Like Manoa, she promises the consolation associated with domestic tragedy: "Life yet hath many solaces, enjoy'd / Where other senses want not their delights / At home in leisure and domestic ease" (915–17). The effect of this theatrical performance of the passions—which is perceived as such by Samson—is to intensify his "uncompassionate anger" (818), his resistance to the theatrical temptation of pity.

Unlike Manoa and Dalila, Harapha does not pretend to offer consolation. Instead, he represents a theatrical or parodic version of Samson's own uncompassionate anger. Parodic because it is clearly motivated by vainglory, which Samson conjectures is related to Manoa's Hobbesian fear for his own self-preservation. At the same time, Samson accuses Harapha of "feigned shifts" (1116) and of mere aesthetic contemplation: "Cam'st thou for this, vain boaster, to survey me [?]" (1227). And, when Harapha mirrors back to Samson his earlier despair, telling him: "Presume not on they God, whate'er he be / Thee he regards not, owns not, hath cut off" (1156–57), Samson replies by rejecting despair for a renewed conviction of God's "final pardon" (1171).

These three encounters function as plays-within-the-play, minidramas in which the very fact of imitation serves as a principle of countervailing passion. Manoa's and Dalila's representations of pity counteract Samson's self-pity; Harapha's fear, in the words of one Renaissance commentator on Aristotle's *Poetics*, "teaches [Samson] to have no fear of [harm to] the body, and makes [him] perceive within [himself] the force of justice."[57]

But it is above all the encounter with the Philistine messenger that dramatizes the transformation of the passivity of passion into tragic action. Initially, Samson refuses the Philistine command to "play" at work, to "sport with blind activity" (1328):

> Although thir drudge, to be thir fool or jester,
> And in my midst of sorrow and heart-grief
> To show them feats, and play before thir god,
> The worst of all indignities, yet on me
> Join'd with extreme contempt? I will not come.
>
> (1338–42)

In these lines, Samson links his sorrow and heart-grief to the impossibility of genuine action, to the theatrical hollowing-out of agency. Shortly after this, however, he feels rousing motions and agrees to go along with the messenger. Whether rousing motions refers to emotion or divine impulsion, the word "motion" *renders emotion as motion, passion as action.* In this respect, "rousing motions" is a semantic minidrama of the way representation can convert passion to action.

Equally important, rousing motions appear to involve neither pity nor fear. Samson has rejected self-pity and pity for others in his encounters with Manoa and Dalila. He has rejected fear for his self-preservation and despair in his encounter with Harapha. At the same time, what he seems to have learned through all three is the power of theatrical representation to turn passion into action. Thus, immediately after experiencing the rousing motions, Samson acts the part of the fearful and obedient captive; he feigns fear for his life: "Masters' commands come with a power resistless / To such as owe them absolute subjection; / And for a life who will not change his purpose?" (1404–6). In the Messenger's account, Samson's actions are rendered in even more theatrical terms: "he still perform'd / All with incredible, stupendious force" (1626–27); he stood at the pillars "as one who pray'd" (1637). But a crucial part of Samson's newfound understanding of the power of theatrical representation to turn passion into action is a critique of aesthetic contemplation. Thus Samson himself mocks the aesthetic pleasure derived from his own playacting when he addresses the Philistine audience:

> Hitherto, Lords, what your commands impos'd
> I have perform'd, as reason was, obeying,
> Not without wonder or delight beheld.

> Now of my own accord such other trial
> I mean to show you of my strength, yet greater;
> As with amaze shall strike all who behold.
>
> (1640–45)

In other words, the aesthetic responses of wonder, delight, and amazement are fatal when not properly understood—when they are understood as the occasion for mere contemplation rather than action. In contrast, Samson has elevated play or representation to the enabling condition of tragic action. For it is under the cover of playacting that Samson transforms his servitude into an act of political resistance.

In this light, both Manoa's and the Chorus's response to Samson's actions are inadequate. Manoa understands that Samson has escaped from his earlier condition of despair. He understands as well that lamentation and mourning are activities properly reserved to the Philistines. But his plan to build a monument for Samson, with his "Acts enroll'd / In copious Legend, or sweet Lyric song" (1736–37) misreads the genre Samson has brought to conclusion. Manoa's vision of valiant youth being inspired to "matchless valor" construes Samson's actions simply as a humanist example to be imitated rather than an exceptional drama of conscience, while the references to "Virgins . . . bewailing / His lot unfortunate in nuptial choice" (1741–43) returns us again to the world of domestic tragedy, or perhaps even melodrama.

The Chorus also understands that mourning is reserved to Gaza. But, judging by Samson's earlier rejection of the consolations offered by Manoa and Dalila, the Chorus errs in its emphasis on peace and consolation, as well as in its declaration of "calm of mind, all passion spent." This interpretation of catharsis implies that pity and fear have been purged (or, depending on how you read spent: tempered) by witnessing the final action of Samson. But the excesses of pity and fear have been tempered long before this, both in Samson and in the reader. Moreover, "calm of mind, all passion spent" does not invite the audience to move from passion to action. To the contrary, in its antinomian complacency ("All is best, though we oft doubt, / What th' unsearchable dipose" [ll. 1745–46]), the Chorus displaces action from Samson to God: "Oft he seems to hide his face, / But unexpectedly returns / And to his faithful Champion hath in place / Bore witness gloriously" (1749–52). It is God who acts here, bearing witness to Samson, rather than vice versa.[58]

In both cases, we can see how a certain theological complacency goes hand in hand with aesthetic contemplation and the eclipse of agency. I have been arguing, in contrast, that both the explicit subject and intended effect of *Samson Agonistes* is not calm of mind but rather (to return to the language of the prefatory note) the "stirring up" of Samson and the reader by means of imitation. The reader sees the passions of pity and fear well imitated by Manoa, Dalila, and the Chorus, and sees them rejected by Samson. For Samson, aesthetic contemplation, including the aesthetic passions of pity and fear, is undone by the distancing effect of representation. This critique of aesthetic contemplation is not only a theme but an effect of *Samson Agonistes*. Confronted with the deliberate opacity of Samson's rousing motions (which turns passion into action on the level of semantics), the reader is provoked to a sublime activity of interpretation, which is itself rousing. In modern terms, we might say that the aesthetic appearance of totality is extinguished by a strange and fragmentary ostentation that provokes a surplus of interpretation; in Milton's vocabulary, sight is displaced by reading. In either case, the lesson is not one of consolation or aesthetic contemplation but of "fiery virtue rous'd."

As we saw in chapter 9, Renaissance commentators on Aristotle can be divided into those who moralize catharsis as a vehicle of the ethical and political dimension of tragedy and those who emphasize the pleasure we derive from artistry of imitation (Minturno on the one hand and Castelvetro on the other).[59] Milton, I have been suggesting, refuses this either-or. In doing so, he anticipates modern theories of aesthetics as critique, theories that make the alienation effect of representation itself the condition of ethical and political action. In doing so, *Samson Agonistes* may allegorize what Walter Benjamin saw as the historical shift from a world governed by a transcendent God to one mired in immanence. By suppressing motivation, by exacerbating the issue of the criterion of Samson's judgment, Milton demonstrates the internalization of judgment that is a feature of the Reformation conscience. This internalization of judgment represents a kind of historical way station between theology and aesthetics, which we have come to know as the process of secularization. Yet this internalization of judgment also makes available a new kind of autonomy and political agency that is linked to the historical emergence of the autonomous aesthetic artifact. Benjamin writes that "for the theater of profane society . . . the power of salvation and redemption only ever lies in a paradoxical reflection on play and appearance."[60] *Samson Agonistes* is a play in which reflection on the play of representation becomes the enabling condition of both tragic action and political critique.

POLITICAL THEOLOGY AND TRAGEDY

Samson's final decision to pull down the temple is notoriously available to conflicting interpretations. In his final words to the Philistines, Samson distinguishes between his "reason," which has led him to obey their commands, and his "own accord," which now moves him to a different trial of his strength (1641–43). The description of Samson bowing his head "As one who prayed" makes this final "act" of conscience a theatrical performance in all its ambiguity: we are unsure, as Milton certainly intended us to be, whether Samson's political act is one of divine authority or merely human violence. Because it involves an act of faith, deciding this point is ultimately a theological act; yet, the surplus of possible meanings also dramatizes the lack of sure coincidence between politics and theology, human action and divine authority.

From one perspective this conclusion might appear to conform to Milton's argument about tyrannicide in *The Tenure*. Taking up the example of Ehud, the slayer of King Eglon (Judges 3:12–26), Milton argued—against Grotius—that evidence of Ehud's divine inspiration is irrelevant to our understanding of his deed since he acted "on just principles, such as were then and ever held allowable."[61] As Martin Dzelzainis has commented, "a divine command establishes that a given action is lawful but is not itself what constitutes the grounds of its lawfulness; for that we must look to natural reason."[62] In this light Manoa's final judgment that God did not part from Samson but favored and assisted him to the end (1719–20) and the Chorus's belief that God "unexpectedly return[ed] / . . . to his faithful Champion" are also irrelevant (1750–51). For, following *The Tenure* and the first *Defence*, we might surmise that here too Samson's natural reason has justified his exceptional act, above the form of law or custom.

And, yet, the feeling we are left with in the end is not that Samson's act has been rationally justified but that it has been made more mysterious, less accessible to reason, more difficult to imitate; for the lack of coincidence between divine authority and human will is represented both as the condition of action and as violence. On the one hand, Manoa describes Samson's act of fulfilling the prophecy in terms of his imperfect identity: in a world in which all interpretation must be in excess of the law, in which there is no secure foundation for acts of conscience, Samson can only quit himself *like* Samson; he must always be an exception even to himself.[63] On the other hand, the equivocal final scene in which Samson is, in Manoa's words, "over-strong against [him]self" (1590) or, in the words of the Chorus, "self-kill'd / Not willingly" (1664–65), shows that this lack of identity may be experienced as violence. We might even conjecture that Milton intends a dark parody of the union of coercion and consent in contemporary rational theories of political contract. Whereas according to Milton and, in a different way, Hobbes, we consent to be coerced when we transfer our power to the sovereign, Samson's final act shows us that the will is itself a mysterious locus of coercion and consent, the intersection of human decision and divine *arcana imperii*.[64]

If, in contrast to Hobbes, Milton presents the dilemmas of the contracting subject as tragedy, he also—as his readers would have expected—uses tragedy to teach us a lesson about political theology. God is ultimately the sovereign who decides the exception, but in this world Samson's act is open to our proximate interpretation. In this respect, it is very much like those actions of *Paradise Lost* which "do not express their own meaning for either the characters involved or the reader," and in response to which the reader is "radically individualized by being compelled freely to judge."[65] In obscuring the grounds of Samson's decision, Milton puts the reader in Samson's position of deciding the meaning of his act. This interpretive reticence on Milton's part makes reading *Samson Agonistes* an ambivalent experience: for the mixture of attraction and repulsion, coercion and consent, identification and differentiation, that characterizes the spectator's experience of tragic catharsis is here rendered as an interpretive ambivalence as well. Confronted with a Samson who is both judge and victim, and whose grounds for deciding the exception are unknowable, the reader experiences not only pity and fear but what Angus Fletcher has described as "the mixture of pain and pleasure" in the uncertainty of exegesis.[66]

Some readers will resolve this uncertainty by deciding that Samson is an exception who is, for that reason, not to be imitated. Other readers, "like Samson," will read Samson as "a mirror . . . unparallel'd," an example of exceptional commitment that they too can decide to embrace. Like the regicide in the first *Defence* and like Samson in Luther's treatise *On Secular Authority*, Milton's Samson reveals the conditional structure of any exception, which is exemplary if we have the grace to make it so. In a revolutionary gloss on the maxim that "the sovereign is he who decides the exception," Milton implies that it is not the sovereign but the conscientious subject whose task it is to differentiate between positive law and true justice and to act accordingly.[67] The conscientious subject is ideally the true sovereign. The conclusion of *Samson Agonistes* thus illustrates Bishop Sanderson's fears about the revolutionaries' equivocal gloss on the word "people" to the prejudice of the king as "ruler of the nation," but only at the price of turning Samson himself into an example of tragic casuistry: to paraphrase Luther's remarks (quoted earlier) from *On Secular Authority*, Samson experiences the conflicting demands of God's kingdom and the world at one and the same time, outwardly and inwardly; he both suffers evil and injustice and yet punishes the wicked; he both resists evil and yet does not resist it. Whether he thereby "satisfies" the demands of God's kingdom and the world is something neither Samson nor we can know. But it is a question, Milton insists, that we must not fail to ask. Milton's tragedy is a product of this effort to make rational sense of his experience—above all, his experience of covenant and contract in the aftermath of the Restoration.

CHAPTER 11

Conclusion

> Two men, who pull the oars of a boat do it by agreement or convention, tho' they have never given promises to each other.
>
> —Hume, *Treatise* 3.2.2

> The social order is a sacred right which is the basis of all other rights. Nevertheless, this right does not come from nature, and must therefore be founded on conventions.
>
> —Rousseau, *The Social Contract*

IN HIS ESSAY "Of the Original Contract," David Hume ridiculed seventeenth-century contract theory as a preposterously artificial account of obligation. According to Hume, contract theory presupposes that promises are binding, but this presupposition in turn assumes a prior agreement to be bound by one's promises and so on ad infinitum. It is absurd to say that people keep their promises because they have promised to do so. Rather, they keep them because they are embedded in a network of social relations, customs, and conventions: "Two men who pull the oars of a boat do it by agreement or convention, tho' they have never given promises to each other."

The current scholarly consensus is that, in his mockery of contract theory, Hume was taking aim at Locke, while elaborating the insights of Hobbes. This argument is sometimes made in terms of Hobbes's utilitarianism, but the point of similarity I wish to stress is Hobbes's and Hume's shared belief in the constructive power of contract and the constitutive power of language. While Locke retreated from Hobbes's creative fiat of contract theory, Hume's antifoundationalist, conventionalist account of human interaction develops Hobbes's contract theory to its logical conclusion: in the absence of any transcendental guarantees of morality, we are creatures of convention, as it were, all the way down.[1] From this perspective, Hume's attention to the passions, interests, and sentiments—his assertion that "Reason is, or ought to be, the slave of passion"—would also follow in part from his absorption of Hobbes.[2]

It is easy to be sympathetic to Hume's complaint about the artificiality of contract theory, especially given the poststructuralist commonplace that we are creatures of language and of conventions to which we do not consent.[3] Nevertheless, something important is lost when contract theory is assimilated to existing customs and conventions—and that is the critical judgment that is facilitated by the distancing effect of artifice. Even when contract is used as a synonym for Magna Carta and fundamental law in the seventeenth century, the point is that such a contract cannot be equated with the status quo. In this sense, even the notion of a "historical" contract functions as a critical fiction. As George Shelton observes in his book on Hobbes, "the social contract . . . is very close to the legal fiction known as 'quasi contract' which allows the court to act *as if* a contract existed where none in fact did. The purpose of the legal fiction is presumably to see that justice is done in a situation where it otherwise would not have been." For this reason, Shelton argues, Hobbes's fiction of the social contract "is more fruitful than Hume's notion of 'convention.' The latter tells us why we behave the way we do but it is of no help in determining why we *ought* to behave that way."[4] The distance between ought and is creates the space for critical judgment. Knowing when we ought to keep our contracts is also a good rule for knowing when we should not. Although Shelton does not make this point, it is Rousseau rather than Hume who is the inheritor of this understanding of seventeenth-century contract theory as a critical fiction. This is because Rousseau was aware that the social contract was not really a contract between the individual and the people, but instead involved the fictional act of *constituting* the people.[5]

As I have argued, in the early modern period, narrative and poetic fiction are an intrinsic part of contract theory because contract theory sees obligation as an artifact or construct. As such, it presupposes that the story of obligation could always be otherwise and so requires a narrative of how obligation comes about. This story involves an appeal to the subject's passions and interests; more radically, it involves the creation of the subject of passion and interest, the creation of the new psychology of the contracting subject. This creation is both thematic and formal: early modern writers drew on the resources of fiction in composing stories about this new subject; in their linguistic and literary self-consciousness, these authors also appropriated the divine fiat for the secular purposes of human interaction. Similarly, seventeenth-century narratives about the contracting subject treat the passions and interests thematically, but these narratives also engage the passions and interests formally through their appeal to the reader's aesthetic pleasure. For these reasons, I have argued, contract theory plays a pivotal role in the emergence of an autonomous realm of aesthetics.

In *The Ideology of the Aesthetic*, Terry Eagleton argued that the discourse of aesthetics first emerged in the eighteenth century as a way of addressing an ideological dilemma inherent in absolutist power—the necessity of encompassing the subject's world of sensation and feeling without jeopardizing absolute sovereignty. Yet, by attending to or creating the new affective subject, aesthetics ultimately became an instrument of the middle class's struggle for political hegemony:

> From the depths of a benighted late feudal aristocracy [Eagleton is discussing Germany], a vision could be projected of a universal order of free, equal, autonomous human subjects, obeying no laws but those which they gave to themselves. This bourgeois public sphere breaks decisively with the privilege and particularism of the *ancien régime*, installing the middle class, in image if not in reality, as a truly universal subject. . . . What is at stake here is nothing less than the production of an entirely new kind of human subject—one which, like the work of art itself, discovers the law in the depths of its own free identity, rather than in some oppressive external power. The liberated subject is the one who has appropriated the law as the very principle of its own autonomy, broken the forbidding tablets of stone on which that law was originally inscribed in order to write it on the heart of flesh. To consent to the law is thus to consent to one's own inward being. 'The heart,' writes Rousseau in *Emile*, 'only receives laws from itself; by wanting to enchain it one releases it; one only enchains it by leaving it free.'
>
> The ultimate binding force of the bourgeois social order, in contrast to the coercive apparatus of absolutism, will be habits, pieties, sentiments and affections. And this is equivalent to saying that power in such an order has become *aestheticized*.[6]

While such an aestheticizing of the social order could mask coercive relations of power, it could also be a revolutionary concept: "There is a world of political difference between a law which the subject really does give to itself, in radical democratic style, and a decree which still descends from on high but which the subject now 'authenticates.' Free consent may thus be the antithesis of oppressive power, or a seductive form of collusion with it."[7]

As I have shown, although the formal discipline of aesthetics appears only in the eighteenth-century, the affective problematic described by Eagleton first emerges in the context of early modern reflection on the social and political contract. We do not need to wait until Hume and Rousseau to find writers concerned to supplement the abstract discourse of rights with an appeal to the passions and to aesthetic interest. In fact, one argument of this book has been that the seventeenth-century crisis of political obligation generated an intense debate about the role of the passions and aesthetic interest in eliciting consent to the political contract. Moreover, in the seventeenth century, as in the later period, the appeal to aesthetic interest did not simply amount to a mystification of the social order or a fictional form of social control. It also served as a vehicle of radical political dissent.

We have lost our ability to see this aspect of seventeenth-century debates because historically Hobbes won out over Milton. Hobbes's invention of "political science" and, by extension, a marginalized realm of aesthetics helped to produce the modern disciplinary distinction between political theory and literary studies that distorts our view of the seventeenth century. In the aftermath of Hobbes's success, liberalism came to be seen as an ideology of formal equality, and aesthetics was equated with the disinterested, apolitical pleasure the spectator derives from the formal qualities of the work of art. For these reasons, modern liberalism and aesthetics alike have been vulnerable to attacks from twentieth-century critics such as Adorno and Horkheimer who aimed to recover a sense of the critical potential of aesthetic form, of aesthetics as critique.

Modern liberalism has also been vulnerable to the charge that its conception of the individual is thin and that its conception of community is correspondingly impoverished. It's one of the ironies of the history of liberalism that Hobbes described *prepolitical* life in the state of nature as "solitary, poor, nasty, brutish, and short"; and that critics of liberalism have been saying the same thing of liberal *political* life ever since. According to its critics, the liberal remedy was as bad as the problem it was designed to solve. In the seventeenth century, opponents of Hobbes complained that the isolated, self-interested subject of *Leviathan* would have no reason to keep his promises, including his promise to abide by the political contract. And, in the late twentieth century, Michael Sandel objected in a similar fashion to John Rawls that the subject who enters into the liberal political contract is an abstract, decontextualized individual with no ties or allegiances, of no particular age, sex, education, or community. According to Sandel, Rawls gives us a socially, even phenomenologically thin subject who has no basis upon which to make the relevant political choices. The language of liberalism, its modern critics say, is an enervated one—the autonomous subject is an unpromising basis on which to build community—in contrast to the embodied subject of communitarianism, which has appealed to critics of liberalism on both the left and the right.[8]

It's perhaps not surprising that modern critics of liberalism, who are usually not scholars of the seventeenth century, have read early modern contract theory from the vantage point of the twentieth century. From this perspective, the seventeenth-century language of contract may indeed look responsible for the attenuated conception of the political subject and political obligation that has dominated liberal thinking ever since. But, as I have argued in this book, the seventeenth-century subject of contract was not the thin modern subject of formal equality but rather, at one and the same time, a richly imagined "aesthetic" subject of passion and interest, and an artifact of the creative powers of language. From one perspective, the creation of this subject amounted to a celebration of the poetic powers of the artist and political theorist. From another, it anticipated the modern insights of antifoundationalism: in the early modern period, the contracting subject was as much an effect of the conventions of contract as their cause—an individual who was capable of binding himself only because he was first bound by the social and linguistic agreement that promises must be kept.

In the preceding pages, I have told the story of contract in terms of the tension between artifice and voluntary servitude, language and the passions, rather than in terms of modern liberal notions of autonomy and formal equality. I have done so in particular by singling out Hobbes and Milton as representative of two antithetical approaches to the discourse of contract. In both Hobbes and Milton, arguments for contract are predicated on a new conception of natural rights that is inextricable from the motivating power of the passions and the poetic power of the imagination. Both are interested in constructing a subject who consents to be bound, who consents to bind himself. Yet, such consent ideally empowers the revolutionary Miltonic agent, whereas the Hobbesian subject is, ideally, primarily constrained. It is precisely the dialectic between Hobbes and Milton—and the larger cultural developments of which they were a part—that I have tried to recover in the preceding pages.

But why should we rethink the meaning of contract and the resources of liberalism via Hobbes and Milton? Neither is as central to the traditional genealogy of liberalism, as, for example, Locke is. This is to a large extent my point. Each was in some respects conspicuously unliberal by modern standards—Hobbes by virtue of his political absolutism; Milton because of his elitism, his limited toleration for religious differences, and his flirtation with antinomianism. Yet each contributed powerfully to the early modern effort to imagine a new subject of political obligation, the new subject of contract. Not only was the analogy between human making and divine making important to both. Equally important was the imagination of a new kind of embodied subject—an "aesthetic" subject in the root sense of sensory perception—for whom the passions and the imagination were critical faculties in inducing voluntary subjection or resistance to political authority.

In the modern era, we have lost both of these dimensions of contractual thinking. On the one hand, we have left behind Hobbes's sense of the radically creative power of contract. To cite just one example, when John Rawls resurrected the metaphor of contract in his own defense of liberalism, he was forced to point out to his critics that this contract was "a device of representation"—so much do we lack a sense of the relevance of fiction and the imagination to political obligation.[9] On the other hand, we have left behind Milton's sense of the limits of making—which is also a sense of the link between our passions and our capacity for dissent—so much so that it's left to so-called compassionate conservatives to condemn the destructive political consequences of "pure reason" and to reclaim the contribution of the passions and the imagination to political obligation. Mimesis and aesthetics—poetics and the passions—these are the neglected terms in the dry juridical discourse of the later history of liberalism. Yet they were crucial to extricating the seventeenth-century subject from the traditional ties that bind, crucial to the very different anatomies of the political subject offered by Hobbes and Milton. To recover the implicit dialogue between *Leviathan* and *Paradise Lost* is to go some ways toward reconstructing a richer history of the contracting subject—a history that modern liberalism would do well to reclaim.

Notes

CHAPTER 1
INTRODUCTION

1. On the shift from status to contract, see Henry Sumner Maine, *Ancient Law* (London, 1906); Max Weber, *Economy and Society*, ed. Günther Roth and Claus Wittich, trans. Ephraim Fischoff et al., 2 vols. (Berkeley, 1978); Perry Miller, *The New England Mind: The Seventeenth Century* (1939; Boston, 1954), 399; Michael Walzer, *Revolution of the Saints* (Cambridge, Mass., 1968), 73 and 236; Donald W. Hanson, *From Kingdom to Commonwealth: The Development of Civic Consciousness in English Political Thought* (Cambridge, Mass., 1970), esp. chap. 10; L. C. Knights, *Drama and Society in the Age of Jonson* (London, 1937). In "Drama and Society in the Age of Jonson: An Alternative View," *Renaissance Drama*, n.s., 13 (1982): 103–29, Don E. Wayne cautions that Henry Sumner Maine's use of the terms status and contract "has been effectively repudiated because of its normative and evolutionist assumptions," but he also notes that "the terms continue to be used descriptively in the field of jurisprudence and by social and intellectual historians" (104, n4). I return to Weber in note 58. On the transition from the pact of subjection to the pact of association, see Otto Gierke, *Natural Law and the Theory of Society, 1500–1800*, trans. Ernest Barker, 2 vols. (Cambridge, 1934); A. P. D'Entrèves, *Natural Law*, 2nd ed. (London, 1970); J. W. Gough, *The Social Contract*, 2nd ed. (Oxford, 1967); Ernest Barker, *Social Contract* (Oxford, 1947).

2. Friedrich Nietzsche, *The Genealogy of Morals*, in *The Birth of Tragedy and The Genealogy of Morals*, trans. Francis Golffing (Garden City, N.Y., 1956), 2.7, p. 201 (Luther and Calvin); 2.17, p. 219 (contract); 1.16, 185–86 (Rome vs. Israel). On Nietzsche's friendship with his older colleague Jacob Burckhardt in Basel, see Lionel Gossman, *Basel in the Age of Burckhardt* (Chicago, 2000).

3. Hunton is quoted in Derek Hirst, *Authority and Conflict: England, 1603–1658* (Cambridge, Mass., 1986), 88; Robert Filmer, *Observations on Aristotle's Politics*, in *Patriarcha and Other Writings*, ed. Johann P. Sommerville (Cambridge, 1991), 251.

4. Filmer, *Observations Concerning the Originall of Government*, in *Patriarcha and Other Writings*, ed. Johann P. Sommerville (Cambridge, 1991), 184 (emphasis added). Filmer's ironic use of Hobbes's vocabulary was pointed out to me by Bernadette Meyler. On contract as a sign of frayed or changing social relations, see Michael Walzer, *Revolution of the Saints* (Cambridge, Mass., 1965), chap. 6.

5. Cited in Nigel Smith, *Literature and Revolution in England, 1640–1660* (New Haven, 1994), 104.

6. See Keith Thomas, "Cases of Conscience in Seventeenth-Century England," in *Public Duty and Private Conscience in Seventeenth-Century England*, ed. John

Morrill, Paul Slack, and Daniel Wolff (Oxford, 1993), 30: "Traditional maxims about buying and selling or lending or borrowing appeared archaic as the economy diversified and credit became univeral." The same could be said of traditional maxims about the mutual love of husband and wife, sovereign and subject, in domestic and political contract. As Tony Tanner has argued in a different context, contract presupposes as well the world of rampant passion—of broken promises of fidelity. See his *Adultery and the Novel: Contract and Transgression* (Baltimore, 1979).

7. Rev. Charles Herle, *A Fuller Answer to a Treatise written by Doctor Ferne* (1642), 14; Butler, *Characters and Passages from Notebooks*, 292; both cited by Christopher Hill, *Society and Puritanism in Pre-Revolutionary England* (London, 1964), 412 and 414. See also Susan Staves, *Players' Scepters: Fictions of Authority in the Restoration* (Lincoln, Neb., 1979), chap. 4, "Oaths and Vows," on Butler's skepticism about oaths.

8. Following Christopher Hill, Jonathan Scott, in *England's Troubles: Seventeenth-Century English Political Instability in European Context* (Cambridge, 2000), claims that what was truly revolutionary about the English civil war were the achievements of the English "radical imagination" (35).

9. In *The Ideology of the Aesthetic* (Oxford, 1990), Terry Eagleton argues that the liberal conception of the autonomous individual is reflected in the rise of aesthetics, with its focus on the autonomous work of art. My argument differs from Eagleton's in attending to the role of artifice and in exploring the prehistory of the eighteenth-century conjunction of liberalism and aesthetics. I return to this conjunction in the conclusion to this book. For a very different argument about the relationship between seventeenth-century politics, including contract theory, and the rise of aesthetics, see Timothy J. Reiss's discussion of the invention of literature as a vehicle of a Cartesian "analytico-referential" discourse in *The Meaning of Literature* (Ithaca, 1992), esp. 73, 91, 84, 95.

10. While reason of state justified the exception in the sphere of government, casuistry addressed the exceptional case in the realm of self-government. Together these discourses articulated something like the Foucauldian problem of "governmentality." See Michel Foucault, "Governmentality," in *The Foucault Effect*, ed. Graham Burchell, Colin Gordon, and Peter Miller (Chicago, 1991):

> Government as a general problem seems to me to explode in the sixteenth century, posed by discussions of quite diverse questions. . . . [These questions of the government of souls, lives, children, and the state, lie] at the crossroads of two processes: the one which, shattering the structures of feudalism, leads to the establishment of the great territorial, administrative, and colonial states; and that totally different movement which, with the Reformation and the Counter-Reformation, raises the issue of how one must be spiritually ruled and led on this earth in order to achieve eternal salvation.
>
> There is a double movement, then, of state centralization on the one hand and of dispersion and religious dissidence on the other: it is, I believe, at the intersection of these two tendencies that the problem comes to pose itself with this particular intensity, of how to be ruled, how strictly, by whom, to what end, by what methods, etc. There is a problematic of government in general. (86–87)

In "Omnes et singulatim: Towards a Criticism of Political Reason," in *The Tanner Lectures on Human Values, 1981*, ed. Sterling M. McMurrin (Salt Lake City, 1981), 225–54, Foucault also links these two tendencies in early modern governmentality to reason of state and casuistry or what he calls political rationality and pastoral power. In general, however, Foucault associates contract theory with the older, juridical notion of sovereignty, while he sees governmentality as a precursor of his own notion of discipline. In the early modern period, however, the problem of government and the related discourses of contract are not so easily domesticated.

11. Aristotle does discuss the role of language in founding government in the *Politics*, trans. Ernest Barker (Oxford, 1957), at 1253a10–12, and he also expresses a preference for constitutional rule over absolutism; but neither of these views leads Aristotle to assert that consent to a contract is a necessary precondition of society or of political association. Rather, political association is natural (1252b8). Aristotle also rejects a purely contractual view of the polis in *Politics*, 1280b10. In *Rhetoric*, 1376b10, Aristotle was predictably more pragmatic about contracts, arguing that "most business relations—those, namely, that are voluntary—are regulated by contracts, and if these lose their binding force, human intercourse ceases to exist." This passage was, however, cited by Cicero and others to illustrate the moral law that promises should be kept. See *De officiis*, 3.17.70. On the relationship between speech and promising, see Aristotle, *Nicomachean Ethics*, book 4, 1127a15, on truthfulness; book 5, 1131b25–1132b20. On Aquinas, see *De regimine principum*, 1.6, in *The Political Ideas of Thomas Aquinas*, ed. Dino Bigongiari (New York, 1953), 191. In *Natural Law and Political Thought* (Washington, D.C., 1971), Paul E. Sigmund argues that "there is no reference in Aquinas to consent of the ruled as a requirement for political legitimacy. Aquinas mentions cases in which a free community has a right to legislate for itself . . . and favors a limited popular role in government . . . but he describes monarchical rule as most in accord with nature" (44–45).

12. See James Gordley, *The Philosophical Origins of Modern Contract Doctrine* (Oxford, 1991), who argues that the Aristotelian virtues of promise keeping, liberality, and commutative justice are essential components of neoscholastic and, indeed, of any coherent contract doctrine.

13. On the differences between late scholastics and a fully developed contract theory, see Gierke, *Natural Law and the Theory of Society*; Gough, *Social Contract*; and Quentin Skinner, *The History of Political Thought*, 2 vols. (Cambridge, 1978), 2:157, as well as 2:161–62, on the use of consent. See Gough, *Social Contract*, 70–71, on Suárez's use, though infrequent, of the language of contract to describe the relationship of sovereign and subject.

14. The terms were often used interchangeably in the sixteenth and early seventeenth centuries. See *Oxford English Dictionary*, s.v. "assent" and "consent." The first definitions of "assent" are: "To give the concurrence of one's will; to agree to (a proposal); to comply with (a desire)."

15. For a lively brief history of these oaths, see William Kerrigan, *Shakespeare's Promises* (Baltimore, 1999), chap. 1.

16. Article 37, in David Cressy and Lori Anne Ferrell, *Religion and Society in Early Modern England: A Sourcebook* (London, 1996), 69.

17. Richard Hooker, *Of the Laws of Ecclesiastical Polity*, ed. A. S. McGrade and Brian Vickers (London, 1975), 1.10.4 (common consent), 8.2.11.

18. Ibid., 1.10.8.

19. See Donald W. Hanson, *From Kingdom to Commonwealth* (Cambridge, Mass., 1970); Arthur B. Ferguson, *The Articulate Citizen and the English Renaissance* (Durham, N.C., 1965); Edmund Morgan, *Inventing the People* (New York, 1988).

20. See Gough, *Social Contract*, 56, 60.

21. The more extreme versions of patriarchalism and divine right theory have themselves been seen as a response to the incursions of contract theory against traditional conceptions of obligation, rather than the other way around. See, for example, Gordon J. Schochet, *Patriarchalism in Political Thought* (New York, 1975), 55–56; and Johann P. Sommerville, *Politics and Ideology in England, 1603–1640* (London, 1986).

22. Sommerville, *Politics and Ideology in England*, 71.

23. See Francis D. Wormuth, *The Origins of Modern Constitutionalism* (New York, 1949), chap. 9. By "people," I mean of course male citizens.

24. John Lilburne in the *Whitehall Debates*, in *Puritanism and Liberty*, ed. A.S.P. Woodhouse (London, 1992), 129.

25. Woodhouse, *Puritanism and Liberty*, 34 (Everard), 10 (Wildman).

26. Ibid., 27 (boundless and endless), 130 (wills, lusts, and passions), 26 (great foundation of justice).

27. Hobbes, *De cive*, book 1, chap. 8, p. 102; *Leviathan*, 26.184. The best study of the centrality of the will to contract theory is Patrick Riley, *Will and Political Legitimacy* (Cambridge, Mass., 1982). Other studies that discuss the antinomies between rationalism and voluntarism in early modern contract theory include Gierke, *Natural Law and the Theory of Society*; Barker, *Social Contract*; and the works cited in note 33. For an earlier discussion of the problems created by thinking of the will and intellect as autonomous faculties in seventeenth-century moral discourse, see Anthony Levi, *French Moralists: The Theory of the Passions, 1585–1649* (Oxford, 1964), 27, 198–200, 316.

28. On the materialist challenge to Aristotle in the seventeenth century, see Susan James, *Passion and Action* (Oxford, 1997). On the new appeal to passions and interests, see Albert O. Hirschman, *The Passions and the Interests: Political Arguments for Capitalism before Its Triumph* (Princeton, 1977); and John Guillory, "Milton, Narcissism, Gender: On the Genealogy of Male Self-Esteem," in *Critical Essays on John Milton*, ed. Christopher Kendrick (New York, 1995), 194–233. On early modern materialism, see also Max Horkheimer, "Materialism and Morality," *Telos* 69 (1986): 85–118. This essay was orginally published in 1933 and draws on Wilhelm Dilthey's account of the Renaissance. There is, of course, an extensive secondary literature on theories of materialism in seventeenth-century science, which I cannot take account of here.

29. Hobbes, *De cive*, 1.2.1.

30. In addition to Hirschman, *Passions and Interests*, see J.A.W. Gunn, *Politics and the Public Interest in the Seventeenth Century* (London, 1969); and Gunn, "Interest Will Not Lie: A Seventeenth-Century Political Maxim," *Journal of the History of Ideas* 29 (1968): 551–64.

31. On Nedham, see Jonathan Scott, *Algernon Sidney and the English Republic, 1623–1677* (Cambridge, 1988), 112.

32. According to Riley in *Will and Political Legitimacy,* seventeenth-century theories of contract were caught on the horns of a dilemma. Consent involves the will, and the will has both a moral and a psychological meaning. The moral meaning assumes that the will is based on reasons; the psychological meaning assumes that it is based on causes. In the first case, the will involves rational choice, but it is unclear what motivates the will; in the second case, the will is already determined by antecedent factors, and it is thus unclear what the role of reason is. Contract or consent theory thus becomes the locus of a set of antinomies between rationalism and voluntarism, or voluntarism and determinism. For similar arguments, see Michael Lessnoff, *Social Contract* (Houndsmill, England, 1986); and David Gauthier, "The Social Contract as Ideology," *Philosophy and Public Affairs* 6 (1977): 130–64.

33. On this conception of mimesis, see Paul Ricoeur, *The Rule of Metaphor,* trans. Robert Czerny with Kathleen McLaughlin and John Costello (Toronto, 1977); and the works cited in note 40.

34. In *Politics and Vision* (Berkeley, 1960), Sheldon S. Wolin discusses the shared assumptions, on the part of Machiavelli, Luther, Calvin, and Hobbes, regarding "the plasticity of human arrangements and the efficacy of the human will" (243). He goes on to discuss Hobbes in particular as "the Great Artificer" and offers a sensitive analysis of the linguistic focus of Hobbes's political thought (246). Yet for Wolin, as for others who note the voluntarism of early modern political thought, this concern with artifice ultimately signals a decline of political philosophy and the rise of the social. I address this argument later.

35. See, for example, Pico della Mirandola, *Oration on the Dignity of Man*, in *The Renaissance Philosophy of Man*, ed. Ernst Cassirer, Paul Oskar Kristeller, and John Herman Randall Jr. (Chicago, 1948), 224–25; Philip Sidney, *A Defence of Poetry*, ed. J. A. Van Dorsten (Oxford, 1975), 23–25.

36. On this phrase, see, among others, Terence Ball, "Hobbes' Linguistic Turn," *Polity* 17 (1985): 740–41: "When we say that modern philosophy generally, and political philosophy in particular, has taken a linguistic turn, we do not mean merely that philosophers are nowadays interested in investigating the nature and functions of language, for that has been a perennial concern (*vide* Plato's *Cratylus*). Roughly, we might say that the linguistic turn began with the realization that our language does not merely mirror the world but is instead partially constitutive of it. Our concepts and categories are not ultimately reducible to names or labels to be affixed to independently existing phenomena or forms of life. On the contrary, reality—particularly political reality—is to a very considerable degree linguistically or conceptually constructed. The material out of which our common world is made are the concepts, categories, discriminations, divisions, designations and differentiations to be found in the language we speak."

37. Charles Taylor, *Sources of the Self* (Cambridge, Mass., 1989), 186, 197.

38. Amos Funkenstein, *Theology and the Scientific Imagination from the Middle Ages to the Seventeenth Century* (Princeton, 1986), 334, 335 (discussing Hobbes in particular). See also Antonio Pérez-Ramos, *Francis Bacon's Idea of Science and the Maker's Knowledge Tradition* (Oxford, 1988); Bloch, *Natural*

Law and Human Dignity, trans. Dennis J. Schmidt (Cambridge, Mass., 1986), 55 (on the mathematical model of constructive knowledge in the seventeenth century); and Francis Oakley, *Omnipotence, Covenant, and Order* (Ithaca and London, 1984), esp. chap. 3.

39. In chapters 16 and 24 of the *Poetics*, Aristotle described mimesis in terms of the drawing of inferences. Both in the *Poetics* and the *Rhetoric*, such inference often turned on a rhetorical syllogism, which gains its force from cultural assumptions or rhetorical conventions rather than from a strictly logical process of deduction. On this point, see also note 42. The *Poetics* also makes it clear that literary verisimilitude does not perfectly conform to the logical criteria of probable judgment, because literature traffics in deception and disguise, plausible impossibilities rather than implausible possibilities. Aristotle, *Poetics*, trans. James Hutton (New York, 1982), chap. 25, 1461b.

40. On the social contract of genre, see Fredric Jameson, *The Political Unconscious* (Ithaca, 1981), 106. On the contract of mimesis in the Aristotelian tradition, see Ricoeur, *The Rule of Metaphor*; Terence Cave, *Recognitions: A Study in Poetics* (Oxford, 1988); and Christopher Prendergast, *The Order of Mimesis* (Cambridge, 1986), 216, 233–34. Also relevant to thinking about the contract of genre and the poetic dimension of political contract is the very distinguished body of criticism that links poetic and legal fiction; see, among others, Kathy Eden, *Poetic and Legal Fiction in the Aristotelian Tradition* (Princeton, 1986); Ian Maclean, *Interpretation and Meaning in the Renaissance: The Case of Law* (Cambridge, 1992); and Lorna Hutson, "The 'Double Voice' of Equity and the Literary Voices of Women," in *"This Double Voice": Gendered Writing in Early Modern England*, ed. Danielle Clarke and Elizabeth Clarke (London, 2000), 142–63. I return to these links in the chapters that follow.

41. One example Cave gives is of the sixteenth-century story of Martin Guerre, where it is unclear whether the wife's "recognition" of her long-lost husband has been coerced or not: "Recognition, then, in this 'true story,' is not the recovery for good or ill of certain knowledge, nor the reassuring restoration of the coordinates of kinship and social position. It unmasks a crisis, a perpetual threat of imposture on the one hand and arbitrary law and coercion on the other. It is also—as the parallel [with the recognition scene in] the *Odyssey* suggests—sexually disquieting" (*Recognitions*, 14–15).

42. In book 1 of the *Rhetoric* Aristotle classifies as atechnical proofs signs such as "laws, witnesses, contracts, torture, and oaths" (Cave, *Recognitions*, 246)— atechnical because the orator finds them ready-made: they are not a product of his rhetorical art, although he may draw on them to make his case. In chapter 16 of the *Poetics* Aristotle tells us that recognition (one of three elements of the tragic plot) involves probable reasoning about similarly atechnical signs of identity, and in chapter 24 he relates such inartistic proofs to paralogism, that is, to probabilistic or faulty reasoning.

43. Prendergast, *Order of Mimesis*, 49–50.

44. Ibid., chap. 7, esp. 216–17, describing Ricoeur and himself, on the one hand, and Barthes, Derrida, Lyotard et al., on the other.

45. The phrase "criticism and compliment" is taken from Kevin Sharpe, *Criticism and Compliment: The Politics of Literature in the England of Charles I* (Cambridge, 1987). On the politics of genre in this period, see, among others, Annabel

Patterson, *Censorship and Interpretation* (Madison, Wis., 1984); Lois Potter, *Secret Rites and Secret Writing: Royalist Literature, 1641–1660* (Cambridge, 1989); David Quint, *Epic and Empire* (Princeton, 1993); Smith, *Literature and Revolution*; and David Norbrook, *Writing the English Republic* (Cambridge, 1999).

46. On Milton and Senecan tragedy, see Smith, *Literature and Revolution*, 17. Smith also discusses the conventions of contemporary newsbooks. In thinking about the exchange between Hobbes and Davenant, I have benefited from reading an unpublished essay by Annabel Patterson.

47. Bloch, *Natural Law and Human Dignity*, 55.

48. Aristotle uses this phrase to describe the realm of prudential deliberation in the *Nicomachean Ethics* and the *Rhetoric*, a sphere that Renaissance critics also associated with literature. See my *Rhetoric, Prudence, and Skepticism in the Renaissance* (Ithaca, 1985).

49. As all seventeenth-century men and women knew, in the Hebrew Bible God established a covenant with Noah and "every living creature of all flesh" (Genesis 6:18). In Genesis 17, God extended an everlasting covenant to Abraham and to "his seed after him"; while in Galatians 4:24, Jesus reinterpreted the covenant of Mount Sinai as a covenant of bondage in contrast to the new covenant of freedom. See also Exodus 19, where God announces his political covenant with the Jewish people, and Exodus 34: 6–7, where God renews the covenant that the Jews have broken by worshiping the golden calf; Joshua 24:25; Jeremiah 31:31; Galatians 3:15; and Hebrews 8:10.

50. I discuss Ciceronian rhetoric and the *lex regia* in chapter 2.

51. Versions of this argument have been put forward by both historians and political philosophers, including Ernst Bloch, C. B. Macpherson, Carole Pateman, John Rawls, Robert Nozick, James Tully, and others. Needless to say, the argument is developed at length by some and primarily assumed or mentioned in passing by others. Some, like Bloch, Macpherson, and Pateman, advance this argument about the seventeenth century only then to critique its putatively liberal assumptions from a Marxist or feminist perspective. Some, like Rawls, draw on seventeenth-century contract theory but specifically take issue with the Hobbesian formulation of contract theory as raising "special problems." Others, like Tully, criticize the Marxist economic interpretation of early modern contract theory, insisting that contract theory in this period responded to a crisis of political obligation rather than to economic change. And still others, like Mary Ann Glendon, attribute some of the deficiences of the modern liberal conception of rights to its early modern formulations. But in each case, seventeenth-century contract theory is seen as the founding moment in the history of liberalism. See David G. Ritchie, "Contributions to the History of the Social Contract Theory" in *Darwin and Hegel, and Other Philosophical Essays* (London, 1893); Bloch, *Natural Law and Human Dignity*; C. B. Macpherson, *The Political Theory of Possessive Individualism* (Oxford, 1962); George Sabine, *A History of Political Theory*, 4th ed. (Hinsdale, Ill., 1973); John Rawls, *A Theory of Justice* (Cambridge, Mass., 1971); Robert Nozick, *Anarchy, State, and Utopia* (New York, 1974); Carole Pateman, *The Sexual Contract*; John Dunn, "Political Obligation and Political Possibilities," in *Political Obligation in its Historical Context* (Cambridge, 1980), 241–301; James Tully, "After the Macpherson Thesis," in *An Approach to Political Philosophy:*

Locke in Contexts (Cambridge, 1993), 71–95; Susan Moller Okin, *Women in Western Political Thought* (Princeton, 1979), esp. 197–201; Jean Bethke Elshtain, *Public Man, Private Woman* (Princeton, 1981), esp. chap. 3; Mary Ann Glendon, *Rights Talk* (New York, 1991); Jeremy Waldron, "Theoretical Foundations of Liberalism," *Philosophical Quarterly* 37 (1987): 127–50; David Boucher and Paul Kelly, eds., *The Social Contract from Hobbes to Rawls* (London, 1994). See also the introduction to John Rawls, *Political Liberalism* (New York, 1993), which traces some of the roots of modern liberalism to early modern developments. The extensive scholarship on Locke's contribution to liberalism is obviously also relevant, but cannot be canvassed here.

52. See J.G.A. Pocock, *The Machiavellian Moment* (Princeton, 1975), esp. 370–72 and 396–400, on Hobbes. In addition to spawning a whole revisionist history of early modern political thought, this work has been widely criticized for its omissions and its overreaching. See, among others, Isaac Kramnick's important article "Republican Revisionism Revisited," *American Historical Review* 87 (2983): 629–64, which questions the relevance of Pocock's model of republicanism to Anglo-American politics after 1760.

53. Joyce Appleby, *Liberalism and Republicanism in the Historical Imagination* (Cambridge, Mass., 1992); Alan Houston, *Algernon Sidney and the Republican Heritage in England and America* (Princeton, 1991); Scott, *Algernon Sidney and the English Republic*; Kramnick, "Republican Revisionism Revisited," esp. 662–63. See also Steve Pincus, "Neither Machiavellian Moment nor Possessive Individualism: Commerical Society and the Defenders of the English Commonwealth," American Historical Review 103 (1998): 703–36; and the recent book by Quentin Skinner, *Liberty before Liberalism* (Cambridge, 1998), in which Skinner revises some of his earlier work on republicanism by arguing for a neo-Roman theory in which individual liberty is inseparable from the free state (whether a monarchy or republic).

54. By the language of contract, then, I mean not only the variety of discourses early modern speakers and writers drew on and the variety of words they used to convey the notion of the political contract. (These included Roman law, natural law jurisprudence, humanist rhetoric, covenant theology, marriage and domestic relations, and the common law. The range of vocabulary included words such as covenant, compact, pact; in Latin, *foedus, pactum, conventus, societas.* The penumbra surrounding contract inevitably included consent and promise.) I also mean the struggle over the meaning of each of these terms.

On the linguistic permeability of terms such as contract, covenant, and pact in the early modern period, see Harro Höpfl and Martyn P. Thompson, "The History of Contract as a Motif in Political Thought," *American Historical Review* 84 (1979): 914–44, esp. 927: "the family of contract-synonyms—a family composed of the terms of covenant, compact, contract, pact, paction, treaty, bargain, and agreement as well as their equivalents in Latin (*foedus, pactum,* or *pactio,* and *contractus*) or other langauges (*Vertrag, Bund, traicté, pacte,* and the like." "The synonymity of these terms in the sixteenth and seventeenth centuries is confirmed by the translating habits of the time and also by contemporary dictionaries" (n11). In *Ideas of Contract in English Political Thought in the Age of Locke* (New York and London, 1987), Martyn P. Thompson argues that contract was used in political writings "as a synonym for, or in conjunction with, other legal notions like trust, stipulation, capitulation, covenant, compact, and even coronation oath and law itself. But equally often, when occasions appeared to suit, writers left the realm of law and legal analogy and considered the term much more loosely as a synonym for promises, bargains, compromises, barriers, or agreements" (13). Recently, political scientists have attempted to discuss contract theory as a multivalent discourse in the Pocockian sense; see Boucher and Kelly, *The Social Contract Tradition from Hobbes to Rawls.*

55. For earlier, still useful studies of the relations between contract theory and literature in the early modern period, see Wayne, "Drama and Society in the Age of Jonson"; Staves, *Players' Scepters*; Carol Kay, *Political Constructions: Defoe, Richardson, and Sterne in Relation to Hobbes, Hume, and Burke* (Ithaca, 1988). Recently, literary historians interested in the common law have begun to discuss the link between economic contract and political contract in the early modern period. See Lorna Hutson, "Not the King's Two Bodies: Reading the 'Body Politic' in Shakespeare's *Henry IV*, Parts 1 and 2," in *Rhetoric and Law in the Early Modern Period*, ed. Victoria Kahn and Lorna Hutson (New Haven, 2001), 166–98. The most distinguished book-length account of contract in recent years, Luke Wilson's *Theater of Intention: Drama and Law in Early Modern England* (Stanford, 2000), focuses primarily on the common law discourse of economic contract, and only briefly discusses its overlap with notions of political contract. In this vein, see also the earlier article by Charles Spinosa, "Shylock and Debt and Contract in *The Merchant of Venice*," *Cardoza Studies in Law and Literature* 5 (1993): 65–85.

56. Annabel Patterson, *Early Modern Liberalism* (Cambridge, 1997).

57. Nancy Armstrong and Leonard Tennenhouse, *The Imaginary Puritan: Literature, Intellectual Labor, and the Origins of Personal Life* (Berkeley, 1992).

58. This tradition descends from Nietzsche's *Genealogy of Morals* and from certain of Weber's arguments. Nietzsche is important because he called attention to the radically aesthetic dimension of contract theory, in the sense of a fiction that underwrites the notion of an autonomous agent. Weber is important because he described the transition from a traditional society to a modern one partly in terms of a new will-centered conception of the individual, and a new understanding of contract as creating rather than reflecting rights and obligations. Also important in Weber's analysis was the development of formal rationality, which plays less of a role in my account. See Max Weber, *The Protestant Ethic and the Spirit of Capitalism*, trans. Talcott Parsons (New York, 1958); and *Economy and Society.* As Weber recognized, contracts in the sense of legally enforceable, voluntary agreements had existed "even in the earliest periods and stages of legal history," but he distinguished between the status contracts of traditional societies and the purposive contracts of modern societies (*Economy and Society*, 2:671–72). Among other differences, status contracts presuppose "norms that are assumed to be an inherent feature or component of the world itself," whereas purposive contracts rest on the assumption that norms are produced. On this point, see Anthony T. Kronman, *Max Weber* (London, 1983), 21, 104, 143. Equally important to Weber's genealogy of modernity was the divine covenant underlying Judeo-Christian notions of God and personal salvation. In *The Protestant Ethic* Weber located the intersection of the purposive contract and the divine covenant

in the early modern period and argued that the Protestant ethic fostered both the habit of calculation and the affective disposition that were conducive to capitalism. The crucial point for my argument is that both the divine covenant and the purposive contract share a will-centered conception of the individual.

59. Leo Strauss, *The Political Philosophy of Hobbes*, trans. Elsa M. Sinclair (1936; Chicago, 1963), 110: "From the outset [Hobbes] sought to answer the question of the best form of State with regard not to man's essential being and the place occupied by him in the universe, but to experience of human life, to application, and therefore with particular reference to the passions." On aesthetics, see ibid., 161, n2. For a more positive assessment of the way Hobbes's contract theory anticipates the eighteenth-century discipline of aesthetics, see Howard Caygill, *Art of Judgment* (London, 1989). In contrast to the argument I develop in this book, Caygill's reading of Hobbes focuses on the similarities between the frontispiece to *Leviathan* and the Kantian problematic of unifying a manifold.

60. Both in *The Human Condition* and in *The Origins of Totalitarianism*, Arendt singled out Hobbes as the figure who ushered in this modern way of thinking. See Hannah Arendt, *The Human Condition* (Chicago, 1958), e.g., 294–304; Arendt, *The Origins of Totalitarianism* (San Diego and New York, 1951), 139–47, 155–57. Arendt's attitude toward making is ambivalent. At the same time that she condemns the reduction of action to fabrication, she also emphasizes the role of artifacts in commemorating the world of action. See *The Human Condition*, 95. Moreover, in *On Revolution* (New York, 1963), Arendt celebrates the revolutionary creation of a new social and political order, which she associates with the theory of the social contract (a theory whose origins she locates in the eighteenth century).

61. Jürgen Habermas, "The Classical Doctrine of Politics," in *Theory and Practice*, trans. John Viertel (Boston, 1974), 41–81, quoting from 41, 43, 62, 47. A similarly negative reading of the eighteenth-century liberal discourse of contract is implicit in Adorno and Horkheimer's *Dialectic of Enlightenment*, trans. John Cummings (1944; New York, 1969). Here the formal equality that is central to the liberal notion of the political contract is also a crucial part of the instrumental rationality of the Enlightenment, which reduces quality to quantity: "[N]umber became the canon of the Enlightenment. The same equations dominate bourgois justice and commodity exchange. . . . Bourgeois society is ruled by equivalence. It makes the dissimilar comparable by reducing it to abstract quantities."

62. Habermas, *Theory and Practice*, 45. Building on this argument, other scholars have argued that the eclipse of politics and of hermeneutic power affected literary history as well. Although neither Arendt nor Habermas devoted much attention to literature, it has become a cliché of intellectual history that the conflation of politics and poetics in instrumental reasoning was accompanied by the simultaneous emergence and marginalization of the realm of aesthetics, now conceived of as a noncognitive realm of pleasurable experience. See Adorno and Horkheimer, *Dialectic of Enlightenment*: "To the Enlightenment, that which does not reduce to numbers, and ultimately to the one, becomes illusion; modern positivism writes it off as literature" (7). Modern scholars on both the left and right have lamented the baleful consequences of this putative reduction of the political to the social and the corresponding rise of the aesthetic. Both camps have seen Hobbes's protoliberal politics of power as the forerunner of the unliberal Nietzsche; both

have seen purely instrumental reasoning as the dialectical progenitor of what one might call an aesthetic modernity—a modernity, in the account of Alasdair MacIntyre, "after virtue." See Alasdair MacIntyre, *After Virtue* (Notre Dame, 1981). On aesthetic modernity, see Jürgen Habermas, *The Philosophical Discourse of Modernity*, trans. Frederick Lawrence (Cambridge, Mass., 1987), esp. "The Entwinement of Myth and Enlightenment: Max Horkheimer and Theodor Adorno" (106–30). On the reduction of the political to the social, see also Wolin, *Politics and Vision*, esp. chaps. 9–10. For a more appreciative analysis of the rise of the aesthetic in the seventeenth century, one that is compatible with my argument, see Michael McKeon, "Politics of Discourses and the Rise of the Aesthetic in Seventeenth-Century England," in *Politics of Discourse*, ed. Kevin Sharpe and Steven N. Zwicker (Berkeley, 1987), 35–51.

63. In "Virtues, Rights and Manners," in *Virtue, Commerce, and History* (1985; Cambridge, 1995), J.G.A. Pocock argued that the protoliberal notion of contractual obligation was inattentive to questions of motivation that could only be answered by republicanism: "It has long been the principal criticism of the liberal synthesis that because it defined the individual as right-bearer and proprietor, it did not define him as possessing a personality adequate to participation in self-rule" (45). In Pocock's formulation, the question of participation in self-rule could only be answered by republicanism, with its attention to virtue, community, and character.

64. See MacIntyre, *After Virtue*.

65. Blair Worden, "Andrew Marvell, Oliver Cromwell, and the Horatian Ode," in *Politics of Discourse*, ed. Kevin Sharpe and Steven Zwicker (Berkeley, 1987), 178; Steven Zwicker, "Politics and Literary Practice in the Restoration," in *Renaissance Genres*, ed. Barbara Kiefer Lewalski (Cambridge, Mass., 1986), 274. See also Zwicker, *Politics and Language in Dryden's Poetry: The Arts of Disguise* (Princeton, 1984); and his *Lines of Authority: Politics and English Literary Culture, 1649–89* (Ithaca, 1993). The epistemic shift at the Restoration is defined in terms of the emergence of probability, the neoclassical view of the socially constructed nature of knowledge, and the inevitable mediation of experience by contingent signs. Although the preoccupation of method is seen to be compatible with divergent political programs—the conservatism of Chillingworth or the political radicalism of Locke—the shared concern with probable inference is said to distinguish the 1660s from the extremism of the 1640s. For a similar argument regarding the shift in attitudes toward language after the civil war, see Richard W. F. Kroll, *The Material Word* (Baltimore, 1991).

66. David Hume, quoted in Louis I. Bredvold, *The Natural History of Sensibility* (Detroit, 1962), 22.

67. Barker, *Social Contract*, viii, vii.

CHAPTER 2
LANGUAGE AND THE BOND OF CONSCIENCE

1. On *nudum pactum*, see A.W.B. Simpson, *A History of the Common Law of Contract* (Oxford, 1987), 381–93. In general, Roman law held that *nuda pacta*

were not binding but then went on to make some exceptions (e.g., stipulation), whereas canon law held that *nuda pacta* were binding.

2. John Selden, *Table Talk*, ed. Edward Arber (Philadelphia, 1972), 40–41 (s.v. "Contracts"). This is a comic version of the scene between the two murderers of Clarence in Shakespeare's *Richard III*, where one says to the other, "When [Richard] opens his purse to give us our reward, then thy conscience flies out" (1.4.122–23).

3. Selden, *Table Talk*, 41.

4. Ibid., 65 (emphasis added).

5. Ibid., 39.

6. There is considerable scholarly debate about whether early modern notions of natural law depart in any significant ways from classical or medieval notions. In his classic work, *Natural Law and the Theory of Society*, trans. Ernest Barker, 2 vols. (Cambridge, 1934), Otto Gierke argued for a departure. See also Knud Haakonssen, *Natural Law and Moral Philosophy, from Grotius to the Scottish Enlightenment* (Cambridge, 1996); Richard Tuck, *Natural Rights Theories* (Cambridge, 1979); Tuck, *Philosophy and Government, 1572–1651* (Cambridge, 1993); Tuck, "The 'Modern' Theory of Natural Law," in *The Languages of Political Theory in Early Modern Europe*, ed. Anthony Pagden (Cambridge, 1987), 99–122; R. S. White, *Natural Law in English Renaissance Literature* (Cambridge, 1996); Jonathan Scott, *Algernon Sidney and the English Republic, 1623–1677* (Cambridge, 1988); J. H. Burns, ed., with the assistance of Mark Goldie, *The Cambridge History of Political Thought, 1450–1700* (Cambridge, 1991), esp. 66–94, 561–656; and Ian Shapiro, *The Evolution of Rights in Liberal Theory* (Cambridge, 1986). Scholars emphasizing continuity include Brian Tierney, *The Idea of Natural Rights: Studies on Natural Rights, Natural Law and Church Law, 1150–1625* (Atlanta, 1997), who argues that modern theories of natural right developed in the twelfth century; James Gordley, *The Philosophical Origins of Modern Contract Doctrine* (Oxford, 1991); Johann Sommerville, "From Suarez to Filmer: A Reappraisal," *Historical Journal* 25 (1982): 525–40; Sommerville, *Politics and Ideology in England, 1603–1640* (London, 1986), e.g., 12–17; and (despite its misleading title) Sommerville, "Selden, Grotius, and the Seventeenth-Century Intellectual Revolution in Moral and Political Theory," in *Rhetoric and Law in Early Modern Europe*, ed. Victoria Kahn and Lorna Hutson (New Haven, 2001), 318–44.

7. J. B. Schneewind, "Pufendorf's Place in the History of Ethics," *Synthèse* 72 (1987): 130.

8. There had of course been precursors of the contractual view of government in Roman law, in the conciliarist arguments of the high Middle Ages, the work of neoscholastic Spanish theologians, and the monarchomach treatises of the late sixteenth century. What distinguished seventeenth-century Protestant accounts of natural law and the contract of government was a more atomistic or individualistic account of human nature, a diminished sense of confidence regarding the legibility of natural law, and a correspondingly greater preoccupation with human arrangements and agreements. Haakonssen stresses the diminished legibility of natural law in Protestant accounts in *Natural Law and Moral Philosophy*, 24–26.

9. Christopher Hill, *Puritanism and Revolution* (London, 1958; 1995), 19: the war "roused the intensest excitement in England and created a profound cleavage of opinion over questions of foreign policy." On the political situation in the new Dutch republic, and Grotius's role as the associate of the Arminian Oldenbarnevelt, see Tuck, *Philosophy and Government*, chap. 5.

10. See Jonathan Scott, "The Law of War: Grotius, Sidney, Locke and the Political Theory of Rebellion," *History of Political Thought* 13 (1992): 565–85, here 566. According to Scott, only Machiavelli rivaled Grotius as a continental influence on English thought during this period. *De jure belli ac pacis* was frequently republished in the following decades; an abridged English translation appeared in 1654 and was reissued the next year. But Grotius was well known in England even before the 1654 edition of *De jure*. John Selden first began to think about natural rights in relation to Grotius's *Mare liberum*, a defense of freedom of the seas. During the war, Grotius's arguments were used by parliamentary critics of the king (see chapter 4). The presbyterian Samuel Rutherford criticized Grotius in *Lex, Rex*, while appropriating some of his arguments to legitimate resistance to Charles I. The puritan clergyman Richard Baxter quoted Grotius in *A Holy Commonwealth* (1659) in defense of resistance and, in particular, of his own actions during the English civil war.

On Filmer, see J. P. Sommerville, Introduction to Robert Filmer, *Patriarcha and Other Writings* (Cambridge, 1991), xiii, xliii. For Grotius's familiarity with Hobbes, see Hugo Grotius, *Epistolae, Quotquot reperiri potuerunt*, 951–52 (a comment to the effect that *De cive* was a royalist work), cited by Johann Sommerville, "Lofty Science and Local Politics," in *The Cambridge Companion to Hobbes*, ed. Tom Sorell (Cambridge, 1996), 247. On Hobbes's knowledge of Grotius, see Tuck, *Philosophy and Government*, 282, 305; Johann Sommerville, *Thomas Hobbes: Political Ideas in Historical Context* (New York, 1992), 3, 13, 16–17. On Milton's meeting with Grotius, see William Riley Parker, *Milton: A Biography*, 2 vols. (Oxford, 1968), 1:169–70. On Robert Sidney, see Scott, *Algernon Sidney and the English Republic*, 54–58. For Rutherford, see Samuel Rutherford, *Lex, Rex: The Law and the Prince* (London 1644), quest. XV ("Whether the King be under a Covenant, and how?"), esp. 110, where Rutherford refers to *De jure belli*, 2.11–13. For Baxter's borrowings from Grotius, see the arguments in chap. 12 of his *A Holy Commonwealth*, ed. William Lamont (Cambridge, 1994); Grotius is explicitly mentioned in chap. 13, p. 223. On the reception of Grotius in England, see Tuck, *Natural Rights*, chaps. 4–8; Tuck, *Philosophy and Government*, chaps. 5–6.

11. As though to emphasize the rhetorical occasion of conflict Grotius made *controversiae* (controversies), the first word of chapter 1. To the early modern reader it would have conjured up not only contemporary religious and political controversies but also rhetorical exercises on both sides of a question, as in the elder Seneca's *Controversiae*, thereby emphasizing the inextricability of discursive and political conflict. Grotius then went on to argue from common linguistic usage that war had come to mean "not a contest but a condition," just as Hobbes would argue in *Leviathan*. See Grotius, *De jure belli*, 1.1, 1.2.1–2; and Hobbes, *Leviathan*, 13.88: "For WARRE, consisteth not in Battell onely, or the act of fighting; but in a tract of time, wherein the Will to contend by Battell is sufficiently known."

J. B. Schneewind, *The Invention of Autonomy* (Cambridge, 1998), 72, also notes that *controversiae* is the first word of chapter 1.

12. Cicero, *De inventione*, 1.1.2–1.2.3; see also Cicero, *De oratore*, 1.8.33–34.

13. *Marcus Tullius Ciceroes thre bokes of duties*, trans. Nicolas Grimalde, ed. Gerald O'Gorman, (Washington, D.C., 1990), 71. For this use of *societas*, see Cicero, *De re publica*, 1.25.39; 4.3.3; Cicero, *De officiis*, 1.4.12; Cicero, *De legibus*, 1.9.27, 1.13.35. For Stoic arguments about natural sociability and natural law, see *De re publica*, 3.22.33; *De legibus*, 1.10.29–30; 1.15.42–1.17.47 (although Cicero also discusses the illegibility of natural law here).

14. See Cicero, *De re publica*, 3.3.2, on men being joined together "iucundissimo . . . sermonis vinclo" (by the most pleasant bond of speech).

15. See also Cicero, *De officiis*, 1.16.50 ("Eius autem vinculum est ratio et oratio"), and 1.17.53–1.18.54.

16. Grotius, *De jure belli*, prolegomena, para. 11.

17. Here I take issue with Richard Tuck, who sees Grotius as responding in part to contemporary currents of skepticism. See Tuck, *Philosophy and Government*, chap. 5. There is considerable debate in the secondary literature on whether "etiamsi daremus" is simply reiterating a scholastic trope or whether, in the context of *De jure*, it functions to highlight Grotius's "secularism and secularizing effect." See, among others, Knud Haakonssen, "Hugo Grotius and the History of Political Thought," *Political Theory* 13 (1985): 239–65, esp. 249; and, contra, Anton-Hermann Chroust, "Hugo Grotius and the Scholastic Natural Law Tradition," *New Scholasticism* 17 (1963): 101–33; Charles S. Edwards, *Hugo Grotius: The Miracle of Holland* (Chicago, 1981). My own view is that, even though the phrase can be found earlier, its strategic function—in particular, its use to combat conflict arising from confessional differences—is decisively new.

18. Hobbes is an exception. In *Leviathan*, chaps. 14 and 15, natural laws are derived hypothetically from natural rights.

19. Thus Grotius imagined individuals in the state of nature as naturally sociable; but rather than defining sociability in terms of objective natural law, he equated it with the noninterference in others' exercise of their subjective rights, including above all the right of self-preservation. On *socialitas*, see Grotius, prolegomena to *De jure belli*, paras. 6 and 8: "This maintenance of the social order . . . is the source of law properly so called. To this sphere of law belong the abstaining from that which is another's, the restoration to another of anything of his we may have, together with any gain which we may have received from it; the obligation to fulfill promises, the making good of a loss incurred through our fault, and the inflicting of penalties upon men according to their desserts" (para. 8). See also Haakonssen, "Hugo Grotius and the History of Political Thought," 242, on Grotius's definition of natural law in terms of negative justice rather than positive virtue.

20. See *De jure belli*, 1.1.10—1.1.17. On this distinction, which derived from the Stoic distinction between the law of nature and the positive law of individual states, and was known to the church fathers, see Ernest Sirluck, *CPW*, 2:24.

21. This distinction was known to Grotius's scholastic predecessors. What was not scholastic in *De jure belli* was Grotius's description of the *origin* of society

in a social contract, as well as his intense interest in the historically, culturally, and linguistically diverse practices through which rights are articulated and enforced.

22. Grotius, *De jure belli*, 2.2.2.4–5. On pactum, see 2.2.2.5, 1.1.10.4.

23. Grotius, *De jure belli*, 1.4.7.

24. Grotius, *De jure belli*, 2.6.1.1, Hobbes, *Leviathan*, 13.90. In moving from property to sovereignty in this way, Grotius was influenced by the Roman law notion of transferrable property (which included immaterial rights), as well as by the Roman law maxim of the *lex regia*, according to which the emperor derived his power from the people. This notion of transfer or alienation would resurface in later English discussions of political rights. It would also be an important linchpin between political and literary notions of alienation and exchange.

25. On governments having origins in sources other than the will of the people, see 1.3.8–9; on *coetus*, see 1.14.1: "Est autem Civitas coetus perfectus liberorum hominum, juris fruendi & communis utilitatis causa sociatus." Cicero uses the term *coetus* in *De re publica*, 1.24.39.

26. Grotius, *De jure belli*, 2.6.4, 1:171; but such consent is not necessarily revocable—see 1.3.8.

27. Cicero, *De legibus*, 3.9; Grotius, *De jure belli*, 1.4.7. On the shewbread, see 1.4.7.1; on individual resistance, see especially 1.4.7.4. Peter N. Miller discusses Grotius's indebtedness to Cicero's arguments about *salus populi* in *Defining the Common Good: Empire, Religion, and Philosophy in Britain* (Cambridge, 1994), although he does not discuss Cicero's contractual account of the state or his remarks about language itself as a *societas* or bond of association.

28. Grotius, *De jure belli*, 2.6.5, 3.7 and 3.8, concern the rights acquired in war over the conquered, and thus implicitly take up the right to transfer one's allegiance to a new ruler.

29. See Joshua 9:15 and *De jure belli*, 2.13.4.2.

30. Grotius, *De jure belli*, prolegomena, para. 7; 3.19.2.1, and Cicero, *De officiis*, 3.24.92–3.25.95.

31. Grotius, *De jure belli*, prolegomena, para. 7.

32. See Grotius, *De jure belli*, 3.19.2.1, and Cicero, *De officiis*, 3.24.92–3.25.95.

33. Grotius, *De jure belli*, 3.19.1.3: "Nam verum eloquendi obligatio est ex causa."

34. See Cicero, *De inventione*, 1.2.3. In para. 2 of the prolegomena to *De jure belli ac pacis*, Grotius refers directly to Cicero in a way that suggests that he is one of the sources of Grotius's title: "Cicero justly characterized as of surpassing worth a knowledge of treaties of alliance, conventions, and understandings of peoples, kings, and foreign nations; a knowledge, in short, of the whole law of war and peace [*in omni denique belli jure & pacis*]." The editor refers the reader to Cicero's speech *For Balbus*, 6.15.

35. See Grotius, *De jure belli*, prolegomena, para. 28.

36. Hence the large place given in Grotius to the rules for the interpretation of contracts—a feature usually not seen in late scholastic treatises and probably traceable to humanist commentaries on Roman law, with their heightened attention to questions of language and interpretation. On early modern legal interpretation, see note 37.

37. On humanist jurisprudence, see Donald R. Kelley, *History, Law, and the Human Sciences* (London, 1984); Kelley, *The Human Measure: Social Thought in the Western Legal Tradition* (Cambridge, Mass., 1990); Kathy Eden, *Hermeneutics and the Rhetorical Tradition* (New Haven, 1997); and Ian Maclean, *Interpretation and Meaning in the Renaissance: The Case of Law* (Cambridge, 1992). Maclean demonstrates a pervasive concern in Renaissance legal texts with objective and subjective criteria of interpretation, the first focusing on the meaning of the words and the second on the intention of the speaker. He also shows that this distinction is untenable: although most Renaissance authors assume "the priority of thought over language," they also assert "the impossibility of thought without language" (146). Intention, that is, is only accessible through language, through the interpretation of words that takes the form of other words. While focusing on civil law, Maclean also demonstrates the existence of the same concerns in Suárez's theological treatise on law and in English legal thought, and comments, "This is on the one hand not surprising, as Roman law provides a precedent for legal thinking for canonists and common lawyers alike and supplies many maxims useful to both; on the other hand, it leaves the modern historian with the question whether the similarities of approach arise out of a common legal outlook, or a common crisis about language which affected Renaissance thinkers at more or less the same time" (202). Maclean asserts that both explanations are likely.

Maclean also demonstrates the greater concern in Renaisssance texts than in their medieval predecessors with the determination of subjective intention. "*Verba*, according to Aristotle and Cicero, are mental symbols or tokens (*notae animi*) representing concepts which are common to all men. . . . By the late Renaissance, on the authority of the Corpus [Juris Civilis] and of writers on forensic rhetoric, the definition of *verba* has been extended to read 'notae rerum declarantes animi voluntatisque passiones et motus' (symbols of things which express the passions and movements of the mind and will). The introduction of subjective meaning is significant. . . . Its apparent exclusion in the medieval period permitted the elaboration of a logic which treated only *intellectus* or thoughts and ignored the word as an expression of feelings (*motus animi*) or perception (*sensus, species*)" (160–61).

My reading of Grotius bears out Maclean's observations. Grotius and many of his contemporaries argued both that the subject's intention was crucial to the binding force of political and legal contracts, and that intention was constrained or dictated by the form of the contract itself. By this, they seemed to mean something different from the scholastic view that the emphasis on intention is compatible with objective obligations attendant upon the essence of a particular contract; rather, for early modern contract theorists the form of the contract is viewed as a constraint on wayward intention and equivocation.

38. Grotius, *De jure belli*, 2.16.1.1 (emphasis added); see 2.13.1.1–2.13.5.

39. See Harold J. Berman, *Law and Revolution: The Formation of the Western Legal Tradition* (Cambridge, Mass., 1983), 247.

40. This characteristically early modern tension between subjective intention and objective meaning—the objective constraints of language—is also apparent in Grotius's discussion of promises in book 2, chapter 11 of *De jure belli*. In this chapter Grotius argued against the French jurist Connanus's view that some

material proof or consideration is necessary for an agreement to be binding. But even here, where Grotius is defending the canon-law principle that we are bound by our bare promises (promises without consideration), he focuses not simply on the necessary representation of the promise in language but also on the way language constrains our meaning in ways we may not intend. I discuss this chapter in "Early Modern Rights Talk," *Yale Journal of Law and the Humanities* 13 (Summer 2001): 391–411.

41. Robert Filmer, "Observations upon H. Grotius *De jure belli & pacis*," in *The Originall of Government*, in *Patriarcha and Other Writings*, ed. Johann Sommerville (Cambridge, 1991), 220–21; Grotius, *De jure belli*, 1.4.7.3. Although written in the 1630s, the "Observations" was published in 1652.

42. Filmer, *Originall of Government*, 221; Grotius, *De jure belli*, 1.4.7.4.

43. Filmer, *Originall of Government*, 215, 233, 234. Although Filmer does not make explicit the link between property and proper meaning, his argument that property and government depend on the suppression of equitable interpretation implies as much.

44. See J. H. Baker, "The Superior Courts in England, 1450–1800," in *Oberste Gerichtsbarkeit und Zentrale Gewalt im Europa der Frühen Neuzeit* ed. Bernhard Diestelkamp (Cologne, 1996), on the phenomenal increase in legal actions for debt in this period: "At the beginning of our period, the Common Pleas was dealing with about 1,000 to 2,000 cases a year in which the defendant appeared. By 1640, the figure was over 20,000. Over three quarters of actions in the first half of the seventeenth century were for the recovery of debts" (83). On the cultural divergence "from the moral fundamentalism of earlier economic values," see Keith Wrightson, *Earthly Necessities* (New Haven, 2000), quoting Misselden (204).

45. See Corinne Weston, "England: Ancient Constitution and Common Law," in *The Cambridge History of Political Thought, 1450–1700*, ed. J. H. Burns (Cambridge, 1991), 374–410, here 390. The classic account is that of J.G.A. Pocock, *The Ancient Constitution and Feudal Law*, rev. ed. (Cambridge, 1987), although his thesis regarding the ahistorical nature of the common-law mind has been subsequently challenged. See also Paul Christianson, "Young John Selden and the Ancient Constitution, ca. 1610–18," *Proceedings of the American Philosophical Society* 128 (1984): 271–315; Sommerville, *Politics and Ideology in England*; Janelle Greenberg, "The Confessor's Laws and the Radical Face of the Ancient Constitution," *English Historical Review* 1044 (1989): 611–37; Glenn Burgess, *The Politics of the Ancient Constitution* (University Park, Pa., 1992); William Klein, "The Ancient Constitution Revisited," in *Political Discourse in Early Modern Britain*, ed. Nicholas Phillipson and Quentin Skinner (Cambridge, 1993), 23–44. On the Norman Yoke, which is discussed in many of these works, see also Christopher Hill, "The Norman Yoke," in his *Puritanism and Revolution* (London, 1958), 50–122.

46. On this notion of a public person, see Christopher Hill, "Covenant Theology and the Concept of 'A Public Person,' " in *The Collected Essays of Christopher Hill*, 3 vols. (Amherst, Mass., 1986), 3:300–24. Hill quotes Mason on p. 308. Hill also quotes Derek Hirst on the Jacobean parliament's "stridently assertive, if incoherent, emphasis on the fact of representation," in contrast to the "relatively infrequent" assertion of representation by Elizabethan parliaments (307).

47. Richard Helgerson notes this contrast in his excellent chapter on Coke in *Forms of Nationhood: The Elizabethan Writing of England* (Chicago, 1992), 84. As Helgerson points out, James cited the maxim *Rex est lex loquens* in his parliamentary speech of 1607 (317, n34).

48. Ibid., 93, 91. On Coke, see also A. F. Pollard, *The Evolution of Parliament* (London, 1920); and William Holdsworth, *Some Makers of English Law* (Cambridge, 1938), lecture 6 on Coke.

49. On the crisis of faithfulness, see Lorna Hutson, *The Usurer's Daughter* (London, 1994); on the economy of obligation, see Craig Muldrew, *The Economy of Obligation: The Culture of Credit and Social Relations in Early Modern England* (New York, 1998).

50. Quentin Skinner, *The Foundations of Modern Political Thought*, 2 vols. (Cambridge, 1978), 2:57. St. German's *Doctor and Student* was first published in Latin in 1528 and then in English in 1530 and 1531.

51. In the *Nicomachean Ethics*, trans. Martin Oswald (Indianapolis, 1962), 5.10, 1137b20–25, Aristotle defined equity as the corrective to the generality of the law: "So in a situation in which the law speaks universally, but the case at issue happens to fall outside the universal formula, it is correct to rectify the shortcoming, in other words, the omission and mistake of the lawgiver due to the generality of his statement. Such a rectification corresponds to what the lawgiver himself would have said if he were present, and what he would have enacted if he had known (of this particular case)."

52. T.F.T. Plucknett and J. L. Barton, eds., *St. German's Doctor and Student* (London, 1974), xx and, on promises, ix. In early modern England, Chancery was one institutional home of equity, for the chancellor could hear appeals of decisions handed down by the courts of common law. During this period, Chancery developed into one of the regular courts, with an increasing volume of business, and "equity" in this context came to refer to a fairly settled body of legal precedents.

In the following paragraphs, I draw on the introduction by Plucknett and Barton, and Stuart E. Prall, "The Development of Equity in Tudor England," *American Journal of Legal History* 8 (1964): 1–19. On the frequent reprinting and widespread influence of St. German, see Prall, 3. I quote St. German from the edition of William Muchall (Cincinnati, 1875; rpt., Union, N.J., 1998). The Doctor links equity and conscience on p. 44. On the relations between equity and conscience, and St. German's borrowings from earlier works of casuistry, see Simpson, *Contract*, 316–26, 387–405.

53. Such contracts had not been treated as breach of promise in the church courts because they had not involved formal swearing before a church representative. On economic expansion in this period, see Joyce O. Appleby, *Economic Thought and Ideology in Seventeenth-Century England* (Princeton, 1978); and Muldrew, *Economy of Obligation*. Although D. C. Coleman, *The Economy of England, 1450–1750* (Oxford, 1977), chap. 4, points to the scarcity of evidence regarding how much trade grew in the second half of the sixteenth century, Wrightson, *Earthly Necessities*, chap. 7, argues for "the likelihood of economic expansion and increased production on a scale that was rare elsewhere in Europe in this period [1580–1650] outside the Netherlands" (160).

54. Plucknett and Barton, eds., *Doctor and Student*, xxiii—xxv; Prall, "The Development of Equity in Tudor England," 5. On Chancery and equity, see also J. H. Baker, *An Introduction to English Legal History*, 3rd ed. (London, 1990), 232–33, and St. German, *Doctor and Student*, 42–43, 49.

55. St. German, *Doctor and Student*, 175, 177; Simpson, *Contract*, 387–91.

56. On "consideration," see St. German, *Doctor and Student*, 176, 178–79; and note 59. As R. H. Helmholz notes, "There was a controversy among canonists about whether a simple promise, *nudum pactum*, gave rise to an action," that is, was legally actionable. See his "Assumpsit and *Fidei Laesio*," *Law Quarterly Review* 91 (1975): 406–32, here 406. Helmholz traces the similarities between the canon law notion of *causa*, the inducement or reason for a contractually binding promise, and the common law notion of consideration (which St. German begins to adumbrate here). Plucknett and Barton, *Doctor and Student*, argue that for St. German the enforceability of a promise depended "upon facts which can be proved in evidence" but that he uses the term "consideration" in a not yet fully technical sense (lvi–lvii).

57. On this point, see Plucknett and Barton, eds., *Doctor and Student*, xxv.

58. I return to this seventeenth-century reception of St. German in chapter 4.

59. The term "consideration" appears in sixteenth-century decisions. For further discussion of "the nascent 'doctrine' of consideration," see J. H. Baker, "New Light on *Slade's Case*," *Cambridge Law Journal* 29 (1971): 218; Baker, "The Place of *Slade's Case* in the History of Contract," *Law Quarterly Review* 74 (1958): 381–98, esp. 386–87; Baker, *English Legal History*, 374–408; P. S. Atiyah, *The Rise and Fall of Freedom of Contract* (Oxford, 1979), 139–64; Simpson, *Contract*, 295–315 (on *Slade's Case*), 316–488 (on consideration). Simpson argues that consideration should not be confused with the idea of quid pro quo: "[T]he conception of consideration was not that of a price for a promise, but a reason for a promise. So conceived, the natural question to ask is whether there is or is not a good reason for the promise" (446).

60. Coke is cited in Baker, "*Slade's Case* in the History of Contract," 303. Executory refers to not yet executed promises.

61. See David Harris Sacks, "The Promise and the Contract in Early Modern England," in *Rhetoric and Law in Early Modern Europe*, ed. Victoria Kahn and Lorna Hutson (New Haven, 2001), 28–53; Hutson, *The Usurer's Daughter*, 140–42; Hutson, "The 'Double Voice' of Equity and the Literary Voices of Women," in *"This Double Voice": Gendered Writing in Early Modern England*, ed. Danielle Clarke and Elizabeth Clarke (London, 2000), 142–63; and Constance Jordan, *Shakespeare's Monarchies* (Ithaca, 1997), 76–78.

62. On consideration and equity, see Simpson, *Contract*, 328, 381–85, 390.

63. See also ibid., 317, 324–25, on other constraints on the actionability of promises, such as reliance and benefit.

64. According to Baker, "1602 may be regarded as the date whence the modern law of contract traces its life as a single entity" (*English Legal History*, 394). In the voluminous literature on the history of contract law, however, scholars only rarely argue for the more general cultural significance of assumpsit. Those who do include Hill, "Covenant Theology"; Lorna Hutson, " 'Not the King's Two Bodies': Reading the 'Body Politic' in Shakespeare's *Henry IV*, Parts 1 and 2," in

Rhetoric and Law in Early Modern England, ed. Victoria Kahn and Lorna Hutson (New Haven, 2001), 182–83; Sacks, "The Promise and the Contract"; Muldrew, *Economy of Obligation*; Luke Wilson, *Theaters of Intention* (Stanford, 2000). In *Rise and Fall*, Atiyah discusses the relationship between early modern notions of a legal contract and the social contract in chap. 3. For the cultural and political implications of Slade's case, see Don E. Wayne, "Drama and Society in the Age of Jonson: An Alternative View," *Renaissance Drama*, n.s., 13 (1982): 103–29; Jordan, *Shakespeare's Monarchies*, 77–78; Charles Spinosa, "Shylock and Debt and Contract in *The Merchant of Venice*," *Cardoza Studies in Law and Literature* 5 (1993): 65–85; Luke Wilson, "Ben Jonson and the Law of Contract," in *Rhetoric and Law in Early Modern Europe*, ed. Victoria Kahn and Lorna Hutson (New Haven, 2001), 143–65.

65. On consideration as contrary to the will theory of contracts, see Simpson, *Contract*, 374; Simpson also argues against the economic explanation of consideration, 487–88. In Simpson's view, the doctrine of consideration assumes that a promise simply reinforces a preexisting obligation; widespread cultural ideas of obligation, rather than any immediate economic interests, shaped the doctrines of assumpsit and consideration. See also Atiyah, *Rise and Fall*, 147: the doctrine of consideration was "a reflection of a moral ideal, not some amoral commerical practice." In "The Promise and the Contract," Sacks argues that will theory and consideration go together as two steps of making a contract: the internal intention and the external signs of the intention. Lon C. Fuller and Melvin Aron Eisenberg, in their extraordinarily lucid "Note on the History of Contract in the Common Law," link the development of the doctrines of assumpsit and consideration to the development of a market economy: "It is . . . not difficult to see why the development of open markets for the sale and purchase of goods should lead to a recognition of the binding effect of executory exchanges," that is, exchanges that both parties agree to perform at some future time. See *Basic Contract Law*, 6th ed. (St. Paul, Minn., 1996), 1061.

66. Simpson, *Contract*, 488, 457.

67. Coke is quoted in Baker, *English Legal History*, 395.

68. See Sacks, "The Promise and the Contract," on how *Slade* exemplifies a more general cultural skepticism about the validity of oaths (38). Sacks also argues that *Slade* and the doctrine of consideration depart from Aristotelian assumptions about intention and promises. See also Michael Lane, "Law and Consciousness in Early Seventeenth Century England," in *1642: Literature and Power in the Seventeenth Century* (Essex, 1981), who describes the development of contract law in this period as having to do "with the external and objective nature of a bargain as opposed to the metaphysics of a promise" (279).

69. Cited in Sacks, "The Promise and the Contract," 39. Morice is speaking of the ex officio oath rather than the oath of compurgation, but as Sacks argues, Coke made similar arguments against the oath of compurgation or wager of law in his reporting of Slade's Case.

70. On the origins and nature of covenant theology in England, see Leonard J. Trinterud, "The Origins of Puritanism," *Church History* 20 (1951): 37–57; John von Rohr, "Covenant and Assurance in Early English Puritanism," *Church History* 341 (1961): 195–203; von Rohr, *The Covenant of Grace in Puritan*

Thought (Atlanta, Ga., 1986); Richard Muller, "Covenant and Conscience in English Reformed Theology: Three Variations on a 17th Century Theme," *Westminster Theological Journal* 42 (1980): 308–34; Lyle Bierma, "Federal Theology in the Sixteenth Century: Two Traditions," *Westminster Theological Journal* 45 (1983): 304–21; Donald K. McKim, "William Perkins and the Theology of the Covenant," in *Studies of the Church in History: Essays Honoring Robert S. Paul,* ed. Horton Davies (Allison Park, Pa., 1988): 85–99; Hill, "Covenant Theology," 3:300–24. John Dykstra Eusden, *Puritans, Lawyers, and Politics in Early Seventeenth-Century England* (New Haven, 1958), argues that the first three decades of the seventeenth century were the "seed time" for covenant theology, which flourished in the 1630s and 1640s.

Covenant theology in the 1590s may also have served as a bulwark against more radical sectarian tendencies. As David Zaret has argued in *The Heavenly Contract* (Chicago, 1985), "puritan covenant theology was a modified Calvinism that provided more room for individual initiative [than Anglicanism] but channeled it in directions that did not threaten the pastoral authority of clerics in a comprehensive church" (163). Covenant theology emphasized the bond between the individual conscience and God, even as it aimed to bind that conscience to the reformed church.

71. Perkins, quoted in the introduction to *The Work of William Perkins*, ed. Ian Breward (Appelford, England, 1970), 39.

72. See William Perkins, *Treatise Tending unto a Declaration Whether a Man Be in the Estate of Damnation or the Estate of Grace* (London, 1595).

73. Perry Miller, "The Marrow of Puritan Divinity," in *Errand into the Wilderness* (New York, 1964), 74; Miller, *The New England Mind: The Seventeenth Century* (1939; Boston, 1961), 401–8; Hill, "Covenant Theology," 303. On contract as indicating the importance of consent, see Zaret, *Heavenly Contract*, 170–71.

74. William Perkins sometimes represented the covenant of works as a prelapsarian legal covenant by which Adam earned eternal life through works, and sometimes as the postlapsarian moral law or Decalogue. On natural law, see William Perkins, *A Discourse of Conscience*, in *William Perkins*, ed. Thomas F. Merrill (Nieuwkoop, the Netherlands, 1966): "Morall law . . . is contained in the Decalogue or ten commandments; and it is the very law of nature written in all mens hearts (for substance, though not for the manner of propounding) in the creation of man" (11); "as for the law of nature though it affoarde indeede some direction; yet it is corrupt, imperfect, uncerten: and whatsoever is right and good therein, is contained in the written word of God" (42).

75. William Perkins, *Commentaries on Galatians*, cited by von Rohr, "Covenant and Assurance," 196; Deuteronomy was referred to as the "book of the covenant."

76. Von Rohr, *The Covenant of Grace*, 49; von Rohr, "Covenant and Assurance," 195. See also Miller, *New England Mind*, chap. 13. Miller writes that "the Covenant, its origin, its progressive unfolding, was thus the meaning of history and that which made intelligible the whole story of mankind" (378).

77. Sibbes is quoted by Zaret, *Heavenly Contract*, 168; see also 156. For other comparisons between the heavenly contract and human contracts, see William Ames, *Conscience with the Power and the Cases thereof* (London, 1639), chap.

42, "Of Contracts"; Joseph Hall, *Resolution and Decisions of Divers Practiall Cases of Conscience* (London, 1650), see the First Decade, "Cases of Profit and Traffique"; Richard Baxter, *Christian Directory* (1673), esp. chap. 19 on contracts. Although, as Christopher Hill has cautioned, "we cannot be precise about causal links, since the feudal contract, with its very different social context (the oath of loyalty and the coronation oath), had been familiar long before the rise of protestantism"; nevertheless, the "actual content of covenant theology suggests that it was influenced by the growing significance of contracts, and of the debtor-creditor relationship, in the economic life of society as capitalism developed." See Hill, "Covenant Theology," 300–301.

78. William Perkins, *Treatise of Vocations*, in *The Work of William Perkins*, ed. Ian Breward (Appleford, England, 1970), 473–74, 475–76. Against this background one can begin to see Milton's Satan, tortured by his "debt immense of endless gratitude" (*PL*, 4.51), as a creature of perverse literalism, still trying to reckon his account with God. For Perkins, Ball, Preston, Milton, and others, by contrast, accounting functioned as a sublime rhetorical figure designed to move the sinner to faith.

79. William Gouge, *A Learned and Very Useful Commentary On The Whole Epistle to the Hebrews* (1655, published posthumously); quoted in Zaret, *Heavenly Contract*, 156. In his *Discourse of Conscience*, 6, Perkins even went so far as to describe conscience itself as a kind of internal covenant or contract that the individual was incapable of observing. For Perkins, conscience was an intellectual faculty of judgment separate from the will. In order for conscience to give testimony or judge, it needed to be separate from what is judged. But what was it that made "conscience give judgment" in the first place? Before conscience binds the sinner, Perkins tells us, *conscience itself must be bound to act like conscience*, and this happens only by God's will. The assent to the Gospel, the covenant with God, thus presupposed a prior, internal covenant of conscience that was itself enabled by God. In this light, it is interesting to note that, when Nietzsche discusses the notion of conscience in *The Genealogy of Morals*, he compares it with a contract just as Perkins does. In Nietzsche's analysis, the ability to make contracts is not simply the effect of conscience but also its cause: the ability to keep one's promises presupposes a kind of internal contract that constitutes the conscientious and "calculable" ethical subject. See *The Genealogy of Morals* in *The Birth of Tragedy and The Genealogy of Morals*, trans. Francis Golffing (Garden City, N.Y., 1956), Second Essay, esp. 2.1–2.19.

80. Perkins, *A Golden Chain*, in *The Work of William Perkins*, ed. Ian Breward (Appleford, England, 1970), 213. This text was first published in Latin as *Armilla aurea* in 1590, and shortly thereafter translated into an expanded English version. Burroughs is quoted in Hill, "Covenant Theology," 306. In *The Parable of the Sower and of the Seed* (1623), Thomas Taylor argued that "The earnest confirms the seller, that he shall receive the whole price . . . so the gift of regeneration confirms us that we shall receive whatever is promised in the covenant." Timothy Rogers assured his readers that, "Whereas we only by our sins were debtors to him," by the covenant of grace "he is not only become a merciful creditor to us, content to release the debts of our sins, but also by his promise become our debtor." See Thomas Taylor, *The Parable of the Sower and the Seed* (1623), 283;

Timothy Rogers, *The Righteous Mans Evidence for Heaven* (1632), 197–98; cited in Zaret, *Heavenly Contract*, 168, 175, 177. Baker defines a bond (or obligation) of debt as "a deed containing an acknowledgment that a sum of money was owed by the 'obligor' to the 'obligee' "; an "earnest" was partial payment of a debt; see his *English Legal History*, 368, 434. For discussions of indenture, see John Ball, *Treatise of the Covenant of Grace* (London, 1645), 199; and John Preston, *The New Covenant* (London, 1630), 323, 329; and the examples cited by Hill, "Covenant Theology," 306; Miller, *New England Mind*, 389–90.

81. William Ames, *The Marrow of Sacred Divinity* (London, n.d.), 70.

82. Trinterud, "Origins of Puritanism," 45.

83. George Downame, *The Covenant of Grace* (London, 1631), 89–90. See also p. 114: "As for that obedience, or service, which is extorted from men by servile feare, because it is forced, it is but momentany [*sic*]. For no violent thing is of continuance, and being momentany, it is but counterfeit."

84. Bulkeley, Preston, and Perkins are quoted by Hill, "Covenant Theology," 304, 305.

85. John Preston, *Life Eternall* (London, 1631), 86; cited by von Rohr, "Covenant and Assurance," 201; see also the quotations in Zaret, *Heavenly Contract*, 171–72, on the conditional nature of the covenant.

86. Ball, *Treatise of the Covenant of Grace*, 5.

87. Ibid., 24, 29, 7.

88. Perkins, *A Golden Chain*, chap. 19, p. 211.

89. See Perkins, *Golden Chain*, 211, 212, 214.

90. See Downame, *Covenant of Grace*, 1, 8–9, on assertory and promissory oaths or covenants. The first states the unalterable truth and the second articulates a promise and a condition that the individual believer may fulfill. See also Preston, *New Covenant*, 7, 24, 29, 180–81, 365, 458.

91. Christopher Hill's observation can serve as a gloss: "Protestant sacramental doctrine bears the same relation to medieval catholic doctrine as credit does to a metal currency, Marx long ago pointed out. Faith becomes the more important as external material aids to grace (the counters of salvation) lose their usefulness. . . . in entering into or renewing a covenant it was essential that the intention should be sincere" ("Covenant Theology," 302).

92. Ball, *Treatise of the Covenant of Grace*, 179 and 84.

93. Preston, *New Covenant*, 321–22 (emphasis added).

94. See Ian Maclean, *Interpretation and Meaning in the Renaissance: The Case of Law* (Cambridge, 1992), 177, on the casus omissus.

95. See also *The Westminster Confession of Faith* for covenant theology's emphasis on intention and sincerity; good works done with bad intention are not acceptable to God: *The Humble Advice of the Assembly of Divines, Now by Authority of Parliament sitting at Westminster* (London, 1647), reprinted in *The Creeds of Christendom*, 3 vols., ed. Philip Schaff (New York, 1877), 3:635, 637, 639. See Barbara Kiefer Lewalski, *Protestant Poetics and the Seventeenth-Century Religious Lyric* (Princeton, 1979), esp. 73 on Protestants' "new attention to the metaphorical power of language" (73). In addition to the numerous quotations in Lewalski, see also Ames, *Marrow*, 9, on how God and his essence are known only "figuratively."

96. Perkins, *Golden Chain*, cited in Lewalski, *Protestant Poetics*, 80.

97. Ames, *Marrow*, 184; see 162. Lewalski, *Protestant Poetics*, links Protestant attention to the figurative language of Scripture to Calvin's position on the sacraments (77).

98. Such walking and working would in turn be assimilated to the politically charged puritan metaphors of warfaring and pilgrimage. See Lewalski, *Protestant Poetics*, 92–93; and Michael Walzer, *The Revolution of the Saints* (Cambridge, Mass; 1975), among others.

99. Ames, *Conscience with the Power and the Cases thereof*, 55.

100. On legalism, see Max Weber, *The Protestant Ethic and the Spirit of Capitalism*, trans. Talcott Parsons (New York, 1958), 123, 165; Miller, *New England Mind*; and Gerhard Oestreich, *Neostoicism and the Early Modern State* (Cambridge, 1982), 141–53. On partial regeneration, see Miller, "Marrow," 74.

101. See, for example, Perkins, *Discourse of Conscience*, 37–38: "[W]ee see also what notorious rebels those are, that beeing borne subjects of this land, yet choose rather to die then to acknowledge (as they are bound in conscience) the Kings Majestie to bee supreame governour under God in all causes and over all persons."

102. Miller, *New England Mind*, 412.

CHAPTER 3
THE PASSIONS AND VOLUNTARY SERVITUDE

1. On the prominence of a new language of passion and interest in this period, see Albert Hirschman, *The Passions and the Interests* (Princeton, 1977); J.A.W. Gunn, *Politics and the Public Interest in the Seventeenth Century* (London, 1969); Richard Tuck, *Philosophy and Government, 1572–1651* (Cambridge, 1993); and Peter N. Miller, *Defining the Common Good* (Cambridge, 1994).

2. Hobbes, *De cive*, 1.2.1, p. 33. Whereas Filmer worried that the voluntarism of contract would dismantle all natural social relations, Hobbes worried that it might not dismantle them enough. In the following pages, "servitude" always refers to an irrational act of subordination, whereas "subjection" refers to a rational act of subordinating oneself.

3. The ambivalent feminization of the subject of contract would be played out in different ways in the literature of Protectorate and the Restoration, as I discuss in chapters 7–10.

4. Grotius, *De jure belli*, prolegomena, para. 28.

5. Grotius, *De jure belli*, prolegomena, paras. 6–7, 16.

6. Grotius, *De jure belli*, 1.4.7.

7. Grotius, *De jure belli* 1.2.2.1–2.

8. See Cicero, *De inventione*, 1.1.2–1.2.3; *De oratore*, 1.5.17, 1.46.202, 1.51.220, 1.52.224, 2.42.178–2.44.216. See also Quintilian, *Institutio oratoria*, 2.33.185–2.53.216, and book 6. For early modern readers, Cicero's pragmatic treatment of the passions as sources of political argument would have been reinforced by Aristotle's discussion of the passions in the *Rhetoric*, esp. book 2. In this text the passions are thoroughly inflected by rhetorical convention. They are rhetorical constructs or commonplaces that reflect the typical ways people conceptualize and speak about their own experience. Orators need to know about these

topoi or habits of speech, Aristotle tells us, not because they are true (though Aristotle ascribes a degree of probability to them) but because they are convincing sources of argument.

9. Just as fear for one's self-preservation is a legitimate kind of coercion, so in other cases as well coercion is not incompatible with consent, as when a people grants its consent to a conqueror, either immediately or by "tacit acceptance" (2.4.14: "ex voluntate tacita").

10. Grotius, *De jure belli*, 1.3.8.1, citing Exodus 21:6.

11. Grotius, *De jure belli*, 1.4.7; see 2.6.5. It is undoubtedly because Grotius believed that an individual's fear of violent death could legitimate rebellion that he emphasized (like all of his contemporaries) that positive law "fails of its outward effect unless it has a sanction behind it" (prolegomena, para. 19)—unless it is supplemented by the sovereign's coercive power of the sword. If coercion is still necessary, what then is the role of consent? The obvious answer is that it turns merely physical coercion into moral coercion: it legitimates the force of law. See prolegomena, sect. 18 toward the end.

12. Grotius, *De jure belli*, 2.11.7.2 (citing *Nicomachean Ethics*, 3.1). Aristotle's text was frequently cited or alluded to in early modern discussions of fear and duress in ordinary contracts, in manuals of casuistry, and elsewhere.

13. For examples of fear that are not legitimately compelling, see Grotius, *De jure belli*, 2.11.7; 2.12.10; 2.13.15; 2.17.17; 2.19.4.

14. Grotius, *De jure belli*, 2.5.27.1.

15. Grotius, *De jure belli*, 1.3.13.

16. Grotius, *De jure belli*, 2.5.9.3–4. The word for association is either "consociatio" (2.5.8.1; 2:234) or "societas" (2.5.17.1, 2:249). Grotius explicitly distinguishes between subjection and association at 2.5.8.1. Grotius does not address the domestic or political implications of association in contrast to subjection. But it may be significant that, right after this, Grotius argues for the legitimacy of divorce (2.5.9.4). Although he says nothing about the specific right of the wife to divorce the husband, the language of association rather than subjection suggests husbands and wives might be equally empowered to initiate divorce.

17. "For it is written, that Abraham had two sonnes, the one by a bondmaid, the other by a freewoman. But he who was of the bondwoman was borne after the flesh: but hee of the freewoman, was by promise. Which things are an Allegorie: for these are the two Covenants; the one from Mount Sinai, which gendereth to bondage, which is Agar. For this Agar is mount Sinai in Arabia, and answereth to Jerusalem, which now is, and is in bondage with her children. But Jerusalem which is above is free, which is the mother of us all" (cited in Barbara Kiefer Lewalski, *Protestant Poetics and the Seventeenth-Century Religious Lyric* [Princeton, 1979], 120). As Lewalski notes of the scriptural hermeneutics taken up by Protestant commentators, "the sinful state is often seen as a debtor's servitude, a state of bondage, the slavish bearing of heavy burdens, while the regenerate condition is that of release from debts and bondage and liberation from slavery." Lewalski mentions Romans and Galatians (90–91). She also discusses the importance of marriage as a scriptural metaphor for the New Covenant.

18. William Perkins, *Treatise Tending unto a Declaration Whether a Man Be in the Estate of Damnation or the Estate of Grace* (London, 1595).

19. Ibid., 3–4.

20. Ibid., 43–46.

21. Ibid., 162.

22. Ibid., 166, 170.

23. William Perkins, *A Discourse of Conscience*, in *William Perkins*, ed. Thomas F. Merrill (Nieuwkoop, the Netherlands, 1966), 39.

24. On the wounds of conscience, see ibid., 3, 72; see also 43, 59, 71–72; Perkins, *Whole Treatise of Cases of Conscience*, in *William Perkins*, ed. Thomas F. Merrill (Nieuwkoop, the Netherlands, 1966), 81. See Friedrich Nietzsche, *The Geneology of Morals* in *The Birth of Tragedy and The Genealogy of Morals*, trans. Francis Golffing (Garden City, N.Y., 1956), Second Essay, esp. 2.7, 2.16, and 2.23. Linking the Judeo-Christian and especially Reformation discourse of conscience to the problem of voluntary servitude, Nietzsche argued that conscience first results from the "slave revolt" against aristocratic morality, a morality predicated on the assertion of power and the equation of power with positive value. Slave morality, by contrast, derives its values indirectly and by negation: the weak direct their rancor against the strong and ultimately against themselves. The will to power constitutes the self by turning against the self, binding the self by a kind of voluntary servitude. Rather than asserting their power, the slaves assert their impotence, but in this paradoxical assertion lies the possibility of sublime transcendence, according to which masochism or "self-crucifixion" (2.23) becomes evidence of conscience, of one's higher spiritual vocation. Conscience is thus from the outset bad conscience, "inflict[ing] itself," in Calvin's words, "with dread at its own guilt." See John Calvin, *Institutes of the Christian Religion*, trans. John T. McNeill, 2 vols. (Philadelphia, 1960), book 1, chap. 15, 1:184.

25. Perkins, *Discourse of Conscience*, 49.

26. Ibid., 22.

27. Ibid., 10, 11, 72 (lambe of God). On assent, see pp. 21, 39–40.

28. John Preston, *The New Covenant* (London, 1630), 119, 118, 529, on true fear.

29. Ibid., 127 and 128.

30. Ibid., 319; John Ball, *A Treatise of the Covenant of Grace* (London, 1645), 94, 118. Later, Ball contrasted the Old Testament to the New in similar terms: God at first "gave his Law with signes of Majesty, glory, and terrour, yea of anger and displeasure against sin and wickednesse. But the new Testament was given with manifest tokens of love, favour and free mercy, God being reconciled in the Son of his love" (164).

31. Ball, *Treatise of the Covenant of Grace*, 265.

32. Richard Sibbes, "The Faithful Covenanter," in *The Complete Works of Richard Sibbes, D.D.*, ed. Alexander Balloch Grosart, 6 vols. (Edinburgh, 1868), 6:12, 18.

33. Perkins, *Discourse of Conscience*, 34–35. Grotius gave the same example of the shewbread in *De jure belli*, 1.4.

34. Perkins, *Discourse of Conscience*, 22.

35. Ibid., 11.

36. Ibid., 35.

37. Ibid., 23; see also 26, 37. Perkins still attempts to support the magistrate's authority.

38. See Lowell Gallagher, *Medusa's Gaze* (Stanford, 1991) on the potentially disruptive effects of casuistry in the Elizabethan period.

39. William Ames, *Conscience with the Power and the Cases thereof* (London, 1639), 153–69.

40. Ibid., 166.

41. See also William Ames, *The Marrow of Sacred Divinity* (London, n.d.), who notes that "political society" was established by God but its precise form was "left to [the] liberty" of the people to determine (309).

42. Ames, *Conscience with the Power and the Cases thereof*, 164, 166, 168, 164.

43. Jeremy Taylor, *Ductor Dubitantium* (1671; London, 1696), 524.

44. Ames, *Conscience with the Power and Cases thereof*, 164; Perkins, *Works* (1609–13), 1: 762, cited in Christopher Hill, "The Norman Yoke," in *Puritanism and Revolution* (London, 1958), 65.

45. George Downame, *Treatise of the Covenant of Grace* (London, 1631), 50 and 71; William Allen, *A Discourse of the Nature, Ends, and Difference of the Two Covenants* (London, 1673), 88, 167, 193.

46. Allen, *A Discourse of . . . the Two Covenants*, 195, [191], 198, 197. Paradoxically Allen makes this last point about the lability of the passions by insisting that self-love will always lead to obedience: "What Rebel is there, or Nature so bad, that would not be won to leave off rebelling against his Prince, and to love and please him, upon undoubted assurance, that by so doing he should not only be pardoned, and restored to favor, but also preferred to the greatest honour and happiness?" A fortiori we will obey God (200). But this comparison only points up the possible conflict between fear of the sovereign and fear for one's soul, as Hobbes among others pointed out.

47. Ian Breward, ed., *The Works of William Perkins* (Appleford, England, 1970), says "no precise date can be assigned to this work" (443). Perkins's general point was that these two callings were compatible; only in very rare cases would one's calling as a Christian come into conflict with the specific obligations of one's office in life. Thus Perkins introduced his argument with the example of the specific calling of the slave or bondman, which he took pains to insist was a literal, not a metaphorical condition.

48. William Perkins, *A Treatise of the Vocations or Callings of Men*, in *The Works of William Perkins*, ed. Ian Breward (Appleford, England, 1970), 446, 449, 453.

49. Ibid., 454, 457–58.

50. Marriage of course was a scriptural metaphor for the relationship of Christ to his church, as well as a divinely instituted covenant in its own right.

51. The quotations in this paragraph are taken from *Christian Oeconomie*, in *The Works of William Perkins*, ed. Ian Breward (Appleford, England, 1970), 436.

52. See Perkins, *A Golden Chain*, in *The Works of William Perkins*, ed. Ian Breward (Appleford, England, 1970), 210, 216; *Christian Oeconomie*, in the

same volume, 429. Strictly speaking, Perkins uses "contract" to refer to "espous-als," whereas marriage refers to "the solemn manifestation of the contract" (*Christian Oeconomie*, 420).

53. See Lewalski, *Protestant Poetics*, on marriage as a metaphor for charitable intepretation.

54. Perkins, *Epieikeia*, in *The Works of William Perkins*, ed. Ian Breward (Appleford, England, 1970), 485–86, 482. On the equation of equity with con-science, see my discussion in chapter 2.

55. It is perhaps for this reason that, in *Christian Oeconomie*, the contrast between wives and slaves shifts again, and wives begin to look more like natural slaves. Although slaves may eventually find their freedom, the same is not true of the wife, Perkins insists, for she is both naturally and voluntarily subordinate.We can detect a similar instability in William Gouge's treatment of the wife's passions in his manual, *Domesticall Duties*. I discuss Gouge in " 'The Duty to Love': Pas-sion and Obligation in Early Modern Political Theory," *Representations* 68 (1999): 84–107.

56. This paragraph relies on Hill, "The Norman Yoke," 50–122; quotations are taken from pp. 59, 62, 64.

57. James I, *The Trew Law of Free Monarchies*, in *The Political Works of James I*, ed. Charles Howard McIlwain (Cambridge, Mass., 1918), 62, 63.

58. Lucy Hutchinson, *Memoirs of the Life of Colonel Hutchinson*, ed. N. H. Keeble (London, 1995), 62. For James's remark about Buckingham, see Derek Hirst, *Authority and Conflict: England, 1603–1658* (Cambridge, Mass., 1986), 97.

59. See Linda Levy Peck, *Court Patronage and Corruption in Early Stuart En-gland* (London, 1990), and Peck, ed., *The Mental World of the Jacobean Court* (Cambridge, 1991); and R. Lockyer, *Buckingham* (London, 1981).

60. Quoted in Charles Gray, "Reason, Authority, and Imagination: The Juris-prudence of Sir Edward Coke," in *Culture and Politics: From Puritanism to the Enlightenment*, ed. Perez Zagorin (Berkeley, 1980), 50, n12.

61. Coke is quoted in Johann P. Sommerville, *Politics and Ideology in England, 1603–1640* (New York, 1986), 93. See also ibid., 107. Some of Coke's legal deci-sions in the first decade of the seventeenth century have also been construed as limiting the power of Parliament, for example, Coke's decisions in Bonham's Case (1608) ("the common law will control the acts of Parliament and sometimes ad-judge them to be utterly void") and Calvin's Case (1609) ("the law of nature cannot be changed or taken away" and "should direct this case"). Some scholars, however, have interpreted these decisions "as stating a principle of judicial con-struction by a lower court of law enunciated by 'the High Court of Parliament' rather than the assertion of a general right of judges to strike down parliamentary legislation." See Paul E. Sigmund, *Natural Law in Political Thought* (Washington, D.C., 1971), 101.

62. On the alliance between common lawyers and MPs, see among others John Dykstra Eusden, *Puritans, Lawyers, and Politics in Early Seventeenth-Century England* (New Haven, 1958); Sommerville, *Politics and Ideology*, chap. 3; Glenn Burgess, *The Politics of the Ancient Constitution* (University Park, Pa., 1993).

63. *State Trials*, 2:382.
64. *State Trials*, 2:382, 388.
65. *State Trials*, 2:383 (emphasis added).
66. *State Trials*, 2:389.
67. See Francis Oakley, *Omnipotence, Covenant, and Order* (Ithaca and London, 1984), esp. chap. 4.
68. *State Trials*, 2:395 (Bacon); 399, 402 (Davies).
69. Emphasis added; see *State Trials*, 2:407, 411, 412, 420, 419 (bondage).
70. James I, *Trew Law of Free Monarchies*, 59.
71. I quote Cowell from Johann P. Sommerville, "History and Theory: The Norman Conquest in Early Stuart Political Thought," *Political Studies* 34 (1986): 255.
72. *State Trials*, 2:479, 486.
73. *State Trials*, 2:505–6.
74. See Sommerville, *Politics and Ideology*, 94; Annabel Patterson, *Early Modern Liberalism* (Cambridge, 1997), 1–2. Sommerville quotes Wentworth (101).
75. Carole Pateman, *The Sexual Contract* (Stanford, 1988), and Don Herzog, *Happy Slaves: A Critique of Consent Theory* (Chicago, 1989), are two important exceptions. Richard Tuck also briefly discusses slave contracts in *Natural Rights Theories* (Cambridge, 1979).

CHAPTER 4
IMAGINATION

1. There was an important precedent for this development in the reign of James. As Margaret Judson has remarked, "Whenever the king needed money, as he always did in the seventeenth century, he had to bargain with his subjects," and such bargaining led both James and the MPs to think of their negotiation with the king as economic contracts. In 1610 Lord Salisbury, James's representative to Parliament, proposed the "Great Contract," according to which the king would cede control of wardships in exchange for annual support and a one-time grant of subsidies. But this effort to secure a fixed annual income for the king had the unintended effect of suggesting that a contract was the right metaphor for the political relationship between the king and his subjects. Francis Bacon perceived the destabilizing effects of this rhetoric and in 1614 he "advised the king that he ought to treat the M.P.s strictly as 'counsellors' rather than as 'merchants and scholars' who, Bacon implies, cheapen wares and debate precedents. 'In the last Parliament his Ma[jesty] took upon him the person of a merchant, and they took upon them the persons of purchasers and contractors.' " Bacon's concerns proved to be prophetic. When the negotiations over the Great Contract failed, James imposed new taxes, which in turn generated new grievances, and an ever increasing desire, on the part of Parliament, to debate precedents and curb royal power by the implied contract of the common law. This in turn set the stage for Charles's own financial negotiations. See Margaret Judson, *The Crisis of the Constitution* (New Brunswick, 1949), 72 and chap. 3 in general; Luke Wilson, *Theaters of Intention: Drama and Law in Early Modern England* (Stanford, 2000), 121. On

the "Great Contract," see also Christopher Hill, *The Century of Revolution, 1603–1714* (New York, 1961), chap. 4, esp. 41–42.

2. *Proceedings in Parliament, 1628*, 6 vols., ed. Robert C. Johnson, Maija Jansson Cole, Mary Frear Keeler, and William B. Bidwell, vols. 1–4: *Commons Debates, 1628* (New Haven, 1977), 2:296, 3.

3. *Commons Debates, 1628*, 2:16, 56 (Seymour), 342 (Selden).

4. The king's *Answer* was written by Colepepper and Falkland. On the *Answer*, see Corinne C. Weston, *English Constitutional History and the House of Lords* (London, 1965); Weston and Janelle R. Greenberg, *Subjects and Sovereigns: The Grand Debate over Legal Sovereignty in Stuart England* (Cambridge, 1981); J.G.A. Pocock, *The Machiavellian Moment* (Princeton, 1975), 361–65; Pocock, "Interregnum and Restoration," in *The Varieties of British Political Thought, 1500–1800*, ed. Pocock, with Gordon J. Schochet, and Lois G. Schwoerer (Cambridge, 1993), 146–79.

5. For two good accounts of the legal difference between a promise and a contract in the early modern period, see E. Allan Farnsworth, "The Past of a Promise: An Historical Introduction to Contract," *Columbia Law Review* 69 (1969): 576–603; and David Harris Sacks, "The Promise and the Contract in Early Modern England: Slade's Case in Perspective," in *Rhetoric and Law in Early Modern Europe*, ed. Victoria Kahn and Lorna Hutson (New Haven, 2001), 28–53.

6. On reliance and expectation, see Farnsworth, "The Past of a Promise," esp. 594–99. The distinction between the promise and the contract has not been recognized in the usual histories of political thought. In a representative survey of Western political theory, George Sabine articulated what is still the critical consensus about seventeenth-century notions of the new political subject, the subject of the political contract. In a classic statement of liberal doctrine, Sabine wrote: "[W]hat seemed [axiomatic] to nearly all [seventeenth-century] thinkers . . . was that an obligation, to be really binding, must be freely assumed by the parties bound. . . . It was this conviction which made all obligation appear under the guise of a promise; what a man promises he may reasonably be held to, since he has himself created the obligation by his own act" (*A History of Political Theory*, 4th. ed. [Hinsdale, Ill., 1973], 398). Sabine captures one strand of seventeenth-century thinking about the political subject but neglects the equally important counterargument or counternarrative. In the counternarrative I want to recover, the focus is not the autonomous subject who conceives of all obligation "under the guise of a promise"—the subject who is then demystified by modern critics such as Nietzsche—but rather on the way the subject who promises is himself a product of a social, political, and linguistic contract.

7. Glenn Burgess, *The Politics of the Ancient Constitution* (University Park, Pa., 1996), 189. Hobbes discusses Parliament's complaint about Shipmoney in *Behemoth*, 36–38, 60. John Adair, *A Life of John Hampden* (London, 1976), gives a good account of the parliamentary discussions of Shipmoney as a continued source of offense in 1640. He also discusses the fate of the Shipmoney judges who voted for the king. Five Knights also had an afterlife in the revolutionary period: see J. H. Baker, *An Introduction to English Legal History*, 3rd ed. (London, 1990): "When the Long Parliament abolished the Star Chamber in 1641, it

took care to reverse the effect of the *Five Knights' Case* and to guarantee *habeas corpus* as a remedy in case of committal by the king or the Council" (540).

8. *State Trials*, 3:45. All quotations in this section are from this volume.

9. On this point, see St. John, arguing for Hampden (*State Trials*, 3:881): "[W]e are [not] to run to extraordinary [means], when the ordinary means will serve the turn. . . . The Common Law is the common reliever of persons wronged; that in Chancery is extraordinary, and therefor no man can sue there, when he may have remedy at common law." See Judson, *The Crisis of the Constitution*, chap. 4, and Burgess, *Politics of the Ancient Constitution*, chap. 7. Burgess argues that the two cases illustrate the use of "civil law languages of absolute prerogative to answer questions of a common law nature" (194; see also 211).

10. Ironically, the form of the Petition dramatized the conflict between the royal prerogative and the common law. In seventeenth-century England, a petition was not a public statute, "the highest kind of man-made law in England." It was instead a formal request to the king, indicating that the Commons still had to plead for its rights, not simply assert them as a matter of law. The fact that this declaration of rights was made in the form of a petition, however, may have been one of the keys to its eventual acceptance by the majority of Lords as well as the king. See Judson, *The Crisis of the Constitution*, 258–59.

11. Cited in ibid., 262.

12. See *State Trials*, 3:1162.

13. Pym and Mason are discussed by Johann P. Sommerville, "History and Theory: The Norman Conquest in Early Stuart Political Thought," *Political Studies* 34 (1986): 258. Pym's speech is excerpted in J. P. Kenyon, *The Stuart Constitution* (Cambridge, 1966), 16–18; Mason is cited in Johnson et al., *Proceedings in Parliament, 1628*, 3:528.

14. On the notion of reliance in early modern contract disputes, see A.W.B. Simpson, *A History of the Common Law of Contract* (Oxford, 1987), 465–70. Reliance on a promise to one's detriment might also be construed as a kind of consideration in this period. See Lon L. Fuller and Melvin Aron Eisenberg, *Basic Contract Law* (St. Paul, Minn., 1996), 1062. For a similar argument in the Ship-money Case, see St. Johns's remarks in *State Trials*, 3:1272: "Breach of Trust, though in a private person, and in the least things, is odious among all men; much more in a public person, and in things of great and public concernment, because great trust binds the party trusted to greatest care and fidelity."

15. See Grotius on binding promises in chapter 2.

16. See Henry Parker, *Observations upon some of his Majesties Late Answers and Expresses* (London, 1642), 4: "The word *Trust* is frequent in the Kings Papers, and therefore I conceive the King does admit that his interest in the Crowne is not absolute, or by a meere donation of the people, but in part conditionate and fiduciary." For a good brief history of the language of trust and trusteeship in this period, up to Locke, see J. W. Gough, "Political Trusteeship," in his *John Locke's Political Philosophy* (Oxford, 1956), 136–71; see also F. W. Maitland, "Trust and Corporation," in *Selected Essays* (Cambridge, 1936), 141–222, who argues for the legal origins of the idea of political trusteeship.

17. See also Robert Mason, MP, commenting on additions the Lords wanted to make to Petition of Right, "The next word is 'trusted,' which is very ambiguous,

whether it mean trusted by God only as a conqueror, or by the people also, as kings which are to govern by laws *ex pacto* [made by agreement]. In this point I will not presume to venture" (cited in Derek Hirst, *Authority and Conflict: England, 1603–1658* [Cambridge, Mass., 1986], 88).

18. Charles first proposed the extension in 1628 but withdrew it in response to parliamentary opposition. He restored the tax in 1634 and extended it to inland counties in 1635. See Adair, *John Hampden*, 56.

19. Ibid., 53–54.

20. See *State Trials*, 3:1011, 1149 ("imminent danger"), 903 ("sudden danger"). In the context of the economic argument, Selden's *Mare clausum* was invoked to support the claim that the king had dominion over the seas and thus the right to do what was necessary to protect this dominion (see, e.g., 3:928, 1023, 1210, 1226).

21. Adair, *John Hampden*, attributes this to Sir George Croke (or Crooke), justice of the King's Bench and a Buckinghamshire fellow countryman to John Hampden (121).

22. *State Trials*, 3:45. For other mentions of reason of state or *salus populi*, see 3:56, 144–45, 149 (and *jus gentium*), 167, 174, 841, 903, 926, 960, 967, 1005, 1059, 1066–67, 1085, 1221, 1254–55, 1260. These references do not include the many mentions of "pretended necessity."

23. See also Serjeant Ashley in the Five Knights Case, *State Trials*, 3:149: "In like manner it is the Law of State; when the necessity of state requires it, they do and may proceed to natural equity." See also 3:1026 on the king's ruling by "natural equity"; 858–59 (where equity is used to justify the people's sharing the common burden of military defense: "Onus defensionis, quod omnes tangit, per omnes debet supportari"), 878 (where St. John turns this around: " 'quod omnes tangit ab omnibus approbatur'; the Charge must be borne by all, so it must be approved by all"), 1019, 1026, 1260, and 1293 (on "the excessive growth of courts of reason and conscience"). The equation of the king's prerogative with equitable judgment was also made in Bates' Case. See chapter 3.

24. On slaves, villeins, and bondmen, as opposed to freemen, see, e.g., *State Trials*, 3:64, 74, 129–30; 1129–30, 1147, 1263, 1293–95, 1303. For criticism of reason of state, see 3:174; also 3:44. Constance Jordan discusses the notion of political servitude with reference to the Commons' debates regarding taxation in 1610 in *Shakespeare's Monarchies* (Ithaca, 1997), 181–87.

25. Cited in Judson, *The Crisis of the Constitution*, 272.

26. See Sir William Jones, speaking for the king, in Shipmoney: "It must not be every kind of fear and rumour that must draw this kind of burden upon the subjects; but such a danger as the king in his understanding perceiveth doth require a speedy defense. . . . That the king is sole judge of this danger, and how to prevent and avoid it, is not to be literally understood, for we are his judges deputed, but our judgment flows from him" (*State Trials*, 3:1184). See also Henry Parker's casting aspersions on the king's "just fear" of Sir John Hotham who refused him entrance to Hull: "The Parliament conceives that the King cannot apprehend any just fear from Sir John Hotham, or interpret the meer shutting of *Hull* gates or the sending away of Arms and Ammunition in obedience to both

Houses, to be any preparation for Warre and Invasion against him at *York*" (*Observations*, 43). On the problem of just fear, see chapter 3.

27. On St. John, see Adair, *John Hampden*, 115. See Holborne in *State Trials*, 3:972: "If you allow such a prince power extraordinary, and make him judge of the occasion . . . in such cases, he hath no restraint, but his will."

28. Crawley sounds like Eve in the separation colloquy in *Paradise Lost*. I return to Eve's arguments in chapter 9.

29. For other references to St. German, see *State Trials*, 3:1085, 1162, 1211, 1225, 1249.

30. Adair, *John Hampden*, 121, where Crooke is spelled Croke. Crooke also said he would follow "God's direction and my own *conscience*" in deciding the case (emphasis added).

31. See Judson, *The Crisis of the Constitution*, 124, on the paradox of trying to make the case for absolutism in a court of law. See also Burgess, *Ancient Constitution*, chaps. 7–8, on this confusion of the languages of royal prerogative and the common law.

32. Clarendon is quoted in *State Trials*, 3:1255. For his earlier remarks about the Shipmoney trial, see 3:1282, where he impugns the "vulgar fears" of the judges, who "delivered up the precious forts they were trusted with, almost without assault" (1282).

33. As Serjeant Ashley observed during the debates over the Petition of Right, "if the State prevail, it gains absolute Sovereignty, but loses the Subjects not their Subjection, for Obedience we must yield, though nothing be left but Prayers and Tears; but it loses the best Part of them, which is their Affections, whereby Sovereignty is established and the Crown firmly fixt on His Royal Head." Ashley is quoted by Judson, *The Crisis of the Constitution*, 251.

34. Once news of the Shipmoney decision reached the inland shires, there was widespread resistance to paying. According to Adair, *John Hampden*, "by 1640, only a third of Ship-Money was received by the Treasurer of the Navy, and sheriffs in almost every county encountered resistance to it" (124).

35. See Ernest Sirluck, who locates the shift in the Militia ordinance, and shows how Charles I referred to an earlier speech by Pym on the supremacy of law (*CPW*, 2:15–17).

36. Burgess describes Parker as a "propagandist for the coalition of peers and gentry that came to control the Long Parliament" (*Ancient Constitution*, 187). In 1642, after being in the employ of Parliament's Committee of Safety, he became secretary to the army and its commander Essex. (He later served as secretary to Cromwell.) On Parker, see also Michael Mendle, *Henry Parker and the English Civil War* (Cambridge, 1995); Richard Tuck, *Philosophy and Government, 1572–1651* (Cambridge, 1993), chap. 6, esp. 226–33.

37. William Haller, *Liberty and Reformation in the Puritan Revolution* (New York, 1955), 73.

38. Henry Parker, *The Case of Shipmony briefly discoursed* (London, 1640), 26–27. For Parker's remarks on *salus populi*, see p. 7. Parker also mentions the Shipmoney Case in his *Observations, upon Some of His Majesties Late Answers and Expresses* (London, 1642), 3.

39. See *CPW* 2: 23. Sirluck points out that Parker was the first to use the language of natural law and contract to defend parliamentary sovereignty (25). On Parker's career at the time of the *Observations*, see Mendle, *Henry Parker and the English Civil War*, 19. On his "parliamentary absolutism," see Mendle, chap. 4. On Parker's use of French monarchomach arguments, see Quentin Skinner, *Liberty before Liberalism* (Cambridge, 1998), chap. 1, esp. n65.

40. Parker, *Observations*, 1.

41. Ibid., 34; Robert Filmer, *Observations concerning the Originall of Government*, in Filmer, *Patriarcha and Other Writings*, ed. Johann P. Sommerville (Cambridge, 1991), 201.

42. Parker also calls attention to the difficulty of using "natural law" as a standard of judgment in *The Contra-Replicant* (London, 1643), 6.

43. Parker, *Observations*: "meere private opinion" (25); "vertue of representation" (15, 45). In response to the question of "who shall judge?" Parker answers "the people," by which he means Parliament, "for the Parliament is indeed nothing else, but the very people it self artificially congregated, or reduced by an orderly election, and representation, into such a Senate, or proportionable body" (18).

44. On the argument from intention, see Parker, *Observations*, 28–29; on natural law, see pp. 42–22.

45. As Ernest Sirluck argued in *CPW*, vol. 2, in the struggle with the king over the militia ordinance, "Parliament was being goaded into taking the final step that would carry it from the old concept that it 'declared' law to the modern concept that it makes law" (21).

46. Quoted in Sommerville, *Politics and Ideology*, 74; see Cicero, *Pro Milone*, 4.11.

47. See Parker, *Observations* 3, 20, 22–23, 35, on trust; and 13, 25, 36, on conscience. Turning the king's language of trust to a legal trust, Parker argues, "wee must not think that it can stand with the intent of any trust, that necessarie defence should be barred, and naturall preservation denied to the people" (20).

48. In Parker's "history" of human government, even Nimrod is not the exception but the rule. Although to Parker and his contemporaries Nimrod was a figure for the tyrant, "that force by which he did prevail, can hardly be supposed to be it self wholly forced" (ibid., 44). Successful force will always by definition be legitimated by consent.

49. Grotius is also cited in Henry Parker, *Jus populi* (London, 1644), on pp. 11, 55, 66–67, and much of the discussion of slavery on pp. 36–42 could have come from Grotius.

50. On self-preservation, see Parker, *Jus populi*, e.g., 20, 28, 42.

51. Not coincidently, the first edition of Milton's *Doctrine and Discipline of Divorce*, which I discuss in chapter 8, was published shortly after this.

52. See also Parker, *Observations*: "[I]t is not just or possible for any nation so to inslave it selfe, and to resigne its owne interest to the wil of one Lord, as that that Lord may destroy it without injury, and yet to have no right to preserve it selfe" (8).

53. Sirluck, *CPW* 2:35. Sirluck adds that Hobbes may instead have been influenced by his two friends. On the authorship of *An Answer to a Printed Book Intituled Observations* . . . (Oxford, 1642), see, in addition to Sirluck, Richard

Tuck, *Natural Rights Theories* (Cambridge, 1979), 101n; Richard Tuck, *Philosophy and Government, 1572–1651* (Cambridge, 1993), chap. 6. Digges's *The Unlawfulnesse* was published posthumously; see Tuck, *Philosophy and Government,* 274.

54. Although Parker devotes only a small part of his treatise to affective questions, he does associate absolute rule with fear and limited government with love: "[S]ome men think it a glorious thing to be able to kill, as well as to save, and to have a kinde of a Creators power over Subjects: but the truth is, such power procures much danger to ill Princes, and little good to any; for it begets not so much love as fear in the subject, though it be not abused; and the fear of the subject does not give so perfect a Dominion as love" (*Jus populi,* 41).

55. See *Answer,* 44: "[H]aving made such a bargain, which might have been profitable, I have no right to recall it, when it appears disadvantageous." The example of the Gibeonites was frequently cited to illustrate the principle that promises should be kept. See Grotius, *De jure belli,* 2.13.4.

The argument of the *Answer* is even more clever than I have suggested: while distinguishing between the prudential motive of self-preservation from the religious obligation of conscience, the authors conflate religious obligation with an otherworldly self-interest: it is rational to keep one's promises not only because we are morally commanded to do so but because we stand to gain something greater than mere life. Hobbes tries to refute this argument about other-worldly self-interest in books 3 and 4 of *Leviathan.*

56. Parker, *Observations,* 174.

57. Just as the *Answer* denies conscience to the parliamentarians, so it attributes the people's unreliability not to their consciences but to their imaginations and affections.

58. Dudley Digges, *The Unlawfulnesse of Subjects taking up Armes against their Soveraigne, in what case soever* (n.p., 1643), 19.

59. Ibid., 167–68. The phrase "Law of feares" appears on p. 167.

60. The contrary view that the office of the king is separable from his person can only legitimate regicide. With uncanny prescience, Digges parodies the argument Milton would make for executing the king in *The Tenure of Kings and Magistrates:* "Though we kill him, it is no fault, because violence was offered only to his person, not to his authority" (32).

61. George Hickes, *A Discourse of the Soveraign Power* (London, 1682). "We may observe," he wrote, "what an absurd doctrine it is, and how disagreeable to Christian divinity, to assert that the sovereign Power is radically and originally seated in the People, and derived from them upon the Prince" (19).

CHAPTER 5
VIOLENCE

1. See J. W. Gough, "Political Trusteeship," in *John Locke's Political Philosophy* (Oxford, 1956), 150, quoting S. R. Gardiner, *Constitutional Documents of the Puritan Revolution,* 3rd ed. (Oxford, 1906), 376: The king told the court that he could not "submit to your pretended authority without violating the trust I have from God for the welfare and liberty of my people."

2. It would be left to *Eikon Basilike*—the text ostensibly by Charles imprisoned by the parliamentary forces—to make the case, posthumously, for the extralegal rhetoric of martyrdom.

3. Cited in C. V. Wedgwood, *Trial of Charles I* (London, 1964), 161.

4. Ibid., 135.

5. John Ball. *A Treatise of the Covenant of Grace* (London, 1645), 56.

6. John Downame, *The Christian Warfare* (1634), 117; John Angier, *An Helpe to Better Hearts* (1647; sermons delivered before 1640), 308; quoted by David Zaret, *The Heavenly Contract* (Chicago, 1985), 144.

7. Perry Miller, *The New England Mind: The Seventeenth Century* (Boston, 1961), 412.

8. Cornelius Burges, "The First Sermon, Preaced to the Honorable House of Comons now assembled in Parliament at their Publique Fast. Novemb. 17. 1640" (London, 1641), 56, 57. The sermon is reprinted in Robin Jeffs, ed., *The English Revolution*, 34 vols. (London, 1970–72), I: *Fast Sermons to Parliament*, vol. 1, November 1640–November 1641 (London, 1970–71). Here and following page references to Jeffs are to the facsimile seventeenth-century text.

9. Burges, "The First Sermon," 44 (emphasis added).

10. James C. Spalding, "Sermons before Parliament (1640–49) as a Public Puritan Diary," *Church History* 36 (1967): 28. On these sermons, see also Ethyn Williams Kirby, "Sermons before the Commons, 1640–42," *American Historical Review* 44 (1939): 528–48; John F. Wilson, *Pulpit in Parliament* (Princeton, 1969); Michael Walzer, *The Revolution of the Saints* (Cambridge, 1968).

11. See Spalding, "Sermons before Parliament," 26; and Wilson, *Pulpit in Parliament*, chap. 7, who distinguishes between prophetic and apocalyptic strains of eschatology within civil war puritanism. Prophetic preachers (Burges, Marshall) emphasized agency and reformation; apocalyptic preachers (Hugh Broughton, Thomas Brightman, Joseph Mede) emphasized divine intervention. As Spalding notes, this prophetic interpretation was buttressed by the Elizabethan John Foxe's *Acts and Monuments* (popularly known as the *Book of Martyrs*), which interpreted the history of Protestant England as an elect nation in light of the Exodus narrative.

12. See Patricia Parker, "The Metaphorical Plot," in her *Literary Fat Ladies* (New York, 1987), 36–53.

13. See Terence Cave, *Recognitions* (Oxford, 1988), 48–49. Kathy Eden discusses the parallels between the construction of metaphor and the tragic plot in *Hermeneutics and the Rhetorical Tradition* (New Haven, 1994), 24–26; and in *Poetic and Legal Fiction in the Aristotelian Tradition* (Princeton, 1986), 71. In Aristotle's *Poetics* metaphors "uncover some unforeseen familiarity between two seemingly unrelated entities" (25). In this sense, the successful "metaphorical plot," like the tragic plot, involves a process of inference. Like tragic form, the surprising effects of metaphor presuppose the equitable judgment of the author and facilitate it in the reader. Moreover, the best metaphors will produce surprise as do the tragic devices of reversal and recognition. Yet, the force of metaphor is not always so easily domesticated. Like the tragic plot, the metaphorical plot may

also involve the illogical, the unexpected, even a moment of violence or coercion— the unnatural yoking of images together.

14. Stephen Marshall, "A Sermon Preached before the Honourable House of Commons, now assembled in Parliament, At their publike Fast, November 17. 1640" (London, 1641), 17. The sermon is reprinted in Jeffs, *The English Revolution*, 1:103–52. Gardiner described Marshall as the "mouthpiece of the Presbyterian party"; see S. R. Gardiner, *History of the Great Civil War*, 4 vols. (rpt., Gloucestershire, 1991), 1:228.

15. Marshall, "A Sermon Preached," in Jeffs, *The English Revolution*, 1:30, 31–32.

16. Ibid., 22–23 (emphasis added).

17. Ibid., 44, 49, 48.

18. *The Grand Remonstrance* (presented to the king December 1, 1641), in *The Puritan Revolution: A Documentary History*, ed. Stuart E. Prall (New York, 1968), 45–75.

19. Ibid.: Five Knights and Shipmoney cases (52–54), Star Chamber (55), the common law (57), Scotland (59), Strafford and Ireland (60), taxation "without consent in Parliament" (65).

20. Clarendon is cited in Kirby, "Sermons," 541. The original reference is to Clarendon, *History of the Rebellion* (Oxford, 1725), 2:22–23.

21. Stephen Marshall, "Meroz Cursed, Or a Sermon preached to the Honourable House of Commons, At their late Solemn Fast, Febr. 23, 1641" (London, 1641), 18, 19.

22. Ibid., reprinted in Jeffs, *The English Revolution*, vol. 2.1:26 (emphasis added).

23. Gardiner, *Civil War*, 1:234.

24. Wilson, *Pulpit in Parliament*, 170. "The Solemn League and Covenant" is reprinted in Prall, *Puritan Revolution*, 103–7.

25. Although or perhaps because the Covenant articulated, among other things, a compromise between the Presbyterians and Independents in England, it served in the long run to emphasize their divisions. In the immediate context, however, it strengthened the parliamentary cause against the king. See Gardiner, *Civil War*, 1:235–36.

26. See John Goodwin, *The Great Interest of States & Kindgomes* (London, 1645), a sermon preached before Commons, February 25, 1645. Goodwin reads the book of Revelation as a prophecy of the destruction of the Roman Empire, a "*Tragy-comedy*, which begins with a Kingdome to be won by conquest, [Rev. 6:8] and ends with the *Coronation of a King*, and the *marriage of his Bride*: and all between, is but the removing of all such lets and impediments" (37).

27. Joseph Caryl, "Of the Nature, Solemnity, Grounds, Property, and Benefits of a Sacred Covenant" (London, 1643), 26.

28. John Brinsley, "The Saints Solemn Covenant with their God" (London, 1644), e.g., 3.

29. Thomas Coleman, "The Christians Course and Complaint" (London, 1643). On the Covenant, see ibid., 43, 64, 66, 68.

30. Thomas Coleman, "The Christians Course and Complaint," waiting (18); false inferences (19); "God dislikes the meanes" (19); backsliding (27–28).

31. Ibid., 49. By 1645, however, Coleman was utterly disenchanted not only with the king but also with the Presbyterians. In a sermon aptly entitled "Hopes Deferred and Dashed" (London, 1645), preached on Job 11:20, he cast the civil war as a conflict between "a praying Army" and "a dissembling Adversary" (19). In doing so, he signaled his allegiance to the New Model army of Cromwell and Ireton as opposed to the Presbyterians and Parliament. See p. 25: "Lay no more burden of government upon the shoulders of Ministers."

32. Jeremiah Burroughs, "The Glorious Name of God, the Lord of Hosts. Opened in two Sermons . . . Vindicating the Commission from this Lord of Hosts, to Subjects, in some case [*sic*], to take up Arms" (London, 1643). This question whether the subject could take up arms against the king was, of course, debated much earlier than this. See, among other tracts, Henry Ferne, *The Resolving of Conscience*; William Bridge's answer to Ferne, *The Wounded Conscience*; Charles Herle, *A Fuller Answer to . . . Dr. Ferne* (all published in 1642); and Dudley Digges, *The Unlawfulnesse of Subjects taking up armes against their Soveraigne in what case soever* (1643), discussed in chapter 4.

33. Burroughs, "Lord of Hosts," 35 (various forms of government); 38, 68 ("covenant or compact"); 30 (precedent and *salus populi*); 32 (Samson); 93 (eternal life). Hobbes would also object to Burroughs's recommendation of using the fear of God to counteract other fears: "A spirit of true courage hath all its fears swallowed up in the fear of God; it hath learned to feare nothing but God; and in order to God [*sic*], it sets the fear of God against all other fears" (102).

34. Contemporary accounts tell of spectators scrambling to get a bloody scrap of the king's clothing. See Wedgwood, *Trial of Charles I*. But there is a way in which the image foreshadows royalist accounts of the regicide as well: the executed Charles is a Christlike martyr, but this logic of martyrdom predicts his eventual triumph as Christ victor.

35. See Wilson, *Pulpit in Parliament*, 51, 58, 196; and 200, on violence; Walzer, *Revolution of the Saints*; Kirby, "Sermons," 545: "The comparison of the task of the commons to the rebuilding of the temple by the Israelites, which is found in many of the sermons, suggested that which would have been almost treasonable had the comparison been carried to its logical conclusion."

36. In his *Commentary on Saint Paul's Epistle to the Galatians* (1531), Luther had opposed spiritual matters to civil policy, insisting that "in civil policy obedience to the Law must be severely required. There nothing must be known as concerning the Gospel, conscience, grace, remission of sins, heavenly righteousness, or Christ himself, but Moses only, with the Law and the works thereof." In the *Institutes of the Christian Religion* (1559) Calvin had similarly distinguished between the spiritual and the political kingdoms: "Through this distinction it comes about that we are not to misapply to the political order the gospel teaching on spiritual freedom, as if Christians were less subject, as concerns outward government, to human laws, because their consciences have been set free in God's sight" (book 3, chap. 19, sec. 15). William Perkins reiterated the compatibility of Christian liberty and magistracy. Perkins, Luther, and Calvin are cited in *CD*, 538, n31. As Milton noted, however, in *The Tenure of Kings and Magistrates*, Luther and Calvin did at points justify resistance on the part of "lesser magistrates," though not of individual subjects (243–46).

37. Hobbes, *Leviathan*, 4.31; see also 5.36.

38. Hobbes, *Behemoth*, 144. Hobbes implies that humanistic learning is dangerous chiefly when applied to scriptural exegesis, for preachers can incite the common people to rebellion in a way that the scholar in his study cannot: "Common people know nothing of right or wrong by their own meditation; they must therefore be taught the grounds of their duty, and the reason why calamities ever follow disobedience to their lawful sovereigns. But to the contrary, our rebels were publicly taught rebellion in the pulpits" (144).

39. *The Tenure* would have been particularly distasteful to Hobbes if he read it. We know that Hobbes knew some of Milton's work because he mentions Milton's *Defence of the English People* in *Behemoth*, 163–64: "A" remarks, "About this time came out two books, one written by Salmasius, a Presbyterian, against the murder of the King; another written by Milton, an Independent, in answer to it." "B" responds: "I have seen them both. They are very good Latin both, and hardly to be judged which is better; and both very ill reasoning, hardly to be judged which is worse; like two declamations, *pro* and *contra*, made for exercise only in a rhetoric school by one and the same man. So like is a Presbyterian to an Independent."

40. Milton, *CD*, 155. As supporting evidence, Milton cited the biblical account of Jonah's prophecy to the citizens of Nineveh that, unless they repented, the city would be destroyed (Jonah 3:4). Although, when the citizens repented, Jonah was angry with God that the prophecy did not come to pass, in Milton's reading this outcome proved that the divinely inspired prophecy was not predictive but rather performative and conditional upon the citizens' response: "For if the decrees of God quoted above, and others of the same kind which frequently occur, were interpreted in an absolute sense without any implied conditions, God would seem to contradict himself and be changeable" (*CD*, 156; see also *CD*, 160). Later in the treatise, Milton described the decree of general rather than specific predestination as conditional as well:

[T]he principle of predestination is founded upon a condition,—*whosoever hath sinned, him will I blot out*. This is announced more fully in the enforcement of the legal covenant, Deut. vii. 6–8. where God particularly declares his choice and love of his people to have been gratuitous; and in v.9. where he desires to be known as *a faithful God which keepeth his covenant and mercy*, he yet adds as a condition, *with them that love him and keep his commandments*. (*CD*, 178).

I quote here from the Sumner translation in John Milton, *Complete Poems and Major Prose*, ed. Merritt Y. Hughes (Indianapolis, 1958), 920, because I prefer the translation of "pactum" as covenant rather than compact.

41. Milton, *CD*, 180.

42. Milton, *CD*, 536; *PL*, 12.300–306.

43. Milton, *CD*, 523–24, 536, 590. See also *CD*, 581–82: "Each passage of scripture has only a single sense, though in the Old Testament this sense is often a combination of the historical and the typological. . . . The right method of interpreting the scriptures [requires] . . . knowledge [of the] distinction between literal and figurative langauge." Milton does not simply equate the spiritual sense with

the figurative sense; he does, however, argue that an understanding of figurative language is an effect of a spiritual interpretation of Scripture.

44. Milton's view of the inseparability of the covenant, figurative interpretation, and ethical responsibility is also apparent in his discussion of the sacraments. Because the covenant of grace is conditional, it serves to demystify the sacraments. No sacrament is efficacious in itself; rather, the power of the sacraments depends on the faith of the believer. In practice, this amounts to a recognition of the figurative dimension of Scripture, including such phrases as "this is my body." For, according to Milton, a sacrament is not itself a covenant but rather "a sign of the covenant." "Failure to recognize this figure of speech in the sacraments, where the relationship between the symbol and the thing symbolized is very close, has been a widespread source of error, and still is today." Thinking tropologically serves to place the ethical burden where it belongs: not on the sacrament alone but on the individual agent and believer. See Milton, *CD*, 555. Maurice Kelley, the editor of *CD*, traces Milton's position on the sacraments in part to William Ames (see the notes to book 1, chap. 27).

45. These passages from *The Representation* are taken from Arthur Barker, *Milton and the Puritan Dilemma* (Toronto, 1941), 142–43.

46. In "The Politics of *Paradise Lost*," in *Politics of Discourse*, ed. Kevin Sharpe and Steven N. Zwicker (Berkeley, 1987), Mary Ann Radzinowicz makes a related point about Milton's use of Scripture in *Paradise Lost*: "He reads Scripture seeking its rational interpretation. Satisfied that he has rightly judged the significance of this or that occasion, his interpretation does not become the precedent to which current affairs are made conformable; rather, the free use of reason in an act of interpretation becomes the precedent, the mode by which current affairs are judged" (207). "So it is with all Milton's political instances involving scriptural scenarios in *Paradise Lost*. In them Scripture is history and not authority; no interpretation is coercive; no public policy comes with God's fiat behind it to overrule freedom" (208).

47. *Tenure CPW*, 3: 191, 194, 229–33. Milton also discusses the king's and the Presbyterians' violation of the Solemn League and Covenant in *Eikonoklastes* (*CPW*, 3:593–97).

48. *Tenure*, 227.

49. Ibid., 232–33; 236 (fals prophecy).

50. See *Tenure*, 193. See Seneca, *De clementia*, 2.5.1. The debate over the catharsis clause is comprehensively treated by Bernard Weinberg, *History of Literary Criticism in the Italian Renaissance*, 2 vols. (Chicago, 1961), and Baxter Hathaway, *The Age of Criticism: The Late Renaissance in Italy* (Ithaca, 1962), 205–302. I take up the political implications of pity in chapters 8–10.

51. *Tenure*, 195 (double contradictory sense); 232 (plotting and contriving).

52. Ibid., 197 (meere useless bulke); 193 (ancient slavery).

53. Ibid., 235, 242. The first edition of *The Tenure* ended with this prayer and the reference to Meroz. See the end of *The Tenure* for the use of military metaphors for the act of interpretation.

54. Ibid., 198. For other instances of the language of right, see 199, 202–3, 206–7, 209, 211–12, 214, 218, 220, 221, 225, 227, 234, 236.

55. Ibid., 200.

56. Ibid., 202.

57. Ibid., 207. As Hughes notes in his edition of Milton, *Complete Poems and Major Prose*, "Deuteronomy 17:14 and I Samuel 8 had been interpreted adversely to popular rights by Grotius in *De Jure Belli et Pacis* II, iv, 3" (206, n68). For Hobbes's interpretation of 1 Samuel 8, see *Leviathan*, 35.446, 40.508–10, 42.541. Hobbes reads 1 Samuel as evidence that God was the Jews' literal king, before they abandoned him and chose another.

58. *Tenure*, 206–7.

59. Ibid., 208; *CD*, 160; *PL*, 3.99.

60. Grotius, *De jure belli*, 1.4.7. See *Tenure*, 213, n85.

61. *Tenure*, 215, 216. See Grotius, *De jure belli*, 1.4.19.4.

62. To support this argument, Milton turned to 1 Peter 2:13 and Romans 13, which were regularly cited by royalists to justify monarchical power and absolute obedience to the crown. According to Milton, Romans' "There is no power but of God" was compatible with Peter's description of government as a "human ordinance," because Romans was not simply a statement of fact but a test of human judgment, an exercise in deliberating about the best way to achieve "common peace and preservation." The people have the "liberty therfore and right" to "dispose of [sovereign power] by any alteration as they shall *judge* most conducing to the public good" (*Tenure*, 212, emphasis added).

63. *Tenure*, 211.

64. See Hobbes, *Leviathan*, 4.31; see 5.36 and chap. 17.

65. *Tenure*, 190.

66. See *PL*, 12.97–101: "Yet sometimes Nations will decline so low / From vertue, which is reason, that no wrong, / But Justice, and some fatal curse annext / Deprives them of thir outward libertie / Thir inward lost. . . ."

67. *Tenure*, 229–30.

68. Ibid., 229, n139.

69. Ibid., 233, 190–92.

70. See William Kerrigan, *The Sacred Complex: On the Psychogenesis of "Paradise Lost"* (Cambridge, Mass., 1983) on the similarity between prophecy and "good metaphors": "One cannot crack the meaning of a good metaphor by recourse to values already affixed to either of its terms. . . . Tradition is decisive for the meaning of dead metaphors. By their very anomaly, good metaphors are prophetic—troublers of stability" (94).

71. *Oxford English Dictionary*, s.v. "tenure."

72. See Richard Helgerson, *Forms of Nationhood* (Chicago and London, 1992), 91.

73. Edward Coke, *Institutes*, book 1, chap. 1, sec. 1, of the *First Institute*. I owe this reference to William Klein.

74. *Tenure*, 221.

75. Ibid., 204.

76. Ibid., 237, 236. This idolatrous interpretation of political contract is also one of the subjects of Milton's *Eikonoklastes*. Milton attacks the Presbyterian understanding of the Solemn League and Covenant in the introduction and in chap. 28, where he speaks of "men so quell'd and fitted to be slaves by the fals conceit of a Religious Covnant" (*CPW*, 3:347, and 595; see 593–97).

77. J.G.A. Pocock, *The Ancient Constitution and Feudal Law*, a reissue with retrospect (Cambridge, 1986); Christopher Hill, *Puritanism and Revolution* (London, 1958), 58–125. In *Tenure* Milton discusses the Norman Conquest (201); the "ancient constitution" (220); the "right of ancient laws and Ceremonies" (225). He also traces "the most fundamental and ancient tenure that any king of England can produce or pretend to" not to William the Conqueror but to the year 446, when the British people elected a king after the Romans had relinquished their right of conquest (221).

78. See Pocock, *Ancient Constitution*, 119–20. At the same time, because the royalists did not want to base the monarchy's claim to legitimacy simply upon the right of (the Norman) conquest, they also argued for the irrevocable consent of the people (as James I does in *The Trew Law of Free Monarchies*) and they even borrowed the language of the ancient constitution and "the immemorial custom of England" (*Ancient Constitution*, 151) to defend absolute monarchy.

79. Pocock, *Ancient Constitution*, 318, 317, 320. Pocock argues that the ancient constitution argument was used by conservative Presbyterians from 1647 on.

80. *Tenure*, 220 (emphasis added).

81. Ibid., 237.

82. Ibid., 256.

83. In the historiography of the seventeenth century, the critique of precedent was sometimes linked to an ahistorical language of rights. But this critique could also be construed as allowing a fuller immersion in history or openness to the possibility of historically new actions, new voices, as it is in *Tenure*. On the critique of precedent as a sign of the crisis of the common law, see Glenn Burgess, *The Politics of the Ancient Constitution* (University Park, Pa., 1992), 223.

84. *Tenure*, 193, 194. On antinomianism, see Michael Fixler, *Milton and the Kingdoms of God* (London, 1964), chap. 4, esp. 146; and William Haller, *Liberty and Reformation in the Puritan Revolution* (New York, 1955), 341–58.

85. *Tenure*, 237–38.

86. Ibid., 199, 253, 254, 220.

87. Milton acknowledged the possible abuse of the language of reason of state in *Paradise Lost* when he referred to "necessity / The Tyrant's plea" (*PL*, 4.393–94).

88. Compare Henry Parker who, in *The Contra-Replicant* (London, 1643), defended reason of state as the legitimate use of extralegal means to preserve the state in times when the ordinary workings of the law are not enforced or will not suffice: "Lawes ayme at *Justice*, Reason of state aimes at *Safety*. . . . To deny to Parliament recourse to reason of State in these miserable times of warre and danger [is] to deny them self-defence" (24–25).

89. Sedgwick (pp. 6 and 11) is quoted by Hill, "Covenant Theology," 16. Fixler also discusses Sedgwick in *Milton and the Kingdom of God*, 151–52.

90. See Florence Sandler, "Icon and Iconoclast," in *Achievements of the Left Hand*, ed. Michael Lieb and John T. Shawcross (Amherst, 1974), 168: "When Milton . . . justifies the regicide court as acting with the authority of the people, he offends the good parliamentarian by refusing to recognize the distinction between a free House of Commons and a Rump sitting at the behest of the Army, and he

aligns himself with the small group of extremists who are prepared to force the actual forms of the law to fit their own arbitrary version of the 'fundamental law.' "

91. Friedrich Nietzsche, *The Genealogy of Morals*, in *The Birth of Tragedy and the Genealogy of Morals*, trans. Francis Golffing (Garden City, N.Y., 1956), 2.1, 2.2, p. 190: "A man who wishes to dispose of his future in this manner must first have learned to separate necessary from accidental acts; to think causally; to see distant things as though they were near at hand; to distinguish means from ends. In short he must have become not only calculating but himself calculable, regular even to his own perception, if he is to stand pledge for his own future as a guarantor does." "The task of breeding an animal entitled to make promises involves . . . the preparatory task of rendering man up to a certain point regular, uniform, equal among equals, calculable."

92. Ibid., 2.3, p. 192, on "Mnemotechnics"; pp. 192–93, "Whenever man has thought it necessary to create a memory for himself, his effort has been attended with torture, blood, sacrifice"; "pain [is] . . . the strongest aid to mnemonics."

93. *Tenure*, 238. Milton's forceful interpretation of God's covenant as a political contract paradoxically provides a mirror image of the "mingling of force and covenant" that royalists found so distasteful in Hobbes's *Leviathan*. See Pocock, *Ancient Constitution*, 164.

94. See *Tenure*, 194, against "disputing presidents [precedents]," and Kerrigan, *Sacred Complex*, 94, quoted earlier in note 70.

CHAPTER 6
METALANGUAGE

1. Hobbes's *Elements of Philosophy*, the English version of *De corpore*, was published in 1656. See also the remarks on method in the "Preface to the Readers" of *De cive*.

2. See Thomas Hobbes, *English Works*, ed. Thomas Molesworth, 11 vols. (London, 1839–45), 1:10; and J.W.N. Watkins, *Hobbes' System of Ideas* (London, 1965), chap. 3.

3. Hobbes, *Leviathan*, 26.191 (natural law), and 16.111. See the famous passage in 21.150 on the revolutionary effects of reading Aristotle, Cicero, and other Roman celebrators of liberty. See also 12.225–26.

4. On mimetic desire, see René Girard, *Deceit, Desire, and the Novel* (1966; rpt., Baltimore and London, 1981); and Girard, *Violence and the Sacred*, trans. Patrick Gregory (Baltimore, 1977), 143–68. According to the structure of mimetic desire, passion is never spontaneous, but always a matter of imitation; the rival in the romance plot is only apparently an obstacle but actually the precondition of the hero's desire. In fact, what the hero desires is to be like his rival, to take his place, which of course means to kill him (although, if he does, the hero's desire will be frustrated since it was always a desire for his enemy, a desire to imitate his desire). In this model, imitation can be deadly; at the very least, it is a source of conflict.

5. On "love and duel," see Hobbes, *Elements*, 63.

6. Like Hobbes's contemporaries, Hegel criticized Hobbes's account of human nature; see Hegel's remarks on "the law of the heart and the frenzy of self-conceit" in *The Phenomenology of Spirit*, trans. A. V. Miller (Oxford, 1977), 221. On

Hegel's reading of Hobbes, see Patrick Riley, *Will and Political Legitimacy* (Cambridge, Mass., 1982), 180–81; and Leo Strauss, *The Political Philosophy of Hobbes* (Chicago, 1936), 57–58. In *Revolution of the Saints* (Cambridge, Mass., 1965), Michael Walzer describes radical puritanism's transformation of the knight errant into the bureaucratic officeholder (72, 136).

7. See Hobbes, *De cive*, chap. 12.

8. See the chart at the end of chapter 9 of *Leviathan* (61), where Hobbes defines ethics as reasoning about "the passions of men" and politics or civil philosohy as reasoning about the rights and duties of subject and sovereign.

9. On the tensions between Hobbes's voluntarism and determinism, or between his deductive scientific method and his materialism, see, among others, Leo Strauss, *Natural Right and History* (Chicago, 1953), 166–202, esp. 173; and John Dewey, "The Motivation of Hobbes's Political Philosophy," in *Thomas Hobbes in His Time*, ed. Ralph Ross, Herbert W. Schneider, and Theodore Waldman (Minneapolis, 1974), 24–25.

10. For treatments of Hobbes's emphasis on poesis or construction, see, among others, Sheldon S. Wolin, *Politics as Vision* (Boston, 1960), chap. 8; Howard Caygill, *Art of Judgement* (Oxford, 1989), 13–16; Amos Funkenstein, *Theology and the Scientific Imagination from the Middle Ages to the Seventeenth Century* (Princeton, 1986), 334–36; Andrejz Rapaczynski, *Nature and Politics: Liberalism in the Philosophies of Hobbes, Locke, and Rousseau* (Ithaca, 1987), ix, 8, 109, 115–16. None of these treatments, however, considers Hobbes's relation to contemporary literary culture or his analysis of mimetic desire.

11. I owe this information to Sears McGee of the University of California, Santa Barbara. In *Essex the Rebel* (Lincoln, Neb., 1970), Vernon Snow discusses the royalist lampooning of Essex (343) but does not mention this incident. He does mention that Essex owned a copy of "*Amadis de Gaul*, the bible of chivalry-conscious knights and nobles" (187).

12. Hobbes, *Behemoth*, 112.

13. As Hobbes remarked in *Leviathan*, glory "maketh men invade . . . for trifles, as a word, a smile, a different opinion, and any other signe of undervalue, either direct in their Persons, or by reflexion in their Kindred, their Friends, their Nation, their Profession, or their Name" (13.88). Although the word Hobbes uses here is "glory," the examples he gives suggest that it is identical with vainglory or self-love.

14. See, for example, Jeremy Burroughs's sermon, dedicated to Essex, "The Glorious Name of God, The Lord of Hosts. Opened in two Sermons . . . Vindicating the Commission from this Lord of Hosts, to Subjects, in some case [*sic*] to take up Arms." (London, 1643), 93: "Those are fittest to venture their lives in fight, who are able to see beyond life, to see what is on the other side of the shore of this mortality, even eternall life and glory."

15. In addition to Lois Potter, *Secret Rites and Secret Writing: Royalist Literature, 1641–1660* (Cambridge, 1989), chap. 3, see Ananbel Patterson, *Censorship and Interpretation* (Madison, Wis., 1984), chap. 4; and Kevin Sharpe, *Criticism and Compliment: The Politics of Literature in the England of Charles I* (Cambridge, 1987), 95–96. For examples of the republican use of romance, see Nigel Smith, *Literature and Revolution in England, 1640–1660* (New Haven, 1994),

246–49. Here seventeenth-century writers would have been influenced by the many reprintings of Sidney's *Arcadia*, which not only provided contemporaries with a gripping narrative of chivalric adventures but also kept the figure of Sidney, the exemplary Protestant poet and military hero, foremost in their minds.

16. On this point, see, for example, Fredric Jameson, *The Political Unconscious* (Ithaca, 1981), 103–51.

17. Quoted by Merritt Y. Hughes, ed., in John Milton, *Complete Poems and Major Prose* (Indianapolis, 1958), 793, n28 (to *Eikonoklastes*).

18. Potter, *Secret Rites*, 73. In "Romance, Probability, and Politics in England, 1650–1720" (Ph.D. diss., Princeton University, 1995), Christopher Hughes cites the passage about King Arthur in a discussion of the puritan use of romance to suggest improbability of the royalist cause (75).

19. Hobbes, *Elements*, 50–51.

20. Hobbes, *Elements*, 63. On false prophets, see the very next chapter (11) in the *Elements*, esp. 67.

21. Davenant's preface to *Gondibert* and Hobbes's response appear in J. E. Spingarn, *Critical Essays of the Seventeenth Century*, 3 vols. (Oxford, 1908), 2: 1–67. The quotation about Davenant's avoidance of the Spenserian model of romance are taken from Colin Burrow, *Epic Romance* (Oxford, 1993), 241. See *Elements*, chap. 9, for Hobbes's analysis of how love, "the great theme of poets" (59), is often an expression of the desire to master others.

22. See Hobbes, *Elements*, 61, where Hobbes defines "the excellency of FANCY" as "finding unexpected similitudes in things," "from [whence] proceed those grateful similes, metaphors, and other tropes." By metaphorical thinking, I mean this reasoning by analogy or similitude.

23. See Hobbes, *Leviathan*, 8.50.

24. See Hobbes, *Leviathan*, 8.53.

25. See Hobbes, *Leviathan*, 5.19. In chapter 12 of *Leviathan*, on religion, Hobbes argues that, when individuals have no knowledge of first causes, they "feign unto themselves, severall kinds of Powers Invisible; and . . . stand in awe of their own imaginations; . . . making creatures of their own fancy, their Gods." In a devastating survey of "the innumerable variety of Fancy," Hobbes reduces religion to a species of poetry concerning "Feare of things invisible" (*Leviathan*, 12.75). On the comparison between religion and poetic feigning, see also 12.79. Hobbes asserts that it is impossible not to believe "there is one God eternall," but we cannot have any "Idea, or Image of him" (12.74–75).

26. See Hobbes, *Leviathan*, 14.197, 18.230.

27. On Hobbes's interpretation of conscience as a metaphor, see Karen S. Feldman, "Conscience and the Concealments of Metaphor in Hobbes's *Leviathan*," *Philosophy and Rhetoric* 34 (2001): 21–37. Once Hobbes reduces conscience to a matter of opinion, it comes under the jurisdiction of the sovereign. Effecting his own metaphorical transfer from the private realm of conscience back to the public realm of knowing together, Hobbes asserts that: "the Law is the publique Conscience, by which [the subject] has already undertaken to be guided. Otherwise, in such diversity, as there is of private Consciences, which are but private opinions, the Common-wealth must needs be distracted, and no man dare

to obey the Soveraign Power, farther than it shall seem good in his eyes" (*Leviathan*, 29.233).

28. This mimesis is not Platonic but Aristotelian; see note 33. In his treatise *On the Sublime*, Longinus quotes God's creative "fiat" as an example of sublime discourse. Note also how Hobbes's comparison of the establishment of the commonwealth to the divine "fiat" complicates his argument about contract, for God is not a party to a contract when he creates the world; he is instead an absolute sovereign. This may be an example (and there are others, as many critics have noted) of the way in which something like sovereign power—including the sovereign power to define and constrain our interpretation of our passions—is a precondition of the contract of government, which is itself a precondition of sovereign power. In other words, although a covenant is an agreement, the model of the covenant is the divine institution.

29. Hobbes, *De cive*, chap. 17, sect. 28, p. 232.

30. See also the chart of the several kinds of knowledge in chapter 9 of *Leviathan*, where Hobbes derives "the *Science* of JUST and UNJUST" from "Contracting," which is in turn one of the "Consequences of Speech" (61). I have discussed Hobbes's attitude toward language in *Rhetoric, Prudence, and Skepticism in the Renaissance* (Ithaca, 1985), chap. 6.

31. See Strauss, *Political Philosophy of Hobbes*, 169.

32. See Hobbes, *Leviathan* 5.36.

33. Here, too, this productive conception of mimesis is Aristotelian rather than Platonic. See Paul Ricoeur, *The Rule of Metaphor*, trans. Robert Czerny with Kathleen McLaughlin and John Costello (Toronto, 1977), 198, citing Aristotle's *Poetics* 1410b, 1459a: "The same operation that lets us 'see the similar' also 'conveys learning and knowledge through the medium of the genus. . . .' But if it is true that one learns what one does not yet know, then to make the similar visible is to *produce* the genus *within* the differences, and not elevated beyond differences, in the transcendence of the concept." See also Christopher Prendergast, *The Order of Mimesis* (Cambridge, 1986), 21, 225, 233; and the discussion of Ricoeur and Aristotle on the productive power of metaphor in Joel Altman, " 'Preposterous Conclusions': Eros, *Enargeia*, and the Composition of *Othello*," *Representations* 18 (1987): 137.

34. In its formal sublation of particular interests, this hermeneutical contract is closer to what the eighteenth-century will call aesthetic interest than it is to the mathematical sciences.

35. See Hobbes, *Leviathan*, 6.38.

36. See Hobbes, *Leviathan*, 6.45.

37. On this point, see John T. Harwood's introduction to *The Rhetorics of Thomas Hobbes and Bernard Lamy* (Carbondale, Ill., 1986), 28.

38. See Hobbes, *Leviathan*, 13.87: Men *believe* themselves equally endowed "in the faculties of body, and mind" and "From this equality of ability, ariseth equality of hope in the attaining of our Ends. And therefore if any two men desire the same thing, which nevertheless they cannot both enjoy, they become enemies." In a classic illustration of mediated desire, desiring the same object is not a simple function of scarcity but of the opinion of equality, and it is precisely this perception of one's likeness to another (this perception of shared desire) that gives rise to

enmity. On the role of opinion in the state of nature, see Richard Tuck, "Hobbes's Moral Philosophy," in *The Cambridge Companion to Hobbes*, ed. Tom Sorell (Cambridge, 1996), 184–85; and David Johnston, *The Rhetoric of Leviathan* (Princeton, 1986), 77–78.

39. See Hobbes, *Leviathan*, 13.87. On Hobbes's use of the term diffidence, Bernard Gert observes (without commenting on the implications of this observation for Hobbes's argument), "It may simply be that it is because Hobbes wanted to use the passion of fear as one of the 'passions that incline men to peace' (*Lev.* ch. 13, *EW* III, 116) that he decided to use a different word when he wanted a passion that led to war." See Gert, "Hobbes's Psychology," in *The Cambridge Companion to Hobbes*, ed. Tom Sorell (Cambridge, 1995), 161.

40. Strauss, *Political Philosophy of Hobbes*, 11, 26.

41. See ibid., on Hobbes's belief that reason is impotent, whence the necessity of focusing on the motivating power of fear, but also on Hobbes's redefinition of fear itself as rational (15–16). See also Gert, "Hobbes's Psychology," 164: "All of the premises about human nature, which Hobbes claims are true of all persons and which he uses in arguing for the necessity of an unlimited sovereign, are in fact statements about the rationally required desires, and not, as most commentators have taken them, statements about the passions." As I have been arguing, they are both—which is why Hobbes can use fear to get us out of the state of nature and also why this solution is vexed.

42. *Leviathan*, 10.66 (dishonorable fear); 4.31 (fear as the beginning of wisdom). Paradiastole—the rhetorical redescription of vice as virtue, of fear as wisdom—is not only the problem Hobbes sets out to remedy (as Quentin Skinner has argued); it is also Hobbes's solution. See Quentin Skinner, "Thomas Hobbes: Rhetoric and the Construction of Morality," *Proceedings of the British Academy* 76 (1991): 1–61; and Skinner, *Reason and Rhetoric in the Philosophy of Hobbes* (Cambridge, 1996).

43. See Hobbes, *Leviathan*, 14.95. A number of critics have noted how Hobbes's language here suggests the doctrines of assumpsit and consideration. See P. S. Atiyah, *Promises, Morals, and the Law* (Oxford, 1981), 13, 178–39; Craig Muldrew, *The Economy of Obligation: The Culture of Credit and Social Relations in Early Modern England* (New York, 1998), 321–25; and David Harris Sacks, "The Promise and the Contract in Early Modern England: Slade's Case in Perspective," in *Rhetoric and Law in Early Modern Europe*, eds. Victoria Kahn and Lorna Hutson (New Haven, 2001), 43–44.

44. See J. L. Austin, "Performative Utterances," in *Philosophical Papers*, ed. J. O. Urmson and G. J. Warnock, 3rd ed. (Oxford, 1979), 233–52, esp. 241, where Austin distinguishes performative utterances and statements from "acting a play or making a joke or writing a poem—in which case it would not be seriously meant and we shall not be able to say we seriously performed the act concerned."

45. Although Austin famously distinguished between constative and performative utterances, utterances that refer to an existing state of affairs or utterances that bring a new state of affairs into existence, he then went on to dismantle his own distinction, by declaring that "stating something is performing an act just as much as is giving an order"—a concession Hobbes would have appreciated ("Performative Utterances," 51). Other scholars have noted the similarity be-

tween Hobbes's account of obligation and Austin's theory of performatives. See, for example, Geraint Parry, "Performative Utterances and Obligation in Hobbes," *Philosophical Quarterly* 17 (1967): 246–53; David Bell, "What Hobbes Does with Words," *Philosophical Quarterly* 19 (1969): 155–58; and Terence Ball, "Hobbes' Linguistic Turn," *Polity* 17 (1985): 740–60.

46. See Otto Gierke, *Natural Law and the Theory of Society, 1500–1800*, trans. Ernest Barker, 2 vols. (Cambridge, 1934), 1:79–84 on Hobbes as the culmination and destruction of the earlier tradition of natural law.

47. See also Hobbes, *Leviathan*, 20.138, 21.146–47.

48. See Hobbes, *Leviathan*, 15.101: "[T]he nature of Justice, consisteth in keeping of valid Covenants: but the Validity of Covenants begins not but with the Constitution of a Civill Power."

49. See Hobbes, *Leviathan*, 12.84, 29.223–24.

50. See Hobbes, *Leviathan*, 15.108–9. It is, however, misleading to think one has a business transaction with the sovereign because the model for the sovereign's relation to subject is not an ordinary contract but the divine covenant. Like God, the sovereign is not literally bound to perform his part but binds himself. This is apparent in Hobbes's analysis of commutative and distributive justice (15.105–6).

51. See Hobbes, *Leviathan*, 26.187, and my comments in chapter 3.

52. Augustine, Aquinas, and canon lawyers on the "just price" had made the same point, but in Hobbes's mouth the effect was to do away with any absolute standard of moral value, including divine law. Samuel Pufendorf makes this objection to Hobbes in *De jure naturae et gentium*, trans. C. H. Oldfather and W. A. Oldfather (Oxford, 1934), 8.4.13.

53. Hobbes, *Leviathan*, 15.105; 10.63. In the *Nicomachean Ethics* (book 5; 1130b–1131a), Aristotle defined commutative justice as justice that rectifies inequalities, and is accordingly governed by arithmetical proportion; distributive justice is justice according to individual merit and is governed by geometrical proportion (the greater the merit, the greater the reward).

54. Hobbes, *Leviathan*, 26.185, 199 ("dreams and fancies"), 189.

55. Thomas Hobbes, *A Dialogue Between a Philosopher and a Student of the Common Laws of England*, ed. Joseph Cropsey (Chicago, 1997); see pp. 86–87 for the Student's quotations of St. German. On Hobbes and St. German on equity, see Sharon K. Dobbins, "Equity: The Court of Conscience or the King's Command, the Dialogues of St. German and Hobbes Compared," *Journal of Law and Religion* 9 (1988): 113–49.

56. In all of this it is important to see that, although Hobbes used the accepted conventionality of the economic contract to point up the quid pro quo of the political contract, the problem of economic contract was for Hobbes a lesser version of the more general problem of political obligation. In his view, the subjectivity of value was a general problem in the state of nature—and the primary cause of civil war. This was a political problem before it was an economic problem or, to put it another way, the economic contingency of value was simply an offshoot of this more general epistemological and affective dilemma. Thus in *Behemoth*, his history of the civil war, Hobbes traced the causes of the conflict to ideology, passion, and opinion rather than economic self-interest. And in *Leviathan*, he made it clear that the sovereign's enforcement of political contract was the precondition of that eco-

nomic "Liberty to buy, and sell, and otherwise contract with one another" (*Leviathan*, 21.148); see *Leviathan*, chap. 24, for most of what Hobbes has to say about economic contract. See also Stephen Holmes, introduction to *Behemoth*, viii; and Holmes, *The Passions and Constraint* (Chicago, 1995), chap. 3.

57. This is a typical rhetorical move in *Leviathan*. Hobbes appears most deferential to God just when he deprives him of any temporal jurisdiction. In a related discussion of commutative and distributive justice, Hobbes rejects the view that distributive justice has to do with merit, which only God can determine: "Merit . . . is not due by Justice; but is rewarded of Grace onely." As a result, "Distributive Justice," which Hobbes also calls equity, is defined as "the Justice of an Arbitrator" (15.105).

58. Hobbes, *Leviathan*, 15.109. For a similar analysis of Hobbes's defense of the golden rule, see George Shelton, *Morality and Sovereignty in the Philosophy of Hobbes* (New York, 1992), chap. 2. For a compatible reading of Hobbes's understanding of natural law, see Norberto Bobbio, *Thomas Hobbes and the Natural Law Tradition*, trans. Daniela Gobetti (Chicago, 1993).

59. See Hobbes, *Leviathan*, 26.188, 16.192.

60. Hobbes, *Leviathan*, 15.101. Compare Grotius, *De jure belli*, 1.1.9, and prolegomena, para. 11.

61. James had even on occasion referred to a contract of subjection by which the people consented to absolute subordination. See James's *The Trew Law of Free Monarchies*, in *The Political Works of James I*, ed. Charles Howard McIlwain (Cambridge, Mass., 1918), 59.

62. See *Leviathan* 17.117, 18.123.

63. See, for example, Walzer, *Revolution of the Saints*, 159–60. This view of Hobbes was already promulgated in the seventeenth century. See Samuel Mintz, *The Hunting of Leviathan* (Cambridge, 1962), 124–46; and Mark Goldie, "The Reception of Hobbes," in *The Cambridge History of Political Thought, 1450–1700*, ed. J. H. Burns with Mark Goldie (Cambridge, 1991), 589–615.

64. *Leviathan*, 19.130; see 18.121–22, 22.156.

65. On Hobbes as a Reformation theologian, see Leopold Damrosch, "Hobbes as Reformation Theologian: Implications of the Freewill Controversy," *Journal of the History of Ideas* 40 (1979): 339–52.

66. George Lawson, *An Examination of the Political Part of Mr. Hobbs his "Leviathan"* (London, 1657), 146.

67. Johann P. Sommerville, *Thomas Hobbes: Political Ideas in Historical Context* (New York, 1992), 71.

68. See Carole Pateman, *The Sexual Contract* (Stanford, 1988), 50.

69. On this point, see the brilliant analysis by Pateman in ibid., 43–50.

70. Goldie, "Reception of Hobbes," quoting John Bramhall, *A Defence of True Liberty . . .* (1655), 182.

71. Ralph Cudworth, *The True Intellectual System of the Universe*, ed. René Wellek, 2 vols. (1678; rpt., New York, 1978), vol. 2, "The Contents," gloss on "Page 893, 895." See also p. 699 on the conflation of right and force in *Leviathan*.

72. Cited by Jean Hampton, *Hobbes and the Social Contract Tradition* (Cambridge, 1986), 10.

73. Cudworth, *True Intellectual System*, 698.

74. John Bramhall, *The Catching of Leviathan or the Great Whale* (London, 1658), 498. This text is bound with and appears after Bramhall's *Castigations of Mr. Hobbes* and the pagination is continuous. On synteresis, see p. 201.

75. James Tyrrell, *A Brief Disquisition of the Law of Nature . . . As also His Confutations of Mr. Hobb's Principles, put into another Method*, 2nd ed. (London, 1701), xl (emphasis added).

76. John Eachard, *Mr Hobbs's State of Nature Considered* (London, 1672), ed. Peter Ure (Liverpool, 1958), 45, 68.

77. Bramhall, *The Catching of Leviathan or the Great Whale*, 571, 509 (the good woman's fear), 519 (better not worse; mutual defense; fidelity and loyalty).

78. Edward, Earl of Clarendon, *A Brief Review and Survey of the Dangerous and pernicious Errors to Church and State in Mr. Hobbes's Book entitled Leviathan* (London, 1676), 6. See also 16–17: "Amongst the many excellent parts and faculties with which Mr. *Hobbes* is plentifully endowed, his order and method in Writing, and his clear expressing his conceptions in weighty, proper, and significant words, are very remarkable and commendable; and it is some part of his Art to introduce, upon the suddain, instances and remarques, which are the more grateful, and make the more impression upon his Reader."

79. Ibid., 18–19.

80. There were precedents for this emphasis on contingency and political machinations in popular prose romances of the late sixteenth and earlier seventeenth centuries. In sixteenth-century England, Italian romance in particular symbolized the potentially dangerous connection between romance and artful deception, between the imitation of the passions and rhetorical technique, which was negatively associated with the pursuit of self-interest. This self-interest could take an erotic or political form, and sometimes both—hence the Elizabethan scholar Roger Ascham's warning against "bawdie books . . . translated out of the Italian tongue." Ascham implied that the reading of romances gives rise to faithlessness in love and went on to observe that the rhetorical manipulation of the passions "in Circes court" is closely linked to the pursuit of self-interest and faction at the royal court. Romance, Ascham suggested, does not simply represent the old world of aristocratic relations but the new world of the Italianate rhetorician: the arriviste, the pretender, the seducer and the fraud. See Ascham, *The Scholemaster*, ed. R. J. Schoeck (Ontario, 1966), 67, 72. I return to the topic of romance in chapters 7–9.

81. Tyrrell, *A Brief Disquisition*, 323.

82. Cudworth, *True Intellectual System*, 894–95, 97 (mispaginated; this page follows 84).

83. Ibid., 654. Hobbes himself seems at times to have felt that *Leviathan* was a philosophical fantasy or fiction. At the end of book 2 of *Leviathan* he wrote that he was "at the point of believing this my labour, as uselesse, as the Commonwealth of *Plato*; for he also is of opinion that it is impossible for the disorders of State, and change of Governments by Civill Warre, ever to be taken away, till Soveraigns be Philosophers" (31.254). And Filmer seconded this view in a sarcastic vein when, in *The Anarchy of a Limited or Mixed Monarchy* (in *Patriarcha and Other Writings*, ed. Johann P. Sommerville [Cambridge, 1991]) he criticized Hobbes's "platonic monarchy": "The book hath so much of fancy that it is a better piece of poetry than policy" (157).

84. See the Introduction to *Leviathan* for Hobbes's injunction to "nosce te ipsum." The moment of recognition in the romance plot often turns on what Aristotle in the *Rhetoric* called inartistic signs, on paralogism or faulty inference. It is striking in this context that Hobbes explicit conceives of his "know thyself" as a remedy for faulty inference. See p. 141 above.

85. It may be for that reason that, in *The Elements*, Hobbes echoes the contemporary language of marriage contracts. He insists that, when political right is transferred, it must be not only "*de futuro*" but also "*de praesenti*" (83). *De praesenti* vows referred to marriage vows that were binding in the present; *de futuro* vows were vows of betrothal, binding the couple to marry at some future time. See p. 336, n.12, below. On the gender dimension of Hobbes's argument, see also Strauss, *Political Philosophy of Hobbes*, and Holmes, *Passions and Constraint*. Strauss argues that Hobbes, like Plato, criticizes traditional equations of manliness with military valor. Holmes mentions Hobbes's appreciation of the church's "unmanning" of subjects by inculcating Christian meekness (96). On the effiminacy of the Hobbesian subject, see also Harvey C. Mansfield, "Virilité et libéralisme," *Archives de philosophie du droit* 41 (1997): 25–42.

86. In *The Origins of Totalitarianism* (New York, 1951), Hannah Arendt also challenged Hobbes's putative "realism." She went on to suggest that Hobbes's emphasis on power politics and the passions anticipated the novel. See pp. 155–57, 140–41. Arendt would not, however, agree with the defense I have offered of Hobbes's deduction of natural law.

CHAPTER 7
GENDER

1. William Cavendish was also a nephew of the earl of Devonshire, who employed Hobbes as a secretary and tutor to the earl's son.

2. On the relation between the marriage contract and the sexual contract, see Carole Pateman, *The Sexual Contract* (Stanford, 1988), 3–7, 54, 90. Pateman discusses the erotic and coercive underside of seventeenth-century theories of contractual obligation, arguing that the liberal model of political contract assumed a prior contract of sexual subordination: sexual inequality is the occluded yet enabling condition of supposedly gender-neutral theories of political obligation.

3. The text of *The Contract* is cited from Margaret Cavendish, *The Description of the New Blazing World and Other Writings*, ed. Kate Lilley (New York, 1992). The following quotations are taken from p. 4.

4. The "scandal" of fiction is discussed later in this chapter. I take the term from Terence Cave, *Recognitions: A Study in Poetics* (Oxford, 1988), 1–24; see also Christopher Prendergast, *The Order of Mimesis* (Cambridge, 1986).

5. See Mary Lyndon Shanley, "Marriage Contract and Social Contract in Seventeenth-Century Political Thought," *Western Political Quarterly* 32 (1979): 79–91; Constance Jordan, "The Household and the State: Transformations in the Representation of an Analogy from Aristotle to James I," *Modern Language Quarterly* 54 (1993): 307–26; and Margaret R. Sommerville, *Sex and Subjection: Attitudes to Women in Early-Modern Society* (London, 1995). Jordan argues that

James preferred the comparison of a king to a father rather than husband, and that the husband-wife analogy often functioned to mitigate the rigors of absolutism.

6. Henry Ferne, *Conscience Satisfied: That there is no warrant for the Armes now taken up by Subjects* . . . (Oxford, 1643), 12; cited in Shanley, "Marriage Contract and Social Contract," 81. Royalist defenders of absolute sovereignty (including James I in *The Trew Law of Free Monarchies*) also used the argument from conquest (or coercion) but even here consent functioned to ratify the conqueror's rule.

7. Shanley, "Marriage Contract and Social Contract," also makes this point, 82–85.

8. Henry Parker, *Observations upon Some of His Majesties Late Answers and Expresses* (London, 1642), 19.

9. Henry Parker, *Jus populi* (London, 1644), 1–2.

10. N. T., *The Resolver Continued: Or, A Satisfaction to some Scruples about the Putting of the Late King to Death* (London, 1649); cited by Elizabeth Skerpan, *The Rhetoric of Politics in the English Revolution, 1640–1660* (Columbia, Mo., 1992), 147.

11. As I argued in chapter 6, consent also has an important role to play in Hobbes's theory, according to which we consent to be coerced by the sovereign. Crucially, however, in Hobbes's model the sovereign is not a party to the contract, and so there is no relationship of mutual consent betweeen subject and sovereign.

12. For the common distinction between spousal contracts *de futuro* (promises to marry at some future time), and *de praesenti* (an exchange of vows that constitutes marriage in the present moment, preferably but not necessarily, according to canon law, with witnesses and solemnization in church), see Henry Swinburne, *A Treatise of Spousals, or Matrimonial Contracts: wherein all the Questions relating to that Subject are ingeniously Debated and Resolved* (London, 1686), facsimile rpt. in *Marriage, Sex, and the Family in England, 1660–1800*, 44 vols., ed. Randolph Trumbach (New York and London, 1985), vol. 3. The treatise was written in the early years of the seventeenth century, although it was not published until later. Under the rubric of "Questions about Marriages or Spousals contracted by Children," Swinburne discusses a case that anticipates the plot of *The Contract*: one party is in minority, the other not; the older party doesn't wait for the younger to reach majority and marries another. Legal opinion is divided, according to Swinburne, about whether the older party is bound by the spousal contract; Swinburne argues that the older party's second marriage is good, because the minority of the first party made the contract only a spousal *de futuro* (34–36). On marriage contracts, see also Ralph A. Houlbrooke, *The English Family, 1450–1700* (London, 1984), chap. 4; Martin Ingram, *Church Courts, Sex and Marriage in England, 1570–1640* (Cambridge, 1987), chaps. 4–6. All the major casuists of the seventeenth century (William Perkins, William Ames, Joseph Hall, Richard Baxter, Robert Sanderson, and Jeremy Taylor) discussed "matrimonial cases."

13. See Keith Thomas, "Cases of Conscience in Seventeenth-Century England," in *Public Duty and Private Conscience in Seventeenth-Century England*, ed. John Morrill, Paul Slack, and Daniel Wolff (Oxford, 1993), 46. The moral ambiguity of domestic cases was undoubtedly aggravated by the upheaval in gender relations that Cavendish and other women experienced during the civil war

and its aftermath. Cavendish herself dramatized this upheaval in *Bell in Campo*, a play written sometime after *The Contract*, in which a troop of Amazons helps the Kingdom of Reformation defeat the Kingdom of Faction, in the process securing a royal decree for the equality of husband and wife in marriage. See Cavendish, *Plays written by the thrice Noble . . . Lady Marchioness of Newcastle* (London, 1662), 588, where the Lady Victoria argues that women are "fit to be Copartners in [men's] Governments." The decree about new marital relations appears on p. 631. While utterly traditional in some respects—women are to have control over servants and household provisions—it also stipulates that women "shall sit at the upper end of the Table above their Husbands," "keep the purse," and "go abroad when they will, without controul, or giving of any account thereof."

Both here and in *The Contract* Cavendish may be registering a more general change "in the conceptualization of the marriage contract in the course of the seventeenth century." If in 1640 "to contract a marriage was to consent to a status which in its essence was hierarchical and unalterable," by 1690 "the terms of the [marriage] contract . . . were [themselves] negotiable" (Shanley, "Marriage Contract and Social Contract," 79; see Houlbrooke, *English Family*, 35).

14. Douglas Grant, *Margaret the First: A Biography of Margaret Cavendish, Duchess of Newcastle* (Toronto, 1957), 132. See also the more recent biography by Kathleen Jones, *A Glorious Fame: The Life of Margaret Cavendish* (London, 1988); and the discussion of Cavendish in Sara Heller Mendelson, *The Mental World of Stuart Women* (Brighton, England, 1987).

15. Cavendish moved to France with the court of Henrietta Maria in 1643. Sir William Cavendish went into exile in 1645 after being defeated by the Parliamentary army at Marston Moor in 1644. In *The Life of . . . William Cavendish, Duke, Marquess, and Earl of Newcastle* (London, 1667) Cavendish recounts a number of conversations between her husband and Hobbes. See also Margaret Cavendish, *Philosophical Letters* (London, 1644), 47, 492. The first part of this text offers a commentary on chapters 1–6 of *Leviathan* and parts of Hobbes's *Elements*. The phrase quoted comes from p. 492.

16. See Kevin Sharpe, *Criticism and Compliment. The Politics of Literature in the England of Charles I* (Cambridge, 1987); Erica Veevers, *Images of Love and Religion: Queen Henrietta Maria and Court Entertainments* (Cambridge, 1989); and Martin Butler, *Theatre and Crisis, 1632–42* (Cambridge, 1984). According to Sharpe, Charles I's tastes did not preclude "political debate and discussion" and "love was the metaphor, the medium, through which political comment and criticism were articulated in Caroline England" (39). A politics of love was of course also important in the reigns of Elizabeth and James, as we see from contemporary drama, poetry, and political debate. Veevers is interesting on the difference between the Elizabethan and Caroline rhetorics of love (73–74, 186–91).

In discussing the politics of love in the 1630s, both Sharpe and Butler have emphasized that "marriage was the ultimate relationship of equals in love" (Sharpe, *Criticism and Compliment*, 288); but as I have already argued, marriage was a favorite metaphor for royalist politics because it emphasized hierarchy as well as mutuality, subordination as well as consent. Thus, to use an example cited by Sharpe, the king in Davenant's *The Fair Favorite* who has mastered his tyrannical passion may have learned to love his subjects, but he is not, as a result, their equal; the idealized marriage of Charles and Henrietta Maria may signify harmony and stability, but no one would assume that this was predicated on the equality of husband and wife, let alone ruler and ruled.

17. On the Caroline masque, see Veevers, *Henrietta Maria*, and Sharpe, *Criticism and Compliment*, chap. 5. According to contemporary theorists, if epic was traditionally defined by heroic action, the principal action of romance often took the form of marriage; see the preface to English translation of Scudéry's *Ibrahim*.

18. Montague's work is discussed by Lois Potter, *Secret Rites and Secret Writing: Royalist Literature, 1641–1660* (Cambridge, 1989), 79–80. Although Potter does not discuss the language of contract, she does observe that "romance allows the major religious differences between the king and queen, and the hostility between their two countries, to be glossed over by the myth of a love which transcends conflict" (80). See also Veevers, *Henrietta Maria*, 39–47; Sharpe, *Criticism and Compliment*, 39–44.

19. For two stimulating discussions of the development of the early modern notion of character, see Edmund Leites, "Casuistry and Character," in *Conscience and Casuistry in Early Modern Europe*, ed. Edmund Leites (Cambridge, 1988), 119–33; and James Tully, "Governing Conduct," in the same volume, 12–71. Leites argues that in the late seventeenth century casuistry was displaced by the idea of autonomous moral character, but that the call to rely on one's own conscience and judgment could be seen as a covert way of having people control themselves in accord with state interest. Leites connects this new "interest in the moral will, [and] non-legal concern over the conduct and character of daily life" with the development of prose fiction, especially the novel (132). On the connection between casuistry and the novel, see also George Starr, *Defoe and Casuistry* (Princeton, 1971). Tully traces the development of "a new practice of governing conduct . . . in the period from the Reformation to the Enlightenment" (12), one that was opposed to the older, potentially subversive idea of conscience. In some ways analogous to Foucault's notion of discipline, this mode of governing conduct is internalized in "mental habits and physical conduct" (70). For a related discussion of contract in the context of the novel, see Nancy Amstrong, *Desire and Domestic Fiction* (Oxford, 1985). Armstrong argues that contract declined as a model for political relationships because of contradictions in the theory, but had a different fate in the novel, where the social contract lived on as the sexual contract; the female gendering of subjectivity through the novel in turn had important political consequences.

20. See Richard Fanshawe, trans., *Il Pastor Fido or the Faithful Shepherd* (London, 1647). In the list of characters, Silvio is described as "contracted to Amarillis." See also pp. 210 ("compact") and 211 ("contract").

21. In *The Dialogic Imagination*, ed. Michael Holquist and trans. Caryl Emerson (Austin, 1981), M.M. Bakhtin discusses the Greek "adventure novel of ordeal," in which "from the very beginning, the love between the hero and heroine is not subject to doubt; this loves remains *absolutely unchanged* throughout the entire novel" (89). Bakhtin remarks on the relevance of this "chronotope" to the seventeenth-century: "In the seventeenth century, the fates of nations, kingdoms and cultures were also drawn into this adventure-time of chance, gods and villains, a time with its own specific logic. This occurs in the earliest European historical

novels, for example in de Scudéry's *Artamène, or the Grand Cyrus*, in Lohenstein's *Arminius and Tusnelda* and in the historical novels of La Calprenède. Pervading these novels is a curious 'philosophy of history' that hands over the settling of historical destinies to an extratemporal hiatus that exists between two moments of a real time sequence" (96).

22. There is, of course, a gender dimension to this argument, for it is only the female protagonist whose yielding to a final kiss is described as "a willing No; an Act / mixt of Conquest and Compact" (Fanshawe, *Pastor Fido*, 209–10).

23. On "the law of the heart," see Terry Eagleton, *The Ideology of the Aesthetic* (Cambridge, Mass., 1990), chap. 2. Annabel Patterson, *Censorship and Interpretation* (Madison, Wis., 1984), 174–76, also discusses the relevance of Fanshawe's translation to the events of the civil war, although she does not comment on the narrative strategy of Guarini's text or the issues of coercion and consent. See also Potter, *Secret Rites*, 85–90.

24. Patterson, *Censorship and Interpretation*, 184. Patterson describes the characteristics of Heliodoran romance as "the survival of chaste and faithful love in the face of all odds; wild adventures and coincidences in an uncivilized environment, where piracy and shipwreck symbolized human and natural anarchy; and a significant difference from chivalric romance, with its casual adulteries and elaborate rituals" (163), noting that this kind of romance could of course be combined with other strains of romance.

25. As Potter has suggested in *Secret Rites*, during the civil war Charles I and his son were themselves romance or tragicomic heroes to their supporters. In fact, "the two Charleses acted out virtually every role available to a ruler in romance or drama: the disguised lover, the husband parted from his wife/kingdom, the loving father of his country, the sacrificial victim, the wandering prince" (107). This romance vocabulary persisted: the Boscobel tracts, which recounted the escape of Charles II to Holland after the Battle of Worcester, describe the events in romance terms as "a history of Wonders," and praise God for contriving such "a Miracle"; see *Boscobel: or The History of His Sacred Majesties Most Miraculous Preservation after the Battle of Worcester 3 Sept. 1651* (London, 1660), "To the Reader."

26. I discuss the royalist romances of Herbert and Sales in chapter 9. For a discussion of the greater realism of character in French romance and its relation to what I have been calling casuistical debate, see Nigel Smith, *Literature and Revolution in England, 1640–1660* (New Haven, 1994), 241–46. esp. 243: "Like the confession of experience or spiritual autobiography, action is described retrospectively, and is that which leads up to the moments of stasis when debate and decision-making take place." For the "decidedly feminist impulse" of French romances, see Patterson, *Censorship and Interpretation*, 186–89.

27. Cavendish was not alone in attempting to reform romance from within: see Patterson, *Censorship and Interpretation*, on the critique of romance and arcadianism in prose romances of the 1650s and 1660s. William Cavendish's prefatory poem to *Natures Pictures* also calls attention to Margaret's reformation of romance: "Gallants and ladies, what do ye lack? pray buy. / Tales à la mode, new fashioned here do lie, / So do romancies . . . / . . . / But these are innocent" (quoted in Grant, *Margaret the First*, 152–53).

28. See Paul Salzman, *English Prose Fiction, 1558–1700* (Oxford, 1984), 240, on the opposition between English prose romances and the Hobbesian picaresque of power seeking after power. In *Politics and Ideas in Early Stuart England* (London, 1989), Kevin Sharpe echoes Salzman, arguing that "the rogue tradition and the anti-romance were the mode of a new society of commerce, interest and experimental science and philosophy" (264). Much of Cavendish's work complicates this distinction because it uses romance to rehabilitate romance as a genre capable of addressing the new society of commerce, interest, and so on. See Michael McKeon, *The Origins of the English Novel, 1600–1700* (Baltimore, 1987), who discusses Viktor Shklovsky's notion of defamiliarization as a paradigm for the dialectical development of genre (12). Cavendish's parody of romance is a perfect example of such generic critique and revision.

29. Cavendish, *The Contract*, 9. For Jonson's strictures about the spectacular component of the masque, see his preface to *Hymenaei* in Ben Jonson, *Selected Masques*, ed. Stephen Orgel (New Haven, 1970). William Cavendish was a patron of Jonson in the 1630s. See Anne Barton, "Harking Back to Elizabeth: Ben Jonson and Caroline Nostalgia," *ELH* 48 (1981): 706–31; and Timothy Raylor, " 'Pleasure Reconciled to Virtue': William Cavendish and the Decorative Scheme of Bolsover Castle," *Renaissance Quarterly* 52 (1999): 402–39.

30. The author continues, "I have had a care likewise to deal in such sort, as the faults, which great ones have committed in my History, should be caused either by love, or by ambition, which are the noblest of passions, and that they be imputed to the evill counsell of flatterers; that so the respect, which is alwaies due to Kings, may be preserved." See Madeleine de Scudéry, "The Preface," to *Ibrahim*, trans. Henry Cogan (London, 1652).

31. See Cavendish, *The Contract*, 19–20 (a discrete and sober man), 20 (force, consent to marry), 22 (like a prisoner), 23 (bound in gratitude).

32. See ibid., 24–25. While the lady declares that when she is married she will be obedient to her husband (22), love in these scenes licenses disobedience, specifically disobedience to her uncle's rules for her conduct.

33. See ibid., 28 (never come near me more), 29 (traitor to gratitude), 29 (you cannot want an owner). In the story of the "She-Ancoret" in *Natures Pictures drawn by Fancies Pencil to the Life* (London, 1656), the question is posed "Whether it were lawful for a King to lay down his Scepter and Crown?" The She-Ancoret responds, "Princes that voluntarily lay down their Royal Dignity, do either express some infirmity in Power, or weakness of Understanding, or imperfect Health of Body, or Effeminacy of Spirits, or doting Affection, or Vainglory. . . . neither the Laws of Honour or Religion allow it; nor can I perceive Morality approves it" (634–35).

34. Cavendish, *The Contract*, 31. On the maxim "interest will not lie," see Albert O. Hirschman, *The Passions and the Interests* (Princeton, 1977), esp. 50. Not only does the viceroy break off his wooing of the lady; he then proceeds to woo the duke's own wife (33).

35. On this fear, see Potter, *Secret Rites*, 108.

36. Cavendish, *The Contract*, 37.

37. On Chariclea, see Cave, *Recognitions*, 17–22.

38.   Canon law would have upheld the validity of the duke's current marriage, which had already been consummated, rather than the *de futuro* spousal contract of a minor which, as Swinburne argues, is not binding without the adult consent of both parties.

39.   Cavendish, *The Contract*, 39 (a promise), 40 (where right is not), 40 (he cannot be free).

40.   Ibid., 41.

41.   Ibid., 42 (sought pleasure), 43 (excuse the faults), 43 (willingly submits).

42.   On Henry Parker, see my discussion in chapter 4. In *The Matter of Revolution* (Ithaca, 1996), John Rogers makes a related argument about the political implications of Cavendish's shift from the scientific theory of Hobbesian, mechanist atomism to vitalism: "[T]he philosopher . . . who holds this view of self-moving matter, frees herself from a resignation to the physics—and the corollary masculinist ethics—of the rule of force." Instead, vitalism allows for an emphasis on consent, which draws near to what Rogers calls protoliberal political principles and to what I have been describing as parliamentary principles. Elsewhere Rogers refers to the "anti-authoritarian, republican structure of [Cavendish's] vitalist philosophy." See also Marina Leslie, "Evading Rape and Embracing Empire in Margaret Cavendish's *Assaulted and Pursued Chastity*," in *Menacing Virgins: Representing Virginity in the Middle Ages and Renaissance*, ed. Kathleen Coyne Kelly and Marina Leslie (Newark, Del., 2001), 179–97, who discusses the political implications of *Assaulted* and comes to conclusions similar in some respects to my own.

43.   For the history of arguments about chastity, see Leslie, "Evading Rape and Embracing Empire." Grotius mentions Chariclea in *De jure belli ac pacis*, 2.1.7.

44.   Cavendish, *Assaulted and Pursued Chastity*, in *The Description of the New Blazing World and Other Writings*, ed. Kate Lilley (New York, 1992), 52; this is typical of Cavendish's syntax.

45   Cavendish, *The Contract*, 87. On "sex-right" and Filmer, see Pateman, *The Sexual Contract*, chap. 4.

46.   Cavendish, *Assaulted*, 69 (common people were slaves), 79 (grant liberty to their slaves), 88–90, 92, 95 (prisoner of war vs. slave), 104–6 (love and voluntary subjection).

47.   The counselor's politic advice also has relevance to the queen, who is suffering from unrequited love and addresses a poem to the gods about the power of feigning for better and worse: "Must all your Works consist in contradiction? / Or do we nothing enjoy but Fiction? / The Mind is nothing but Apprehension, / 'Tis not a Thing, unless it hath Dimension. / But O you powerful Gods, by your Decree, / Can of Nothing a Something make to be: / Then make me Something, grant me my Delight, / Give me my lover, or destroy me quite" (*Assaulted*, 102–3). William Cavendish's advice to the young Charles II is available in a modern edition: *Ideology and Politics on the Eve of the Restoration: Newcastle's Advice to Charles II*, ed. Thomas P. Slaughter (Philadelphia, 1984).

48.   In "Evading Rape and Embracing Empire," Leslie discusses Cavendish's attempts to reconcile the narratives of political restoration and female emancipation.

49. Most political theorists of the sixteenth and seventeenth centuries believed that "a queen could be subject to her husband in relation to marriage and the family, [while] being 'superior in relation to political government.' " On the issue of queens regnant as wives, see Margaret R. Sommerville, *Sex and Subjection*, 57–59, 174, 212, 220; here 59.

50. On the social construction of gender in *Assaulted and Pursued Chastity*, see Kathryn Schwarz, "Chastity, Militant and Married: Cavendish's Romance, Milton's Masque," *PMLA* 118 (2003): 270–85, esp. 280–82.

51. Cave, *Recognitions*, 46.

52. On these two interpretations of the contract of genre and social contract, see my discussion in chapter 1 and Christopher Prendergast, *The Order of Mimesis*, 49–50, and chap. 7.

53. On the prominence of tragicomedy in royalist literature of the 1650s, see Potter, *Secret Rites*, who describes it as "the dramatic manifestation of romance"; and Smith, *Literature and Revolution*, 76–87. The genres of romance and tragicomedy were often linked in the sixteenth and seventeenth centuries.

54. On Cavendish's imagining herself as a sovereign, see Catherine Gallagher, "Embracing the Absolute: The Politics of the Female Subject in Seventeenth-Century England," *Genre* 1 (1988): 24–39. Gallagher argues that "much in Cavendish's texts suggests that the absolutist desire, the desire to be the sovereign monarch, itself derives from a certain female disability: not from her inability to be a monarch but from her inability to be a full *subject* of the monarch. Of the two available political positions, subject and monarch, monarch is the only one Cavendish can imagine a woman occupying" (27).

55. *The Contract*, 22 (power, authority, and commands), 29 (unheard of malice). In this respect, *The Contract* conforms to the formal characteristics Patricia Parker has ascribed to romance in *Inescapable Romance* (Princeton, 1979). On the advantage to women of prolonging the negotiations of the spousal contract, see Susan B. Iwanisziw, "The Place of Women in Early Modern English Closet Drama" (Ph.D. diss., University of Pennsylvania, 1994), who argues that the "liminal state of 'espousal' . . . conferred a certain sexual agency upon women along with the property rights of an unmarried woman. And it is this matrix of sexual agency, material properties and legal rights that creates the romantic plots of early modern English pastoral tragicomedies" (248).

56. Sheldon Wolin, *Hobbes and the Epic Tradition of Political Theory* (Berkeley, 1970), 22. Epic, in Wolin's characterization, involves elements of romance: he notes the "uneasy tension" between Hobbes's heroic impulse, which defines "a hostile world" in "epical terms," and "a scientific impulse which required that mystery and romance be dropped out of the world so that ratiocination and utility could be made the main business" (32).

57. In *The Life of William Cavenish*, Margaret Cavendish portrays her husband as a gentleman and soldier, one whose devotion to Charles I and Charles II was uncontaminated by considerations of personal self-interest: "He never minded his own interest more than his loyalty and duty, and upon that account never desired nor received anything from the Crown to enrich himself, but spent great sums in his Majesty's service. . . . He never repined at his losses and suffer-

ings, because he lost and suffered for his King and country." The duke's old-fashioned values of honor and loyalty in the midst of the civil war are explicitly contrasted to those who have "politic designs," which "tend more to interest than justice" (93, 129).

58. As Hume was to write some eighty years later in his essay, "Of the original contract," any acquiescence or consent that is truly voluntary is also, precisely for that reason, precarious. See *Essays, Moral, Political, and Literary*, ed. Eugene F. Miller (Indianapolis, 1987), 465–87. I return to Hume in the conclusion.

59. Smith, *Literature and Revolution*, 235, makes this point about Hobbes's fear and the accuracy of his insight into the fictional dimension of politics.

CHAPTER 8
EMBODIMENT

1. See *CD*, 1.10, p. 351. On Milton and covenant theology, see John T. Shaw-cross, "Milton and Covenant: The Christian View of Old Testament Theology," in *Milton and Scriptural Tradition*, ed. James H. Sims and Leland Ryken (Columbia, Mo., 1984), 160–91; Joseph E. Duncan, *Milton's Earthly Paradise* (Minneapolis, 1972), esp. 132–48.

2. *CD*, 1.10, pp. 352, 353; 1.11, p. 384; *PL*, 10.751, and 759. On Milton's commonplace view of the prohibition as "conditional," and as "an unwritten, embryonic Mosaic law," see Jason P. Rosenblatt, "Milton's Chief Rabbi," *Milton Studies* 24 (1988): 62–63. Rosenblatt further argues that Milton adopts Selden's conflation of Edenic, Mosaic, and natural laws, according to which natural laws oblige because they are God's command. But Milton is not as skeptical of the powers of reason as Selden: in *CD* he distinguishes between the natural law of reason in Eden and the divine prohibition as command.

3. Milton follows Selden in seeing marriage as a civil contract. See *CPW*, 7:299, and Rosenblatt, "Milton's Chief Rabbi," esp. 47–48.

4. On the political context of the Divorce Tracts, and the influence of Parker et al., see Arthur Barker's *Milton and the Puritan Dilemma* (Toronto, 1942), 63–120; William Haller, *Milton and the Puritan Dilemma* (New York, 1955), chap. 3; and Ernest Sirluck, introduction to *CPW*, vol. 2 (New Haven, 1959).

5. Writing in response to the Presbyterian Herbert Palmer's criticism of *The Doctrine*, Milton noted that he could have drawn his arguments for the natural law principle of revoking one's consent and for the greater liberty of the New Testament in comparison with the Old from Palmer's own *Scripture and Reason Pleaded for Defensive Armes* (1643). See Sirluck, *CPW*, 2:47, 49, 152–53; and Milton, "To the Parliament" (preface to *Tetrachordon*), in *CPW*, 2:582.

A number of scholars have located a crucial shift in Milton's thinking about natural law in the Divorce Tracts, especially *Tetrachordon*. Sirluck argued for the revolutionary implications of Milton's distinction—"borrowed from parliamentary apologetics"—between primary (prelapsarian) natural law and secondary (postlapsarian) natural law. In fact, this distinction could be found in earlier writers, but Sirluck's point is that it was put to new uses in the 1640s. In particular, according to Sirluck, Milton used this distinction "to prevent Christians from being held to a higher moral duty than that imposed by [secondary] natural law," the law of necessity or self-preservation (157, 132). On the revolutionary reinterpretation of natural law in parliamentary pamphlets, see also Sirluck, 52, 130–35. On the shift in Milton's hermeneutics, see Dayton Haskin, *Milton's Burden of Interpretation* (Philadelphia, 1994). In *Milton and the Puritan Dilemma*, Barker anticipated the arguments of Sirluck and Haskin but with a slightly different emphasis. For Barker, what was most revolutionary about Milton's argument in the Divorce Tracts, especially *Tetrachordon*, was the claim that, after the fall, the primary law of nature was rewritten on the hearts of good men, who could then judge according to their own reason what was permitted by divine and natural law (114–17, 169). In "Christian Liberty in Milton's Divorce Pamphlets" *MLR* 35 (1940): 153–61, Barker argued that in the second edition of *The Doctrine* and *Tetrachordon*, we see Milton making his way toward the view of *Christian Doctrine* that "the law in the heart is conscience, and conscience alone in a Christian governs the will" (160). I agree with Barker that Milton effectively conflates the secondary law of nature with the primary law written on the hearts of good men, and thus the law with the gospel.

    6. See *The Doctrine*, *CPW*, 2:343, on "the tyranny of usurpt opinions."

    7. Hobbes, *Elements*, Epistle dedicatory.

    8. Annabel Patterson has discussed the contradictory logic of *The Doctrine* in narrative and biographical terms, delineating a "grammar of self-division" in Milton's shifting portrayal of himself as both heroic warrior and abandoned husband, active and passive. See her "No Meer Amatorious Novel?" in *John Milton*, ed. Patterson (London and New York, 1992), esp. 95. But whereas Patterson emphasizes the plot of frustration in *The Doctrine*—"When we get what we thought we wanted we no longer want it. . . . *The Doctrine and Discipline of Divorce* is . . . a special case of the renunciative novel" (100)—I would like to stress the positive vision behind this renunciation or divorce. For a compatible positive interpretation of the labor of interpretation in *The Doctrine*, see also Haskin, *Milton's Burden of Interpretation*, chap. 3.

    9. See Barker, *Milton and the Puritan Dilemma*, on Milton's reading of Ames (17 and 367, n97).

    10. Milton refers to Perkins in *The Doctrine*, *CPW*, 2:317 and 320, to Grotius on 238, 329, 335, 344, and Selden on 350.

    11. Like Grotius and Selden, Milton reconciles divine law and the secondary law of nature through the notion of God's permission. See *The Doctrine*, *CPW*, 2:354, on "permissive liberty."

    12. William Perkins, *A Discourse of Conscience*, in *William Perkins, 1558–1602*, ed. Thomas F. Merrill (Nieuwkoop, the Netherlands, 1966), 8 (conscience as notary), 10 (as magistrate or jailer), 32 (as judge).

    13. In *The Political Theory of Possessive Individualism* (Oxford, 1962), C. B. Macpherson argued Hobbes's and Locke's contract theory presupposes a protocapitalist notion of property in one's person. See Janel M. Mueller, "On Genesis in Genre: Milton's Politicizing of the Sonnet in 'Captain or Colonel,' " in *Renaissance Genres*, ed. Barbara Kiefer Lewalski (Cambridge, Mass., 1986), for a related argument regarding the "connection between liberty, political identity, and property [in] . . . Milton's political consciousness" (236).

    14. *The Doctrine*, *CPW*, 2:239, 240, 249, 270, 280, 326.

15. Christ's command concerning marriage "can be no new command, for the Gospel enjoyns no new morality, save only the infinit enlargement of charity. . . . Those commands therfore which compell us to self-cruelty above our strength, so hardly will help forward to perfection that they hinder & set backwards in all the common rudiments of Christianity" (*The Doctrine, CPW*, 2:330–31). See John Guillory, "Milton, Narcissism, Gender: On the Genealogy of Male Self-Esteem," in *Critical Essays on John Milton*, ed. Christopher Kendrick (New York, 1995), 194–233, on "the problem of legitimizing self-love, of negotiating its discursive relations to 'pride' and 'glory' in Milton and in the period in general" (220). For Nietzsche's remarks on self-cruelty and asceticism, see *The Genealogy of Morals*, in *The Birth of Tragedy and The Genealogy of Morals*, trans. Francis Golffing (Garden City, N.Y., 1965), esp. 2.22 and 23, pp. 225–28, and the Third Essay, devoted to ascetic ideals.

16. On the tie between contractualism and masculinism in the divorce tracts, see also Mary Nyquist, "The Genesis of Gendered Subjectivity in the Divorce Tracts and in *Paradise Lost*," in *Re-membering Milton*, ed. Mary Nyquist and Margaret W. Ferguson (New York and London, 1987), 99–127, esp. 114, 124. For a helpful discussion of the concept of intention and the role of woman as dangerous supplements to Milton's argument in *The Doctrine*, see Stanley Fish, "Wanting a Supplement: The Question of Interpretation in Milton's Early Prose," in *Politics, Poetics and Hermeneutics in Milton's Prose*, ed. David Loewenstein and James Grantham Turner (Cambridge, 1990), 41–83.

17. Ernest Sirluck calls this Milton's "axiom" in his introduction to *The Doctrine, CPW*, 2:147.

18. See *The Doctrine, CPW*, 2:276, for a similar ellipsis: "So every covnant between man and man, bound by oath, may be call'd the covnant of God, because God therin is attested. So of marriage he is the author and witnes." Milton's famous allegory of Eros and Anteros also suggests that the marriage contract is between men (2:254–55); on this passage, see Patterson, "No Meer Amatorious Novel," 97.

19. Samuel Pufendorf, *De jure naturae et gentium*, trans. C. H. Oldfather and W. A. Oldfather (Oxford, 1934), 6.1.24. In *The Reformation of the Subject: Spenser, Milton, and the English Protestant Epic* (Cambridge, 1995), Linda Gregerson discusses the homoerotic dimension of Milton's patriarchalism in *Paradise Lost* (173–74).

20. See Guillory, "Milton, Narcissism, Gender," on the disappearance of the body in male self-esteem, which is analogous to the disappearance of sex—or the degrading of it in favor of the intellectual activity of interpretation—in *The Doctrine*; and Annabel Patterson, "No Meer Amatorious Novel," esp. 97, on Milton's ambivalence about heterosexual sex in *The Doctrine*.

21. Terry Eagleton, *The Ideology of the Aesthetic* (Oxford, 1990), 19. I return to this passage in chapter 11. See G.W.F. Hegel, *The Philosophy of History*, trans. J. Sibree (New York, 1956), on the Reformation: "Man himself has a conscience; consequently the subjection required of him is a free allegiance" (423). Here we see that it is not the economic contract that is central to Milton's conception of the husband's self-realization in marriage but the theological covenant: whereas

the former is based on alienable property in oneself, the latter anticipates what Eagleton has called aesthetic ideology.

22. For a related insight into Satan's dilemma, though without reference to the language of contract, see Marshall Grossman, *"Authors to Themselves": Milton and the Revelation of History* (Cambridge, 1987), 35: "God supplies the context of all actions by creating the universe." Satan rejects this context and "By denying divine creation, he, in effect, challenges the medium of discourse." "Under the metaphors of discourse and authorship that control the presentation of subjectivity in *Paradise Lost*, Satan is a monologuist, who attempts self-affirmation by negating the very language in which the self is constituted" (35).

23. See *Paradise Lost*: "the sole Command, / Sole pledge of his obedience" (3.94–95); "But of the Tree whose operation brings / Knowledge of good and ill, which I have set / The Pledge of thy Obedience and thy Faith" (8.323–25); "The only sign of our obedience left" (4.428). I discuss the prohibition as a sign in "Allegory and the Sublime in *Paradise Lost*," in *Milton*, ed. Annabel Patterson (London and New York, 1992), 185–201.

24. In *The Reformation of the Subject*, Gregerson makes a related point when she reads Milton's meditation on likeness in the context of English Reformation iconoclasm, as well as in the context of Lacanian psychoanalysis. She explores the development of the self through "specular recognition scenes" (6), the education of subject through process of construing likeness, and revision of likeness. She does not, however, discuss the subject of contract.

25. William Perkins, *Epieikeia: or a Treatise of Christian Equity and Moderation* in *The Works of William Perkins*, ed. Ian Breward (Appleford, England, 1970), 503. Cf. *PL*, 10.771–73, Adam: "why delays / His hand to execute what his Decree / Fix'd on this day?" On narrative dilation, see Patricia Parker, *Inescapable Romance* (Princeton, 1979); "The Metaphorical Plot," in *Literary Fat Ladies* (New York, 1986, 36–53); "Dilation and Delay: Renaissance Matrices," *Poetics Today* 5 (1984): 519–35; and "Shakespeare and Rhetoric: 'Dilation' and 'Delation' in *Othello*," in *Shakespeare and the Question of Theory*, ed. Patricia Parker and Geoffrey Hartman (London, 1985), 54–84.

26. On narrative and rationality, see Paul Ricoeur, "Mimesis and Representation," *Annals of Scholarship* 1 (1981): 15–32; "On Interpretation," in *Philosophy in France Today*, ed. Alan Montefiore (Cambridge, 1983), 175–97. See also Christopher Prendergast, *The Order of Mimesis* (Cambridge, 1986), 233.

27. On Eve voluntarily submitting to Adam as the submission of desire to paternal law, see Nyquist, "The Genesis of Gendered Subjectivity," 99–127, esp. 122–23. See also Janet E. Halley, "Female Autonomy in Milton's Sexual Poetics," in *Milton and the Idea of Woman*, ed. Julia Walker (Champaign, Ill., 1988), 230–53, reprinted in the Norton edition of *Paradise Lost*, ed. Scott Elledge (New York, 1993), 661–74; and John Rogers, *The Matter of Revolution* (Ithaca, 1996), 208–9.

28. William Gouge, *Domesticall Duties* (London, 1622), 25–26, 269–70. I discuss Gouge in " 'The Duty to Love': Passion and Obligation in Early Modern Political Theory," *Representations* 68 (1999): 83–107.

29. Dudley Fenner, *Artes of Logike and Rethorike* (Middleburg, 1584); cited by Patricia Parker, *Literary Fat Ladies* (New York, 1987), 108. As Parker points

out, Fenner was drawing on Cicero, *De oratore*, 3.41.165. On metaphor as the rhetorical equivalent of recognition, see Terence Cave, *Recognitions: A Study in Poetics* (Oxford, 1988), 48–49 (discussing Ricoeur, Frye, and Parker). According to Cave, the structure of metaphor parallels the structure of plot: metaphor is "a linguistic mode of disguise or temporary deception leading to the revelation (recognition?) of *likeness amid difference*" (emphasis added).

30. For related arguments, see Carole Pateman, *The Sexual Contract* (Stanford, 1988); Nyquist, "The Genesis of Gendered Subjectivity," 114, 124. For other helpful readings of the gender dimension of Miltonic subjectivity, see Guillory, "Milton, Narcissism, Gender"; and Gregerson, *The Reformation of the Subject*, who argues that the postlapsarian subject is female.

31. Whereas Gouge and other writers of manuals of "domesticall duties" insisted that husbands did not need to be instructed in self-love or the desire to govern but did need to be urged to love their wives, Milton portrays Adam as loving Eve to excess and failing to govern, despite her lesser likeness to God.

32. See James Turner, *One Flesh: Paradisal Marriage and Sexual Relations in the Age of Milton* (Oxford, 1987), on Adam's crude anthropomorphism (276).

33. The *Oxford English Dictionary* tells us "approve" could mean demonstrate or assent to as good. In support of the first meaning, it cites Hobbes, *Leviathan*, chap. 5: "We demonstrate or approve our reckonings to other men." "Approved" in the sense of "pronounced good; justified, sanctioned, commended, esteemed," is illustrated by a quotation from *Paradise Lost*: "To stand approv'd in sight of God" (6.36).

34. Michael Walzer, *The Revolution of the Saints* (Cambridge, Mass., 1965), 194–95.

35. See Terence Cave, *Recognitions*, on Castelvetro and Denores (69–70). In chapter 5, Cave contrasts the conventional family plot of Aristotelian recognition to "the plot of the psyche." In the former, "the recovery of identity is primarily the restitution of an authorized set of family, social, and perhaps also political relations." In the plot of the psyche, by contrast, priority is given to the individual, to internalized self-recognition and the recognition of moral truth (229). On romance in *Paradise Lost*, see, among others, Parker, *Inescapable Romance*; David Quint, *Epic and Empire* (New Haven, 1993); and, especially, Colin Burrow, *Epic Romance* (Oxford, 1993).

36. *Areopagitica*, in *CPW*, 2:527.

37. See Tony Tanner, *Adultery in the Novel: Contract and Transgression* (Baltimore and London, 1978), chap. 1.

38. We may even detect an anticipation of Adam's plaintive, even resentful reply to God: "thy terms too hard" (10.751).

39. See William Empson, *Milton's God* (London, 1965), 75; Mary Ann Radzinowicz, "The Politics of *Paradise Lost*," in *Politics of Discourse*, ed. Kevin Sharpe and Steven Zwicker (Berkeley, 1987), 204–29, commenting in part on *PL*, 3.341: "God shall be All in All." More recently, in *The Matter of Revolution*, Rogers has argued that materialist vitalism and, with it, a decentralized proto-liberal cosmos and divinity, is at odds with Hobbesian mechanism and a personal, absolute God in *Paradise Lost* (see, e.g., 113). According to Rogers, Milton briefly entertains the possibility that creation contains an element of inert, recalcitrant

matter (130–43; *PL*, 2, on chaos, and 7.233–41, on "dregs"). Ultimately, however, Rogers sees Milton's materialist vitalism as a defense of agency, as against Hobbesian mechanism. I argue later that the agency of the contracting subject is in tension with material embodiment throughout *Paradise Lost*, that Milton focuses on embodiment as a limit as well as a condition of human agency.

40. Cf. Cave, *Recognitions*, chap. 2, on Renaissance interpretations of Aristotelian pity and fear as the characters' as well as the audience's.

41. See Burrow, *Epic Romance*, 285. My reading takes issue with Guillory, "Milton, Narcissism, and Gender," who argues that the difference between Eve's fall and Adam's is that the first is shadowed by psychological determinism, while the second is characterized by ethical voluntarism, and this is typical of the gender system of the poem as a whole (226). While there is some truth to this distinction, I believe Milton deliberately complicates it, giving Eve the heroic role and Adam the feminized bond of nature and the passion of pity.

42. *Areopagitica*, in *CPW*, 2:527.

43. If Eve demonstrates the antinomy of coercion and consent, and the contribution of the passions and the imagination to a Hobbesian restless seeking after power, Adam demonstrates the coexistence of coercion and consent, which is to say the contribution of the passions and the imagination to the human experience of obligation.

44. This argument is complicated by Eve's contrition and sympathy after the fall, in contrast to Adam's recriminations. On Eve and sympathy, see Kevis Goodman, " 'Wasted Labor?' Milton's Eve, the Poet's Work, and the Challenge of Sympathy," *ELH* 64 (1997): 415–46.

45. My formulation echoes and deliberately alters Grotius's "etiamsi daremus": even if we were to concede that God did not exist, there would still be natural rights and natural law. See chapter 2.

CHAPTER 9
SYMPATHY

1. *His Majesties Most Gracious Speech, Together with the Lord Chancellors, to the Two Houses of Parliament; On Thursday the 13 of September, 1660* (London, 1660), 11–12; quoted in Andrew Shifflett, *Stoicism, Politics, and Literature in the Age of Milton* (Cambridge, 1998), 97.

2. Percy Herbert, *Certaine Conceptions, or Considerations . . . upon the Strange change of Peoples, Dispositions and Actions in these latter times* (London, 1650), 78, 79.

3. Ibid., 80, 250.

4. Ibid., 115–19 (bonds of trust), 148–59 (breach of contract).

5. Ibid., 148–59 (breach of contract), 162 (interest and commodity), 170 (romance), 252 (subjecting one's will).

6. Of course, royalists were not the only ones concerned to analyze the causes of the civil war in the 1650s. For a brief survey of commonwealth historiography, see Lois Potter's introduction to Francis Osborne, *The True Tragicomedy formerly Acted at Court* (New York, 1983). Potter discusses the shared royalist and parliamentarian "concern to explain the downfall of the House of Stuart" by

reference to James's prodigality, which in turn gave rise to Charles's forced loans (xxv, xxxiii).

7. On the theme of consolation in royalist literature of the 1650s, see Derek Hirst, "The Politics of Literature in the English Republic," *Seventeenth Century* 5 (1990): 137–38. Hirst's main point, which I agree with, is that royalist literature in this period was not so much withdrawn as polemical and politically engaged, and that "the components of the nation's literary culture became the subject of angry argument" (136).

8. *Cloria* and *Theophania* were published anonymously; Brathwaite used the pseudonym of Castalion Pomerano. Brathwaite was a poet who was known for his pastoral romances in verse and prose, as well for *The English Gentleman* (1630, 1641, 1652) and *The English Gentlewoman* (1631, 1641). The *Dictionary of National Biography* tells us he "is said to have served on the royalist side in the civil war" (*DNB*, s.v. Brathwaite, Richard, 1142). Unlike Herbert and Brathwaite, Sales seems to be a pseudonym. The authorship is contested, but at least one critic has speculated that *Theophania* was written by Edward Hyde, later earl of Clarendon. See A. H. Shearer, "*Theophania*: An English Political Romance of the Seventeenth Century," *Modern Language Notes* 31 (1916): 74. The secondary literature on these romances is slight. On *Cloria* and *Panthalia*, see Annabel Patterson, *Censorship and Interpretation* (Madison, Wis., 1984), chap. 4. See also Benjamin Boyce, "History and Fiction in *Panthalia: or the Royal Romance*," *JEGP* 57 (1958): 477–89; Nigel Smith, *Literature and Revolution, 1640–1660* (New Haven, 1994), 233–50; Paul Salzman, *English Prose Fiction, 1558–1700* (Oxford, 1985), chap. 11; and the introduction to Paul Salzman, *An Anthology of Seventeenth-Century Fiction* (Oxford, 1991). For the criticism of arcadianism, see in addition to Patterson, Salzman, and Smith, Lois Potter, *Secret Rites and Secret Writing: Royalist Literature, 1641–1660* (Cambridge, 1989), esp. chap. 3.

9. The foregoing summarizes the lucid argument of Earl R. Wasserman, "The Pleasures of Tragedy," *ELH* 14 (1947): 283–307; the quote appears on p. 288. See also Baxter Hathaway, "The Lucretian 'Return upon Ouselves,'" *PMLA* 62 (1947): 672–80; and Eric Rothstein, "English Tragic Theory in the Late Seventeenth Century," *ELH* 29 (1962): 306–23.

10. I discuss the difference between these two emotional responses later in the chapter.

11. There are, of course, other reasons why prose romance of the 1650s looks the way it does, including intrageneric influences such as Sidney's *Arcadia*, Barclay's *Argenis*, French romance, and Heliodorus (whom I discuss later). In *Sir Philip Sidney: Rebellion in Arcadia* (New Brunswick, N.J., 1979), Richard McCoy discusses the influence of Sidney on critics of Charles I, as does Dennis Kay in his preface to *Sir Philip Sidney: An Anthology of Modern Criticism* (Oxford, 1987). But Sidney's reputation and work were also appropriated by royalists in the 1650s, including not only the authors of *Cloria*, *Panthalia*, and *Theophania*, but also, for example, Thomas Blount in his *Academie of Eloquence* (1654); see Hirst, "Politics of Literature," 143–44. For the circulation of manuscripts of the *Arcadia* prior to the civil war, see H. R. Woudhuysen, *Sir Philip Sidney and the Circulation of Manuscripts, 1558–1640* (Oxford, 1996). On the Hobbesian and Machiavellian elements of Sidney's political analysis in the different versions of

the *Arcadia*, see Maurice Evans's introduction to Sidney's *The Countess of Pembroke's Arcadia* (London, 1977), 27–40. For a fuller analysis of the politics of *Arcadia*, see Blair Worden, *The Sound of Virtue: Philip Sidney and Elizabethan Politics* (New Haven, 1996). On Barclay, see Amelia Sandy, "Secret Agents: Politic Ideology and Jacobean Romance" (Ph.D. diss., Princeton, 1997).

12. Leo Strauss, *The Political Philosophy of Hobbes* (1936; Chicago, 1963), 161, n2.

13. The phrase is taken from Hugh Trevor-Roper, "The General Crisis of the Seventeenth Century," in *Crisis in Europe, 1560–1660*, ed. Trevor Aston (New York, 1965), 93.

14. Hirst, "Politics of Literature," 147 (statecraft), 149 (delegitimation). It is in this context that Hirst takes issue with Annabel Patterson's influential account of royalist romance: "Might we not read the proliferation of romances in the 1650s not . . . as testimony to the effectiveness of censorship but as political prescription, when in the minds of many, force rather than nobility and virtue appeared to dominate the body politic?" (148).

15. I am thinking in particular of Albert Hirschman's important argument. I return to Hirschman in the conclusion to this chapter.

16. [Percy Herbert], *The Princess Cloria: or, The Royal Romance* (London, 1661), Cloria and Roxana (202); Creses (203). Creses goes on: "All smart, grief, and discontents, is encreased by want of action and too much leasure for consideration; so, I must conclude, that it is a great deal easier for a person to dye fighting in the Field, though he should be cut assunder in a thousand pieces, then to endure a long and tedious captivity, which is *Euarchus* present condition" (203). In a later conversation, a chaplain urges the imprisoned Charles to display his "heroical virtues . . . by a majestick patience in your outward sufferings."

17. Ibid., 346.

18. Ibid., 392 (Arethusius), 204 (Creses).

19. Ibid., 73, 74. For further discussion of the legitimacy of politic dissimulation, see, e.g., 390–91.

20. Ibid., 59.

21. Ibid., 62 (Osiris), 507 (Creses).

22. Ibid., 334.

23. Ibid., 140 (affection stronger than interest), 551–52 (people of Lydia), and 542 (desperate passions). On the distemper of the passions, see also, e.g., 13, 28, 106, 189, 499, 423.

24. Ibid., 500–501. For other recommendations of wise compliance, see 230, 373.

25. Patterson, *Censorship and Interpretation*, sees the recommendation of compliance as a contribution to the engagement controversy (195). On neo-Stoic constancy, see Gordon Braden, *Renaissance Tragedy and the Senecan Tradition: Anger's Privilege* (New Haven, 1985); Shifflett, *Stoicism, Politics, and Literature in the Age of Milton*; and Reid Barbour, *English Epicures and Stoics* (Amherst, 1998). Braden comments on the way the Stoic's display of virtue may paradoxically manifest itself as theatricality. In contrast, wise compliance suggests that constancy can itself be feigned for political ends. Here constancy draws near to a kind of Tacitean or Machiavellian shrewdness. Lipsius's *De constantia* and *Politi-*

corum . . . libri sex (both of which were translated into English in the seventeenth century) were important vehicles of these Tacitean and Machiavellian insights.

26. See Cicero, *De officiis*, 2.6.22–2.7.23: "But, of all motives, none is better adapted to secure influence and hold it fast than love; nothing is more foreign to that end than fear. For Ennius says admirably: 'Whom they fear they hate. And whom one hates, one hopes to see him dead.' " Alluding to the recent assassination of Julius Caesar, Cicero drew the obvious political moral: "[F]ear is but a poor safeguard of lasting power; while affection [benevolentia], on the other hand, may be trusted to keep it safe for ever."

27. Herbert, *Cloria*, 608, 601.

28. See ibid., 82, 191ff., on the balancing of royal prerogative and the subject's freedom. It is significant in this regard that the subtitle of the 1661 edition refers to the romance's "Political Notions, and singular Remarks of Modern Transactions," for transactions in this period meant negotiations, business dealings, agreements, or covenants.

29. See ibid., 445, where Charles II/Arethusius "hoped the instability of things, would of necessity at last bring him to his Rights." As Salzman, "*Cloria*," points out, Charles II does not regain his throne by military virtue but by means of romance contingency (243).

30. See John J. Winkler, "The Mendacity of Kalasiris and the Narrative Strategy of Heliodorus' *Aithiopika*," *Yale Classical Studies* 27 (1982): 93–158. Winkler observes, "Reflections such as these on the crazy-quilt of Life and whether a friendly designer or a brute force is behind it have the value of self-advertizements for the author, since the novelist will be most successful on his own terms if we regard his story as one of impossible odds and plausible resolutions, that is an elegant mediation between the hopelessness of a world governed by malevolent or indifferent tyche and the confidence of a world mysteriously orchestrated by providence" (126). See also 152–54, on the providential conclusion of the plot. Heliodorus was well known in the early modern period. Even taking this into account, the similarities between the two texts are remarkable. Winkler's entire discussion provides an uncanny analysis of the narrative strategies of *Cloria*.

On the influence of Heliodorus in the early modern period, see Alban K. Forcione, *Cervantes, Aristotle, and the "Persiles"* (Princeton, 1970), 49–87; Merritt Y. Hughes, "Spenser's Debt to the Greek Romances," *Modern Philology* 23 (1925–26): 67–76; Margaret Doody, *The True Story of the Novel* (New Brunswick, N.J., 1996), chaps. 10–11.

31. Winkler, "The Mendacity of Kalasiris," 152.

32. The mediating term is, of course, craft which can signify craftiness or artifice/artfulness.

33. Interestingly, the author of the preface expresses doubt concerning the aesthetic appeal of *Cloria*'s digressions in a time of political upheaval. Ordinarily, "the many Descriptions of Countreys, Places, and Triumphs" would satisfy the human desire for variety. But in the present crisis the author wonders "Whether the hair-brain'dness of the present world, will give leasure enough to most, to dwell upon any thing at all, much less to practise Heroical Vertues with such a constant settledness as is necessary, being the chief intention of the Authour (as I

conceive) in writing of this *Romance*." Here the author may be suggesting that the sheer length of the romance is well suited to "the hairbrain'dness of the present world": if romance doesn't speak to our passions, it will at least try our patience and so educate us to constancy and voluntary subjection.

34. Thus I strongly disagree with Smith, who argues in *Literature and Revolution* that Herbert's goal is "to make his reader experience a stoical expulsion of all emotions" (239).

35. Marchamont Nedham, *The Case of the Commonwealth of England Stated*, ed. Philip A. Knachel (Charlottesville, 1969); James I, *Trew Law of Free Monarchies*, in *Political Works of James I*, ed. Charles McIlwain (Cambridge, Mass., 1918).

36. *Cloria* thus does not conform to Potter's description of many post-regicide romances: "[T]he typical romance plot, in which elaborately intertwining intrigues are resolved by quasi-miraculous means, corresponds to a view of life which, of necessity, became that of many royalists after 1651" (*Secret Rites*, 109). Although "wise compliance" could be described as "a waiting policy" (ibid.), these romances also educate the reader to the need to create the Restoration.

37. Patterson, *Censorship and Interpretation*, also comments on the way the preface provides "a suggestive account . . . of the interpretive act, poised as it is in this genre between esthetic and political experience," but she links the "esthetic" dimension of *Cloria* with the semantic "indeterminacy" that results from the author's refusal to provide a key to the political allegory (196–97). As should already be clear, although I agree with many of Patterson's points, I do not see the aesthetic or the "artfully difficult" (Patterson, 197) dimension of *Cloria* or other, contemporary romances as a consequence of political censorship.

38. Smith, *Literature and Revolution*, 237.

39. *Panthalia* was composed when Richard Cromwell was still the head of government but published shortly after his abdication. The entry in the stationer's register shows it was first addressed to Parliament and only afterward fitted out with a postscript and frontispiece showing an image of Charles II. See Boyce, "History and Fiction in *Panthalia*," 478, n3.

40. In *Theatre and Crisis* (Cambridge, 1984) Martin Butler explores this nostalgia in English plays from the 1630s to 1641 (see esp. 195–205).

41. [Richard Brathwaite], *Panthalia: or the Royal Romance. A Discourse stored with infinite variety in relation to State-Government and Passages of matchless affection gracefully interveined, and presented on a Theatre of Tragical and Comical State, in a successive continuation to these times* (London, 1659), 23 (domestick love; emphasis added); 29 (causeless fears).

42. Ibid., 39 (tilts), 39–40 (Carpet-Knights), 43 (state service), 41 (Basilius), 37 (Ismenia).

43. Ibid., *Panthalia*, 88. See 103 on the connection between degenerate pursuit of pleasure and equally debased pursuit of self-interest on the part of Rosicles's "senatours."

44. Ibid., 86.

45. Ibid., 98.

46. Ibid., 99, 101.

47. Ibid., 101–2 (emphasis in the original).

48. Ibid., 112.

49. On this connection between the new market economy and the fear of clandestine marriage, see Lorna Hutson, *The Usurer's Daughter* (London, 1994).

50. Brathwaite, *Panthalia*, 176 (commodity), 177–78 (affections). *Acolastus* was the title of a neo-Latin play by Fullonius, which was translated by John Palsgrave in 1540 and used as school text.

51. Brathwaite, *Panthalia*, 180–81; see also 203 (conjugall tyranny), 205.

52. Ibid., 248 (Strafford), 181. According to Matthew Black, *Richard Brathwait* (Philadelphia, 1928), Strafford's family bestowed patronage on Brathwaite (87).

53. This is not noted in any of the secondary literature on *Panthalia* with which I am familiar. For Cicero's recommendations regarding the political uses of love, see note 26. In *The Prince*, Machiavelli had countered that it was much safer to be feared than loved (chap. 17). For a thorough history of the romance passion of pity in early modern romance and epic, see Colin Burrow, *Epic Romance* (Oxford, 1993). Burrow argues that after 1620 "many epic poems appear to abandon the civic concerns which had led Spenser to attempt to weld the opposing motives of love and honour into a single force, and turn to the internal regimen of the passions as the chief activity for the heroic mind" (147–48). See 237–38 on Cowley's positive association of pity with the royalist cause, and 274 on later seventeenth-century depictions of Charles II as a romance Aeneas, pitying his subjects and showing clemency.

54. Seneca, *De clementia*, 2.5.1. Seneca associates pity with effeminacy in this same passage: "And so it is most often seen in the poorest types of persons; there are old women and wretched females who are moved by the tears of the worst criminals, who, if they could, would break open their prison."

55. See the excellent discussion of clemency in Shifflett, *Stoicism, Politics, and Literature in the Age of Milton*, esp. 76–78, 95–100. Shifflett discusses the relevance of *De clementia* to discussions regarding the Act of Oblivion. See also Shifflett, " 'How Many Virtues Must I Hate': Katherine Philips and the Politics of Clemency," *Studies in Philology* 94 (1997): 103–35; and Barbour, *English Epicures and Stoics*, 166. In *Poetic and Legal Fiction* (Princeton, 1986), Kathy Eden argues for "the transmission of pity and fear into Christian poetic theory and practice indirectly through Christian ethics, rather than directly through the domination on Aristotle's authority of literary matters." But she stresses that this "points to an even more profound continuity in the Aristotelian tradition [of the similarities between poetic and legal fiction]. Even without the argument of the *Poetics*, fiction continues to share its peculiar psychology with the law and in particular with the relation between the Old and New Law" (156).

56. Brathwaite, *Panthalia*, 264 (State-Theatre), 251, 273–74. See Hobbes's comparison of individuals in the state of nature to mushrooms in *De cive*, 1.8.

57. Brathwaite, *Panthalia*, 296.

58. Patterson's comment on Brathwaite's representation of the Caroline court may be relevant here: "As the English civil war could, from one perspective, be seen to have been caused by effeminacy, by the feminization of culture, so romance, in Brathwaite's opinion, was a form that history should *not* have taken" (*Censorship and Interpretation*, 201). See also Brathwaite's *The Schollers Medley, or An*

Intermixt Discourse upon Historicall and Poeticall Relations (London, 1618), where he urges the reading of ancient historians and the avoidance of "Don Quixotte transformed into a Knight with the Golden Pestle" (Black, *Brathwait*, 144).

59. Brathwaite, *Panthalia*, 299. See Seneca, *De clementia*, 1.5.7: "To save life is the peculiar privilege of exalted station"; 1.18.1: "No glory redounds to a ruler from cruel punishment—for who doubts his ability to give it?—but, on the other hand, the greatest glory is his if he hold his power in check."

60. Brathwaite, *Panthalia*, 301.

61. Shakespeare, *Macbeth*, 1.4.12–13.

62. Brathwaite, *Panthalia*, 302. There were numerous other sources, besides Seneca, for the association between mercy and equity. St. German's dialogue *Doctor and Student*, discussed in chapter 2, is one influential early modern source. On the relation between pity and equity in the Aristotelian and Christian traditions, see Eden, *Poetic and Legal Fiction*, esp. 28, 100–102, 156. Charicles's invitation echoes King James's royal motto "Pro me (se mereor) in me."

63. [William Sales], *Theophania: Or Severall Modern Histories represented by way of Romance: and Politickly Discours'd upon* (London, 1655), 114. There is now a modern edition of *Theophania*, edited by Renée Pigeon (Ottawa, 1999).

64. I want to acknowledge here reading Ian McLellan's unpublished manuscript on *Theophania*, which has shaped my understanding of the political context of this work. See also the excellent introduction by Pigeon, especially pp. 37–45. Pigeon argues that "*Theophania*'s author espouses a moderate royalist position, asserting via Synesius the need for negotiation betweeen the royalist and the parliamentarian followers of Essex, *Theophania*'s Cenodoxius" (37).

65. Sales, *Theophania*, 105.

66. Ibid., 104 (slavish obedience), 114 (politick maxims).

67. Ibid., 152 (resistless power of love), 165 (emphasis added).

68. Ibid., 168.

69. Ibid., 169–70; cf. 183 on the shipwreck of civil war.

70. Ibid., 187. There is some dispute whether Corastus stands for Fairfax (as McLellan believes) or Cromwell (as Shearer and Pigeon argue). On this point, see note 86.

71. Ibid., 193.

72. Ibid., 191–92; see 37 on the horrid effects of sympathy.

73. See Pigeon, ed. *Theophania*, 42–43: "Cenodoxius's narrative locates the genesis of the war in the personal indignation suffered by the nobility and affronts offered them by the monarchy; Synesius, in contrast, sees his country's problems as stemming from the failure of the constitution to clarify where that power should lie, thus allowing 'public affairs' to be 'swayed by the interests or inclinations of particular persons.' He finds the genesis of the war not in the personal failings of those involved, but in the nature of the institutions which permit corruption to flourish." Pigeon, following Harold Tomlinson, aligns these two positions with those of Edward Hyde (later earl of Clarendon) on the one hand, and Harrington on the other.

74. Sales, *Theophania*, 193 (the syntax is faulty in the original).

75. Ibid., 190 (politick maximes), 196 (protection).

76. Leicester was in France from 1636 to 1642. Jonathan Scott discusses the influence of Tacitus, Bodin, and Grotius on Leicester, who frequently cites them in his private writings; see *Algernon Sidney and the English Republic, 1623–1677* (Cambridge, 1988), 45. McLellan refers to this passage in Scott. Grotius's *Politick Maxims* was published in London in 1654, a year before *Theophania* appeared in print.

77. Quoted in Scott, *Algernon Sidney*, 58. On the second Earl of Leicester's library, see Germaine Warkentin, "The World and the Book at Penshurst: The Second Earl of Leicester (1595–1677) and His Library," *Library* 20 (1998): 325–46.

78. Sales, *Theophania*, 32 (posture), 36 (courtship). None of the critical accounts I am familiar with mention these scenes.

79. Ibid., 36–37.

80. Ibid., 38.

81. Along with the ekphrasis typical of Greek romance, Sidney is an important influence here. In his introduction to the Penguin *Countess of Pembroke's Arcadia* (London, 1977), Maurice Evans discusses Sidney's method of description, which "keeps us at a distance from the action, so that tragedy is turned into spectacle and admiration aroused in place of pity and fear" (18). Many treatises of Renaissance poetics also emphasized the aesthetic effects of admiration and wonder. Finally, in his commentary on *De clementia*, Calvin argues that pity is admirable and cites Cicero's *Pro Ligurio*: "Nothing is so dear to the people as kindness, and none of your many virtues arouses such admiration and such pleasure as your pity" (12.37); see *Calvin's Commentary on Seneca's De Clementia*, ed. Ford Lewis Battles and André Malan Hugo (Leiden, 1969), 361 (comment on *De clementia* 2.4).

82. Sales, *Theophania*, 191, mispagination for 200.

83. Thomas Hobbes, *Leviathan*, chap. 13, p. 87.

84. Sales, *Theophania*, 202. There is a precedent in Sidney's *Arcadia* where the shared love of Urania maintains friendship between rival shepherds Strephon and Claius (ed. Evans, 64).

85. See Pigeon, ed., *Theophania*, who notes that "the general viewpoint expressed in the text appears most appropriate to 1645. Charles I (Antiochus) still lives, as does the third earl of Essex (Cenodoxius)" (13). She goes on to quote Shearer: "There would have been no point to a large part of the book had not Essex still been living" (Pigeon, 14; Shearer, "Theophania," 72). The question remains why the text was published in 1655. Shearer argues that it was done to discredit the Commonwealth (73) but, because he identifies Corastus with Cromwell, he is then unable to explain why Cromwell appears in a sympathetic light. If, however, Corastus is Fairfax, as I believe, *Theophania* could both discredit the Commonwealth and represent sympathy rather than military virtue as the bond of obligation and key to the Restoration.

Terry Eagleton discusses the aestheticizing of politics in the early eighteenth century in *The Ideology of the Aesthetic* (Oxford, 1990). Nancy Armstrong develops a related argument regarding the sublimation of arguments about political obligation in the novel in *Desire and Domestic Fiction* (Oxford, 1987). Prose romance of the 1650s anticipates both of these developments. For the later fortunes of sympathy, and its relation to theatricality in the eighteenth century, see David Marshall, *The Surprising Effects of Sympathy* (Chicago, 1988).

86.   Brathwaite, *Panthalia*, 42–43.

87.   Carol Kay, *Political Constructions: Defoe, Richardson, and Sterne in Relation to Hobbes, Hume, and Burke* (Ithaca, 1988), 278, 270, quoting Edmund Burke, *Reflections on the Revolution in France*. For an argument that builds on Kay, see Claudia Johnson, *Equivocal Beings: Politics, Gender, and Sentimentality in the 1790s* (Chicago, 1995), 13: "Sentimentality renders Hobbes's absolute sovereign superfluous. Because the subjects of the state are sensitive to each other's approval and disapproval—craving the former and avoiding the latter—they observe and sustain shared customs without requiring the intervention of authoritarian rule."

88.   Albert O. Hirschman, *The Passions and the Interests: Political Arguments for Capitalism before Its Triumph* (Princeton, 1977).

89.   Brathwaite argues that princely clemency will "redeem the time" in *Panthalia*, 299, 302; the phrase echoes Hal's famous speech in Shakespeare's *Henry IV, Part I*. Potter, *Secret Rites*, comments on the desire on the part of royalists to turn the future Charles II into a kind of Prince Hal figure who will reconcile the worlds of court and tavern, king and kingdom (103–4).

CHAPTER 10
CRITIQUE

1.   See Grotius, *De jure belli*, 3.7.5.1: " 'The name of slaves [*servi*],' says Pomponius, 'comes from the fact that commanders are accustomed to sell prisoners and thereby to save them [*servare*] and not to kill them.' " On the Restoration context of *Samson Agonistes*, see, among others, Christopher Hill, *Milton and the English Revolution* (Harmondsworth, England, 1977), 428–50; Laura Lunger Knoppers, *Historicizing Milton: Spectacle, Power, and Poetry in the Restoration* (Athens, Ga., 1994); Nicholas Jose, "*Samson Agonistes*: The Play Turned Upside Down," *Essays in Criticism* 30 (1980): 124–50; Steven N. Zwicker, "Milton, Dryden, and the Politics of Literary Controversy," in *Culture and Society in the Stuart Restoration*, ed. Gerald MacLean (Cambridge, 1995), 137–58; Blair Worden, "Milton, *Samson Agonistes*, and the Restoration," in the same volume, 111–36; Sharon Achinstein, "*Samson Agonistes* and the Drama of Dissent," *Milton Studies* 33 (1996): 133–58. *Samson Agonistes* is quoted from John Milton, *Complete Prose and Major Poems*, ed. Merritt Y. Hughes (1957; Indianapolis, 1984).

2.   On the relevance of Grotius to Samson's status as slave in *Samson Agonistes*, see the superb analysis of Leonard Tennenhouse, "The Case of the Resistant Captive," *South Atlantic Quarterly* 95 (1996): 919–46. Joseph Wittreich offers a different account of the influence of Grotius on *Samson Agonistes*, by attending to Grotius's biblical commentary on Judges. See his *Shifting Contexts: Reinterpreting Samson Agonistes* (Pittsburgh, 2002).

3.   For Milton and his contemporaries, the judgment about whether one should keep or break one's contracts was a matter of conscience. But, in a kind of infinite regress of contract theory, conscience itself involved an internal con-

tract. In his *Discourse of Conscience*, in *William Perkins*, ed. Thomas F. Merrill (Nieuwkoop, the Netherlands, 1966), William Perkins described conscience itself as a kind of internal covenant or contract, which the individual was incapable of observing. See chap. 2, n41.

4. As Arthur Barker noted long ago, although in principle the law of nature or right reason was different from divine grace, in practice "that theoretical distinction was difficult to preserve, especially when reason and faith, natural and spiritual law, were together involved in the dispute over the rights of conscience." In radical puritan thought, reasoning about the exception on the basis of natural law and the inner promptings of grace came to involve far more than "the mere natural law of self-preservation": at stake was the relationship of unwritten natural law to the law of the spirit and thus, I would add, the power and authority of reason itself. Arthur E. Barker, *Milton and the Puritan Dilemma* (Toronto, 1942), 148–49.

5. On the similarity between the arguments of Hobbes and some defenders of the Restoration, see Achinstein, "*Samson Agonistes* and the Drama of Dissent." For a superb reading of *Samson Agonistes* in terms of the contrasting views of Hobbes and Milton on natural law, see Catherine Gimelli Martin, "The Phoenix and the Crocodile: Milton's Natural Law Debate with Hobbes Retried in the Tragic Forum of *Samson Agonistes*," in *The English Civil Wars in the Literary Imagination*, ed. Claude J. Summers and Ted-Larry Pebworth (Columbia, Mo., 1999), 242–70.

6. On Milton's critique of the theatrical spectacle of the Restoration, see Knoppers, *Historicizing Milton*; and David Loewenstein, *Milton and the Drama of History* (Cambridge, 1990).

7. See Milton, *The Reason of Church Government*, in *CPW*, 1:818. Milton thus engages contemporary arguments about the use of one passion (or interest) to counteract the deleterious political effects of another. Unlike modern historians of political thought such as Albert Hirschman, however, Milton is as concerned with the countervailing force of mimesis and aesthetic interest as he is with political interest narrowly construed. See Albert O. Hirschman, *The Passions and the Interests: Political Arguments for Capitalism before Its Triumph* (Princeton, 1977).

8. Christopher Hill cites a number of the references to Samson in contemporary political debate in *Milton and the English Revolution*, 428–30. See also Joseph Wittreich, *Interpreting "Samson Agonistes"* (Princeton, 1986), chap. 4.

9. In *The Casuistical Tradition* (Princeton, 1981), Camille Wells Slights notes that "The maxim *salus populi suprema lex* was invoked variously in Henry Parker, *Observations upon some of his Majesties Late Answers and Expresses* (1642); in Samuel Rutherford, *Lex, Rex* (1644); in John Goodwin, *Right and Might Well Met* (1648); in Milton, *The Tenure of Kings and Magistrates* (1649); and in Thomas Hobbes, *Leviathan* (1651). Robert Sanderson devotes two of his ten lectures on casuistry to explaining it. See *Several Cases of Conscience Discussed in Ten Lectures* (1660)" (276, n26).

10. Carl Friedrich, *Constitutional Reason of State* (Providence, 1957), 4.

11. On the link between reason of state and *arcana imperii*, see Ernst H. Kantorowicz, "Mysteries of State," *Harvard Theological Review* 48 (1955): 65–90;

Francis D. Wormuth, *The Royal Prerogative, 1603–1649* (1939; rpt., Port Washingon, N.Y., and London, 1972); Jonathan Goldberg, *James I and the Politics of Literature* (Baltimore, 1983).

12. Wormuth, *Royal Prerogative*, 74. James I argued: "These are unfit Things to be handled in Parliament, except your King should require it of you: for who can have Wisdom to judge of Things of that Nature, but such as are daily acquainted with the Particulars of Treaties, and of the variable or fixed Connexion of Affairs of State, together with the Knowledge of Secret Ways, Ends and Intentions of Princes, in their several Negotiations?" (75).

13. Quoted by Johann P. Sommerville, *Politics and Ideology in England, 1603–1640* (London, 1986), 167–68.

14. Coke is cited by Wormuth, *Royal Prerogative*, 78; Browne is cited by Sommerville, *Politics and Ideology*, 166.

15. Quoted in Richard Tuck, *Philosophy and Government, 1572–1651* (Cambridge, 1993), 234.

16. John Milton, *A Defence of the English People*, in *CPW*, 4.1:317–18.

17. Ibid., 397, 459.

18. Parker, *The Contra-Replicant* (London, 1642): "For if it be lawfull for both Houses of Parliament to defend themselves, it must of necessity follow, that they may and must imprison, levye moneyes, suppresse seditious preachers, and make use of an arbitrary power according to reason of state, and not confine themselves to meere expedient of Law" (29).

19. *Bishop Sanderson's Lectures on Conscience and Human Law*, ed. Christopher Wordsworth (London, 1877), 273–74, 278. See 278–79 on the interpretation of "people" in the phrase *salus populi* as excluding the king: "I observe . . . that the word *people* . . . may be taken either *collectively*, as it includes the whole community of the State, the sovereign and the *subjects* together; or *disjunctively*, as it implies the *subjects only*. . . . It is therefore a most dangerous mistake (not to call it a malicious design) to wrest and to apply what is said of the people *collectively* in the *first sense*, as it includes the *whole community* [including the king], to the *people* in the *latter* acceptation, as it signifies the *subjects only*, to the exclusion of the sovereign." Sanderson's lectures were delivered in 1647.

20. John Goodwin, *Right and Might Well Met* (London, 1648), 15.

21. *The Question concerning Impositions*, cited in Wormuth, *Royal Prerogative*, 72. Wormuth notes "the book was written toward the end of the reign of James I, but was not published until 1656." According to Wormuth, the "three great constitutional issues in the period 1600–1660" all involved the crown's appeal to reason of state: "the king's right to levy impositions, decided in Bate's Case (1606); the king's right to arrest for reason of state without alleging a cause, decided in the Five Knights' Case (1627); the king's right to levy taxes without the consent of Parliament, on the plea of necessity, decided in Hampden's case (1638)."

22. *The Reason of Church Government*, in *CPW*, 1:858–59; *Defence of the English People*, in *CPW*, 4:401–2. See also the reference to Samson in *Areopagitica*, in *CPW*, 2:557–58.

23. See George Mosse, *The Holy Pretence: A Study in Christianity and Reason of State from William Perkins to John Winthrop* (Oxford, 1957); Carl

Friedrich, *Constitutional Reason of State*, esp. chap. 4; and Michael Walzer, *The Revolution of the Saints* (Cambridge, Mass., 1965).

24. At least since Weber, the idea that Protestantism (particularly Calvinism) fostered a rational view of this worldly activity has been a familiar one. Weber famously argued for the connection between Protestantism and capitalism; but others have modified his views by extending them—and claiming that they apply chiefly—to the sphere of politics. See Walzer, *Revolution of the Saints*; Hirschman, *The Passions and the Interests*, who argues that Weber's account of the rise of capitalism needs to be supplemented by attention to specifically political arguments; and Friedrich, *Constitutional Reason of State*, esp. chap. 4.

25. Quoted in Friedrich, *Constitutional Reason of State*, 57.

26. "Whether Soldiers, too, Can Be Saved" (1526), in *Luther's Works*, 55 vols., ed. Jaroslav Pelikan and Helmut T. Lehmann; vol. 46, ed. Robert C. Shultz (Philadelphia, 1967), 135.

27. John Guillory explores the relevance of the doctrine of the calling to *Samson Agonistes* in "The Father's House: *Samson Agonistes* in Its Historical Moment," in *Milton*, ed. Annabel Patterson (London, 1992), 202–25.

28. Perkins is also cited by Guillory, "The Father's House," who is also interested in the instability of the notion of calling as vocation or work in Luther and Perkins, and the tension between general and specific predestination—the called and the elect—in Calvin; but his chief concern is the way this instability adumbrates a bourgeois conception of the individual.

29. See Walzer, *Revolution of the Saints*, following George Mosse.

30. See Christopher Hill, "Covenant Theology and the Concept of 'A Public Person,' " in *The Collected Essays of Christopher Hill*, 3 vols. (Amherst, 1986), 3: 300–324. Hill shows that the criteria for defining a public person were themselves a subject of debate: for some a public person was someone who held a representative public position, such as being a member of Parliament; for others "the godly were public persons because Christ was a public person, and they were part of Christ" (18). On the fear that casuistry would create rebellious subjects during Elizabeth's reign, see Lowell Gallagher, *Medusa's Gaze* (Stanford, 1991), 77–80.

31. Luther, *On Secular Authority*, in *Luther and Calvin on Secular Authority*, ed. Harro Höpfl, Cambridge Texts in the History of Political Thought (Cambridge, 1991), 15. See also 16: "It is in this way that all the saints have borne the Sword from the beginning of the world: Adam and his descendants, Abraham when he saved Lot. . . . And Moses, Joshua, the Children of Israel, Samson, David, and all the kings and princes of the Old Testament acted in the same way." As the translator points out, the German title of Luther's treatise, *Von Weltlicher Oberkeit*, is ambiguous: *Oberkeit* is "an abstract term meaning either the status of having authority or power" (xxxii).

32. Luther, *On Secular Authority*, 16, 18, 22.

33. It is thus not surprising that Samson's meditations involve some of the standard cases of casuistry (marriage with an infidel, attending forbidden rites, suicide), as well as what Perkins described as "the greatest [case of conscience] that ever was: how a man may know whether he be the child of God, or no" (quoted by Slights in *The Casuistical Tradition*, 293). Although Slights discusses the links between *Samson Agonistes* and traditional cases of conscience, she

stresses that these are "less important than Samson's gradual enlightenment about how to resolve moral problems" (292). On *Samson Agonistes* as a drama of the will, see William Kerrigan, "The Irrational Coherence of *Samson Agonistes*," *Milton Studies* 22 (1986): 217–32.

34. On either-or reasoning in *Samson Agonistes* and its transformation into both-and by the end of the tragedy, see Joseph Summers, "The Movements of the Drama," in *The Lyric and Dramatic Milton*, ed. Joseph Summers (New York, 1965), 157–60. See also Edward Tayler, *Milton's Poetry: Its Development in Time* (Pittsburgh, 1979), who writes that *Samson Agonistes* is a Christian tragedy because "Samson guided solely by God is not 'tragic,' as Samson guided solely by himself is not 'Christian' " (121).

35. Stanley Fish, "Question and Answer in *Samson Agonistes*," *Critical Quarterly* 11 (1969), notes that the Chorus tries to make Samson "a particular instance of a general and implacable truth" (242). He also notes the way the Chorus turns Samson's unparalleled condition into a parallel, that is, an example, in "Spectacle and Evidence in *Samson Agonistes*," *Critical Inquiry* 15 (1989): 559–60.

36. On the Chorus's fideism, see Joan S. Bennett, "Liberty under the Law: The Chorus and the Meaning of *Samson Agonistes*," *Milton Studies* 12 (1978): 141–63.

37. I borrow the term "negative dialectics" from Theodor Adorno and Max Horkheimer, who used it to refer to a method of dialectical thinking that is not teleological but instead engages in an "immanent critique" of the status quo. Here I want to suggest that Samson engages in a kind of immanent critique of others' arguments from authority, showing that any positive term contains its own negation: dialectical thinking is reasoning about the exception (or the difference at the heart of any identity) because it turns positive terms into their own negation ("at variance" with themselves, 1585). As I suggest later, in showing that every positive term can turn into its opposite, dialectical thinking also suggests a kind of equivocation.

38. In "Milton's *Samson* and the 'New Acquist of True [Political] Experience' " *Milton Studies* 24 (1989), Barbara Kiefer Lewalski remarks, "In some ways there seems little to choose between Dalila's proclaimed motives and Samson's own, since his marriage [was] intended to advance Israel's cause against the Philistines. Samson, however, challenges Dalila's relativism by appealing to widely shared human values. With all the polemic of the English civil war echoing in the background, he flatly denies ultimate authority to civil and religious leaders, or to *raison d'état*" (241). This is true in the obvious sense that "ultimate" authority in Milton's universe always resides with God. But as I am arguing, there is another sense in which Samson does not at all reject reason of state: he simply redefines it as critical reasoning about the exception. As this redefinition suggests, in arguing from reason of state Dalila is not so much Samson's opposite as she is his parodic double. On this point, see Joan S. Bennett, " 'A Person Rais'd': Public and Private Cause in *Samson Agonistes*," *Studies in English Literature* 18 (1978): 156. Slights, *The Casuistical Tradition*, 277, also notes Dalila's false reasoning about the public good.

39. Martin, "The Phoenix and the Crocodile," 255.

40. In "Milton's *Samson*," Lewalski notes that "Samson's responses [to Harapha] echo the basic radical Puritan (and Miltonic) justifications . . . [including] appeals to the natural law, which always allows rebellion against conquerors" (243); but she doesn't see the relevance of these remarks to Samson's exchange with Dalila. Bennett, however, does in " 'A Person Rais'd.' "

41. Slights, *The Casuistical Tradition*, 280.

42. Ibid., 285, quotes Ames on how subjection doesn't necessarily imply obedience. Even the general rule of nonresistance was qualified by scriptural passages stating that (in cases of conflict) one should always obey God, not man. For Luther's and Calvin's arguments for passive obedience or nonresistance, as well as their remarks justifying active resistance by lesser magistrates against unjust rulers, see Quentin Skinner, *The Foundations of Modern Political Thought*, 2 vols. (Cambridge, England, 1978), esp. 1:191–238.

43. Summers, "Movements," also makes this point about the ambiguity of "life."

44. See Stephen Marshall, "Meroz Curs'd," cited in chapter 5. Martin, "Phoenix and Crocodile," also notes the relevance of Marshall's pun to *Samson Agonistes*. Martin provides a wonderful analysis of Samson's un-Hobbesian puns throughout the poem; see esp. 260–62.

45. For a sixteenth-century illustration of this fear, see the *Arte of English Poesie* (1589), in which George Puttenham gives examples of *amphibologia* or ambiguous speech, which is associated with rebellion. On this association, see also Steven Mullaney, "Lying Like Truth: Riddle, Representation, and Treason in Renaissance England," *ELH* 47 (1980): 32–47. The role of equivocation in *Samson Agonistes* may explain the echoes of *Macbeth*: lines 34, 82, 605.

46. Hobbes, *Leviathan*, chap. 38.

47. Milton, *Defence*, *CPW*, 4.1:374.

48. In "Spectacle and Evidence," Stanley Fish notes that when Samson says, "I with this messenger will go along" (1384), the will "stands not for the fixed position of a fully formed and independent self but for a self 'willing' to have its configurations transformed by a future it cannot read" (579). For Fish, this amounts to a shift in emphasis from Samson's final act of pulling down the temple to his decision to go with the messenger. In my reading, both actions involve decisions which are equally mysterious.

49. In book 8, sect. 9 of the *Confessions*, Augustine describes the effect of sin as the inability "ex toto velle": literally, to will completely; quoted in Charles Taylor, *Sources of the Self* (Cambridge, Mass., 1989), 185.

50. There is a distinguished body of secondary literature on Milton's revision of Aristotle. See in particular Paul R. Sellin, "Sources of Milton's Catharsis: A Reconsideration," *Journal of English and German Philology* 55 (1961): 712–30; John Arthos, "Milton and the Passions: A Study of *Samson Agonistes*," *Modern Philology* 69 (1971–72): 209–21; John M. Steadman, " 'Passions Well Imitated': Rhetoric and Poetics in the Preface to *Samson Agonistes*," in *Calm of Mind*, ed. Joseph Anthony Wittreich Jr. (Cleveland, 1971), 175–208; and in the same volume, Raymond B. Waddington, "Melancholy against Melancholy: *Samson Agonistes* as Renaissance Tragedy," 259–88; Annette C. Flower, "The Critical Context of the Preface to *Samson Agonistes*," *Studies in English Literature* 10 (1970): 409–28.

51.   As Hughes noted in Milton, *Complete Poems and Major Prose*, although Milton does not explicitly cite Minturno in the preface to *Samson*, he seems to have subscribed to a similar view of the complicated, politically bracing homeo-pathic effect of tragedy. See Giacopo Mazzoni, *On the Defense of the Comedy of Dante*, trans. Robert L. Montgomery (Tallahassee, 1983), 105–6; Antonio Minturno, *L'arte poetica*, in *Literary Criticism from Plato to Dryden*, ed. Allan H. Gilbert (Detroit, 1962), 290; see also p. 289. In his note on the preface to *Samson Agonistes*, Hughes observes that Minturno "came close to Milton's 'agonistic' conception by adding that tragedy is properly a kind of spiritual athletic discipline like the hard physical training of the Spartans, and that it trains men to endure reversals of fortune" (549, n3). Other Italian Renaissance commentators also noted that tragedy could police the passions, while implying (in some cases despite themselves) that it could also channel them into a potentially subversive Stoicism. See Baxter Hathaway, *The Age of Criticism: The Late Renaissance in Italy* (Ithaca, 1962), 205–302, on the debate about catharsis.

52.   On the Dutch critic Daniel Heinsius's possible influence on Milton in this regard, see Sellin, "Sources of Milton's Catharsis."

53.   Steadman, " 'Passions Well Imitated,' " and Flower, "Critical Context," call attention to Milton's understanding of the delight that results from imitation as a means (rather than simply accompaniment) of purgation but do not explore the implications of this emphasis on imitation for a reading of *Samson Agonistes*.

54.   On *Samson Agonistes* as a mimesis of the government of the passions by reason, see Mary Ann Radzinowicz, *Towards "Samson Agonistes"* (Princeton, 1978), chap. 3; and "The Distinctive Tragedy of *Samson Agonistes*," *Milton Studies* 17 (1980): 249–80.

55.   See C. M. Bowra's complaint that "Samson's fault is stressed so strongly that we hardly pity him, and if we feel any fear, it is less for him than for the Philistines"; Bowra is cited in Milton, *Complete Poems and Major Prose*, 546. See also A.S.P. Woodhouse, "Tragic Effect in *Samson Agonistes*," in *Milton: Modern Essays in Criticism*, ed. Arthur E. Barker (New York, 1965), 447–66, esp. 463, on how the end mitigates our sense of tragedy since we don't feel sorry for the death of the Philistines.

56.   Cited by Eric Rothstein, "English Tragic Theory in the Late Seventeenth Century," *English Literary History* 29 (1962): 313.

57.   Giambattista Guarini, *The Compendium of Tragicomic Poetry*, cited in *Literary Criticism from Plato to Dryden*, ed. Allan H. Gilbert (Detroit, 1962), 518.

58.   But see William Flesch, "Reading, Seeing, and Acting in *Samson Agonistes*," in *Critical Essays on John Milton*, ed. Christopher Kendrick (New York, 1995), 130–46, on the attenuated conception of action here: "There's something strangely passive about what God has done—he's done what we've done, he's been a witness. . . . The emphasis is on witness, rather than intervention" (133).

59.   Earl R. Wasserman, "The Pleasures of Tragedy," *ELH* 14 (1947): 283–307.

60.   Walter Benjamin, *The Origin of German Tragic Drama*, trans. John Osborne (London, 1977), 81–82.

61.   Milton, *The Tenure of Kings and Magistrates*, in *CPW* 3:215–16.

62.   Martin Dzelzainis, ed., in Milton, *Political Writings* (Cambridge, 1991), xv.

63. In this sense, Milton's Samson does live up to one seventeenth-century etymology of his name as "there a second time." William Riley Parker, *Milton's Debt to Greek Tragedy in "Samson Agonistes"* (1937; rpt., Hamden, Conn., 1963), 13, n35.

64. Here we might remember Milton's reference in the preface to *Samson* to Paraeus's commentary on the tragedy of Revelation. As Barbara K. Lewalski argued in "*Samson Agonistes* and the Tragedy of the Apocalypse," *PMLA* 85 (1970), Paraeus was not alone among Protestant commentators in "locat[ing] the tragedy of Revelation in the sufferings and agons of the Church under Antichrist: 'the forme of this Prophesie . . . representeth Tragicall motions and tumults of the adversaries against the Church of Christ' " (1051). Samson, in this light, is not so much a type of Christ, as he is a warfaring saint who, "under the conditions of this life . . . cannot escape suffering and death, or the knowledge that [his] own guiltiness deserves it" (1062).

65. Carrol B. Cox, "Citizen Angels: Civil Society and the Abstract Individual in *Paradise Lost*," *Milton Studies* 23 (1987): 165–96, here 176.

66. Angus Fletcher, *Allegory*, quoted by Neil Hertz, "The Notion of Blockage in the Literature of the Sublime," in *The End of the Line: Essays on Psychoanalysis and the Sublime* (New York, 1985), 47. Fletcher observes that this "intellectual tension, [which accompanies] the hard work of exegetical labor," "is nothing less than the cognitive aspect of ambivalence which inheres in the contemplation of any sacred object. Whatever is *sacer* must cause the shiver of mingled delight and awe that constitutes our sense of 'difficulty' " (47).

A number of critics have commented on what I would like to call the double focus of *Samson Agonistes*. A.S.P. Woodhouse argues that Milton presents Samson as armed both with "celestial vigor" and "plain heroic magnitude of mind"; and that the poem represents the human tragedy of Samson's martyrdom, before it subsumes the human into a larger, providential scheme ("Tragic Effect in *Samson Agonistes*," *University of Toronto Quarterly* 28 [1959]: 205–22, esp. 213, 221). Virginia R. Mollenkott makes a similar argument about Milton's presentation of Samson as both an instrument of God and a flawed human individual in "Relativism in *Samson Agonistes*," *Studies in Philology* 67 (1970): 89–103. In *Prophetic Milton* (Charlottesville, Va., 1974), William Kerrrigan observes that Samson's "tragedy poses one pair of alternatives that can never collapse into harmony." Commenting on the lines "doubtful whether God be Lord, / Or *Dagon*," he writes, "This 'Or' cannot be compromised. What the catastrophe of *Samson* divides, [only] the Apocalypse will clarify once and for all" (250); *Samson* dramatizes "the 'brotherly dissimilitudes' of *Areopagitica*" (253).

67. Carl Schmitt, *Political Theology*, trans. Georg Schwab (Cambridge, Mass., 1988), 5.

CHAPTER 11
CONCLUSION

1. On Hume's antifoundationalism, see, for example, Annette Baier, *Postures of the Mind* (Minneapolis, 1985), 174–206. On the relationship between Hume and Hobbes, see George Shelton, *Morality and Sovereignty in the Philosophy of*

Hobbes (New York, 1992); 219–22; Carol Kay, *Political Constructions: Defoe, Richardson, and Sterne in Relation to Hobbes, Hume, and Burke* (Ithaca, 1988); and William Kerrigan, *Shakespeare's Promises* (Baltimore, 1999), 19–20. Perhaps another sign of Hume's total absorption of contract theory is his turn from the traditional philosophical genre of the treatise to the literary genres of the essay and autobiography. On this turn, see John Mullan, *Sentiment and Sociability: The Language of Feeling in the Eighteenth Century* (Oxford, 1988).

    2. David Hume, *A Treatise of Human Nature*, ed. L. A. Selby-Bigge (Oxford, 1968), 2.3.3, p. 415.

    3. See, for example, Christopher Prendergast, *The Order of Mimesis* (Cambridge, 1986): "[T]he contract of language is not one that is entered into by autonomous and sovereign speakers"; "no speaker has the right to recede from the contract . . . except at the price of ceasing to be a speaker at all" (37).

    4. Shelton, *Morality and Sovereignty in the Philosophy of Hobbes*, 176.

    5. See Louis Althusser, "Rousseau: The Social Contract (the Discrepancies)," in *Montesquieu, Rousseau, Marx: Politics and History*, trans. Ben Brewster (London, 1972), 113–60, esp. 160.

    6. Terry Eagleton, *The Ideology of the Aesthetic*, (Oxford, 1990), 19, 20.

    7. Ibid., 27.

    8. Michael Sandel, *Liberalism and the Limits of Justice* (Cambridge, 1982), critiquing John Rawls, *A Theory of Justice* (Cambridge, Mass., 1971).

    9. John Rawls, *Political Liberalism* (New York, 1996), xxxi.

Index

Adorno, Theodor, 282, 294n.61, 294–
295n.62, 360n.37
aesthetics, 7, 8, 20, 23, 24, 26, 254, 272,
280–284
aesthetic interest, 26, 225, 226–227, 232,
238, 246, 248–251, 280–284
affection. *See* passions
agency, 55, 65, 112, 180, 274–275,
347–348n.39
Allen, William, 69–70
Ames, William, 50, 68–69
Appleby, Joyce, 21
Aquinas, St. Thomas, 9, 156
arcana imperii, 255, 277
Arendt, Hannah, 24, 294n.60, 335n.86
Aristotle, 9, 92, 133, 156, 192, 234, 271,
276; *Nicomachean Ethics*, 43, 62,
302n.51, 332n.53; *Poetics*, 17, 124,
141, 216, 225, 238–239, 249, 290n.39;
Politics, 287n.11, *Rhetoric*, 141,
290n.42, 308n.8
Armstrong, Nancy, 23, 338n.19
artifice, 25, 56, 57, 103–104, 135–136,
138, 225, 271, 282–284
assumpsit, 46–47, 155
Austin, J. L., 155–156, 331n.44, 331n.45

Bacon, Sir Francis, 46
Bakhtin, M. M., 338–339n.21
Ball, John, 52–53, 67
Banks, Sir John, 92
Barker, Arthur, 357n.4
Barker, Ernest, 28
Bates' Case, 75–76, 258
Benjamin, Walter, 276
Berlin, Isaiah, 214–215
Bloch, Ernst, 19, 291n.51
Bodin, Jean, 245
Bradshaw, John, 113
Braithwaite, Richard, 20, 224; *Panthalia*,
224, 227, 233, 234–241, 247, 249
Bramhall, John, 167
Bulkeley, Peter, 51
Burckhardt, Jacob, 2, 285n.2
Burges, Cornelius, 114–115, 132, 162

Burke, Edmund, 250
Burroughs, Jeremiah, 114, 119–120
Burrow, Colin, 220
Butler, Samuel, 4

calling, Protestant notion of, 260–262, 267
Calvin, John, 2, 120, 239, 261, 322n.36
Caryl, Joseph, 118
Castelvetro, Lodovico, 216
casuistry, 8, 14, 68, 84, 180, 186, 188,
225, 261, 286n.10
catharsis, 276, 278
Cave, Terrence, 116, 192, 216, 320–
321n.13, 346–347n.29, 347n.35
Cavendish, Margaret, 6, 20, 26, 172–195,
226; *Assaulted and Pursued Chastity*, 172–
173, 176, 180, 181, 189–195; *The Contract*, 172–195, 225; on love, 171–174,
185, 187–188, 194; on romance, 172–174,
177–189; on subjection, 190–191
Cavendish, William, 171, 176, 191, 194
Chillingworth, William, 104
Cicero, 16–17, 34–35, 38, 61, 92, 158,
230, 299n.27, 299n.34, 308n.8; *De oratore*, 17; *De officiis*, 17, 34–35; *De inventione*, 34–35
Clarendon, Edward Hyde, earl of, 94–95,
117, 169
coercion, 58, 62, 77, 176, 187, 190, 194–
195, 198, 205, 218, 309n.11
Coke, Edward, 41–42, 46–47, 74, 87–90,
129, 160, 161, 255
Coleman, Thomas, 119
commerce, 76
common law, 41–48, 59, 83, 84, 86–88,
96, 159–161, 186
conscience, 7, 8, 32, 43, 67–68, 100–101,
103, 104, 106–107, 146–147, 159, 189,
199, 202, 207, 240, 254–255, 278,
310n.24, 356–357n.3
consent, 9, 13, 20, 39, 58, 73–79, 97–
98, 100, 104–105, 109, 128, 151, 165,
173, 176, 182, 187, 190, 194–195, 198,
200–201, 204, 211, 289n.32, 309n.11,
336n.11; instability of, 57–59

consideration, 4–5, 46–47, 155, 159
constitutionalism, 6
contract: breach of, 3, 44–45, 83, 85, 107, 155–156, 162, 197, 201–202, 222, 224, 356–357n.3; contingency of, 32; fictional quality of, 6, 85, 138; language and, 1, 5, 34–35, 56, 292n.54, law and, 42; limits of, 197; metaphor of, 8, 19, 54, 95–104, 111, 122, 123; of conscience, 306n.79; of genre, 15–20, 192; of metaphor, 54, 122, 204; of mimesis, 18, 141, 147–51, 192, 196, 216; psychology of, 13–15, 57–58, 271, 280–284; secular notion of, 5; sexual, 26,172, 208, 335n.2; voluntarism of, 14, 78–79. See also economic contract, marriage contract
covenant, 12, 18, 26, 33, 105, 114, 123, 254, 263, 330n.28; as metaphor, 54; metaphor of, 49–50; of grace, 49, 52, 201, 204; of works, 49, 52, 196, 305n.74; religious notion of, 5, 123. See also divine convenant
covenant theology, 5, 6, 20, 22, 25, 48–55, 59, 64–73, 114–115, 158–159, 198, 201
Crawley, Edward, 93
Cromwell, Oliver, 11, 132
Cudworth, Ralph, 167, 169, 170

Davenant, William, 18, 142–143
Davies, Sir John, 258–259
debt, 44–45, 66
Denores, Giason, 216
Descartes, 13, 225
desire. See passions
determinism, 16, 220–222
Digges, Dudley, 3, 104–110
divine covenant, 48–52, 71, 78, 196–197, 198, 219–220, 208, 219, 222, 253; as testament, 50, 55. See also covenant
divorce, 199–200
domestic relations, 10, 102–103
Downame, George, 52, 67, 114
Dzelzainis, Martin, 277

Eachard, John, 168
Eagleton, Terry, 280–281, 286n.9
economic contract, 43–48, 84, 88, 332n.56. See also contract, marriage contract
Engagement controversy, 14

English civil war, 2, 4, 6, 25, 27, 34, 95, 120, 135, 176, 179, 197, 227, 234
equity, 43–45, 53–55, 68, 72, 91, 123, 133, 200–201, 302nn.51, 52; and reason of state, 40–41
Essex, third earl of, 138–39, 140, 235, 237, 241–46

fabrication, 15, 35
Falkland, Lucius Cary, second Viscount,104
Fanshawe, Sir Richard, 178–180
fear, 62, 67, 93–94, 107–108, 124–125, 141, 151, 170, 187, 198, 226, 250, 309n.9; of God, 66; of violence, 13, 26, 61, 135, 151–154, 163, 171, 250, 309n.11; servile v. filial, 69
Ferne, Henry, 174–175
Filmer, Robert, 3, 40–41, 58, 195, 285n.4, 308n.2
Five Knights Case, 86–87, 91, 113, 116
Fleming, Chief Baron,
Fletcher, Angus, 278
Fortescue, John, 10
Foucault, Michel, 16, 286–287n.10
Friedrich, Carl, 255

Galileo, 135
gender, 22, 59, 70–72, 102, 111, 165–166, 170, 172–195, 205–207, 236, 335n.85
general will, 23
genre, 15–20, 22, 177, 181, 185–186, 188, 193, 216, 228, 232, 234, 254, 290n.40
Glanville, John, 88
Glendon, Mary Ann, 291n.51
Goodwin, John, 257–258
Gouge, William, 50, 210
government, origins of, 96, 125, 134, 296n.8
governmentality, 286–287n.10
Grand Remonstrance, 116–117
Great Contract, the (1610), 313n.1
Grotius, Hugo, 8, 25, 34–41, 60–64, 70, 105, 110, 120, 127, 128, 155, 158, 163, 164, 189, 221, 245–246, 252; Filmer on, 40–41; on government, 36; on linguistic contract, 38–39; on private property, 36; on resistance, 37
Guarini, Battista, 178–179

habeas corpus, 78, 86
Habermas, Jürgen, 24, 294–295n.62

Hakewill, William, 76
Hall, John, 140
Hampden, John, 90–95, 117
Harrington, James, 21, 169
Heath, Robert, 87, 91
Hegel, G.W.F., 136
Heinsius, Daniel, 271
Heliodorus, 179, 186, 189, 231
Herbert, Percy Sir, 20, 180, 223–224, 227–234; *Certaine Conceptions*, 223–224; *The Princess Cloria*, 227–234
Herle, Charles, 4, 256
Hickes, George, 110–111
Hill, Christopher, 73
Hirschman, Albert, 17, 250
Hirst, Derek, 226
Hobbes, Thomas, 4, 27, 58, 120–170, 171, 194, 224, 225, 252, 255, 266–267, 270, 279–284, 294–295n.62; absolutism of, 155, 163–166; and Grotius, 163–164; and his critics, 166–170; and mathematics, 19, 135; and St. German, 161; and the liberal tradition, 20–25, 121, 138, 243; 279–284; *De cive*, 13, 14, 104, 135, 149, 197; *De corpore*, 184; *Dialogue between a Philosopher and Student of the Common Laws of England*, 161; *Elements of Law*, 104, 141, 142, 145, 148; *Elements of Philosophy*, 135, 197; *Leviathan*, 4, 6, 7, 14, 16, 18, 19, 26, 108, 121, 128, 135–170, 171, 184, 187, 194, 215, 243, 247, 269, 271, 282, 284; materialism of, 6, 7, 137, 167, 225; on common law, 159–161; on conscience, 329n.27; on covenant theology, 158–159; on economic contract, 332–333n.56; on fear, 141, 151–152, 157, 163, 171, 182; on imagination, 144–145; on language, 135–138; on metaphor, 150; on obligation, 137, 160, 163; on romance, 140–147, 150, 169; on science, 148–149; on the laws of nature, 151, 155, 157, 162–164; on the origins of government, 134; on the passions, 151–152, 171–174; on women, 165–166
Homer, 17
homo faber, 24
Hooker, Richard, 10
Horkheimer, Max, 282, 288n.28, 294n.61, 294–295n.62, 360n.37
Houston, Alan, 21
Hugenots, 10

Hume, David, 8, 28, 279, 280, 281, 343n.58
Hunton, Philip, 2

imagination, 93, 104, 107–108, 136, 144–145, 152–153
interest, 13, 47, 97
Ireton, General, 12

Johnson, Samuel, 204
Jonson, Ben, 18
judgment, 127

Kay, Carol, 250
Kramnick, Isaac, 21

Lawson, George, 165
Leveller Agreement of the People, 11
liberalism, 20–25, 279–284; and possessive individualism, 20, 21
liberty, negative, 214–215; spiritual, 70–71
Lilburne, John, 12
linguistic contract, 34, 37–39, 149, 168
linguistic turn, 16, 289n.36
Littleton, Sir Edward, 91, 92
Locke, John, 8, 21, 279
love, politics of, 171–174, 181, 187, 198, 211, 215, 229–230, 237, 250, 337–338n.16
loyalty oaths, 4
Lucretius, 225, 249
Luther, Martin, 2, 5, 120, 260, 261–262, 267, 278, 322n.36

Machiavelli, Niccolò, 2, 5, 21, 297n.10
Maclean, Ian, 300n.37
Macpherson, C. B., 1, 20, 291n.51, 344n.13
Magna Carta, 42, 83, 84, 86, 88, 90, 114, 129, 280
Maine, Henry Sumner, 1, 285n.1
Marshall, Stephen, 114, 116–117, 132
Martin, Catherine Gimelli, 266–267
Mason, Robert, 89
marriage contract, 3, 10–11, 26, 63–64, 99, 102–103, 109, 165, 172–195, 196–207, 219–220, 229, 238, 243, 335n.85, 336n.12; marriage contract, and the Engagement controversy, 176–177, 184–185. *See also* contract, economic contract
materialism, 6–7, 13–15, 137–138, 167–168

Mazzoni, Giacopo, 271
metaphor, 92, 99, 108, 115–116, 123, 128,
    131, 133, 150, 198, 320–321n.13, 346–
    347n.29
Militia Ordinance, 11
Miller, Perry, 55
Milton, John, 5, 19, 120–133, 252–278,
    282–284; Areopagitica, 216, 220, 221,
    270; Defence of the People of England,
    256, 257, 259, 269, 277, 278; Eiko-
    noklastes, 18, 125, 140, 216; material-
    ism of, 7; Of Education, 271; On Chris-
    tian Doctrine, 121, 127, 196, 197; on
    conscience, 202, 207; on fear, 214–221;
    on freedom, 203; on gender, 198–222;
    on love, 204–205; on marriage, 4; on
    metaphor, 120–33, 150; on natural law,
    343–344n.5; on obligation, 131; on regi-
    cide, 120–133, 222, 253, 256, 277, 278;
    on republicanism, 3, 27; on resistance,
    130–131, 222; on sacraments, 324n.44;
    on Scripture, 324n.46; on the marriage
    contract, 196–207, 219–222; on the pas-
    sions, 199–201, 205–222; on tyranny,
    128; Paradise Lost, 23, 25, 26, 121,
    127, 132, 188, 197, 198, 201, 205, 207–
    222, 278, 284; Samson Agonistes, 26,
    103, 118, 119, 133, 222, 252–254, 262–
    278; Tetrachordon, 199; The Doctrine
    and Discipline of Divorce, 14, 26, 175,
    198–208, 218, 220; The Reason of
    Church Government, 18, 259; The Ten-
    ure of Kings and Magistrates, 3, 7, 14,
    26, 112, 121–133, 253, 256, 277
mimesis, 15, 17, 137–139, 141–142, 147–
    153, 163, 192, 196, 208–214, 216, 218,
    225, 241, 244, 246, 270–272, 280–284,
    290n.39, 327n.4, 330n.28, 330n.33
mimetic desire, 140, 146, 149, 152–154,
    215, 244, 246–47
Minturno, Antonio, 271
Misselden, Edward, 41
Montague, Walter, 178
moral law, 85, 103, 156, 207

natural law, 3, 5, 6, 22, 33–34, 36, 37, 44,
    60, 84, 86, 96–100, 110, 117, 122, 155,
    156, 196–197, 200–201, 207, 253, 255,
    267, 296n.8
natural rights theory, 5, 7, 33–41, 48, 59,
    78, 97, 100–101, 109, 152, 155, 156,
    197, 283

Nedham, Marchamont, 14
Nietzsche, Friedrich, 2, 66, 133, 205,
    285n.2, 293–294n.58, 294–295n.62,
    306n.79, 310n.24, 327n.91
nominalism, 16
Norman Conquest, 73, 77, 109, 125, 130
Nozick, Robert, 291n.51
nudum pactum, 31–32, 46, 295n.1

obligation, 1, 2, 8, 11, 19, 21, 24, 28, 31,
    34, 47, 56, 61, 84, 95–96, 99–101, 111,
    131, 135, 160, 163, 171, 184, 194–195,
    216–217, 221, 229, 253; and romantic
    love, 182–184; constructed nature of,
    37, 280–284; domestic, 4, 171; mini-
    malist account of, 33; psychology of, 22

paralogism, 17, 141, 145, 192, 217,
    290n.42
Parker, Henry, 3, 25, 84–85, 95–104, 132,
    175, 188, 198, 199, 256, 257; Observa-
    tions upon Some of His Majesties Late
    Answers and Expresses, 3, 84–85, 96–
    100, 175; Jus Populi, 100–104; The
    Case of Shipmoney briefly discoursed,
    96; The Contra-Replicant, His Com-
    plaint to His Majestie, 256
Parker, Patricia, 116
passions, 5, 58, 59, 61, 65, 104, 106–107,
    110, 137, 140, 142, 144, 149–150, 179,
    182, 187, 197, 213, 220, 229–230, 238,
    250–251; and interests, 1, 13, 57, 151,
    194–195, 226, 242, 250, 280–284; insta-
    bility of, 77–78
Pateman, Carole, 206, 291n.51
patriarchy, 103, 195
Patterson, Annabel, 22, 180
Perkins, William, 25, 48–54, 65–66, 68–
    73, 114, 128, 206, 260; A Golden
    Chain, 52, 54, 72; Christian Oeconomie,
    72; Consolations for Troubled Con-
    sciences, 65; Discourse of Conscience,
    66, 68, 202; Epieikeia, 72; Treatise of
    the Vocations or Callings of Men, 50,
    70–72; Whether a Man Be in the Estate
    of Damnation or the Estate of Grace,
    50, 52, 65
Petition of Right (1628), 88–90, 255
Phillips, Sir Robert, 87
pity, 124–125, 216, 220, 22, 226, 234–
    241, 247, 249, 253
Plato, 148, 213

Plutarch, 109
Pocock, J.G.A, 21, 24, 292n.52, 295n.63
poetics, 16, 17; and contract, 15
Ponet, John, 10
positive law, 98–100, 110, 122, 253, 255
Post-Nati, case of, 74
Potter, Lois, 139
power, 101
predestination, 64
Preston, John, 51–54, 67, 114, 197
promises, 3, 4, 31–32, 38, 46–47, 52, 85–
    86, 89, 186, 262, 279, 314n.6
property, 36, 45, 61, 84, 86, 91, 203
prophecy, 26, 263, 113–120, 123
Protestant Reformation, 8
public person, 42, 51, 132
Pufendorf, Samuel, 206–207
Putney debates, 11–12
Pym, John, 89

Quintilian, 17

Rapin, René, 225, 272
Rawls, John, 282, 283, 291–292n.51
reason, 24, 213, 216–217
reason of state, 8, 12, 37, 76, 84, 90–92,
    96, 102, 107, 132,199, 253–262, 266–
    270
regicide, 120–133, 253, 256, 277, 278
republicanism, 21
resistance, right of, 85, 100, 105, 130–131,
    222
rhetoric, 17
Roman law, 19, 39
romance, 20, 26, 136, 139–141, 169–170,
    172–174, 177–189, 192–195, 216, 224–
    228, 232–236, 241–242, 248–251,
    334n.80, 339n.24; political dangers of,
    138
Rousseau, Jean-Jacques, 23, 63, 104, 179,
    280, 281
royal prerogative, 73–78, 85–89, 91, 255,
    258–259

Saint Augustine, 270
Sales, William, 20, 180, 224; *Theophania*,
    224, 227, 241–251
salus populi. *See* reason of state
Sandel, Michael, 282
Sanderson, Bishop William, 257, 278
Scott, Jonathan, 21, 297n.10
Sedgwick, William, 132

Selden, John, 31–32, 58, 84
self-interest, 60, 103, 171, 179, 192, 238
self-love, 13, 107, 205, 208, 215, 222
self-preservation, 12, 33, 96, 101, 106–
    107, 109, 110, 123, 155, 163, 185, 199,
    215, 222
Seneca, 124, 239, 247, 353n.54
sentimentality, 8, 250, 252
servitude, voluntary, 25, 58, 64, 66–67, 73,
    78, 104, 119, 122, 196, 197, 199, 207,
    213, 271–272
Shakespeare, William, 186, 187, 188
Shanley, Mary, 175
Sharpe, Kevin, 139
Shelton, George, 280
Shipmoney Case, 86–87, 90–95, 96, 113,
    116
Sibbes, Richard, 67
Sidney, Algernon, 21
Sidney, Philip, 18, 139, 216, 235, 329n.15,
    349n.11
Sidney, Robert, second earl of Leicester, 34,
    241, 245
Simpson, A.W. B., 47
Skinner, Quentin, 21, 292n.53
Slade's Case, 45–47, 85, 94, 155, 159
slave contract, 60–64, 99, 165
slavery, 59, 60–64, 70, 103, 125,
    190–191
Solemn League and Covenant, 118, 122,
    124
Spinoza, Benedict de, 13
St. German, 43–45, 94, 161
St. John, Oliver, 93
Starkey, Thomas, 73
Strauss, Leo, 23, 24, 148, 149, 226
Suárez, Francisco, 32
subjection, voluntary, 58, 59, 60–67, 73,
    78, 190–191, 207, 230–232, 235
Summa theologica, 24
sympathy, 223–251

Tacitus, 245
Tanner, Tony, 218
Taylor, Charles, 16
Taylor, Jeremy, 69
Tennenhouse, Leonard, 23
theology, political, 278
Tolstoy, Leo, 181
tragedy, 18, 20, 216, 225–226, 239, 243,
    248–250, 252–278, 254, 270–278
trust, 88–90, 99

Tully, James, 291n.51
Tyrrell, James, 167–170

vainglory, 138, 142, 146, 153–154, 221, 224, 243–244, 249
violence, 112–113, 120–133, 162, 189–190, 193, 277
voluntarism, 14, 16, 73–79, 163–165, 207–215, 220–222. *See also* will

Waller, Edmund, 92–93
Walzer, Michael, 1, 215
Weber, Max, 1, 47, 293–294n.58

Wedgwood, C. V., 113–114
Weston, Corinne, 42
Whitehall debates, 11
Wildman, John, 12
will, 58, 98, 106, 109, 133, 151–152, 205, 216, 221, 289n.32, 304n.65. *See also* voluntarism
Winkler, John J., 231
Wolin, Sheldon, 194, 289n.34, 342n.56

Yelverton, Sir Henry, 77

Zwicker, Steven, 27